On This Day

ON THIS DAY

A Collection of Everyday Learning Events and Activities for the Media Center, Library and Classroom

ELAINE J. HAGLUND   MARCIA L. HARRIS

Center for Teaching
The Westminster Schools

LIBRARIES UNLIMITED, INC.
Littleton, Colorado
1983
Junior High Library
Westminster Schools

P 371.3
Haglund

LIBRARIES UNLIMITED, INC.
P.O. Box 263
Littleton, Colorado 80160

Library of Congress Cataloging in Publication Data

Haglund, Elaine.
   On this day.

   Bibliography: p. 454
   Includes index.
   1. Holidays--United States--Handbooks, manuals,
etc. 2. Displays in education--Handbooks, manuals,
etc. 3. Teaching--Aids and devices--Handbooks,
manuals, etc. 4. Schools--Exercises and recreations
--United States--Handbooks, manuals, etc.
5. Instruction materials centers--United States--
Handbooks, manuals, etc. 6. Library exhibits--Hand-
books, manuals, etc. I. Harris, Marcia L.,
1951-   . II. Title.
LB3525.H33 1982   371.3'07'8   82-13960
ISBN 0-87287-345-5

B + T 27.50
7/5/84

Libraries Unlimited books are bound with Type II nonwoven material that meets and exceeds National Association
of State Textbook Administrators' Type II nonwoven material specifications Class A through E.

On This Day is dedicated to learners of all ages and to the teachers, librarians, substitute teachers, parents, school administrators, specialists, teacher aides, youth-group leaders, and cross-age tutors upon whose innovative use of the book its success largely depends.

TABLE OF CONTENTS

PART 1
Events and Activities Section

PART 2
Extra-Know-How Section

PART 3
Task Card Section

PART 4
Reproducible Section

PART 5
Sample Packet—Student Folders Section

FOREWORD

FROM ONE OUTSIDE LOOKING IN

On This Day developed out of a deep commitment to students. Through this book, it is hoped that young people will evolve potential abilities through all of their senses, by becoming aware and expressing what they, as persons, are all about. The intent is for students to experience the process of *learning how to learn* and to have the satisfaction of success by feeling good about themselves—a celebration of their wholeness. In using this book, readers are encouraged not only to accept, but to stress, divergent ways of thinking and processing activities. The idea is to provide ways for the student "to let out what is inside," rather than for the teacher "to put in what 'should be there.' " It is assumed by the authors that qualities of uniqueness and genius lie within each human being; one of the implicit goals of this book, therefore, is to reach those students who learn differently and those who respond to alternatives due to their own individuality.

I believe that this book will be best used if students are active rather than passive learners. They must be free to work and interact with each other. They must be able to experiment, take initiative, develop independence, test their ideas, and, most importantly, to take responsibility for their own direction. *It is not the material itself, but how the material is interpreted and presented, that is crucial.* The following premises, therefore, are offered for implementing the material within the book.

- Teaching needs to allow for the freeing of people rather than the controlling of them, for the uncovering of concepts rather than the covering of a stipulated body of material, and for the process of revealing rather than of concealing.

- Teaching must be a helping relationship rather than a system of telling people what is good for them.

- People will learn more easily, rapidly, and effectively if they help make the important decisions about their learning.

- The most important perceptions an individual has are those he/she has about himself/herself. One's self-concept is one of the most, if not *the* most, important single influences affecting a learner's behavior.

- People learn and grow even more quickly if they are not afraid to make mistakes. They can be more creative more often if they can risk making errors and do not have to worry about the "What'd ja get?" factor of grading.

- The "product-certainty" principle of only one right answer to a question is antithetical to the process of learning.

- Freedom, latitude, and self-responsibility are bred in an environment of trust and acceptance.

- Learning occurs best when the student is ready to learn according to where he/she is, rather than where teachers think he or she should be.

- Learning is likely to be optimal when there is a balanced stimulation of both hemispheres of the brain. The inventive, metaphoric, and integrative potential of the right brain and the objective, verbal, and linear functions of the left brain need to be equally developed.

This book is intended to assist teachers, librarians, and others in fulfilling the purpose of education, as derived from the word "educe"—to draw forth, bring out.

This is a fun, warm book. Enjoy ...

Fred Baker, Ph.D.
Professor, Central Michigan University

ACKNOWLEDGMENTS

The authors wish to extend a special note of appreciation to:

Stephen L. Harris, Marcia's husband, for his ongoing cooperation and for his having suggested the title;

Raymond C. Snyder for his valuable suggestions and untiring efforts in readying the manuscript;

Dr. Robert W. DeGrasse for his computer expertise and personal tenacity in preparing the index;

the many family members and special friends for their ideas and kind support;

the reference librarians for their resourcefulness and willing assistance—

all of whom helped make this book possible.

INTRODUCTION

On This Day is a chronological listing of personalities, places, and events; it is based on the idea that every day is the anniversary of several incidents, many of which are relevant to human accomplishments that have gone unacknowledged. The primary intent of the book is to serve as a source for motivating students to learn how to learn—how to retrieve and productively use information. The "knowledge explosion" has created an exponential growth of data—information which is of little value without students' knowing how to locate and gather the material. In response to this situation, *On This Day* is designed to stimulate students' interest in further exploring the book's various topics through media, library, and other resources.

Through assorted, open-ended suggestions, the book also purposes to generate much creativity and divergent thinking among the students who participate in the activities. The contents provide much opportunity for initiative and resourcefulness through the various recommended projects and those the students supplement and design themselves. By citing certain historical occasions and by observing their significance each day with students, there is an opportunity to inspire thoughts, images, and feelings which may lead to imaginative and innovative solutions. Similarly, by introducing selected personalities, students are led to an understanding that the human potential has been strengthened by the combined energies of many men and women of diverse ethnic and national backgrounds—many of whom took risks by digressing from the norm.

Another purpose of the book is to make history come alive for young people. It is hoped that the text will help translate historical facts, which by nature are interdisciplinary, into meaningful application, thereby assisting teachers and school librarians in integrating a variety of subject areas within the curriculum. Additionally, with the emphasis on American history, one of the objectives is to free the content, as much as possible, of national biases in our nation's history.

On This Day is divided into five parts, each of which is described below.

Part 1: The Events and Activities Section, the major part of the book, is a chronological listing of events for each day of the month. Each month begins with the origin of the month's name, the astrological sign, the flower, and descriptions of month-long observances, special weeks, and variable dates within the month. Each daily listing is followed by suggested ways for presenting the information in the main entry and by cross-references to other activity sections of the text.

Part 2: The Extra-Know-How Section covers three subsections—General Topics, Data-Detail, and Address Listing. "General" includes four areas (Biography, States Admitted to the USA, Resource Person, and Conducting a Survey); when it is suggested in part 1 to refer to one of these areas in the Extra-Know-How Section, the purpose is to provide additional techniques for using the information in the entry—*not* to supply additional content information. It is the Data-Detail subsection which offers the reader information which is supplemental to that provided in the entry; the Address Listing offers an alphabetized directory of organizations and agencies to which the reader can write for additional information relating to the entry.

Part 3: The Task Card Section offers a large number of activities which can be used either separately or in conjunction with the entries in part 1.

Part 4: The Reproducible Section presents a variety of worksheets and diagrams arranged in numerical order to correspond with the events listed in part 1.

Part 5: The Sample Packet—Student Folders Section presents directions and worksheets to enable teachers and librarians to develop an individualized contract-based program, utilizing student folders, in relationship to the main text.

Appendices present subject arrangement of persons listed in the book, as well as a bibliography of reference works. A comprehensive index is included to facilitate the location of specific data and the process of cross-referencing.

The more detailed sections and subsections of the book—in particular, Data-Detail in the Extra-Know-How Section, the Task Card Section, the Reproducible Section, and the Sample Packet—Student Folders Section—have individual contents listings to facilitate location of entries within those divisions. These listings are not included in the main Table of Contents at the beginning of the book.

The series of events and activities which are listed and described in the book are the outcome of many years of collecting data, along with several "dry run" experiences with both students and other teachers. Even though no formal criteria existed for the selection of entries, what remains in the book are those items which worked well with our students and our colleagues. As with most books to be used within the public sector, there is minimal reference to religious observances. Concerted attention was given to balancing the frequency of various ethnic minority entries; also, credit is assigned to individuals' national origin of birth. Despite the focus on American history, the basic orientation is that of multiculture and world-mindedness. In general, item selection was based upon traditional events and known personalities, but with a generous input of lesser-known individuals and events—those items which were considered to blend, as well as supplement, the conventional curriculum.

The information contained in each entry was considered to be accurate by virtue of its having appeared in at least two sources. However, when numerous resources were consulted, discrepancies of a day or so were often found. This factor, of course, can and should be a basis of learning for students, in that a number of reasons contribute to disparities that appear in records, such as differential time zones, human error, and so on. If and when discrete differences in dates are discovered, students should be encouraged to research in a number of sources to determine the date which is, based upon frequency, the most appropriate. In general, nearly all information in the book was documented in a major reference work, as listed in Appendix E, and then confirmed by another source. All of the citations appearing in the Reference Sources in Appendix E have been carefully reviewed; most, if not all, are readily available and well suited to preadolescent and adolescent students.

The intended readership includes teachers, librarians, and media specialists, along with recreation personnel, other community youth leaders, and "trivia buffs." Depending upon the individual using the book, the volume can function as a reference tool in nearly any setting or as a manual for the contract approach in the schools, as suggested in the final section (Sample Packet—Student Folders) of the book. *On This Day* can also serve as a catalyst for stimulating theme ideas for various programs and parties in schools, libraries, hospitals, campgrounds, club meetings, and family settings. The book is written to accommodate young people with various interests, needs, and levels of learning and ability. The intent, once again, is to encourage a broad range of students to investigate information from a wide world of sources—both print and nonprint media, people, and agencies. Although the activities are centered in the upper elementary and junior high level, the expectation is that they will be used flexibly for adaptation to all age levels.

On This Day was primarily conceived as an instructional tool for teachers and school librarians, complete with an organized contract-based arrangement in part 5, the Sample Packet—Student Folders Section. However, the book can be effectively used as a reference or resource text that can simply be referred to weekly, monthly ... or every day. The activities which are listed in the book are not necessarily intended as total class projects; rather, the book may serve as a source of ideas for small group or individual work. Therefore, in selecting the events to be observed each month, it is recommended that certain students with particular interests be considered; such individual attention may well pique a student's interest in school. Also, as students' birthdays are observed throughout the year, the citing of events on the day of their birth may well add historical significance to the celebration of their special day. Regardless of how the book is used, students should be encouraged to supplement and update the contents with their own entries—information which they have gleaned from their learning activities or from current events that occur throughout the year. Additionally, in following the suggested activities of the book, caution must be taken to assure the safety of all participants, such as being aware that the nature of certain activities may not be suitable for all youngsters in every setting.

On This Day will be most effectively used if a particular month's events and activities are examined beforehand. The leader, or a group of students, can select those events considered appropriate to the particular group. An Events Center can be organized. A large monthly calendar, highlighting important historical events of the month, might be posted within the center. A wide variety of reference books, such as various almanacs, a set of encyclopedias, and related audiovisual resources could be made accessible in the center for in-depth investigation of the month's events. And, as various *On This Day*-related projects and creative efforts are completed throughout the month, they, too, can be featured in or around the Events Center.

Ideally, the Events Center would be the opening focus for the school day, following the morning's routine procedures. Committees could assume responsibility for presenting a short version of the "You Are There" format. Or, a radio spot-broadcast could be taped beforehand, as follows:*

---

*Encourage students to design their own format for announcements.

This is Radio K-I-D-S   1110 on your radio dial.*

Today is Monday, January 4, 1982. Today marks history for the following events:

- Sir Isaac Pitman, born 1813
- Jacob Grimm, born 1785
- Louis Braille, born 1809
- Utah admitted to the USA as the forty-fifth state, 1896
- Ralph Bunche became the first black appointed as an official of the U.S. State Department

See the Events Center for activities for this day. And be ready at 10:30 a.m. for our guest speaker from the Braille Institute.

This is <u>(student's name)</u> on K-I-D-S News, on location in <u>(room #)</u> <u>(name of school and city)</u>.

In whatever way readers choose to use the book, it is hoped that its contents will prove to be both enlightening and fun. Information may be copied for classroom use. *On This Day* is meant as one more teaching aid to help young people discover, or rediscover, the joy of learning.

---

*"K" is a West Coast radio transmitting call-letter; the choice of station number can be made according to the age level of students, just as "1110" in the above example is intended to refer to 11- and 10-year-old students.

P A R T   1

EVENTS AND ACTIVITIES
SECTION

JANUARY

The Roman god, Janus, allegedly had two faces which allowed him to look both to the future and to the past. January was named after Janus because the month was thought to be an interim period between one season's end and another's beginning. (Because the ancient Roman year formerly began in March — until 46 B.C. — January was not originally the first month of the year.)

Birthstone: Garnet
Flower: Carnation

Use the Find-a-Word Reproducible to preview happenings in January. (See Reproducible Section.)

MONTH-LONG OBSERVANCES

March of Dimes Month

Investigate and discuss the history of the March of Dimes; write to the March of Dimes National Foundation. (See Address Listing in Extra-Know-How Section.)

Contact a local chapter office of the March of Dimes Foundation concerning the possibility of getting a speaker or film for class.

Research the disease poliomyelitis; investigate how Jonas Salk's antipolio serum and Albert Sabin's polio vaccine have significantly lessened the danger of the disease.

(See activities under September 20, "Sister Elizabeth ....")

Guitar Month

Use Reproducible #1 to study the diagram for parts of a guitar.

Invite a class member or resource person to play the guitar. (See Resource Person Data in Extra-Know-How Section.)

Explore the history of the guitar, as related to other string instruments.

Look through catalogs for pictures of guitars; discuss different types of guitar-like instruments.

Obtain recordings of various types of guitar music — classical, folk, jazz, rock.

National Blood Donor Month

Discuss the value of blood donations.

Introduce a study of the circulatory system; include Dr. William Harvey's historic discovery in 1628 of the direction of blood flow in arteries and veins.

Write to the American Association of Blood Banks for further information. (See Address Listing in Extra-Know-How Section.)

Trace the derivation of the word, "polymorphonuclearleukocyte" (multishaped nucleus within a white blood cell).

(See activities under February Month-long Observances, "Heart Month" and March 15, "First blood ... " and April 1, "William Harvey ... " and April 8, "Harvey Cushing ....")

National Egg Month

Investigate the nutritional value of eggs; discuss the effect of eggs' cholesterol content on the human body; compare egg substitutes with the egg.

Trace the tradition of egg decorating in various countries.

Find out why decorated eggs are significant in the celebration of Easter.

Determine how to identify a hard-boiled egg from an uncooked egg, without cracking the shell.

Exchange various recipes containing eggs.

Experiment with eggshell mosaics for an art project.

Write to the Poultry and Egg National Board for information. (See Address Listing in Extra-Know-How Section.)

Examine an egg and consider various alternative uses of the egg.

SPECIAL WEEKS

National Ski Week (second Friday)

Invite a local ski-shop merchant or ski enthusiast to talk with the class.

Investigate the development of skiing.

(See Data-Detail in Extra-Know-How Section, "Skis — History.")

Make a ski-related diorama.

Nurses' Week (second week)

Invite the school nurse to talk about nursing as a career for both men and women; explore the various specialities, such as pediatric nursing, psychiatric nursing, etc. Also ask the visitor to speak about nutrition and food preparation as related to the prevention of certain diseases such as botulism.

Discuss the profession of nursing as one which is parallel, as opposed to subordinate, to that of physicians.

Investigate the various roles of nurses as separate from a health-care facility (private nurse, industrial nurse, school nurse).

International Printing Week (includes January 17)

Use filmstrips, films, or books to investigate the history of the printing press.

Break into small groups in order to make lists of all the ways in which printing is used, i.e., food packaging, posters, advertisements, greeting cards.

Use Task Card #1 to enrich students' printing-related vocabulary.

Discuss how books are printed and bound.

Examine the parts and process of a duplicating machine.

Obtain a miniature printing press or rubber stamp set to be used at a learning center on printing.

Set up a learning center for students to make their own letter-stencil kits. (Suggested materials: tagboard, scissors, pencils, master set of letters).

Use Task Card #2 to do a vegetable printing art lesson.

Conduct an art lesson in which students can design book covers.

Consider the impact the printing press had upon the dissemination of knowledge. Write to the Library of Congress for the leaflet "The Gutenberg Bible." (See Address Listing in Extra-Know-How Section.)

Write to Hunt Manufacturing Co. for the booklet "Lettering and Print Making Kit," and/or write to Carter's Ink Co. for the booklet "Lettering with a Felt Tip Marker." (See Address Listing in Extra-Know-How Section.)

(See activities under May 11, "Ottmar Mergenthaler ....")

YMCA Week (Sunday of last full week of the month)

Write to the National Council of YMCA. (See Address Listing in Extra-Know-How Section.)

Contact the local YMCA regarding its scheduled activities.

VARIABLE DATES

Chinese New Year (January or February)

Investigate the Asian calendar.

Find out how the Chinese typically celebrate the holiday.

Read *Twelve Years, Twelve Animals*, by Yoshiko Samuel, to understand the Asian custom of assigning animal names to years; also enjoy *Mei-L'ei*, by Thomas Handforth.

Collegiate and professional football bowl games (New Year's Day to mid-month)

DAYS OF THE MONTH

January 1

New Year's Day

Paul Revere, American Revolutionary patriot, born 1735
(See Biography Data in Extra-Know-How Section.)
Obtain a copy of Longfellow's poem "The Midnight Ride of Paul Revere" and share it with the class.
Write to Revere Copper and Brass, Inc. for information on Paul Revere. (See Address Listing in Extra-Know-How Section.)

First fire insurance issued, 1735
Discuss the purpose of carrying insurance policies.
Investigate the terms: premium, deductible, policy, coverage, annuity.

Betsy Ross, American flagmaker, born 1752
(See Biography Data in Extra-Know-How Section.)
Discuss the fact that Betsy Ross is now generally discredited as the first national flagmaker.
Use Task Card #3 to learn more about the background of the American flag.

Official U.S. flag raised for the first time, 1776
Discuss flag-protocol: how flags are displayed, raised, lowered, and folded.
Write to John Hancock Mutual Life Insurance Co. for the booklet "Flags of the U.S.A." (See Address Listing in Extra-Know-How Section.)
Write to Snibbe Publications, Inc. for the booklet "Old Glory." Cost $1.00. (See Address Listing in Extra-Know-How Section.)
(See Data-Detail in Extra-Know-How Section, "U.S. Flag and Flag Day—History.")

Reformatory for juvenile delinquents established, 1825
Discuss practices of rehabilitation versus punitive measures.
Investigate various "training before trouble" programs in the juvenile justice system.

First American fire engine operated, 1853
Encourage students to obtain pictures of old-time fire engines; compare and contrast the old vehicles with modern ones.
Invite students to design an "ideal" fire engine.

First U.S. income tax law enacted, 1862
Discuss the purpose of income tax; make a list of other types of revenue—sales tax, gasoline tax, property tax.
Investigate the terms: tax shelter, tax-deductible, dependent, tax write-off.
Find out which levels of government (local, county, state, federal) are responsible for collecting which taxes.

Emancipation Proclamation issued by Abraham Lincoln, 1863
Discuss the dynamics of freedom-without-preparation-for-freedom as related to post-Civil War America.
Write to Giant Photos, Inc. for a reproduction of the Emancipation Proclamation. (See Address Listing in Extra-Know-How Section.)

U.S. Parcel Post Service begun, 1913
Set up a learning center on "How to Wrap a Package." Provide supplies such as boxes, paper, tape, and string.
Interview a parcel post truck driver in order to learn about the work as a potential job.

First air-conditioned office building opened, 1928
Investigate the principles of air-conditioning.
Discuss how air-conditioning and other environmental influences affect employee productivity.
Brainstorm ideas for energy sources for air-cooling systems.

Newspaper issues first put onto microfilm by newspaper industry, 1936
Visit the local library in order to view newspapers or other data on microfilm.

First uniform system of birth certificate registration created in the U.S., 1949
Invite students to find their own birth certificates and examine them.

January 2

Save the Pun Day
Investigate what a pun is; find samples of puns.
Invite students to write original puns.

U.S. Constitution ratified by Georgia, thus making it the fourth state, 1788
(See States Admitted to the USA Data in Extra-Know-How Section.)

First junior high school opened in the United States, 1910
Interview a person who is a junior high school student, teacher, or administrator.
Discuss the differences among elementary, junior high, middle, and senior high schools. Contrast American school levels with those in various other countries.

Isaac Asimov, Russian-American science fiction writer/scientist, born 1920
(See Biography Data in Extra-Know-How Section.)
Discuss the meaning of the term: Sci-Fi.
Explain that Asimov is both a scientist and a writer; read one of Asimov's science fiction stories.

January 3

First patent for oleomargarine issued, 1871
Use Task Card #4 to learn how to make butter and to contrast it to oleomargarine.

Artificial drinking straws patented, 1888
Investigate the development of straws.
Conduct a straw art lesson; place a small amount of colored, thinly mixed tempera paint on one-half of a folded sheet of paper. With a straw, blow the paint around the half-a-sheet space; then fold the sheet together to create a mirror design.

John R. R. Tolkien, English author and scholar, born 1892
(See Biography Data in Extra-Know-How Section.)
Read *The Hobbit* to enjoy the fantasy characters created by Tolkien.

March of Dimes Campaign established, 1938
(See activities under January Month-long Observances, "March of Dimes Month.")

Bobby Hull, Canadian ice hockey player, born 1939
(See Biography Data in Extra-Know-How Section.)
Study hockey rules; write to Cosom (Div. of I.T.T. Thermotech) for the booklet "Safe-T-Play Hockey Rule Book." (See Address Listing in Extra-Know-How Section.)
Invite a hockey player to come to class to share further information about the game of hockey.
Use Task Card #5 for activities related to hockey.

Alaska admitted to the United States as the forty-ninth state, 1959
(See States Admitted to the USA Data in Extra-Know-How Section.)
(See activities under March 30, "Alaska purchased ... " and September 10, "Alaska awarded.")

January 4

Jacob Grimm, German philologist, born 1785
(See Biography Data in Extra-Know-How Section.)
Read and enjoy Grimm's Fairy Tales.
Discuss the meaning of "philologist."
(See activities under February 24, "Wilhelm Karl ....")

Louis Braille, French inventor of printing and writing system for the blind, born 1809
(See Biography Data in Extra-Know-How Section.)
Contact the local Braille Institute for information.
Invite a blind person (or a hard-of-seeing person) or a person who types Braille to come to class.

Write to the American Foundation for the Blind for the two booklets "Louis Braille" and "Understanding Braille." (See Address Listing in Extra-Know-How Section.)

Obtain some form of Braille script from the local Braille Institute or from the local library.

Introduce the book *Follow My Leader*, by James Garfield, concerning seeing-eye dogs.

Use Task Card #6 to aid class members in taking a "blind walk."

Read the book *To Catch an Angel*, by Robert W. Russell.

Contact a local chapter of Lion's Club, International; invite a representative to talk about the organization's projects for the blind.

Read the book *Louis Braille: The Boy Who Invented Books for the Blind*, by Margaret Davidson; find out how Braille became blind at the age of 3 and then later developed the Braille system, a method based upon a night writing system used by the French soldiers at that time.

Discuss various innovative technical instruments that are being marketed, i.e., an electronic sensory transmitter which detects high-frequency sounds designed to be received by the ears of hard-of-seeing or blind individuals to guide them; brainstorm other similar ideas.

Organize an aluminum/tin can or newspaper drive to collect money; with the proceeds, consider donating a group gift of a Braille book for a blind child (approximately $10 through the local Braille Institute). Encourage students to think further about the satisfaction of giving; suggest to students at their next birthday or gift-giving time to request a Braille book certificate to give, in turn, to a blind child through the Braille Institute.

Sir Isaac Pitman, English creator of a shorthand system (based on phonetic rather than orthographic principles), born 1813

(See Biography Data in Extra-Know-How Section.)

Note the variety of shorthand methods.

Invite the school secretary to the classroom to demonstrate one method of shorthand.

(See activities under June 17, "Robert Gregg ....")

First appendectomy performed, 1885

Survey the class as to how many students have had appendectomies.

Conduct a discussion concerning the appendix and other parts of the body which are not needed for a functioning body.

Familiarize students with the suffixes: itis (inflamation) and ectomy (cutting out).

Utah admitted to the United States as the forty-fifth state, 1896

(See States Admitted to the USA Data in Extra-Know-How Section.)

Ralph Bunche became the first black appointed as an official of the U.S. State Department, 1944

Trace the accomplishments of Ralph Bunche to learn why he was awarded the Nobel Prize.

January 5

George Washington Carver Day (honors the American black scientist on the anniversary of his death in 1943)

Investigate the life of Geroge Washington Carver.

Use Task Card #7 to learn how to make peanut butter.

Read the book *A Word Is a Flower: The Life of George Washington Carver*, by Alik.

King Camp Gillette, inventor of the modern razor, born 1855

(See Biography Data in Extra-Know-How Section.)

Obtain pictures of all U.S. presidents; find out how many of the presidents wore beards.

Hold a "Draw a Beard" contest.

(See activities under March 18, "Electric dry ....")

Nellie Tayloe Ross took the oath of office as the first female governor in the United States (Wyoming), 1925

Investigate the circumstances in which Ross became governor.

Find out what U.S. government position she later held.

January 6

Joan of Arc, French saint and national heroine, born 1412

(See Biography Data in Extra-Know-How Section.)

Define the term: canonization; find out what is involved for one to become canonized.

Haym Solomon, American Jewish patriot, died 1785

Explain that Solomon petitioned the Board of Censors to do away with the religious oath required of public servants; discuss the implications involved in the situation.

Investigate Solomon's contribution to the American Revolution.

Carl Sandburg, American poet and biographer of Abraham Lincoln, born 1878

(See Biography Data in Extra-Know-How Section.)

Explain that Sandburg was the recipient of two Pulitzer awards; find others who have been honored with this award.

Obtain the recording of Carl Sandburg reading his own work, "Poems for Children."

Enjoy reading a copy of Sandburg's *Rootabaga Stories*; encourage students to break into small groups to analyze the meaning of a particular poem; tape record a reading for the whole class.

New Mexico admitted to the United States as the forty-seventh state, 1912

(See States Admitted to the USA Data in Extra-Know-How Section.)

The "Four Freedoms" speech delivered by Franklin Delano Roosevelt, 1941

Invite a student to obtain a copy of the speech, dress up as FDR, and deliver the speech.

Discuss the speech and its relevance today (freedom from want, from fear, of religion, and of speech and expression).

January 7

First commercial bank opened (Philadelphia), 1782

Invite a representative from a local commercial bank to the classroom to explain various bank books (checkbooks, deposit slips), banking procedures, and the terms: principal and interest.

Use Reproducibles #2 and #3 to learn how to write a check.

Arrange a classroom model banking system.

Introduce vocabulary words such as deposits, withdrawals, accounts.

Take a field trip to a bank.

Use Task Card #8 for bank activities.

(See activities under March 6, "National Bank ....")

First American presidential election held, 1789

Trace the development of presidential elections, i.e., how ballots were originally gathered, how the electoral college began, what the purpose of primary elections is.

Millard Fillmore, thirteenth president of the United States, born 1800

(See Biography Data in Extra-Know-How Section.)

Find out the background of the Compromise of 1850 which was passed during Fillmore's administration.

Panama Canal, "the path between the seas," opened to traffic, 1914

Discuss the challenge of uniting different levels of water—inland lakes and rivers with sea-level water; trace the problems of yellow fever and the medical triumph of Walter Reed and William Gorgas.

Use Task Card #9 to create a mini-canal lock from milk cartons.

Write to Panama Canal Information Office for the booklet "The Panama Canal and the Canal Zone." (See Address Listing in Extra-Know-How Section.)

Discuss the significance of the treaty which transferred control of the canal from the United States to Panama.

January 8

World Literacy Day

Obtain copies of children's literature from other countries, written in English or in the native languages, and related alphabets.

Discuss the words: literate, illiterate, functional literacy.

Refer to an almanac to find literacy rates throughout the world; compare and contrast the rates of industrially developed nations with those of industrially developing nations. Make a graph of the findings.

Eleventh Amendment to the U.S. Constitution ratified, 1918
(See Data-Detail in Extra-Know-How Section, "Amendments to the U.S. Constitution.")

Bobby Fisher, won the U.S. chess championship for the first time at the age of 14, 1958
Use Reproducible #4 for "Chess Test."
Learn how to play chess; *The Programmed Methods for Learning to Play Chess*, by M. W. Sullivan, is a recommended resource.
Investigate the history of the game of chess.
Hold a class chess tournament; invite senior citizens to participate.
Ask students to design their own chess pieces.
Visit convalescent homes and suggest playing a game of chess.
Trace Fisher's record of achievement in both U.S. and international competition.

January 9

U.S. Constitution ratified by Connecticut, thus making it the fifth state, 1788
(See States Admitted to the USA Data in Extra-Know-How Section.)

First U.S. balloon flight launched by Blanchard Jean Pierre, 1793
Investigate the dynamics of balloon flight.

Carrie Lane Chapman, American suffrage-reformer, born 1859
(See Biography Data in Extra-Know-How Section.)

Richard M. Nixon, thirty-seventh president of the United States, born 1913
(See Biography Data in Extra-Know-How Section.)
Review Nixon's presidency and the events surrounding his resignation.
(See activities under August 8, "First U.S. President ....")

Har Gobird Khorana, American-Pakistani biochemist, born 1922
(See Biography Data in Extra-Know-How Section.)
Explain that biochemistry is a science dealing with the life processes of plants and animals. Find out the function of enzymes; discuss the area of chemical imbalances and their effects on the human body.
Invite a biochemist to class to learn more about the training of a biochemist.

Countee Cullen, American poet, died 1940
Investigate biographical information about Countee Cullen.
Use Task Card #10 to become familiar with the style of his poetry.

Joan Baez, American folksinger, born 1941
(See Biography Data in Extra-Know-How Section.)
Obtain a book of her songs; analyze the meaning of the words of her music.
Enjoy listening to various recordings of her music.

U.N. Headquarters opened in New York City, 1951
Use Reproducible #5 to study the countries of the United Nations.
Ask students to make flags of the United Nations.
Explore the history and functions of the United Nations.
Show a film or filmstrip of the United Nations.
Write to the United Nations for information and literature. (See Address Listing in Extra-Know-How Section.)
Investigate the requirements for becoming a guide or an interpreter in the United Nations building.
Stage a mock-meeting of the U.N. Security Council or General Assembly.
Write to UNESCO for the publication "Educational Toys and Games." (See Address Listing in Extra-Know-How Section.)
(See activities under October 24, "United Nations ....")

January 10

Ethan Allen, hero of the American Revolution, born 1738
(See Biography Data in Extra-Know-How Section.)
Trace the background of the Green Mountain Boys, of which Allen was the leader.

Common Sense, a pamphlet setting forth arguments for American independence from England, published by Thomas Paine, 1776
Discuss the courage involved in publicly declaring one's political values through written publication.
(See activities under January 29, "Thomas Paine ....")

Standard Oil Company incorporated by John D. Rockefeller, 1870
Explore the development of large corporations in the late nineteenth century which led to the Sherman Antitrust Act of 1890 and the Clayton Antitrust Act of 1914.
Search through magazines for products that use oil or are derived from petroleum products.
Compare and contrast off-shore platform drilling and on-shore rig-drilling processes and equipment.
Discuss oil: 1) as an international commodity of energy and 2) as an ecological issue.
Investigate the newspaper for the price of shares in oil stock.
Invite a petroleum engineer or geologist to discuss oil drilling and careers in the field of petroleum engineering; inquire about the jargon used in the field.
Find out the purposes of a drilling rig or derrick; find out also the reasons for constructing a well head in the completion of a well.
Encourage students to draw a subsurface contour map and a subsurface cross-section of an oil and gas field.

League of Nations formed in Geneva, Switzerland, 1920
Investigate what the Fourteen Points were in President Woodrow Wilson's proposal.

Edward Brooke sworn in as the first popularly elected black U.S. senator, 1968
Investigate the qualifications required to become a U.S. senator and other data concerning the position.

Last issue of *The Saturday Evening Post* published, 1969
Discuss the duration of the magazine's publication (1822-1969).
Create a class magazine, or do a mock version of *The Saturday Evening Post.*

January 11

Alexander Hamilton, American statesman, born 1757
(See Biography Data in Extra-Know-How Section.)

Rhubarb first shipped from London to the United States, 1761
Pass out pieces of rhubarb and eat as a carrot stick.
Use Task Card #11 to make Strawberry-Rhubarb Sauce.

St. John A. MacDonald, first Canadian prime minister, born 1815
(See Biography Data in Extra-Know-How Section.)
Investigate the official titles and roles of the main leadership positions in Canada's national government; find out other information about Canada, such as its major products, cities, languages, and provinces.

Milk sold in bottled containers for the first time, 1878
Use Task Card #12 concerning a study of dairy processing.

Report that cigarette smoking is hazardous to health submitted by the U.S. Surgeon General, 1969. (Note: first recorded use of tobacco for smoking purposes is November 15, 1492.)
Invite a physician to discuss the health hazards involved in smoking.
Conduct a study concerning a family member or friend who smokes, in terms of the financial cost of smoking each year.
Introduce a role-play to discourage peer pressure toward smoking.
Write to the Center for Disease Control for the pamphlet "Chart Book on Smoking, Tobacco, and Health." (See Address Listing in Extra-Know-How Section).
(See activities under March Variable Dates, "National Stop ....")

January 12

Charles Perrault, French writer, born 1628
(See Biography Data in Extra-Know-How Section.)
Explain that Charles Perrault and his son are credited with having first written down the Mother Goose tales that had formerly only been passed on by word of mouth; enjoy reading all types of folklore and fairy tales.
Discuss the differences between oral tradition and written data.

John Hancock, American Revolutionary patriot, born 1737
(See Biography Data in Extra-Know-How Section.)
Discuss the size and general visibility of Hancock's signature on the Declaration of Independence and how one's "John Hancock" has come to be synonymous with one's signature.
Invite students to practice writing their own signatures in different styles.
Obtain a book on graphoanalysis and discuss handwriting analysis.

Johann Pestalozzi, Swiss educational reformer, born 1746
(See Biography Data in Extra-Know-How Section.)

First United States public museum established, 1773
List and design exhibits for a museum of the future, based upon classroom and household items which may later be obsolete, such as a manual pencil sharpener, chalkboard erasers.
Discuss the purposes and costs of maintaining museums; stage a debate on the topic: "Museums are a worthwhile public expenditure."
(See activities under March 17, "National Gallery ... " and April 13, "New York's ... " and November 8, "Louvre, the ....")

Frank Gerber, American manufacturer and founder of the firm, Gerber Products Co., born 1873
(See Biography Data in Extra-Know-How Section.)
(See activities under April Special Weeks, "National Baby ....")

Jack London, American adventure writer, born 1876
(See Biography Data in Extra-Know-How Section.)
Obtain a copy of *The Call of the Wild* and share it with the class.
Create book jackets which would be appropriate for London's books.

First X-ray produced, 1896
Obtain X-rays from a physician, hospital technician, or dentist.
Investigate the careers of an X-ray technician and of a radiologist and roentgenologist by inviting such medical personnel to class.
Draw a facsimile of an X-ray by rubbing white chalk on black paper.
(See activities under March 27, "William Roentgen ....")

James Farmer, U.S. civil rights leader, born 1920
(See Biography Data in Extra-Know-How Section.)

First woman U.S. senator, Hattie Caraway, elected 1932
Find out which state Hattie Caraway represented.
Investigate the qualifications required to become a U.S. senator, as well as other data about the position.

Brinks Robbery solved, 1956
Investigate the robbery incident and portray it by means of a puppet show, a role-play, or other medium of expression.

January 13

Stephen Foster Memorial Day
Investigate the life of Stephen Foster.
Introduce several of Foster's songs to the class.
Explain that the first publisher of his music printed his name wrong; ask students to consider what feelings Foster may have had about this.
Discuss what a minstrel show was; create new sets of lyrics which would be more contemporarily appropriate.

Write to the Stephen Foster Memorial for the short biography "Stephen Collins Foster." (See Address Listing in Extra-Know-How Section.)
(See activities under July 4, "Stephen Foster ....")

Horatio Alger, American writer of boys' stories which depict success against great odds, born 1834
(See Biography Data in Extra-Know-How Section.)

Accordion music instrument patented, 1854
Invite a music teacher or student who plays the accordion to demonstrate the instrument.
Obtain a recording of accordion music for folk dance or square dancing; enjoy learning a new dance together.
Present an accordion-fold paper project.

Alfred C. Fuller, founder of the Fuller Brush Company, born 1885
(See Biography Data in Extra-Know-How Section.)
Explain that Fuller is credited with having started the first mass-market door-to-door selling; discuss the pros and cons of door-to-door sales.

J'accuse, Emile Zola's classic defense of the Dreyfus Affair published in Paris, 1898
(See Data-Detail in Extra-Know-How Section, "The Dreyfus Affair.")
Explain the case of Alfred Dreyfus and discuss the factor of unjust accusations; relate these dynamics to playground and classroom incidents.
Discuss the fact that many books have historically served to affect and effect social change.

Robert C. Weaver, first black cabinet member, appointed, 1966
Investigate the various cabinet positions in the federal government.
Find out more specifically how the president of the United States determines cabinet appointments.

January 14

Benedict Arnold, American Revolutionary general and traitor, born 1741
(See Biography Data in Extra-Know-How Section.)
Use Task Card #13 to extend concepts concerning traitors.

First Caesarian operation or section performed successfully in a hospital (erroneously assumed to be named for Julius Caesar who allegedly was born by this method), 1794

Albert Schweitzer, Alsatian humanitarian and missionary/physician to Africa, born 1875
(See Biography Data in Extra-Know-How Section.)
Discuss the terms: humanitarian, missionary-physician.
Determine where the Alsace part of western Europe is and then locate it on a globe or map.

Assembly-line production inaugurated in America by Henry Ford, 1914
Organize an assembly-line project, using a number of students to complete the work (sorting, collating, stapling, stacking papers).
Discuss the factor of boredom that often accompanies assembly-line jobs and what effect this factor has upon workers.

Pentagon building completed, 1943
Ask students to write the Pentagon to obtain information concerning the architecture of the building. (See Address Listing in Extra-Know-How Section.)

January 15

First screw-clamp skate patented, 1866
Discuss the changes in skates to their present form as shoe-skates.
Invite students to bring in their skates and do tricks on their skates.
Visit a roller-skating rink.

"Donkey" emblem of the Democratic Party first published, 1879
Investigate the background of the symbol.
Draw the Democratic Party symbol.

Suggest that students design another symbol they believe would be appropriate for the Democratic Party.
(See activities under September 27, "Thomas Nast ....")

First dental gold inlay described, 1907
(See activities under February Special Weeks, "National Children's ....")

Edward Teller, Hungarian-American scientist, born 1908
(See Biography Data in Extra-Know-How Section.)

Martin Luther King, Jr., U.S. civil rights leader and recipient of the Nobel Peace Prize, born 1929
(See Biography Data in Extra-Know-How Section.)
Encourage students to write an "I Have a Dream" essay, based on King's speech, involving themselves or a social cause.
(See activities under April 4, "Rev. Dr. ....")

First solar-heated, radiation-cooled house built, 1955
Discuss solar heating/energy and architectural innovations which allow for the use of solar heat and light.
Investigate other uses of solar energy, such as the sun-powered *Challenger* which flew over the English Channel—a flight of 230 miles; find out the speed at which the plane flew, as well as other details about how the plane operated on sun-generated electricity.

January 16

World Religion Day
Make a chart with the class concerning the different religions and religious sects of the world in order to appreciate the extent of varying beliefs in the world; with the use of a map or globe, attempt to locate the geographical origin of each belief system.

U.S. Civil Service established, 1883
Investigate the history of the civil service.
Invite a civil service employee to visit the class to explain the Civil Service Examination and what particular job opportunities are available through the civil service.

Dizzy Dean, American baseball player, born 1911
(See Biography Data in Extra-Know-How Section.)
Discuss how nicknames (such as "Dizzy") originate.
Develop a class list of professional personalities known by their nicknames.

January 17

Benjamin Franklin, American statesman, printer, scientist, and writer, born 1706
(See Biography Data in Extra-Know-how Section.)
Make a class list of Franklin's inventions.
Introduce the book *Ben and Me*, by Robert Lawson.
Obtain a copy of *Poor Richard's Almanac* and enjoy reading the sayings, i.e., "The things which hurt instruct"; "'Tis easier to prevent bad habits than to break them."

Automatic film developing machine patented, 1928
Invite a camera enthusiast or a local merchant from a camera shop to discuss film with the class; ask the quest to bring samples of different size films (16mm, 35mm, etc.); encourage the students to examine the film to speculate on the use of the sprocket holes.
Use Task Card #14 to learn how to make a movie without a camera.
(See activities under September 4, "First roll-film ....")

U.S. Navy submarine *Nautilus* launched, 1955.
Investigate the dynamics of what keeps a submarine submerged and how a submarine operates.
Discuss a few aspects of living in a submarine for a long period of time.
Find out the meaning of the prefix "sub"; make a class list of other words with "sub," in which the three letters reflect the same meaning as they do in the word "submarine."

Write a group creative story about a submarine adventure.

Explore various aspects of the Trident submarine program—the "Supersubs" designed to replace the Polaris and Poseidon submarines.

January 18

Peter Roget, English lexicographer, born 1779
(See Biography Data in Extra-Know-How Section.)
Find out the background of the word "lexicographer."
Use Reproducible #6 in order to learn about a thesaurus.

Daniel Webster, American statesman, attorney and orator, born 1782
(See Biography Data in Extra-Know-How Section.)
Expose students to the word "orator"; encourage students to present a speech or participate in a debate.

A. A. Milne, British writer of children's books, born 1882
(See Biography Data in Extra-Know-How Section.)
Explain that Milne wrote books for and about his son, Christopher Robin, and about his son's stuffed animals; enjoy *The House at Pooh Corner* and other selections.

Danny Kaye, American performer, born 1913
(See Biography Data in Extra-Know-How Section.)

Formulation of a peace treaty begun by world leaders at Versailles, following the end of the First World War, 1919
Investigate who the "Big Four" were in the negotiations.
Locate the city of Versailles on a globe or map and identify which country it is in.
Trace the background of the famous palace of Versailles.

Muhammad Ali (Cassius Clay), American boxer, born 1942
(See Biography Data in Extra-Know-How Section.)
Examine the rules and history of boxing.
Find out what types of officials are present at most boxing matches; name at least five pieces of boxing equipment; investigate the meaning of boxing-related abbreviations, such as ABA, WBC.
(See activities under March 8, "Muhammad Ali ....")

January 19

James Watt, Scottish inventor of a particular type of steam engine, born 1736
(See Biography Data in Extra-Know-How Section.)
Explain that a unit of energy, the watt, was named after James Watt; investigate further what is meant by the terms: watt, kilowatt, kilowatt hour.

Robert E. Lee Day (established for the birth date of the Confederate general in the American Civil War, born 1807)
(See Biography Data in Extra-Know-How Section.)

Edgar Allan Poe, American writer, born 1809
(See Biography Data in Extra-Know-How Section.)
Read aloud, with suspense, *The Pit and the Pendulum*.
Listen to a reading of "The Raven" and draw scenes which might be inferred from the description.

Process for the tin-canning of food patented, 1825
Collect different cans; make a comparison-study of differences in size, shapes, labels, etc.
Create a unique label for a real or an imagined canned food.

Paul Cézanne, French painter, born 1839
(See Biography Data in Extra-Know-How Section.)
Examine prints of Cézanne's art work; notice the artist's use of vivid color and his skill in creating depth through shadows and outlines; invite students to create either a landscape or still-life painting.

January 20

U.S. Presidential Inauguration Day (since 1937)
Find out the meaning of the word "inauguration."
Hold a simulated inauguration ceremony for a class officer.

Red Jacket (Otetiani or Sagoyewatha), American Indian, died 1830
(See Biography Data in Extra-Know-How Section.)

First U.S. basketball game played, 1892
(See Data-Detail in Extra-Know-How Section, "Basketball—History.")
Invite another class to play a game of basketball; stress sportsmanship and basketball "etiquette."

U.S. Medicare Bill signed, 1966
Hold an open-ended discussion concerning the purposes of medical insurance; ask students to consider what a financial burden a catastrophic medical bill would be for most families.
Explore governmental medical services in other economically developed countries.
Explain that the term "medicare" is a neologism—a new word in the vocabulary of a language; invite students to originate various neologisms concerning care programs for school equipment, such as "Deskare."
(See activities under July 1, "Medicare put ....")

U.S. hostages freed by Iran after 444 days of captivity, 1981
Explain that several of the hostages reported that among the things they missed during their captivity were hearing the baseball scores and eating certain foods. Ask students to list things which they believe they would miss were they not able to have them.
Review the Israeli hostage episode at Entebbe, Uganda; compare this situation with that of Iran.
Discuss what the purpose is in holding people as hostages.
Try to imagine the hardships and the aftereffects that a hostage might experience; write a story in the first person, describing a fictional hostage environment and the personal feelings that may be evoked as a result of being held as a hostage.
Read *The Diary of Anne Frank* to learn why one might become a self-imposed prisoner.

January 21

First day of the zodiac period, Aquarius, the Water Carrier (through February 19)
(See Data-Detail in Extra-Know-How Section, "Notes on Astrology.")

Envelope-folding machine patented, 1853
Use Reproducible #7 to learn how to make an envelope.
Discuss the various types of envelopes, i.e., self-adhesive, self-addressed, window envelopes; ask students for suggestions for new and improved envelopes.

Kansas City saloon raided by Carrie Nation, 1901
Investigate the incident as related to Carrie Nation's views concerning temperance.

Law requiring automobile operator's licensing first effected, 1937
Find out more information—the "who, what, when, where, why"—provided by the law.
Obtain a driver's license and examine it in detail.
Investigate state requirements for obtaining an operator's license.

January 22

U Thant, former United Nations Secretary General, born 1909
(See Biography Data in Extra-Know-How Section.)
(See activities under January 9, "U.N. Headquarters ....")

Joseph Wambaugh, American author and police detective, born 1937
(See Biography Data in Extra-Know-How Section.)

Explain that Wambaugh was a member of a metropolitan city police department and subsequently wrote about his former experiences as a policeman; encourage students to write a detective story, using an actual case as the theme for the fictional story.

Invite a member of the local police detective squad to visit class to talk about a career in law enforcement.

January 23

First M.D. degree ever earned by a woman in the United States received by Elizabeth Blackwell, 1849
Investigate the qualifications required for becoming a medical doctor.
Design a "shingle" which could be hung outside a physician's office.
Make a class list of the various types of medical specialists there are.

Humphrey Bogart, American actor, born 1899
(See Biography Data in Extra-Know-How Section.)

Twenty-fourth Amendment to the U.S. Constitution ratified, 1964
(See Data-Detail in Extra-Know-How Section, "Amendments to the U.S. Constitution.")

January 24

Gold discovered in California, 1848
Use Task Card #15 to learn about panning for gold.
Write to the U.S. Department of Interior for the booklet "Gold." (See Address Listing in Extra-Know-How Section.)

"Eskimo Pie" patented, 1922
Enjoy "Eskimo Pies" together.
Collect the leftover popsicle sticks to do an original art project.

Maria Tallchief, American Indian ballerina, born 1925
(See Biography Data in Extra-Know-How Section.)

Jackie Robinson elected as the first black to the National Baseball Hall of Fame, 1973
Investigate this historic incident.
(See activities under April 10, "Jackie Robinson ....")

January 25

Robert Burns, Scottish poet, born 1759
(See Biography Data in Extra-Know-How Section.)
Introduce the song "Auld Lang Syne."
Discuss dialect writing; encourage interested students to create a poem with the dialect of their choice.
Talk about the meaning of Burns' words: "Oh wad some power the giftie gie us, to see oursel's as ithers see us!"

Dan Rice, American circus clown, born as Daniel McLaren, 1823
(See Biography Data in Extra-Know-How Section.)
Consider what the life of a professional clown might be; design and act out a clown routine.
Invite a make-up artist to class to discuss the tricks of the trade.
(See activities under August Special Weeks, "National Clown ....")

Felix Mendelssohn's wedding march first played publicly, 1858
Obtain a recording of the march and share with the class; decide whether this piece of music has traditionally served as the processional or the recessional at weddings.

First U.S. local community's water fluoridated, 1945
Discuss the process of fluoridation and the conflicting opinions concerning its use.

January 26

Australia Day (celebrated for the day that Sydney, Australia was founded, 1788)
On globe or map, locate "The Land Down Under."

Mary Mapes Dodge, American writer, born 1831
(See Biography Data in Extra-Know-How Section.)
Introduce the book *Hans Brinker and the Silver Skates.*

Michigan admitted to the United States as the twenty-sixth state, 1837
(See States Admitted to the USA Data in Extra-Know-How Section.)

First electrical dental drill patented, 1875
Invite students to share their feelings about their visits to dentists.
Consider the alternatives to professional help, as in other nations.

Douglas MacArthur, American World War II general, born 1880
(See Biography Data in Extra-Know-How Section.)

Eartha Kitt, American singer, born 1928
(See Biography Data in Extra-Know-How Section.)

Jules Feiffer, American political cartoonist, born 1929
(See Biography Data in Extra-Know-How Section.)
Find samples of Jules Feiffer cartoons and share with class.
Discuss the influence of political cartoons and other forms of social commentaries.

January 27

Wolfgang Mozart, Austrian composer, born 1756
(See Biography Data in Extra-Know-How Section.)
Explain the term "child prodigy" by virtue of Mozart's composing music for the harpsichord at the age of five and of his playing the violin, organ, and harpsichord as a small child before the empress of Austria.
Enjoy recordings of Mozart's music.

Lewis Carroll, English writer, born 1832
(See Biography Data in Extra-Know-How Section.)
Discuss the words: pseudonym, penname; find out Carroll's birth-given name.
Introduce *Alice in Wonderland.*

Samuel Gompers, American co-founder of what became the American Federation of Labor, born 1850
(See Biography Data in Extra-Know-How Section.)
Relate labor-management disputes by discussing conflicting interests at a school or family level.

Incandescent lamp patented by Thomas Edison, 1880
Investigate the parts of a light bulb.

First magnetic tape recorder created, 1948
Discuss the use of magnetic tapes and the many ways in which tape recorders have changed data-gathering/dissemination practices.
Examine various types of recorders, such as reel-to-reel, eight-track, cassette, and others.

Terramycin first dispensed, 1950
Discuss the word "antibiotic"; find other words with the prefix "anti" (against) or with the word unit "bio" (life). Consider why a type of medicine would be called "anti-life."
Make a class list of various other antibiotic medicines.

U.S. astronauts killed by fire in *Apollo* spaceship, 1967
Compare the degree of courage involved in being a twentieth-century astronaut to that of being a sixteenth-century sea explorer.

Trace the derivation of the word "astronaut."
Write a science fiction story.

January 28

First telephone switchboard put into operation, 1878
Discuss the job of a telephone or switchboard operator.
Investigate the school's telephone and intercom arrangement.
Take a field trip to a business office in which students are able to view a switchboard operator at work.

Arthur Rubinstein, Polish-American piano virtuoso, born 1887
(See Biography Data in Extra-Know-How Section.)

Jackson Pollack, American modern art painter, born 1912
(See Biography Data in Extra-Know-How Section.)
Share samples of Pollack's work. Investigate the techniques of Pollack's painting; invite students to try similar techniques.

U.S. Coast Guard founded by Congress, 1915
Invite a Coast Guard recruiter to visit the class to provide information about the Coast Guard as a career and its various services.

First American Jew appointed to the U.S. Supreme Court (Louis Brandeis), 1916
Find out the procedure by which one is appointed to serve on the Supreme Court.

First U.S. ski tow operated, 1934
Enjoy exchanging personal experiences about former trips on a ski tow.
Complete an unfinished story: "Jean was going up the ski tow and ...."

First photograph bounced off the moon, 1960
Use Task Card #16 to make a papier-mâché model of the moon.

Vietnam War ended after 11 years at war, 1973
Locate Vietnam on a map or globe; trace the history of Indochina.
Discuss the causes and effects of the Vietnam War.

January 29

Thomas Paine, American patriot/writer, born 1737
(See Biography Data in Extra-Know-How Section.)
Explain that the day was formerly celebrated in Paine's honor as "Common Sense Day" to encourage the use of good sense in appreciating and protecting the rights of all people.
Consider Paine's quote, "These are the times that try men's souls"; discuss "trying times" in terms of the revolutionary period and the present time.
(See activities under January 10, "Common Sense ....")

William McKinley, twenty-fifth president of the United States, born 1843
(See Biography Data in Extra-Know-How Section.)
(See activities under September 6, "President McKinley ....")

Kansas admitted to the United States as the thirty-fourth state, 1861
(See States Admitted to the USA Data in Extra-Know-How Section.)

Baseball's American League organized, 1900
List the teams currently in the American League.
Investigate and recreate emblems or insignia of each team in the American League.
Make an exhibit of baseball cards, featuring American League players, past and present.
Use Task Card #17 for information about score-keeping in baseball.
Use Reproducible #8 about baseball facts.
(See activities under February 2, "Baseball's National ....")

Eighteenth Amendment to the U.S. Constitution ratified, 1918

(See Data-Detail in Extra-Know-How Section, "Amendments to the U.S. Constitution.")

Investigate the history of prohibition, the subject of the amendment.

Discuss such topics as the possible places for people to have stored "moonshine" and what it would be like to have prohibition at the present time; talk also about moderation as opposed to abuse of privileges.

Find out the background of the term "speakeasy."

Ice-cream cone rolling machine patented, 1924

(See Data-Detail in Extra-Know-How Section, "Ice-Cream Cones—History.")

Explain that ice cream has been eaten since the first century in Rome, but that it did not appear in America until the late 1700s; enjoy the book *Peanuts, Popcorn, Ice Cream, Candy and Soda Pop and How They Began*, by Solveig P. Russell.

Enjoy ice-cream cones together.

Invite students to suggest and draw various new ideas for ice-cream cones—different shapes, flavors, and colors.

Use Task Card #18 for ice-cream recipes.

(See activities under July 23, "Ice-cream ....")

First baseball players elected to the National Baseball Hall of Fame, 1936

Write to the National Baseball Hall of Fame and Museum to: 1) inquire as to what qualifications are needed for election into the Hall of Fame; 2) request a membership roster. (See Address Listing in Extra-Know-How Section.)

January 30

Osceola, American Indian leader, died 1838

(See Biography Data in Extra-Know-How Section.)

Franklin Delano Roosevelt, thirty-second president of the United States, born 1882

(See Biography Data in Extra-Know-How Section.)

Discuss the significance of Roosevelt's unprecedented number of terms in presidential office; investigate the subsequent congressional action limiting the executive tenure to two terms in office (Twenty-second Amendment to the U.S. Constitution).

Investigate the various "alphabet soup" agencies of Roosevelt's New Deal program, such as WPA and others.

Explain that "FDR" refers to the same man as Franklin Delano Roosevelt; encourage students to think of how they might be known were they to become famous.

Discuss Roosevelt's statement, "The only thing we have to fear is fear itself." Suggest that students talk about fears that they may have in common.

Adolf Hitler appointed chancellor of Germany by Paul von Hindenburg, 1933

Investigate the life of Adolf Hitler and the background of the Nazi Party.

Find the meaning of such German words as: Der Führer, Reichstag, *Mein Kampf*, Reich.

"The Lone Ranger" first broadcast, 1933

Obtain a recording of the "William Tell Overture" from Rossini's opera to share with the class.

Discuss ways in which radio braodcast stations arrange for and produce sound effects.

Examine the term "Hi-yo, Silver"; consider other terms which radio and TV have made famous.

January 31

Franz Schubert, Austrian composer, born 1797

(See Biography Data in Extra-Know-How Section.)

Introduce Schubert's Symphony in B Minor ("The Unfinished Symphony") and other selections of his compositions.

Find out what German "Lieder" are and what connection Schubert had to this type of music.

Jackie Robinson, first black elected to the National Baseball Hall of Fame, born 1919

(See Biography Data in Extra-Know-How Section.)

(See activities under January 24, "Jackie Robinson ... " and April 10, "Jackie Robinson ....")

First U.S. satellite, *Explorer I,* **launched at Cape Canaveral (Cape Kennedy), Florida, 1958**
    Design satellites; make models from papier-mâché or styrofoam, and hang them. (Review Task Card #16 to find out how to work with papier-mâché.)

Santa Barbara oil spill in California occurred, 1969
    Draw individual panoramic pictures or a class mural of ocean scenery; then discuss the effect of an oil slick on such an area's sea life, as well as on other eco-system factors.

Total eclipse of the moon occurred, 1972
    Discuss the words: eclipse, solar, lunar, planetary bodies, heavenly bodies.
    Investigate the possibilities of predicting the occurrences of eclipses; find out the difference between a total eclipse and a partial eclipse.

FEBRUARY

The word, "February," has its origin in Februare, *a Latin word which means "to purify or cleanse." Because the Romans staged an animal purification ceremony at this time of the year, they chose a name which reflected this particular ritual.*

Birthstone: *Amethyst*
Flower: *Violet*

Use the Find-a-Word Reproducible to preview happenings in Feburary. (See Reproducible Section.)

MONTH-LONG OBSERVANCES

Heart Month

Obtain a model of a heart from within the school or from a nearby college; examine the model and discuss the physiology and the anatomy of the heart. Compare and contrast the traditional "heart shape" with the shape of the heart organ.

Invite a representative of the local American Heart Association to visit the class, or write the American Heart Association for information. (See Address Listing in Extra-Know-How Section.)

Ask students to campaign against America's No. 1 killer—cardiovascular disease—by making posters for exhibits in the local community.

Encourage students to obtain model building kits with body parts—available at major toy stores—in order to become more familiar with the total circulatory system.

Use Reproducible #9 to learn about the parts of the heart.

(See activities under January Month-long Observances, "National Blood ... " and March 15, "First blood ... " and April 1, "William Harvey ... " and December 3, "First successful ....")

American History Month

Make a timeline mural of American history.

Show a variety of American history films.

Invite the school or local librarian to share various fiction and nonfiction books which reflect the history of America; encourage interested students to research and cross-reference various data in order to challenge "misinformation" which has been perpetuated in various history books. Invite students to contact publishers about their documented findings regarding particular personalities or events.

Discuss what the responsibilities of a historian are; find out what "historiography" means.

Use Reproducibles #10 and #11 for a timeline project.

Look for notable Americans in Appendices A-D.

American Music Month

Invite students to make a timeline of musical history in America.

Make a class chart which lists different types of music, i.e., rock, rhythm and blues, classical.

Study different types of musical instruments through the use of pictures or actual instruments.

Encourage students to share music on instruments they have learned to play.

Use Task Card #19 to enjoy music further.

Use Reproducible #12 for games related to music.

SPECIAL WEEKS

National Children's Dental Week (first Sunday)

Write to the American Dental Association to obtain information. (See Address Listing in Extra-Know-How Section.)

Ask students to interview a dentist to discuss dental caries as a major health problem in America; find out why in some countries people do not suffer as many cavities as in America.

Hold a class discussion concerning feelings (apprehensions or otherwise) in regard to a visit to a dentist's office.

Investigate dentistry, past and present; consider dental health in terms of preventative dentistry.

Invite a dentist, dental hygienist, or dental technician to come and share information about the dental profession. Ask about various other specialists in the field of dental health.

Use Task Card #20 for activities about the teeth.

National Crime Prevention Week (week of Lincoln's birthday)

Study the history and functions of the Federal Bureau of Investigation.

Initiate a comparison study on crime rates in major metropolitan areas, both domestically and internationally.

Invite a law enforcement officer to discuss crime, i.e., felony vs. misdemeanor and crime detection/prevention.

Use Reproducible #13 to study the practice of fingerprinting and other means of identification.

Discuss proposals for ways to prevent rule-breaking in the classroom and school.

Suggest independent projects in which interested students can research historically famous crimes, such as that of Al Capone or the Brinks Robbery. Discuss professional vs. amateur crimes.

Conduct a survey on opinions concerning firearm controls. (See Conducting a Survey Data in Extra-Know-How Section.)

Arrange for a debate on the following topic: "Capital Punishment Is a Justifiable Practice."

(See activities under May 10, "J. Edgar Hoover ... " and May 19, "First Fingerprint ....")

Black History Week (includes February 12, Lincoln's birthday, and February 14, the birthday of Frederick Douglass)

Plan a learning center which depicts the accomplishments of black Americans.

Obtain the books *The Black Experience in Children's Books* (a bibliography) and *Important Dates in Afro-American History*, by Lee Bennett Hopkins.

Write to the Association for Study of Negro Life and History; also write to Fitzgerald Publishing Co., Inc. for information about purchasing *Golden Legacy Black History Comics*. (See Address Listing in Extra-Know-How Section.)

Brotherhood Week (week of Washington's birthday)

Ask students to cut out magazine pictures which illustrate people from different cultures; collages can be made from the cut-outs.

Invite the school or local librarian to present books representative of the commonalities, as well as the differences, among people.

Discuss the difference between prejudice (attitudes/feelings) and discrimination (behavior).

Write to the National Conference on Christians and Jews for information concerning brotherhood. (See Address Listing in Extra-Know-How Section.)

Discuss the phrase, "The common good of the entire human family."

(See activities under March Special Weeks, "International Education ... " and December Special Weeks, "Human Rights ....")

Future Farmers of America Week (Saturday before February 22)

Contact a resource person, perhaps through the local 4-H Club, to discuss with the class the purposes of the organization.

Draw a mural depicting farm life.

Make a class list of the various types of farms to clarify the various specializations of farming.

Create a story describing life on a farm.

Discuss or encourage independent projects concerning government subsidies, parities, surplus crops.

Write for information to the National Future Farmers of America Center (See Address Listing in Extra-Know-How Section.)

(See activities under October Special Weeks, "National 4-H ....")

National Pencil Week (last full week, beginning Sunday)

Investigate how the pencil was created by writing to the Lead Pencil Manufacturer Association. (See Address Listing in Extra-Know-How Section.)

Ask students to design a "wonder pencil."

Introduce a personification exercise by suggesting to students that they make their pencils come alive; then have them describe what they experience in their "pencil lives."

Invite students to imagine what school would be like without pencils.

Hold up a pencil and challenge students to conjure as many ideas as possible of how a pencil could be alternatively used.

(See activities under March 30, "Pencil with ... " and November 19, "Machine with ....)

National Engineer's Week (last full week, beginning Sunday)

Make a class list concerning various types of engineers and choose one type of engineer to invite to the class (construction, electrical, mechanical, etc.).

Organize groups to research and interview representatives from one of each of the major engineering professions.

Make a field trip to a place of industry to investigate the workplace of an engineer.

National Salespeople's Week (last full week, beginning Sunday)

List various commodities that are sold.

Invite students to make a persuasive speech to sell a real or fictional product.

Use Task Card #21 to learn about merchandising.

Ask students to conduct a survey revealing how many salespeople, retail or wholesale, are in their families; conduct a school-wide survey to learn how many school parents are involved in the field of sales. (See Conducting a Survey Data in Extra-Know-How Section.)

Discuss what the students consider to be qualities of a successful sales personality.

VARIABLE DATES

Washington's Birthday (third Monday)

(See Biography Data in Extra-Know-How Section.)

Ash Wednesday

Investigate the background of Ash Wednesday as related to the Lenten season.

Chinese New Year (January or February)

(See activities under January Variable Dates, "Chinese New Year.")

Shrove Tuesday or Mardi Gras

Research the various ways in which Shrove Tuesday is celebrated throughout the Christian world, along with the names by which it is known.

Leap Year (only years in which this date occurs are years in which the last two digits are divisible by four)

Find out the purpose for having introduced the idea of an extra day.

Encourage students to figure out which turn-of-the-century years were leap years and to establish a formula representing the method they use.

DAYS OF THE MONTH

February 1

First session of the U.S. Supreme Court held, 1790

Obtain a picture or diagram of the Supreme Court building; construct a facsimile out of sugar cubes or other materials.

Research a list of chief justices, past and current.

Re-enact a previously held court case that is of particular interest to the group.

Explore the process of becoming a justice and the length of tenure.

First Dental College incorporated, 1840

(See Feburary Special Weeks (above), "National Children's Dental Week.")

Victor Herbert, American composer, born 1859

(See Biography Data in Extra-Know-How Section.)

Enjoy recordings of Herbet's music, particularly "Babes in Toyland."

"Battle Hymn of the Republic" published by Julia Ward Howe, 1862

Explain that the words were written to the music of the old song "John Brown's Body."

Find out the setting which caused Howe to write the words; discuss the meaning of the verses.

Invite students to write their own words to the same melody.

First automobile insurance policy in the United States issued, 1898

Invite an insurance company representative to the class; ask that the guest bring several blank policy forms so that groups of students can draw up a simulated policy on a car.

Discuss no-fault insurance; find out what public liability and property damage insurance is. Hold a debate: "Every driver should be legally required to carry public liability and property damage insurance."

Consider the immediate responsibilities one has at the scene of an automobile accident, aside from medical concerns.

Clark Gable, American actor, born 1901

(See Biography Data in Extra-Know-How Section.)

Langston Hughes, American writer, born 1902

(See Biography Data in Extra-Know-How Section.)

Examine and share selections of his poetry; in particular, examine his poems for children in *Don't You Turn Back: Poems by Langston Hughes*, by Lee Bennet Hopkins.

First U.S. federal penitentiary building completed, 1906.

Discuss past and current prison conditions and proposals for prison reform.

Explore the various governmental levels of penal institutions (city, county, state, federal).

Discuss corporal punishment, extra labor, isolation, and deprivation of privileges as related to long-term changes in behavior.

February 2

Groundhog Day

Find out why this day is designated as "Groundhog Day."

(See Data-Detail in Extra-Know-how Section, "Goundhog Day—History.")

New Amsterdam incorporated as a city, 1653

Find out what current city represents the area that once was New Amsterdam.

(See activities under May 11, "Peter Stuyvesant ....")

First coeducational college in the United States incorporated, 1834.

Define the term "coeducational."

Ask students' opinions concerning having classes of either all girls or all boys.

Discuss what the public reaction might have been in 1834 concerning the concept of coeducation; explain that in many parts of the world girls are still not necessarily expected to attend school.

Treaty of Guadalupe Hidalgo, an agreement which gave New Mexico and California to the United States, signed 1848

Make a map of the territory ceded to the United States as a result of this treaty.

Fritz Kreisler, Austrian-American violinist/composer, born 1875

(See Biography Data in Extra-Know-How Section.)

Enjoy recordings of Kreisler's violin playing and compare it with the violin playing of Jascha Heifetz or other great violinists.

Baseball's National League formed, 1876

Make a class list of the member teams in the National League.

Obtain a copy of the book *How Baseball Began*, by LeGrand.

Review Task Card #17 for further information about baseball.

Review Reproducible #8 for a baseball quiz sheet.

(See activities under January 29, "Baseball's American ....")

James Joyce, Irish novelist, born 1882

(See Biography Data in Extra-Know-How Section.)

Find out the literary components of a novel.

Crown-cork bottle cap patented, 1892

Collect crown-cork bottle caps and compare them to bottle caps currently used.

Ask students to bring bottle caps of their favorite drinks; then design original caps for the drinks.

Encourage students to create a project using a collection of bottle caps.

Jascha Heifetz, Russian-American violinist, born 1901

(See Biography Data in Extra-Know-How Section.)

Enjoy recordings of Heifetz's violin playing.

Discuss why the violin is considered to be among the more difficult instruments to play.

Ethyl gasoline patented, 1923

Explore the differences among ethyl, regular, and unleaded gasolines.

Find out the background of the three basic arrangements in station managership: 1) oil company's total ownership and managership; 2) independent distributors; 3) independent dealers.

Conduct a survey of the students' parents to learn which gasoline companies' stations are the most frequented. (See Conducting a Survey Data in Extra-Know-How Section.)

Examine several credit cards; invite students to design a credit card for a fictitious or existing petroleum company.

February 3

First U.S. paper money issued, 1690

Obtain a picture or copy of the first American paper money; share with the class.

Examine a current paper bill and identify the items printed on it, such as the serial number, Federal Reserve Seal and letter, annual series number, check letter, face plate number, and U.S. Treasury Seal.

Find out whose picture is represented on the 1, 5, 10, 20, 50, 100, 500, 1,000, 5,000, 10,000, 100,000 dollar U.S. currency bills.

Ask students to design their own money; encourage the use of different denominations from those which are currently typical.

Invite students to bring to class any collections of paper money from other countries; compare and contrast the sizes, colors, etc.

Write to the U.S. Department of the Treasury for the booklet "Facts about U.S. Money." (See Address Listing in Extra-Know-How Section.)

(See activities under July 10, "Smaller-sized U.S. ....")

Horace Greeley, founder of the *New York Tribune*, born 1811

(See Biography Data in Extra-Know-How Section.)

Discuss the significance of Greeley's suggestion, "Go west, young man," in terms of advice in the nineteenth century; consider what type of similar message might be suggested to young people in the twentieth century.

Elizabeth Blackwell, first woman in the United States to be granted a medical degree, born 1821

(See Biography Data in Extra-Know-How Section.)

Obtain a copy of *Women Who Shaped History*, by Henrietta Buckmaster, to learn about other notable women.

(See activities under January 23, "First M.D. degree ....")

Fifteenth Amendment to the U.S. Constitution ratified, 1870

(See Data-Detail in Extra-Know-How Section, "Amendments to the U.S. Constitution.")

Felix Mendelssohn, German composer, born 1890

(See Biography Data in Extra-Know-How Section.)

Enjoy recordings of Mendelssohn's music.

Norman Rockwell, American illustrator, born 1894

(See Biography Data in Extra-Know-How Section.)

Encourage students to look in magazines and books for samples of Rockwell's designs; analyze his style and message of human interest.

James Michener, American writer, born 1907

(See Biography Data in Extra-Know-How Section.)

First income tax levied according to one's wealth, 1913
Introduce a microeconomics unit in which students have control over their own expenditures, earnings, and savings; incorporate an income tax structure into the overall plan of activities.
Discuss the concept and purpose of taxation/revenue-gathering.

Sixteenth Amendment to the U.S. Constitution ratified, 1913.
(See Data-Detail in Extra-Know-How Section, "Amendments to the U.S. Constitution.")

Betty Friedan, feminist, born 1921
(See Biography Data in Extra-Know-How Section.)
Trace the legislative history of the Equal Rights Amendment.

February 4

Confederate States of America formed, 1861
Draw a map of the Confederate States of America; include a drawing of the Confederate flag on the map.

George Washington named president of the United States by the electoral college, 1789
Investigate how the electoral college functions and what the possibilities are for reforming its alleged inequities.

Philippine insurrection against the United States led by Emilio Aquinaldo, 1899
Trace the relationship between the Spanish American War and the USA's control of the islands.
Locate on a globe or map where the Philippine Islands are; find out approximately how many thousand islands there are in the Republic of the Philippines; investigate the country's development since its independence in 1946—its languages and government.

Charles A. Lindbergh, American aviator, born 1902
(See Biography Data in Extra-Know-How Section.)
Write to the Smithsonian Institution for the booklet "Charles A. Lindbergh and the Spirit of St. Louis." (See Address Listing in Extra-Know-How Section.)
Find out why Lindbergh was called the "Flying Fool."
(See activities under May 20, "Charles Lindbergh ... " and June 11, "First U.S. ....")

First Winter Olympic Games held, 1932
Trace the record of geographical areas in which winter games have been held; find out the requirements a city or area must meet in order to host a winter Olympics competition; discuss the reasons that a city chooses to host a major function such as the Olympics.
Organize an "Olympic Games" meet appropriate to the school setting; use class flags or other appropriate means of identifying group and individual participants; stress the attitude of sportsmanship.
Write to the U.S. Olympic Committee for the booklet "The Olympic Games." (See Address Listing in Extra-Know-How Section.)
(See activities under April 6, "First modern ....")

United Service Organization (USO) established, 1941
Find out what the purpose of the organization has been.
Discover the name of the famous USO club in Los Angeles during World War II.
Investigate which entertainers have voluntarily toured overseas with the USO.

February 5

Roger Williams, colonial clergyman and founder of Rhode Island, first arrived in colonial America, 1631
Explain that Williams came to America for religious freedom but was banished from Massachusetts for his beliefs; evaluate both the concept and the reality of religious freedom in modern America.

First gas company in America incorporated, 1817
Write to the Federal Power Commission for information. (See Address Listing in Extra-Know-How Section.)
Find out what the responsibilities are of the public utility commissions in each state.
Brainstorm ways in which state and federal governments might organize to maximize energy reserves.

Adlai Stevenson, American statesman, born 1900
(See Biography Data in Extra-Know-How Section.)
Discuss his comment: " ... rather (we) light candles than curse the darkness."
Investigate the relationship between a-hole-in-the-shoe and Adlai Stevenson.

Hank Aaron, American baseball player, born 1932
(See Biography Data in Extra-Know-How Section.)
Explain that Hank Aaron "topped" Babe Ruth's homerun record; discuss the following topic: "If you could 'top' a present world record, what would you like it to be? Why?"
Read the autobiography *Aaron,* by Henry Aaron, with Furman Bisher; explain that celebrities often work with a writer to publish an "as told to" autobiography.

February 6

U.S. Constitution ratified by Massachusetts, thus making it the sixth state, 1788
(See States Admitted to the USA Data in Extra-Know-How Section.)

Babe Ruth, American baseball player and "homerun king," born 1895
(See Biography Data in Extra-Know-How Section.)
Investigate how the nickname of "Babe Ruth" developed out of the given name of "George Herman."

Spanish-American War terminated, 1900
(See activities under April 21, "Spanish-American ....")

Ronald Reagan, fortieth president of the United States, born 1911
(See Biography Data in Extra-Know-How Section.)
(See activities under March 30, "President Ronald ....")

February 7

Eleventh Amendment to the U.S. Constitution ratified, 1795
(See Data-Detail in Extra-Know-How Section, "Amendments to the U.S. Constitution.")

Charles Dickens, English novelist, born 1812
(See Biography Data in Extra-Know-How Section.)
Share selections of Dickens' works, i.e., *David Copperfield, Oliver Twist, A Christmas Carol*; discuss the term "scrooge" as derived from Dickens' fictional character, an infamous people-hater.

First ballet performed in America, 1827
Invite interested students to do a presentation of ballet skills.
Investigate a list of the more commonly used ballet-related French terms.

Laura Ingalls Wilder, author of the "Little House" books, born 1867
(See Biography Data in Extra-Know-How Section.)
Explain that Wilder did not begin writing her books until the age of 65.
Arrange a reading table which features a number of Wilder's books.

Alfred Adler, Austrian psychiatrist, born 1870
(See Biography Data in Extra-Know-How Section.)

Sinclair Lewis, American writer who was the first American to win the Nobel Prize for literature, born 1885
(See Biography Data in Extra-Know-How Section.)
Explain that Lewis won his greatest acclaim for writing in the area he knew best, the American Midwest; invite students to write a story about a topic or area with which they are most familiar.

February 8

Jules Verne, French science fiction writer, born 1828
(See Biography Data in Extra-Know-How Section.)

Encourage students to create their own science fiction stories.

Start a group science fiction "progressive story," the phases and phrases of which are created by progressing from one person to the next.

Envelope-folding and gumming (adhesive) machine patented, 1898

Review Reproducible #7 to learn how an envelope is made.

(See activities under January 21, "Envelope-folding ....")

Boy Scouts of America incorporated, 1910

Invite a member of the Boy Scouts to share information about the organization.

Investigate the history of the Boy Scouts, nationally and internationally.

Find out how Boy Scout uniforms look, as represented by countries from all over the world.

Birth of a Nation, film directed by D. W. Griffith, premiered in Los Angeles, 1915

Explain that the film portrayed the human relationships between a northern and a southern family during the American Civil War and Reconstruction period.

Discuss the term and concept, "white supremacy"; consider whether supremacy of any group over another is a valid ethic.

Investigate the history of the Ku Klux Klan; explain that the name derives from the Greek word *kuklos*, meaning "band" or "circle."

February 9

William Henry Harrison, ninth president of the United States, born 1773

(See Biography Data in Extra-Know-How Section.)

U.S. Weather Service established, 1870

Introduce information about barometers, thermometers, meteorology.

Cut out the weather section from the newspaper; ask students to note the areas in the world where the lowest and highest temperatures for the day have been recorded; find these areas on a globe.

Ask students to find the percentage of accurate predictions that the "weatherman" generally makes.

Select volunteers to develop a weather forecast presentation, as if on television or radio.

Create a cloud chart, using cotton balls to identify the four types of clouds.

Ask students to find out the "who, what, when, where, why" of the U.S. Weather Service.

Write to the Taylor Instrument Co. for the booklet "Instructions for Home Weather Forecasting." (See Address Listing in Extra-Know-How Section.)

Earthquake in California occurred, 1971

Discuss emergency procedures in the event of an earthquake.

Explain that earthquakes have commonly occurred in the "Pacific Fire Ring," but that they also have occurred in inland and coastal areas all over the world.

Research the causes of earthquakes and whether earthquakes are predictable; if predictable, discuss what measures could be taken in advance to reduce loss of life and damage to property, i.e., how might high-rise structures be evacuated quickly, how could water levels in dams be lowered rapidly, how might nuclear power plants be closed down immediately?

Discuss earthquake damage relative to other catastrophes, i.e., hurricanes (typhoons), tornadoes, cyclones, tidal waves.

Write to the U.S. Dept. of Interior, Geological Survey for the booklet "Earthquakes." (See Address Listing in Extra-Know-How Section.)

(See activities under March 27, "Alaska earthquake ... " and April 18, "San Francisco ....").

Halley's Comet due to return, 1986

Investigate the cycle of Halley's Comet

Find out about the causes and the structure of comets.

February 10

Canada surrendered to Great Britain by France (Treaty of Paris), 1763

Initiate a study on Quebec, the one remaining French culture province in Canada; hold a debate on the following topic: "Quebec should become independent from the rest of Canada."

Ira Remsen, American chemist who discovered chemical sweetener (saccharine), born 1846
(See Biography Data in Extra-Know-How Section.)
Discuss the possible advantages and disadvantages of artificial sweeteners.
(See activities under October 18, "Use of ....")

First fire extinguisher patented, 1863
Promote a discussion as to what the components of a fire extinguisher are and how one operates.
Invite a representative from the fire department to discuss fire prevention measures.
(See activities under April 1, "First salaried ....")

First "singing telegram" delivered, 1933
Encourage students to compose a telegram to another student; collect the communications and invite the writer to sing the message.
Use the telegram reproducible for practice in telegram writing. (See sample Folder Section.)
Write to Western Union Corp. for the booklet "Western Union—On the Frontier of Communication since 1851." (See Address Listing in Extra-Know-How Section.)

February 11

National Science Youth Day
Hold a science fair in the classroom or school.
Write to the Thomas Crowell Co. for the booklet "Teacher's Guide to Easy Tested Experiments." (See Address Listing in Extra-Know-How Section.)

First hospital in America opened in Philadelphia, 1751
Explain that the word "hospital" derives from the word *hospitālis,* which means "house" or "institution for guests."
(See activities under May Special Weeks, "National Hospital ....")

Thomas Alva Edison, American inventor, born 1847
(See Biography Data in Extra-Know-How Section.)
(See Data-Detail in Extra-Know-How Section, "School Record of Thomas Edison.")

February 12

First puppet show in America commercially staged, 1738
Discuss the many types of puppets (marionettes, finger puppets, humanettes, stocking puppets, etc.).
Encourage students to create and stage a puppet show.
(See activities under April 24, "Tony Sarg ....")

Abraham Lincoln, sixteenth president of the United States, born 1809
(See Biography Data in Extra-Know-How Section.)
Investigate the following information about Lincoln: 1) the incident in which Lincoln's corpse was stolen; 2) the similarities between Lincoln and John F. Kennedy; 3) the fact that Lincoln had Marfan's Syndrome; 4) personal characteristics of Lincoln's wife and children.
Obtain a copy of *Abraham Lincoln Joke Book,* by Beatrice Schenk de Regniers.

Charles Darwin, British naturalist and author of *Origin of the Species,* born 1809
(See Biography Data in Extra-Know-How Section.)
Research the details of the famous Scopes Trial in which a public school teacher was convicted for having taught Darwin's theory of evolution, contrary to state statute (Clarence Darrow, defense attorney, vs. William Jennings Bryan, prosecuting attorney).
(See activities under March 23, "Law banning ....")

Randolph Caldecott, English artist, born 1846
(See Biography Data in Extra-Know-How Section.)
Obtain a list of the Caldecott award-winning books from the local or school librarian; the award is granted each year to a selected illustrator of a children's book. Enjoy one of the books.

Explain that Caldecott illustrated books that authors had written; discuss other fields in which illustrators are needed, i.e., the commercial graphic artists for layouts in advertising and public relations, for specialty diagrams in medical textbooks, etc.

(See activities under November Special Weeks, "National Children's ... " and November 1, "Authors' Day.")

Baseball catcher's mask patented, 1878

Examine a catcher's mask; discuss the benefits and disadvantages of it.

Consider the significance of the catcher's position—the "quarterback" of the baseball team.

John L. Lewis, American labor leader, born 1880

(See Biography Data in Extra-Know-How Section.)

National Croquet League established, 1880

Obtain a croquet set; explain the rules and etiquette, and play the game.

Judy Blume, American author, born 1938

(See Biography Data in Extra-Know-How Section.)

Obtain copies of several of Blume's books for young people.

Yalta Conference agreement announced, 1945

Discuss the significance of the following decisions: 1) Russia's agreement to enter the war in the Pacific; 2) Russia's influence in the organization of the Polish government.

Locate on a map or globe where Yalta is.

February 13

Oldest public school in America established (Boston Latin School), 1635

Investigate what one-room school houses were like.

Divide a piece of large drawing paper in half; invite students to sketch a one-room school house on one half and a modern classroom on the other half.

Find out when schools in the local area were built.

First magazine in the United States, *American Magazine,* published, 1747

Make a class list of the names of all the magazines with which students are acquainted.

Discuss subscription vs. newsstand purchasing of journals.

Consider various magazine-related vocations: photographer, writer, editing staff, printer, distributor.

Create a class magazine entitled "Playground" or a name of the class' choice; include news and views of the playground.

"Blue Danube Waltz" first performed in Vienna, 1867

Obtain recordings of various Viennese waltzes and teach the waltz step.

Explain that the city of Vienna (Wien, in German) reached its height as a center of art in the eighteenth, nineteenth, and early twentieth centuries; make a list of other composers from the Vienna area.

Consult a German dictionary to figure out the meaning of "Wiener Wald."

Grant Wood, American painter, born 1892

(See Biography Data in Extra-Know-How Section.)

Expose students to the artist's famous painting "American Gothic."

February 14

St. Valentine's Day

(See Data-Detail in Extra-Know-How Section, "Saint Valentine's Day—History.")

Use Task Card #22 to learn how to make heart-shaped cookies.

First apple parer patented, 1803

Discuss the function of an apple parer.

Encourage students to design an instrument which might aid them in their daily chores or activities.

Write to the Washington State Apple Commission for the booklet "The Story of Washington Apples." (See Address Listing in Extra-Know-How Section.)

Use Task Card #23 for activities using apples.

Frederick Douglass, American abolitionist, born 1817
(See Biography Data in Extra-Know-How Section.)
Discuss the meaning and significance of the word "abolitionist."

Christopher Latham Sholes, inventor of an early typewriter, born 1819
(See Biography Data in Extra-Know-How Section.)
Trace the development of the typewriter; consider how the typewriter has affected communication.
Ask students to find out about typewriters that exist for languages with different orthographies, such as for Russian or Greek alphabets or for Chinese ideographs.
Invite a typewriter salesman to demonstrate new models of typewriters or word processors.
(See activities under April 12, "First portable ….")

Oregon admitted to the United States as the thirty-third state, 1859
(See States Admitted to the USA Data in Extra-Know-How Section.)

Jack Benny (Benny Kubelsky), American actor/comedian, born 1894
(See Biography Data in Extra-Know-How Section.)

First voting machine approved in the United States, 1899
Promote a discussion on voting: secret ballots, hand-raising, current national voting processes, futuristic vote-retrieval systems.
(See activities under February 15, "First election ….")

Arizona admitted to the United States as the forty-eighth state, 1912
(See States Admitted to the USA Data in Extra-Know-How Section.)
Find out what percentage of Arizona land is federally owned.

February 15

Galileo, Italian astronomer, born 1564
(See Biography Data in Extra-Know-How Section.)
Explain that Galileo ushered in the concept and practice of "scientific method," thereby shocking those who followed Aristotelian logic; consider the ridicule that Galileo experienced for exploring unpopularly held scientific theories. Discuss the statement, "We cannot discover new oceans unless we have the courage to lose sight of the shore."
Write to Edmund Scientific Co. for the booklet "Astronomy and You." (See Address Listing in Extra-Know-How Section.)
Explain that Galileo upset his contemporaries by confirming the Copernican theory that the earth moves around the sun; ask students to consider a theory that might currently shock people; discuss whether students think that most people would be open to changing their attitudes about their theories.
Obtain the book *Galileo and the Magic Numbers*, by Sidney Rosen, to find out about Galileo's other accomplishments.

Mustard first advertised as a prepared food in the United States, 1768
Make a class list of types of mustard; find out the various ways that people use mustard today.
Bring a mustard plant to class for students to examine.
Explain that mustard powder has been used to prepare mustard plasters, heat penetrating pads for the body; discover other vegetation which has been used for medicinal purposes.

First election ballot printed in the United States, 1799
Hold a private-ballot election, with voting booths, for class officers and monitors.
(See activities under February 14, "First voting … " and June 30, "Twenty-sixth Amendment.")

Cyrus McCormick, American inventor, born 1809
(See Biography Data in Extra-Know-How Section.)
Find out the different farm machines that McCormick invented; trace what the essential elements were in his reaper which proved to be such a significant contribution to agricultural machinery.
(See activities under May 17, "Grain reaper ….")

Susan B. Anthony, leader of the woman suffrage movement, born 1820
(See Biography Data in Extra-Know-How Section.)

Invite students to design a Susan B. Anthony postage stamp.

Investigate women's voting rights throughout the world.

Find out why the U.S. government chose to mint a coin (the Susan B. Anthony dollar) along with the dollar paper notes.

First adhesive postage stamps introduced in the United States, 1842

Discuss the postage stamp as a means of prepayment for service to be rendered.

Find out why stamps purchased in a machine may cost more than those purchased at the counter at a post office.

Encourage students to bring their stamp collections to share.

(See activities under November Special Weeks, "National Stamp ....")

First national college for the deaf opened, 1857

Find out the location of the college.

Invite a resource person to demonstrate sign language.

Investigate ways, other than sign language, that deaf-mutes receive and express language.

Show a film or television program without turning on the sound; discuss afterwards with the viewers what dynamics they had to depend upon to derive meaning from the interaction.

(See activities under September 23, "Hearing aid ....")

Alfred North Whitehead, British mathematician and philosopher, born 1861

(See Biography Data in Extra-Know-How Section.)

Explain that, as a mathematician and philosopher, Whitehead was very involved with the field of logic; present various games related to logical thinking, such as the commercial game "Mastermind."

Discuss Whitehead's comments: "Analyzing the obvious has produced some of man's most dramatic accomplishments"; "Ideas won't keep; something has to be done about them."

Ian Keith Ballantine, publisher who helped develop the paperback book industry, born 1916

(See Biography Data in Extra-Know-How Section.)

Discuss the advantages and disadvantages of paperback books.

Investigate the various paperback book order clubs.

February 16

National New Idea Day

Introduce the group-process technique of brainstorming for new ideas, a process whereby any and all ideas are accepted; encourage students to suggest ideas, such as automatic desk cleaners, moving sidewalks, automatic chalkboard cleaners, all of which are run by solar energy.

Henry Adams, American historian, born 1838

(See Biography Data in Extra-Know-How Section.)

Invite students to compile a scrapbook with captions on any historical event or on any topic which may be meaningful, i.e., family events.

Discuss the necessity of a professional historian's accuracy of data; consider also the ethics involved in historical research; find out some of the difficulties encountered in investigating oral tradition.

Benevolent and Protective Order of Elks established, 1868

Invite a member of the local Elks chapter to discuss the purpose of the organization (they advocate charity, justice, brotherly love, and faithfulness).

Edgar Bergen, American ventriloquist, born 1903

(See Biography Data in Extra-Know-How Section.)

Discuss the terms: dummy, ventriloquist; refer to the dictionary for the background of the word "ventriloquist."

Invite a ventriloquist to perform.

Nylon first patented in the United States, 1937

Ask students to bring in various items made of other synthetic materials.

Investigate the "who, what, when, where, why" and the effects of nylon production.

(See activities under May 15, "Women's long ....")

February 17

Rene Theophile Larnnec, French inventor of the stethoscope, born 1781
(See Biography Data in Extra-Know-How Section.)
Obtain a stethoscope and demonstrate its use; discuss various other instruments used for biofeedback, such as a thermometer and more elaborate mechanisms.
Invite a physician to class to demonstrate a variety of medical instruments.

Montgomery Ward, mail-order merchant, born 1843
(See Biography Data in Extra-Know-How Section.)
Discuss the advantages of mail ordering for residents of rural areas; find out the differences between mail-order businesses and other retail arrangements.
Obtain several mail-order catalogues; develop a math lesson in terms of purchase orders; complete a mail-order form.

Thomas J. Watson, Jr., American business executive and founder of IBM Corporation, born 1874
(See Biography Data in Extra-Know-How Section.)
Investigate the various kinds of machines manufactured by the International Business Machines Corporation.

American Parent Teacher Association founded, 1897
Invite to class an officer from the executive board of the school's PTA (or equivalent organization).

Marian Anderson, first black employed as a member of the New York Metropolitan Opera Company, born 1902
(See Biography Data in Extra-Know-How Section.)

Geronimo (Goyathlay), American Indian leader, died 1909
(See Biography Data in Extra-Know-How Section.)
Share with the class *Geronimo's Story of His Life.*

February 18

Pilgrim's Progress by John Bunyan published, 1678
Find out the meaning of "muckrake" as Bunyan used it in "Man with a Muckrake."

First opera in America performed, 1735
Obtain a children's opera recording; discuss the story beforehand and then play it.
Print a simple statement on the chalkboard; ask the students to read the words aloud; then ask them to repeat the words as if they were singing them in an opera (to demonstrate lyrics put to music).
Explain why many operas are written in languages other than English; discuss the difficulties of translating lyrics in a musical score.

Alessandro Giuseppe Antonio Anastasio Volta, Italian physicist and discoverer of the electric battery, born 1745
(See Biography Data in Extra-Know-How Section.)
Find out what a "volt" is as related to electricity.
Begin a study unit on all types of batteries.

Jefferson Davis, president of the Confederate States of America, inaugurated, 1861
Outline on a U.S. map the states that were part of the Confederacy.
Discuss Davis' quote, "All we ask is to be let alone," in view of Civil War issues.

Andrés Segovia, Spanish classical guitarist, born 1894
(See Biography Data in Extra-Know-How Section.)
Review Reproducible #1 concerning the parts of a guitar.
Enjoy a recording of Segovia's music.
(See activities under January Month-long Observances, "Guitar Month.")

Sholom Aleichem, Jewish-Yiddish writer, born 1895
(See Biography Data in Extra-Know-How Section.)

Luis Muñoz-Marín, Puerto Rican leader who was the first Puerto Rican governor elected, born 1896
(See Biography Data in Extra-Know-How Section.)
Discuss the issue of whether or not Puerto Rico should become the fifty-first state of the United States.

Planet Pluto discovered, 1930
Investigate the discovery of Pluto's and Neptune's crossing of each other's paths.

Robert Oppenheimer, American atomic physicist, died 1967
Conduct a discussion regarding scientific ethics (technical progress vs. human preservation and quality of life).
Obtain a copy of *Buckminster Fuller to Children of Earth*, by Cam Smith, and share it with the class.
Write to the U.S. Atomic Energy Commission for the booklet series on atomic pioneers. (See Address Listing in Extra-Know-How Section.)

February 19

Nicholas Copernicus, Polish astronomer, born 1473
(See Biography Data in Extra-Know-How Section.)
Explain that Copernicus is famous for having rejected the geocentric theory of the universe, a theory proposed by Ptolemy in the second century A.D. He believed that the sun is at the center of a large system in which the earth is only one of several planets revolving around it; many believe that this reversal of thought signaled the passage from the medieval to the modern world.
Construct a model of the solar system.
Discuss the concept of "light years"; consult the dictionary to trace the background of words such as "astronomy," "geocentric."

Ohio admitted to the United States as the seventeenth state, 1803
(See States Admitted to the USA Data in Extra-Know-How Section.)

Lydia Estes Pinkham, patent medicine manufacturer, born 1819
(See Biography Data in Extra-Know-How Section.)
Explain that Pinkham created concoctions for ailments but that the medicinal value was questioned.
Ask students to create a concoction for a particular ailment.
Make a study of the various types of patent medicines available for a certain illness.
Create a commercial for a particular patent medicine.

Phonograph machine, the "Talking Machine," patented by Thomas Edison, 1878
Find out about the original wax cylinder recordings.
Encourage students to bring in their favorite records to play; talk about such terms as: long-play, stereophonic, quadraphonic high-fidelity, amplifier, and others; suggest that students develop new words which might be appropriate with future advances in sound production.
(See activities under May 20, "Emile Berliner ....")

First statewide teachers strike held, 1968
Ask students to make a class list of what they consider likely concerns that teachers might have; discuss with them the implications of a teacher strike in their own school.

February 20

First day of the zodiac period, Pisces, the Fish (through March 20)
(See Data-Detail in Extra-Know-How Section, "Notes on Astrology.")

John Glenn Day (commemorates the United States' having orbited a person around the earth).
Invite students to design spacecraft out of cardboard boxes; hold a name contest for the most original and appropriate names.
(See activities under July 18, "John H. Glenn ....")

U.S. Federal Post Office established, 1792
Take a field trip to the local post office or invite a representative to discuss various facets of mail delivery.
Investigate the current management arrangement of the U.S. Postal Commission—quasi-responsibility to the U.S. Congress.
Discuss other agencies for the distribution of messages and packages, public or private.

First hydraulic electric elevator patented, 1872

Develop a class list of local buildings which have automatic elevators; make a separate column for attendant-run elevators.

Discuss the following topic: "Elevators are an over-use of energy vs. elevators are a necessity."

First toothpick manufacturing machine patented, 1872

Use Task Card #24 to create a toothpick-art project.

Sidney Poitier, American actor, born 1927

(See Biography Data in Extra-Know-How Section.)

First black umpire in organized baseball hired (in 1966 became first black in a major league), 1952

Investigate the requirements to become a career umpire in professional baseball.

February 21

Popcorn first introduced to American colonists, 1630

Make and enjoy popcorn with the class; discuss the process of corn-popping; find out the relative food value in popcorn.

Create popcorn mosaics; attempt to find colored kernels.

Obtain a copy of *The Popcorn Dragon*, by Catherine Woolly, or a copy of *100 Pounds of Popcorn*, by Hazel Krantz.

Write to the Popcorn Institute for pamphlets about popcorn. (See Address Listing in Extra-Know-How Section.)

First sewing machine patented in the United States, 1842

Obtain a sewing machine and discuss the mechanical principles; consider also the workings of a treadle machine.

Encourage students to participate in a sewing project for the classroom or school (beanbags for the kindergarten or a class flag)—a school-wide "sewing bee."

(See activities under July 9, "Elias Howe ....")

First burglar alarm installed, 1858

Discuss the various types of burglar alarms and the variety of places where they are positioned.

Investigate the feedback process involving various persons/agencies, once an alarm is sounded.

First female dentist in the United States, Lucy B. Hobbs, graduated, 1866

Discuss various concerns regarding the selection of a dentist, such as personal qualities and professional specializations.

August Von Wasserman, German bacteriologist, born 1866

(See Biography Data in Extra-Know-How Section.)

Explain that Wasserman developed a diagnostic test for a type of venereal disease and that this Wasserman test is required to obtain a marriage license.

Investigate the dramatic increase of cases of venereal disease.

First telephone directory issued, 1878

Compile a classroom or school-wide telephone directory; encourage students to write street names with consonants only, as in regular telephone directories; yellow pages may also be included by soliciting advetising from real or fictitious agencies.

Discuss the advantages and disadvantages of listing one's name in a telephone directory.

Find out if husbands and wives may enter separate listings at no extra charge.

Consult the yellow pages of a directory and trace various cross-listings.

Use Task Card #25 to understand further the use of the telephone directory.

Washington Monument dedicated, 1885

Obtain a picture of the monument and share it with the class; find out the history of the structure's development.

Introduce the word "obelisk" and relate the term to the monument.

Washakie, American Indian leader, died 1900
    (See Biography Data in Extra-Know-How Section.)
    Discuss the words of his epitaph: "Always loyal to government and his white brothers."

First camera patented to photograph, develop, and print pictures on photo paper, 1947
    Obtain a Polaroid® camera and take class pictures.
    Use Task Card #26 to understand the development process and what a pinhole camera is.

Malcolm X, leader of the black militant movement, died 1965
    Investigate the life of Malcolm X.
    (See activities under May 19, "Malcolm X ....")

People's Republic of China visited by President Richard Nixon (February 21-28), 1972
    Discuss the significance of "state visits"; consider the international and domestic implications of opened diplomatic relations between the United States and People's Republic of China.

February 22

George Washington, first president of the United States, born 1732
    (See Biography Data in Extra-Know-How Section.)

First "Five and Ten Cent" store established by F. W. Woolworth, 1879
    Ask students to pretend they are managers of a retail dimestore; outline inventory areas, design a floorplan, a store logo, and window display.
    Choose 10 items from the inventory list which would not have been sold in 1879.
    (See activities under April 13, "F. W. Woolworth ....")

Frederick Chopin, Polish-French composer and pianist, born 1810
    (See Biography Data in Extra-Know-How Section.)
    Obtain recordings of Chopin's music and enjoy listening.

February 23

George Frederick Handel, German-English composer, born 1685
    (See Biography Data in Extra-Know-How Section.)
    Play a recording of Handel's oratorio "The Messiah" and his orchestral suite "Water Music"; note that his other suite "Fireworks Music" was played on the eve of England's royal wedding of His Royal Highness Prince Charles and Lady Diana Spencer in Hyde Park.
    Explain that Handel was buried in Westminster Abbey, England's shrine for coronations and the burial of kings and other distinguished individuals.

First total-process cotton mill produced in the United States, 1813
    Ask students to bring to class various items that have been made from cotton.
    Obtain a sample of the cotton plant to examine the seeds and the boll-capsules of the vegetable fiber which are spun into thread.
    Investigate which states are the greatest cotton producers; find out how agriculturists combat boll weevils.
    Write to the U.S. Department of Agriculture, Cotton Division, for the booklet "The Story of Cotton." (See Address Listing in Extra-know-How Section.)

Battle of the Alamo fought, 1836
    Discuss the Mexican people's justification for the battle.
    Relate the phrase "Remember the Alamo" to the Texans' victory at San Jacinto six weeks later.
    Make a diorama representing the mission in San Antonio where the battle was fought.

First process for the manufacture of aluminum devised, 1886
    Make a class list of items which are made primarily from aluminum.

Quanah (Quanah Parker), American Indian leader, died 1911
    (See Biography Data in Extra-Know-How Section.)
    Explain that Quanah established Indian schools; discuss his belief that the "only way to survive was by the ways of the white man."

U.S. flag raised on Mt. Surabachi, Iwo Jima, by the U.S. Marines (portrayed in famous photograph of World War II), 1945

Encourage interested students to conduct research on Japan in terms of the country's minimal land base and population pressures, as a historical basis for the country's military aggression.

First mass inoculations with Salk antipolio serum begun, 1954

Discuss the process of inoculation and the condition of immunity.

(See activities under January Month-long Observances, "March of ....")

Twenty-fifth Amendment to the U.S. Constitution ratified, 1967

(See Data-Detail in Extra-Know-How Section, "Amendments to the U.S. Constitution.")

February 24

Wilhelm Karl Grimm, one of the German "Brothers Grimm," born 1786

(See Biography Data in Extra-Know-How Section.)

Share selections of Grimm's fairy tales.

Invite students to create their own fairy tales, individually or with a friend.

(See activities under January 4, "Jacob Grimm ....")

Act of Congress first ruled unconstitutional by the U.S. Supreme Court in the *Marbury vs. Madison* case, 1803

Discuss the implications of the "checks and balances" system in U.S. government; draw diagram to illustrate the three sectors of authority — executive, judicial, and legislative.

Winslow Homer, American artist, born 1836

(See Biography Data in Extra-Know-How Section.)

Examine selections of the artist's work.

U.S. Steel Corporation incorporated, 1901

Discuss terms such as: cartel, magnates, multinational corporations, mergers.

Name other large corporations which developed at this time and led to the Clayton Antitrust Act of 1914.

First presentation by "Voice of America" broadcast, 1942

Discuss the purpose of "Voice of America"; make a mock broadcast for a foreign country of the class' choice.

February 25

First national quarantine legislation in America enacted, 1799

Explain the concept of "quarantine"; hold a simulated quarantine, i.e., prevent a segment of the class from participating in recess.

First electric printing press patented, 1837

(See activities under January Special Weeks, "National Printing ....")

Pierre Renoir, French post-impressionist painter, born 1841

(See Biography Data in Extra-Know-How Section.)

Find out the meaning of "impressionism" as a period in art history.

Examine prints of the artist's work.

U.S. Bureau of Engraving and Printing authorized, 1862

(See activities under February 3, "First U.S. ....")

First black (Hiram R. Revels) elected to the U.S. Senate, 1870

Find out which state elected Revels.

Compare and contrast the requirements to become a U.S. senator with those of a U.S. representative.

(See activities under September 27, "Hiram Rhoades ....")

Enrico Caruso, Italian tenor, born 1873

(See Biography Data in Extra-Know-How Section.)

(See activities under February 18, "First Opera ....")

Sixteenth Amendment to the U.S. Constitution ratified, 1913
(See Data-Detail in Extra-Know-How Section, "Amendments to the U.S. Constitution.")

First state gasoline tax levied in the United States, 1919
Investigate the reason for a gasoline tax and how the collected revenue is used.
Find out which state was the first to levy this tax.

George Harrison, British musician, born 1943
Use Task Card #27 for activities to portray the Beatles.

February 26

Victor Hugo, French writer, born 1802
(See Biography Data in Extra-Know-How Section.)
Discuss Hugo's comments: "It is no more possible to prevent thought from reverting to an idea than the sea from returning to the shore"; "It is through fraternity that liberty is saved."
Explain that Victor Hugo has been recognized as having written the longest sentence in literature—a sentence with 823 words covering three printed pages.

Buffalo Bill (William Frederick Cody), American plainsman, scout, and showman, born 1846
(See Biography Data in Extra-Know-How Section.)
Find out the origin of Cody's nickname.
Encourage students to enjoy the western folklore of the United States.

First U.S. subway opened in New York, 1870
Explain the meaning of the prefix "sub"; find other words with that prefix.
Conduct a discussion about the advantages and disadvantages of rapid transit.

First glass-blowing machine in the United States introduced, 1895
Make a class list of items which are made of glass; discuss the diminished use of glass in view of the invention of plastic; create a second list of glass items which cannot be replaced by plastic.
Talk about the fact that glass-blowing is not normally a lifelong career due to the heavy stress upon the lungs of a glass-blower; think of various occupational hazards in other fields of work.
Compare and contrast the materials and methods in producing blown glass (liquid base), cut glass, and lead-cut glass; find out the relative financial values placed upon these three types of glass.
Write to Libby-Owens Ford Glass Co. for the booklet "Glass, the Miracle Worker"; also write to the Glass Container Manufacturer Institute, Inc. for the "Story of Glass Containers." (See Address Listing in Extra-Know-How Section.)

Grand Canyon National Park established, 1919
Discuss the dynamics of river erosion (Colorado River).
Obtain a photo of the canyon and encourage students to paint their own watercolor versions.
Enjoy listening to a recording of Ferde Grofe's "Grand Canyon Suite."
(See activities under March 1, "Yellowstone National ....")

Twenty-second Amendment to the U.S. Constitution ratified, 1951.
(See Data-Detail in Extra-Know-How Section, "Amendments to the U.S. Constitution.")

February 27

Henry Wadsworth Longfellow, American poet, born 1807
(See Biography Data in Extra-Know-How Section.)
Enjoy reading selections of Longfellow's poetry, such as "Paul Revere's Ride."

Hugo Black, U.S. Supreme Court justice, born 1886
(See Biography Data in Extra-Know-How Section.)
Investigate the career of a judge.
Invite a clerk from a local court to visit the classroom to talk about the various governmental levels of the courts, jury selection, and court-related jobs, such as court reporters.

David Sarnoff, American broadcaster, born 1891
   (See Biography Data in Extra-Know-How Section.)

John Steinbeck, American writer, born 1902
   (See Biography Data in Extra-Know-How Section.)
   Discuss the point that Steinbeck wrote about his own area of Salinas, California; invite students to write a short story set in their local area.

February 28

Bachelor's Day (in non-leap years)
   Discuss stereotypes which may be held about bachelors; ask students about the advantages and disadvantages of being a bachelor; hold a similar discussion in terms of females.
   (See activities under December 20, "Bachelor Tax ....")

U.S. Republican Party founded, 1845
   Discuss the "two-party" system in America.
   Find examples of Thomas Nast's symbol of the Republican Party.
   Consider that conservatism and conservation reflect similar meanings; discuss the terms as related to the conserving of natural resources.

Linus Pauling, American scientist, born 1901
   (See Biography Data in Extra-Know-How Section.)
   Explain that one of Pauling's discoveries is vitamin C; introduce a unit on vitamins.

Mario Andretti, Italian-American race-car driver, born 1940
   (See Biography Data in Extra-Know-How Section.)
   Design a race car that Mario Andretti might drive; exhibit the drawings.

February 29

Bachelor's Day (in leap years)
   (See activities under February 28, "Bachelor's Day.")

John Phillip Holland, Irish-American inventor of the submarine, born 1844
   (See Biography Data in Extra-Know-How Section.)
   Trace the history of submarines.
   (See activities under January 17, "U.S. Navy ....")

MARCH

When Julius Caesar revised the calendar in 46 B.C., he moved the beginning of the year from March to January, therefore altering the numerical sequence of the months. March, originally the first month, became the third month. March is generally considered a month with stormy weather at the outset, followed by mild weather near the end. Perhaps the month was named after the God of War, Mars, due to the month's turbulent beginning. Writers tend to describe March as signifying springtime—longer days and a period of renewal.

Birthstone: *Bloodstone or Aquamarine*
Flower: *Daffodil/Jonquil*

Use the Find-a-Word Reproducible to preview happenings in March. (See Reproducible Section.)

MONTH-LONG OBSERVANCES

Red Cross Month

Study the history of the Red Cross; write to the American National Red Cross for information. (See Address Listing in Extra-Know-How Section.)

Invite a representative from the local Red Cross chapter to class to discuss who the Red Cross serves and what its basis of financial support is.

Investigate the names of the Red Cross in other languages.

(See activities under May 8, "Jean Henry ... " and December 25, "Clara Barton ....")

Hamburger Month

Discuss hamburger (ground round or ground beef) substitutes.

Find out the history of the hamburger sandwich.

Bring favorite recipes to class in which ground beef is an ingredient.

Tour a franchise fast-food establishment.

Ask students to design their own hamburger franchise business—original ideas concerning the building, the theme, and the menu.

Create and cook a nutritious luncheon menu, with hamburger as part of the main course.

Brainstorm names for hamburgers and include descriptions, i.e., "Nude-burger—nothing on it."

Discuss other sources of protein for one's diet.

Write to Hunt-Wesson Kitchens for the booklet "Hamburger—Umpteen Different Ways for Ten Good Reasons." (See Address Listing in Extra-Know-How Section.)

Lent

Discuss pre-Lenten activities that are held throughout the Christian world, i.e., Mardi Gras in France, Fasching in Germany.

Youth Art Month

Sponsor a school-wide art contest with different categories according to ages and various art-media.

(See activities under January 12, "First United ... " and March 17, "National Gallery ... " and April 13, "New York's ... " and November 7, "Museum of ... " and November 8, "Louvre, the ....")

Pickle Month

Obtain a copy of *101 Pickle Jokes*, by Bob Vlaci; read a joke each day of the month.

Discuss the various types of fruits and vegetables which most often are pickled; investigate what the pickling process is.

(See Data-Detail in Extra-Know-How Section, "Information about Pickles.")

Write to Pickle Packers International, Inc. for further information about pickles. (See Address Listing in Extra-Know-How Section.)

(See Data-Detail in Extra-Know-How Section, "Love Ballad to My Love, the Great Pickle.")

Discuss the meaning of the expression "to be in a pickle"; try to figure out the origin of the phrase.

Use Task Card #28 for various activities related to pickles.

National Easter Seal Campaign

Write to the National Easter Seal Society for information. (See Address Listing in Extra-Know-How Section.)

Discuss the difference, if any, between buying seals for a campaign and simply making a contribution to charities.

National "Let's Go Fly a Kite" Month

Introduce the song from Walt Disney's *Mary Poppins*, "Let's Go Fly a Kite."

Investigate kites from all over the world, particularly Japan where kites may be so enormous as to require eight to ten people to maneuver them; discover the various shapes in which kites can be made, such as box kites, star kites, fish kites, and plane surface kites.

Discuss the meaning and origin of the expression, "Go fly a kite."

Conduct a school-wide kite contest; include categories such as "Most Unusual Tail," "Most Comical Kite," "Kite with the Most Moving Parts," "Kites Made with Adult Assistance."

SPECIAL WEEKS

National Weights and Measures Week (March 1)

Write for information to Weights and Measures Associates. (See Address Listing in Extra-Know-How Section.)

Use Reproducible #14 for copy of metric measuring license.

Return-the-Borrowed-Book Week (March 1)

Encourage students to return all borrowed books.

Find the statistic which reflects the highest recorded library book fine.

National Procrastination Week (first week of the month—unless postponed)

Discuss "procrastination" and ask students to list their own habits of procrastination, if any.

Suggest to students that they procrastinate in acknowledging this particular week!

Discuss the quote by Edward Young: "Procrastination is the thief of time; collar him!"

National Peanut Week (first Wednesday)

Pass out different kinds of peanuts for the students to taste.

Hold various peanut races (holding a peanut on a spoon, rolling a peanut with one's nose, etc.).

Review Task Card #7 on how to make peanut butter.

International Education Week (second week)

Contact a local chapter of the Rotary Club and request that a member come to speak about international study opportunities.

Invite several foreign students to speak about their own countries (contact the school district and local churches that might be sponsoring foreign students).

Write to the American Field Service and/or Experiment in International Living for information about international education exchanges. (See Address Listing in Extra-Know-How Section.)

(See activities under February Special Weeks, "Brotherhood Week ....")

Girl Scout Week (including March 12)

Invite a Girl Scout in the class or school to describe the activities and purposes of the Girl Scouts and related groups.

Design an original box and label it to hold Girl Scout cookies.

Save Your Vision Week (first Sunday)

Write to the American Optometric Association for information. (See Address Listing in Extra-Know-How Section.)

Discuss various types of corrective lenses; design a pair of glasses.

Investigate topics such as visual acuity/perception and eye diseases.

Introduce a unit on the eye and eye care; encourage students to experiment at home with a mirror—finding their tear ducts and watching their pupils contract and dilate according to the amount of light in the room; ask students to find out why newborn infants do not blink or tear in the first weeks of life.

(See activities under March 29, "First eye ... " and May 9, "First eye ....")

Campfire Girls Birthday Week (Sunday of last full week of the month)

Invite a Campfire Girl to visit the class to describe her organization.

Sing songs that are traditionally sung around a campfire.

Discuss how to build and extinguish a campfire.

Design a layout of a camp (nature center, stables, lake, etc.).

Discuss the fact that Campfire Girls is now a coeducational organization.

National Wildlife Week (third Sunday)

Write to the National Wildlife Federation to obtain a list of endangered species and other information. (See Address Listing in Extra-Know-How Section.)

Check out various naturalist journals from the library and share with the class.

Paint a wildlife scene.

Investigate the related careers of naturalists, forest rangers, taxidermists, photographers, painters.

National Smile Week (March 21)

Discuss the nonverbal communication of a smile: what is it that causes one to smile? Does it take more muscles to smile or to frown? Does a smile or a blanket deliver more warmth? What does smiling with one's eyes mean? Does a smile mean the same thing in all cultures?

Use Task Card #29 to introduce a unit on smiling.

(See activities under August Special Weeks, "National Smile ....")

National Poison Prevention Week (third Sunday)

Discuss the symbol of poison, the misuses of toxins, antitoxins, and antidotes.

Write to the National Association of Retail Druggists for the "NARD Poison Prevention Kit." (See Address Listing in Extra-Know-How Section.)

VARIABLE DATES

Spring, or vernal, equinox (on or about March 21)

Discover why it is that day and night are equal during this time.

Enjoy poetry and art which reflect the season of spring.

Use Task Card #30 for activities about spring.

Passover (Jewish holiday, occasionally in March)

National Stop Smoking Week

Invite a physician to class to describe the physical dangers of smoking.

Investigate the disease of emphysema.

Write to the American Cancer Society for information about lung cancer. (See Address Listing in Extra-Know-How Section.)

Check the printed wording on each package of cigarettes as related to a health warning.

Discuss the comment of Benjamin Franklin, " 'Tis easier to prevent bad habits than to break them"; ask students to think of habits they have that are difficult to break.

(See activities under January 11, "Report that ....")

DAYS OF THE MONTH

March 1

Articles of Confederation adopted, 1781

Explain that the document served as the "Constitution" for the thirteen colonies, one which needed to be replaced by the U.S. Constitution which assigned more power to the central government; find out what a constitution is and what its purpose is.

First U.S. Census begun, 1790

Conduct a school-wide population census with categories such as gender, age, and others. (See Conducting a Survey Data in Extra-Know-How Section.)

(See activities under April 1, "U.S. population ....")

Ohio admitted to the United States as the seventeenth state, 1803

(See States Admitted to the USA Data in Extra-Know-How Section.)

Nebraska admitted to the United States as the thirty-seventh state, 1867

(See States Admitted to the USA Data in Extra-Know-How Section.)

Yellowstone National Park created by the U.S. Congress, 1872

Suggest that students make a diorama of certain areas of Yellowstone National Park.

Discuss various types of recreation areas, i.e., national parks, national monuments, state parts.

Write to the U.S. Department of Interior for further information. (See Address Listing in Extra-Know-How Section.)

Glenn Miller, American band leader, born 1904

(See Biography Data in Extra-Know-How Section.)

Find out how Miller was able to buy his first trombone at the age of 13.

Obtain recordings of his music and teach a few of the swing-style dance steps.

View, if possible, the film *The Glenn Miller Story* (1953).

(See activities under December 15, "Glenn Miller ....")

Dinah Shore, American singer/actress, born 1917

(See Biography Data in Extra-Know-How Section.)

Peace Corps of the United States established, 1961

Invite a representative from the local Peace Corps Action office to learn more about the admission requirements and activities of Peace Corps volunteers.

Ask students which country/language they would choose were they to become Peace Corps volunteers – and for what reasons.

Find out the names of comparable organizations in other countries.

March 2

Law which banned the import of slaves enacted by the U.S. Congress, 1808

Investigate this law as it relates to the Civil War.

First school for the blind in America established in Massachusetts, 1829

Describe the environment, physical and otherwise, if a school were designed for the benefit of blind students.

(See activities under January 4, "Louis Braille ....")

Independence from Mexico declared by Texas, 1836

Review the history of Texas; create a chart or poster showing all the flags that have flown over the state.

U.S. Department of Education created, 1867

Explain that in most countries, the federal office of education has considerable authority; discuss the American concept of state and local school board jurisdiction.

Find out the various means by which the U.S. government does affect local schools.

Name of JELL-O® coined by the wife of its inventor, P. B. Wait, 1897

Explain that JELL-O is a dessert made from gelatin; gelatin had been used since the 1600s, but not until 1897 was it packaged as a dessert.

Exchange various gelatin recipes; try making a gelatin mold.

Use Task Card #31 for activities using JELL-O.

Theodore Seuss Geisel (Dr. Seuss), American author/illustrator, born 1904

(See Biography Data in Extra-Know-How Section.)

Discuss the point that Seuss' first book was rejected many times before it was finally accepted.

Talk about the possibilities of translating nonsense words into other languages.

Introduce the word "onomatopoeia" (the use of words whose sounds suggest the sense); find examples of onomatopoeia in Dr. Seuss' books. Invite students to create their own examples of onomatopoeia.

Desi Arnaz, Cuban-American actor, born 1907
(See Biography Data in Extra-Know-How Section.)

Time **magazine** first published, 1923
Bring in several *Time* magazines as well as other similar weekly news magazines; compare and contrast the magazines' formats.
Introduce the topic: "If you were on the editorial staff of the magazine, whom would you choose to be selected as the cover subject for the 'Person of the Year'?" Ask students to justify their choices.
Investigate what personality has appeared the most times on the cover of *Time*.
Make a facsimile copy of *Time* magazine, as related to the school community.

March 3

Girls' Day (celebrated in Japan)
Explain that individual birthdays are less celebrated in Japan than they are in America; this holiday serves as every Japanese girl's birthday. (See May 10 for Boys' Day); find out how the day is celebrated in Japan.
Encourage interested students to explore more of the customs in the Japanese culture.

George M. Pullman, founder of the Pullman Palace Car (railway car) Co., born 1831
(See Biography Data in Extra-Know-How Section.)
Ask students if anyone has taken a train trip and used or observed the "Pullman" berths for sleeping.
(See activities under September 1, "First Pullman ....")

Florida admitted to the United States as the twenty-seventh state, 1845
(See States Admitted to the USA Data in Extra-Know-How Section.)

Alexander Graham Bell, Scottish-American scientist, born 1847
(See Biography Data in Extra-Know-How Section.)
Explain that Bell originally worked with mute people; during this time he accidentally discovered a method of transmitting sound through vibrations—a discovery which led to the transmission of the human voice over the telephone; investigate how a telephone operates.
Discuss what it would be like if the telephone had not been invented; extend the discussion to brainstorming about various future media for interpersonal commuication.
Ask students to make a list of Bell's many inventions.
Investigate telephones designed for the hard-of-hearing; find out what other types of telephones there are, i.e., conference phones.
Contact the local American Telephone & Telegraph Co. for the booklet "Alexander Graham Bell and How the Telephone Works."

First U.S. postage stamps authorized, 1847
Encourage students to share their stamp collections.
Ask students to design and draw their own postage stamps.
(See activities under November Special Weeks, "National Stamp ....")

First woman lawyer, Belva Ann Lockwood, to have practiced before the U.S. Supreme Court, 1879
Investigate the subject of the case which Lockwood argued before the Court.

Robert Flemming, Jr., black patent holder of a type of guitar, born 1886
(See Biography Data in Extra-Know-How Section.)
Review Reproducible #1 to learn the parts of a guitar.

U.S. Forest Service established, 1905
Investigate the career of a forest ranger or naturalist.
Discuss the meaning of the saying, "You can't see the forest for the trees."
Encourage students to research the many different types of trees found in the United States and their specific locales.
Present an art project with a forest as the theme.
Write to the U.S. Department of Interior for particular information about the U.S. Forest Service. (See Address Listing in Extra-Know-How Section.)

Star-Spangled Banner officially accepted as the U.S. national anthem, 1931
Play a recording of the song; discuss the meaning of the words.
Obtain recordings of national anthems from other countries.
Discuss the word "anthem" in terms of celebration or praise.
Ask students: "If you could choose from all the music available, which song would you select as the national anthem of the United States?"

March 4

Former U.S. Presidential Inauguration Day (until 1937)
Make a list of the U.S. presidents who were inaugurated on this day.
(See activities under January 20, "U.S. Presidential ....")

Constitutional government of the United States initiated, 1789
Find out how many states were needed to ratify the Constitution in order for it to become effective.

Vermont admitted to the United States as the fourteenth state, 1791
(See States Admitted to the USA Data in Extra-Know-How Section.)

Confederate flag raised, 1861
Obtain a copy of the flag or a photograph, and display it in the classroom; discuss its significance.

Knute Rockne, famous Notre Dame football coach, born 1888
(See Biography Data in Extra-Know-How Section.)
Ask interested students to draw diagrams of Rockne football strategies, i.e., forward pass and fast, deceptive plays.

First international copyright agreement established, 1891
Explain what a copyright is; locate copyright dates in various books.
(See activities under May 31, "U.S. Copyright ....")

U.S. Department of Labor created, 1913
Investigate who the current cabinet secretary of labor is.

March 5

Crispus Attucks Day (in honor of the first black "American" to die in pre-Revolutionary War events, in the Boston Massacre, 1770

Gerhard Mercator, Flemish geographer and cartographer, born 1512
(See Biography Data in Extra-Know-How Section.)
Consult a dictionary to analyze the words: geographer, cartographer.
Discuss the display maps with the Mercator projection.
Use Reproducibles #15 and #16 to understand more about Mercator projections.

William Oughtred, British mathematician and inventor of the slide rule, born 1575
(See Biography Data in Extra-Know-How Section.)
Obtain a slide rule to show to the class; investigate the functions of the slide rule; consider its significance in view of the appearance of computers.

James Merritt Ives, American painter and lithographer, born 1824
(See Biography Data in Extra-Know-How Section.)
Explain that Ives and Nathaniel Currier depicted America during its westward expansion; they never intended that their prints be works of art. However, history has indicated that they were among America's first pictorial reporters; in effect, their lithographs provided a graphic means of bringing news in the form of pictures to the people.
Write to Esmark, Inc. for information concerning the free loan of a color/sound film entitled "The Legacy of Currier and Ives." (See Address Listing in Extra-Know-How Section.)
(See activities under March 27, "Nathaniel Currier ....")

First woman ever placed on the FBI "Ten Most Wanted" List, 1969
Encourage students to check bulletin boards in local public buildings for personalities wanted by the federal government.

March 6

Michelangelo (Buonarroti), Italian painter and sculptor, born 1475
(See Biography Data in Extra-Know-How Section.)
Enjoy the illustrations of Michelangelo's works, such as the *Pieta* and *David* in the book *The World of Michelangelo,* by Robert Coughlan.
Introduce an art project of creating clay statues.

Dred-Scott Case upholding slavery decided upon by the Supreme Court, 1857
Discuss the significance of this decision upon Civil War developments.
Investigate which amendment to the Constitution nullified the Supreme Court decision.

First American automobile driven on the streets of Detroit by Charles Brady King, 1896
Suggest that students create a timeline showing the development of the automobile industry in America.
Find out the reason American automobiles have been driven on the right-hand side of the street; also trace the background of the driver's seat being positioned on the left side of the car.
Write to the Motor Vehicle Manufacturers Assoc. of the U.S., Inc. for the "Bulletin Board Kit — Automobile"; also write to General Motors Corp. for the booklet "Automobile Story." (See Address Listing in Extra-Know-How Section.)

Ed McMahon, television announcer, born 1923
(See Biography Data in Extra-Know-How Section.)

Frozen foods (individually packaged products) patented by Clarence Birdseye, 1930
Consider the impact of frozen foods on lifestyles.
Design an appropriate logo and label for frozen food packages.
Investigate taste and nutrition elements as they are affected by freezing fresh vegetables over an extended period of time.

National Bank Holiday proclaimed by Franklin D. Roosevelt, 1933
Discuss the Depression; examine the significance of having closed bank operations and gold transactions for four days.
Use Task Card #8 for activities on banking skills.
(See activities under January 7, "First commercial ....")

March 7

Burbank Day (in commemoration of the birth date of the horticulturist, Luther Burbank, born 1849)
Consult the dictionary to analyze and define the word "horticulture."
Use Task Card #32 to learn more about horticulture.

Telephone patented by Alexander Graham Bell, 1876
(See activities under March 3, "Alexander Graham Bell ....")

First coin-operated locker patented, 1911
Determine what a coin-operated locker is (used at airports, bus stations).
Introduce a lesson in which the students are to imagine a fictitious locker (#S-3203) and develop a story about it, in any medium of expression.

Transatlantic radio/telephone service begun between New York and London, 1926
Trace in detail the development of transoceanic communication — from cable to wireless transmission towers to satellites.
(See activities under May Month-long Observances, "National Radio ....")

March 8

National Women's Day
(See activities under August 26, "Nineteenth Amendment ... " and October 29, "National Organization ....")

Oliver Wendell Holmes, U.S. Supreme Court justice, born 1841
(See Biography Data in Extra-Know-How Section.)
Discuss the following statements by Holmes: "Bigotry is like the pupil of the eye; the more light you pour on it, the more it will contract"; "The great thing in this world is not so much where we stand, as in what direction we are moving."

First dog license law passed in the United States (New York State), 1894
Investigate the local city and state rulings regarding dog licenses.
Design an original dog license and dog tag.

Muhammad Ali (Cassius Clay) defeated by Joe Frazier in the world heavyweight boxing championship bout, 1971
Discuss boxing as a sport with regulations, as opposed to free-for-all fighting; explain that the sport of boxing dates back to 3000 B.C. in Mesopotamia; find out which official match was the last of bare-knuckle boxing.
Ask students to find the weight classifications for the following categories: heavyweight, light heavyweight, middleweight, welterweight, lightweight, featherweight, bantamweight, flyweight in professional and amateur boxing.
Investigate the history, scoring, and rules of boxing.

March 9

Amerigo Vespucci, Italian navigator, born 1851
(See Biography Data in Extra-Know-How Section.)
Explain that America's name is derived from "Amerigo"; ask students to name a country in terms of their own names.
Discuss the value of Vespucci's contribution, that of evolving a system for computing nearly exact longitude.

Artificial teeth first patented by Charles Graham, 1822
Discuss the reasons why people need artificial teeth (dentures) and how they are designed specifically for each person.
Review Task Card #20 for activities about teeth.

Leland Stanford, American railroad builder, politician, and philanthropist, born 1824
(See Biography Data in Extra-Know-How Section.)
Investigate the vast financial holdings Stanford held in the mining industry.

Confederate currency authorized, 1861
Obtain pictures of Confederate money.
Discuss what "greenbacks" were and why they were put into circulation.

Conflict between the *Monitor* (Union Navy) and the *Merrimac* (Confederate Navy) ships occurred, 1862
Ask students to trace the development of the term "ironclad ships" and why the term was used for the *Monitor* and the *Merrimac.*

Howard Hathaway Aiken, American mathematician who invented the first modern digital computer (Mark I), born 1900
(See Biography Data in Extra-Know-How Section.)
Explain that Aiken's computer weighed 35 tons, was 51 feet long, and could only compute arithmetic.
Investigate various computer software to learn about computers' current capabilities.
(See activities under March 11, "Vannever Bush ... " and December 28, "John Van Neumann ....")

March 10

Lillian D. Wald, American Jewish social worker, born 1867
(See Biography Data in Extra-Know-How Section.)
Invite a social worker to explore the field of social work as a career.

Salvation Army established in the United States, 1880
Invite a representative from the Salvation Army to discuss the purpose of the organization.

Harriet Tubman, an escaped slave and abolitionist, died 1913
Investigate the life of Harriet Tubman.
Find out how Harriet Tubman was able to free over 300 slaves.

March 11

Blizzard of '88, record snowstorm in northeastern part of the United States, occurred, 1888
Encourage the development of a creative writing story as related to the occurrence of a blizzard.
Find out how frostbite affects the body.
Encourage students to recall and relate when they were uncomfortably cold.
Find out the coldest temperatures in which human beings are able to survive.

Vannever Bush, one of the early inventors contributing to computer technology, born 1890
(See Biography Data in Extra- Know-How Section.)
Trace the early development of computers.
Invite a computer sales representative to talk about various forms of computers; ask the guest to bring an actual computer with examples of accompanying software.
Create a list of the potential uses of computer technology.
Visit a computer center and enroll in a computer language course; study the design of a video game.

Lawrence Welk, American bandleader, born 1903
(See Biography Data in Extra-Know-How Section.)

Ralph Abernathy, American civil rights leader, born 1926
(See Biography Data in Extra-Know-How Section.)

March 12

First steam engine used, 1755
Explain that a steam engine is a machine to convert heat energy into mechanical energy; invite interested students to describe the process and mechanisms in detail.

Louis Prang, creator of the first commercial greeting card in America, born 1824
(See Biography Data in Extra-Know-How Section.)
Invite students to bring various greeting cards to class, examine them, and then create their own.

First parachute jump from an airplane occurred, 1912
Obtain a parachute; examine the fabric and how a parachute is made.
Compare parachute jumping to skydiving.
Use Task Card #33 in order to participate in class parachute activities.
Discuss the statement: "Minds are like parachutes; they function only when open."
Order the film "Pack Your Own Chute," the theme of which is being self-responsible for one's own life; order from the University of California Extension Media Center (Ramic Production from California). (See Address Listing in Extra-Know-How Section.)
(See activities under October 1, "First American ....")

Girl Scouts of America formed, 1912
Trace the history of the organization back to England.
(See activities under March Special Weeks, "Girl Scout ....")

First sound-on-film motion picture demonstrated, 1923
Show a film with the sound turned almost off to demonstrate the viewing of a film without sound.
Stimulate discussion and an investigation as to where the sound is located on film.

First "Fireside Chats" held by Franklin Delano Roosevelt, 1933
Discuss Roosevelt's purpose in speaking informally to the American people on the radio.

Edward Albee, American playwright, born 1928
(See Biography Data in Extra-Know-How Section.)

Liza Minnelli, American actress, born 1946
(See Biography Data in Extra-Know-How Section.)
(See activities under June 10, "Judy Garland ....")

March 13

Joseph Priestley, English theologian and scientist who discovered oxygen, born 1733
(See Biography Data in Extra-Know-How Section.)
Investigate the chemical element of oxygen.
Use Task Card #34 concerning oxygen and water.

"Uncle Sam" cartoon published, 1852
(See Data-Detail in Extra-Know-How Section, "Uncle Sam — History.")

Impeachment proceedings initiated against Andrew Johnson, 1868
Investigate the impeachment process in the United States.
Explain that the Senate failed to convict Andrew Johnson; find out who would have succeeded Johnson had the Senate been successful.

First earmuff patented, 1877
Design a creative set of earmuffs; describe the material, colors.
Create sets of earmuffs that would be particularly appropriate for certain famous personalities.
Consider other protections for the face or head against cold weather, such as masks, nose-cozies.

World system of standard time, based on Greenwich Mean Time, established by International Conference, 1884
Locate Greenwich, England on a map or globe; investigate what the term "prime meridian" means.
Use Task Card #35 to gain ideas concerning time.

March 14

First cotton gin patented by Eli Whitney, 1794
Invite interested students to explore how the machine worked.
Find out what effect the cotton gin had on slavery.
Introduce a unit on textiles.
(See activities under February 23, "First total-process ... " and December 8, "Eli Whitney ....")

First U.S. War Bond authorized, 1812
Discuss the purpose of war bonds and other government savings bonds; design a bond for a particular cause.

Albert Einstein, German-American theoretical physicist and Nobel Prize winner, born 1879
(See Biography Data in Extra-Know-How Section.)
(See Data-Detail in Extra-Know-How Section, "Comments on Albert Einstein."
Investigate Einstein's contributions of his theory of relativity and his work regarding the conversion of matter into energy, a contribution that was basic to the development of further nuclear research.
Discuss Einstein's statement, "The next war will be fought with stones."
(See activities under July 16, "First atomic ....")

First National Bird Reservation in the U.S. established, 1903
Visit a bird sanctuary.
Use Reproducible #17 concerning the study of birds.
Write to the American Nature Study Society for information on birds; ask for the booklet "Birds of Your Neighborhood — How to Study Them." (See Address Listing in Extra-Know-How Section.)
Explain the molting process of birds, whereby the feathers of birds disappear at regular intervals and are replaced by new plumes; most birds molt and replace the long feathers of the wing one by one so that the wing has sufficient feathers for flight at any time. Ducks are an exception; encourage students to research the plumage process of ducks.
(See activities under April 26, "John James ....")

March 15

Ides of March, Julius Caesar assassinated, 44 B.C.
Discuss the ominous association with the "Ides of March."
Obtain a simple version of *Julius Caesar*, by Shakespeare; read and act out the play; discuss Shakespeare's famous quote, "Beware the Ides of March."

Andrew Jackson, seventh president of the United States, born 1767
(See Biography Data in Extra-Know-How Section.)
Discuss the concepts involved in "Jacksonian democracy."
Find out why Jackson was called "Old Hickory."

Maine admitted to the United States as the twenty-third state, 1820
(See States Admitted to the USA Data in the Extra-Know-How Section.)

Escalator patented by Jesse Reno, 1892
Describe and discuss escalators in comparison with elevators; brainstorm ideas for a verticle people-carrier that might be more energy-efficient.
(See activities under August 9, "Escalator first ....")

First commercial airfield in the United States established by Lyman Gilmore, 1907
Find out where the airfield was established.
Explain that Gilmore is considered by some historians to have been the first person to fly an airplane (May 15, 1902)—more than a year before the Wright Brothers' first flight; investigate the situation to decide which event deserves to be considered the first successful airplane flight.
(See activities under December 17, "First powered ....")

First formal presidential press conference held by Woodrow Wilson, 1913
Discuss the different style that each U.S. president has brought to press conferences; consider the issue of how much information a president should divulge.
Stage a mock press conference.

First blood bank in America established, 1937
Investigate what is involved in donating blood; consider the pros and cons of paying donors for their blood.
Find out the rebuilding process of one's blood supply when blood is given.
Explain the process of how blood is stored and reinjected: Blood is taken from veins of a well person; a machine separates the plasma from the other parts of the blood; then it is frozen into a dry powder and stored; when needed, sterile water is added to convert it into a liquid again, ready to be reinjected.
Encourage interested students to make a detailed study of the four types of blood: Groups O, A, B, AB; investigate what Rh negative blood is.
Find out what Charles Drew contributed to knowledge about blood transfusions.
(See activities under January Month-long Observances, "National Blood ... " and February Month-long Observances, "Heart Month ... " and April 1, "William Harvey ....")

March 16

James Madison, fourth president of the United States, born 1751
(See Biography Data in Extra-Know-How Section.)

George Ohm, German scientist, born 1787
(See Biography Data in Extra-Know-How Section.)
Find out what contributions Ohm made to science.

Negro newspaper *Freedom's Journal,* first published, 1827
Discuss various facets of freedom from the Negroes' viewpoint of that time.
Encourage students to serve as journalists; ask them to submit articles which may have been printed in the journal.

First fertilizer law in America enacted, 1871
    Investigate the benefits and dangers of chemical fertilizers.

Federal Trade Commission organized, 1915
    Explain that the commission serves to maintain fair trade practices among merchandisers.
    Discuss situations in which students or their families have found merchants not responsible business people in terms of their goods and services.
    Investigate a local consumer complaint; inquire from a local protection agency what can be done to guard the consumer from special vested interest groups and industrial lobbyists.

Jerry Lewis, American actor, born 1921
    (See Biography Data in Extra-Know-How Section.)

First liquid-fueled rocket developed in the United States by Robert Goddard, 1926
    Investigate the development of rocketry in various countries.

March 17

St. Patrick's Day
    (See Data-Detail in Extra-Know-How Section, "Saint Patrick's Day—History.")

Gottlieb Daimler, German engineer and "Father of the Automobile," born 1834
    (See Biography Data in Extra-Know-How Section.)
    Investigate how Daimler adapted the internal combustion engine to wheeled vehicles.
    Encourage students to design a modern automobile.
    (See activities under March 6, "First American ....")

First postage-canceling machine patented, 1863
    Distribute a number of envelopes with canceled stamps; discuss the purpose of canceling stamps.

First glider flight in America occurred, 1894
    Use Task Card #36 to learn how to make gliders.
    Discuss the sport of hang gliding.

First practical submarine in America launched, 1898
    (See activities under January 17, "U.S. Navy ....")

Campfire Girls of America organized, 1912
    (See activities under March Special Weeks, "Campfire Girls ....")
    Discuss the origin of the group's watchword "Wohelo" (from the first two letters of the words, "work, health, and love"). Invite students to create additional watchwords following this pattern. (The watchwords can relate to themselves.)

Rudolf Nureyev, Russian ballet dancer, born 1938
    (See Biography Data in Extra-Know-How Section.)
    Discuss the rigorous preparation for the physical development of the body.
    Consider Nureyev's decision to relinquish his Russian citizenship to defect to the United States; find the names of others who have chosen to do the same.

National Gallery of Art, Washington, DC, opened, 1941
    Introduce various art appreciation activities; write to Giant Photos for catalogue of inexpensive art prints. (See Address Listing in Extra-Know-How Section.)
    See activities under January 12, "First United ... " and April 13, "New York's ... " and November 7, "Museum of ... " and November 8, "Louvre, the ....")

March 18

Norbert Rillieux, black scientist who invented a sugar refining method, born 1806
    (See Biography Data in Extra-Know-How Section.)
    Find out how sugar is refined.

Investigate the negative effects that sugar consumption can have upon the human body.

Select 10 commercial breakfast cereals; compare the sugar content of each.

Grover Cleveland, twenty-second and twenty-fourth president of the United States, born 1837

(See Biography Data in Extra-Know-How Section.)

Discuss the fact that Cleveland was the first U.S. president to have served two nonconsecutive terms; investigate whether any other president has been elected to nonconsecutive terms since that time.

Rudolph Diesel, German engineer who developed the diesel internal combustion engine, born 1858

(See Biography Data in Extra-Know-How Section.)

Discuss the advantages and disadvantages of diesel engines.

Investigate the process of internal combustion as a process separate from the use by engines.

Electric dry shaver patented, 1931

Discuss social attitudes towards beards throughout history.

Ask students to find out how many different brands of electric shavers are on the market by researching various consumer guides.

Find out the ways which people shaved before electric shavers were available.

Obtain a mustache cup and talk about its use.

Ask students to find pictures of male faces in magazines and then draw mustaches and beards on the faces.

(See activities under January 5, "King Gillette ... " and November 6, "First electric ....")

Plastic lenses for cataract patients fit, 1952

Investigate what cataracts are.

Find out what new treatments there are for cataract patients.

Invite an ophthalmologist to visit the class to discuss various malfunctions of the eye.

Initiate a study of the eye and eye care.

Explore the careers of an optician, optometrist, oculist, ophthalmologist.

(See activities under March Special Weeks, "Save Your Vision Week.")

March 19

Swallows allegedly return to Mission San Juan Capistrano (first recorded in 1776)

Discuss the phenomenon of a predictable return date each year.

Investigate the background of this particular California mission, approximately halfway between San Diego and Los Angeles.

Pursue a bird study of the swallow, i.e., habitat, mating procedures, special features of the bird.

Paint pictures of swallows.

First bank robbery in American occurred, 1831

Investigate how bank security has improved since 1831.

Write an exciting story involving a bank robbery.

William Jennings Bryan, American orator and political leader, born 1860

(See Biography Data in Extra-Know-How Section.)

(See activities under February 12, "Charles Darwin ....")

Irving Wallace, American author, born 1916

(See Biography Data in Extra-Know-How Section.)

Explain that Wallace authored the book called *The Book of Lists*; examine a copy of this book of trivia items and then encourage students to create their own similar lists.

March 20

Earth Day

Use Task Card #37 for Earth Day activities.

(See activities under April Special Weeks, "Earth Week ....")

Harriet Beecher Stowe's novel *Uncle Tom's Cabin* **published, 1852**
Discuss the impact of the story on the United States in the year leading up to the Civil War.
Obtain a children's version of *Uncle Tom's Cabin* and share it with the class. (The novel holds the record for being the most-sold book, other than the *Bible*, up to that period of time.)

Jan Matzeliger, inventor of a machine which made possible the mass production of shoes, born 1883
(See Biography Data in Extra-Know-How Section.)
Ask students to make an informal survey of shoe styles; determine which is the most popular style; discuss the value of mass production in order to meet style demands.
Invite a shoe repair person to class to discuss how a shoe is made; find out whether the field of shoe repair has a future since mass production allows for some types of shoes to be manufactured almost as cheaply as they can be repaired.
Hold a shoe scramble outside in which all students' shoes are mixed in one large pile; at the signal, all students are to scramble to find their own shoes, put them on, and tie them. (Discuss strategies beforehand; the object is for all to finish with their own pair of shoes.)
Write to Footwear Bureau of Canada for the booklet "Neatfeet." (See Address Listing in Extra-Know-How Section.)
(See Data-Detail in Extra-Know-How Section, "Shoes — History.")

B. F. Skinner, American psychologist, born 1904
(See Biography Data in Extra-Know-How Section.)
Encourage interested students to explore the field of behavior modification and stimulus-response experiments.

Carl Reiner, American writer, born 1922
(See Biography Data in Extra-Know-How Section.)
Investigate the career of a comedy writer.

March 21

First day of the zodiac period Aries, the Ram (through April 19)
(See Data-Detail in Extra-Know-How Section, "Notes on Astrology.")

First day of spring (on or about March 21)
(See activities under March Variable Dates, "Spring or Vernal ....")
Review Task Card #30 for activities on spring.

Johann Sebastian Bach, German composer of baroque music, born 1685
(See Biography Data in Extra-Know-How Section.)
Explain that Bach composed music for the harpsichord and clavichord before the pianoforte or piano became popular; due to the limitations of those instruments (no pedal to sustain tone and small keyboards that made chords difficult), Bach ingeniously created the "fugue" — multiple melodies intertwined with one another, note for note, in perfect mathematical coordination.
Invite interested students to investigate, in greater detail, Bach's many other contributions, such as the influence of his fingering system for the keyboard; define terms such as oratorio and cantata, as created by Bach for the organ, stringed instruments, and voice; find out the connection between Bach's baroque ensembles and the modern counterparts of jazz groups.

Benito Juárez, Mexican statesman known as the "Mexican Washington," born 1806
(See Biography Data in Extra-Know-How Section.)

Phyllis McGinley, American writer, born 1905
(See Biography Data in Extra-Know-How Section.)
Investigate the career of a children's author.
Obtain copies of McGinley's books and share them with the class.

John D. Rockefeller, III, grandson of the Standard Oil industrialist, John D. Rockefeller, born 1906
(See Biography Data in Extra-Know-How Section.)
Investigate two of the Rockefeller family's most noted philanthropies — the endowment of the University of Chicago and the Rockefeller Foundation.

Find out how foundation and trust funds are perpetuated; define the term "endowment."
(See activities under July 8, "John D. Rockefeller ... " and "Nelson Rockefeller ....")

March 22

Sir Anthony Van Dyck, Flemish portrait painter, born 1599
(See Biography Data in Extra-Know-How Section.)
Locate the area on a map that currently represents where Flanders was; find out what language was spoken in Flanders.
Explain that Van Dyck produced a series of etched portraits called the "Iconography"; define the terms: icon, iconography, iconoclast.
Find out the process through which one gains the title of "Sir."

British Stamp Act against the American colonists enforced, 1765
Research the background of the phrase "taxation without representation."

Robert A. Millikan, American physicist, born 1868
(See Biography Data in Extra-Know-How Section.)
Investigate the career of a physicist.

Karl Malden, American actor, born 1913
(See Biography Data in Extra-Know-How Section.)

Marcel Marceau, French pantomimist, born 1923
(See Biography Data in Extra-Know-How Section.)
Define the following words: mime, pantomime, mimic.
Invite students to practice the art of mime and pantomime.
Play the game "Charades."

Grand Coulee Dam first operated, 1941
Discuss what the purpose of a dam is.
Locate where the Grand Coulee Dam is; find out which river was harnessed through the construction of the dam.

March 23

World Meteorology Day
(See activities under February 9, "U.S. Weather ....")

"Give me liberty or give me death" speech delivered by Patrick Henry, 1775
Discuss the significance of the message; consider the risk involved in having made such a public declaration.

Rivet patented, 1794
Discuss the area of language and culture; explain that certain Eskimo groups are known to have multiple words to describe snow conditions, whereas highly technologic societies as America have developed extended vocabulary for areas of technical knowledge, such as for fasteners (rivet, zipper, button, snap, hook-and-eye, safety pins, clips).

Fannie Farmer, cooking expert and creator of the level measurement, born 1857
(See Biography Data in Extra-Know-How Section.)
Begin a unit on measurement.
Experiment with recipes using inexact or estimated measurements.
Attempt to obtain a copy of Farmer's original cookbook and review the recipes.

First cable car patented, 1858
Investigate the operating principles of a cable car.
(See activities under August 1, "First cable ....")

Erich Fromm, American psychologist/writer, born 1900
(See Biography Data in Extra-Know-How Section.)

Discuss the concept of "escape from freedom" as related to a sense of responsibility that accompanies freedom; relate the idea to privileges and self-responsibilities within the classroom and home settings.

Discuss Fromm's statement: "The highest form of human activity is inactivity."

Joan Crawford, American actress, born 1908
(See Biography Data in Extra-Know-How Section.)

Law banning the teaching of evolution adopted by the state of Tennessee, 1925
Read *Inherit the Wind*, by Jerome Lawrence and Robert Lee, and then invite students to enact the Scopes Trial.

Discuss the reasons that a state would regulate what is to be taught in the public schools.

Wernher von Braun, German-American rocket engineer, born 1912
(See Biography Data in Extra-Know-How Section.)

Name other German scientists who came to America, following World Wars I and II, who continued to contribute their expertise.

March 24

John Wesley Powell, American geologist/anthropologist, born 1834
(See Biography Data in Extra-Know-How Section.)

Investigate the career of a geologist or anthropologist.

Explain that Powell was the first director of the U.S. Bureau of Ethnology and was responsible for the first classification of American Indian languages; trace the background of the word "ethnology."

Bring to class copies of the journals *Ethnology* and *American Anthropologist*.

Right to vote won by the women of Canada, 1837
Ask interested students to develop a comparative chart of dates concerning women suffrage movements throughout the world.

Find out when women in the United States gained the right to vote.

Consult a dictionary to define "suffrage."

Andrew Mellon, American financier and U.S. secretary of the treasury, born 1855
(See Biography Data in Extra-Know-How Section.)

Discuss the fact that Mellon was raised in a financially successful family but that he continued gainful investments throughout his life; through his development of the Union Savings Bank, he gained control of coal, railroad, steel, waterpower, oil, and aluminum enterprises.

Investigate Mellon's other areas of benefaction besides his extensive philanthropy to the National Gallery of Art in Washington, DC.

Discovery of the tubercle bacillus announced by Robert Koch, 1882
Find out what disease is related to this discovery and what benefit accrued by having isolated the germ of the disease formerly called "consumption."

Investigate current methods of detecting the germ in human beings.

Discover what the career of a medical researcher would be like.

(See activities under November Month-long Observances, "Christmas Seal ... " and December 11, Robert Koch ....")

Steve McQueen, American actor, born 1930
(See Biography Data in Extra-Know-How Section.)

Twenty-sixth Amendment to the U.S. Constitution ratified, 1971
(See Data-Detail in Extra-Know-How Section, "Amendments to the U.S. Constitution.")

March 25

James Braid, Scottish surgeon who established the reality of hypnotism, died 1860
Investigate the modern application of hypnosis; in particular, find out how hypnosis relates to the field of medicine.

Discuss the potential benefits of being able to self-hypnotize.

Gutzon Borglum, American sculptor and creator of the Mt. Rushmore figures, born 1867
(See Biography Data in Extra-Know-How Section.)
Obtain a picture of the Mt. Rushmore Memorial; discuss how Borglum arrived at the decision as to which personalities to portray.
(See Data-Detail in Extra-Know-How Section, "Mount Rushmore Description.")

Arturo Toscanini, Italian conductor, born 1867
(See Biography Data in Extra-Know-How Section.)
Investigate how one prepares for a career as a conductor.
Make a list of famous conductors throughout the world, past and present; find out with which symphonies current conductors are associated.

Aretha Franklin, American singer, born 1942
(See Biography Data in Extra-Know-How Section.)

Commercial production of colored television sets begun, 1954
Use Task Card #38 to study television further.

Record of first five-time world boxing championship achieved by Sugar Ray Robinson, 1958
(See activities under March 8, "Muhammad Ali ....")

March 26

Lifeboat patented, 1845
Design an ocean liner with lifeboats strategically placed.
Write a creative story revealing an exciting adventure in which lifeboats are needed.

Adhesive and medicated plaster patented, 1845
Consider what bandages were like before they were made adhesive.

Commercial motion picture film first manufactured by George Eastman, 1885
Examine different sizes of motion picture film or study about them.
Write a class letter to Eastman-Kodak Co. for further information about film. (See Address Listing in Extra-Know-How Section.)
Investigate what new advances are being made in the development of film.

Robert Frost, American poet and four-time winner of the Pulitzer Prize, born 1875
(See Biography Data in Extra-Know-How Section.)
Obtain copies of Frost's poetry and share with the class.
Discuss the following lines from Frost's poem "The Road Not Taken" and consider what it means to be an individualist: Two roads diverged in a wood
And I—I took the one less traveled by
And that has made all the difference.

Walt Whitman, American poet, died, penniless, 1892
Investigate the life and times of Whitman.
Obtain a copy of the poem "O Captain! My Captain!"; share it with the class and discuss the meaning.
Learn why Whitman was called "the good gray poet."

Tennessee Williams, American playwright, born 1911
(See Biography Data in Extra-Know-How Section.)

Fire involving the Triangle Shirt-Waist Factory occurred, 1911
Explain that the fire caused 147 deaths and many injuries and that the incident served as the forerunner of factory safety and protection regulations.
Discuss what a "sweatshop" might have been like to work in and whether this type of workplace still exists in the United States; investigate current fire safety rules in buildings around the community.
Review school fire-drill procedures.

Statue of "Popeye, the Sailor" erected by the spinach-growers of Crystal City, Texas, 1937
Discuss how celebrities, real or fictitious, influence people's buying habits, i.e., Fred Flintstone Vitamins.®

Plant and tend a garden of spinach seeds.
Discuss various uses of spinach: salad, soufflé, and various recipes containing the term "Florentine."
Find out how many students like or dislike spinach.

Polio vaccine introduced by Jonas Salk, 1953.
(See activities under January Month-long Observances, "March of ....")

March 27

Edward M. Bannister, American negro painter of land- and seascapes, born 1828
(See Biography Data in Extra-Know-How Section.)
Explain that Bannister's art work was awarded a first prize-gold medal at the Centennial Exposition in Philadelphia, 1876; however, he was only able to claim the award after competing artists insisted that Bannister not be racially discriminated against.

William Roentgen, German physicist, born 1845
(See Biography Data in Extra-Know-How Section.)
Discuss how scientists occasionally chance upon a discovery, which is what happened in Roentgen's discovery of the X-ray.
Obtain copies of X-rays and share with class; discuss how medicine has benefited from X-rays.
Investigate the careers of an X-ray technician and that of a physician-radiologist.
Write to the Food and Drug Administration for the booklet "We Want You to Know about Diagnostic X-rays." (See Address Listing in Extra-Know-How Section.)
Use Task Card #39 for X-ray art.
Find out how uranium functions in the production of high-energy X-rays.
(See activities under January 12, "First X-ray ....")

Otto Wallach, German chemist, born 1847
(See Biography Data in Extra-Know-How Section.)
Explain that Wallach researched ethereal oils and the identification of alicyclic (organic) compounds, chemicals which were important to the modern perfume industry.
Make a list of commonly known perfumes.
Find out the chemical differences among perfume, cologne, and fragrant toilet water.
Investigate the career of a chemist or chemical engineer.

Corkscrew patented, 1860
Discuss what the purpose of a corkscrew is and what innovations have replaced the original designs.
Ask students to create other novel type openers for containers.

Edward Steichen, photographer/editor, born 1879
(See Biography Data in Extra-Know-How Section.)
Obtain a copy of *Family of Man* and share it with the class; discuss how photographs can evoke compassion, humor, etc.; consider the statement, "A picture is worth a thousand words."

Ferde Grofé, American composer, born 1892
(See Biography Data in Extra-Know-How Section.)
Obtain pictures of the Grand Canyon, as well as a recording of Grofé's "Grand Canyon Suite."

First cherry trees planted in Washington, DC, 1912
Obtain a picture of Washington, DC with the cherry trees in blossom.
Find out who was responsible for the massive planting of cherry trees in the nation's capital city.
Develop an art creation of cherry trees in blossom.
Find out how double-petaled cherry blossoms were developed.

Nathaniel Currier, American artist, born 1918
(See Biography Data in Extra-Know-How Section.)
Obtain copies of Currier and Ives pictures; discuss the particular technique of lithography art; invite students to paint their own pictures of nineteenth-century America.
(See activities under March 5, "James Merritt ....")

Alaska earthquake occurred, 1964
Investigate the relationship among earthquakes, tidal waves, and other geologic-lunar-related phenomena.
(See activities under April 18, "San Francisco ....")

March 28

Raphael, Italian painter of the Renaissance, born 1483
(See Biography Data in Extra-Know-How Section.)
Obtain prints of Raphael's work, such as *The Three Graces* and the *Sistine Madonna*.
Find out about other artists who lived during the Renaissance.

First washing machine in the United States patented by Nathaniel Briggs, 1797
Obtain a washboard and demonstrate its use; discuss the various ways clothes were washed before the development of automatic washers and dryers.

Child-labor Law, restricting the ages of the worker, approved in Pennsylvania, 1848
Discuss the rationale for the law at that time but the possible disadvantages of such a law at the present time.

First hospital ambulance service introduced, 1866
Discuss the occupation of an ambulance driver and of a paramedic.
Investigate what the inside of an ambulance looks like; explore the communication system between an ambulance and an emergency room of a hospital.

Spyros Panagiates Skouras, Greek-American motion picture executive and creator of 20th Century Fox Studios, born 1893
(See Biography Data in Extra-Know-How Section.)
Investigate certain aspects of moviemaking, such as the "Movieola."
Write a movie script, and film the action.
Write the Academy of Motion Picture Arts and Sciences for information, such as how the "Oscar" derived its name, when the first Academy Awards were granted, and who the most recent winners were. (See Address Listing in Extra-Know-How Section.)

First lethal execution by gas authorized in America, 1921
Hold a debate on the following topic: "The Death Penalty Should Be Abolished."
Consult a dictionary for the background of the word "lethal."

First microfilm reading device introduced, 1922
Discuss what microfilm is and its advantage for storage; explore the differences between microfilm and microfiche.
Take a field trip to a local library that has a microfilm or microfiche reader; assist students in learning how to use the machines.

Breakdown of nuclear power plant's reactor at Three Mile Island (Middletown), occurred in Pennsylvania, 1979
Explain that the Nuclear Regulatory Commission warned of a possible core meltdown—a catastrophic event that could mean major loss of life; hold a debate on the topic of nuclear reactors.
(See activities under December 2, "First atomic ....")

March 29

John Tyler, tenth president of the United States, born 1790
(See Biography Data in Extra-Know-How Section.)

Federal highway, the "Great National Pike," authorized, 1806
Discuss why the thoroughfare was also called "The Great Highway of Western Migration."
Obtain a map of the United States and trace the national highway from Cumberland to St. Louis (approximately follows U.S. Highway 40).
Trace the background of the word "turnpike."

First eye hospital incorporated, 1822
Investigate the career of an eye surgeon.

Make a study of the functions and structure of the eye.

Develop a list of the more commonly known eye diseases and malfunctions; list also the corrective procedures. (Consult a dictionary to find the meaning of the prefix, "mal"; also find the meaning of the prefix, "bene"; make two separate lists of other words which have these prefix-related meanings, i.e., "malign" and "benign").

Oscar F. Mayer, American meat packer and founder of Oscar Mayer & Company, born, 1859
(See Biography Data in Extra-Know-How Section.)
Discuss the various cuts of meat from a variety of animals.
Check the labels on cans of meat to find out the ingredients inside.

Pearl Bailey, American singer/actress, author, born 1918
(See Biography Data in Extra-Know-How Section.)

Julius and Ethel Rosenberg and Morton Sobel convicted of World War II espionage conspiracy, 1951
Investigate the background of their espionage activities, as related to secret atomic research.
Discuss the fact that many nations maintain intelligence agencies; find out more about the work of America's CIA (Central Intelligence Agency).
Find out the derivation and meaning of "espionage."

Twenty-third Amendment to the U.S. Constitution ratified, 1961
(See Data-Detail in Extra-Know-How Section, "Amendments to the U.S. Constitution.")

March 30

National Shut-in Day
Find out the meaning of a "shut-in."
Investigate which local groups arrange for people to visit "shut-ins"; consider how valuable television has been for people who are in rest homes or hospitals.
Visit a convalescent home and plan a program to be performed.

Francisco José de Goya, Spanish artist, born 1756
(See Biography Data in Extra-Know-How Section.)
Obtain prints of the artist's work and share them with the class.

Anesthesia first used during surgery, 1842
Investigate the careers of an anesthetist and of a physician-anesthesiologist.
Discuss the actual role that the anesthesiologist serves in an operation; explore what other procedures were used before anesthesia was introduced.
Find out the derivation of the word "anesthesia."
Consider why malpractice insurance is particularly essential for an anesthesiologist to carry.

Incubator for eggs patented, 1843
Obtain or build an incubator for eggs to demonstrate how chickens hatch.
Discuss the question, "Which comes first—the chicken or the egg?"
Investigate other types of incubators.

Vincent Van Gogh, Dutch artist, born 1853
(See Biography Data in Extra-Know-How Section.)
Obtain prints of the artist's paintings and discuss his varying style throughout various periods of his life.
Invite students to learn more about the style which is characteristic of Van Gogh's work and then try to recreate it in their paintings.
Discuss Van Gogh's statement: "The best way to know life is to love many things."

Pencil with attached eraser patented, 1858
Hand out new pencils, as students earn them by helping others or by doing chores.
(See Data-Detail in Extra-Know-How Section, "History of Writing Instruments."
Think about the comment, "To err is human, but when the eraser runs out ahead of the pencil, you're overdoing it."
(See activities under February Special Weeks, "National Pencil ... " and November 19, "Machine which ....")

Alaska purchased from Russia by the United States, 1867

Discuss the background of the term "Seward's Folly."

Introduce a study of Alaska that stresses the state's wealth in terms of wildlife, timber, oil, and fishing industries.

Explore the history of the Alaskan pipeline, in view of energy needs vis-á-vis ecological imbalances; draw a map of Alaska with the pipeline crossing south from Prudhoe Bay to Valdez.

Find out what international agreements with Canada have been necessary concerning the extension of gas lines from Alaska through Canada.

Find out how far the western-most point of Alaska is to Russia.

Write the Alaska Division on Tourism for a teacher's kit on Alaska. (See Address Listing in Extra-Know-How Section.)

(See activities under June 16, "Alaska gold ... " and September 10, "Alaska awarded ....")

Fifteenth Amendment to the U.S. Constitution ratified, 1870

(See Data-Detail in Extra-Know-How Section, "Amendments to the U.S. Constitution.")

Warren Beatty, American screen actor, born 1937

(See Biography Data in Extra-Know-How Section.)

President Ronald Reagan shot in an attempted assassination, 1981

Investigate the incident and discuss the issues surrounding handgun control; hold a debate concerning whether handgun control laws should be established.

Find out which other U.S. presidents were victims of assassination attempts.

Examine the historical coincidence that every U.S. president elected in a year divisible by 20 has died in office; find out who these seven presidents were.

Investigate the circumstances which allegedly led to the curse that the Shawnee Indians invoked upon William Henry Harrison and the U.S. government—the "Indians' Revenge" for the U.S. government's unfair seizure of their lands.

March 31

René Dèscartes, French philosopher, mathematician, and scientist, born 1596

(See Biography Data in Extra-Know-How Section.)

Discuss what Dèscartes meant by, "I think, therefore I am" (*Cognito ergo sum*).

Consider Dèscartes' statement, "One thing that cannot be doubted is doubt itself."

Explain that the theories and teachings of Dèscartes are termed "Cartesian"; find out what other contributions are Cartesian in origin.

Explore why it is that philosophers are often mathematicians as well.

Franz Josef Haydn, Austrian composer, born 1732

(See Biography Data in Extra-Know-How Section.)

Obtain recordings of Haydn's music and invite students to create drawings in response to the music.

Robert Wilhelm Bunsen, German scientist, born 1811

(See Biography Data in Extra-Know-How Section.)

Investigate why the Bunsen burner is unique.

Bring a Bunsen burner to class and conduct a simple chemistry experiment with the burner.

First electric street lighting installed in the United States, 1880

Discuss the advantages and disadvantages of street lighting.

Encourage students to draw a picture of a street in three sections to depict three periods of time in the development of street illumination: lamplighters, electric lighting, and a futuristic form of energy-saving lighting such as "solar light at night."

Eiffel Tower in the city of Paris, France completed, 1889

Investigate the various statistics about the development of the tower which made it a significant engineering feat.

Find out how the tower derived its name.

Original daylight saving time begun, 1918

Discuss the advantages and disadvantages of "saving" daylight time; mention the various careers that are significantly affected by the change.

Review Task Card #35 concerning activities on time.

Investigate the reason for changing March 31, the original initial day of daylight saving, to that of the fourth Sunday in April.

Cesar Chávez, labor union organizer of the United Farm Workers, born 1927

(See Biography Data in Extra-Know-How Section.)

Hold a debate relating to the pros and cons of labor unions.

Discuss what leadership skills or personal qualities are needed to organize a group of people.

Discover what the term "boycott" means.

First black selected as an astronaut, Edward J. Dwight, Jr., 1962

Find out what training is necessary to become an astronaut.

Learn what the purpose of Dwight's space flight was; draw a picture depicting this particular space mission.

Richard Chamberlain, American actor, born 1935

(See Biography Data in Extra-Know-How Section.)

APRIL

April, as the fourth month of the year, originates from Aprilis, *the Latin word meaning "to open." The interpretation is thought to refer to the opening or budding of spring blossoms.*

Birthstone: *Diamond or Zircon*
Flower: *Sweetpea/Daisy*

Use the Find-a-Word Reproducible to preview happenings in April. (See Reproducible Section.)

MONTH-LONG OBSERVANCES

National Automobile Month

Arrange for a class contest on the design of a futuristic automobile.

Make a class list of foreign and domestic automobiles that are available.

Discuss different types of engines, i.e., V6, V8; find out why "V" is used to refer to the number of cylinders.

Investigate the career of an automotive mechanic.

(See activities under March 6, "First American automobile ... " and March 17, "Gottlieb Daimler ....")

Cancer-Control Month

Invite a representative from the local chapter of the American Cancer Society to visit the class.

Write to the American Cancer Society to obtain literature on the types of cancer, warning signs, and preventative measures. (See Address Listing in Extra-Know-How Section.)

Consider one definition of cancer—anything harmful or corruptive that spreads and destroys, as related to the disease.

Explain that pathology is the science of the origin, nature, and course of disease; discuss the fact that medical researchers have contained such fatal diseases as yellow fever, malaria, cholera, pneumonia, diphtheria, smallpox, poliomyelitis, measles, tuberculosis, and many others; find out which of the above diseases were basically eradicated by preventative immunization, rather than through "cures" of medication and care after the fact.

Discuss the point that immunization often involves the process of inoculation by which an individual is injected with a very minor form of the germ; consider the body processes which operate to build up an immunity to the disease.

Define the terms: carcinogen, remission, malignant, tumor.

Investigate the profession of a pathologist.

SPECIAL WEEKS

National Laugh Week (week of April first)

Invite students to bring a joke to class.

Discuss what makes people laugh and consider the different forms of humor, i.e., exaggeration, pun (play on words), satire, timing; consider the point that humor varies according to different languages and cultures.

Arrange for a "Crazy Day" in which everyone wears crazy clothes if they wish to do so.

Discuss the following comments: "Laughter is a tranquilizer with no side effects"; "He laughs best, who laughs last"; "The day you grow up is the day you can laugh at yourself."

(See activities under June Special Weeks, "National Humor ....")

National Library Week (second Sunday)

Acknowledge the librarian at the school or local library.

Introduce library skills and the Dewey Decimal System; investigate the purpose and services of the Library of Congress.

Explain the resource of the reference librarian; ask a librarian to expose students to the variety of reference volumes.

Invite students to conduct a survey of students' favorite library books, by grade level. (See Conducting a Survey Data in Extra-Know-How Section.)

Investigate the career of a librarian and the many different types of librarians.

Encourage students to do a book report. (See Book Report in Sample Packet Section.)

(See activities under April 9, "First American ... " and November 1, "Authors' Day ....")

National Coin Week (third Sunday)

Invite students to bring their coin collections to class; examine both domestic and foreign coins, past and present, and "proof sets" for given years.

Investigate the derivation of the word "numismatic."

Write to the American Numismatic Association. (See Address Listing in Extra-Know-How Section.)

(See activities under April 2, "Establishment of ... " and July 31, "Cornerstone Laid ... " and August 2, "First Lincoln ....")

National Secretary Week (last full week)

Acknowledge the secretaries of the school in a special way.

Explore the topic of why the occupation of a secretary in the U.S. has been gender-linked with females.

Earth Week (third week)

Review Task Card #37 for activities about the earth.

Discuss the statement: "Whatever his accomplishments, his sophistication, his artistic pretentions, man owes his very existence to a six-inch layer of topsoil—and the fact that it rains."

National Garden Week (week including April 22)

Plant an indoor or outdoor vegetable or flower garden.

Discuss the tips, tricks, and techniques of creating a garden.

Study the principles of hydroponic gardening.

Make a study of types of flowers and their parts.

Trace the background of the word "horticulture."

Review Task Card #32 for activities on planting.

Bike Safety Week (Monday of third full week)

Discuss the purpose of registering bikes; conduct a survey as to how many bikes in the school are registered. (See Conducting a Survey Data in Extra-Know-How Section.)

Write to Aetna Life and Casualty Insurance Co. for the booklet "Bicycle Safety." (See Address Listing in Extra-Know-How Section.)

Use Task Card #40 for activities on bicycles.

Pan American Week (week including April 14)

Contact the Pan American Union to obtain information. (See Address Listing in Extra-Know-How Section.)

Encourage students to make a map of the Western Hemisphere; trace the approximate route of the original plan for the Pan American Highway.

Write to the Organization of American States for the booklet "Program Aids." (See Address Listing in Extra-Know-How Section.)

(See activities under April 30, "Organization of ... " and November Special Weeks, "Latin America ... " and December 2, "Pan American ....")

National YWCA Week (Sunday of last full week in April)

Contact the local YWCA to find out what activities and services are available.

Discuss the principles upon which both the YWCA and the YMCA are formed.

Chemical Progress Week (mid-month)

Obtain a chemistry set; discuss laboratory materials, equipment, vocabulary; discuss the steps of the scientific method; conduct an experiment.

Discuss the term "progress" as related to environmental concerns.

Investigate the career of a chemist.

Canada—U.S. Goodwill Week (Sunday including April 27)

Design a study unit on the 10 provinces of Canada.

Investigate the major international crossings between the United States and Canada, both by land and water.

Discuss the various reciprocal customs which exist between the two countries, i.e., foreign postage rates are not necessary on letters between the two countries.

Consider the importance of cooperative relations between countries that are contiguous to one another.

Investigate the province of Quebec to learn the background of how a French province developed along with the English-speaking provinces; find out if both French and English are considered to be official languages in Canada.

National Baby Week (usually last Saturday)

Ask students to discuss with family and relatives what the student was like as an infant.

Examine the nutritional needs of babies; discuss the pros and cons of bottle-feeding.

Invite students to talk about their baby siblings.

Share baby pictures to see if other students can identify who the picture represents.

Review guidelines for effective babysitting.

Find out at what age babies' tear ducts begin to produce tears.

Consider the necessities and the luxuries for baby care.

Obtain pictures of babies growing up in other countries; notice the commonly practiced custom of mothers' carrying their child on their backs.

Invite a pediatrician to class to speak about pediatrics as a career.

Write to Gerber Products Company for information. (See Address Listing in Extra-Know-How Section.)

VARIABLE DATES

Baseball season begins (first or second Monday)

Encourage students to bring in newspaper clippings from sports pages.

Make classroom baseball predictions for the season.

Draw team insignia of favorite teams in either the American or National Leagues.

Encourage students to coach one another on learning the terms for the following box score terms: E.R. = earned runs; A.B. = at bat; H = hits; I.P. = Innings pitched; R.B.I. = runs batted in; S.O. = strike out; B.B. = base on balls; R. = runs; D.H. = designated hitter.

Investigate the careers of a professional baseball player or baseball club manager.

Review Task Card #17 for activities on baseball.

Review Reproducible #8 concerning baseball trivia.

(See activities under January 29, "Baseball's American ... " and "First baseball ....")

Master's Golf Tournament (week which includes first or second Thursday)

Use Task Card #41 for the study of golf.

Motion picture industry Academy Awards evening

Write to the Academy of Motion Picture Arts and Sciences for information concerning the background of the Oscar award; inquire also about the various categories for which the awards are given and who the Oscar winners of the past have been. (See Address Listing in Extra-Know-How Section.)

Invite students to list their current nominations for each category and then conduct an election.

Encourage students to watch the award presentation, with parental/guardian permission.

National Artichoke Week (any week, beginning on Thursday)

Find out where the "Artichoke Capital of the World" is and where the artichoke was first cultivated.

Bring in an artichoke, explain how it is cooked, served, and eaten.

Create a project with an artichoke; develop a vegetable puppet; write an ode to an artichoke; draw a stylized artichoke.

Write to the California Artichoke Advisory Board for information. (See Address Listing in the Extra-Know-How Section.)

Daylight Saving Time (last Sunday)

Discuss the purpose of implementing daylight saving time.

Remind students, in terms of resetting their clocks, "You 'spring' forward and 'fall' back."

Use a map to point out a specific area in the United States; once clocks are reset, specify a time and ask students to figure out the time in various other time zones.

(See activities under March 31, "Original Daylight ....")

Passover (usually in April) — a Jewish holiday commemorating the deliverance of the Jewish people from slavery in Egypt

Holy Week (usually in April, sometimes in March)
   Palm Sunday, Holy (Maundy) Thursday, Good Friday, Easter Sunday

DAYS OF THE MONTH

April 1

April Fools' Day
   Use Reproducible #18 for learning to follow the rules.
   Use Reproducible #19 for Logic Test to teach students not to be fooled.
   (See Data-Detail in Extra-Know-How Section, "April Fools' Day—History.")

William Harvey, English physician who partially described the system of human blood circulation, born 1578
   (See Biography Data in Extra-Know-How Section.)
   Explain that Harvey's discovery was only possible because he ventured to experiment on live animals rather than on human cadavers; his findings were revolutionary to the field of medicine in that he determined that arteries carry blood *away* from the heart and that veins carry it *toward* the heart, and that the same blood is pumped round and round the body.
   Consider why a significant part was missing from Harvey's description of the body's flow of blood. (The network of millions of capillaries and their vital functions were not noticed by the naked eye of Dr. Harvey for he lived long before the invention of the microscope.)
   Study the flow of blood in the circulatory system as vitally related to other systems and parts of the body.
   Investigate the background of the term "intravenous"; find out one of the reasons for the intravenous process (to inject the blood system with glucose following surgery in order to save the "shocked" body from having to produce its own glucose and other nourishment.
   Research blood-sugar levels as related to the body conditions of hypoglycemia and diabetes. Investigate the process of glucose-tolerance tests.
   Examine in greater detail the technique of coronary arteriography (exploratory photograph)
   (See activities under January Month-long Observances, "National Blood ....")

Otto von Bismarck, creator of the German Empire, born 1815
   (See Biography Data in Extra-Know-How Section.)
   Investigate the meaning of "Iron Chancellor."
   Research the background of the Austro-Prussian War.

First salaried fire department organized, 1853
   Investigate the careers of those involved with fire prevention fighting at all levels—municipal, county, state, and federal.
   Invite a representative from the local fire department to visit the class to discuss the extended responsibilities of fire departments.
   Find out whether the local community sponsors a volunteer fire fighting organization.
   Develop a class list of compound words beginning with "fire"; then consult a dictionary to augment the list.
   Consider what the significance of the discovery of fire was on human civilization.
   Explore various fire and smoke alarm systems found in homes and public buildings.
   (See activities under October Special Weeks, "Fire Prevention ....")

First U.S. wartime conscription law enacted, 1863
   Find out what "conscription" means.
   Discuss the conscription law of that time, whereby a recruit could send a replacement; consider the difference between a deserter and a bonafide conscientious objector.
   Explore the advantages and disadvantages of both a volunteer defense force and that of armed forces by conscription.
   (See activities under September 16, "Selective Service ... " and October 29, "Men drafted ....")

Abraham Maslow, American psychologist, born 1908
   (See Biography Data in Extra-Know-How Section.)
   Explore the significance of Maslow's revolutionary approach to psychology—to use the mentally/emotionally healthier, as opposed to the mentally/emotionally weaker, as a model.

Investigate the preparation and the careers of a psychoanalyst, psychiatrist, psychologist, and related professions.

Find out the derivation of the term "psyche."

First movie censorship board established, 1913

Show a film and "censor" it by cutting off the sound or image at various intervals.

Discuss what censorship is, who is granted the right to determine censorship decisions, and why a censorship board is considered by some to be necessary; consider how censorship and the First Amendment to the U.S. Constitution (freedom of belief and expression) conflict.

Talk about the purpose of cinema ratings of X, R, PG, and G.

First telephone switchboard with Braille markings used, 1928

Review what a switchboard is; investigate the technology of Braille markings on a switchboard.

Discuss how inventions help to provide employment and other opportunities for the handicapped.

Brainstorm other innovations that might aid any individual who, for one reason or another, has varying needs (such as left-handed people or those with severe or profound handicaps).

Debbie Reynolds, American actress, born 1932

(See Biography Data in Extra-Know-How Section.)

Ali MacGraw, American actress, born 1939

(See Biography Data in Extra-Know-How Section.)

U.S. Population census taken, 1970

Investigate how a population census is taken.

Consult an almanac to compare the U.S. population to that of other countries; make U.S. comparisons of age, ethnic, gender groups.

Design estimation problems based upon census information; for example, if there were 205 million Americans in 1970 and 210 million in 1974, what is the predictable U.S. population for later years?

April 2

International Children's Book Day

Use Task Card #42 for activities about books.

(See activities under April Special Weeks, "National Library ....")

Establishment of the U.S. Mint authorized by Congress, 1792

Bring a variety of U.S. coins to class; ask students to place a coin under paper and rub over it with the side of a lead pencil; detect the markings on the rubbings and discuss the significance of the *S*, the *D*, and of the coins with no letter marking.

Examine the various persons who are commemorated on different denominations of coins; look at the various wordings on the coins, i.e., "In God We Trust" and *E Pluribus Unum*; find out the meaning of the Latin term.

Show a film on the minting of money.

(See activities under April Special Weeks, "National Coin ... " and May 16, "First U.S. ... " and July 31, "Cornerstone laid ....")

Hans Christian Andersen, Danish folktale writer, born 1805

(See Biography Data in Extra-Know-How Section.)

Celebrate the day with a birthday party for H. C. Andersen; ask students to dress as characters from Andersen's tales and to act out the parts.

Obtain a copy of *Hans Christian Andersen*, by Hedvig Collin, and enjoy it with the students.

Frederic Auguste Bartholdi, French sculptor who created the Statue of Liberty, born 1834

(See Biography Data in Extra-Know-How Section.)

(See activities under October 28, "Statue of Liberty ....")

Process for refining aluminum patented by Charles M. Hall, 1899

Discuss the significance of the metallic element's light weight.

Make a class list of products and various industries which make use of the lightweight quality of aluminum.

U.S. Congress asked by President Woodrow Wilson to declare war on Germany, 1917

Discuss U.S. government procedures for declaring war; review the three branches of government, as well as the system of checks and balances.

Investigate the attitude of the American public toward going into World War I.

Find out why World War I was referred to as "the war to end all wars."

April 3

Washington Irving, American author, born 1783 (pseudonym—Diedrich Knickerbocker)

(See Biography Data in Extra-Know-How Section.)

Enjoy the tales of "Rip Van Winkle" and "The Legend of Sleepy Hollow."

Encourage students to write a creative story about the following topic: "If I Were to Fall Asleep Today and Awaken in the Year 2000, What Would the General Environment Be Like?"

Edward Everett Hale, American author and clergyman, born 1822

(See Biography Data in Extra-Know-How Section.)

Obtain a copy of *Man without a Country* (or the film) and share it with students. (Explain that the character, Philip Nolan, and the plot are fictitious.)

Discuss what it would be like to be banished from one's own country and never be allowed to receive news about the country.

Coffee mill patented, 1829

Bring various types of coffee beans for the students to examine.

Review the various approaches to making coffee, i.e., percolator, instant powder or freeze-dried, capsule, brewed, commercial vending machine.

On a map of the world, color in the areas where coffee is grown; explain that coffee is one of the most universal beverages of the world, although it is prepared and served differently.

Emile Zola, French social reformer and novelist, born 1840

(See Biography Data in Extra-Know-How Section.)

(See activities under January 13, "*J'accuse*, Emile ....")

First Pony-Express service begun, 1860

Find out why the Pony Express lasted only 37 days.

Discuss the advantages and disadvantages of the Pony Express.

Hat-blocking and shaping machine invented, 1866

Encourage students to examine history books for various styles of old-fashioned hats.

Hold a "Design Your Own Hat" contest.

Trace the derivation of the word "millinery."

Discuss the progression of social customs as related to the wearing of hats by both men and women.

Ask students to bring in various hats and to role-play the person who would fit the hat.

Sergei Rachmaninoff, Russian composer and pianist, born 1873

(See Biography Data in Extra-Know-How Section.)

Obtain recordings of his music and share with the class.

Jesse James, American outlaw, died 1882

Investigate the life and times of Jesse James.

Suggest that students read books about Jesse James.

Introduce the art of ballad writing; encourage students to write a ballad about life in the American old west.

(See Biography Data in Extra-Know-How Section.)

"The American Creed," by William Tyler, written, 1917

(See Data-Detail in Extra-Know-How Section, "The American Creed"; analyze the words and message of the creed.)

Invite students to create their own creeds as members of a family, students in a classroom, or citizens of the world.

Marlon Brando, American actor, born 1924

(See Biography Data in Extra-Know-How Section.)

Jane van Lawick-Goodall, English ethologist, born 1934
　　(See Biography Data in Extra-Know-How Section.)
　　Explain that an ethologist scientifically studies animal behavior.
　　Find out in what countries Goodall conducted most of her work; locate these areas on a map or globe.
　　Investigate the following topics: what animals, in particular, that Goodall studied; the name of a famous anthropologist with whom Goodall worked and what his accomplishments were.
　　Trace the circumstances surrounding Goodall's death.

Marshall Plan enacted by the United States following World War II, 1948
　　Investigate the background of the European Recovery Program.
　　Discuss how the Marshall Plan has served as a precedent for peacetime programs following military conflicts.

April 4

Dorothea Lynde Dix, American writer and social reformer, born 1802
　　(See Biography Data in Extra-Know-How Section.)
　　Break into small groups and discuss ideas concerning reforms of a social nature within the school and/or community.

U.S. flag, with 13 stripes and many stars, adopted by Congress, 1818
　　Conduct a class project to determine which star represents which state in order to develop a list of the order in which states were admitted to the United States. (Begin with the fourteenth state.)
　　(See Data-Detail in Extra-Know-How Section, "U.S. Flag and Flag Day—History.")

Linus Yale, inventor and lock manufacturer, born 1821
　　Investigate various kinds of locks.
　　Invite a representative from the local police department to talk about security.
　　Write a story about locks, keys, and keyholes.
　　Find out information about lock-related topics, such as master keys or about the origin of the name "skeleton key."

Pierre Monteux, French-American conductor, born 1875
　　(See Biography Data in Extra-Know-How Section.)
　　(See activities under March 25, "Arturo Toscanini ....")

Arthur Murray, American dance instructor, born 1895
　　(See Biography Data in Extra-Know-How Section.)

Rhodes Scholarships established, 1902
　　Research the background and purpose of the scholarship.
　　Design a simple application form; ask students to pretend to apply, and then invite a "selection committee" to choose the candidate.
　　Discuss how money for scholarships is continually generated.
　　(See activities under November 11, "Independence from ....")

Vitamin C isolated by C. G. King after five years of research, 1932
　　Make a list of the foods that contain vitamin C.
　　Investigate some of the claims relating to the usefulness of vitamin C.

North Atlantic Treaty signed, 1949
　　Research which countries signed the treaty and the reasons why NATO was organized.
　　Explain that NATO is an acronym; trace the derivation and meaning of the word "acronym."

Rev. Dr. Martin Luther King, Jr., American civil rights leader, assassinated, 1968
　　Investigate the life and times of Martin Luther King.
　　Discuss the word "assassination" and how it differs from the word "murder."
　　Obtain a recording of King's speech, "I Have a Dream," and analyze its message.
　　(See activities under January 15, "Martin Luther ....")

April 5

Wedding of John Rolfe and Pocahontas held, 1614
Enjoy a story about the life of Pocahontas or about this period of early America.

Act of veto first used by President Washington, 1792
Explain the background of the word "veto" (Latin for "I forbid").
Discuss the process of vetoing as related to the system of checks and balances in American government.

First American chamber of commerce established, 1768
Find out the purposes of chambers of commerce.
Invite a local merchant who is a member of the local chamber to speak to the class about the organization.

Cider mill patented, 1806
Investigate how a cider mill works.
Bring in apple cider and invite students to sample-taste it.
Discuss cider as a formerly popular beverage in comparison with the current consumption of soft drinks; compare nutrition values of selected carbonated drinks and ciders.

Joseph Lister, English surgeon and founder of antiseptic surgery, born 1827
(See Biography Data in Extra-Know-How Section.)
Discuss hygiene and sanitary procedures in hospitals.
Explain that the commercial product "Listerine" derived its name from Dr. Lister; invite students to think of other products, real or fictitious, whose names refer to researchers and/or their discoveries.
Investigate the amount of bacteria in one's mouth.
Trace the derivation of the term "antiseptic."
Investigate the career and preparation required of a surgeon or medical researcher.

Robert Smalls, American slave hero, born 1839
(See Biography Data in Extra-Know-How Section.)
Explain that Smalls escaped to freedom and later was elected a congressman; obtain a copy of *Captain of the Planter*, by Dorothy Sterling, to trace the daring escape made by Smalls.

Booker T. Washington, teacher and social reformer, born 1856
(See Biography Data in Extra-Know-How Section.)
Write to Tuskegee Institute for information concerning its founder. (See Address Listing in Extra-Know-How Section.)

Bette Davis, American actress, born 1908
(See Biography Data in Extra-Know-How Section.)

Herbert von Karajan, Austrian conductor, born 1908
(See Biography Data in Extra-Know-How Section.)
(See activities under March 25, "Arturo Toscanini ....")

First balloon tire produced, 1923
Obtain a balloon-tube tire and take out the inner tube; observe the buoyancy factor of an inflated inner tube in water.
Investigate the principles of tubeless tires.

First human lung successfully removed, 1933
Present a lesson on the lungs—their care, anatomy, and physiology.
Find out the meaning of the words "anatomy" and "physiology."
Investigate such lung diseases as bronchitis, emphysema, cancer, and tuberculosis.
Learn about the purposes of an iron lung; find out the cost for private use in the home.

Idea of a "hotline," direct emergency communications link with the United States, first accepted by the USSR, 1963
Discuss the significance of maintaining a "hotline" with Russia; find out specifically where the terminals are and whether the system has ever been used in emergencies; consider what other countries might be potential "hotline" communicators.
Relate how the intercom system within a school, supermarket, or department store is a similar arrangement.

April 6

Harry Houdini, American magician and locksmith, born 1874
(See Biography Data in Extra-Know-How Section.)
Explain that Houdini took his name from the famous French magician Jean Houdini and that he died on Halloween; investigate the professional life of Houdini—the intricacies of his famous escape-artist/locksmith performances.
Invite interested students to perform magic tricks for the class.
Talk about the phrase, "The hand is quicker than the eye."
Check out library books on magic and set up a display of books and magic materials.
Define the following magician-related words: prestidigitator, wizard, sorcerer, conjurer; write a story with a magician serving as the central character.
Investigate the area of mental telepathy.

Lincoln Steffens, American journalist, born 1866
(See Biography Data in Extra-Know-How Section.)
Investigate the career of a journalist and other press-related fields.
Introduce skills of journalism, i.e., accuracy in reporting facts, differentiation between editorialized writing and news reporting, "eye-catching" human interest titles, headlines, and captions; culminate the study with the publication of a class or school newspaper.
(See activities under June 7, "Freedom of ....")

First modern Olympic Games in Athens, Greece, won by the United States in unofficial competition, 1896
Use Task Card #43 for activities concerning Olympic Games.
(See activities under February 4, "First winter ....")

North Pole reached by Robert E. Perry and Matthew Henson, 1909
Examine on a globe where the North Pole is; discuss what life would be like "on top of the world."
Read *Ahdoolo! The Biography of Matthew B. Henson*, by Floyd Miller.

World War I entered into by the United States against Germany, 1917
Investigate the causes and effects of World War I; find out why the term "world" was used when not all nations of the world were involved.
Discuss the concept, "The war to end all wars," as World War I was thought to be.
Investigate the Americans' generally unified response to the war.
Consider the thoughts, feelings, and experiences of German-American immigrants who had not lived long in their new country and perhaps still had family and friends in "the old country."

April 7

World Health Day (annual commemoration of the founding of WHO—World Health Organization, 1948)
Discuss the level of health and nutrition around the world; find out more about the stated goal of WHO: "Attainment of all peoples of the highest level of health."
Set up exhibits concerning various diseases and the effects of malnutrition, due partly to the unequal distribution of resources; consider the need for health and nutrition education in industrially developed nations where the availability of abundant resources could maximize the levels of health.
Ask various committees to present programs on particular areas of hygiene and health care.
Write to the Pan American Health Organization for the booklet "The World Health Organization." (See Address Listing in Extra-Know-How Section.)

William Wordsworth, English poet, born 1770
(See Biography Data in Extra-Know-How Section.)
Investigate what a "sonnet" is.
Find out what is meant by "poet laureate"; make a list of those besides Wordsworth who have been accorded this honor.

Walter Winchell, American columnist and news commentator, born 1897
(See Biography Data in Extra-Know-How Section.)
Discuss the role of a news commentator and columnist as opposed to that of a news reporter; investigate each as a potential career.

Hold a debate on the controversial issue of whether the press corps should be forced to reveal its sources of information when reporting a news story.

Ravi Shankar, Asian-Indian musician, born 1920
(See Biography Data in Extra-Know-How Section.)
Obtain recordings of Indian sitar music and enjoy listening to selections.
Introduce a picture of the musical instrument, the sitar; explain that it is similar to a lute and that it is made from a gourd.
Find out whether an international set of abstract symbols is used in written music so as to be mutually understandable throughout the world.

Dag Hammarskjold, from Sweden, elected Secretary General of the United Nations, 1953
Research the organizational structure of the United Nations.
(See activities under January 9, "U.N. Headquarters ... " and July 29, "Dag Hammarskjold ....")

April 8

Florida first explored by a European (Spanish), Juan Ponce de León, 1513
(See Biography Data in Extra-Know-How Section.)
Document through research that the "Fountain of Youth" he allegedly found is merely legend.

First American-Jewish congregation convened in New York City, 1780 (Spanish and Portuguese Synagogue, Shearith Israel)
Trace the history of Judaism in the United States

Harvey Cushing, American neuro-brain surgeon and Pulitzer Prize author, born 1869
(See Biography Data in Extra-Know-How Section.)
Investigate the preparation required and career of a neuro-brain surgeon.
Discuss the point that Cushing's medical advances were possible, partly due to the fact that anesthesia had already been introduced; consider how one discovery, invention, or accomplishment is often dependent upon earlier achievements.
Explain that Cushing developed an instrument to measure blood pressure; find out the purpose of blood pressure readings; learn the specialized term for a blood pressure cuff (sphygmomanometer); trace the derivations of "sphygmo" (pulse) and "meter" (instrument that measures)—"pulse-measurer."
See activities under January Month-long Observances, "National Blood ....")

Mary Pickford, Canadian actress, born 1893
(See Biography Data in Extra-Know-How Section.)

Sonja Henie, American ice skater and child actress, born 1912
(See Biography Data in Extra-Know-How Section.)
Invite students to share experiences about ice-skating, both on outside and indoor rinks.
Discuss the technology and energy sources needed to prepare and maintain a massive piece of ice indoors.

Seventeenth Amendment to the U.S. Constitution ratified, 1918
(See Data-Detail in Extra-Know-How Section, "Amendments to the U.S. Constitution.")

April 9

First American town-supported "free" public library established, 1833
Discuss the fact that lending libraries are not found in every country.
Invite a public librarian to class to discuss library operations at the local library; find out the differences between the catalog system of the Library of Congress and that of the Dewey Decimal arrangement.
Investigate library science as a career; find out the various kinds of research librarians there are in such specialized fields as medical, legal, business, educational, theological, etc.
Review Task Card #42 for activities with books.
(See activities under April Special Weeks, "National Library ... " and November 1, "Authors' Day ....")

Robert E. Lee, General of the Confederate Army in the American Civil War, surrendered to General Ulysses S. Grant, General of the Union Army, at Appomattox Courthouse, 1865

Locate the city of Appomattox on a U.S. map.

Obtain a copy of the surrender letter and a copy of the picture depicting the signing of the surrender document. Encourage students to role-play the event.

Write to John Hancock Mutual Life Insurance Co. for the booklet "Robert E. Lee." (See Address Listing in Extra-Know-How Section.)

First dried milk patented, 1872

Bring powdered milk and demonstrate how it is liquefied; arrange for a taste-test to compare it with prepared milk from a carton; discuss the advantages and disadvantages of both forms.

James William Fulbright, U.S. senator, born 1905

(See Biography Data in Extra-Know-How Section.)

Investigate the Fulbright-Hays "Awards Abroad Program" for educational activities that "enable the government of the United States to increase mutual understanding between the people of the U.S. and the people of other countries."

(See activities under February Special Weeks, "Brotherhood Week ....")

Golf Hall of Fame in the United States established, 1941

Discuss urban planning in terms of "green belts" and recreation areas.

Review Task Card #41 for activities on golf.

Make a name list of the individuals chosen to the Golf Hall of Fame.

First United States astronauts selected, 1959

Trace the derivation of the term "astronaut."

Discuss the point that Russia's Sputnik spacecraft feat in 1958 stimulated a more intense U.S. interest in space science; trace the development of the funding record of the National Science Foundation as related to this period of time.

Investigate the career preparation to become an astronaut.

Ask students to choose a member of the class who they believe would be an effective astronaut—and to give justification for their choices.

Astrodome, a roofed stadium in Houston, Texas opened, 1965

Encourage students to draw an indoor stadium as an architectural design lesson.

Discuss the advantages and disadvantages of the astrodome and its astroturf.

April 10

First U.S. patent law adopted, 1790

Find out what a patent is; discuss how a patent is obtained and what its duration is. (Currently, a patent must be renewed after 17 years.)

Invite students to bring to class items which have patent numbers on them; arrange the items in sequential order of their patent numbers.

Write to the U.S. Patent Office for booklets on patents and trademarks. (See Address Listing in Extra-Know-How Section.)

Explain that patents protect inventions; trademarks protect the names or identifying designs for goods and services, and copyrights protect literary and artistic works; find out the symbols, if any, for patents, trademarks, and copyrights.

Discuss the following statements: "The impulse to invent is nearly as strong as the instinct to survive" (Buckminster Fuller); "If the mountaineer climbs 'because it's there,' the inventor invents because it's *not* there but ought to be"; "The world is moving so fast these days that the person who says it can't be done is usually interrupted by someone doing it."

Invite a representative from the local chapter of the Inventor's Assistance League to class; inquire about prepatent procedures and how an inventor makes contact with marketing agencies.

Discuss the phrase, "Necessity is the mother of invention."

Matthew C. Perry, American naval officer who opened Japan to world trade, born 1794

(See Biography Data in Extra-Know-How Section.)

Investigate Japan's 200-year isolationist policy in which Japan remained closed to the world in nearly every dimension; discuss whether in the modern world of communication systems such a national policy is likely; identify areas of the world which do remain relatively out of contact with "mainstream" communication systems.

Research Japan's economic development since Perry's visit to Japan in 1853-1854.

William Booth, English evangelist and founder of the Salvation Army, born 1829
(See Biography Data in Extra-Know-How Section.)
Invite a member of the Salvation Army to class to discuss the organization.
(See activities under May Special Weeks, "Salvation Army ....")

Joseph Pulitzer, American journalist and newspaper owner, born 1847
(See Biography Data in Extra-Know-How Section.)
Investigate the seven types of Pulitzer awards in journalism and letters.
Make a list of individuals who have received the Pulitzer Prize award since 1917; include the specific field for which they received the award.

First safety pin patented by Walter Hunt, 1849
Draw a safety pin and discuss the ingenuity of its design; consider what might have been used for fastening before the advent of the safety pin.
Make a class list of alternative ways a safety pin could be used.
Discuss various types of pins, i.e., class pin, corsage pin, hat pin; consider the meaning of the term "pinpoint"; use it in a sentence.

Catamaran patented, 1877
Investigate in detail what a catamaran is and its principle of balance.
Encourage students to write an adventure story about sailing on a catamaran; illustrate the story.

Synthetic rubber produced, 1930
Identify what rubber is; make a class list of the uses of rubber today.
Find out how crude or natural rubber is collected from the "Para" rubber plant; investigate in detail what latex is and how it is sometimes processed to prevent coagulation; find out in what form most rubber is shipped to manufacturing centers in the United States; name the continent that produces the most rubber plants or rubber trees.
Explore whether any amount of natural rubber is used in producing synthetic rubber; name the materials from which most synthetic rubber is derived.
Investigate whether natural or synthetic rubber has more advantages.
Trace the derivation of the term "synthetic."
(See activities under June 15, "Vulcanized rubber ....")

Jackie Robinson, the first black in a major baseball club recruited by the Brooklyn Dodgers (National League), 1947
Explain to students that Jackie Robinson was subjected to racial discrimination, particularly at that time of his career, but allegedly tempered his reactions in order to remain in the major leagues; ask students to respond to this.
(See activities under January 24, "Jackie Robinson ....")

First three-dimensional motion pictures featured in America, 1953
Discuss three-dimensional images as opposed to those with two dimensions.
Obtain a manual viewer, a stereoscope, designed for use of 3-D cards and share with the class.
Use Task Card #44 for 3-D art activity.

April 11

Charles Evans Hughes, U.S. secretary of state and chief justice of the U.S. Supreme Court, born 1862
(See Biography Data in Extra-Know-How Section.)
Research the extent of power that is authorized the chief justice.

American Society for the Prevention of Cruelty to Animals chartered in New York State, 1866
Contact a representative from the local chapter to discuss the purposes of the organization; find out why there are regulations concerning the burial of animals and what the regulations are.
Investigate other similar groups—the Humane Society or a local animal shelter organization.

Interview a pet store merchant for ideas about the care of pets.

Explore a local supermarket to determine an approximate percentage of the shelf space used for pet food; hold a debate concerning the topic of using natural resources to feed pets before providing for the malnourished people of the world.

Find out by interviewing those who travel whether the practice of keeping pets is very typical around the world; if so, in which countries, and whether the animals are allowed or welcomed into places of business.

Define the term "vivisection"; discuss the pros and cons of this practice.

Use Task Card #45 for ideas about organizing a pet show.

U.S. Price Regulation Law enacted, 1941

Use Task Card #46 to learn about the practice of price controls.

Oveta Culp Hobby sworn in as first secretary of the U.S. Department of Health, Education, and Welfare, 1953

Discuss the needs which led to the establishment of this governmental agency.

Find out the year in which the position of secretary (of the Department of HEW) became a presidential cabinet post; also, trace how this particular department has changed.

Investigate how many women have served on U.S. presidential cabinets.

April 12

Henry Clay, American statesman, born 1777

(See Biography Data in Extra-Know-How Section.)

Research the following topics: Missouri Compromise, Compromise of 1850, and the "War-Hawk."

Analyze Clay's words, "I'd rather be right than President"; associate the meaning of this message with situations in the classroom.

Fireproof safe patented, 1833

Consider the ways in which a safe can be broken into; encourage students to brainstorm and design a foolproof safe. (Discuss the background of the term "foolproof"); consider whether any container can be made "fail-safe" or totally free from harm or damage.

Invite an attorney to class; consult him or her about which type of items and personal documents are recommended to be placed in a safe deposit box.

Talk about the word "safe" as it refers to a steel or iron box; think about the many other uses of the word.

First Civil War battle fought at Fort Sumter in the harbor of Charleston, South Carolina, 1861

Use Task Card #47 to play a game related to the Civil War.

First catcher's mask worn by James Tyng and called a "birdcage" by Frederick Thayer (Tyng's coach), 1877

Discuss the advantages and disadvantages of this type of mask.

List other safety or protection devices designed for sports.

Design safety devices for various events.

First portable typewriter patented, 1892

Obtain a typewriter and examine it; ask students to change the ribbon; discuss different features of both nonelectric and electric typewriters.

Consider how keyboards differ with various alphabets and writing systems throughout the world; for instance, do Asians have typewriters to type the many hundreds of ideograph symbols?

Investigate how typewriters have become more sophisticated in terms of more complex information processing.

Hold a typing contest based upon time and accuracy.

Compose a class story by progressive "turns" on the typewriter; invite students to enter a letter or word(s) to follow what has already been written.

(See activities under February 14, "Christopher Latham ... " and May 16, "First typewriter ... " and September 14, "Typewriter ribbon ....")

Lily Pons, French-American opera singer, born 1904

(See Biography Data in Extra-Know-How Section.)

Investigate the career of an opera singer.

Discuss what opera is; choose an opera and familiarize the students with the story in terms of acts and scenes; enjoy a recording of the opera.

Investigate the various voice qualities and vocal ranges of soprano, lyric soprano, mezzo-soprano, alto, contralto, tenor, baritone, base.

Franklin Delano Roosevelt died 1945

Discuss the impact of Roosevelt's death upon the world.

Investigate what a cerebral hemorrhage is; trace the derivation of the two words.

(See activities under January 30, "Franklin Delano Roosevelt ....")

First significant "rock and roll" recording "Rock around the Clock" distributed, 1954

Obtain the recording and play it for students; encourage them to move their whole bodies to the music.

Invite students to create their own "rock and roll" music by making up lyrics and then accompanying their statements with rhythm instruments.

Yuri Gagarin, Russian astronaut, became the first person to orbit the earth, 1961

Discuss ways in which world powers might cooperate in advancing technical knowledge; explore the term "synergistic energies."

Discuss the pros and cons of space exploration. One of the benefits is that in the process of searching the "world beyond" the learned insights and technologies may directly improve conditions on earth; consider the opposite view that the expenditure is not warranted when there are more pressing priorities.

Illustrate the various levels or spheres through which a spacecraft travels.

Space shuttle *Columbia* launched, 1981

Obtain a model of the space shuttle and construct it.

Discuss the advantages and possibilities of a reusable space craft.

Write a fictional dialog describing the communication between the astronauts and the members of the ground control staff.

April 13

Thomas Jefferson, third president of the United States, born 1743

(See Biography Data in Extra-Know-How Section.)

Explain that Jefferson was the first president inaugurated in Washington, DC—the city which he had helped to plan.

Research Jefferson's various accomplishments as a statesman—the principal author of the Declaration of Independence and a foreign diplomat; include a study of his social-political philosophy.

Make a list of Jefferson's other pursuits in the fields of architecture, science, and education; identify the five foreign languages which he spoke.

Find a picture of Jefferson's home, Monticello, and recreate it by drawing a picture of it. Investigate Jefferson's own inventions which he incorporated into his home, such as the dumbwaiter, a special air-circulation system, and the seven-day clock; find out how long it took to build Monticello and also what the name means.

F. W. Woolworth, American merchant, born 1852

(See Biography Data in Extra-Know-How Section.)

Discuss with students their preferences—whether to work for someone or to be "one's own boss"; consider the risks of investing one's money, the responsibility of financially succeeding when a significant shift in the social-economic situation could lead to bankruptcy, and the reality of no paid vacations or assured retirement benefits. Consider also the many advantages—freedom to implement one's own ideas and the sense of personal accomplishment.

Invite students to design a sign plate or business logo, using their own names for their own places of business.

(See activities under February 22, "First 'Five ....' ")

New York's Metropolitan Museum of Art, the largest art museum in the United States, founded, 1870

Obtain copies of famous art in order to expose students to many different styles and media; write to Giant Photos for catalogs of inexpensive prints. (See Address Listing in Extra-Know-How Section.)

Read the Newbery Award-winning book *From the Mixed-Up Files of Mrs. Basil E. Frankweiler,* by Elaine L. Konigsburg.

(See activities under January 12, "First United ... " and November 7, "Museum of ....")

J. C. Penney's first store opened in Kemmerer, Wyoming, 1902

Discuss the concept of free or private enterprise as opposed to state-owned businesses.

Introduce various retailing-related careers, i.e., window designing, advertising, selling, merchandise buying, store managing, credit and personnel supervising.

(See Data-Detail in Extra-Know-How Section, "Resource Guide for Vocational and Professional Guidance.")

Note: Many J. C. Penny retail stores lend and give educational materials on a variety of topics to classroom teachers as a public service to the community.

Jefferson Memorial in Washington, DC dedicated, 1943

Obtain a picture of the memorial.

Trace the background of the construction of the memorial.

(See activities above, "Thomas Jefferson ....")

April 14

Pan American Day (in commemoration of the founding of the Pan American Union in 1890)

(See activities under April Special Weeks, "Pan American ....")

First edition of Noah Webster's dictionary copyrighted, 1828

(See Data-Detail in Extra-Know-How Section, "How Webster Created the Dictionary.")

Distribute dictionaries to students; conduct fun dictionary games.

Find out what is involved in obtaining a copyright and what the purpose of copyrighting is.

(See activities under October 16, "Noah Webster ....")

Arnold Toynbee, English economic historian, born 1852

(See Biography Data in Extra-Know-How Section.)

Abraham Lincoln assassinated by John Wilkes Booth, 1865

Research and then re-enact the incident—from the shooting in the theater to the death of Booth.

Investigate the Reconstruction period following the Civil War; consider the many intense issues involved in reuniting a separated nation; trace the many corruptive activities, such as the Ku Klux Klan and the "carpetbaggers," which only led to new dimensions of white control over the blacks. Find out the meaning of "emancipation" and "enfranchisement."

Anne Sullivan, American educator and companion to Helen Keller, born 1866

(See Biography Data in Extra-Know-How Section.)

Brainstorm ideas of how to teach a student who is both blind and deaf.

(See activities under June 27, "Helen Keller ....")

British luxury-liner named the *Titanic* sunk, 1912

Obtain a picture of the ship; discuss its various features.

Conduct a choral reading of the words to the song "The *Titanic*"; then lead the students in a speech ensemble (reading roles).

Explain that the ship hit an iceberg; investigate what an iceberg is; discuss the phrase, "It's only the tip of the iceberg."

Create a story about being on a ship that is sinking; emphasize and develop in detail the feelings of fear that would be experienced; share with the class.

Obtain a copy of the book *The Titanic, the Psychic and the Sea*, by Rustie Brown.

Investigate who the Titans were in Greek mythology in order to understand why the ship was named the *Titanic* and why it was considered to be unsinkable.

International Civil Aviation Organization established, 1947

Discuss the reasons for chartering such an organization.

April 15

U.S. income tax filing deadline day

Obtain copies of income tax forms; encourage students to experiment with filling out the forms.

Discuss the purpose of income tax; consider other means of gaining tax revenue, i.e., state, county, property, and sales taxes.

Ask students how well they respond to long-term deadlines as opposed to working better under pressure at the last minute.

National Hostility Day

Discuss the term "hostility"; make a class list of what makes various people angry, frustrated, or hostile; consider safe means by which individuals might vent their anger, i.e., talking over a problem, hitting a punching bag or pillow.

Leonardo da Vinci, Italian Renaissance artist and scientist, born 1452

(See Biography Data in Extra-Know-How Section.)

Investigate the term "renaissance."

Obtain copies of the painting *Mona Lisa*; find out what the word "fresco" refers to and then examine Leonardo da Vinci's famous fresco *The Last Supper*.

Explore the variety of pursuits and abilities which da Vinci's many accomplishments represent in the fields of human physiology and transportation.

Insulin made available for use in America, 1928

Find out what insulin shock is; discuss the value of insulin and the ways in which insulin is administered.

Discuss the self-discipline involved in being a diabetic.

Investigate how laboratory analysts are able to learn so much from a relatively small amount of blood in a blood test.

(See activities under November Special Weeks, "Diabetes Week ... " and November 14, "Frederick Grant ....")

Levi Strauss Company ordered to give back 33¢ to customers for having price-fixed their products, 1981

Trace the circumstances surrounding this court order; discuss whether companies should be forced to return money for having price-fixed their products.

Design a new style of jeans.

Find out what symbol is used on the Levi Strauss label and what the significance of the symbol is.

Investigate how Levi Strauss created the jeans that have become so famous.

April 16

Wilbur Wright, American inventor and aviator, born 1867

(See Biography Data in Extra-Know-How Section.)

(See activities under December 17, "First powered ....")

Charlie (Charles S.) Chaplin, English actor, born 1889

(See Biography Data in Extra-Know-How Section.)

Obtain copies of Charlie Chaplin films, either from a local library or from Blackhawk films. (See Address Listing in Extra-Know-How Section.)

Ask students to mirror another's hand and arm motions; when class becomes proficient, add appropriate music (as might have accompanied silent films).

Book-of-the-Month Club started, 1926

Explain what the Book-of-the-Month Club is and talk about other subscription clubs that operate in a similar way.

Encourage students to pretend they are the editorial board for decisions regarding which children's books are to be selected; ask that they arrange for a year's plan of selections, based upon group consensus, covering a variety of types of books from the school or local library.

April 17

William Chauncy Camp, American football player called "Father of Football," born 1859

(See Biography Data in Extra-Know-How Section.)

(See activities under May 3, "Johnny Unitas ....")

Statute requiring fire escapes on tenement buildings enacted, 1860

Ask students to listen and respond to oral directions given only once: 1) "Make a quick drawing of a brick building with a fire escape"; 2) "add to the scene a fire in the building"; 3) "depict a person going down the fire escape."

Lead into a discussion about fire escapes, emergency fire exits, and other building safety requirements; discuss modern smoke detection and alarm systems.

(See activities under April 1, "First salaried ....")

Thornton Wilder, American novelist, born 1897
(See Biography Data in Extra-Know-How Section.)

Gregor Piatigorsky, Russian-American cellist, born 1903
(See Biography Data in Extra-Know-How Section.)
Investigate the career of a concert musician.
Obtain a cello; examine the sounds and structure of the instrument.
Study other string instruments.

April 18

Paul Revere Day (marks the alleged midnight ride to warn colonists that the British were coming into an area outside of Boston, 1775)
Enact the incident after reading H. W. Longfellow's poem "The Midnight Ride of Paul Revere."
Consider other historical events made more famous through authors' interpretations.
Explain that Revere was also the first American to build a copper-rolling mill to produce roll sheet copper; find out where copper is found in the United States and how it is now produced.
(See activities under January 1, "Paul Revere ....")

Clarence Darrow, American criminal lawyer who defended both John Scopes and Leopold-Loeb, born 1857
(See Biography Data in Extra-Know-How Section.)
Read *Clarence Darrow for the Defense*, by Irving Stone.

San Francisco devastated by earthquake and fire, 1906
Discuss why fire so often follows an earthquake and therefore compounds the damage.
Investigate what a seismograph is; discuss technology's potential in predicting earthquakes.
Research terms such as "Pacific ring of fire" and "fault."
Obtain from the local library a recording of the narration of the fire (Standard Oil Broadcasting Series, "Turn of the Century," Side A, "The Progressive Era").
(See activities under February 9, "Earthquake in California ... " and March 27, "Alaska earthquakes ....")

First crossword puzzle book published in America, 1924
Obtain a copy of a crossword puzzle, appropriate to the age level, or make up an original puzzle using students' names.
Use Reproducible #20 for a sample crossword puzzle.
(See activities under November 5, "Crossword puzzles ....")

First laundromat, called a washateria, opened in Fort Worth, Texas, 1934
Consider the ways clothes were washed prior to washing machines.
Devise story problems in math as related to the number of laundromats and the people who use them.
Think of other services which might operate as laundromats, such as coin-operated film developing studios, and create names appropriate to the function.

April 19

Battle of Lexington, the start of the American Revolutionary War, begun, 1775
Obtain a toy capgun-rifle and walk into the room and fire a shot; lead into a discussion about Ralph Waldo Emerson's words, "the shot heard 'round the world."
Share Ralph Waldo Emerson's entire poem about this incident.
Discuss the terms: revolutionary and loyalist.
Investigate what other major revolutionary wars have been fought in the world.

American Revolutionary War ended, 1783
Discuss the point that the date of the war's end was the anniversary of its beginning.
Consider the spirit in which the Declaration of Independence was written in 1776; then talk about the close of the war and the reality of having to establish an independent nation.

Battle of Warsaw Polish Ghetto begun, 1943

Obtain copies of two books: *Twenty Plus Ten*, by Clare Bishop, and *Escape from Warsaw* (original title, *Silver Sword*), by Ian Serraillier, and share with the class.

Discuss the significance of the battle in which the Jews fought the German Nazi occupiers.

April 20

First day of the zodiac period, Taurus, the bull (through May 19)

(See Data-Detail in Extra-Know-How Section, "Notes on Astrology.")

Carpet loom patented, 1837

Obtain rug samples from local retailer; as a class project, weave the samples together to form a throw rug for a reading center in the classroom.

Find out how carpets were made prior to the creation of the carpet loom.

Use Task Card #48 for activities on weaving and looms.

Daniel C. French, American sculptor of the Lincoln Memorial, born 1850

Obtain a picture of the Lincoln Memorial and share with the class.

Show the film "Face of Lincoln" and encourage interested students to recreate a sculptured form of Lincoln.

Investigate the career of a sculptor-artist.

Sol Harry Goldberg, American manufacturer of the Hump Hair Pin Company, born 1880

(See Biography Data in Extra-Know-How Section.)

Explain that Goldberg created irregular lines in the hairpin—an innovation which improved the product and expanded the hairpin industry.

Invite students to create hairpin sculptures.

Adolf Hitler, German dictator, born 1889

(See Biography Data in Extra-Know-How Section.)

Define and compare the terms: dictatorship and autocracy.

Trace Hitler's rise to power; investigate his anti-Semitic views and Nazism as described in his book *Mein Kampf* (*My Struggle*).

Radium isolated by Marie and Pierre Curie, 1902

Find out what radium is and what its current uses are; investigate what the abbreviation and element number are for radium; discuss what the differences are between discovering an element and isolating it.

Explain that the husband-wife team was awarded the Nobel Prize for their work with radium and polonium; later Marie Curie won a second Nobel award, making her the first person to have received the Nobel Prize twice; find out for what achievement she won the second award.

Investigate what field the Curies' daughter, Irene Curie Jolio, entered and for what accomplishment she was also awarded the Nobel Prize.

(See activities under November 7, "Marie Curie ....")

April 21

Friedrich Froebel, German educator and founder of the Kindergarten (children's garden), born 1782

(See Biography Data in Extra-Know-How Section.)

Ask students to recall their kindergarten experiences and how they would teach if they were kindergarten teachers.

Arrange for a cross-age tutoring experience with kindergarteners.

Charlotte Brontë, English novelist, born 1816

(See Biography Data in Extra-Know-How Section.)

John Muir, American naturalist, born 1838

(See Biography Data in Extra-Know-How Section.)

Locate Muir Woods National Monument.

Use Task Card #49 for further information about conservation and ecology.

Spanish-American War begun, 1898
Investigate whether Theodore Roosevelt's famous charge up San Juan Hill on horseback is historically accurate. (Consult *The Dictionary of Misinformation* by Tom Burnam.)
Research the outcomes of the war as to the decisions concering Cuba, Guam, Puerto Rico, and the Philippines.

Brazilia created as the capital of Brazil, 1960
Locate Brazilia on a map and research the development of the new city in South America's largest country.

April 22

Immanuel Kant, German philosopher, born 1724
(See Biography Data in Extra-Know-How Section.)
Ask interested students to try to explain the following contradiction: "Space and time are infinite and yet they are finite."
Explore why it is that philosophers are often also mathematicians.

Vladimir Lenin, Russian revolutionary, born 1870
(See Biography Data in Extra-Know-How Section.)
Investigate bolshevism and the Russian Revolution of 1917.

First bicycle trip around the world begun, 1884
Chart several possible routes on a world map.
Arrange for a day in which bicycles can be brought to school to be decorated and entered into a bike parade.
Review Task Card #40 for bicycle activities.

First section of the Oklahoma Territory opened to homesteaders in the American land rush, 1889
Research what the Homestead Act of 1862 was; find out why the U.S. government encouraged homesteading.

Poison gas used by German forces in World War I, 1915
Obtain a gas mask and discuss how and why it is used.
Inquire about the various types of toxic gases and also about antitoxins used in defense.

Television broadcast of Senate hearings against Senator Joseph R. McCarthy begun, 1954
Investigate the circumstances leading to these proceedings.

April 23

William Shakespeare, English poet and dramatist, born 1564
(See Biography Data in Extra-Know-How Section.)
Use Task Card #50 concerning activities about Shakespeare and his times.
Obtain a copy of *Shake Hands with Shakespeare*, by Albert Cullum; with the student scripts, produce a play or a Shakespeare festival.
Read *Shakespearean Sallies, Sullies, and Slanders: Insults for All Occasions*, by Ann McGovern (editor).
Obtain recordings of Shakespeare's more famous plays—with the environmental sound effects.

James Buchanan, fifteenth president of the United States, born 1791
(See Biography Data in Extra-Know-How Section.)

Sanford Ballard Dole, American statesman and first president of the Republic of Hawaii, born 1844
(See Biography Data in Extra-Know-How Section.)
Consult the *Standard Poor's Register of Corporations, Directors, and Executives* to gain information about the Dole Pineapple Company.

Sergei Prokofiev, Russian composer, born 1891
(See Biography Data in Extra-Know-How Section.)
Enjoy a recording of "Peter and the Wolf," by Prokofiev.

Shirley Temple, American actress, born 1928
(See Biography Data in Extra-Know-How Section.)
Discuss Shirley Temple as a child star and later as Shirley Temple Black with a position in government.

Obtain the book of *The Shirley Temple Treasury: Stories from Movies That Made Her Famous.*
Talk about fads, i.e., Shirley Temple dolls and hairstyles.

April 24

First regularly issued American newspaper, the Boston *Newsletter***,** published, 1704
Introduce a unit on the newspaper. (Check with local newspaper for an educational kit.)
Tour the local newspaper production office.
Create a classroom or school newsletter.
Discuss the massive daily consumption of newsprint throughout the world in respect to the natural resources required to produce the paper.
Use Task Card #51 for additional ideas about newspapers.
(See activities under April 29, "William Randolph ... " and October Special Weeks, "National Newspaper ....")

Library of Congress established in Washington, DC, 1800
Discuss the significance of the Library of Congress.
(See activities under April Special Weeks, "National Library Week" and under April 9, "First American ....")

Soda fountain patented, 1833
Investigate the technology behind a soda fountain.
(See Data-Detail in Extra-Know-How Section, "Soft Drinks—History.")
Find out how to make a soda; ask students to create their own sodas, listing creative ingredients and assigning appropriate names to the sodas.

Tony Sarg, German puppeteer, born 1882
Obtain books on puppets to investigate the world of puppetry.

Irish Easter Rebellion against British rule begun, 1916
Compare and contrast America's revolutionary war and Ireland's rebellion to British rule.
Investigate the economic and religious basis for the continual strife between Northern Ireland and the Republic of Ireland (Eire).

Barbra Streisand, American actress, born 1942
(See Biography Data in Extra-Know-How Section.)
Obtain recordings of Streisand's singing; listen to the music and analyze the meaning of the words.
Ask students to consider what it is like to rise to her status as a famed actress.

April 25

St. Lawrence Seaway opened, 1959
Locate the St. Lawrence River on a map and discuss the significance of the "ship path" to the sea.

Guglielmo Marconi, Italian physicist and Nobel Peace Prize winner, born 1874
(See Biography Data in Extra-Know-How Section.)
Investigate the structure and uses of the wireless telegraph.
Trace Marconi's earlier achievements with electromagnetic waves to the transmitted long-wave signals in transatlantic communication and modern radio.
Encourage interested students to study the radio as to different types, how they are made, and how they basically operate.

Ella Fitzgerald, American singer, born 1918
(See Biography Data in Extra-Know-How Section.)
Enjoy selections of the singer's recordings.

First Seeing Eye dog in America presented, 1923
Explain what a seeing eye dog is; specify that a purebred female German shepherd is proved to be the most effective for this purpose.
Investigate how the dogs are trained, the cost of a dog for a blind person, and what a dog is trained to do.
Invite a representative from the local chapter of the Lion's Club, an organization that sponsors work-for-the-blind and sight conservation causes.

Contact the local Braille institute for further information about seeing eye dogs.
Review Task Card #6 for a variation of the "Blind Walk."

April 26

John James Audubon, American artist/ornithologist, born 1785
(See Biography Data in Extra-Know-How Section.)
Obtain pictures of Audubon's paintings and display them.
Investigate the word "ornithologist."
Write to the National Association of Audubon Societies for information. (See Address Listing in Extra-Know-How Section.)
Check out copies of the *Audubon Magazine* and books about birds from the local library.
Encourage students to become bird-watchers by noticing and recording characteristics about birds that they observe.
Introduce watercolor lessons on birds.
Present the book *Let's Discover Birds in Our World*, by Ada and Frank Graham, Jr.
Review Reproducible #17 for activities about birds.
(See activities under March 14, "First National ....")

Charles Francis Richter, American seismologist, born 1900
(See Biography Data in Extra-Know-How Section.)
Explain that Richter developed the Richter Scale, a device for measuring earthquake intensity; investigate the current use of the scale.
In a world almanac, check the location and frequency of earthquakes throughout the world; find what area is referred to as "the Pacific Ring."
Find out what a "fault" is and locate the major faults in the world.
Discuss what destructive forces are associated with earthquakes.
Make a chart of various earthquakes and identify each with a number from the Richter scale.
(See activities under February 9, "Earthquake in ....")

Carol Burnett, American actress, born 1935
(See Biography Data in Extra-Know-How Section.)

April 27

Ferdinand Magellan, Portuguese navigator, killed in the Philippines, 1521
(See activities under September 20, "Voyage around ....")

Samuel F. B. Morse, American inventor and artist, born 1791
(See Biography Data in Extra-Know-How Section.)
Research Morse's other accomplishments besides the invention of the telegraph and the design of the Morse code.
Expose students to the system of the Morse code; ask students to bring in flashlights to use for sending secret messages; suggest that students also try tapping messages with their fingers.

Ulysses S(impson) Grant, eighteenth president of the United States, born 1822
(See Biography Data in Extra-Know-How Section.)
Find out Grant's original name.

Walter Lantz, American cartoonist, born 1900
(See Biography Data in Extra-Know-How Section.)
Find out who can most effectively imitate the laugh of Woody Woodpecker.
Encourage students to create their own cartoon characters.
Investigate the career of a cartoon artist.

First U.S. Social Security payment made, 1937
Discuss what Social Security is.
Explore the significance of one's Social Security number; suggest that students ask to see their parents' Social Security cards to examine them.
Discuss possible alternatives to the current Social Security funding.

Edward R. Murrow, American news commentator and interviewer, died 1969
Investigate what Murrow's technique and style were in interviewing people.
Suggest that students prepare a list of questions and then interview a classmate or an adult in the school.

April 28

Arbor Day
Use Task Card #52 concerning Arbor Day activities.
Check out books from the library with scientifically drawn illustrations, as well as books with artists' stylized versions of trees; also introduce the books *Trees and How We Use Them,* by Tillie Pine and Joseph Levine, and *Once There Was a Tree: The Story of the Tree, a Changing Home for Plants and Animals,* by Phyllis Busch, and *The Giving Tree,* by Shel Silverstein.
Conduct a fund-raising drive to purchase a small tree to be planted on the school grounds.

James Monroe, fifth president of the United States, born 1758
(See Biography Data in Extra-Know-How Section.)
Research the significance of the Monroe Doctrine.
Explain that Monroe was the only president other than Washington to run unopposed; find out if that was true of both of the elections in which he was a candidate.

U.S. Constitution ratified by Maryland, thus making it the seventh state, 1788
(See States Admitted to the USA Data in Extra-Know-How Section.)

Mutiny on the British ship, the *H.M.S. Bounty*, organized, 1789
Draw a picture of the *H.M.S. Bounty*; discuss what "H.M.S." means.
Define the term "mutiny" and discuss the significance of the act of mutiny.
Read with the class *Mutiny on the Bounty,* by Charles Nordhoff and James N. Hall.
Discuss the thought: one can postpone mutiny by dividing the group into opposing forces.

Addressograph patented, 1896
Discuss what an addressograph serves to do.
Obtain a plate from a local merchant; consider the value of an addressograph machine to a business person.

Lionel Barrymore, American actor, born 1878
(See Biography Data in Extra-Know-How Section.)
Compare and contrast the various skills involved in stage acting and those of screen acting.

Vaccine for yellow fever announced, 1932
Investigate what yellow fever is, what a vaccine is, what the process is by which a vaccine serves to combat disease, and what the various ways are of administering vaccines.
Examine the life and times of Walter Reed, who helped in the development of the vaccine, and of William Gorgas, who demonstrated in the Panama Canal Zone that yellow fever could be eradicated through mosquito control.

April 29

William Randolph Hearst, American journalist and publisher, born 1863
(See Biography Data in Extra-Know-How Section.)
Explain the extent of Hearst's news empire (30 big daily papers and magazine/motion picture interests).
Introduce the term "yellow journalist," a derisive expression describing journalists who print the sensational aspect of an event to draw attention.
Ask if any student has visited Hearst Castle at San Simeon, California; if so, invite the student to share impressions of the visit.
(See activities under April 24, "First regularly ... " and October Special Weeks, "National Newspaper ....")

Duke Ellington, American musician, born 1899
(See Biography Data in Extra-Know-How Section.)
Enjoy selections of Ellington's recordings; discuss his style; encourage interested students to find out how he altered the entire pattern of jazz.

Casey Jones, engineer of Illinois Central's Cannonball Express, rode to his death, 1900
　　Obtain a recording of the classic folk song; introduce the legend of Casey Jones by listening to the words.

Emperor Hirohito of Japan, born 1901
　　(See Biography Data in Extra-Know-How Section.)
　　Trace the history of "emperor worship" in Japan prior to World War II.

Zipper patented by Gideon Sundback, 1913
　　Bring several zippers to class; discuss the different types of zippers, how they are sewn in, and the correct way to use them.
　　Discuss the expression, "Elevators are like zippers; they're great when they work and distressing when they don't." Think of other items that fit this description.
　　Examine today's clothing articles and consider how they might have been made without a zipper; create ideas for future possibilities of fastening clothing.
　　(See activities under March 23, "Rivet patented ....")

Nazi concentration camp at Dachau, Germany liberated by U.S. troops, 1945
　　Acquaint students with what a concentration camp is by sharing suitable passages from the book *Man's Search for Meaning*, by Viktor Frankl.
　　Discuss the fact that two memorial sites of this camp exist—in Dachau and in Israel.

April 30

Walpurgis Night, spring celebration in Scandinavia
　　Discuss the beginning of long days and short nights in the Northern Hemisphere.
　　Research various ways in which spring is celebrated throughout the world; look for commonalities.
　　Review Task Card #30 for activities about spring.

George Washington sworn in as the first American president, 1789
　　Ask students to re-enact the presidential swearing-in.
　　Analyze the words of the presidential oath of office; ask students to write an appropriate oath for a school officer and stage a swearing-in ritual.

Louisiana admitted to the United States as the eighteenth state, 1812
　　(See States Admitted to the USA Data in Extra-Know-How Section.)

Regularly scheduled television programs begun in America, 1939
　　Review Task Card #38 for further study of television.

Organization of American States established, 1948
　　Research the background and membership of the organization.
　　Compare the purposes of the organization to those of the Pan American Union.
　　Write to the Organization of American States for further information. (See Address Listing in Extra-Know-How Section.)
　　(See activities under April Special Weeks, "Pan American ... " and November Special Weeks, "Latin America ... " and December 2, "Pan American ....")

Saigon, Vietnam surrendered to Communist forces, 1975
　　Locate Saigon on the map or globe.
　　Discuss the impact of this event; find out the background and duration of the Vietnam War.

MAY

Maia, the Roman goddess of spring and fertility, is considered the background figure for the name of May. However, some scholars suggest that May's name is derived from majores, *the Latin word for "older men." Just as June is dedicated to youth, so is May associated with older people. Even today in the United States, the month of May is designated as Senior Citizen Month.*

Birthstone: Emerald
Flower: Lily of the Valley

Use the Find-a-Word Reproducible to preview happenings in May. (See Reproducible Section.)

MONTH-LONG OBSERVANCES

Senior Citizen Month

Hold a Senior Citizen visitation day; encourage the visitors to sign up for volunteer work in the school; find out particular skills that they may be willing to share with the class.

Conduct a discussion on what a senior citizen is, on whether retirement at 65 should be mandatory, and how best the talent and experience of senior citizens can be utilized.

Discuss how nutrition, medical science, and other factors have helped to extend the years of longevity; use an almanac to compare longevity in America with other countries and with America in 1900.

Find out the percentage of people living in America who are less than 65 as compared with the percentage of people who are over 65 years of age.

Visit a home where a number of senior citizens live.

(See activities under September 15, "Respect for ....")

National Radio Month

Investigate the history of the radio.

Write to the National Association of Broadcasters for information on radio broadcasting. (See Address Listing in Extra-Know-How Section.)

Obtain recordings of old radio shows and share them with the class.

Discuss the skill of listening in contrast to the combined skills of watching/listening to television.

Obtain a simple radio kit and build it.

Find out about short-wave radios, transistor radios, AM/FM radios, police, and citizen-band radios.

Discuss futuristic uses and styles of radios.

(See activities under April 25, "Guglielmo Marconi ....")

National Correct Posture Month

Study the bones of the body, posture, and carriage.

Write to the American Chiropractic Association for *Posture Activity Book* or to Reedco, Inc. for the booklet of "Basic Posture Patterns." (See Address Listing in Extra-Know-How Section.)

Initiate a posture program.

National Bike Month

Decorate bicycles and organize a bicycle parade; arrange for many different classifications.

Review Task Card #40 concerning the parts of a bike.

(See activities under April Special Weeks, "Bike Safety ... " and June 26, "Bicycle patented ....")

Hearing and Speech Month

Invite the speech/hearing specialist to class to discuss the field and profession of speech and language pathology.

Find out the ways in which deaf people learn to communicate.
(See activities under September 23, "Hearing aid ....")

Salad Month

Create a salad bar by asking students to bring recipes; make the salads and enjoy eating the various types of salads that have been created.

Concoct an original salad or salad dressing and design an appropriate container for it.

Mental Health Month

Make a class list of characteristics which constitute a mentally healthy individual.

Encourage interested students to pursue a study of Abraham Maslow's conceptual contributions to the field of mental health.

Find out about the volunteer possibilities in the local mental health association.

Investigate the mental health-related professions.

SPECIAL WEEKS

National Music Week (usually first Sunday)

Revitalize the music program in the classroom; consider various approaches, such as students sharing their music abilities.

Review Task Card #19 for music activities and Reproducible #12 for music games.

National Goodwill Week (first Sunday)

Encourage students to clean out their closets and contribute their belongings to the Goodwill Industries or other charitable organizations.

Relate to students the purposes of the Goodwill Industries; discuss the term "goodwill."

National Be Kind to Animals Week (usually first Sunday)

Invite students to design posters with "kindness to animals" as the theme.

Review Task Card #45 for ideas on organizing a pet show.

(See activities under April 11, "American Society ....")

Salvation Army Week (second Monday)

Find out what led to William Booth's having founded the organization; compare the purposes of the Salvation Army with those of the Goodwill Industries.

Invite a representative from the Salvation Army to talk about the organization.

National Hospital Week (Sunday including May 12)

Explain that the word "hospital" derives from the word *hospitalis*, pertaining to a "house" or "institution for guests."

Take a field trip to a local hospital; interview a hospital administrator and any other career people involved with the regulating of hospital procedures; investigate the routine for entering the hospital; inquire about emergency room policies.

Discuss hospital costs and hospitalization insurance.

Find out about the sophisticated technology which is housed in a hospital.

Define the term "out-patient ward."

Explore the various private/public health or hospital facilities in the local area.

Police Week (week including May 15)

Discuss the area of public safety; make a list of the ways in which the police force serves the community.

Visit a police station; investigate the possibilities of taking "police rides."

Invite a police officer to class to discuss public safety and law enforcement.

(See activities under August 12, "First police ....")

National Transportation Week (including the third Friday)

Create a mural on the evolution of transportation from the wheel to the supersonic transport and futuristic vehicles.

Discuss the public and private transportation systems in the local community and the potential or rapid transit systems in the large metropolitan areas.

Brainstorm various ideas for people-carriers.

Define the term "drayage."

Explore the combined industries of rail and road, i.e., the practice of piggy-backing (railroad cars carrying trucks).

International Pickle Week (next to last Thursday of the month)

Review Task Card #28 for various activities about pickles.

(See activities under March Month-long Observances, "Pickle Month.")

World Trade Week (Sunday, including May 22)

Discuss international dependence, according to various natural resources.

Obtain and use a social studies simulation game concerning world trade.

Discuss the merits of having a universal system of measurements; study the metric system.

Compare the different size measurements used for clothing and other commodities in various countries.

Encourage students to check the Sunday newspapers for the various monetary exchange rates throughout the world.

Investigate fair trade laws as they may particularly relate to the interests of students; discuss what "balance of trade" is.

(See activities under March 16, "Federal Trade ....")

National Realtor Week (third or fourth Sunday)

Discuss various types of real estate, such as residential, commercial, and income property.

Explore newspaper advertisements for property for sale.

Investigate the general procedure for buying and/or selling a house.

Bring a loan application and a rental agreement form to class for students to see.

Find out the meaning of such terms as: down payment, mortgage payment, assumed loans, negative income, escrow.

Invite a realtor to class to discuss real estate as a career.

Write to the National Association of Real Estate Boards for more information. (See Address Listing in Extra-Know-How Section.)

VARIABLE DATES

Kentucky Derby (usually first Saturday of the month)

Use Task Card #53 for information on racetracks.

Discuss past winners and the current contenders for the race.

Make a chart which traces various records that have been achieved in the Kentucky Derby.

(See activities under May 17, "First Kentucky ... " and August 19, "Willie Shoemaker ....")

Pulitzer Prize Awards (first Monday)

Ask students to contribute their best piece of written work; select a review board to choose the winner; conduct an awards ceremony.

Investigate the background of the awards; find out how many specific areas there are for which the Pulitzer awards are given.

Mother's Day (second Sunday)

Create a special gift for the classroom mother.

Review the economic conditions of the Depression years and explain that both Mother's Day and Father's Day were supposedly created by merchants at that time for the purpose of stimulating the economy through the purchases of gifts.

Encourage students to think of what their mothers or guardians would most appreciate as a gesture from the students; suggest they consider alternative gift ideas, such as a favor they could do for them or an arranged experience their mothers/guardians could enjoy alone or with the family.

Use Task Card #54 for additional activities for Mother's Day.

International Science and Engineering Fair (first week)

Discuss the advantages of joint international efforts in science.

Consider the point that science, music, and art tend to be the fields which carry with them a cross-cultural and international sharing; discuss that the reason may be that these respective fields have a more or less common set of symbols with which to communicate, exchange, and appreciate one another's accomplishments; define "*lingua franca*" as related to this point.

Investigate the Nobel Peace Prize as an award which has fostered the recognition of international pursuits, particularly in science.

Hold a school-wide science fair.

National Congress of Parents and Teachers Meeting (third or fourth Sunday)

Invite a representative from the local parents' group to speak to the class about the organization; consider the possibility of joint projects between the student body and the parent group.

National Emmy Awards (mid-month)

Investigate the history of the Emmy awards.

Invite students to make their own choices of current best television actor-actress performances.

Armed Forces Day (third Saturday)

Investigate the various career possibilities within the armed services.

Discuss the pros and cons of voluntary service as opposed to conscription practices.

Indianapolis 500-mile Auto Race (Memorial Day weekend)

Invite students to bring in their miniature racing cars and conduct their own "500-foot" races.

Discuss the significance of the checkered flag that is used.

Investigate the past winners and the current contenders.

Make a graph which indicates various records that have been achieved in this particular racing event.

Memorial Day (generally the last weekend)

(See Data-Detail in Extra-Know-How Section, "Memorial Day — History.")

DAYS OF THE MONTH

May 1

Law Day

Discuss international, federal, state, county, and city laws briefly; then stress school rules by introducing students to the educational code as published by the particular state.

Make a class list of words similar in meaning to the word "law" (rule, statute, ordinance, etc.).

Invite a law enforcement officer, an attorney, and/or a judge to discuss their careers.

(See activities under May 11, "Justinian, Byzantine ... " and August 21, "American Bar ....")

May Day (originally celebrated by the Druids and Romans)

Use Task Card #55 for directions on how to make a maypole and May baskets for a circle dance.

Introduce an alternate interpretation to May Day. Find out the background of a "May Day" call for help.

Louis Marie Chardonnet, French chemist and inventor of rayon (the first artificial fiber), born 1839

(See Biography Data in Extra-Know-How Section.)

(See activities under September 30, "Rayon, a synthetic ....")

First Wild West show, staged by Buffalo Bill, 1883

Investigate what Buffalo Bill's birth-given name was.

Find out the differences and similarities between a Wild West show and a rodeo, if any.

Obtain a roll-cap pistol and use it dramatically in class; motivate the students to create their own Wild West show. (Instruct students as to how to use the gun safely.)

Enjoy a book together about Buffalo Bill and/or other personalities and aspects of America's frontier life.

Kate Smith, American singer, born 1909

(See Biography Data in Extra-Know-How Section.)

Empire State Building dedicated in New York City, 1931

Find out what the current tallest building in America is.

Review Reproducible #21 for math activities related to the Empire State Building.

Participating U.S. railroads delegated their passenger services to Amtrak, a quasi-government subsidized railroad, 1971

Discuss the background and the significance of this negotiation.

Take a local field trip on the train.

Investigate railroad-related careers.

Ask students to bring Amtrak railroad models to share.

May 2

Hudson's Bay Co. chartered in England, 1670

Investigate the purposes of the Hudson Bay Co.

Write creative stories about North American Indians and the fur traders.

Catherine the Great, Empress of Russia, born 1729

(See Biography Data in Extra-Know-How Section.)

Make a class list of titles or terms which indicate royalty and/or political leadership.

General Henry M. Robert, developer of Robert's "Rules of Order," born 1837

(See Biography Data in Extra-Know-How Section.)

Explain that Robert adapted the rules of procedure used in the U.S. House of Representatives for the general use in less formal group meetings.

Obtain the reference booklet "Parliamentary Procedure at a Glance," by O. Garfield Jones; conduct a class meeting, according to Robert's "Rules of Order"; appoint an interested student as parliamentarian.

Benjamin Spock, American physician and author of *Baby and Child Care,* born 1903

(See Biography Data in Extra-Know-How Section.)

Investigate the career of a pediatrician and compare it with that of an obstetrician.

Encourage students to ask their parents if they were influenced by the views expressed in Dr. Spock's book.

Bing Crosby, American singer and actor, born 1904

(See Biography Data in Extra-Know-How Section.)

First jet airplane passenger service begun by Great Britain between London and Johannesburg, South Africa, 1952

Illustrate the development of jet aircraft; discuss the advantages and disadvantages of supersonic jets.

Baseball record set by Stan Musial (five homeruns in one day in two games), 1954

Invite students to hit as many balls, as far as possible, until they fail to hit the ball (no pitcher is to be used).

Ask students to make up and solve math story-problems using baseball terminology and situations.

May 3

Niccolo Machiavelli, Italian statesman, born 1469

(See Biography Data in Extra-Know-How Section.)

Define and discuss the term "Machiavellian."

First medical school in colonial America established in Philadelphia, 1765

Find out the requirements to get into medical school.

Invite a medical student to class to discuss his career pursuit.

Compare the requirements of earlier schools to those of today's institutions of higher learning.

Encourage students to read the diplomas and degrees which may be framed on the walls of their phsyicians' offices.

Make a list of the various types of medical doctors (specialists).

Jacob Riis, American journalist and philanthropist who exposed the degradation of the tenement districts of New York City, born 1849

(See Biography Data in Extra-Know-How Section.)

Define and discuss the term "tenement district."

Discuss the opportunity that a journalist has to expose certain corruptive elements in society; consider also the courage involved in the risk of publicly divulging information which could, in turn, result in harmful acts by the parties found guilty.

Golda Meir, former prime minister of Israel, born 1898

(See Biography Data in Extra-Know-How Section.)

Explain that Golda Meir immigrated to Palestine and lived on a kibbutz with her husband; find out what a kibbutz is.

Investigate the formation of the state of Israel and its history since 1948.

Find out what other women have served as heads of state.

First U.S. air passenger service begun, 1919

Create a mural representing the development of passenger airplanes.

Trace the route on a map or globe of this first air passenger flight.

Pete Seeger, American folksinger, born 1920

(See Biography Data in Extra-Know-How Section.)

Obtain recordings of Seeger's music and enjoy listening with students.

Encourage students to create children's folk songs.

Johnny Unitas, American football player, born 1933

(See Biography Data in Extra-Know-How Section.)

Invite a football player or coach from the local high school to talk about rules and safety regulations in football.

Investigate the history of the composition of footballs—from pigskin to cowhide to that of materials currently used for footballs.

Check out football films, discuss football purposes and strategies; enjoy books about the game and about famous players.

Play a flag football game.

(See activities under October 18, "Football rules ....")

May 4

American Comedy Day

Invite students to watch a situation comedy on television; the following day discuss the various forms of comedy, i.e., exaggeration and the depiction of commonly known daily frustrations.

Discuss the ability to be able to laugh at oneself.

Bring joke books to class.

Consider the asset of a sense of humor as opposed to taking life too seriously, negatively, or suspiciously.

Enjoy comical skits through the use of "paper bag dramatics"; put several items and a printed word in each bag; ask students to break into small groups and make use of each item in the group's bag to create a skit according to a theme represented by the printed word.

Obtain films with comic motif from the library or through Black Hawk Films. (See Address Listing in Extra-Know-How Section.)

(See activities under April Special Weeks, "National Laugh ... " and June Special Weeks, "National Humor ....")

Horace Mann, American educator, born 1796

(See Biography Data in Extra-Know-How Section.)

Find out what Horace Mann's contributions were to American education.

Thomas Huxley, British marine-biologist and grandfather to Aldous Huxley, born 1825

(See Biography Data in Extra-Know-How Section.)

Investigate the careers of a marine-biologist or of an oceanographer.

(See activities under June 22, "Julian Huxley ....")

Four students killed by National Guard troops at Kent State University, Kent, Ohio, 1970

Investigate the incident as closely as possible; ask interested students to present a case for either the students or for the National Guardsmen.

May 5

Cinco de Mayo (Mexican holiday commemorating the victory over the French at the Battle of Puebla, 1867)

Investigate the causes and effects of the Battle of Puebla.

Find out ways in which this holiday is traditionally celebrated.

Soren Kierkegaard, Danish philosopher, born 1813
(See Biography Data in Extra-Know-How Section.)
Discuss what a philosopher does and what it means to philosophize.

Karl Marx, German social philosopher, born 1818
(See Biography Data in Extra-Know-How Section.)

John Batterson Stetson, American hat manufacturer, born 1830
(See Biography Data in Extra-Know-How Section.)
Make a list of various types of hats and their purposes; create a class display of pictures of hats.
Design an original hat.
Encourage students to bring in unusual hats and conduct a hat parade.

Nicola Sacco and Bartolomeo Vanzetti arrested for robbery, 1920
Discuss the issue of possible innocence, regardless of incriminating evidence; relate this incident to the classroom situation.

Carnegie Hall opened in New York City, 1891
Investigate the career of a professional musician.
Find out the background of the name of Carnegie Hall.

Gwendolyn Brooks became the first black to win the Pulitzer Prize, 1950
Investigate the life and times of Gwendolyn Brooks.
(See activities under April 10, "Joseph Pulitzer ... " and June 7, "Gwendolyn Brooks ....")

Federal Republic of Germany declared a free sovereign nation, 1955
Investigate Germany's nation status in the early post-World War II era; discuss the reasons for the designated limitations during this period.

May 6

Sigmund Freud, Austrian psychiatrist, born 1856
(See Biography Data in Extra-Know-How Section.)
Find out the meaning of psychoanalysis; discuss the term, "Freudian slip."

Robert E. Perry, American explorer, born 1856
(See Biography Data in Extra-Know-How Section.)
Examine a globe to trace Perry's exploration; investigate his adventures in arriving at the North Pole.

Amadeo Peter Giannini, founder of the Bank of Italy, the forerunner of the Bank of America, born 1870
(See Biography Data in Extra-Know-How Section.)
Trace the development of the Bank of America.
Invite a representative from the Bank of America to discuss career opportunities in the field of banking.

Orson Welles, American actor, director, and producer, born 1915
(See Biography Data in Extra-Know-How Section.)

Willie Mays, American baseball player, born 1931
(See Biography Data in Extra-Know-How Section.)
Celebrate the day by holding a "stolen-base" contest.

Works Progress Administration (WPA) begun, 1935
Explain Roosevelt's plan to create employment during the Depression years in order to stimulate the economy; consider what effect a similar plan might have on the current economic scene.
Investigate the types of jobs that were available through the WPA.

Hindenburg **disaster** occurred, 1937
Discuss the word "dirigible."
Obtain a book about the event; ask a student to role-play the act of the on-the-scene newscaster; find out why the newscaster lost his job following the event.

Roger Bannister, British track star, became the first person to run a mile in less than four minutes (3:59:4), 1954
Ask students to attempt to run a mile and record their timing.

May 7

Robert Browning, English poet, born 1812
(See Biography Data in Extra-Know-How Section.)
Invite students to write a love poem to either an inanimate object or to a plant, animal, or person. (See Data-Detail in Extra-Know-How Section, "Love Ballad to My Love, the Great Pickle.")
Examine selections of Browning's poetry; ask students to discuss the various types of affection described by the word "love": puppy-love, family love, friendship love, romantic love, infatuation, love for a pet, brotherly or spiritual love; consider the Greek word *agape*, defined as the highest form of love—for one's fellow human beings.
Discuss the significance of love-hate relationships—strong feelings as opposed to apathy.
Think about the various ways in which love is expressed to family or friends.
Invite students to write a statement about the emotion of love.

Johannes Brahms, German composer, born 1833
(See Biography Data in Extra-Know-How Section.)
Obtain recordings of "Brahms' Lullaby"; discuss the mood which is created by the music; consider various synonyms for the term "lulling."

Peter I. Tschaikovsky, Russian composer, born 1840
(See Biography Data in Extra-Know-How Section.)
Obtain recordings of his music, including such contrasts as the "1812 Overture" with "Sleeping Beauty," "Swan Lake," and "The Nutcracker"; while listening, experiment with coordinating gross motor drawings with the various sweeps and dynamics of the music.

American Medical Association established, 1847
Discuss the significance of a professional code of ethics; consider the difference between a group-defined set of principles from within the profession as opposed to imposed regulations outside the profession; talk about the word "integrity" (personal or professional).
Examine the advantages and disadvantages of professional organizations.
Hold a debate on high medical costs and the possibility of greater governmental control and responsibility.

Edwin Herbert Land, American inventor of first Polaroid Instant Camera, born 1909
(See Biography Data in Extra-Know-How Section.)
(See activities under February 21, "First camera ... " and August 12, "Portable moving ....")

Lusitania, British liner, sunk by German submarine, 1915
Investigate the incident and discuss the significance of it as related to World War I.

French forces in Indochina defeated, 1954
Investigate what facets of French culture have remained in Vietnam and in other areas of Southeast Asia.
Find out which countries comprise Indochina.

May 8

World Red Cross Day
Write to the American National Red Cross for information. (See Address Listing in Extra-Know-How Section.)
Contact a representative from the local Red Cross chapter to come talk with the class.
Make a poster of the various Red Cross symbols used throughout the world; find out why the International Red Cross does not recognize the Israeli Red Cross symbol of the Magen David (Star of David), while allowing other nations to use different symbols.
(See activities under March Mongh-long Observances, "Red Cross ....")

Mississippi River discovered by the first European, Hernando DeSoto, 1541
Research specific data about the Mississippi River, i.e., length, depth, as related to other rivers on the North American continent.
Investigate geographic-related terms, such as: alluvial fan, flood plain, river delta.
Enjoy the book *Life on the Mississippi*, by Mark Twain.
Ask students to think about life along the Mississippi in terms of growing up there; create poems and drawings about the environment.

Jean Henry Dunant, Swiss founder of the Red Cross, born 1828
 (See Biography Data in Extra-Know-How Section.)
 Find out Dunant's city of birth; discover what language is spoken in that part of Switzerland; learn to pronounce Dunant's first name in that language.
 (See activities under May 8, "World Red Cross Day.")

Harry S Truman, thirty-third president of the United States, born 1884
 (See Biography Data in Extra-Know-How Section.)
 Explain that Truman had wished to have a middle name; in its place, he chose merely the letter *S* (in effect, a middle name); ask students what they would choose to do if they did not have a middle name.
 Investigate the dynamics of the election in which Truman defeated Thomas Dewey for the presidency.
 Discuss Truman's comment: "There's nothing new except the history we haven't read."

VE Day, 1945
 Discuss the impact of this event on current world affairs.
 What does the term "VE" mean?

May 9

First newspaper cartoon published in America, 1754
 Examine newspaper cartoons, sociopolitical as opposed to others.
 Differentiate between cartoons and the "comics."
 Invite students to create their own cartoons.

James Pollard Espy, American meteorologist, born 1785
 (See Biography Data in Extra-Know-How Section.)
 Define the term "meteorology."
 Investigate the career of a meteorologist.
 Organize a meteorology center in the classroom.
 (See activities under February 9, "U.S. Weather ....")

John Brown, American abolitionist, born 1800
 (See Biography Data in Extra-Know-How Section.)
 Define the word "abolitionist"; trace the derivation of the word.
 Find out the significance of John Brown's raid on Harpers Ferry, Virginia.
 Obtain a copy of the words and music of the song, "John Brown's Body" and discuss the meaning of the words.
 (See activities under December 2, "John Brown ....")

North Pole viewed from an airplane by Richard E. Byrd and Floyd Bennet, American aviators, 1926
 Examine on a globe where the North Pole is; investigate and discuss its longitude and latitude lines.
 Consider whether there is vegetation in the North Pole area.
 Compare polar-route flight distances as opposed to those of mid-Atlantic crossings to Europe.

Pancho Gonzales, American tennis player, born 1938
 (See Biography Data in Extra-Know-How Section.)
 (See activities under July Special Weeks, "Let's Play ....")

First eye bank opened in New York, 1944
 Consider what an eye bank is; investigate what the requirements are for either donating or receiving the cornea of an eye.
 Present a lesson on the anatomy and physiology of the eye.
 Discuss various colors of the eye; invite interested students to research eye color as related to Mendel's genetic theory of dominant and recessive genes.
 Invite a specialist to visit the class—an ophthalmologist, optometrist, oculist, or optician.
 Find out what an "ophthalmoscope" is.
 (See activities under March Special Weeks, "Save Your ....")

May 10

Boys' Day (celebrated in Japan)

Explain that individual birthdays are less celebrated in Japan than they are in America; this holiday serves as every Japanese boy's birthday. (See March 3 for "Girls' Day.")

Investigate the custom of flying huge paper carps from poles on this day.

Confederate Memorial Day (observed in a few southern states)

Encourage interested students to research information on the Confederacy and report back to the class.

Review Task Card #47 to play a game concerning the Civil War.

Sir Thomas Johnstone Lipton, founder of Lipton Tea Company, born 1850

(See Biography Data in Extra-Know-How Section.)

Explore the various types of teas; discuss the special teas that are used for medicinal purposes.

Review Task Card #30 to learn how to make solar tea.

Locate where tea is grown in various parts of the world and how the leaves are harvested.

Investigate the custom of "high tea" as it is observed in Great Britain.

First transcontinental railroad in America completed at Promontory, Utah, 1869

Trace the routes of the Central Pacific and the Union Pacific Railways to the meeting point at Promontory.

Conduct a discussion concerning the golden spike and the significance of train transportation in American history from earlier times up to the present.

Investigate what life as a railsman may have been like at that time; find out the ethnic make-up of the various railroad workers.

J. Edgar Hoover selected as head of the Federal Bureau of Investigation, 1923

Review Reproducible #13 for an activity about fingerprinting.

Write to the FBI for booklets and brochures. (See Address Listing in Extra-Know-How Section.)

(See activities under February Special Weeks, "National Crime ... " and May 19, "First Original ....")

First planetarium in the United States opened in Chicago, 1930

Take a field trip to a planetarium, if possible.

Pose the question: "Why are planetariums established and maintained?"

Study the stars and various constellations.

Investigate what telescopes are; obtain a telescope and discuss what high-powered lenses and prisms are.

Various books burned by the Nazi Party throughout Germany, 1933

Review the social-political situation in Germany at that time.

Explore the meaning and purpose of censorship; discuss whether any official representing governmental, industrial, professional, or other interest groups has the right to monitor literature, films, radio and TV programs, and press reports; investigate the interpretations of the First Amendment to the U.S. Constitution as related to this issue.

Discuss the dynamics involved in the process of "unwanted attention through sensational removal," thus often creating the reverse response; an example is the "forbidden fruit" notion, whereby prohibiting or protesting sometimes only intensifies one's wish or pursuit of that which is being denied.

May 11

Justinian, Byzantine emperor who created and codified Roman law, born 483

(See Biography Data in Extra-Know-How Section.)

Explain that the word "justice" is derived from Justinian's name; find out what the term "Byzantine" represents.

Review the Roman Code of Law; compare and contrast with modern laws.

Inquire of the students: "If the rules of fairness were to be named after one of you, what might they be called?"

Design a code of fairness for the classroom and school.

(See activities under May 1, "Law Day.")

Peter Stuyvesant, Dutch colonist, declared governor of New Amsterdam, 1647

Investigate what the current name is of the city that replaced New Amsterdam; find out the purchase price that was paid for New Amsterdam.

Trace the development of that area from the beginning to the current time; find out various statistics about the cost of rental space in the high-priority areas of the city.

Minnesota admitted to the United States as the thirty-second state, 1858
(See States Admitted to the USA Data in Extra-Know-How Section.)

Ottmar Mergenthaler, American inventor, born 1854
(See Biography Data in Extra-Know-How Section.)
Explain that Mergenthaler developed the first line-of-type machine, with a keyboard, which cast solid lines of type. ("Linotype" is the trademark name.)
(See activities under January Special Weeks, "International Printing ....")

Irving Berlin, American composer, born 1888
(See Biography Data in Extra-Know-How Section.)
Obtain recordings of Berlin's music and enjoy listening.

Salvador Dali, Spanish artist, born 1904
(See Biography Data in Extra-Know-How Section.)
Discuss the form of art known as "surrealism"; obtain art prints of Dali's and other surrealists to exemplify this art form.
Invite students to experiment with creating surrealistic drawings.

Glacier National Park created by Congress, 1910
Make a geological study on glaciers.
Create a chart and accompanying map of the national parks in the United States and in the world.
(See activities under March 1, "Yellowstone National ....")

May 12

Edward Lear, American poet, born 1812
(See Biography Data in Extra-Know-How Section.)
Examine samples of Lear's poetry, such as "The Owl and the Pussycat"; present *The Complete Nonsense Book,* as edited by Lady Strachey.
Explain that Lear wrote many limericks; introduce the limerick form of five-line poetry: the first, second, and fifth lines rhyme, and the second and third lines may or may not rhyme.

> There was a young man from Frisco
> Who tried to learn the Disco;
>   His legs were so short
>   He could not cavort
> And had to flee to San Bernardino.

Share other limericks and invite students to create their own.

Florence Nightingale, English nurse and hospital administrator, born 1820
(See Biography Data in Extra-Know-How Section.)
Consider why she was called "Lady of the Lamp" during the Crimean War.
Investigate nursing as a career for both men and women; find out about the position of hospital administrator and other health-related positions.

Burt Bacharach, American composer, born 1929
(See Biography Data in Extra-Know-How Section.)
Invite students to play some of his recordings.

May 13

Jamestown, first permanent English settlement in America, founded, 1607
Locate Jamestown on a map (formerly on a peninsula that is now an island).
Write to Jamestown Williamsburg, Department of Educational Programs, for further information. (See Address Listing in Extra-Know-How Section.)

War declared on Mexico by the U.S. Congress, 1846
 Investigate on a map the present international boundary of Mexico and the United States; find out the causes leading to the four-year Mexican War.

George Nicholas Papanicolaou, American physiologist, born 1883
 (See Biography Data in Extra-Know-How Section.)
 Explain that Papanicolaou developed a test for diagnosing cervical cancer (the Pap smear); discuss the point that he made his discovery in 1928 but that his work was ignored until 1940.
 Investigate the career of a physiologist.

Ernest L. Thayer's poem, "Casey at the Bat," recited by DeWolf Hopper, 1888
 Obtain a copy of the poem and read it to the class.
 Review some of the parody works on this poem.
 Invite students to write a poem or story describing a time when they were at bat and what the outcome was.
 Talk about the necessity of team work in sports activities. Discuss the problems that may develop when relying on one particular person or when blaming a loss on one person.
 Introduce students to a variety of games from *The New Games Book* and other activities produced by the New Games Foundation.

Joe Louis, American prizefighter, born 1914
 (See Biography Data in Extra-Know-How Section.)
 (See activities under January 18, "Muhammad Ali ....")

May 14

Gabriel Daniel Fahrenheit, German physicist, born 1686
 (See Biography Data in Extra-Know-How Section.)
 Investigate the many different types of temperature scales and their relative measurements—Fahrenheit, Centigrade, Kelvin, and Réaumur.
 Find out why Fahrenheit substituted mercury for alcohol in his thermometer.
 Present a lesson concerning the formula for converting centigrade temperatures to fahrenheit, and the reverse.

Thomas Gainsborough, English portrait and landscape painter, born 1727
 (See Biography Data in Extra-Know-How Section.)
 Obtain a copy of "The Blue Boy" and share with the class.

Thomas Wedgewood, British inventor of camera techniques, born 1771
 (See Biography Data in Extra-Know-How Section.)
 Review Task Card #26 to learn how to make a pinhole camera and other activities.

U.S. Women's Army Auxiliary Corps (WAAC) established, 1942
 Investigate the careers of women in the U.S. Army.
 Find out what nations maintain female defense forces.

Israel declared an independent nation, 1948
 Investigate the current boundaries of Israel; compare its area and population to various states in the United States.
 (See activities under November 2, "Balfour Declaration ....")

May 15

Frank Baum, American author, born 1856
 (See Biography Data in Extra-Know-How Section.)
 Ask students to read and enact parts of *The Wonderful Wizard of Oz*; find out the names of the other 13 tales of Oz.
 Investigate the two different pen names used by Baum.

Pierre Curie, French co-discoverer of radium, born 1859
 (See Biography Data in Extra-Know-How Section.)
 See activities under April 20, "Radium isolated ...."

U.S. Air Mail service begun, 1818
Investigate the advantages and drawbacks of airmail service.

Ellen Church became first airline stewardess (United Airlines), 1930
Write to various commercial airlines to learn about the careers of flight attendants.
Design an outfit for a flight attendant, male or female.

Women's long nylon stockings first merchandised in America, 1940
Discuss what material was used for hosiery prior to nylon.
Trace the validity of the point that chemical science is capable of producing "run-less" hose that would appeal to women, but that the industry has not done so for fear of the decline in business. Ponder other advances that may be withheld from the public for similar reasons; discuss the term "throw-away culture."
Suggest that students experiment with putting nylon hosiery in the freezer to test whether the hosiery's durability is increased.
Use Task Card #56 for ideas that make use of nylons.

May 16

Phillip D. Armour, American meat-packing executive, born 1832
(See Biography Data in Extra-Know-How Section.)
Explain that Armour was the first person to use refrigerated cars to ship meat across the country; he was also the first to can meat products.
Ask students to make a list of the various canned meat products that are available.
(See activities under March 29, "Oscar F. Mayer ....")

First U.S. five-cent piece minted and circulated, 1866
Invite students to bring in their coin collections and books (annual guidebooks and grading publications); examine the variety of designs among nickels; encourage students to scrutinize the minute differences found among coins.
Investigate how coins are originally dispatched and circulated.
Invite students to design their own five-cent pieces.
Write to the American Numismatic Association for further information on coins. (See Address Listing in Extra-Know-How Section.)
(See activities under April Special Weeks, "National Coin ....")

First typewriter with immediately visible print patented, 1893
Consider the disadvantages prior to this invention of not being able to view the typed page until it was finished.
Obtain a typewriter and encourage students to practice spelling lessons on the typewriter.
Investigate the advantages of an electronic typewriter and/or word processor.
(See activities under April 12, "First portable ... " and September 14, "Typewriter ribbon ....")

First Oscar Awards of the Academy of Motion Picture Arts and Sciences presented, 1929
Make a timeline of Oscar winners.
(See activities under April Variable Dates, "Academy Awards ....")

May 17

Edward Jenner, English physician, born 1749
(See Biography Data in Extra-Know-How Section.)
Explain that Jenner was the originator of the inoculation with cowpox virus for the purpose of immunizing against smallpox; define the word "inoculation" and discuss the process as an inventive way to prevent the spread of disease.
(See activities under May 26, "Smallpox epidemic ....")

New York Stock Exchange established, 1792
Encourage interested students to bring in the financial page from their local newspaper in order to discuss the field of stocks and investments—the terminology and the concepts; suggest that students listen to stock market reports on the radio and TV; remind students to watch for sudden fluctuations in the market and to try to determine the reason.
Use Task Card #57 to learn more about the stock exchange.

Grain reaper patented by Cyrus McCormick, 1834

Investigate the original reaper machine and its subsequent improvements, such as the combine.

Explain that during the early years of McCormick's reaper business, the demand was greater than he could supply, so he chose to license various manufacturers in other areas; this arrangement proved unsatisfactory because McCormick could not have quality control on the product bearing his name. He proceeded to consolidate his operations in one large factory in Chicago, the fastest growing western city at that time.

Discuss the meaning of the saying, "Sow and you shall reap," as related to McCormick's hard work and success.

Consider the various marketing reasons for his success—a credit system and a warranty service; in addition, he promoted his products through exposure at county fairs, public relations programs, and advertising with testimonials from satisfied customers.

(See activities under February 15, "Cyrus McCormick ... " and June 21, "Functional wheat ....")

First Kentucky Derby horse race held at Churchill Downs, 1875

Find out the meaning of the following horse racing-related terms: purse, gelding, handicapping, sprint, route, turf, bug, totalization board, filly, mare, colt.

Investigate the different types of horse racing the horse racetracks.

Explore what the advantages and disadvantages might be in having a racetrack in one's community.

Write to the American Quarterhorse Association for pamphlets on horse racing. (See Address Listing in Extra-Know-How Section.)

Review Task Card #53.

(See activities under May Variable Dates, "Kentucky Derby ... " and August 19, "Willie Shoemaker ....")

Racial segregation in public schools declared unconstitutional by the U.S. Supreme Court, 1954

Discuss the point that mandated decisions take time to be accepted and enforced in that human attitudes and behavior do not automatically change; trace various Supreme Court decisions and substantiate the approximate time span between the date of the ruling and the time of its being a widely accepted practice.

Differentiate and discuss the terms: integration, desegregation.

May 18

Walter Gropius, German-American architect, born 1883

(See Biography Data in Extra-Know-How Section.)

Investigate the designs of the Bauhaus School in Chicago, the school with which Gropius is associated.

Research the architectural accomplishments of other architects, such as Mies van der Rohe, Le Corbusier, and I. M. Pei.

(See activities under June 8, "Frank Lloyd Wright ....")

First steamboat passed through the Panama Canal, 1914

(See activities under January 7, "Panama Canal ....")

U.S. Selective Service Act passed, 1917

(See activities under April 1, "First U.S. wartime ....")

Tennessee Valley Authority (TVA) hydraulic power system authorized, 1933

Investigate other examples of hydroelectric plants in America.

Find out the other purposes and outcomes of the TVA, other than the generation of energy for that area.

Trace the derivation of the prefix "hydra-" or "hydro-."

Capital punishment authorized by U.S. federal law, 1934

Hold a debate concerning the pros and cons of capital punishment.

Head of the Lochness Monster first "discovered," 1964

Ask students to research in various newspapers in the library for reports about the Lochness Monster, as well as about "Sasquatch" (Big Foot) in America's Northwest, or about the "Abominable Snow Man" in the Himalaya region of Asia; when the data are gathered, ask students whether they believe the monsters do, in fact, exist.

May 19

Johns Hopkins, American philanthropist, born 1795
(See Biography Data in Extra-Know-How Section.)
Write to Johns Hopkins University for information about the university. (See Address Listing in Extra-Know-How Section.)

Electric fire alarm system patented, 1857
Make a location map which indicates particular areas where there are fire alarms and extinguishers in the school.
Discuss the problem of false alarms.
(See activities under April 1, "First salaried ....")

Boys' Club of America organized, 1906
Investigate the background and purposes of this organization.

First criminal conviction using fingerprints as evidence occurred, 1911
Explain that it is believed that the Chinese used thumbprints before the birth of Christ; a method of identifying fingerprints in the Western world was developed in 1858 by Sir William Herschel; currently, fingerprint characteristics can be converted into digital computer language through a print scanner which "looks at" an unidentified fingerprint and matches it with prints in the FBI files.
Investigate to what degree the court system in America relies on assistance from graphologists (handwriting analysts) to determine the validity of signatures as related to charges of forgery.
Review Reproducible #13 for activities about fingerprinting.
(See activities under May 10, "J. Edgar Hoover ... " and February Special Weeks, "National Crime ....")

National quotas for immigration into the United States established by Congress, 1921
Explain about the industrial revolution in the late nineteenth century which brought about widespread emigration from western and eastern Europe; discuss the government's decision to establish quotas and its effect upon immigrants.
Arrange a social problem for the students to solve in order for them to understand more fully about quotas: "I have just two tickets for entrance to Disneyland (or a substitute area); what criteria should be used to make the decision as to which two students are to receive the tickets and be admitted?"
Trace the derivation and meaning of the words "immigration" and "emigration"; use them each in appropriate sentences.

Malcolm X, black leader, born 1925
(See Biography Data in Extra-Know-How Section.)
Investigate the lives of other black leaders by sending to Fitzgerald Publishing Co. for the Golden Legacy series of comics. (See Address Listing in Extra-Know-How Section.)
Explain that many Muslims took the letter *X* as a last name to replace the family names formerly assigned by white owners to their slaves.
(See activities under February 21, "Malcolm X ....")

Calaveras County Frog-Jumping Jubilee held, 1928
Discuss this event and recreate a similar competition by obtaining frogs and conducting a contest.
Introduce the game of "Leap Frog."

First woman, Jacqueline Cochran, to fly faster than the speed of sound, 1953
Investigate what the speed of sound is and how the speed of sound is measured.

May 20

First day of the zodiac period, Gemini, the Twins (through June 20)
(See Data-Detail in Extra-Know-How Section, "Notes on Astrology.")

Dolly Madison, White House hostess (1801-1809) and U.S. First Lady (1809-1817), born 1768
(See Biography Data in Extra-Know-How Section.)
Investigate the role that Dolly Madison played in rescuing the many pieces of art and public papers during the White House fire of 1812. (Find a print of the famous Gilbert Stuart painting of George Washington, one of the many art works that she was able to save; share with the class.)

Fountain pen patented, 1830

Compare and contrast fountain pens and ball-point pens.

Find out the variety of pen points that a draftsman uses; investigate if there are specialized pen points for left-handed writers.

Write to the Parker Pen Co. to obtain information on the history of pens. (See Address Listing in Extra-Know-How Section.)

(See Data-Detail Section in Extra-Know-How Section, "History of Writing Instruments.")

Émile Berliner, American inventor, born 1851

(See Biography Data in Extra-Know-How Section.)

Explain that Berliner invented the flat "platter" phonograph record.

Trace the development of the record industry.

Invite students to bring in their favorite records to enjoy with the group.

(See activities under February 19, "Phonograph machine ... " and August 12, "Phonograph invented ....")

Homestead Act signed by President Lincoln, 1862

Investigate the purpose behind the act; define the term "homesteading."

Ask students where they would most like to homestead if they had their choice.

International Bureau of Weights and Measurements established, 1875

Discuss the significance of a universally accepted system of weights and measures among trading nations of the world.

Obtain a copy of a weights and measurements table from an encyclopedia, mathematics book, or cookbook; begin a study unit on weights and measurements.

Write to Weights and Measures Associates for further information. (See Address Listing in Extra-Know-How Section.)

Review Reproducible #14 to complete the metric license fill-in exercise.

First driver arrested for speeding, Jacob German, New York City, 1899

Record various students' estimates of what the speed limit was and then find out the answer.

Investigate the schedule for fines for speeding tickets in the local community.

Introduce safe-driving information by contacting the local police department or automobile clubs.

Moshe Dayan, Israeli leader, born 1915

(See Biography Data in Extra-Know-How Section.)

Charles Lindbergh's flight, the first solo flight across the Atlantic Ocean, begun, 1927

Investigate the name of Lindbergh's airplane and where it is currently located.

Find out what happened in Lindbergh's personal life, following this major feat; discuss the advantages and disadvantages of fame.

Discuss the term "solo," and then ask students to suggest activities they would or would not like to do solo.

Compare the instrument panel of Lindbergh's plane (from a photograph) to that of current small private planes.

Define the terms: gyroscope, tachometer, pitch indicator, compass, altimeter, bank indicator.

Read selected parts from Lindbergh's book *The Spirit of St. Louis*, for which he won the Pulitzer Prize; also obtain a copy of *Ride on the Wind*, by Alice Dalgliesh, and share with students.

(See activities under February 4, "Charles A. Lindbergh ... " and June 11, "First U.S. Distinguished ....")

Amelia Earhart's first solo flight across the Atlantic Ocean begun, 1932

Investigate Earhart's other flights and the outcome of the attempted flight around the world.

Use Task Card #58 for activities on Earhart and on flight.

(See activities under July 2, "Amelia Earhart ... " and July 24, "Amelia Earhart ....")

Pan American Airlines' transatlantic passenger service begun, 1939

Investigate what the passenger capacity was of these early passenger planes.

Write to Pan American World Airways for information on the variety of careers in the airline industry. (See Address Listing in Extra-Know-How Section.)

Investigate the number of current varied flight paths across the Atlantic by checking a flight schedule book and a map of charted flights at a local travel bureau.

First heliport on top of a hotel established in Fort Worth, Texas, 1953

Discuss what a heliport is and its purpose.

Encourage students to draw a hotel with their own hotel-top innovations.

May 21

Albrecht Dürer, German artist, born 1471
(See Biography Data in Extra-Know-How Section.)
Obtain copies of his painting and sculptures, then share and enjoy them with the class.
Explain that Dürer created a self-portrait; invite students to make their self-portraits.

American National Red Cross founded by Clara Barton, 1881
(See activities under May 8, "World Red ....")

Raymond Burr, American actor, born 1917
(See Biography Data in Extra-Know-How Section.)
Ask students to enact a mystery case in the style of the "Perry Mason" television show, or pretend to play the part of the police chief in a wheelchair, as formerly portrayed by Burr in the television show "Ironsides."

"Crime of the Century" (Leopold-Loeb murder case) committed, 1924
(See Data-Detail in Extra-Know-How Section, "Leopold-Loeb Story.")
Introduce ballad writing. (See Data-Detail in Extra-Know-How Section, "The Ballad of Poor Innocent Bobby.")

May 22

National Maritime Day (commemorates the start of the first trans-Atlantic voyage of the first U.S.-built steamship, the *Savannah*, in 1819)
Obtain a model kit of the *Savannah* and arrange an interest center in which students can construct the model.
Define the word "maritime."

First life insurance policy issued in America, 1761
Invite an insurance agent to class to discuss life insurance.
Obtain policies from various insurance companies; compare and contrast the terms and benefits.
Write to Bankers Life for the booklet "How to Select the Right Life Insurance Company." (See Address Listing in Extra-Know-How Section.)

Aaron Burr's trial for treason begun, 1807
Define and discuss the term "treason."
Investigate the situation which led to the political leader's trial; trace the outcome of the court's decision.

Richard Wagner, German opera composer, born 1813
(See Biography Data in Extra-Know-How Section.)
Obtain recordings of Wagnerian operas, i.e., *Lohengrin* or *The Flying Dutchman*, and enjoy listening to the drama of the legends.
(See activities under July Variable Dates, "Wagner Festival ....")

Sir Arthur Conan Doyle, British writer, born 1859
(See Biography Data in Extra-Know-How Section.)
Introduce Conan's literature character, Sherlock Holmes, through library books or comics.
Obtain the film "The Hound of the Baskervilles" from the local film library.
Discuss the various elements in developing effective mystery stories; invite students to create a mystery story.

Sir Laurence Olivier, English actor and director, born 1907
(See Biography Data in Extra-Know-How Section.)

Janet Guthrie, American race-car driver, informed that she was the first woman to qualify for the Indianapolis 500 race, 1977
(See activities under May Variable Dates, "Indianapolis 500-mile ....")

May 23

Carl Linnaeus, Swedish naturalist and "Father of Botany," born 1707
(See Biography Data in Extra-Know-How Section.)

Conduct a study on plants, introducing such aspects as photosynthesis and parts of a plant.

Write to the Botannical Society of America for the booklet entitled "Botany as a Profession." (See Address Listing in Extra-Know-How Section.)

Review Task Card #32 for activities about horticulture.

He also is credited for having founded modern taxonomy by having devised a systematic classification; find out the difference between "genus" and "species."

Eyeglass bifocals patented by Benjamin Franklin, 1785

Find out the many other accomplishments of Franklin.

Discuss the purpose of multifocal lenses.

U.S. Constitution ratified by South Carolina, thus making it the eighth state, 1788

(See States Admitted to the USA Data in Extra-Know-How Section.)

First nursery school in America founded, 1827

Discuss the purposes of nursery schools then and now; find out the differences, if any, among nursery schools, preschools, day-care or child-care centers.

Investigate the career of a nursery school teacher or director.

Visit a nearby nursery school; make a presentation, such as a puppet show.

Invite students to write a story about what happened to them in nursery school, true or fictitious.

First U.S. veterinary school established, 1879

Invite a veterinarian to class to discuss the preparation as a physician and his/her career of treating animals.

Find out how many schools of veterinary medicine there are in America.

Mt. Everest, the highest mountain in the world, scaled by the first woman, a Japanese housewife, 1975

Find out who first successfully climbed Mt. Everest and how many have done so since that time.

Locate Mt. Everest; find out what country it is in; investigate the heights of Mt. Everest, in both feet and meters; make a list of other high mountain peaks with their locations and heights; develop a chart or diagram to report the findings.

Discuss the comment: "It isn't the mountains ahead that wear you out; it's the grain of sand in your shoe."

May 24

Empire Day, celebrated throughout British-related areas of the world in honor of the anniversary of Queen Victoria's birth date.

Discuss the meaning of the term "empire."

List the various empires throughout world history.

Ask students to imagine what their empire would be like and then to write a play script or story about that empire.

Enjoy the fiction story, *Star Wars — The Empire Strikes Back* (book and/or film).

Manhattan Island purchased from the Indians by Peter Minuit, Dutch colonial leader in America, 1626

Explain that Minuit was the director-general of Holland's North American settlements, known as New Netherlands; during the first year of his rule, he purchased Manhattan Island from a council of Indian chiefs for trinkets worth 60 guilders (Dutch money), equal to about $24 at that time; invite students to re-enact the incident.

First telegraph message ("What hath God wrought?") transmitted by Samuel F. B. Morse, American inventor, 1844

Differentiate between a telegraph message and a telegram; find out the meaning of the prefix "tele."

Ask students to draw the name of a classmate and tell a message to the class telegraph agent; the agent is to transcribe the voiced message onto a message-gram and then distribute it to the intended class member.

(See activities under April 27, "Samuel F. B. Morse ....")

Exploration of the Grand Canyon begun by John W. Powell, American geologist, 1869

Conduct a study on the Grand Canyon, including such geological terms as: mountain-building, erosion, uplift, Archeozoic era.

Investigate the career of a geologist.

Use Task Card #59 for more information on geology.

(See activities under February 26, "Grand Canyon ....")

Brooklyn Bridge in New York City opened, 1883
  Discuss the concept that a straight line is the shortest distance between two points.
  Suggest that students bring in various pictures of bridges; ask them to draw their own bridges, using fundamentals of perspective drawing.

First temperance society in America formed, 1893
  (See activities under January 21, "Kansas City ....")

First strike settlement in America mediated by the Department of Labor, 1913
  Introduce a simulation game on labor-management relations.
  Investigate the development of unions in America; find out the background of the American Federation of Labor (AFL) and the Congress of Industrial Organizations (CIO), now merged.
  (See activities under November 13, "First known ....")

First U.S. foreign service created, 1924
  Investigate what preparation is needed for a career as a foreign diplomat or ambassador.

First major league night baseball game in the United States held (Cincinnati vs. Philadelphia), 1935
  Discuss how night lighting has expanded the possibilities of all spectator sports.
  Find out the advantages and disadvantages of artificial lighting and of sunlight from the viewpoints of both the players and the spectators.

Bob Dylan, American singer, born 1941
  (See Biography Data in Extra-Know-How Section.)
  Obtain recordings of Dylan's music and enjoy with the class; encourage students to write poetry in a style similar to Dylan's.

First coin-operated automatic food dispenser in America (Food-o-Mat) installed, 1945
  Discuss the advantages and disadvantages of these machines.
  Invite students to design an automatic food machine that stocks nutritious foods and has many mechanical conveniences.

First moving sidewalk in America installed, 1954
  Discuss the benefits and disadvantages of a moving sidewalk.
  Query students as to an ideal location for a moving sidewalk.

First house in the United States with a nuclear bomb shelter built, 1959
  Discuss the reason for bomb shelters; find out where the local community bomb shelters are.

May 25

African Liberation Day (commemorates the formation of the Organization of African States, 1963)
  Study the various nations, languages, and ethnic groups within Africa; find out whether nation-states' lines were drawn in terms of ethnic-group boundaries or not.
  Define and discuss such terms as: colonialism, imperialism, white man's burden, white supremacy, multinational corporations.
  Make a list of nations that have declared their independence from European powers and identify the European nation associated with each.

Ralph Waldo Emerson, American essayist, philosopher, and poet, born 1803
  (See Biography Data in Extra-Know-How Section.)
  Read with the class excerpts from "Self-Reliance."
  Investigate what is meant by the term "transcendentalism."
  Consider the following statements by Emerson:
      "The only way to have a friend is to be one."
      "They can conquer who believe they can."
      "Fear always springs from ignorance."
      "Life is a perpetual instruction in cause and effect."
      "What is a weed? A Plant whose virtues have not yet been discovered."

Gasoline engine patented, 1844
Discuss the impact of this invention and also the advantages and disadvantages of the gas engine.
Invite students to bring in model kits of car engines with which to work.
Observe a gas engine operating in an automobile; compare a V6 and V8 engine.

Beverly Sills, American opera star, born 1929
(See Biography Data in Extra-Know-How Section.)
Investigate the career of an opera singer.
(See activities under February 18, "First opera ... " and April 12, "Lily Pons ....")

Babe Ruth's last homerun hit, 1935
Ask students to line up and hit the ball (either pitched or not) as far as they can, trying to match the distance of Babe Ruth's last homerun.
(See activities under February 6, "Babe Ruth ....")

First noncommercial educational television program in America broadcast, 1953
Compare and contrast various aspects of commercial and noncommercial television.
Investigate how noncommercial stations are subsidized.

May 26

Smallpox epidemic in America occurred, 1721
Discuss what smallpox is and how it has nearly been eliminated in America.
Ask students where on their bodies they have been vaccinated.
(See activities under May 17, "Edward Jenner ....")

John Wayne, American actor, born 1907
(See Biography Data in Extra-Know-How Section.)

May 27

First witchcraft execution in America witnessed, 1647
Investigate the historical practice of witchcraft and the Salem witch trials.
Define and discuss the term "exorcism."
(See activities under June 10, " 'Witches' hanged ....")

Cornelius Vanderbilt, American railroad magnate and philanthropist, born 1794
(See Biography Data in Extra-Know-How Section.)
Investigate the direct railway route that was laid by the New York Central Railroad.
Define and discuss the term "philanthropist"; explain that Vanderbilt donated land as a legacy to Columbia University.
Find out where both Columbia and Vanderbilt universities are.

Piano patented, 1796
Invite a piano shop owner or piano tuner to come to discuss types of pianos and how pianos work.
Interview a piano tuner to find out how a piano is tuned; inquire as to what training or abilities are needed to be a piano tuner.
Investigate which instruments, similar to the piano, preceded the piano.
Invite students who play the piano to present a song to the class.

Louis Agassiz, Swiss-American ichthyologist, born 1807
(See Biography Data in Extra-Know-How Section.)
Define and trace the derivation of the word "ichthyologist"; pronounce the word.
Introduce a unit on ichthyology.

Amelia Bloomer, American suffragette who introduced "bloomers" for women to wear, born 1818
(See Biography Data in Extra-Know-How Section.)
Find out what bloomers are, how they are worn, and what the social impact was when they were introduced.

Discuss the various changes in dress and grooming throughout history; talk about conventions and nonconformity in dress and why there are usually some forms of dress codes in schools.

Survey the class as to whether dresses or long pants on women are preferred and which the girls prefer to wear.

Julia Ward Howe, American social reformer for women's rights, born 1819

(See Biography Data in Extra-Know-How Section.)

Explain that Julia W. Howe wrote the words to "The Battle Hymn of the Republic."

(See activities under February 1, "Battle Hymn ....")

Vincent Price, American actor, born 1912

(See Biography Data in Extra-Know-How Section.)

Explain that Vincent Price learned to change his original speech pattern and intonation to fit the various acting parts he played.

Invite students to make a presentation, using different voice modulation and tone; ask them to try to imitate someone.

Golden Gate Bridge in San Francisco opened, 1937

Find out why the Golden Gate Bridge represented such an engineering feat.

(See activities under May 24, "Brooklyn Bridge ....")

May 28

First labor law prohibiting employment of women enacted, 1879

Find out the reasons for this law and its significance in contrast to current women's movements.

Pure Food Law in the United States enacted, 1881

Explain that the purpose of the law was to remove harmful products from the market in order to protect the consumer; comment also upon the point that Upton Sinclair's book *The Jungle* aided in rallying interest in the law's passage.

Write to the U.S. Food and Drug Administration for the booklet "Food Labels." (See Address Listing in Extra-Know-How Section.)

Discuss the problem of overprotection by authorities and the subsequent decrease in free choice.

(See activities under June 26, "First pure ....")

James Francis Thorpe ("Jim"), American Indian Olympic athlete, born 1888

(See Biography Data in Extra-Know-How Section.)

Explain that Thorpe won medals in the pentathlon and decathlon events, but that the medals were taken away due to a technicality regarding amateur status.

Obtain the film "Jim Thorpe: All American" for a review of his life and struggles.

First talking picture entirely in color produced, 1929

Show a film, turn off the sound, and later discuss various impressions of viewing a film without sound.

Locate where the sound factor is on film.

Dionne quintuplets born, 1934

Conduct a mock TV interview with the parents of the newborn children.

Discuss the word "quintuplets"; ask which words are used for groups of three, four, and six children.

Consider what it would be like to grow up as a twin or a sibling in a multiple-birth grouping; explain that there are groups called "twin-liberation" that are organized to aid in self-identity.

Find out the difference between fraternal and identical twins.

First animated three-dimensional technicolor cartoon created by Walt Disney, 1953

Contact Walt Disney Films for a collection of Disney cartoons and share them with the class. (See Address Listing in Extra-Know-How Section.)

Discuss cartoon animation and the term "three-dimensional."

Review Task Card #44 for 3-D art activity.

Obtain a book describing how animated films are produced; try creating a simple animated film.

May 29

Patrick Henry, American statesman, born 1736
(See Biography Data in Extra-Know-How Section.)
Obtain a copy of Henry's famous speech and ask interested students to present it dramatically to the class.
Explain that Patrick Henry was criticized by many as being a radical; name current personalities who are thought to be radical but who might one day be considered as heroes, as in Patrick Henry's case.
(See activities under March 23, "Give me ....")

U.S. Constitution ratified by Rhode Island, thus making it the thirteenth state, 1790
(See States Admitted to the USA Data in Extra-Know-How Section.)

First American nautical school established in Massachusetts, 1827
Find out the derivation of the word "nautical."
Study various terms, i.e., "starboard," "port," "stern," bow"; compare distances of a knot and a mile or kilometer.

Wisconsin admitted to the United States as the thirtieth state, 1848
(See States Admitted to the USA Data in Extra-Know-How Section.)

Bob Hope, British-American actor and comedian, born 1903
(See Biography Data in Extra-Know-How Section.)
Discuss the fact that Hope traveled overseas to perform shows for military personnel.
Encourage students to present jokes in the style of Bob Hope.

Benny Goodman, American musician, born 1910
(See Biography Data in Extra-Know-How Section.)
Invite a student-clarinetist to explain and demonstrate his/her musical instrument.
Obtain recordings of Goodman's music and enjoy them with the class.
Compare the sounds and appearances of the clarinet and oboe; name other woodwind instruments.

John F. Kennedy, thirty-fifth president of the United States, born 1917
(See Biography Data in Extra-Know-How Section.)
Write to Columbia Pictures for the Super 8 film, "John F. Kennedy, Man of Courage, 1917-1963." (See Address Listing in Extra-Know-How Section.)
Read selections from Kennedy's book *Profiles in Courage*, for which he received the Pulitzer prize.
Discuss Kennedy's statement in his inaugural address, "All this will not be finished in the first one hundred days ... nor in the life of this Administration, nor even perhaps in our lifetime on this planet. But let us begin." Talk about another of Kennedy's quoted comments: "Fear not to negotiate, but never negotiate out of fear."
(See activities under November 22, "John F. Kennedy ....")

U.S. President's Flag adopted, 1916
Obtain a picture of the President's Flag and ask students to recreate a drawing of it; or encourage students to design a new flag for the office of U.S. president.

May 30

Joan of Arc, French saint and national heroine, burned at the stake, 1431
Find out the reasons why a national heroine would be burned at the stake.
Investigate the word and process of "canonization."

First corporation in America chartered, 1650
Discuss what a corporation is and how it legally differs from various forms of partnerships.
Explore the development of large corporations which led to the Sherman Antitrust Act of 1890 and the Clayton Antitrust Act of 1914.
Use Task Card #60 for further information about corporations.

Countee Cullen, American poet, born 1803
(See Biography Data in Extra-Know-How Section.)
Review Task Card #10 to become familiar with Cullen's poetry.

Manual ice-cream freezer patented, 1848
Review Task Card #18 on how to make ice cream.

First automobile accident in America recorded, 1896
Obtain statistics for auto accidents in the local community and in the nation.
Invite a representative from a local motor vehicle department or state highway patrol office to discuss the various reasons for auto accidents and the need for people to drive defensively.
(See activities under May 20, "First driver ....")

Hall of Fame for Great Americans established, 1901
Ask students to agree upon a list of the 10 most deserving candidates to the Hall of Fame; invite students to arrange the process by which they are to achieve consensus, as well as to decide upon the criteria for selecting candidates of the past or present.
Read the book *The 100: A Ranking of the Most Influential Persons in History*, by Michael H. Hart.

First Workman's Compensation in America created, 1908
Explore the meaning of "compensation" as related to working conditions.
Stage a debate concerning the pros and cons of such a provision.

Indianapolis Speedway opened, 1911
Investigate the history of the speedway.
(See activities under February 28, "Mario Andretti ... " and May Variable Dates, "Indianapolis 500 ....")

May 31

U.S. Copyright Law signed, 1790
Ask students to check their books for copyright dates.
Discuss what the purpose is of a copyright.
Encourage students to write to the Register of Copyright to find out how to obtain a copyright and also to request a copy of the copyright regulations regarding the reproduction of copyrighted materials. (See Address Listing in Extra-Know-How Section.)
Use Task Card #61 for further information on copyrighting.
(See activities under March 4, "First international ....")

Walt Whitman, American poet, born 1819
(See Biography Data in Extra-Know-How Section.)
Examine selections of his poetry, particularly "Leaves of Grass."
(See activities under March 26, "Walt Whitman ....")

First Arctic expedition organized, 1853
Look on a world globe to locate where the Arctic region is.
Investigate the various types of ethnic groups who live in the Arctic, as well as the variety of vegetation and animal life found there.

Sheet-asphalt pavement patented, 1870
Discuss how this achievement changed road construction; find out current processes of road construction.
Investigate the various ways in which revenue is collected for highway maintenance (turnpike and expressway tolls, gasoline tax, etc.); find out how trucks and other large vehicles are assessed for their heavy use of the roads.
Write to the Asphalt Institute for the booklet "Magic Carpet – The Story of Asphalt." (See Address Listing in Extra-Know-How Section.)

Joe Namath, American football player, born 1943
(See Biography Data in Extra-Know-How Section.)

JUNE

It is generally accepted that the month of June was named for Juno, *the patron goddess of marriage. However, some authorities believe that the name was taken from* juniores, *the Latin word for male youths, because the month of June in Rome was dedicated to young men.*

Birthstone: Pearl
Flower: Rose

Use the Find-a-Word Reproducible to preview happenings in June. (See Reproducible Section.)

MONTH-LONG OBSERVANCES

Dairy Month
Investigate the various types of milk and milk products.
Review the contributions of Gail Borden to the dairy industry.
Write to the National Dairy Council for information about the dairy industry. (See Address Listing in Extra-Know-How Section.)
Discuss the popularity of yogurt and natural raw-culture products.
Exchange recipes which have dairy products as the ingredients.
Review Task Card #4 for information on how to make butter.
Review Task Card #12 to learn the steps involved in milk distribution.
Review Task Card #18 to learn how to make ice cream.
(See activities under June 4, "Roquefort Cheese ....")

National Rose Month
Investigate how many types of roses there are, the growth stages of a rose, and the care of roses; think of occasions that might be particularly appropriate to send roses.
Trace the derivation and define the words "anthropomorphism" and "personification"; ask students to personify a rose, both in body movement and in verbalization. ("How would you feel as part of a bouquet at a wedding?" "Would you rather be somewhere else than at a wedding?")
Write to the Pasadena Tournament of Roses Association for information concerning the use of roses in the Rose Parade. (See Address Listing in Extra-Know-How Section.)
Write to the American Rose Society for more data on roses. (See Address Listing in Extra-Know-How Section.)

Italian Heritage Month
Obtain a map of Europe; locate Italy and its principal cities.
Make a list of names of Italians who became famous in art, music, and science.
Explain that pasta—flour and water food—is the basic national dish in Italy. Foods made from pasta include spaghetti, ravioli, macaroni, and vermicelli; ask students to illustrate a chart with names to identify the pastas.
Present a noodle and glue art lesson.
Write to the Italian Historical Society of America for more information about Italy. (See Address Listing in Extra-Know-How Section.)

SPECIAL WEEKS

National Humor Week (first Sunday)
Ask the school librarian to make up a display of humorous books to be enjoyed.

Discuss the following comments: "To be a humorist, one must see the world out of focus" (P. G. Wodehouse). "Humor is the sudden disruption of thought, the conjoining of unlikely elements" (S. J. Perelman). Talk about various other elements which make up humor.

Write to George Q. Lewis for particular information on humor. (See "Lewis" in Address Listing in Extra-Know-How Section.)

(See activities under April Special Weeks, "National Laugh ... " and January 2, "Save the Pun ....")

National Little League Baseball Week (second Monday)

Write to Little League Baseball for information. (See Address Listing in Extra-Know-How Section.)

Invite a Little League official or coach to class for a discussion about sportsmanship.

Hold a debate on whether girls should be admitted to Little League or should initiate their own league.

(See activities under August Variable Dates, "Little League ....")

Let's Play Golf Week (first Saturday)

Obtain a set of golf clubs and equipment; ask various students to help explain the various clubs; make a class list of golf-related vocabulary.

Visit a driving range or golf course and report the impressions.

Investigate the career of a golf professional.

Review Task Card #41 for activities on golf.

(See activities under April 9, "Golf Hall ....")

VARIABLE DATES

National Spelling Bee (first Monday)

Hold a class or all-school spelling bee for those who wish to participate.

Ponder the point that some individuals spell better in writing than in oral expression.

Write to Scripps-Howard Newspapers for additional information on spelling bees. (See Address Listing in Extra-Know-How Section.)

Father's Day (third Sunday)

Use Task Card #62 for activities on Father's Day.

(See activities under May Variable Dates, "Mother's Day,")

Summer Solstice (on or about June 21)

Explain that "solstice" means "sun stands still"; ask students to investigate the scientific explanation of solstice and relate it to the sun's standing still.

National Marble Tournament (third week)

Obtain a copy of the *Great American Marble Book*, by Ferretti, concerning the history and types of marbles, marble vocabulary, and various marble games.

Hold a marble tournament; encourage students to bring in their own marble collections.

Present a marble art lesson: place marbles in a covered pan of boiling water; cook until they crack open; dry the pieces and glue them in interesting designs on colored paper or masonite board.

DAYS OF THE MONTH

June 1

Jacques (also Père) Marquette, French missionary and explorer of the Great Lakes region in America, born 1637

(See Biography Data in Extra-Know-How Section.)

Obtain a map of the Great Lakes region; identify and label each of the lakes; investigate the pollution factor of the Great Lakes.

Write to the Northern Great Lakes Area Council for the booklet "Adventure North to the Great Lakes-Area Map." (See Address Listing in Extra-Know-How Section.)

Write to various chambers of commerce in cities on the Great Lakes to locate several favorite fishing areas.

Kentucky admitted to the United States as the fifteenth state, 1792

(See States Admitted to the USA Data in Extra-Know-How Section.)

Tennessee admitted to the United States as the sixteenth state, 1796
  (See States Admitted to the USA Data in Extra-Know-How Section.)

Brigham Young, Mormon leader, born 1801
  (See Biography Data in Extra-Know-How Section.)
  Discuss the reasons for the Mormon's move west; if it was for religious freedom, then inquire further as to why a nation partially founded upon the desire for religious freedom perhaps found other facets of the Mormon's lifestyle which were not acceptable. (Investigate the term "polygamy.")
  Find out the other name by which the Mormon Church is known.

Marilyn Monroe, American actress, born 1926
  (See Biography Data in Extra-Know-How Section.)
  Discuss the advantages and disadvantages of being a celebrated personality.

June 2

Grover Cleveland (first U.S. president to be married in the White House) married the youngest First Lady in history (22 years old), 1886
  Make up a fantasy, as a class, as to what a wedding in the White House would be like; then, find out the details of the actual wedding ceremony and who it was that Cleveland married.

Johnny Weismuller, American swimmer/actor, born 1904
  (See Biography Data in Extra-Know-How Section.)
  Discuss the many career opportunities available to successful athletes.

American Indians granted citizenship by Congress, 1924
  Trace the history of the Native Americans' plight since the arrival of Europeans.
  Investigate current Native American organizations that are mobilized to improve their own welfare, as differentiated from the functioning of the U.S. Bureau of Indian Affairs.
  Make a list of various North American Indian groups.
  Scrutinize a map to find place names which are Native American in origin.
  Define and trace the derivation of the word "ethos"; choose a Native American group and investigate its general ethos and cosmology and compare with other classmates' findings about other groups.

Battle of Warsaw Ghetto ended, 1943
  (See activities under April 19, "Battle of Warsaw ....")

June 3

Florida claimed for Spain by Hernando DeSoto, Spanish explorer, 1539
  Investigate the life of DeSoto and his explorations.
  Trace the history of Florida's political status being transferred to the United States; write to the Florida Department of Commerce for the booklet "Florida History." (See Address Section in Extra-Know-How Section.)
  Make a chart that lists other European explorers' ventures into the North and Central American continents during the fifteenth and sixteenth centuries, including the areas and dates of exploration.

Dutch West India Company chartered by the Dutch Republic (a process by which the Dutch Republic was given trading rights in the area of New Netherlands, including what is now New York), 1621
  Find out other areas in which the company had trading rights.
  Investigate information, as a separate but related topic, about the Dutch West Indies.

Jefferson Davis, U.S. Confederate leader, born 1808 (celebrated as a holiday in some southern states)
  (See Biography Data in Extra-Know-How Section.)
  (See activities under February 18, "Jefferson Davis ....")

Charles Richard Drew, black American surgeon, born 1904
  (See Biography Data in Extra-Know-How Section.)
  Explain that Drew worked to develop blood banks and also studied the area of blood preservation.
  Read *Important Dates in Afro-American History,* by Lee Bennett, to learn about other black leaders and their contributions.

Explain that Drew had a tragic accident and died, largely because he was refused a blood transfusion in an all-white hospital.

(See activities under March 15, "First Blood ....")

United States Reserve Officers Training Corps (ROTC) established by Congress, 1916
Find the nearest school or military unit which offers an ROTC program.
Invite a representative from the local unit to discuss the program.

Allen Ginsberg, American poet, born 1926
(See Biography Data in Extra-Know-How Section.)

First American spacewalk accomplished by Major Edward H. White, 1965
Discuss the significance of this feat and the joint efforts and expertise of many individuals to make this achievement possible.

(See activities under January 27, "U.S. astronauts ....")

June 4

Roquefort cheese allegedly discovered in a cave near Roquefort, France, 1070
Obtain samples of Roquefort and Bleu Cheese salad dressings, as well as the cheeses; enjoy a salad and cheese tasting party to compare and contrast the aromas, flavors, and textures.

Write to the Roquefort Association, Inc. for the booklet "Roquefort Chefmanship Recipes." (See Address Listing in Extra-Know-How Section.)

(See activities under October 17, "Charles Herbert ....")

First Ford car wheeled from a brick shed in a residential area of Detroit, Michigan by Henry Ford, 1896
Consider the various feelings that Henry Ford may have experienced as he moved the car out of the shed; reenact the event, portraying Ford as well as the neighbors and their reactions to the unusual scene.

(See activities under July 30, "Henry Ford ....")

Position as first female pilot for a major U.S. air passenger service assigned to Bonnie Tiburzi, 1973
Investigate the training and career of an airline pilot.

June 5

World Environment Day (as established June 5, 1972)
Review Task Card #37 for Earth Day activities.
(See activities under October 16, "World Food ....")

Socrates, Greek philosopher, born 469 B.C.
(See Biography Data in Extra-Know-How Section.)
Explain that Socrates did not write down his thoughts, but that his student, Plato, recorded most of which is now known about Socrates' views; explore the point that Socrates was sentenced to death by his contemporaries who felt his ideas were corrupting the youth at that time.
Discuss Socrates' statement, "Know thyself."

First balloon ascension accomplished in France, 1783
Obtain a can of helium and several balloons from a toy store to inflate balloons; inflate a number of other balloons with air; compare and contrast the flights.
(See activities under June 23, "First U.S. balloon ....")

John Couch Adams, English astronomer and discoverer of the planet, Neptune, born 1819
(See Biography Data in Extra-Know-How Section.)
Explore the career of an astronomer.

John Henry Breck, American cosmetics manufacturer, born 1877
(See Biography Data in Extra-Know-How Section.)
Explore the variety of hair-care products and shampoos that are available in retail stores.
Investigate the variety of careers related to the cosmetology industry.

John Maynard Keynes, British economist, born 1883
(See Biography Data in Extra-Know-How Section.)
Research the significance of Keynesian economics, i.e., "free economy"; explain that Keynes later supported government large-scale economic planning and spending to promote employment.
Consider the various reasons that individuals modify and alter their thinking.

Israeli-Arab Six Day War begun in the Mideast, 1967
Find out the background of the terms "Middle East" and "Near East"; research why the area is sometimes referred to as "the cradle of civilization."
Investigate the geography and history of the Middle East.
Find out the causes and effects of the Israeli-Arab conflict.

Senator Robert F. Kennedy shot in Los Angeles, 1968
Discuss the risks that public figures take in committing themselves to particular viewpoints.
Conduct a biographical study of the Kennedy family and report the findings.

June 6

Nathan Hale, American patriot and military spy, born 1755
(See Biography Data in Extra-Know-How Section.)
Discuss Hale's statement, "I only regret that I have but one life to lose for my country"; ask students about what cause they may feel strongly enough to give their lives; talk about whether people actually sacrifice their lives for their country or if there are other motivations involved.
Investigate the career of an intelligence agent.

YMCA organized in London, 1844
Find other organizations that exist in America but that originated in other countries.
(See activities under January Special Weeks, "YMCA Week.")

First drive-in movie theater opened in America, 1933
Discuss the advantages and disadvantages of a drive-in movie.
Brainstorm ideas as to how drive-in movie parking lots can be utilized during the daytime.
Consider what other types of drive-in enterprises there are.
Consult the newspaper to see what movie is currently featured at the local drive-in theater(s).

June 7

Freedom of the Press Day
Discuss the significance of "freedom of the press" and which amendment to the U.S. Constitution mandates this right.
Write to the Inter-American Press Association for information. (See Address Listing in Extra-Know-How Section.)
Hold a debate concerning both the rights and the disadvantages of reporters withholding information from public safety officers.
Investigate public opinion concerning which major newspaper is considered to be the least biased and most accurate in its reporting.
Define the terms "libel," "slander"; compare and contrast the meanings.
Discuss a reporter's obligation to objective reporting; consider the saying, "As we label, we libel."

Exploration of Kentucky begun by Daniel Boone, 1769
Obtain a map of the southeastern states; find specific areas where Boone is known to have explored, i.e., Cumberland Gap.
Make a shoebox diorama of Daniel Boone, the frontiersman, and his general environment.
(See activities under November 2, "Daniel Boone ....")

George Bryan Brummell (Beau Brummel), wealthy Englishman and man of fashion, born 1778
(See Biography Data in Extra-Know-How Section.)
Explain that Beau Brummel was noted for his fine clothes; invite students to sketch designs of men's clothing which illustrate ingenuity in styling.
Discuss the relative significance of conforming to style and fashion fads.

Paul Gauguin, French artist, born 1848
    (See Biography Data in Extra-Know-How Section.)
    Find out what the terms "impressionist," "post-impressionist," mean as related to the field of art.
    Obtain copies of Gauguin's paintings and share them with the class.

First American pinch-hitter to hit a single in baseball achieved by John J. Doyle, 1892
    Define the terms "pinch-hitter," "single"; discuss the issue of whether using a pinch-hitter is a fair practice.
    Ponder how the term "pinch-hitter" originated; use the term in sentences, as separate from the setting of baseball.

Gwendolyn Brooks, American writer and poet laureate of Illinois, born 1917
    (See Biography Data in Extra-Know-How Section.)
    Explain that Brooks was the first black to win the Pulitzer Prize for poetry; make a list of other blacks who have won a Pulitzer Prize.
    Find out what a "poet laureate" is.
    Obtain a copy of Brooks' book *Bronzeville Boys and Girls,* poems about children living in American inner cities.

June 8

First American-built steamboat launched, 1809
    (See activities under May 22, "National Maritime ....")

Suction-type vacuum cleaner patented by Ives W. McGaffey, 1869
    Obtain a vacuum cleaner to demonstrate how the many fixtures work.
    Discuss the need for other types of heavy-duty vacuum cleaners for garage and industrial areas.
    Talk about other pneumatic devices that exist or are yet to be invented.
    Trace the derivation of the word "pneumatics"; explain that it refers to the branch of physics which deals with the mechanical properties of air and other gases.

Frank Lloyd Wright, American architect, born 1869
    (See Biography Data in Extra-Know-How Section.)
    Present a lesson on architectural forms and terminology.
    Invite a local architect to class to discuss the interpretation of blueprints and the various building regulations of the area.
    Explore the careers of architects and building contractors.
    Obtain a picture of the Guggenheim Museum in New York City and find out why it was considered controversial; encourage students to create their own designs of various public buildings.
    Find out the background of the word "blueprint."

June 9

Amadeo Avogadro, Italian physicist, born 1776
    (See Biography Data in Extra-Know-How Section.)
    Explain that Avogadro coined the word "molecules" and was the first to distinguish between atoms and molecules.
    Begin a study on atoms and molecules.
    Discuss the importance of shared findings among the world's scientists.
    Investigate the career of a physicist.

First "dime novel" in America (*Malaeska: The Indian Wife of the White Hunter,* by Ann Sophia Stevens) published, 1860
    Discuss the advantages and disadvantages of both paperback and hardback books.
    Inform students of the reference book *Books in Print,* published annually and found in most libraries and retail book stores; encourage students to visit a library to become acquainted with the information offered by the book, in its various forms.
    Discuss the current connotation of the term "dime novel."

Cochise, American Indian leader, died 1874
   (See Biography Data in Extra-Know-How Section.)

First American elevated railway established in Chicago, 1883
   Discuss current systems of rapid transit and fantasize about future systems.
   Investigate and evaluate the relative effectiveness of the current Chicago elevated railway; find out why it is referred to as "the L."

Cole Porter, American composer, born 1892
   (See Biography Data in Extra-Know-How Section.)
   Obtain recordings of Porter's music and enjoy listening.

Fred Waring, American music composer/arranger, born 1900
   (See Biography Data in Extra-Know-How Section.)
   Obtain recordings of Waring's music and analyze this style.
   Explain what is involved in arranging music—varied instrumental/vocal orchestrations of an original composition.
   Listen to different recorded arrangements of the same composition.

First U.S. ballistic missile submarine launched, 1959
   Investigate how this vessel was different from former submarines; find out the meaning of the terms "ballistic," "missile."
   (See activities under January 17, "U.S. Navy ....")

June 10

First tornado in America recorded, 1682
   Discuss what a tornado is; find out its causes and effects, and what areas of the country are more commonly affected by tornadoes.
   Find out the differences between a tornado, hurricane, typhoon, and cyclone.

"Witches" hanged at Salem, 1692
   Discuss society's general reaction to individuals who do not culturally conform; consider the dynamics involved in the spread of confirmed fears (whether for substantial reason or not) and the possible effects, based upon the factor of "power in numbers."
   (See activities under May 27, "First witchcraft ....")

Judy Garland, American singer/actress, born 1922
   (See Biography Data in Extra-Know-How Section.)
   Discuss how children occasionally follow in the professional paths of their parents (Liza Minnelli, daughter of Judy Garland).

Alcoholics Anonymous established, 1935
   Explore the topic of various types of addictions; ponder the point of whether there are "positive" addictions.
   Discuss the significance of making a personal commitment to altering one's addiction (the basis of Alcoholics Anonymous) as opposed to being expected to correct one's habits through the decision and responsibility of another party.
   Define the term "anonymous"; discuss the pros and cons of anonymity; fill in the blank of other organizations which are organized along similar premises as Alcoholics Anonymous: _____ Anonymous.
   Invite a representative from AA to discuss various statistics about alcoholism and the various causes and effects of it.

June 11

Kamehameha Day (commemorates the birth of the king who unified the Hawaiian Islands, 1758)
   Prepare a unit study on Hawaii, including its history and geography, in order to understand more fully the dynamics of the various ethnic groups currently living in Hawaii.
   Investigate the terms: Polynesian, Micronesian, Melanesian.

Write to the chamber of commerce of Hawaii for the booklet "Hawaii, the Aloha State." (See Address Listing in Extra-Know-How Section.)

Find out the background of the name "Sandwich Islands.

(See activities under July 7, "Hawaiian Islands ... " and August 21, "Hawaii admitted ....")

Comstock Lode, a silver deposit discovered in Nevada by "Old Pancake" Comstock, 1859

Investigate silver in its various forms—sterling, silver-plate, and its use in mirrors, flatware table service, jewelry, etc.

Make a class list of figurative terms using the word "silver," or forms of it, i.e.: silvery surface, silver lining, silver tongue, silver waves, born with a silver spoon in his/her mouth.

Create a fictional story which would substantiate why Comstock was called "Old Pancake"; share with the class.

Find out if the "Mother Lode" country is associated in any way with the Comstock Lode; find out what type of deposit is found in the "Mother Lode."

Richard Strauss, German composer, born 1864

(See Biography Data in Extra-Know-How Section.)

Create a timeline of the famous musical family.

Obtain recordings of Richard Strauss' opera *Der Rosenkavalier*; study the story and enjoy listening; find out the English meaning of "kavalier."

Jeannette Rankin, first woman to be elected to the House of Representatives, born 1880

(See Biography Data in Extra-Know-How Section.)

Explain that Rankin participated in both the women's suffrage and the pacifist movements; consider the point that she was the only member of Congress who voted against America's entry into either of the world wars; investigate the voting records of various government representatives, regarding either former or current issues, at any level of government.

Jacques Ives Cousteau, French explorer of the oceans, filmmaker and author, born 1910

(See Biography Data in Extra-Know-How Section.)

Explain that Cousteau invented the aqualung for scuba diving. Find out about all types of diving.

Create a story that takes place below sea level.

Obtain Cousteau's books *The Living Sea* and *The Silent World*.

(See activities under July 29, "Charles William ....")

First U.S. Distinguished Flying Cross medal awarded to Charles A. Lindbergh, 1927

Investigate what the significance of the medal is; ask students to find pictures of it; encourage them to create their own designs that would be appropriate to this award.

(See activities under February 4, "Charles A. Lindbergh ... " and May 20, "Charles Lindbergh's ....")

June 12

John Augustus Roebling, Prussian engineer/bridge builder, born 1806

(See Biography Data in Extra-Know-How Section.)

Investigate the technology of a suspension bridge.

Locate on a contemporary map the area to which Prussia refers.

(See activities under May 24, "Brooklyn Bridge ....")

Anne Frank, German Jewish victim of Nazi anti-Semitism, born 1929

(See Biography Data in Extra-Know-How Section.)

Obtain a copy of *Anne Frank: Diary of a Young Girl* and read to the group.

Discuss what it must be like to have to live in hiding; consider also the significance of diary writing for an individual who is forced into hiding. Encourage students to make a habit of journal writing to help them explore their thoughts and concerns.

Baseball Hall of Fame opened in Cooperstown, New York, 1939

(See activities under January 29, "First baseball ....")

Tricia Nixon and Edward F. Cox married at the White House, Washington, DC, 1971
Find out how many children of former U.S. presidents have been married in the White House; identify them.

Baseball players' strike occurred over free agent compensation issues, 1981
Investigate the 1890 Brotherhood League as it relates to the 1981 strike.

June 13

Alexander the Great, King of Macedonia, died 323 B.C.
(See Biography Data in Extra-Know-How Section.)
Ask students to consult or draw a map of the world as it was conceived in 323 B.C.; locate the area to which Macedonia refers and what its current name is.
Discuss what year it would be five years later than 323 B.C., ten years earlier, etc.; figure out if 323 B.C. is considered to be a date in the third or the fourth century B.C.

William Butler Yeats, Irish poet, born 1865
(See Biography Data in Extra-Know-How Section.)
Explain that in Ireland many road signs are written in both English and Gaelic; find out the meaning of Gaelic or Irish-related terms, such as: shillelagh, Erin-go-bragh, Eire, Orangemen.
Study a map of Ireland; investigate the political, economic, and religious divisions among northern Ireland, the Republic of Ireland, and England.
Find out why Ireland is referred to as "The Emerald Isle."

Thurgood Marshall, the first black Supreme Court justice, nominated by President Lyndon Johnson, 1967
Discuss the significance of this nomination.

June 14

Flag Day (commemorates the adoption of the American flag by the U.S. Continental Congress, 1977)
(See Data-Detail in Extra-Know-How Section, "U.S. Flag and Flag Day—History.")
Investigate which U.S. president proclaimed Flag Day as a holiday.
(See activities under January 1, "Betsy Ross ... " and "Official U.S. Flag ... " and December 28, "Pledge of ....")

U.S. Army founded with the authorized recruitment of riflemen by the Second Continental Congress, 1795
Trace the development of U.S. Army uniforms from the beginning; invite students to familiarize themselves with the insignia representing the various military ranks.
Invite an Army recruiting representative to discuss the military as a career.

Harriet Beecher Stowe, American author of *Uncle Tom's Cabin*, born 1811
(See Biography Data in Extra-Know-How Section.)
(See activities under March 20, "Harriet Beecher Stowe's ....")

John Bartlett, compiler of quotations, born 1820
(See Biography Data in Extra-Know-How Section.)
Examine *Bartlett's Familiar Quotations*; recite famous quotes from the book. Play a game of "Who Said?"
Initiate a punctuation study on the use of quotation marks—direct and indirect quotes; discuss the importance of giving credit to the original writer through the use of quotation marks.

Sandpaper patented, 1834
Bring various types of sandpaper to class; explain the proper method of sanding (going with the grain) and identify terms, such as "coarse," "fine."
Create a project which requires sanding for refinement.
Use Task Card #63 for activities with sandpaper.

Diving suit for sub-marine diving patented, 1834
Invite a salesperson from a local sporting goods store to bring in diving apparel and equipment and to explain the purposes of the various items.
Find out what skin-diving is.
Investigate the career of a professional diver; find out what diseases and dangers are unique to the occupation.

California Republic established, 1846

Initiate a unit on California's history prior to its independence from Mexico.

Obtain a picture of the Bear Flag; find out why a bear was chosen as a symbol to represent the republic; encourage students to draw an original bear flag.

Burl Ives, American folksinger/actor, born 1909

(See Biography Data in Extra-Know-How Section.)

First presidential address over the radio, broadcast by Warren Harding, 1922

Find out what the general message of the speech was.

U.S. Voting Rights Act of 1965 enacted, 1965

Explain that the law provided for the elimination of the use of literacy tests as prerequisites for voting; define the term "literacy" and discuss the significance of the law, as related to civil rights issues.

Discuss a related issue regarding the pros and cons of ballots printed in more than one language.

June 15

Magna Carta Day (commemorates the signing of the Magna Carta in England, assuring the practice of feudal traditions, 1215)

Obtain a copy of the Magna Carta; compare and contrast the principles found within this document in comparison with those of the American Bill of Rights.

Invite students to make a literal translation of the term "Magna Carta" (charter).

Examine the background of the feudal system in England.

Kite used by Ben Franklin to prove that lightning contained electric current, 1752

Make a diorama of Benjamin Franklin's flying the kite (include the key and the lightning).

Discuss what is meant by, "Go fly a kite."

Write to the U.S. Atomic Energy Commission for the booklet "Electricity and Man." (See Address Listing in Extra-Know-How Section.)

(See activities under January 17, "Benjamin Franklin ....")

Arkansas admitted to the United States as the twenty-fifth state, 1836

(See States Admitted to the USA Data in Extra-Know-How Section.)

Edvard Grieg, Norwegian composer, born 1843

(See Biography Data in Extra-Know-How Section.)

Find out the name of the Norwegian dramatist whose play formed the basis for Grieg's "Peer Gynt Suite."

Obtain copies of Grieg's music and enjoy listening.

Vulcanized rubber patented, 1844

Investigate how the process was discovered by accident.

Write to the Goodyear Tire & Rubber Co. for two booklets, "Charles Goodyear and the Strange Story of Rubber" and "The Miracle of Rubber," a booklet which provides the history of rubber and its many uses. (See Address Listing in Extra-Know-How Section.)

Explain that used tires are recycled for their oil content which, in turn, is used to make coal burn hotter; investigate the components of tires and identify other recycling possibilities.

Find the definition of "vulcanization" and trace the background to Vulcan, the Roman god; discuss why a vulcan-related term is appropriate for the name of the rubber process; make a list of other mythical gods and assign products and their names which represent each god appropriately. (This exercise is equally suitable with Greek or other mythology systems.)

(See activities under April 10, "Synthetic rubber ... " and December 29, "Charles Goodyear ....")

Celluloid patented, 1859

Find out what celluloid is and name the industry that makes significant use of the substance.

Erik Erikson, German-American psychoanalyst and student of problems found in childhood, born 1902

(See Biography Data in Extra-Know-How Section.)

Discuss the term "student" as used above; consider the concept of lifelong learning; also ponder the point of whether one is ever an "expert in a field" with nothing more to learn.

U.S. Pentagon Papers published by American newspapers, 1971
Investigate what these particular "Pentagon papers" were and the significance of the papers' having been published.

June 16

Elisha Perkins acclaimed for having discovered a rheumatic fever cure, 1741
Find out what rheumatic fever is; write to the American Heart Association for the booklet "Protect Your Child's Heart." (See Address Listing in Extra-Know-How Section.)

Nelson Doubleday, American publisher, born 1889
(See Biography Data in Extra-Know-How Section.)
Explain that Doubleday started the first dollar book club and that he also founded the Literary Guild; investigate the subscription book business.
Explore the career of publishing.
Make a list of current best sellers—both fiction and nonfiction.

Stan Laurel, British film actor, born 1895
(See Biography Data in Extra-Know-How Section.)
Write to Black Hawk Films for the rental or purchase of Laurel and Hardy short films. (See Address Listing in Extra-Know-How Section.)

Alaska gold rush begun, 1897
Prepare a unit on the gold strike; find out why the terms "Klondike" and "sourdough" are associated with the gold rush.
Review Task Card #15 concerning the panning of gold.
(See activities under March 30, "Alaska purchased ... " and September 10, "Alaska awarded ....")

First helicopter flight of sustained time occurred, 1922
Find out how a helicopter works.
Discuss the advantages of the helicopter, along with the high-risk factors involved in flying in a helicopter during military conflicts; investigate various military statistics concerning fatalities related to helicopters.

Russian space flight, *Vostok VI,* carrying the first woman in space, Valentina Tereshkova, launched, 1963
Suggest that students imagine a future feat in space development that they will personally achieve as astronauts; invite them to share their fantasies.
Find out how many students are interested in becoming space astronauts.

June 17

Battle of Bunker Hill begun, 1775
Investigate the background of the battle.
(See activities under April 19, "Battle of Lexington ....")

John Robert Gregg, Irish-American developer of a system of shorthand, born 1867
(See Biography Data in Extra-Know-How Section.)
Define "shorthand"; discuss the fact that the word "shorthand" is a contracted form itself for a "short way of handwriting."
Invite the school secretary to class to discuss various symbols used in shorthand; discuss which of the many systems of handwriting is considered the most common and whether many of the symbols are interchangeable so that one secretary can read another's shorthand.
Encourage students to devise a code or shorthand system for various commonly used words in order to learn to take notes more quickly.
(See activities under January 4, "Isaac Pittman ....")

George Cormack, American cereal manufacturer and founder of General Mills, born 1870
(See Biography Data in Extra-Know-How Section.)
Investigate what products are produced by General Mills.
Design a cereal box.

Igor Stravinsky, Russian composer, born 1882
 (See Biography Data in Extra-Know-How Section.)
 Obtain recordings of Stravinsky's "The Fire Bird" and "Petrouchka" and enjoy listening to particular selections.

Dean Martin, American singer/actor, born 1917
 (See Biography Data in Extra-Know-How Section.)

Prayer or Bible-reading in the public schools banned, 1963
 Discuss which constitutional amendment in the United States substantiates this decision.
 Hold a debate on whether or not prayer or Bible-reading should be allowed in public schools.
 Consider what alternatives there are to a prayer or Bible-reading.
 Discuss whether the parents of children attending private schools should be expected to contribute financially through taxes to the local public schools.

Democratic National Headquarters broken into, 1972
 Investigate the Watergate scandal and why that particular name is associated with the incident.
 List various outcomes that corruption in government has upon the people.

June 18

First bicycle traffic court established, 1936
 Invite a law enforcement officer to present a program on bicycle safety.
 Suggest that students bring bicycles to school; ask one to commit a "safe" infraction of the rules; hold a traffic court trial with attorneys, judge, and jury to decide on conviction or acquittal.
 (See activities under May Month-long Observances, "National Bike ....")

Paul McCartney, British singer, born 1942
 (See Biography Data in Extra-Know-How Section.)
 Review Task Card #27 for activities to portray the Beatles.

June 19

Statue of Liberty delivered to Bedloe's Island, New York, 1855
 Find out from where the statue was arriving.
 Use Task Card #64 for activities on the Statue of Liberty.
 (See activities under October 28, "Statue of ....")

Maximilian, Austrian emperor of Mexico, executed by Mexico, 1867
 Investigate the background of this incident.

Lou Gehrig, American baseball player, born 1903
 (See Biography Data in Extra-Know-How Section.)
 Explain that Gehrig died of a rare form of a spinal paralysis infirmity, amyotrophic lateral sclerosis, which is now called "Lou Gehrig Disease."
 Investigate the generic term "sclerosis."

Nickelodeon movie theater opened in Pittsburgh, 1905
 Encourage students to create names of theaters according to the amount of the entrance fee, as in the case of the Nickelodeon theater.
 Discuss current fees for theaters; conduct market research by comparing the ticket prices of theaters in the local community.

U.S. National Archives established, 1934
 Write to the National Archives Trust Fund Board for information.
 (See Address Listing in Extra-Know-How Section.)
 Investigate the terms: archives, archivist.
 Find out what is housed in the Archives; determine that new methods are being used for data storage and retrieval.

Julius and Ethel Rosenberg executed in Sing Sing Prison, New York, for wartime espionage, 1953
   (See activities under March 29, "Julius and ....")

June 20

Great Seal of the United States, as designed by William Barton, adopted by Congress, 1782
   Ask students to find a picture of the Great Seal; discuss what the motto of the United States means: "E Pluribus Unum."
   (See Data-Detail in Extra-Know-How Section, "Great Seal of the United States of America.")

West Virginia admitted to the United States as the thirty-fifth state, 1863
   (See States Admitted to the USA Data in Extra-Know-How Section.)

Lizzie Borden acquitted in Massachusetts for the murder of her father and stepmother, 1893
   Investigate the background of this famous case.
   Define the terms: acquitted, convicted.

Errol Flynn, American actor, born 1909
   (See Biography Data in Extra-Know-How Section.)

June 21

First day of the zodiac period, Cancer, the Crab (through July 22)
   (See Data-Detail in Extra-Know-How Section, "Notes on Astrology.")

First day of summer (on or about June 21)
   (See activities under June Variable Dates, "Summer solstice ....")

U.S. Constitution put into effect by New Hampshire's ratification, whereby New Hampshire became the ninth state, 1788
   Ask students what percentage of approval was needed in order to put the Constitution into effect if nine of the thirteen states had to ratify it.

Functional wheat reaper patented, 1834
   Investigate how the reaper functions in the cultivation of wheat.
   Make a class list of wheat products that are produced.
   Discuss the importance of wheat, nutritionally and economically.
   Explain that Cyrus McCormick patented a wheat reaper about a month earlier; learn what the requirements are for patenting an invention which is similar to another.
   Find out what a cradle is as related to the harvest of wheat; explain that prior to the reaper, a person with a cradle could harvest about three acres of wheat a day; with the reaper, about 15 to 20 acres could be cut a day; find out the rate of increase that amount represents.
   Investigate what a combine is; learn what the working capacity of today's grain harvester is. Explain that with earlier reapers, several additional processes were necessary once the grain had been cut; examine what the processes were that were eliminated by the combine.
   Research the following terms: scythe, cradle, industrial revolution, homesteader.
   (See activities under February 15, "Cyrus McCormick ... " and May 17, "Grain reaper ....")

Daniel Carter Beard, American illustrator-naturalist and founder of the Boy Scouts of America, born 1850
   (See Biography Data in Extra-Know-How Section.)
   Define the words "flora," "fauna"; find examples of these and illustrate.
   (See activities under February 8, "Boy Scouts ....")

Long-playing microgroove records first demonstrated by Peter Goldmark, 1948
   Compare and contrast current long-playing records with the original 78s and 45s; find out what these numerals represent.
   Discuss current phonograph records; brainstorm ideas for improved records or new ways of recording.

June 22

Pin-manufacturing machine patented, 1832
Discuss the various types of pins and the purposes of each.
Present a pin art lesson: distribute several straight pins to each student; ask students to weave each pin into various points on the paper; then draw lines from point to point by crayola, paint, or chalk.

U.S. Department of Justice established, 1870
Investigate the American judicial system as related to the attorney general, penal institutions, the FBI, the various courts—Supreme, circuit, appellate, county, municipal, etc.

Case of flux cured by Dr. Andrew Still, the first known osteopath in America, 1874
Find out what the disease "flux" is.
Investigate what the term "osteopath" refers to; contrast how an osteopath, orthopedist, and a chiropractor differ professionally.

Sir Julian Huxley, British biologist/writer, born 1887
(See Biography Data in Extra-Know-How Section.)
Make a timeline which charts the accomplishments of the famous Huxley family. (Note that although each individual pursued different fields, each was a published writer.)

June 23

First U.S. balloon flight, made by a 13-year-old boy, occurred, 1784
Refer to *Guinness Book of Records* for statistics about balloon flights.
Enjoy the book *The Red Balloon*, by A. Lamorisse.
Encourage students to use balloons in a creative mode of expression.
(See activities under June 5, "First balloon ....")

First typewriter patented by Christopher Sholes, 1868
(See activities under April 12, "First portable ....")

Lip-reading tournament established, 1926
Encourage students to make a voiceless presentation based upon intended lip-reading by the audience.
Investigate sign language and other correlated techniques of unvoiced communication for the deaf.

Taft-Hartley Act (also known as the Labor-Management Relations Act) enacted, 1947
Encourage students to make a list of labor/management-related terminology and the corresponding definitions, i.e.: open-shop, closed-shop, lock-out, boycott, collective bargaining, injunction.
(See activities under May 24, "First strike ....")

June 24

Eleuthère Irénéé Dupont, French-American chemical manufacturer, born 1771
(See Biography Data in Extra-Know-How Section.)
(See activities under April Special Weeks, "Chemical Progress ....")

Jack Dempsey, American boxer, born 1895
(See Biography Data in Extra-Know-How Section.)
(See activities under March 8, "Muhammad Ali ....")

First reports of flying saucers recorded, 1947
Investigate the various reported events concerning flying saucers.
Create a story, individually or as a class, related to some form of UFOs (unidentified flying objects).
Discuss ways in which the number of fabricated reports to authorities could be minimized.

June 25

U.S. Constitution ratified by Virginia, thus making it the tenth state, 1788
(See States Admitted to the USA Data in Extra-Know-How Section.)

Rose Cecil O'Neill, illustrator, author, and doll designer, born 1874
(See Biography Data in Extra-Know-How Section.)
Find out how the name "Kewpie" originated.
Encourage all students to bring in a great variety of dolls for a doll display.
Create a doll and design clothes for it.
Invite a person who restores dolls to talk about his/her work.

General Custer defeated in his "last stand," 1876
Investigate the name of the area and the name of the Indian group that defeated Custer.
Locate the national monument that is named after Custer.

Korean War begun, 1950
Investigate the country of Korea and find out why America chose to involve itself in the war.
Discuss the terminology "Cold War" as related to the Korean War.

June 26

Bicycle patented, 1819
Write to Earth Action Council for a copy of *The Bicycle Book*, edited by Bob Boethling. (See Address Listing in Extra-Know-How Section.)
Review Task Card #40 for further study on bicycles.
(See activities under May Month-long Observances, "National Bike ... " and April Special Weeks, "Bike Safety ... " and June 18, "First Bicycle ....")

Abner Doubleday, "Father of Baseball," born 1819
(See Biography Data in Extra-Know-How Section.)
Bake a birthday cake in the shape of a baseball in honor of Abner Doubleday; write to Wilton Enterprises for information about special cake pans for many occasions. (See Address Listing in Extra-Know-How Section.)
Review Task Card #17 on baseball scoring.
Review Reproducible #8 on baseball trivia.
Find out what else Abner Doubleday is famous for having developed.

First Pure Food Law enacted, 1848
Find out the provisions of this law.
Write to the Food and Drug Administration for the leaflet "We Want You to Know about Labels on Foods." (See Address Section in Extra-Know-How Section.)
(See activities under May 28, "Pure Food ....")

Last plank placed on the Atlantic City boardwalk, 1870
Discuss what a boardwalk is and the derivation of its name.
Locate Atlantic City on a map; find out significant current information about the city.

Pearl S. Buck, American author of *The Good Earth* and winner of both the Nobel and Pulitzer prizes, born 1892
(See Biography Data in Extra-Know-How Section.)
Explain that Pearl Buck spent much of her early life in China and later wrote about China in a way that has helped to promote greater understanding between the East and the West; discuss how writers effectively write about their own experiences. Invite students to create stories about that with which they are familiar.

U.S. Drug Law enacted, 1906
Explain that on this day, 58 years earlier, a law was passed whereby food was to meet stipulated criteria.
Write to the Food and Drug Administration for the leaflet "We Want You to Know about Today's FDA." (See Address Listing in Extra-Know-How Section.)

Mildred Ella Didrikson Zaharias ("Babe"), American athlete, born 1914
(See Biography Data in Extra-Know-How Section.)

Obtain a copy of her autobiography *This Life I've Led* and share with the class.

Discuss Zaharias' courage and determination throughout her sports activities and her life bout with cancer.

June 27

Mormon leaders, Joseph and Hyrum Smith, killed by a mob, at which time Brigham Young became the Mormon leader, 1844

Discuss the dynamics of mob behavior; define the term "lynching."

Obtain a copy of the book *The Oxbow Incident*, by Walter Van Tilburg Clark, and share with the class.

(See activities under June 1, "Brigham Young ....")

Paul Lawrence Dunbar, American poet, born 1872

(See Biography Data in Extra-Know-How Section.)

Obtain copies of his poetry and enjoy them with the class.

Helen Keller, American blind-deaf author/lecturer, born 1880

(See Biography Data in Extra-Know-How Section.)

Research various statistics related to how many people are multiply/severely handicapped.

Acknowledge the point that Helen Keller gave lectures; discuss how that might be possible since many deaf people are mute; define the term "mute."

Write to the American Foundation for the Blind for the pamphlet "Helen Keller." (See Address Listing in Extra-Know-How Section.)

Investigate the life of Anne Sullivan, Helen Keller's teacher.

Discuss the following comment of Helen Keller: "To be blind is bad, but it is worse to have eyes and not see."

Obtain copies of the two books by Margaret Davidson, *Helen Keller* and *Helen Keller's Teacher.*

(See activities under January 4, "Louis Braille ... " and April 14, "Anne Sullivan ....")

First Newbery Medal awarded to Hendrik Van Loon for the book entitled *Story of Mankind*, 1922

Investigate the priorities and the criteria by which the medals are awarded to the authors of children's books.

Ask a children's librarian for a list of the award winners since 1922; share several of the books with the class; form a review panel of interested students to vote on a choice for a "Supra-Newbery Medal."

(See activities under November Special Weeks, "National Children's ... " and November 1, "Authors' Day ....")

Robert James Keeshan, "Captain Kangaroo" TV actor, born 1927

(See Biography Data in Extra-Know-How Section.)

Design and produce a new children's television show.

June 28

Paul Bunyan Day (commemorates the American folk-hero and his ox, Babe)

Enjoy folk stories about Paul Bunyan; discuss folk heroes from America and elsewhere and create oral or written stories about them.

Richard Rodgers, American composer, born 1902

(See Biography Data in Extra-Know-How Section.)

Enjoy some of Rodgers' musical recordings, such as *Oklahoma* and *South Pacific*, classified as "musicals."

Explain that Rodgers often composed music with Oscar Hammerstein, a librettist and lyricist; define these terms. Ponder the point as to whether it is very likely that two people would work together on a musical production where their talents were more similar and the "division of labor" not as well defined; consider partnerships of all kinds in which strengths and weaknesses/needs are dynamically interdependent.

(See activities under July 12, "Oscar Hammerstein ....")

Panama Canal, in an unfinished state, bought from France by the United States, 1902

Investigate the condition of the canal at this particular point in history.

(See activities under January 7, "Panama Canal ....")

Archduke Ferdinand of Austria assassinated, an event that helped trigger World War I, 1914

Investigate the background of this particular incident; research the social-political situation in Europe at that time.

(See activities under July 28, "War declared ....")

Treaty of Versailles, ending World War I, signed, 1919

Find a copy of the picture depicting this event; find out what the significance of the treaty was and what connection it had to the League of Nations.

(See activities under January 18, "Formulation of ....")

United States-Europe commercial telephone service begun via "Early Bird" satellite, 1965

Ask an interested student to call an overseas operator to find out what the rates are to one or two major cities in Europe.

Trace the history of cross-Atlantic communications and express the findings in a creative medium.

June 29

Peter Paul Rubens, Flemish artist, born 1577

(See Biography Data in Extra-Know-How Section.)

Discuss the word "Flemish," as related to Flanders; investigate the language that was spoken, and locate the area that currently represents medieval Flanders; define the term "medieval."

Obtain prints of Rubens' paintings and share with the class; note the brilliant use of color and movement expressed in his art.

William James Mayo, American physician, born 1861

(See Biography Data in Extra-Know-How Section.)

Write to the Mayo Foundation for information pertaining to the Mayo brothers. (See Address Listing in Extra-Know-How Section.)

Discuss the clinic arrangement whereby all types of physicians practice within one organization.

Luisa Tetrazzini, Italian opera singer, born 1871

(See Biography Data in Extra-Know-How Section.)

Explore the point that many opera singers in Europe are government-subsidized; consider the priority and value system that this practice represents.

Al Smith, first Catholic candidate for the U.S. presidency, nominated by the Democratic Party, 1928

Discuss and substantiate how religious affiliations, as well as gender and ethnic factors, have historically affected politicians' success or failure in elections; document elections which show evidence of current changes in respect to this situation.

June 30

Niagara Falls crossed by Blondin, a French tightrope walker, 1859

Investigate the other feats which Blondin later performed on the tightrope (one of which was cooking an omelette above Niagara Falls).

Talk about the various qualities and abilities that a tightrope walker would be expected to have.

Ada H. Kepley, first woman lawyer to graduate from an accredited law school, 1870

Schedule a visit to witness a courtroom in session.

Invite senior law students from a local university to stage a mock trial in the classroom and to share their law-school experiences.

Gone with the Wind, Pulitzer Prize-winning book, by Margaret Mitchell, published, 1936

Discuss the attention this book received at the outset and the factor of its increased popularity due to the movie versions; think about other films which have led to greater public awareness of a book which preceded the film.

Explore various facets of the life-style in the South as described in the book, such as the social-political situation, fashions, plantation life, customs, and attitudes.

Twenty-sixth Amendment to the U.S. Constitution ratified, 1971

(See Data-Detail of Extra-Know-How Section, "Amendments to the U.S. Constitution.")

Discuss reasons that would substantiate the decision to lower the voting age from 21 to 18.

Invite a representative from the League of Women Voters to discuss issues of pending legislation; find out also about such topics as the procedure and regulations for voter registration, bilingual ballots, "write-in" candidates, and absentee ballots.

(See activities under February 15, "First election ....")

JULY

July, *originally the fifth month in the calendar, was first named* Quintilis, *which means "fifth." However, when Julius Caesar altered the calendar, he renamed the month, his birth month, after himself. Somewhat ironically, the month named after a dictator is the month in which the United States, France, Canada, The Netherlands, and Belgium, among other countries with representative forms of government, celebrate the anniversaries of independence.*

Birthstone: *Ruby*
Flower: *Larkspur*

Use the Find-a-Word Reproducible to preview happenings in July. (See Reproducible Section.)

MONTH-LONG OBSERVANCES

Hot Dog Month
Trace the origin of the hot dog.
Conduct a consumer research project by comparing the ingredients of various brand name hot dogs.

National Barbecue Month
Demonstrate or explain the various types of barbecue techniques, i.e., charcoal, gas, and electric; discuss the advantages of a covered barbecue or of a rotisserie unit.
Trace the background of the word "barbecue."
Plan a class barbecue.

SPECIAL WEEKS

Let's Play Tennis Week (first Saturday)
Introduce the game of tennis and its scoring pattern; think of any similarities to the game of table tennis or ping pong.
Plan a tennis tournament.
Find out the names and awards of various amateur and professional tennis tournaments.
Think about the maintenance factor of preparing and maintaining a lawn for tennis playing.
(See activities under July 10, "Arthur Ashe ... " and August 8, "First Davis ....")

National Safe Boating Week (Sunday of the week including July 4)
Make a class list of the various kinds of boats; illustrate one or more of the boats in a watercolor seascape.
Invite students to share various boating experiences they have had.
Write an exciting adventure story with a nautical theme.
Invite a representative from a local Coast Guard unit to discuss safety regulations as related to boating.

Joke Exchange Week (second Sunday)
(See activities under June Special Weeks, "National Humor ....")

National Softball Week (first half of the month)
Compare and contrast the games of softball, slow-pitch, and baseball.
Organize a softball game between the students and the faculty/staff.
Investigate the softball star from the team, "Queen and Her Court"; explain that the star pitcher had such a unique style of throwing the ball that major league players had difficulty hitting her pitches.
Explain the similarities and differences between the games of slow-pitch and standard softball; play a game of slow-pitch.

VARIABLE DATES

Pennsylvania Dutch Folk Festival (week including July 4)

Explain that the term "Pennsylvania Dutch" is the popularly accepted name for the descendents of Germans, but that it is an erroneous transfer from the original word "Deutsch," meaning "German."

Find out what relationship the Pennsylvania Dutch people have to the Mennonites, Moravians, and Amish peoples.

Investigate the lifestyle of the Pennsylvania Dutch people—language, crafts, customs—as varying from that of "mainstream America"; consider the dynamics involved in preserving a separate lifestyle amid a highly media-oriented society.

Miss Universe Pageant (10-day pageant which begins on a Thursday, first half of the month)

Discuss what a beauty pageant is and how a futuristic pageant might be described, i.e., entries from other planets and galaxies; invite students to draw their choice contestant of the future.

All-Star baseball game (usually a Tuesday)

Ask students to reach consensus on whom they would currently choose to serve on an all-star team in the major leagues; other choices might be offered involving a school all-star team.

(See activities under April Variable Dates, "Baseball season ....")

Berkshire Music Festival (Fourth of July weekend)

Locate the Berkshire area of New England on a map.

Discuss what participant-activities are likely to occur at a summer workshop designed for musicians.

Salzburg Festival (third or fourth weekend)

Explain that Salzburg is the birthplace of Wolfgang Mozart; obtain recordings of Mozart's music and share with the class.

Suggest that students read a biography of Mozart.

Find out the English translation of the placename "Salzburg"; learn why the city was named that and locate it on a map.

(See activities under January 27, "Wolfgang Mozart ....")

Craftsmen's Fair of the Southern Highlands, North Carolina (starts third Monday)

Hold a school-wide craft fair.

Discuss the point that newly developed crafts are always possible and that one is only limited by the limits of one's imagination.

Define such words as "craftsmanship," "crafty," "craft unions."

Mother-of-Twins Club Convention (last half of the month)

Discuss the physiological explanation of twins and the differences between fraternal and identical twins.

Consider what it might be like to be a twin.

Make a survey of twins in the school and/or of students in the school who have twins in their immediate families. (See Conducting a Survey Data in Extra-Know-How Section.)

Find out the frequency factor of multiple births in a given family line.

Make a class list of words which contain the word "twin," such as "twin-engined" "twin bed."

Wagner Festival (starts fourth Friday or Saturday)

Explain that Bayreuth in the state of Bavaria, West Germany, is the birthplace of Richard Wagner and the site of the festival; locate the city on a map of Europe.

Find out how Wagner's name is pronounced (the letter *w* is pronounced as an English *v* in German); think about the fact that certain foreign words retain the same spelling and approximate pronunciation in English, while others undergo changes when translated, such as "München"/"Munich."

DAYS OF THE MONTH

July 1

Canada Dominion Day, commemorating the establishment of the Canadian Confederation, 1867

Review Canadian history to find out what Canada's current relationship is with the government and monarchy of England.

Gottfried Leibnitz, German mathematician/philosopher, born 1646
(See Biography Data in Extra-Know-How Section.)
Explain that logic is the basis for both the fields of philosophy and of math. (Mathematics is the exact study of quantities and magnitudes in an abstract system of ordering data, using self-consistent symbols, which, in turn, is logic.)
Discuss the fact that Isaac Newton and Leibnitz were contemporaneously, but separately, developing a similar significant concept in calculus (that of derivatives) — each man unaware of the other's activity. Consider the point that people the world over have tended to develop similar, but separate, solutions when given the same intellectual conditions (prior body of knowledge) and material needs in the environment. Consider the expression, "Necessity is the mother of invention," as related to this discussion.

Battle of Gettysburg begun, 1863
Locate Gettysburg, Pennsylvania on a map; discuss the historical aspects of the battle; find other Civil War battle sites on the map.
Investigate the background and content of Lincoln's speech; look into the diverse records of American history concerning the preparation of the speech and the type of response it received.
Find out the background of the Mason-Dixon Line; locate it.
(See activities under November 19, "Gettysburg Address ....")

Battle of San Juan Hill begun, 1893
(See activities under April 21, "Spanish-American War ....")

Medicare put into effect in America, 1966
Hold a debate on whether health care programs should be totally subsidized in America by the government.
Find out the eligibility rules of Medicare.
Discuss the significance of a catastrophic accident and the ensuing medical expenses.
(See activities under January 20, "U.S. Medicare ....")

July 2

President James Garfield shot, 1881
Explain that Garfield died on November 19 of the same year.
(See activities under November 19, "James A. Garfield ... " and September 6, "President McKinley ....")

Sherman Antitrust Act passed, 1890
Discuss the significance of the phrase used by Theodore Roosevelt, "malefactors of great wealth."
Explain the background of breaking up industrial monopolies: the antitrust act was based upon reducing the restraint of trade (price-fixing and cartel agreements) rather than simply decreasing "bigness"; one response to antitrust legislation which has changed the nature of corporate bigness has been corporate diversification, a process by which industries can invest capital in other sectors of the economy (i.e., sewing machine companies buying stereo companies); through this process, the basic nature of competition is not disturbed because the market share in each sector does not legally restrain trade.
Hold debates on the following issues:
1) Is there a better way than competition to organize the economic system? (How should economic resources be distributed — through individuals and corporations following their own self-interests *or* through a reasoned analysis of the total social effect of economic decisions?);
2) Should resources be allocated via decentralization or centralized decision-making? (How does the centralization of decision-making affect the market mechanism and the allocation of resources?)

Thurgood Marshall, the first black U.S. Supreme Court justice, born 1908
(See Biography Data in Extra-Know-How Section.)
(See activities under June 13, "Thurgood Marshall ....")

Boston's first million-dollar boxing bout held, 1921
Consider the questions, "Should there be professional boxing?" "Does a boxer deserve a million dollars for a victory?"
(See activities under March 8, "Muhammad Ali ....")

Amelia Earhart, American aviatrix, vanished into the Pacific Ocean, 1937
Research various newspaper accounts of the incident; discuss the variety of opinions and speculations that have ensued since that time.

Review Task Card #58 for activities on Amelia Earhart.
(See activities under May 20, "Amelia Earhart ... " and July 24, "Amelia Earhart ....")

Civil Rights Act signed by President Johnson, 1964
Examine the implications of the following statements: "Your right to swing your arm ends where my nose begins," or, "The sole end for which mankind are warranted, individually or collectively, in interfering with the liberty of action of any of their number, is self-protection" (John Stuart Mill).
Obtain the books *The Law and You*, by Elinor Porter-Swiger; *Up against the Law*, by Jean Strousse; *Youth and the Law*, by Irving J. Sloan.
(See activities under December Special Weeks, "Human Rights ....")

July 3

Samuel de Champlain, French explorer and chief founder of New France, born 1567
(See Biography Data in Extra-Know-How Section.)
Locate the area that is now represented by "New France"; find Lake Champlain on the map also.
Introduce a study on the French province of Canada, Quebec; discuss the advantages and disadvantages of a country with bilingual/bicultural traditions.

George M. Cohan, American playwright and composer, born 1878
(See Biography Data in Extra-Know-How Section.)
Discuss patriotism and Cohan's love of America and the opportunities that vaudeville afforded him; define the term "chauvinist" in terms of being a patriot; discuss the quote, "Our country, right or wrong" (Nicolas Chauvin).
Introduce two of Cohan's songs, "You're a Grand Old Flag" and "Over There."
Obtain a copy of the play *George M.* and act out with the class.
Explain the saying, "He was bitten by the theater bug"; make a list of stage terms and jobs.
Introduce the vaudeville era through pictures and songs.
Obtain recordings of Cohan's music and enjoy listening with the class.

Idaho admitted to the United States as the forty-third state, 1890
(See States Admitted to the USA in Extra-Know-How Section.)

July 4

Independence Day in the United States (also the anniversary date of the death of three American presidents, James Monroe, Thomas Jefferson, and John Adams)
(See Data-Detail in Extra-Know-How Section, "Independence Day [Fourth of July]—History.")
Find out what "birthday gift" on this day was given to America in 1884.

Nathaniel Hawthorne, American writer, born 1804
(See Biography Data in Extra-Know-How Section.)
Obtain copies of his *Wonder Book, Tanglewood Tales,* or *the House of Seven Gables* and share with the class.

Edward Robinson Squibb, physician and manufacturer of pharmaceutical supplies, born 1819
(See Biography Data in Extra-Know-How Section.)
Investigate various controversial pharmaceutical products to learn why the FDA has not yet approved them for use in the United States.
Explore the professions of a pharmacist, chemist, and related careers.
Trace where the local poison control center is and find out what services it offers.
Find out the purpose of "Mr. Yuk" labels and how they may be effectively used in the household. Investigate in what U.S. city "Mr. Yuk" labels originated.

Stephen Foster, American songwriter, born 1826
(See Biography Data in Extra-Know-How Section.)
Obtain recordings of Foster's music or a Stephen Foster songbook to listen to and analyze the verses.
Explain that Foster's knowledge of the Negro was gained from minstrel shows; find out the background of minstrel shows, as performed at that time.
(See activities under January 13, "Stephen Foster ....")

First American hotel to install bathrooms established, 1828
Discuss the variety of conveniences offered by modern hotels.
Ask students to design the ideal hotel in terms of energy-saving considerations.

"America," the song, publicly sung for the first time, 1832
Enjoy singing the song and its many verses.
Encourage students to create new lyrics to the melody, i.e., "My classroom 'tis of Thee ...."

President Calvin Coolidge, thirtieth president of the United States, born 1872
(See Biography Data in Extra-Know-How Section.)
Find out Coolidge's nickname as related to his conservative, quiet manner.

Statue of Liberty presented to the United States by France, 1884
(See activities under October 28, "Statue of ....")

Louis Armstrong, American jazz musician, born 1900
(See Biography Data in Extra-Know-How Section.)
Examine a trumpet and invite a student or other trumpet player to entertain the class.
Obtain a recording of "Hello, Dolly" and share with the students.
Initiate a study on different types of jazz—blues, progressive, Dixieland.

Abigail Van Buren (Pauline E. Friedman), columnist, born 1918
(See Biography Data in Extra-Know-How Section.)
Find out if the "Dear Abby" column is syndicated in the local newspaper.
Explain that the columnist has a sister, Ann Landers, who writes a similar type of column; find out the name of that column.
Discuss why such columns are as popular as they are.
Write a letter to "Dear Abby."

July 5

David G. Farragut, American nine-year-old admiral, born 1801
(See Biography Data in Extra-Know-How Section.)
Investigate why a nine-year-old was given the responsibility of being a naval officer.
Write to Farragut Naval Camps for information. (See Address Listing in Extra-Know-How Section.)

P. T. Barnum, American circus showperson, born 1810
(See Biography Data in Extra-Know-How Section.)
Obtain the film or book *Toby Tyler* and discuss circus life.
Invite students to create their own circus, including animal sideshows, ringmasters, and the appropriate self-made costumes.
Discuss Barnum's statement, "There's a sucker born every minute."

Cecil John Rhodes, founder of the Rhodes Scholarship, born 1853
(See Biography Data in Extra-Know-How Section.)
Investigate the qualifications required to become a Rhodes Scholar.
Trace the development of Rhodes' South Africa Company and his vision of a Cape-to-Cairo railway.
Explain that the territory previously known as Rhodesia, as named after Cecil Rhodes, became the independent country of Zimbabwe in 1980; ask students to locate Rhodesia/Zimbabwe, as well as nearby Zambia, on a map of Africa.
Read about Victoria Falls, David Livingston, the Zambezi River, the great stone ruins of Zimbabwe.
Find out what major language group is represented in this area.
Check out issues of the journals *Southern Africa, Africa,* and *Africa Today* from the library.
Discuss "apartheid" and related issues concerning southern Africa.
Encourage interested students to read *On Trial for My Country*, by Stanlake Samgange.
(See activities under April 4, "Rhodes Scholarships ....")

Dwight Filley Davis, donor of the Davis Cup, born 1879
(See Biography Data in Extra-Know-How Section.)
Explain that the Davis Cup is a prized team trophy in tennis.
Study how the game of tennis is scored and how many sets compose a match.

Free health care effected in England, 1948
Hold a debate on the pros and cons of free health care for everyone.
(See activities under July 1, "Medicare put ....")

July 6

John Paul Jones, American Naval officer, born 1747
(See Biography Data in Extra-Know-How Section.)
Discuss the situation of delayed recognition for heroic acts, as was the case with Jones.
Research the setting in which Jones is quoted as having said, "I have not yet begun to fight."

Harry S Truman Memorial Library opened, 1957
Find out where the building is located.
Discuss the purpose of presidential memorial libraries; ask students to consider what kinds of memorabilia would be found in a memorial library dedicated to one of them.
Investigate what the "Truman Doctrine" was and its significance.
(See activities under May 8, "Harry S Truman ....")

July 7

Pinocchio, a puppet, created by Carl Lornzini (pen name, Collodi), 1881
Enjoy *The Adventures of Pinocchio,* as illustrated by Attillio Mussino.

Marc Chagall, Russian artist, born 1887
(See Biography Data in Extra-Know-How Section.)
Obtain copies of Chagall's prints and share with the class.
Introduce a tissue paper collage lesson to approximate his type of overlay art.

Hawaiian Islands authorized to become a U.S. annexation, 1898
Discuss what territorial possessions are.
Make a class list of current U.S. territorial possessions.
Obtain a map of the Pacific Ocean; measure the various distances from Honolulu to San Francisco, Tokyo, Manila, Jakarta, Hong Kong, Guam, Taipei, Auckland, Sydney, Saipan, and other points.
(See activities under June 11, "Kamehameha Day ... " and August 12, "Hawaii annexed ....")

Leroy "Satchel" Paige, American League baseball pitcher, born 1906
(See Biography Data in Extra-Know-How Section.)
Investigate the racial discrimination which Paige, a black, experienced in trying to be accepted by the National and American leagues.
Find out how the nickname "Satchel" developed.

Ringo Starr, Beatles drummer, born 1940
(See Biography Data in Extra-Know-How Section.)
Review Task Card #27 for activities to portray the Beatles.

July 8

Liberty Bell Day (denotes the day the bell cracked while tolling the death of Chief Justice John Marshall, 1835)
Investigate how much the bell weighs, how it was rung, and how the bell cracked; find out also what the inscription reads.
Research the event for which the bell was being run when it cracked a second time.

Count Ferdinand von Zeppelin, German inventor, born 1838
(See Biography Data in Extra-Know-How Section.)
Find out what kind of an airship a zeppelin is.
Ask students to create their own zeppelins (models or mock airships).
Make a class list of honorary titles assigned to various individuals in Europe.

John D. Rockefeller, American financier, born 1839
(See Biography Data in Extra-Know-How Section.)
Trace the derivation of the term "philanthropist."
Investigate the background of the Rockefeller Foundation.
Write a creative story which begins, "If I were rich ...."
(See activities under July 2, "Sherman Antitrust ... ," as related to the interests of a financier.)
Make a chart identifying Rockefeller's descendants.

William Jennings Bryan's famous "Cross of Gold" speech delivered to the Democratic National Convention, 1896
Find out the background of this speech; ask students to reenact Jennings' presentation.

First Ziegfeld Follies presented, 1907
Encourage students to experiment with various dance movement routines.

Nelson Rockefeller, U.S. vice-president and governor of New York, born 1908
(See Biography Data in Extra-Know-How Section.)
Refer to the entry above which lists the birthday of John D. Rockefeller; make a school survey as to how many students share a birthday with a parent, guardian, or grandparent.
(See Conducting a Survey Data in Extra-Know-How Section.)
(See activities under March 21, "John D. Rockefeller ....")

July 9

Jan Van Eyck, founder of the early Flemish movement in painting, died 1440
Explain that Van Eyck is credited with having greatly perfected the art of oil painting; he was also known for being a master of detail. Obtain a copy of his painting *The Marriage of Giovanni Arnolfini and Jeanne Cenami.* Discuss the symbolism present in the painting, such as the dog (fidelity), the candle (the presence of Christ), and the abandoned slippers (holy ground); note the couple's reflection in the mirror and encourage the students to create a mirror image painting as did Van Eyck.

Doughnut cutter patented, 1872
Obtain a doughnut cutter and demonstrate it.
Visit a doughnut shop and observe the production of doughnuts.
Make doughnuts and enjoy eating them.
Make a class list of the standard types of doughnuts; encourage students to think of names of original doughnut (and doughnut hole) concoctions.
Conduct a survey of students' favorite types of doughnuts. (See Conducting a Survey Data in Extra-Know-How Section.)

Corncob pipe patented, 1878
Obtain corncobs and create corncob pipes, discuss the folklore behind corncob pipes.

Elias Howe, American inventor, born 1890
(See Biography Data in Extra-Know-How Section.)
Explain that Elias Howe invented a sewing machine; develop a sewing center which includes ideas for various sewing projects and lists of various stitches.
Invite a sales representative from a local sewing machine retail store to demonstrate a new machine and various sewing gadgets.
(See activities under February 21, "First sewing ... " and September 10, "Sewing machine ....")

O. J. Simpson, American football player, born 1947
(See Biography Data in Extra-Know-How Section.)
Investigate the differences between college and professional football.

July 10

Sir William Blackstone, English jurist and authority on legal interpretations, born 1723
(See Biography Data in Extra-Know-How Section.)
Encourage students to create a handbook of rules concerning their school environment.
Investigate the practice of jury duty; find out how individuals are selected for particular cases.

James Whistler, American artist, born 1834

(See Biography in Extra-Know-how Section.)

Obtain a print of the famous painting called *Whistler's Mother* and discuss its real title, *A Study of Gray and White.*

Mary McLeod Bethune, black educator and founder of National Council of Negro Women, born 1875

(See Biography Data in Extra-Know-How Section.)

Wyoming admitted to the United States as the forty-fourth state, 1890

(See States Admitted to the USA Data in Extra-Know-How Section.)

David Brinkley, American news commentator, born 1920

(See Biography Data in Extra-Know-How Section.)

Explain that Brinkley and Chet Huntley appeared together on TV news shows; suggest other professional pairs in radio and television; discuss the advantages and disadvantages of such partnerships.

Smaller-sized U.S. paper money printed, 1929

Encourage students to share their paper money collections; if foreign bills are brought, compare the size to American money; examine each bill denomination for the pictured personality and for other details.

Study the functions of the U.S. Bureau of Printing and Engraving, such as the responsibility for phasing out damaged bills and for generating their replacements.

Investigate what measures are in effect to guard against the production of counterfeit currency.

(See activities under February 3, "First U.S. ....")

Arthur Ashe, Jr., black American tennis player, born 1943

(See Biography Data in Extra-Know-How Section.)

Discuss how the application of computers is influencing the world of tennis and other sports.

Make a class list of all the racket games played, both in the United States and in other countries.

Visit a sports equipment store to learn about the varied construction of tennis rackets.

Investigate the varied surfaces on which tennis is played; find out any differences which exist concerning the regulations of each.

Discuss what factors in modern life-style have contributed to an increase of leisure activities.

(See activities under July Special Weeks, "Let's Play ....")

July 11

John Quincy Adams, sixth president of the United States, born 1767

(See Biography Data in Extra-Know-How Section.)

Trace on a timeline the ancestors and descendants of this distinguished American family.

Find out why Adams was elected by the House of Representatives rather than by the electoral college.

Aaron Burr killed in a duel with Alexander Hamilton, 1804

Discuss what a duel is and trace the background of this historic conflict between the two men.

Find out the derivation of the word "truce" and other terms related to duels or battles.

Suggest that students safely re-enact the scene of the duel.

Triborough Bridge in New York City opened, 1936

Explain that the bridge links the boroughs of Manhattan, Bronx, and Queens in New York City; ask students to find out what a borough is and how many boroughs exist in New York City.

Examine a map of New York City to identify the various boroughs and other bridges in the metropolitan area; find out what other constructed transportation links there are with Manhattan Island.

July 12

Julius Caesar, Roman Emperor, born 102 B.C.

(See Biography Data in Extra-Know-How Section.)

Stage the children's version of Shakespeare's *Julius Caesar.*

Initiate a study of the Roman Empire, including architecture, dress, history, and maps drawn at that time.

Josiah Wedgewood, English pottery manufacturer, born 1730
(See Biography Data in Extra-Know-How Section.)
Investigate the various methods and materials from which china is made.
Consider why certain types of ceramic or porcelain ware are referred to as china.
Write to Kiddie Kreations for information regarding students' self-designed pottery discs or plates. (See Address Listing in Extra-Know-How Section.)

Henry Thoreau, American writer, born 1817
(See Biography Data in Extra-Know-How Section.)
Discuss Thoreau's belief that each person reforms society by reforming himself or herself.
Explain that Henry Thoreau lived as a recluse at Walden Pond in Massachusetts; discuss the dynamics of an isolated existence at the present time in terms of what one might miss or gain from the experience.
Find out what the term "transcendentalism" means.
Explain that Thoreau did not pay his taxes during his stay at Walden Pond as an act of passive resistance to the Mexican War; discuss the significance of countering authority due to a commitment to a particular set of personal principles.

George Eastman, American inventor, born 1854
(See Biography Data in Extra-Know-How Section.)
See activities under March 26, "Commercial motion ... " and September 4, "First roll ....")

Paper-bag manufacturing machine patented, 1859
Discuss the point concerning the amount of paper bags used by supermarkets and other retail stores; suggest ways in which the use of paper bags might be diminished for purposes of ecology.
Visit a paper manufacturing company or study about how paper is manufactured.
Invite students to produce various creations from paper bags.

Buckminster Fuller, American architect, born 1895
(See Biography Data in Extra-Know-How Section.)
Investigate the background of Fuller's geodesic dome in terms of its architectural and ecological significance; find out what a geodesic is and what the geometric scheme of Fuller's dome is.
Introduce a study on geometric shapes, such as octahedrons, tetrahedrons.
Discuss the following comments: "When my ideas are needed badly enough, they're accepted; so I just invent, then wait until man comes around to needing what I've invented" (Fuller). "Man is simultaneously becoming an expert and an exile by losing touch with the forces of nature" (Anonymous).
Share the book *Buckminster Fuller to Children of Earth,* by Cam Smith.

Oscar Hammerstein II, American lyricist, born 1895
(See Biography Data in Extra-Know-How Section.)
Investigate the terms "lyricist," "librettist."
Compare or contrast the identifications which follow some names, such as "II," "Jr."; discuss the comment, "Naming a child 'Jr.' is like making the same mistake all over again" (Thomas LaMance).
(See activities under June 28, "Richard Rodgers ....")

Milton Berle, American actor, born 1908
(See Biography Data in Extra-Know-How Section.)

Andrew Wyeth, American artist, born 1917
(See Biography Data in Extra-Know-How Section.)
Obtain prints of Andrew Wyeth's paintings and share with the class.
Obtain the film "World of Andrew Wyeth" from the International Film Bureau and share with the class. (See Address Listing in Extra-Know-How Section.)
Explain that Andrew Wyeth's father was an artist, as is Andrew's son; ask students to name other known personalities whose parents or offspring have followed similar careers.

July 13

Northwest Ordinance of the U.S. Congress established, 1787
Find out which states now represent the geographic area that was involved in the Northwest Ordinance; on a U.S. outline map, color in the area of the Northwest Territory.

Discuss how the interest in maintaining and extending American territory was a contributing factor in the causes of the War of 1812.

Numbering system for patents adopted, 1836
(See activities under April 10, "First U.S. ....")

July 14

Bastille Day (French national holiday commemorating the storming of the Bastille in the French Revolution, 1789)
Find out what the term "Bastille" refers to in this incident.
Explain that shortly after the storming of the Bastille, the feudal system was abolished as a result of the thinking expressed by the phrase, "Liberty, Equality, Fraternity"; investigate what the feudal system was.
(See activities under August 15, "Napoleon Bonaparte ....")

Isolationist Japan opened by Admiral Perry, 1853
(See activities under April 10, "Matthew C. Perry ....")

Tape measure patented, 1868
Introduce the standing broad jump; use a tape measure to record the distance of the jump; create other experiences which involve the use of a tape measure.
Make a class list of other devices which measure flat surfaces.

Billy the Kid, American folklore hero, killed, 1881
Investigate the life and times of Billy the Kid; find out the background of his name.
Enjoy various children's books of western folklore.

Isaac Bashevis Singer, Jewish-American author, born 1904
(See Biography Data in Extra-Know-How Section.)
Share some of his stories and invite students to illustrate them.

Gerald Ford, thirty-eighth president of the United States, born 1913
(See Biography Data in Extra-Know-How Section.)
Discuss the fact that Ford was the only person in U.S. history to have become president without having been nationally elected; investigate the circumstances.

Nicola Sacco and Bartolomeo Vanzetti convicted, 1921
Investigate the world-famous robbery case; hold a mock trial based upon researched information from newspaper records during the trial.
Discuss the issue of possible innocence, regardless of incriminating evidence; relate the issue to a classroom situation.
(See activities under August 23, "Nicola Sacco ....")

July 15

Rembrandt Harmenzoon Van Rijn, Dutch painter, born 1606
(See Biography Data in Extra-Know-How Section.)
Obtain copies of Rembrandt's prints and share with the class.
Examine Rembrandt's art work in terms of his unique use of light and shadow; create art experiences based upon differences in light and shadow.
Find out why this famous painter is known by his first name.

Clement Moore, author of the poem *The Night before Christmas,* born 1779
(See Biography Data in Extra-Know-How Section.)
Obtain a copy of the poem *The Night before Christmas* and share it.
Encourage students to create their own poems based upon the night before another special day, such as "The Night before My Birthday."

July 16

First mission established in California in San Diego by Father Junípero Serra, 1769
Introduce a study of California missions; explain that missions were constructed approximately one day's walk apart, a route which was called "El Camino Real" (the royal highway); find out the number of the U.S. highway that currently represents the original roadway.

Obtain a map of California; find out where each of the missions was located and find each of them on the map; make a list of those missions which are still in existence.

Mary Baker Eddy, founder of the principles of Christian Science, born 1821
(See Biography Data in Extra-Know-How Section.)

Roald Amundsen, Norwegian explorer, born 1872
(See Biography Data in Extra-Know-How Section.)
Explain that Amundsen was the first person known to reach the South Pole; locate Antarctica on a map. Investigate the continent of Antarctica and express the findings in a unique way.
(See activities under December 14, "South Pole ....")

Automatic parking meter installed, 1935
Find out how the revenue derived from parking meters is collected and used.

Discuss various futuristic strategies as related to innovations in parking and other concerns of traffic management.

First atomic test bomb exploded, 1945
Find out where the event occurred.

Discuss the significance of this event in terms of international power and the possible destruction of human life; consider the moral issues involved in the decision to use atomic power for military purposes.

Define the term "détente" and relate its meaning to international power struggles; find out other words which are used similarly.

Investigate how many countries are currently capable of producing atomic bombs.

Explore the uses of nuclear energy in peaceful as well as military application; discuss the pros and cons of using nuclear power.

Write to the U.S. Atomic Energy Commission for the booklet series on atomic pioneers. (See Address Listing in Extra-Know-How Section.)

Find out what uranium is and where and how it is found; learn more about U-235 as a nuclear fuel.

Investigate the implications of the Three Mile Island nuclear reactor incident.

(See activities under August 1, "U.S. atomic ... " and August 6, "First atomic ....")

July 17

Erle Stanley Gardner, American writer, born 1889
(See Biography Data in Extra-Know-How Section.)
Explain that Gardner was the author of the Perry Mason mysteries; find out how many stories he created about Perry Mason.

Encourage students to develop their own mystery story on paper or on a tape recorder.

James Cagney, American actor, born 1904
(See Biography Data in Extra-Know-How Section.)

Phyllis Diller, American comedienne, born 1917
(See Biography Data in Extra-Know-How Section.)

Famous flight by Douglas "Wrong Way" Corrigan begun, 1938
Explain that Corrigan flew out of New York, intending to arrive in California but landed the next day in Dublin, Ireland; find out the facts surrounding this incident and if, in fact, a mistake was made.

Discuss possible outcomes of mistakes—the fact that positive results often occur from such experiences as wrong turn-offs, etc.; list other "mistakes," accidental inventions, or unintended ventures which have made people famous.

Potsdam Conference of Truman, Stalin, and Churchill convened, 1945
    Identify each of the participants and the countries they represented at the conference.
    Investigate the significance of this post-war conference as related to the Yalta Conference and world power politics.

Disneyland in Anaheim, California, opened, 1955
    Locate on a map of the United States where both Disneyland and Disneyworld are.
    Find out what the Disneyland in Japan is called.

July 18

Alfred Binet, French psychologist who devised an intelligence scale, born 1857
    (See Biography Data in Extra-Know-How Section.)
    Explain that Binet's work on mental age (MA) and the scales which he developed were the direct predecessors of contemporary intelligence tests; discuss the advantages and disadvantages of standardized testing.
    Investigate the field of psychology.

Red Skelton, American comedian and actor, born 1913
    (See Biography Data in Extra-Know-How Section.)
    Find out Skelton's birth-given name.

S. I. Hayakawa, American educator, linguistic scientist, politician, born 1906
    (See Biography Data in Extra-Know-How Section.)
    Investigate the field of linguistics.
    Consider Hayakawa's statement: "Dictionaries are history books, not law books"; discuss whether dictionaries are for the purpose of describing how language has generally been used or whether the purpose is to prescribe how language should be used.

John H. Glenn, American astronaut, born 1921
    (See Biography Data in Extra-Know-How Section.)
    Explain that Glenn was the first American to orbit the earth; find out the details of this flight—number of times orbited, the fastest speed, and number of miles.
    (See activities under February 20, "John Glenn ....")

July 19

Samuel Colt, American inventor of the Colt 45 pistol, born 1814
    (See Biography Data in Extra-Know-How Section.)
    Discuss the advantages of the six-shooter "with which the West was won"; trace the history of this particular pistol.
    Obtain a toy model or picture of the gun and show to the class; point out the intricate engraving on the handle.
    Share the book *Weapons, A Pictorial History*, by Edwin Tunis.

Edgar Degas, French artist, born 1834
    (See Biography Data in Extra-Know-How Section.)
    Obtain prints of both Degas' earlier and later art work; analyze the change from a perfectionist style in oils to that of a free-flowing and highly colorful expression.

Bloomers introduced at women's rights convention, 1848
    (See activities under May 27, "Amelia Bloomer ....")

Charles H. Mayo, American medical doctor, born 1865
    (See Biography Data in Extra-Know-How Section.)
    See activities under June 29, "William James Mayo ....")

Sitting Bull forced to surrender, 1881
    Investigate the background surrounding this incident.
    (See activities under June 2, "American Indians ....")

July 20

Neil Armstrong became the first man to land on the moon, 1969
Discuss the significance of this event; review Armstrong's famous comment, "That's one small step for a man, one giant leap for mankind"; encourage students to create an appropriate statement were they to become the first person to step onto other planets or into other galaxies.

Discuss an explorer-astronaut as the human extension of a machine, behind which is a massive amount of technology and combined efforts.

Consider the following thought: "To land an individual on the moon, one needs know-how; to develop and educate a human being, one needs 'be-how.'"

U.S. *Viking I* landed on Mars, 1976
Investigate the planet Mars.

July 21

Jesse James' first train robbery staged, 1873
Invite students to illustrate a train robbery.
Obtain a biographical account of Jesse James and share with the class.
(See activities under April 3, "Jesse James ....")

Ernest Hemingway, American writer who was affectionately called "Papa Hemingway," born 1899
(See Biography Data in Extra-Know-How Section.)
Read aloud the story *The Old Man and the Sea.*
Explore Hemingway's style of short sentences and abbreviated expression.
Find out in which years Hemingway was awarded the Pulitzer Prize and Nobel Prize.

Isaac Stern, Russian-American violinist, born 1920
(See Biography Data in Extra-Know-How Section.)
Enjoy listening to recordings of Stern's music.
Obtain a violin or a picture of one; discuss the intricate parts and how the quality of workmanship affects the tone.

U.S. Veterans Administration established, 1930
Discuss the purpose of this agency; find out the extent of its services, i.e., hospitals, monetary benefits.
Visit a local VA hospital.

President Franklin D. Roosevelt nominated for the fourth term, 1944
Investigate the later congressional action (Amendment 22) which provides for limiting the tenure of executive office to two terms.

July 22

Gregor Mendel, Austrian biologist and religious monk, born 1822
(See Biography Data in Extra-Know-How Section.)
Explain that the Mendelian laws of heredity went unnoticed until others "discovered" them; investigate other contributions or inventions which have not been recognized at the outset.
Suggest that students record various characteristics and color patterns which have been inherited within their own families.
Explore the field of genetics and the Mendelian laws of heredity; discuss the following terms: dominant, recessive.
Explain that Mendel conducted plant breeding experiments in the monastery gardens; find out which vegetable served as the basis for most of his research.
Investigate the career of a biologist; find out the meaning of the word unit "bio" and make a list of words containing "bio."

Emma Lazarus, American poet, born 1849
(See Biography Data in Extra-Know-How Section.)
Explain that words from Lazarus' poem "The New Colossus" are engraved on the pedestal of the Statue of Liberty. ("Give me your tired, your poor ....").

Review Task Card #64 concerning the Statue of Liberty.
(See activities under October 28, "Statue of ....")

Selman Abraham Waksman, Swiss-American microbiologist, born 1888
(See Biography Data in Extra-Know-How Section.)
Explain that Waksman is credited with having coined the word "antibiotic" and that he discovered streptomycin; find out for what infections streptomycin is often prescribed.
(See activities under January 27, "Terramycin ....")

Karl Menninger, American psychiatrist, born 1893
(See Biography Data in Extra-Know-How Section.)
Trace the derivation of the word "psyche"; find the difference in meaning of the following: psychoanalyst, psychometrist, psychologist, psychiatrist.

Stephen Vincent Benét, American poet and twice a recipient of the Pulitzer Prize, born 1898
(See Biography Data in Extra-Know-How Section.)
Share selections of Benét's poetry.

Alexander Calder, American wire sculptor, born 1898
(See Biography Data in Extra-Know-How Section.)
Consult a book on mobiles to understand better the dynamics of balance within a complex structure; invite students to create their own mobiles.
Find out the meaning of the following words and use each in a sentence: mobile, stabile, labile.

John Dillinger, public enemy, shot by G-men, 1934
Discuss what is meant by the term "public enemy."
Investigate the life of John Dillinger.
Make a guess as to what "G-men" means.

July 23

First day of the zodiac period, Leo, the Lion (through August 21)
(See Data-Detail in Extra-Know-how Section, "Notes on Astrology.")

Albert Warner, Polish-American founder of Warner Brothers Productions, born 1884
(See Biography Data in Extra-Know-How Section.)
Investigate how a movie is produced.
Encourage students to create their own movie script, act it out, and film it with a Super 8 movie camera.

Ice-cream cone created by Charles Merchas in St. Louis, Missouri, 1904
(See Data-Detail in Extra-Know-how Section.)
(See activities under January 29, "Ice Cream ....")

Bedloe's Island, site of the Statue of Liberty, changed in name to Liberty Island, 1956
Review Task Card #64 for activities on the Statue of Liberty.
(See activities under October 28, "Statue of Liberty ....")

July 24

Simón Bolívar, South American revolutionist and liberator, born 1783
(See Biography Data in Extra-Know-How Section.)
Discuss the pattern of Bolívar's life: he was born of an aristocratic, slave-holding family, was influenced in Europe by egalitarian philosophers (Rousseau), became a revolutionist/liberator on his return to South America, eventually became the most powerful man in South America—a tyrannical dictator who was hated by many but today is revered as one of the greatest Latin American heroes.

Alexandre Dumas, French writer, born 1802
(See Biography Data in Extra-Know-How Section.)
Introduce Dumas' stories of *The Three Musketeers* and *The Count of Monte Cristo.*

Mormon settlement of Salt Lake City established, 1847

Discuss the factors which led Brigham Young to choose that particular area after the crossing of the country and to declare, "This is the place."

Explore information about Salt Lake City as it exists today.

Investigate the prehistoric background of the Great Salt Lake as a fresh water lake; find out why the lake now is second only to the Dead Sea as having the greatest salinity of any body of water in the world; learn what effect the salt factor has on swimming.

Trace the derivation of the word "salinity."

Amelia Earhart, American aviatrix, born 1898

(See Biography Data in Extra-Know-How Section.)

Make a list of the various flight records established by Earhart.

(See activities under May 20, "Amelia Earhart ... " and July 2, "Amelia Earhart ....")

Famous statement by Baron Pierre de Coubertin delivered at the Olympic Games, 1908

Discuss the quoted comment: "The most important thing in the Olympic Games is not winning but taking part ... the essential thing in life is not conquering but fighting well."

Find out where the Olympic Games were held that particular year.

July 25

Carousel patented, 1871

Obtain pictures of carousels; invite students to design original carousels.

Discuss the word "carousel" as related to other structures—carousel projector, carousel restraurant.

Enjoy a ride on a nearby carousel.

Walter Brennan, American actor, born 1894

(See Biography Data in Extra-Know-How Section.)

Self-governing status of Puerto Rico granted, 1952

Discuss the advantages and disadvantages of remaining a territorial possession as opposed to becoming a state.

Locate Puerto Rico on a map; find out the name of the group of islands of which it is a part; trace Puerto Rico's history.

Andrea Doria, Italian liner, sunk by a collision with the *Stockholm,* a Swedish liner, 1956

Discuss how collisions at sea can be avoided; investigate what type of security equipment has been developed since the time of this accident.

July 26

U.S. Constitution ratified by New York, this making it the eleventh state, 1788

(See States Admitted to the USA Data in Extra-Know-How Section.)

Liberia gained its independence as an African republic from the American Colonization Society, 1847

Investigate the background of the U.S.-Liberian relationship, recognizing that Liberia was founded as a home for freed slaves from the United States.

Discuss the traditions and history of the Liberian peoples who lived in the area before the Americans came; compare their history, before and after the establishment of the colony, with the history of the American Indians.

Find Liberia on a map of West Africa; locate its neighbor, Sierra Leone, a country which also served as a home for freed slaves, those from England—the British counterpart of Liberia.

George Bernard Shaw, Irish dramatist and Nobel Prize winner, born 1856

(See Biography Data in Extra-Know-How Section.)

Investigate some of Shaw's famous quotes: "The worst sin toward our fellow creatures is not to hate them, but to be indifferent to them; that's the essence of inhumanity"; "The more things a man is ashamed of, the more respectable he is"; "There's no love sincerer than the love of food."

Explain that Shaw developed a phonetic English alphabet to eliminate the inconsistencies in spelling and pronunciation; to prove the irregularities, he cited the following: "ghoti" could be read as "fish"—*gh* as in "enough"=*f*; *o* as in "women"=*i*; *ti* as in "nation"=*sh*. Consult a dictionary for its "Table of Common English Spellings" to design similar words with surprise pronunciations.

Carl Jung, Swiss psychiatrist, born 1875
(See Biography Data in Extra-Know-How Section.)
Investigate Jung's contributions as founder of the school of analytical psychology.
Define two of the terms Jung introduced, "extroversion," "introversion."

Aldous Huxley, British writer and author of *Brave New World*, born 1894
(See Biography Data in Extra-Know-How Section.)
Discuss the following comments of Huxley: "Happiness is like coke—something you get as a by-product in the process of making something else"; "There's only one corner of the universe you can be certain of improving and that's your own self."
Encourage students to write a science-fiction story.
(See activities under June 22, "Julian Huxley ....")

U.S. Department of Defense established, 1947
Write to the Pentagon for information concerning the administration and organization of all branches of the Department of Defense. (See Address Listing in Extra-Know-How Section.)
Obtain a picture of the Pentagon building to understand better the meaning of its name.

Suez Canal seized by Egypt, 1956
Investigate the background of this particular event.
(See activities under November 17, "Suez Canal ....")

July 27

Atlantic telegraph cable between England and the United States completed, 1866
Trace in detail the development of transoceanic communication—from cable to wireless transmission towers to satellites.
Find out the length and diameter of the Atlantic cable and how long it took to complete the project.

Leo Durocher, American baseball player, coach, and manager, born 1906
(See Biography Data in Extra-Know-How Section.)
Explain that Durocher was the originator of the saying, "Nice guys finish last"; discuss whether "nice guys" really do finish last.
Consider how poor sportsmanship had an effect on Durocher's career, such as his suspension for a year from major league baseball.
Explore the meaning of coaching as related to all activities; compare the act of coaching as opposed to actually doing the act for someone.

Korean War terminated by an armistice agreement, 1953
Investigate the causes and effects of the war.
Find out why the Korean War was called the "Cold War."
Find on a map of Asia the 38th parallel which separates North and South Korea; find other parallels or meridians which serve as political boundaries in the world.

July 28

Fourteenth Amendment to the U.S. Constitution ratified, 1798
(See Data Detail in Extra-Know-How Section, "Amendments to the U.S. Constitution.")

War declared on Serbia by Austria-Hungary, starting World War I.
Explain that the immediate cause of conflict was the assassination of Archduke Francis Ferdinand of Austria-Hungary by a Serbian nationalist; explore the major causes of World War I that led up to this incident—rising nationalism and the European balance of power alignments.
(See activities under April 6, "World War ... " and June 28, "Archduke Ferdinand ...")

Jacqueline Kennedy Onassis, former American First Lady, born 1929
(See Biography Data in Extra-Know-How Section.)
Explain that Jacqueline Kennedy redecorated the White House; invite students to make suggestions as to how they would redecorate the various rooms in the White House.
Use Reproducible #22 about the interior of the White House.

July 29

Booth Tarkington, American writer and recipient of the Pulitzer Prize, born 1869
    (See Biography Data in Extra-Know-how Section.)
    Obtain a copy of *Penrod* or of *Seventeen* and share with the class.

Alexis de Tocqueville, French liberal politician and writer, born 1877
    (See Biography Data in Extra-Know-How Section.)
    Ask students to pretend that they are writer-historians and suggest that they conduct research on the history of their school.

Charles William Beebe, American naturalist and inventor of the bathysphere, born 1877
    (See Biography Data in Extra-Know-How Section.)
    Explain that although Beebe was noted as a curator of ornithology (the study of birds), he was known for his underwater explorations in the bathysphere; in his steel sphere, Beebe was able to go 3,038 feet below sea level for deep-sea observation.
    Encourage students to create a watercolor painting showing their impressions of the sea.
    (See activities under June 11, "Jacques Ives Cousteau ....")

Benito Mussolini, Italian Fascist dictator, born 1883
    (See Biography Data in Extra-Know-How Section.)
    Trace the development of fascism in Italy and Mussolini's rise to power.
    Find other countries where a different form of fascism is practiced.
    Investigate how fascism differs from communism; find out what is meant by "social Darwinism" as related to fascism.
    (See activities under September 8, "Italy's surrender ....")

Dag Hammarskjold, Swedish statesman and secretary-general of the United Nations and recipient of the Nobel Peace Prize, born 1905
    (See Biography Data in Extra-Know-How Section.)
    Discuss Hammarskjold's statement: "The only kind of dignity which is genuine is that which is not diminished by the indifference of others."
    (See activities under April 7, "Dag Hammarskjold ....")

Marcel Bich, French-American manufacturer of the Bic® pens and lighters, born 1914
    (See Biography Data in Extra-Know-How Section.)
    Discuss the advantages and disadvantages of disposable products.

July 30

First representative assembly in America convened in Jamestown, Virginia, 1619
    Discuss the significance of representative government.
    Suggest that students attend a city council meeting or town meeting.
    Elect a small group of students with the responsibility of organizing a class or school project.
    Explain that over 95 million dollars from the Rockefeller Foundation has helped to restore the Jamestown-Williamsburg historic area; write to Jamestown-Williamsburg, Dept. of Education Programs.
    (See Address Listing in Extra-Know-How Section.)

Emily Brontë, English author of *Wuthering Heights* and various poems, born 1818
    (See Biography Data in Extra-Know-How Section.)

Henry Ford, American inventor, born 1863
    (See Biography Data in Extra-Know-how Section.)
    Invite students to share their model cars or to assemble model car kits.
    Discuss the advantages and disadvantages of assembly-line production; initiate a class project in which students participate on an assembly-line basis, i.e., collating, stapling, and stacking paper.
    Discuss Ford's comment: "Failure is only the opportunity to more intelligently begin again."
    (See activities under October 1, "Model T ... " and June 4, "First Ford ....")

Casey Stengel, American baseball manager of the New York Yankees, born 1891
(See Biography Data in Extra-Know-how Section.)
Consider and discuss the many responsibilities of a baseball club manager.

Vladimir Kosma Zworykin, Russian-American "Father of electronic television," born 1889
(See Biography Data in Extra-Know-How Section.)
Obtain a copy of the book *A Pictorial History of Television*, by Irving Settel and William Laas; invite a group of students to present a report on the information found in the book.
Discover what image was first transmitted on television and the reason it was used.
Obtain copies of various trivia and quiz books and then stage a TV quiz contest.
Discuss the advantages and disadvantages of television viewing.
(See activities under August 13, "John Baird ....")

WAVES, Women's division of the U.S. Navy, created, 1942
Investigate the uniforms worn by the WAVES; suggest that students design uniforms for the women's branch of the military.
Explore the military as a career.

July 31

Spanish Armada attacked by the English, 1588
Explain that the Armada consisted of 130 ships and approximately 30,000 men; trace the events of this fleet that was launched in order to invade England and seize the throne for King Philip II of Spain; name the sea captain who successfully attacked the "invincible" Armada.

First U.S. patent granted to Samuel Hopkins for the potash process in soapmaking, 1790
Find out what other uses there are for potash.
Investigate the wide range of fields for which inventions have been given patents; make a list of the more unusual inventions.
(See activities under April 10, "First U.S. ....")

Cornerstone laid for the U.S. Mint in Philadelphia, 1792
Find out the functions and responsibilities of the mint; discuss why "mint condition coins" are considered more valuable.
Invite students to share their coin collections.
Discuss what a cornerstone is; think of the various local buildings which may have cornerstones.
(See activities under April 2, "Establishment of ....")

Whitney N. Young, U.S. civil rights leader, born 1921
(See Biography Data in Extra-Know-How Section.)

AUGUST

August was originally the sixth month of the year and was called sextilis, *which means "sixth." Augustus Caesar, however, renamed the month for himself; in order to be equal to the number of days in July, he extended the month to 31 days by taking one day from February. Now, just as Augustus Caesar followed Julius Caesar, August follows July.*

Birthstone: Sardonyx or Peridot
Flower: Poppy or Gladiolus

Use the Find-a-Word Reproducible to preview happenings in August. (See Reproducible Section.)

MONTH-LONG OBSERVANCES

Sandwich Month

Explain that the name of sandwich refers to the man who created it—the Earl of Sandwich in England; find out what an "earl" is.

Obtain a copy of a menu from a unique sandwich shop to serve as a model for students to originate ideas for their own creative sandwiches.

Ask students to make a list of their favorite sandwiches and then categorize them under various classifications, i.e., most nutritional, least expensive, types of breads.

National Allergy Month (August 15-September 15)

Invite a physician/allergist to class to discuss his/her profession and various information about allergies.

Analyze the following statement: All people are potentially allergic, dependent upon the time and biorhythm of their bodies in relation to the geographic area or the environment in which they live.

Think about why allergies have recently been referred to as the "Twentieth-Century Illness" or as an "environmental handicap" (due to the abundance of petro-chemical products in the atmosphere).

Ask students to suggest various things to which they would not like to be allergic—and also those things to which they would like to develop allergies; investigate data which indicate that some allergies may be psychologically induced.

(See activities under September Month-long Observances, "National Allergy ....")

SPECIAL WEEKS

National Clown Week (week of August 1)

Explain that workshops are held for people interested in learning the arts of clowning, mime, and body movement—in order to train for performing in hospitals and other areas of social service. For information, write to Holy Fools and the United Methodist Communications. (See Address Listing in Extra-Know-How Section.)

Encourage a group of students to create a clown script and present it, complete with costumes and make-up.

Suggest to students that they write or tape a story on topics such as "The Clown Who Was Happy on the Outside and Sad on the Inside" or "The Funny Clown with a Sad Heart."

Trace the career of Emmett Kelley, as a well-known professional clown.

Write to Clowns of America to subscribe to the monthly magazine *Calliope*. (See Address Listing in Extra-Know-How Section.)

National Smile Week (first Monday)

Present the statement, "It takes only 17 muscles to smile, 43 to frown; conserve energy!"

(See activities under January 2, "Save the ... " and March Special Weeks, "National Smile ... " and April Special Weeks, "National Laugh ... " and June Special Weeks, "National Humor ....")

VARIABLE DATES

Garlic Festival, Gilroy (first weekend)

Locate where Gilroy is on a map of California; find out information about garlic as a cash crop, such as how it is farmed and marketed.

Make a list of foods that are likely to contain garlic; cook a recipe containing garlic.

Find out if garlic is used for purposes other than food seasoning.

Soap Box Derby (second week)

Encourage students to design their own soap boxes and hold a race.

Trace the background and meaning of the word "derby"; make a class list of both real and imagined derbies, i.e., "Skateboard Derby."

American Indian Exposition (third week)

Introduce a unit on American Indians and create group exhibits which reflect the culture of the Native Americans.

Make a list of Native American Indian groups; find where each is located and indicate on an outline map.

Explain that much of the Native American culture has been passed from parents to children through an oral tradition; however, now anthropologists and historians have studied and recorded some of their perceptions of Native Indian culture; find information which would help explain the deeply cyclical and holistic nature of Native American cosmologies.

Enjoy the story of an Indian child through *Island of the Blue Dolphin*, by Scott O'Dell; to help to understand the recording of oral tradition, read *Ten Grandmothers*, by Alice Marriott (Civilization of the American Indian Series), or read one of the books from the Fox Fire series.

Examine the list of Notable American Indians. (See Appendix B.)

Write to American Indian Historical Society, the Association on American Indian Affairs, and Bureau of Indian Affairs. (See Address Listing in Extra-Know-How Section.)

(See activities under June 2, "American Indians ... " and September Variable Dates, "American Indian ....")

Little League World Series (Tuesday of last full week)

Hold a debate on the pros and cons of Little League baseball competition.

Find out what other leagues have been arranged for young baseball players.

Invite a Little League coach to discuss the philosophy and management of Little League.

(See activities under June Special Weeks, "National Little ....")

DAYS OF THE MONTH

August 1

Sports Day

Make a class list of sports in America and of games played in other countries; find out which games are played in several countries, such as soccer ball.

Discuss facets of good sportsmanship, i.e., sensitivity to the feelings of players who make mistakes, losing graciously, putting victory into perspective.

Ask students to choose a game they would like to play, whereby good sportsmanship is to be emphasized.

William Clark, American frontier explorer, born 1770

(See Biography Data in Extra-Know-How Section.)

See activities under August 31, "Exploration of ....")

Francis Scott Key, American writer of the poem *Star-Spangled Banner*, born 1779

(See Biography Data in Extra-Know-How Section.)

Analyze the words of the poem.

Trace the development of how the poem came to be used as the national anthem of America.

(See activities under March 3, *Star-Spangled* ....")

Richard Henry Dana, American writer, born 1815
   (See Biography Data in Extra-Know-How Section.)

Herman Melville, American writer, born 1819
   (See Biography Data in Extra-Know-How Section.)
   Obtain a children's version of *Moby Dick* and share with the class.
   (See activities under October Special Weeks, "International Whale ....")

First cable car in San Francisco introduced by the inventor, Andrew Hallidie, 1873
   Find out what a cable car is and how it works; discuss the advantages and disadvantages of cable cars.
   Make a guess as to why the first cable car was trial-run at five o'clock in the morning.

Colorado admitted to the United States as the thirty-eighth state, 1876
   (See States Admitted to the USA Data in Extra-Know-How Section.)

First shredded wheat biscuits patented, 1892
   Obtain a box of shredded wheat; discuss the process of developing shredded wheat; check the label for the nutritional value.
   Invite students to create a three-dimensional art project using spoon-sized shredded wheat.

First U.S. Army Air Force established, 1907
   Invite a representative from the local recruiting offices to talk about the opportunities in the army or in the air force.
   Obtain a book about military insignia and their significance.
   Invite students to bring model kits of early army air force planes and enjoy building the models.

War declared on Russia by Germany, 1914
   Find out the causes and effects of World War I as related to the various power alliances which were formed.

U.S. Atomic Energy Commission established, 1946
   Define and discuss the terms "atomic energy," "nuclear energy."
   Trace the national backgrounds of several of America's original nuclear scientists.
   Find out what uranium is, where it is found in the world, and in what form it is found.
   Initiate a study on atoms and molecules.
   Investigate how members are selected to serve on the Atomic Energy Commission.
   Stage a debate on nuclear/atomic energy in terms of quality-of-life factors versus national defense and energy needs.
   Discuss the possibilities of a "Solar Energy Commission"; brainstorm other possible sources of energy, i.e., "brain-wave energy," "body-heat energy."
   Write to the U.S. Atomic Energy Commission for the booklet series "Atomic Pioneers." (See Address Listing in Extra-Know-how Section.)
   (See activities under July 16, "First atomic ... " and August 6, "First atomic ....")

August 2

Wild Bill Hickok, American cowboy, ambushed and killed, 1876
   Obtain a book about Hickok and share with the class; find out the background of his name.
   Find synonyms for the word "ambush."
   Encourage students to create western folklore stories.

First Lincoln-head penny issued, 1902
   Find out what, if any, image was engraved on the penny previous to the Lincoln-head penny.
   Invite students to share their penny collections.
   Investigate the coin system in other countries, especially the small denominations of the German pfennig and the British half-penny or the six-pence; find these foreign coins that have less value than a U.S. penny.
   (See activities under April Special Weeks, "National Coin ....")

Twelve-hour working day replaced by the eight-hour day by the U.S. Steel Corporation, 1923
   Investigate the working conditions in the early 1900s and the gradual increase in power of the labor unions in America.

Discuss the possibility of further reduced hours in the work week; consider the effect that decreased working hours per worker may have on society, i.e., increased opportunities for leisure, less unemployment if job positions are to be distributed (more people working fewer hours).

James Baldwin, American writer, born 1924
(See Biography Data in Extra-Know-How Section.)
Discuss Baldwin's statements: "The world is before you and you need not take it or leave it as it was when you came in"; "Not everything that is faced can be changed, but nothing not faced can be changed."

Title of "Reichsfuehrer" of Germany proclaimed by Adolf Hitler, 1934
Find out the meaning of "reich" and of "fuehrer" (führer) in the German language.
Investigate the events which led up to Hitler's proclaiming this title.

August 3

Elisha Graves Otis, inventor and manufacturer of the elevator, born 1811
(See Biography Data in Extra-Know-How Section.)
Discuss the advantages and disadvantages of elevators.
Write a story related to an elevator.
Explore how an automatic elevator operates.

Ernie Pyle, American news cartoonist of World War II, born 1900
(See Biography Data in Extra-Know-How Section.)
Investigate Pyle's involvement with the military and his contributions; examine books of World War II memorabilia and look for prints of Pyle's cartoons.
Investigate the career of a cartoonist.
Introduce a unit on newspaper cartoons; encourage students to create their own cartoons and captions.

First U.S. military airplane bought from the Wright Brothers by the U.S. War Department, 1909
Investigate the features of the plane as compared with modern-day military planes and missiles; compare costs also.

Leon Uris, novelist, born 1924
(See Biography Data in Extra-Know-How Section.)
Briefly describe the contents of Uris' book *The Exodus*; listen to a recording of the music of *The Exodus*; encourage students to parallel certain parts of the story with particular pasages of the music.
Trace the development of the modern state of Israel.

Ninety cadets dismissed from U.S. Military Academy at West Point for cheating, 1951
Explain that most military academies have traditionally set up very strict regulations; discuss the possible reasons for such strictness.
Find out what an honor code is; ask students if they could reveal to the authorities that a friend of theirs had cheated; think about the idea of "guilty by complicity" if one does not report an infraction of the rules.

August 4

John Peter Zenger, American colonial printer and journalist, acquitted, 1735
Explain that Zenger's articles against the provincial administration led to his arrest for libel; investigate the meaning of "libel."
Find out why his acquittal is regarded as having helped establish America's commitment to the freedom of the press.

Percy Bysshe Shelley, British poet, born 1792
(See Biography Data in Extra-Know-How Section.)
Discuss the quote from his poetry: "If winter comes, can spring be far behind?"

Glenn Cunningham, American track star, born 1909
(See Biography Data in Extra-Know-How Section.)
Obtain a copy of the book *Champions All the Way* and read the story of Glenn Cunningham. Discuss the accident which occurred and how Cunningham's determination "beat the odds" so that his legs were spared

amputation. Review the fact that Glenn's brother was killed in the accident; invite students to talk about their feelings as related to their having experienced the death of a family member or close friend.

Organize an exercise club to practice calisthenics; investigate the world of running and jogging.

Virgin Islands purchased by the United States from Denmark, 1917

Locate the Virgin Islands on a globe or map.

Find out how the islands are administered and what a duty-free port means.

August 5

Guy de Maupassant, French writer, born 1850

(See Biography Data in Extra-Know-How Section.)

Share with the class Maupassant's "The Necklace" and discuss its implications.

Spotted Tail (Sinte-galeshka), American Indian leader, assassinated on the reservation, 1881

Investigate the details surrounding this incident.

Cornerstone of the Statue of Liberty laid on Bedloe's Island, 1884

(See activities under October 28, "Statue of Liberty ....")

Clara Bow, American actress, born 1905

(See Biography Data in Extra-Know-How Section.)

Suggest the importance of exaggeration in silent movie acting; encourage students to write a short script and to act it out as if in a silent movie.

Investigate what a Clara Bow hat is, as made famous by the actress.

Neil Armstrong, American astronaut, born 1930

(See Biography Data in Extra-Know-How Section.)

Review Armstrong's historic statement on the moon, "That's one small step for a man, one giant leap for mankind."

Trace Armstrong's pursuits since his historic landing on the moon.

August 6

Alfred Lord Tennyson, English writer, born 1899

(See Biography Data in Extra-Know-How Section.)

Share with the class Tennyson's epic poem *Charge of the Light Brigade*; find out what an epic poem is; investigate with which war the poem is associated.

Sir Alexander Fleming, Scottish discoverer of penicillin, born, 1881

(See Biography Data in Extra-Know-How Section.)

Study penicillin by tracing it from its original form of orange mold to that of a medication; discuss the idea of unknown potential that may lie in certain other waste products.

Ask students how many have had shots of penicillin or if any are allergic to it.

Explain that the discovery of penicillin is a relatively recent achievement; discuss the significance of the following point: approximately ninety percent of all the world's scientists are now alive and that one estimate is that the "new" knowledge turned out every hour equals a book the size of a conventional encyclopedia.

Make a list of other antibiotics or antibacterial medicines.

Lucille Ball, American actress, born 1911

(See Biography Data in Extra-Know-How Section.)

Discuss the significance of the point that Lucille Ball's real-life pregnancy was written into the television script.

English Channel first swum by a woman, Gertrude Ederle, an American, 1926

Find out the length that Ederle swam in this particular achievement.

Consider the training and perseverance represented by this feat; ask students to try to imagine the thoughts and feelings Ederle may have had while swimming that distance; talk about the sense of satisfaction that students may have experienced through some particular accomplishment.

Investigate the records of others who have swum the channel crossing or other long distances.

First atomic bomb dropped by the United States on Hiroshima, 1945

Investigate the ways in which Hiroshima has dedicated itself to world peace, such as the establishment of a museum and various other landmarks in the area of the bombing's epicenter; write to the Japan National Tourist Organization for specific information on Hiroshima and Nagasaki. (See Address Listing in Extra-Know-How Section.)

Research the various events leading to the bombing; hold a debate on the following topic: "Enough warning was given to the Japanese people prior to the bombing."

Obtain the book *Return from Hiroshima*, by Betty Jean Lifton, and share with the class.

(See activities under July 16, "First atomic ... " and August 1, "U.S. Atomic ....")

U.S. Post Office no longer totally controlled by the U.S. Congress, 1970

Investigate the U.S. postal system, past and present.

Conduct a comparison study of various postal systems throughout the world—Germany and Japan, in particular.

Brainstorm ideas of how the postal system could be improved administratively in America.

Refugee flights to the United States suspended by Cuba, 1971

Explain why a developing country cannot afford a mass exodus of its citizens (loss of talent and the educational investment made in its people).

Investigate in an almanac the population changes in the greater Miami area during the 10-year period, 1961-1971; discuss the impact the immigration had upon the service sector of Miami in terms of language differences and other factors.

Locate Cuba on a map or globe; determine the distance between Havana and Miami.

August 7

Whiskey Rebellion staged in western Pennsylvania, 1789

Explain that the event was a protest against the tax on whiskey at that time.

Define what a rebellion is; discuss the pros and cons of rebellious action—peaceful and militant.

Ask students about practices in the classroom or school which they find unfair; discuss ways in which they might effect changes, i.e., through a student council or other organized efforts which might unify their resistance as well as help generate constructive suggestions for change.

Mata Hari (Gertrud Margarete Zelle), Dutch-Indonesian World War I spy, born 1876

(See Biography Data in Extra-Know-How Section.)

Explain that the name "Mata Hari" means "Eye of the Morning"; ask students if they were to choose a spy name for themselves what it would be.

Invite students to imagine themselves as spies and describe the ensuing intrigue in a fictional incident.

Obtain a copy of *Harriet, the Spy*, by Louise Fitzhugh; share with the class.

(See activities under October 18, "Mata Hari ....")

Revolving door patented, 1888

Talk about what a revolving door is—its advantages and its disadvantages (such as for a person in a wheelchair or on crutches).

Consider the various types of doors which have evolved since the revolving door.

Suggest that students design various doors of the future.

Ralph Bunche, grandson of a slave, American statesman and United Nations mediator, born 1904

(See Biography Data in Extra-Know-How Section.)

Investigate the background of Bunche's having received the Nobel Peace Prize (the first black American to have received the award).

First audience-participation television show broadcast, 1941

Trace the history of audience-participation shows, including the Mark Van Doren incident.

Find out what current regulations exist concerning audience-participation shows.

Ask students to consult the local TV guide in order to make a list of the television shows which involve audience participation.

Hold a mock audience-participation show.

Review Task Card #38 concerning activities about television.

U.S. Marines landed on Guadalcanal, 1942
Explain that Guadalcanal was the site of the first major U.S. offensive against the Japanese in World War II; locate Guadalcanal on the map or globe and find out in what group of islands it is situated in the Pacific Ocean.

August 8

Mimeograph process patented by Edison, 1876
Trace the derivation of the word "mimeograph."
Obtain access to a mimeograph machine and demonstrate the process.
Discuss the advantages and disadvantages of the mimeograph process.
Consider other current methods of copy reproduction.

Household refrigerator patented, 1899
Trace the history from early ice-box models to modern refrigerators.
Invite a specialist to explain what the refrigeration process involves.
Make a class list of various refrigerator features of today; encourage students to design futuristic models of refrigerators that include unique conveniences but that are also ecologically sound.

First Davis Cup tennis matches held, 1900
Trace the history of the Davis Cup competition.
Investigate the differences between professional and amateur tennis in terms of rules, regulations, and types of courts.
(See activities under July Special Weeks, "Let's Play ....")

Andy Warhol, American pop artist, born 1931
(See Biography Data in Extra-Know-How Section.)
Examine prints of the artist's work.
Invite students to create Warhol-style posters.

First U.S. president to have resigned from office (resignation submitted by Richard Nixon), 1974
Discuss such a resignation in terms of its effect on the country, the man, and his family.
Investigate the reasons behind Nixon's resignation.
Discuss the various meanings of the words "resignation" and "resigned to"; talk about why a request to resign is considered preferable to being impeached or dismissed.

August 9

First railway steam locomotive in the United States, the Stourbridge Lion, operated for the first time, 1829
Investigate steam in terms of the process which turns vapor into a powerful locomotive force.
Trace the development of trains since 1829; illustrate the findings.
Hold a model-train day exhibit.

James Norris Gamble, American businessman who developed Ivory soap, the first floating soap, born 1836
(See Biography Data in Extra-Know-How Section.)
Write to Procter and Gamble, asking for an annual report, to learn more about the company. (See Address Listing in Extra-Know-How Section.)
Introduce an art project in which students create soap carvings.

Escalator first patented, 1859
Discuss what an escalator is and its advantages and disadvantages.
Find out the meaning of the word "escalate"; create a word for a descending escalator.
Research whether an elevator or an escalator utilizes more energy.
Hold an opinion poll as to which is preferred—an elevator, escalator, or a stairway.
Create a story involving an escalator.
(See activities under March 15, "Escalator patented ....")

William T. Morton, American physician who first used ether as an anesthetic, born 1819
(See Biography Data in Extra-Know-How Section.)
Investigate what ether is, its uses, and the developments in anesthesia since that time.

Explore the careers of an anesthesiologist and of an anesthetist.
(See activities under September 30, "Ether used ....")

Jean Piaget, Swiss psychologist, born 1896
(See Biography Data in Extra-Know-How Section.)
Investigate the stages in child development, according to Piaget.
Find out how many different types of psychologists there are.

Complete electric, self-contained washing machine patented, 1910
Prepare a comparison analysis of various types of washing machines as to various features and costs.
Discuss how clothing was washed prior to the electric machines and how clothing in the future may be cleaned.
Investigate the various washing machine aids, i.e., water softeners, bleaches; discuss their advantages and disadvantages.

Jesse Owens, black U.S. track star, became first individual to win four gold medals in the Olympic Games, 1936
Explain that in one day Owens set three world records and tied another; find out for which events those records were set.
Discuss the motivation factor involved in trying to "top" or to break the record.
Investigate Hitler's attempt to restrict Owens' participation in the Olympic Games in Berlin (because of Owens' being a black).
(See activities under September 12, "Jesse Owens ....")

Atomic bomb dropped by the United States over Nagasaki, Japan, 1945
(See activities under August 6, "First atomic ....")

Gerald Ford sworn in as the thirty-eighth president of the United States, 1974
Discuss the fact that Ford was the first vice-president and president never to have been elected.
Obtain a copy of *Famous First Facts about the Presidents,* by Joseph Kane; share several unusual facts with the class.

August 10

E Pluribus Unum, as the motto of the United States, first suggested by Benjamin Franklin, John Adams, and Thomas Jefferson.
Investigate the meaning of the term; find out on which various items the term is printed.

Missouri admitted to the United States as the twenty-fourth state, 1821
(See States Admitted to the USA Data in Extra-Know-How Section.)

Smithsonian Institution founded, 1846
Find out in what city the Smithsonian is and what types of items it houses.
Ask each student to choose an item out of today's culture and substantiate its value in terms of its being displayed in the Smithsonian a hundred years from now.
Obtain a copy of the *Smithsonian* magazine to share with the class.
Write to the Smithsonian Institution for further information. (See Address Listing in Extra-Know-How Section.)
Consider the purposes of museums and the fact that there are famous museums throughout the world; make a list of the more well-known ones and their locations.

Herbert Hoover, thirty-first president of the United States, born 1874
(See Biography Data in Extra-Know-How Section.)
Discuss Hoover's statement: "Older men declare war, but it is youth that must fight and die."
Find out how Hoover accumulated his wealth to have become a millionaire.

Twenty-seven people killed mysteriously by the Legionnaire's Disease, 1976
Trace the background of this incident in Philadelphia.
Explain that this event halted tourism to Philadelphia during the Bicentennial year, largely because no apparent cause for the disease could be found; elicit opinions from the students as to whether they would have changed their trip plans due to the occurrence.

August 11

Sprinkler head patented, 1874
Investigate how a sprinkler system operates; also explore types of sprinkler systems which have controlled-timing mechanisms.
Consider the impact that wide-range irrigation sprinkler systems have had upon farming and upon the massive consumption of water.

Electric light socket with pull-chain patented, 1896
Explore the development of light fixtures, i.e., twisting the bulb to illuminate it, pulling the chain, using a lamp switch, a wall switch/rheostat.

Alex Palmer Haley, American author, born 1921
(See Biography Data in Extra-Know-How Section.)
Explain that Haley is known for his book *Roots*; discuss the point that the book served to encourage others to trace their backgrounds.
Investigate the field of genealogy.
Encourage students to trace their own roots by creating a family tree.
Introduce an autobiography lesson.

Race riots in Los Angeles (Watts), California, occurred, 1965
Trace the background of this occurrence.

August 12

First police force in the United States established, 1658
Invite a representative from the local police department to discuss law enforcement as a career.
Discuss the many difficult responsibilities of a police officer, such as assisting when a traffic accident has occurred and reporting a fatality to the victim's family.
(See activities under May Special Weeks, "Police Week ....")

Robert Mills, first American-born architect, born 1781
(See Biography Data in Extra-Know-How Section.)
Explain that Mills designed many of the original government buildings in Washington, DC—the U.S. Post Office, U.S. Treasury Building, U.S. Patent Office, and the Washington Monument.
Introduce a lesson on perspective drawing.
Investigate the career of an architect.

Sewing machine patented by Isaac Singer, 1851
Investigate the various models of sewing machines currently on the market; make a list of the more unique accessories.
Brainstorm ideas for futuristic sewing machines.
(See activities under July 9, "Elias Howe ... " and August 12, "Sewing machine ... " and September 10, "Sewing machine ....")

First U.S. patent for an accordion issued to Anthony Faas, 1856
Bring an accordion (or a picture of one) to the class.
Invite an accordionist to the classroom to play the instrument.
Introduce polka music and appropriate dance steps.

Julius Rosenwald, American philanthropist, born 1862
(See Biography Data in Extra-Know-How Section.)
Use Task Card #65 on Rosenwald and his merchandising career.

Phonograph invented by Thomas A. Edison, 1877
Find out how a phonograph operates.
Discuss the various types of needles and recording systems.
Define terms such as: cylinders, monaural, stereophonic, quadraphonic.
Invite interested students to design a recording system of the future, outlining various unique features.
Enjoy students' favorite records.
(See activities under May 20, "Emile Berliner ....")

Cecil B. DeMille, American film director, born 1881
   (See Biography Data in Extra-Know-How Section.)
   Discuss DeMille's style, his movies, and his reputation as a "taskmaster."
   Invite a student to direct a film, using home movie equipment.
   Investigate the variety of careers as related to the motion picture industry.
   Discuss DeMille's statement: "Most of us serve our ideals by fits and starts; the person who makes success of living is the one who sees his goal and aims for it unswervingly."

George Bellows, American painter and lithographer, born 1882
   (See Biography Data in Extra-Know-How Section.)
   Discuss lithography as a form of producing paintings and posters.
   Obtain samples of Bellows' posters.

Hawaii annexed by the United States, 1898
   Define the word "annex"; research the legislative procedures of annexation.
   (See activities under June 11, "Kamehameha Day ....")

First regular air mail service between Washington DC and New York established, 1918
   Investigate the variety of ways and rates to send letters and packages domestically and internationally.

Portable moving picture camera advertised, 1922
   Obtain a movie camera and film each of the students in action.
   Talk about the advantages of a moving picture camera over a camera which takes prints or slides; reverse the discussion to the advantages of slide and print cameras over moving picture cameras.

U.S. evacuation of people of Japanese ancestry completed, 1942
   Explain that 110,000 people were interned in 10 camp areas during World War II; find out the reasons why the U.S. government ordered the evacuation.
   Read *Farewell to Manzanar,* by Jeanne Wakatsuki Houston.

U.S. communications satellite put into orbit, 1960
   Investigate how a communications satellite operates.
   Discuss the emerging uses of the term "satellite" as removed from its association with space technology.
   Talk about complex communication systems in reference to the "shrinking world" concept.

August 13

Lucy Stone, American suffragist, born 1818
   (See Biography Data in Extra-Know-How Section.)
   Obtain the recording of Walt Disney's *Mary Poppins* album and play the song "Sister Suffragette"; discuss the implications of the words.

Sir George Grove, British author of *Dictionary of Music and Musicians,* born 1820
   (See Biography Data in Extra-Know-How Section.)
   Introduce a study of musical instruments, types of music, differences among musical instruments and sounds around the world.
   Invite a musician to class to discuss music as a career.
   (Review Reproducible #12 about music games.)

Annie Oakley, American sharpshooter, born 1860
   (See Biography Data in Extra-Know-How Section.)
   Obtain the recording of "Annie Get Your Gun" and discuss the lyrics, "I can do anything you can do, better."

John Baird, Scottish inventor and the "Father of Television," born 1888
   (See Biography Data in Extra-Know-How Section.)
   Create a timeline depicting the development of television.
   Explain that Baird was the first person to demonstrate television of objects in motion and that he used mechanical scanners, not the electronic scanners of modern television; invite students to find out the difference.
   Review Task Card #38 on various television activities.
   (See activities under July 30, "Vladimir Kosma ... " and December 2, "Peter Carl ....")

Coin telephone patented, 1889

Discuss the convenience factor of pay telephones; consider the labor involved in maintaining them and in collecting the revenue; talk about the expense that vandalism costs in terms of damaged telephones, booths, and disappearing telephone directories.

Find out some interesting statistics associated with telephone booths.

Write a creative story about a telephone booth.

Alfred Hitchcock, English-American film director, born 1899

(See Biography Data in Extra-Know-How Section.)

Obtain a copy of Hitchcock's *Solve It Yourself* mysteries and enjoy reading them with the students.

Discuss Hitchcock's style of unpredictable endings and his sense of timing.

Encourage students to create a mystery story with a surprise ending.

First motorized taxicab in New York City operated, 1907

Create a story involving a taxicab or a taxicab driver (cabby).

Discuss what the daily life of a taxi cab driver in a large city is perhaps like.

Ben Hogan, American golfer, born 1912

(See Biography Data in Extra-Know-How Section.)

Review Task Card #41 for activities related to golf.

Fidel Castro, Cuban revolutionary and leader, born 1927

(See Biography Data in Extra-Know-How Section.)

Trace the history of Cuba to the present time.

First U.S. roller derby opened, 1935

Discuss what a roller derby is and how television has stimulated public interest in the sport.

August 14

Electric meter patented, 1888

Discuss the occupation of a meter reader.

Make a list of electric household appliances; discuss which items are likely to register fewer kilowatts on an electric meter.

Think of various electric meters that are used in industry and technology.

(See activities under January 19, "James Watt ....")

U.S. Social Security Act approved, 1935

(See activities under April 27, "First U.S. Social ....")

International Olympics' first basketball game played, 1936

(See activities under January 20, "First U.S. ....")

World War II ended by Japan's surrender (VJ Day), 1945

Find out the meaning of "VJ."

Discuss who the significant personalities were who signed and witnessed the surrender aboard the *U.S.S. Missouri* (MacArthur, Hirohito, Tojo, etc.).

Investigate the war in the Pacific; draw maps showing Japan, Okinawa, and various north and south Pacific islands that were prominent in World War II.

Discuss the length and terms of the American occupation; investigate what the political, economic, and social conditions were during the years of American occupation (new Japanese Constitution, changed status of the emperor, and a minimum military force).

Trace the economic relationship between Japan and the United States during the postwar years up to the present time.

(See activities under August 6, "First atomic ... " and August 30, "Occupation of Japan ....")

August 15

Napoleon Bonaparte (Napoleon I), Emperor of France, born 1769

(See Biography Data in Extra-Know-How Section.)

Explain that the Napoleonic Wars and the French Revolution broke down the ancient structure of Europe and opened the way for nineteenth-century liberalism.

Obtain a picture of Napoleon and identify his characteristic stance.

Relate the expression, "He met his Waterloo," to Napoleon's fate at the end of his rule of "The Hundred Days."

(See activities under July 14, "Bastille Day ....")

Edna Ferber, writer of the American past and Pulitzer Prize winner, born 1887
(See Biography Data in Extra-Know-How Section.)
Obtain a recording of *Show Boat*, a musical adaptation of her work; enjoy with the class.

Will Rogers and Wiley Post killed in a plane crash, 1935
Investigate who these two men were; encourage students to perform a Will Rogers-Wiley Post program.
Discuss Rogers' statement, "Everybody is ignorant, only on different subjects."

Wartime gasoline rationing terminated in the United States, 1945
Explain the term "rationing" as related to the word "ratio."
Discuss the impact of gasoline rationing and the possibility of overall energy/natural resource rationing for conservation purposes.
Obtain an old ration book or a sign that reads, "Is this trip necessary?"

Woodstock, famous musical rock festival, held, 1969
Discuss the logistics involved in arranging for a festival of that magnitude—security considerations, hygienic facilities.
Hold a rock festival in the classroom (either with instruments or with records).

August 16

George Meany, U.S. labor leader, born 1894
(See Biography Data in Extra-Know-How Section.)
Discuss qualities and skills that are involved in strong leadership, i.e., tapping and unifying the strengths in an organization.
Introduce such terms as: arbitration, settlement, closed shop, management, strike, negotiation, mediation, closed-shop.
Trace the development of labor to the present time.

Gold discovered at Bonanza Creek, Alaska, 1896 (Klondike gold-dig begun two days later).
Review Task Card #15 to learn about panning for gold.
(See activities under March 30, "Alaska purchased ... " and September 10, "Alaska awarded ....")

August 17

Davy Crockett, Indian scout, American frontiersman, army officer, and congressman from Tennessee, born 1786
(See Biography Data in Extra-Know-How Section.)
Obtain a Davy Crockett coonskin cap and bring to class to share.
Play the record "Davy, Davy Crockett, King of the Wild Frontier."
Introduce the autoharp and song bells; encourage students to learn to play these instruments and then play simple accompaniments to American folksongs.

Maiden voyage of Robert Fulton's steamboat, the *Clermont*, **launched,** 1807
Obtain or build a model of the *Clermont*.
Investigate the operating principles of a steamboat.
Discuss the significance of the boat's nickname "Fulton's Folly"; consider the importance of Fulton's quality of persistence.

Wrench patented by Solyman Merrick, 1835
Discuss what a wrench is and make a class list of various types of wrenches and their intended uses.
Think of other ways the word "wrench" is used, i.e., "She wrenched herself loose."

Electric self-starter automobile patented, 1915

Find out how automobiles were formerly put into motion.

Discuss the significance of the self-starter in automobiles.

Trace the background of the word "ignite"; examine modern ignition systems in cars.

Discuss what it means to possess the human quality of being a "self-starter."

August 18

Arrangements for joint defense between the United States and Canada established, 1940

Make a timeline which indicates the various cooperative agreements that Canada and the United States have arranged.

(See activities under April Special Weeks, "Canada – U.S. Goodwill ....")

Virginia Dare, first child of European parents to be born in North America, 1587

Consider what it would be like to be the "first" of anything; encourage students to imagine that of which they would most like to be "first."

Enjoy the book *Famous First Facts*, by Joseph Kane, and *The Book of Firsts*, by Patrick Robertson.

Meriwether Lewis, American explorer, born 1774

(See Biography Data in Extra-Know-How Section.)

(See activities under August 31, "Exploration of ....")

Marshall Field, American merchant, born 1835

(See Biography Data in Extra-Know-How Section.)

Define the terms "merchant," "mercantilism."

Trace the outcome of Field's commercial efforts.

Robert Redford, American actor, born 1937

(See Biography Data in Extra-Know-How Section.)

Investigate Redford's efforts in ecological causes; discuss the significance of a well-known star's interest in a particular social cause.

August 19

National Aviation Day

(See activities under November Month-long Observances, "International Aviation ....")

Seth Thomas, American clock manufacturer, born 1785

(See Biography Data in Extra-Know-How Section.)

Make a class list of types of timepieces.

Design an original timepiece with particular futuristic features.

Take an old watch or clock apart in order to determine how it operates.

Review Task Card #35 on the subject of time.

Bernard Baruch, American statesman, born 1870

(See Biography Data in Extra-Know-How Section.)

Discuss the significance of his title "Elder Statesman."

Orville Wright, American aviator, born 1871

(See Biography Data in Extra-Know-How Section.)

Investigate the first power-driven aircraft of Orville and Wilbur Wright — the dimensions of the plane and the various off-the-ground records achieved by the plane.

Review Task Cards #36 on glider-making and #58 on flight activities.

(See activities under December 17, "First powered ....")

Ogden Nash, American poet, born 1902

(See Biography Data in Extra-Know-How Section.)

Explain that Nash didn't follow the usual rules for grammar and rhythm and yet achieved great success in writing; enjoy such lines as: "The panther is just like the leopard / Except it hasn't been peppered. / If you should see a panther crouch, / Prepare to say, 'ouch'! / Better yet, if called by a panther, / Don't anther."

Discuss Nash's style of verse couplets; encourage students to create their own verses, similar to Nash's style; suggest that they also consider developing malapropisms; find out what a "malapropism" is and where the word came from in literature. (Examples: "Lead the way and we'll precede"; "Wipe out and eradicate redundancy.")

Philo T. Farnsworth, American inventor, born 1906
(See Biography Data in Extra-Know-How Section.)
Explain that Farnsworth discovered the first system for electronic television, called an image dissector.
Obtain the book *A Pictorial History of Television*, by Irvine Settel and William Laas; trace the history of television from Czarist (Tsarist) Russia (1907) where Boris Rosing first experimented with the medium of television.

Willia Shoemaker, jockey, born 1931
(See Biography Data in Extra-Know-How Section.)
Investigate the life and career of a horse-race jockey.
Find out the number of career wins of jockey Willie Shoemaker.
Locate the names of 10 of the most successful thoroughbred jockeys; find out the height and weight of each and determine the averages.
On an outline map of the United States, indicate the geographical area of five of the major racetracks in America.
Define the following terms: thoroughbred, quarter-horse, harness, and steeple-chase racing.
Write to the National Museum of Racing for information on topics, such as weight-handicapping, breeding, training, the cost maintenance of horses, the diet of horses, race-course designs in the United States and elsewhere, among other subjects of interest. (See Address Listing in Extra-Know-How Section.)
Investigate the amount of tax money from horse racing that is contributed annually to state revenue.
Review Task Card #53 for activities related to horse racing.

August 20

Vitus Bering, Danish-born Russian explorer who claimed Alaska for Russia, born 1741
(See Biography Data in Extra-Know-How Section.)
Locate the Bering Sea and the Bering Strait on a map or globe.

Benjamin Harrison, twenty-third president of the United States, born 1833
(See Biography Data in Extra-Know-How Section.)
Investigate how Harrison, the grandson of President William Henry Harrison, lost the election by 100,000 popular votes but became president over Grover Cleveland; see *Famous First Facts about the Presidents*, by Joseph Kane.

August 21

American Bar Association established, 1828
Investigate the various meanings of "bar" as related to the legal profession; explain that there is generally a railing in most courtrooms that separates the general public from the part of the room occupied by the judges, jury, and attorneys; a "barrister" or lawyer is one who is admitted to plead at the "bar" in a courtroom.
Discuss the phrases "to pass the bar" and "to be disbarred."
Contact an attorney from the local American Bar Association to discuss law as a profession.
Discuss the significance of professional associations, i.e., agreed-upon ethical standards.
(See activities under May 1, "Law Day ....")

Slave rebellion led by Nat Turner, 1833
Investigate the outcome of the slaves' rebellion.

Venetian blinds patented, 1841
Discuss what venetian blinds are; find out the origin of the name.
Investigate what variations from the original design have been developed.
Design futuristic window coverings, i.e., those which admit sunshine, store the energy, and generate compounded amounts of solar energy.

Lincoln-Douglas (Stephen Arnold Douglas) debates begun, 1858
Investigate Stephen Douglas' Freeport Doctrine and his ideas regarding "popular sovereignty."

Research the issues of the debates and then simulate them.

Explain that current historians view Douglas as one of the few men in his era with broad national vision; think of various contemporary statesmen whose political positions and contributions may be viewed differently a century later.

Count Basie, American musician, born 1906
(See Biography Data in Extra-Know-How Section.)

Wilt Chamberlain, American basketball player (seven feet, one inch tall), born 1936
(See Biography Data in Extra-Know-How Section.)
Obtain a copy of *Wilt Chamberlain*, by Kenneth Ruden, and share with the class.
Measure heights of students and record growth on a chart; discuss the advantages and disadvantages of being tall.
(See activities under January 20, "First U.S. ....")

Hawaii admitted to the United States as the fiftieth state, 1959
(See States Admitted to the USA Data in Extra-Know-How Section.)
Suggest that students make a list of all 50 states in the order in which they were admitted to the United States. (Note: The first 13 states are generally listed in the order in which each ratified the U.S. Constitution.)
(See activities under June 11, "Kamehameha Day ... " and July 7, Hawaiian Islands ....")

August 22

First day of the zodiac period, Virgo, the Virgin (through September 22)
(See Data-Detail in Extra-Know-How Section, "Notes on Astrology.")

Savannah, the first steamship to cross the Atlantic Ocean, launched, 1818
Determine the distance across the Atlantic Ocean from Savannah, Georgia to various points.
(See activities under May 22, "National Maritime ....")

First international yacht race, won by *The America*, held, 1851
Discuss the structure of yachts; invite students to design their own yachts.

Claude Debussy, French composer of the Impressionist movement, born 1862
(See Biography Data in Extra-Know-How Section.)
Enjoy a recording of "Clair de Lune" or of "La Mer."

Soap in liquid form patented, 1865
Make a class list of the various brands of liquid soaps; conduct a cost analysis, based upon net weight; compare the ingredients on the labels as to which may be more ecologically appropriate; take a survey to find out which brand is used the most by the homes represented in class.
Compare the alleged advantages of particular soaps, i.e., "soft to the hands," "designed to fight grease," or "guaranteed to leave shinier dishes"; invite students to create a liquid coap commercial.
Encourage students to create soap carvings from bars of soap.

Mona Lisa **painting** stolen from the Louvre in Paris (1911) and recovered, 1913
Discuss the motivation involved in the thievery of art work.
Find out what criteria there are in terms of assigning monetary value to pieces of art.
Obtain a print of the *Mona Lisa*; explain that the figure's eyes are said to follow the observer wherever he/she moves.

Ray Bradbury, author, born 1920
(See Biography Data in Extra-Know-How Section.)
Discuss the term "science fiction."
Share several of Bradbury's short stories.

August 23

National Hula-Hoop Championship Day
Discuss the point that a simple invention resulted in a nationally accepted fad; consider the statement, "The secret of financial success is for one to be ready for the opportunity when it comes along."

Obtain hula-hoops and practice various skills; hold a hula-hoop contest.
Obtain the record "Big Blue Marble" and play the song "Hula-Hooping."

Baron de Cuvier, French naturalist who has been known as the "Father of Fossils," born 1769
(See Biography Data in Extra-Know-How Section.)
Discuss what a fossil is and what its value to science is.
Ask students to create their own fossils-for-the-future by pressing an object into freshley poured plaster in small aluminum foil trays; when dry, display the fossils and ask other students to identify the object.
Visit a natural history museum.
Discuss the statement: "Nature abhors sameness—even two blades of grass are different."

Commodore Oliver Hazard Perry, American naval officer, born 1785
(See Biography Data in Extra-Know-How Section.)
Explain that Perry was immortalized by his words at the end of the Battle of Lake Erie, "We have met the enemy and they are ours"; investigate the war to which the Battle of Lake Erie refers; trace the derivation of the word "immortalized."
Find out the name and accomplishments of Perry's brother.

Edgar Lee Masters, American author, born 1869
(See Biography Data in Extra-Know-How Section.)
Share the book *Spoonriver Anthology.*
Explain that a "spoonerism" is a group of words with transposed letters, i.e., "tons of soil" for "sons of toil"; invite students to create their own spoonerisms and to find out the background of the word.

Gene Kelly, American actor/choreographer/dancer, born 1912
(See Biography Data in Extra-Know-How Section.)
Trace the derivation of the word "choreographer."
Ask students to watch for a Gene Kelly film on television and to express their reactions creatively.
Hold a birthday party for Gene Kelly; ask students to choreograph a dance to "Singing in the Rain"; suggest that students dress as particular guest personalities, such as Fred Astaire, Cyd Charisse, Bill "Bojangles" Robinson.

Nicola Sacco and Bartolomeo Vanzetti executed, 1927
Hold a debate: "Capital punishment is necessary in order to maintain law and order."
Investigate the financial costs of maintaining federal and state penal institutions; discuss alternative efforts, designed to rehabilitate convicted criminals and to discourage recidivism.
Discuss the concept of "training-before-trouble" within the family and the juvenile justice system.
(See activities under July 14, "Nicola Sacco ....")

August 24

Washington, DC burned in the War of 1812 by British troops, 1814
Investigate the incident.
Trace the history of the White House since that event.
Review Reproducible #22 concerning the interior of the White House.

Waffle iron patented by Cornelius Swarthout, 1869
Hold a classroom cooking day in which batter cakes of all designs are created.

August 25

Bret Harte, American writer, born 1836
(See Biography Data in Extra-Know-How Section.)
Obtain a copy of a Bret Harte anthology of western stories; share especially "The Outcasts of Poker Flats."

Joshua Lionel Cowen, American inventor of the toy electric train, born 1880
(See Biography Data in Extra-Know-How Section.)
Visit a retail store with model trains; examine various train models.
Introduce a lesson in which students can experiment with drawing to scale.
Investigate the field of miniatures—doll houses and doll furniture.

National Park Service established, 1916

Obtain outline maps of the United States; ask students to locate and mark where each national park is; design an appropriate legend to use for the symbol of a national park, i.e., a tree.

Encourage students to select a national park of their choice and to express their findings to the class in whatever medium they wish.

Discuss the purpose of allocating natural areas to federal, state, or local authorities; consider the effects, in terms of various enterprises, such as the logging industry.

Write to the U.S. Department of Interior for information. (See Address Listing in Extra-Know-How Section.)

(See activities under March 1, "Yellowstone National ....")

Leonard Bernstein, American composer/conductor, born 1918

(See Biography Data in Extra-Know-How Section.)

Investigate the titles of music compositions of Bernstein; obtain videotapes of lessons about music which Bernstein has made for public television broadcasts.

Althea Gibson, women's singles lawn tennis champion, born 1927

(See Biography Data in Extra-Know-How Section.)

(Review activities under July Special Weeks, "Let's Play ....")

(See activities under July 10, "Arthur Ashe, Jr. ....")

First wedding in a parachute occurred, 1940

Write a creative story, imagining a wedding in the air.

Review Task Card #33 for parachute activities at school.

Brainstorm ideas as to other settings where people might hold a wedding.

(See activities under March 12, "First parachute ....")

August 26

Antoine Lavoisier, French chemist who discovered the element of oxygen (independent of J. Priestly who also made the discovery), born 1743

(See Biography Data in Extra-Know-How Section.)

Discuss the term "coeval," which refers here to general developmental stages based upon need and prior conventional wisdom; explain that Priestly and Lavoisier independently, but contemporaneously, discovered oxygen. Extend the meaning of coeval to the various stages in art and other fields that civilizations have passed through at about the same points of their development.

Encourage students to list as many chemical elements and their symbols as they can.

Review Task Card #34 to learn more about oxygen.

Lee DeForest, American radio inventor, born 1873

(See Biography Data in Extra-Know-How Section.)

Investigate how a radio operates.

Discuss what home entertainment was like before television, i.e., radio program serials and situation comedies for which listening skills were more necessary than for television viewing.

Visit a radio station; investigate the use of sound effects used on the air; with the use of a tape recorder, record various sounds intended to simulate other sounds.

Consider how the term "on the air" as related to radio may have originated.

Linotype machine patented by Ottmar Mergenthaler, 1884

(See activities under May 11, "Ottmar Mergenthaler ... " and January Special Weeks, "International Printing ....")

Dr. Albert Sabin, Polish-American discoverer of polio vaccine, born 1906

(See Biography Data in Extra-Know-How Section.)

Discuss the variety of ways in which vaccine is administered—capsules, sugar tablets, intravenous tubes.

Investigate the career of a microbiologist.

Use Reproducible #23 to learn the parts of a microscope.

(See activities under January Month-long Observances, "March of ....")

Nineteenth Amendment to the U.S. Constitution ratified (commemorated as Women's Equality Day), 1920

(See Data-Detail in Extra-Know-How Section, "Amendments to the U.S. Constitution.")

Discuss women in terms of the effect that the inability to vote had upon them as "second-class," disenfranchised citizens.

Simulate a debate which may have been held in 1920: "Women should have the right to vote."

Investigate women's voting rights throughout the world.

Obtain a copy of *Women Who Shaped History*, by Henrietta Buckmaster, to learn more about leaders in the women's suffrage movement.

Play the recording "Free to Be You and Me," by Marlo Thomas.

Examine a list of notable women for bulletin board displays, project ideas, or reports about women. (See Appendix C.)

(See activities under March 8, "National Women's ... " and October 29, "National Organization ....")

August 27

Confucius, ancient Chinese philosopher, born 551 B.C.

(See Biography Data in Extra-Know-How Section.)

Explain that *Confucius* is the Latin form of the word "K'ung-futzu," meaning "Great Master K'ung"; also talk about the idea that Confucius was hardly known throughout most of China, but it was his followers who recorded and spread his teachings.

Obtain a book of Confucius' sayings to enjoy with the class.

Ponder the point of whether this exact date was, in fact, the birth date of Confucius in view of subsequent calendar changes and other factors.

Oil first produced commercially by E. L. Drake, 1859

Locate on a map the chief sources of oil throughout the world.

Investigate costs, surplus, conservation issues, and the transportation of oil.

(See activities under January 10, "Standard Oil ....")

Samuel Goldwyn, Polish-American pioneer in the motion picture industry, born 1882

(See Biography Data in Extra-Know-How Section.)

Investigate the symbol or logo associated with his name and associates.

Obtain a film catalog in order to make a list of Metro Goldwyn Mayer (MGM) productions.

Lyndon B. Johnson, thirty-sixth president of the United States, born 1908

(See Biography Data in Extra-Know-How Section.)

List the various programs legislated under Johnson's Great Society.

August 28

Delaware Bay first discovered by a European, Henry Hudson, 1609

Locate a map where the Delaware Bay is.

Investigate the life of Henry Hudson and his various explorations while seeking "Northwest Passage"; find the Hudson River and Hudson Bay on a map of North America.

Trace the route of the Delaware River leading into Delaware Bay; find out which large city is supplied by water from the Delaware Aqueduct.

Johann Wolfgang Goethe, German writer, born 1749

(See Biography Data in Extra-Know-How Section.)

Discuss Goethe's statement, "Flowers are the hieroglyphics of nature, with which she indicates how much she loves us."

Demonstration held at the Democratic National Convention by the Chicago Seven, 1968

Discuss various means of protest other than violence and brutality.

August 29

First abolitionist newspaper *The Philanthropist* published, 1817

Define the term "abolitionist"; invite students to conjecture on the meaning of the title of the newspaper.

Discuss what influence political publications have upon world affairs.

Create articles for a classroom newspaper which suggest the abolition of certain policies/practices on any issue from the classroom setting to that of a more global perspective.

Wagon brake patented, 1828
Present pictures of various types of wagons and determine where the brakes are.
Investigate the features of modern braking systems; find out what the following terms mean: front-wheel, disc, and power brakes.

Charles F. Kettering, American educator, born 1876
(See Biography Data in Extra-Know-How Section.)
Investigate the purposes of the Kettering Foundation.

First motorcycle patented by the German inventor, Gottlieb Daimler, 1885
Invite students to talk about the various types and names of motorcycles.
Encourage students to bring in motorcycle magazines.
Review safe driving practices for both road and dirt-bike driving.

Joyce Clyde Hall, American manufacturer and founder of Hallmark Cards, born 1891
(See Biography Data in Extra-Know-How Section.)
Explain that Hallmark retail stores are franchised. Find out what a franchise is; make a list of other businesses which are franchised.
Encourage students to design their own greeting cards or to make a collage from old greeting cards.

August 30

Mary Shelley, author of *Frankenstein, or the Modern Prometheus,* born 1797
(See Biography Data in Extra-Know-How Section.)
Illustrate the story of Frankenstein.
Explain that Dr. Frankenstein selectively combined body parts, such as the brain of a prisoner and the heart of an old man, to create the figure of Frankenstein; ask students what physical characteristics they would use to create their fictional figure.
Write a sequel to the Frankenstein novel.
Compare and contrast the early nineteenth-century Frankenstein with the twentieth-century "Six Million Dollar Man" or the "Bionic Woman."

Huey P. Long, American politician, born 1893
(See Biography Data in Extra-Know-How Section.)
See activities under September 8, "Huey P. Long ....")

Roy Wilkins, American civil rights leader, born 1901
(See Biography Data in Extra-Know-How Section.)
Investigate what the letters NAACP represent and find out more about the organization.

Ted Williams, American baseball player, born 1918
(See Biography Data in Extra-Know-How Section.)
Investigate the world of baseball.

Occupation of Japan by U.S. forces begun, 1945
Explain that the U.S. government moved into Japan and changed a significant part of Japan's way of living, such as eliminating "emperor worship" in the schools; stage a debate on whether or not such directives insure long-term alteration of a country's militaristic past.
Write a creative story that portrays the occupation of America by a foreign authority; include many changes in life-style, i.e., school sessions held half-day, six days a week, the ban of church attendance.

Washington-Moscow hotline opened, 1963
Ask students to suggest individuals or cities to which they would like to have a hotline and why.
(See activities under April 5, "Idea of ....")

August 31

Exploration of western America begun by Meriwether Lewis and William Clark, 1803
Obtain a map of America to trace the areas they explored. Create a journal that depicts their possible reactions to their experiences.
Compare the dynamics involved in the Lewis and Clark exploration and modern space exploration.

Maria Montessori, Italian educator, born 1870

(See Biography Data in Extra-Know-How Section.)

Explain that Montessori was the first woman to receive a medical degree in Italy, but that she also implemented educational practices which were considered revolutionary at that time—recognizing children as children, not as little adults, and designing a classroom which was physically scaled to children's sizes and needs.

Explore Montessori's other ideas—the development of individual freedom and initiative and an emphasis upon sense perception and physical coordination.

Motion picture kinetoscope patented by Thomas A. Edison, 1887

Explain that the kinetoscope was a device for viewing through a magnifying lens a sequence of pictures of a changing scene on an endless band of film moved continuously over a light source and a rapidly rotating shutter; encourage students to make their own kinetoscopes.

Locate an appropriate book to learn how to make a film.

Trace the word unit "kine" to "cinema" and find out the meaning of the prefix "kine."

(See Data-Detail in Extra-Know-How Section, "School Record of Thomas Edison.")

Arthur Godfrey, American entertainer, born 1903

(See Biography Data in Extra-Know-How Section.)

Alan Jay Lerner, American composer, born 1918

(See Biography Data in Extra-Know-How Section.)

Enjoy selections from *My Fair Lady* and other musical scores.

Select the lyrics from a play script or television program and create a song that would be appropriate to the script.

Find out with which lyricists and librettists Lerner's name is associated.

SEPTEMBER

September was originally the seventh month of the year; therefore, it was assigned a name from the Latin word, septem, *meaning "seven." Because it is a harvest time in many parts of the world, September is often a month of fairs, exhibitions, and ritualistic celebrations.*

Birthstone: *Sapphire*
Flower: *Aster/Morning Glory*

Use the Find-a-Word Reproducible to preview happenings in September. (See Reproducible Section.)

MONTH-LONG OBSERVANCES

National Allergy Month (August 15-September 15)

Write to the Allergy Foundation of America for information.

Ask a group of students to make a list of all allergies represented by students in the class.

Consider what is involved in tracing the cause of an allergy, the handicaps or inconvenience in having an allergy, and the current preventative measures and remedies used.

Investigate the career of an allergist.

(See activities under August Month-long Observances, "National Allergy ....")

National Better Breakfast Month

Write to the Cereal Institute of America for information. (See Address Listing in Extra-Know-How Section.)

Ask students to chart the foods they have for breakfast over a week's time.

Write to the Kellogg Co. for a class breakfast game kit. (See Address Listing in Extra-Know-How Section.)

Present an art project: ask students to bring in an empty breakfast cereal box and cover it; proceed to make a new design for that particular cereal, including all of the necessary written information.

Ask students which foods commonly eaten for breakfast are also eaten at other meals; also find out if dinner-type or lunch-type foods are eaten at breakfast-time in their homes.

Investigate what people in other countries eat for breakfast, i.e., raw fish in Japan.

Conduct small group research on the four basic food groups and general nutrition.

Consider the word "breakfast" as a compound word to understand how it came to mean a morning meal.

National Pancake and Flapjack Month

Design a menu for a pancake house with creative and original entries, i.e., "Frisbee Flapjack" with special air-whipped butter.

Hold a pancake breakfast for the school staff and parents.

Write to Modern Maid Food Products for information on pancakes. (See Address Listing in Extra-Know-How Section.)

Conduct a survey concerning favorite flavored syrups. (See Conducting a Survey Data in Extra-Know-How Section.)

Find out how maple syrup is retrieved from the trunk of maple trees; hold a taste test between real maple syrup and imitation-flavored maple syrup.

Home-Sweet-Home Month

Conduct a discussion on what makes a home; ask students the differences between a house and a home; think of various words that denote a house or home—domicile, shelter, place of residence, place where "one hangs one's hat," retreat, homestead, dwelling place, stomping ground; place the words under either the heading of "House" or "Home," whichever students consider appropriate.

Suggest that students write a real-life story about their homes and families and that they consider doing something to make their homes more "homey."

Discuss the statements: " 'Mid Pleasures and palaces though we may roam, be it ever so humble, there's no place like home" (John Howard Payne); "Home is the place where, when you have to go there, they have to take you in" (Robert Frost).

SPECIAL WEEKS

Comedy Appreciation Week (usually first Sunday)

Ask students to present something comical (facial gestures, jokes, routines), either individually or in groups.

(See activities under January 2, "Save the ... " and April Special Weeks, "National Laugh ... " and June Special Weeks, "National Humor ....")

National Hispanic Heritage Week (usually second Sunday)

Explain that "Hispanic" refers to the country of Spain and that it is different from that which is native Central or South American.

Initiate a study on Spain and the Iberian Peninsula.

Constitution Week (usually begins September 17)

Write a class constitution designed upon mutually agreed-upon standards.

(See activities under September 17, "Constitution Day.")

National Dog Week (Sunday of last full week)

Make a class list of breeds and types of dogs.

Enjoy various classical stories about dogs; encourage students to write their own creative stories about dogs.

Invite an official from a dog obedience school or a representative from a dog show to discuss dog showmanship; encourage students to bring in their own dogs and hold a dog show.

Design innovative accessories for dogs.

Make a list of words which use "dog" as part of the word, i.e., doghouse.

(See activities under March 8, "First dog ... " and May Special Weeks, "National Be ... " and April 11, "American Society ....")

National Sweater Week (third Monday)

Write to the Knitted Outerwear Foundation for information. (See Address Listing in Extra-Know-How Section.)

Cut out pictures of sweaters from various mail-order catalogs or magazines; make a collage with the pictures.

Set up a knitting learning center; invite an individual with knitting skills to help initiate the center.

Remind students of the importance of putting nametags on belongings; hold a class project in which students bring their sweaters to class during the whole week so that they can be nametagged; once the clothes are labeled, hold a fashion show.

Share-the-Happiness Week (second Sunday)

Invite students to share some happy, "peak" experiences of their lives.

Discuss ways in which people can help others to experience happiness.

Think about the following quoted statements:

"That action is best which procures the greatest happiness for the greatest numbers." (Francis Hutcheson)

"O, how bitter a thing it is to look into happiness through another man's eyes!" (Shakespeare)

"You have no more right to consume happiness without producing it than to consume wealth without producing it."

VARIABLE DATES

Labor Day (first Monday)

Investigate the background of this particular national holiday.

(See Data-Detail in Extra-Know-How Section, "Labor Day—History.")

Autumnal, or fall, equinox (on or about September 21)

Find out the scientific explanation of the autumnal equinox.

Introduce art activities which represent the fall colorings of nature.

American Indian Day (last Friday)
Write to the Association on American Indian Affairs for a listing of books in *Preliminary Bibliography of Selected Children's Books about American Indians*. (See Address Listing in Extra-Know-How Section.)
Conjecture as to why American Indians are not referred to as Indian Americans, following the word order of other ethnic minority group designations (i.e., black Americans, Mexican Americans, Irish Americans, etc.); consider other possibilities, such as "Native Americans."
Examine the list of Notable American Indians. (See Appendix B.)
(See activities under August Variable Dates, "American Indian ....")

Jewish High Holy Days—Rosh Hashanah and Yom Kippur (end of September, early October)
Investigate the significance of these holidays.
Obtain a copy of *Jewish Holidays*, by Betty Morrow and Louis Hartman.
Examine a list of notable Jewish personalities. (See Appendix D.)

DAYS OF THE MONTH

September 1

First plow with interchangeable parts patented, 1819
Discuss what a plow is and the uses of one with interchangeable parts.
Make a class list of items which have interchangeable parts (an arrangement whereby one basic instrument can support or energize several different attachments, i.e., sewing machine or kitchen food mixer with several attachments); make another list of items that are based on the idea that the entire item need not be discarded if only one part is faulty, i.e., tubes in a radio.

First Pullman sleeping car introduced, 1859
Ask students to find pictures and descriptions of a sleeping car; find out about compartments on trains.
Investigate the comparative costs of sitting up in a regular seat, a Pullman arrangement, or a compartment.
Discuss why trains in America no longer carry as many long-distance travelers.

Edgar Rice Burroughs, American writer, born 1875
(See Biography Data in Extra-Know-How Section.)
Introduce the character of Tarzan by sharing book jackets of the Tarzan book series.
Encourage students to practice their Tarzan calls at recess and hold a Tarzan yelling contest.

First female telephone operator hired, 1878
Discuss the role of a telephone operator and the various ways in which a telephone operator's assistance may be requested.

Chop suey concocted and served in New York for the first time, 1896
Explain that the dish was created by a Chinese chef working for a statesman named Li Hung-Chang who was visiting the United States; when asked what the dish was called, the chef replied "Chop Suey"; according to the story, chop suey is the word for "hash" in some parts of China.
Invite students to prepare a meal of chop suey and/or to create an original concoction.
Make a class list of Chinese American foods.
Discuss what other commodities or inventions have been introduced by the Chinese people.

Speed record of 1,817 miles per hour achieved by a U.S. Air Force jet plane, 1974
Compare this speed record with the speed of sound.

September 2

London's Great Fire occurred, 1666
Explain that in 1165 there was the great plague that took about 75,000 lives; in 1666 the Great Fire destroyed most of the city; trace the contributions made by Christopher Wren following these two incidents.
(See activities under October 20, "Christopher Wren ....")

U.S. Treasury Department established, 1789
Investigate the following offices for which the Treasury Department has responsibility: U.S. Secret Service, Bureau of the Mint, Internal Revenue Service, Bureau of Customs, Bureau of Engraving and Printing, Bureau of

Narcotics, Bureau of Public Debt; through small group work, research the responsibilities of each of these bureaus and report the findings; find out how many government employees there are in the U.S. Treasury Department.

Define the terms "comptroller" and "treasurer."

Find out how school monies are budgeted and controlled.

(See activities under February 3, "First U.S. Paper ... " and April 2, "Establishment of ....")

Eugene Field, American journalist and author of children's verses, born 1850

(See Biography Data in Extra-Know-How Section.)

Enjoy Field's verses of "Wynken, Blynken, and Nod" and "Little Boy Blue."

September 3

Edward A. Filene, American merchant, born 1860

(See Biography Data in Extra-Know-How Section.)

Explain that "Filene's Automatic Bargain Basement" is the lower two levels of a large retail store in Boston; discuss the merchandising practice of automatically reducing the prices of unsold items every week or so. (After about three price reductions, unsold items are given to charity.)

Find out why bargain areas in stores are often in the basements.

First Labor Day celebrated as a legal public holiday, 1894

(See Data-Detail in Extra-Know-How Section, "Labor Day—History.")

September 4

Los Angeles, California founded as El Pueblo de Nuestra Señora de la Reina de Los Angeles de Porciúncula, 1781

Research what the translation to English is of the original name.

Investigate the sightseeing areas of Los Angeles; plan and map out an itinerary for a proposed trip to Los Angeles.

Electric lighting power first made available to customers, 1882

Suggest a homework assignment in which students are asked to initiate a "Save Energy Project" by turning off unnecessarily used lights and appliances in the home.

First self-service restaurant in America opened, 1885

Discuss the advantages and disadvantages of self-service restaurants.

Design the food-dispensing area of a cafeteria; use a long piece of butcher paper and divide it into various categories, i.e., salads, vegetables. Invite students to bring their lunches in the form of a dish that would be appropriate to one of the created sign categories; at lunchtime, enjoy exchanging roles as workers or customers in the classroom cafeteria. (Mathematics can be introduced with money and cashier.)

First roll-film camera patented and the Kodak name registered by George Eastman, 1888

Trace the development of the camera and various types of film.

Investigate how one registers a trade name.

Make a list of the various products now bearing the Kodak name.

Invite students to bring their cameras, if possible, and to take photographs for a school photography display.

September 5

First Continental Congress established in Philadelphia, 1774

Investigate what colonies were represented.

Find out how many continental congresses there were and what was accomplished by them.

Jesse James, American outlaw, born 1847

(See Biography Data in Extra-Know-How Section.)

(See activities under April 3, "Jesse James ....")

Crazy Horse (Tashunca-Uitco), American Indian leader, died 1877

(See Biography Data in Extra-Know-How Section.)

First gasoline pump introduced, 1885

Investigate the cost of a gas pump, including its installation; consider the expenditure involved in changing the readings on gas pumps to the metric system.

Ask students to draw a picture of a gas pump, both above surface and below.

Investigate the cost of a gallon of gasoline in 1885 as compared to the current price.

Darryl F. Zanuck, American film director-producer, born 1902

(See Biography Data in Extra-Know-How Section.)

Investigate the career of a film director or producer.

Seventeen Israeli Olympic participants killed during the Olympic team games, 1972

Discuss the incident; consider the dynamics in which innocent people are victimized for a political cause.

Contemplate how this incident ironically conflicted with one of the basic purposes of the Olympic Games—to engender international friendship and cooperation.

September 6

Lafayette (or Marquis de la Fayette, Marie Joseph Paul Ives Roch Gilbert du Motier), French military general and statesman, born 1757

(See Biography Data in Extra-Know-How Section.)

Explain that despite opposition by his government, Lafayette sailed for America to serve in Washington's army and was made a general by Congress; find out what a "mercenary" is and whether Lafayette's role in the American army would be classified as such.

Trace the life of Lafayette once he returned to France and participated in the French Revolution.

Jane Addams, American social reformer, born 1860

(See Biography Data in Extra-Know-How Section.)

Investigate what the purpose of the Hull House in Chicago was.

Obtain a copy of Addams' book *Twenty Years at Hull House* and share with the class.

President McKinley shot by an assassin, 1901

Discuss the word "assassination" and how it differs from the word "murder."

Make a list of presidential assassinations and attempted assassinations; find out what the U.S. government does to protect its presidents, other officials, and their families.

Find out what effect the assassination had upon Theodore Roosevelt and the country; also, research what was done to punish the assassin.

First video recording on magnetic tape, 1958

Obtain a video tape recorder; examine the magnetic tape to learn which part is for voice and which is for picture; enjoy recording various class activities.

September 7

Nickname "Uncle Sam" coined, 1813

Discuss where the nickname is used today (posters, stamps).

Investigate the origin of the nickname.

(See Data-Detail in Extra-Know-How Section, "Uncle Sam—History.")

Anna Mary Robertson Moses ("Grandma Moses"), American painter, born 1860

(See Biography Data in Extra-Know-How Section.)

Explain that the artist did not begin to paint until she was 78 years old; ask students what types of hobbies they may wish to pursue when they are septuagenarians.

J. P. Morgan, American financier, born 1867

(See Biography and Extra-Know-How Section.)

Explain that Morgan was the grandson of the head of a colossal banking and industrial enterprise and the son of John Pierpont Morgan, who headed the first billion-dollar corporation in the world.

Discuss the point that J. P. Morgan helped finance World War I and also dispensed numerous philanthropies; find out if these are distinctly different types of contributions and, if so, how.

Operations of Boulder Dam, later named Hoover Dam, begun in the Colorado River basin, 1936

Find out where the dam is located on a map of the United States; name the reservoir/recreation area that was created; discuss what major areas are served by Boulder Dam.

Investigate how a dam functions and what the purposes of a dam are.

September 8

Anton Dvořák, Czechoslovakian composer, born 1841

(See Biography Data in Extra-Know-How Section.)

Obtain a recording of Dvořák's symphony in E Minor, "From the New World," written while he was in the United States.

Sextuplets, four of whom lived to old age, born in Chicago, 1866

(See activities under May 28, "Dionne quintuplets ....")

Huey P. Long, U.S. senator and governor of Louisiana, shot by a political opponent and died two days later, 1935

Explain that Long promoted a "share the wealth" program but by ruthless and demagogic means; define the word "demagogue"; think of other political leaders throughout the world who have been or are guilty of demagoguery.

Seizure of Warsaw, Poland begun by Nazi forces in World War II, 1939

(See activities under April 19, "Battle of Warsaw ....")

Italy's surrender in World War II announced, 1943

Investigate the events which led to the death of Mussolini (Il Duce) and to Italy's surrender.

Find out the English translation of the word "Il Duce."

(See activities under July 29, "Benito Mussolini ....")

Japanese Peace Treaty signed by 49 nations in San Francisco, 1951

Find out the significance of this treaty in terms of the regulations set up by the surrender agreements which had greatly limited Japan's liberties.

September 9

California Admission Day (commemorates California's admission to the United States as the thirty-first state, 1850)

(See States Admitted to the USA Data in Extra-Know-How Section.)

Name of "United States of America" adopted, 1776

Discuss the meaning of the name in terms of the meaning of the U.S. motto, *E Pluribus Unum.*

Make a map of the 50 states and identify each.

Develop a class list of the ways in which the citizens of the United States of America are united, such as constitutional rights, the English language, etc.

Leo Tolstoy, Russian writer, born 1828

(See Biography Data in Extra-Know-How Section.)

Explain that Tolstoy wrote *War and Peace,* a prose epic novel about the Napoleonic Wars that is considered by many to be one of the greatest novels ever written.

Find out what the components of a novel are and what the term "prose epic" means.

First log-rolling national championships held in America, 1898

Obtain fireplace logs (any logs of approximately equal lengths) and hold a log-rolling contest; explain that this was a major recreation and spectator sport during the nineteenth century in certain parts of the country.

September 10

Sewing machine patented by Elias Howe, 1846

Explain that Howe, as an apprentice-machinist, developed the sewing machine; discuss what an apprentice is and ask students in which fields they might like to serve as apprentices.

Find out how much Howe sold his patent for in England (due to the fact that little interest was shown in his invention in America).

Explain that Howe's machine was a lock-stitch sewing machine; find out what other kinds of sewing machines, if any, had been developed by that time.

Investigate the career of a tailor or of a business person in the garment trades.

(See activities under July 9, "Elias Howe ... " and August 12, "Sewing Machine ....")

Alaska awarded $900 million worth of oil leases, 1969

Investigate what effect this funding has had upon Alaska's economy, standard of living, and general life-style.

Trace the conflict between the oil industry and the environmentalists concerning the Alaska pipeline.

Locate on a map of North America the pathway of the Alaska pipeline and the intended path of the gas line from Alaska through Canada to the United States.

(See activities under January 10, "Standard Oil ... " and March 30, "Alaska purchased ....")

First U.S. coast-to-coast highway completed, 1913

Obtain highway maps and trace a cross-country route, using only the interstate highway system.

(See activities under March 29, "Federal highway ....")

September 11

Manhattan Island first discovered by a European—Henry Hudson, 1609

Locate the Henry Hudson River on a U.S. map; find out the various routes that are currently used to commute to Manhattan Island.

Discuss the remark made by some New Yorkers, "There's nothing west of the Hudson River."

Investigate the various other explorations made by Henry Hudson.

U.S. Department of War established, 1789

Find out what the responsibilities of this department were, which branches of the military service were included, and how extensive its influence was.

Investigate, in a similar way as above, the responsibilities of the current Department of Defense.

William Sydney Porter (pseudonym, O. Henry), American short-story writer, born 1862

(See Biography Data in Extra-Know-How Section.)

Obtain copies of O. Henry's stories; share with the class, especially "The Gift of the Magi" and "The Ransom of Red Chief."

Explain that O. Henry is known for the unexpected endings to his stories; encourage students to create a story with a surprise ending.

Discuss the various reasons for authors' use of pseudonyms.

First artificial aortic valve operation performed, 1952

Contact a medical authority concerning the operation to find out the risks and advantages of such an operation.

Find out other types of prosthetics that are added to the body.

Define what a pacer is and what a by-pass operation is.

(See activities under January Month-long Observances, "National Blood ... " and February Month-long Observances, "Heart Month ....")

First Giant panda born in captivity in China, 1963

Define the term "captivity" as related to animals.

Investigate information concerning panda bears.

September 12

Richard J. Gatling, American inventor of the machine gun, born 1818

(See Biography Data in Extra-Know-How Section.)

Discuss what a machine gun is; compare and contrast its advantages with other types of guns.

Bring in selected books on the history of weapons.

Alfred A. Knopf, American publisher, born 1892
  (See Biography Data in Extra-Know-How Section.)
  Investigate the career of a book publisher.
  Take a field trip to a local book publishing house.
  Present a library research skill lesson: ask students to open a book to the title page and write on an index card the title, author, place of publication, publisher, and date of publication; acquaint students with the various established styles of recording this information.
  Review Task Card #42 on book activities to learn how a book is structured, bound, and prepared for distribution.

Jesse Owens, winner of four Olympic Gold Medals, born 1913
  (See Biography Data in Extra-Know-How Section.)
  Introduce a variety of track and field running skills and activities.
  (See activities under August 9, "Jesse Owens ....")

September 13

Walter Reed, American bacteriologist, born 1851
  (See Biography Data in Extra-Know-How Section.)
  Find out where the Walter Reed Hospital is located.
  (See activities under April 28, "Vaccine for ....")

Milton Hershey, founder of Hershey Candy Company, born 1857
  (See Biography Data in Extra-Know-How Section.)
  Find out about Hershey's philanthropic efforts for children.
  Create a recipe using Hershey products as one of the ingredients.
  Design an original candy bar wrapper.
  Compare the amounts of sugar in a variety of commercial chocolate bars. (Dextrose, glucose, and sucrose all represent sugar content).

John J. Pershing, U.S. commander in chief of the World War I Expeditionary Forces in France, born 1860
  (See Biography Data in Extra-Know-How Section.)

Arnold Schönberg, Austrian-American composer, born 1874
  (See Biography Data in Extra-Know-How Section.)
  Investigate the terms: chords built on fourths, atonality, the twelve-tone scale; obtain recordings of Schönberg's "modern" music and enjoy.

Roald Dahl, British author, born 1916
  (See Biography Data in Extra-Know-How Section.)
  Enjoy reading Dahl's books *Charlie and the Chocolate Factory* and *James and the Giant Peach*.
  Sequence the events of either book through illustrations.
  Practice the art of storytelling by retelling the stories in each book.

First national hog-calling contest held, 1926
  Investigate the various terms relating to hogs and pigs—swine, piglets, sounders, boars, gilts, runts.
  Explain that animals are often categorized according to common characteristics; investigate what characteristic might describe the type of mammal that hogs are (cloven-hoofed).
  Investigate which type of food in America is considered good to feed hogs and which states grow the greatest quantity of that food crop; find this area on a map of the United States.
  Find out what is involved in hog-calling; hold a hog-calling contest, with or without hogs.
  Enjoy the story of *Charlotte's Web*, by E. B. White, and the series of *Freddy the Detective*, by W. F. Brooks.

Revolt at Attica State Correctional Facility in New York ended, 1971
  Investigate the causes of the revolt.
  Discuss prison reform, the issue of punishment vs. rehabilitation measures; define the term "recidivism"; find out the rates of recidivism in both state and federal prisons.

September 14

First light in a lighthouse in America kindled, 1716

Investigate the purpose of a lighthouse.

Present a watercolor lesson of a seascape which includes a lighthouse.

Ask students to imagine together what living in a lighthouse would be like; have the class write a progressive story involving these perceptions.

Gregorian calendar introduced, 1752

Arrange for a math lesson involving the days and months of the year.

Research the various calendars of the world, i.e., the Hebrew calendar which has 13 months; find out when the "new year" is celebrated in various areas throughout the world.

Encourage students to bring unique calendars to class; suggest that students design their own creative calendars which designate the coming events and holidays of the school year.

See activities under October 5, "Gregorian calendar ....")

Frederick Heinrich Alexander Von Humboldt, German geophysicist, naturalist, geographer, and diplomat, born 1769

(See Biography Data in Extra-Know-How Section.)

Explain that Von Humboldt is credited with having organized the study of geography; introduce the study of geography by presenting both the physical and the cultural aspects.

Investigate geography terms such as: cartographer, map projection, elevation, meridians, parallels.

Explore the history of geography and who some of the earlier geographers were, i.e., Erastosthenes and Ptolemy and their respective contributions.

Review Task Card #59 to study more about geography.

Words of the *Star Spangled Banner* written by Francis Scott Key in the War of 1812 during the bombardment of Fort McHenry, 1814

Explain that the melody is taken from an English tune, composed by John Stafford Smith; the song with the words officially became the U.S. national anthem by a presidential order in 1916, confirmed by Congress in 1931.

Obtain a copy of the book *The Story of the Star Spangled Banner*, by Peter Spier.

(See activities under March 3, "*Star Spangled* ....")

Ivan Pavlov, Russian physiologist and Nobel Peace Prize winner, born 1849

(See Biography Data in Extra-Know-How Section.)

Investigate the meaning of "operant conditioning."

Engage in a class project involving the training of an animal, using a reward technique such as food or stroking.

Explain that Pavlov pioneered in the study of the digestive glands; investigate his famous experiment with conditioning the reflexes of the digestive glands.

Discuss the ways in which students in a classroom are already conditioned, such as various reactions to certain bells for recess or the change of classes; think of other ways that individuals are conditioned by stimuli in their daily lives.

Charles Dana Gibson, American illustrator, born 1867

(See Biography Data in Extra-Know-How Section.)

Explain that a "Gibson Girl" was a turn-of-the-century black-and-white picture of a girl on advertising posters.

Investigate the career of an advertising illustrator.

Draw various millinery designs which may have been appropriate for Gibson Girl posters.

Margaret Higgins Sanger, founder of Planned Parenthood, born 1883

Suggest that students write to the United Nations World Health Organization to learn current statistics on the world's population. (See Address Listing in Extra-Know-How Section.)

Find out the year in which a U.S. commemorative stamp was issued in recognition of the family planning movement. Contact a local U.S. Post Office to examine a current edition of *Stamps and Stories* to learn about various events and public figures that have been acknowledged through the issuance of commemorative stamps.

Typewriter ribbon patented, 1886

Obtain a typewriter and suggest that students learn to change a typewriter ribbon.

Discuss the various types of ribbons available—variety of colors, carbon, cartridge, correcting ribbons.

(See activities under April 12, "First portable ... " and May 16, "First typewriter ....")

September 15

Respect for the Aged Day
Suggest that students write a letter to a grandparent or an aged friend.
Talk about facial characteristics which reflect age and character; invite students to draw pictures of how they think they will look when they are elderly.
Discuss what a make-up artist must do "to age" a person or what an actor/actress must take into consideration when representing an older person.
Consider the statement, "Do not resent growing old; many are denied the privilege."
(See activities under May Month-long Observances, "Senior Citizen ....")

James Fennimore Cooper, American author, born 1789
(See Biography Data in Extra-Know-How Section.)
Share some of Cooper's books, i.e., *The Last of the Mohicans, The Deerslayer*, or *The Pathfinder.*

Independence from Spain established by Central American countries, 1821
Initiate a study on Costa Rica, El Salvador, Guatemala, Honduras, and Nicaragua.

William Howard Taft, twenty-seventh president of the United States, born 1857
(See Biography Data in Extra-Know-How Section.)
Trace the background of the custom concerning the president throwing out the first ball to open the baseball season.

First mail-order business in America established, 1871
Discuss the advantages of mail-order catalog purchasing, especially for shut-ins or those who live long distances from metropolitan areas; encourage students also to be aware of the fraud that has been exposed in the mail-order business.
Discuss what is involved in developing a mail-order catalog and processing the various orders, but consider also the advantages of not needing to maintain a retail place of business.
Invite students to bring in various mail-order catalogs and examine them as if they were wish-books for items they can "purchase" by completing the order forms.

Military tank first used by the British army, 1916
Ask students to bring in models or books with pictures of tanks; compare the various styles of tanks in both World War I and World War II.
Talk about the advantages and disadvantages of military tanks.

Anti-Jewish Nuremberg (Nürnberg) Laws enacted, 1933
Explain that the legislation deprived Jews in Germany of their rights, i.e., to own property, to worship in their religion.
Create a similar situation in which certain students are disenfranchised of classroom privileges, due to some arbitrary criterion such as blond hair or the color of clothing. (Prior notification to parents/guardians is advised.)

September 16

World Peace Day
Discuss the word and the concept of "peace"; ask students if they believe sustained world peace is likely; talk about peace in the family and inner peace within individuals.
Explain that peace may be aided by knowledge of others' customs and background; in an effort to stimulate independent study of certain countries, hand a globe to a student; wherever his/her right thumb touches, ask the person to name the country and try to identify one thing known about the country; circulate the globe to others.
Discuss the point that in order to create peaceful relationships, there needs to be a basic respect for others' rights to follow their particular belief systems.
(See activities under December Special Weeks, "Human Rights ... " and February Special Weeks, "Brotherhood Week ....")

Voyage of the *Mayflower* begun, 1620
Investigate what the Mayflower Compact was and chart the voyage of the ship.
Find out the reasons for chartering the trip.
Write a story describing life on board the ship during the crossing.
(See activities under November 19, "*Mayflower* ship ... " and December 21, "Pilgrims landed ....")

Mexico's revolution against Spain begun (celebrated as Mexican Independence Day), 1810
   Investigate the causes of Mexico's rebellion against Spain.
   Create a timeline of Mexico's history.

Francis Parkman, American historian, born 1823
   (See Biography Data in Extra-Know-How Section.)
   Investigate the career of a historian.
   Consider the ethics involved in preserving objectivity and thoroughness in one's research; investigate what "revisionists" are in the field of history (those who reinvestigate the conventional wisdom concerning events in history).
   Invite a group of students to report on the history of the school or of the local area, using the historical method—written records and oral informants; encourage other students to trace the genealogy of their families, using oral tradition as a method.
   Investigate the related careers of an archivist, historiographer, anthropologist, or archaeologist.
   Introduce two conflicting reports of the same historical event, each of which may be valid; encourage students to favor one of the reports and substantiate the reason for the choice.

Selective Service Act passed, 1940
   Discuss the practice of using draft cards and the various responsibilities and classifications involved in the induction process.
   Hold a debate on the following topic: "Defense force quotas are best met through volunteers"; document the data used to substantiate various points.
   Trace the history of compulsory registration for service in the armed forces.
   (See activities under April 1, "First U.S. wartime ... " and October 29, "Men drafted ....")

September 17

Constitution Day and Citizenship Day (commemorates the Constitutional Convention's adoption of the U.S. Constitution, 1787)
   Investigate the requirements for a person to become a naturalized citizen.
   Obtain a copy of the U.S. citizenship test from the local library; mix fun with fact to see whether the class, as a whole, can pass the test.

Friedrich Wilhelm von Steuben, Prussian officer and American Revolutionary War general, born 1730
   (See Biography Data in Extra-Know-How Section.)
   Find out what services von Steuben performed for the Continental Army.
   Discuss why men of von Steuben's status would choose to fight for a cause with another country.

Edgar Mitchell, American astronaut, born 1930
   (See Biography Data in Extra-Know-How Section.)
   Discuss what thoughts and feelings astronauts must experience once they move from a relatively predictable environment to that of "unreal" or "distorted" perceptions of time and space.
   Explain that after Mitchell's return from his space voyage, he became associated with the Institute of Noetic Science in an attempt to examine the inner spaces that he traversed while in outer space. (Note: "Noetic is from the Greek word *noētikós,* of or pertaining to the mind.) Investigate the field of noetic science as it may or may not relate to "noosphere," described by Pierre Teilhard de Chardin as the layer of human awareness that envelops the earth like a psychic biosphere.

First successful separation of Siamese twins performed, 1953
   Discuss why these types of twins are termed "Siamese."
   Obtain a copy of *Very Special People,* by Frederick Drimmer, in order to research various other exceptional births.
   Consider what it would be like to be a Siamese twin.
   Discuss other types of multiple births—identical or fraternal twins; think what it might be like to share one's personal identity; talk about such ideas as dressing alike, being in the same classroom, being confused with one's twin.

September 18

Cornerstone of the capitol building in Washington, DC laid by President Washington, 1794
Find out what a cornerstone is; discuss the significance of a ceremony which marks the laying of a cornerstone of an official building.
Obtain a layout map of Washington, DC from an encyclopedia or textbook; study the locations of various landmarks and important buildings in the area.
Investigate what wording was used on the cornerstone, or else invite students to create an original phrase which would be appropriate on the cornerstone of the nation's capitol.

Samuel Johnson, English writer and the dominating literary figure of his time, born 1709
(See Biography Data in Extra-Know-How Section.)
Find out who the various members of Johnson's prestigious literary club in London were.
Explain that Johnson met his future biographer, James Boswell; discuss whether or not most biographers have met the biographee before writing about the person and if it is advantageous to do so.
Discuss Johnson's comments: "The future is purchased by the present"; "Nothing will ever be attempted if all possible objections must be first overcome."
(See activities under October 29, "James Boswell ....")

September 19

"Dixie," the song by D. D. Emmett, first presented in America, 1859
Introduce the song; analyze the meaning of the words.
Find on a map the general area of "Dixie Land" to which the song refers.
Use Task Card #66 to learn how to make a jug band to accompany the song.

First carpet sweeper patented, 1876
Compare and contrast a carpet sweeper and a vacuum cleaner.
(See activities under June 8, "Suction-type ....")

First animated, talking cartoon picture featured, "Steamboat Willy," 1928
Investigate how the character of Mickey Mouse has changed from the days of "Steamboat Willy" to the present time.
Obtain a recording of "Turkey in the Straw," the background music which set the pace for Mickey Mouse's movements.
Invite students to make a short, animated Mickey Mouse film.

September 20

Voyage around the world begun by Ferdinand Magellan, Portuguese explorer, 1519
Chart Magellan's route around the world; especially note the Strait of Magellan which outlined the path for future voyages before the Panama Canal was built.
Explain that Magellan was headed for the Spice Islands, now known as the Moluccas in Indonesia; find out the significance of the Spice Islands to Europeans; locate the area on a map; trace the history of the Moluccas island group.
Discuss the fact that although Magellan was unable to complete the voyage, one of the five original vessels was able to return to Spain, thus having completed the first circumnavigation of the earth.
Explore the importance of Magellan's voyage that proved the roundness of the earth and that the Americas were continents separate from Asia; ask students to draw a map that represents a flat world with the continents of Europe, Asia, and the Americas connected.

"Old Ironsides," American naval frigate the *Constitution*, launched, 1797
Investigate why the ship was nicknamed "Old Ironsides"; find out where it is now located.
Define the word "frigate."
Obtain a model kit of the ship and build it in the classroom for a long-term construction project.

Electric range patented, 1859

Compare and contrast electric and gas ranges in terms of their respective advantages and disadvantages.

Consult a mail-order catalog for the pricing and the various features of electric ranges and microwave ovens.

Trace the meaning of the word "range" or "cooker" as opposed to the word "stove."

Upton Sinclair, American novelist and Pulitzer Prize recipient, born 1878

(See Biography Data in Extra-Know-How Section.)

Explain that Sinclair's book *The Jungle* contributed to the passage of the Pure Food and Drug Act of 1906; discuss the term "muckraker" and the topic of how books can influence social change.

Sister Elizabeth Kenney, Australian nurse, born 1886

(See Biography Data in Extra-Know-How Section.)

Investigate the polio treatment for which she is known to have developed.

(See activities under January Month-long Observances, "March of Dimes ....")

September 21

First day of fall (on or about September 21)

Discover why it is that day and night are equal during this time.

Find out the difference between the terms "equinox" and "solstice."

Obtain the book *Fall Is Here*, by Dorothy Sterling, and enjoy with the class.

(See activities under September Variable Dates, "Autumn begins ....")

H. G. Wells, British writer, born 1866

(See Biography Data in Extra-Know-How Section.)

Share one of his science fiction books, *The Time Machine*; if possible, obtain the film of the same title from the local library or by contacting a local film distributor.

Encourage students to write a creative story in which a time machine is either taken forward to the future or back into history.

Duryea Motor Wagon Co. incorporated, 1895

Explain that the Duryea Co. was a major forerunner of the entire automobile industry; investigate the original Duryea buggy.

Write a creative story within the setting of the horse and buggy days.

Famed article, "Yes, Virginia, There Is a Santa Claus," published by the New York *Sun*, 1897

(See Data-Detail of Extra-Know-How Section, "Yes, Virginia, There Is a Santa Claus.")

Encourage students to write an editorial, similar in style to this famous one, pertaining to a topic of their choice.

Federal Republic of West Germany established, 1949

Investigate the postwar years of Germany—the unconditioned surrender, the agreements at the Yalta and Potsdam conferences, the Marshall Plan, the status of Berlin under a four-power occupation, the Allied High Commission which led to Germany's becoming a federal parliamentary democracy.

Trace the history of Germany since Konrad Adenauer, West Germany's first chancellor, led a coalition cabinet through the first stages of government.

September 22

Nathan Hale, American Revolutionary War patriot, hanged by the British as a spy, 1776

(See activities under June 6, "Nathan Hale ....")

U.S. Post Office established, 1789

Talk about the words that are inscribed on the main post office building in New York City: "Neither snow nor rain nor heat nor gloom of night stays these carriers from their swift completion of their appointed rounds."

Find out the purpose of the zoning system which started in 1943 and the zip code system which followed in 1963; investigate the details of how zip codes have been assigned.

Write to the U.S. Postal Service for the booklet "History of the U.S. Postal Service." (See Address Listing in Extra-Know-How Section.)

Investigate postal service-related careers.

Michael Faraday, English scientist who discovered electromagnetic induction, the forerunner of electrical machinery for industry, born 1791

(See Biography Data in Extra-Know-How Section.)

Discuss the point that an individual who was primarily self-educated was able to make a discovery which made possible the modern electric and electronic age.

Encourage interested students to explore "Faraday's Laws."

Explain that Faraday was elected as a fellow of the Royal Society; find out the background of the organization and what other distinguished fellows have been elected.

Chen Ning Yang, Chinese-American physicist, born 1922

(See Biography Data in Extra-Know-How Section.)

Review with students the essence of the scientific method.

Visit the school or community library to examine books in the area of science; find the call numbers which are specific to the field of physics.

Invite a physicist to the class, or interview a physicist, to learn about physics, both as a career and as a practical course to study.

September 23

First day of the zodiac period, Libra, the Scales (through October 22)

(See Data-Detail in Extra-Know-How Section, "Notes on Astrology.")

Euripides, Greek dramatist, born 480 B.C.

(See Biography Data in Extra-Know-How Section.)

Explain that Euripides was one of the great dramatic triumvirate that also included Aeschylus and Sophocles; enjoy reading and acting various versions of Greek plays, using *Greek Tears and Roman Laughter,* by Albert Cullum, as a source.

First college commencement in America held at Harvard College, 1642

Discuss the meaning and significance of the word "commencement."

Find out how many students plan to attend and graduate from college.

Investigate the background of such customs as the cap and gown, mortar board, valedictorian, the music "Pomp and Circumstance," and titles such as *summa cum laude* and *magna cum laude.*

William McGuffey, American educator who compiled the six Eclectic Readers', born 1800

(See Biography Data in Extra-Know-How Section.)

Obtain a copy of *McGuffey's Eclectic Reader* and compare it with today's reading in the schools.

Lewis and Clark expedition completed, 1806

(See activities under August 31, "Exploration of ....")

Baseball Rules Code adopted, 1845

Discuss the necessity of consistent rules in all games; relate this idea to playground games.

Ask students to name various changes and rules, such as those of the pinch-hitter and in-field fly.

Planet Neptune accidentally discovered by two German astronomers, 1846

Find out what the "accident" was that led the scientists to having discovered Neptune.

Investigate what other scientific discoveries have occurred by accident.

John Lomax, founder of the American Folklore Society, born 1870

(See Biography Data in Extra-Know-How Section.)

Discuss the term "folklore."

Share various American folklore stories with the class.

Hearing aid for the hard-of-hearing patented, 1879

Write to the Zenith Radio Corporation for a free record, "Getting through, a Guide to Better Understanding of the Hard-of-Hearing"; in particular, listen to Band 4, "An Unfair Hearing Test." (See Address Listing in Extra-Know-How Section.)

Discuss different types of hearing problems.

Initiate a science unit on sound; include terms such as decibel, high, flat frequencies, and experiment with a tuning fork and its effect on other objects.

Invite students to participate in an experiment to prove that most people tend to rely on lip reading and body language to "hear"; ask a student to stand behind a seated individual and pronounce a message or list of words and then proceed to read a similar list or message while standing in close view of the seated person; ask the listener which procedure was easier to listen to.

Discuss the significance of the statement: "People learn about 85% of what they know by listening"; consider the difficulties, if this statement is valid, that are experienced by deaf or hard-of-hearing individuals.

(See activities under February 15, "First national ... " and May Month-long Observances, "Hearing and ....")

Time capsule buried at the World's Fair, 1938

Discuss what a time capsule is.

Fill a cardboard tube with magazine or newspaper cut-outs of famous current events; bury the tube and its contents in a cupboard until the end of the year; share the contents the last week of school. Variation: measure the height of each student, make a class record of the heights and bury it until the end of the year when new measurements are to be made to compare the growth patterns.

Walter Lippmann, American political writer, born 1889

(See Biography Data in Extra-Know-How Section.)

Discuss the significance of the freedom to express and publish political thoughts and viewpoints.

Mickey Rooney, American actor, born 1922

(See Biography Data in Extra-Know-How Section.)

Consider the advantages and disadvantages of being part of a "minority" group—that of short people; consider the ways in which Rooney capitalized upon his short stature.

September 24

John Marshall, fourth chief justice of the U.S. Supreme Court, born 1755

(See Biography Data in Extra-Know-How Section.)

Explain that Marshall opposed states' rights doctrines; investigate the significance of "states' rights" and hold a debate that might have been engaged in between John Marshall and Thomas Jefferson, a proponent of states' rights.

U.S. Office of Attorney General created and the U.S. Supreme Court authorized, 1789

Investigate the responsibilities of the office of attorney general.

(See activities under February 1, "First session ....")

September 25

Pacific Ocean "and all shores washed by it" claimed by Vasco Núñez de Balboa for Spain, 1513

Trace the route Balboa followed on his exploration to the Pacific; find an account of the march across the isthmus which is now Panama.

Compare in detail the geographic terms "isthmus" (a narrow strip of land bordered on both sides by water, connecting two larger bodies of land) and "strait" (a narrow passage of water connecting two larger bodies of water).

Find out the reason for Balboa's choice in naming the ocean he claimed for Spain; explain that Balboa claimed all shores of the Pacific Ocean but that he had only viewed a small part of the eastern shore of the ocean.

Twelfth Amendment to the U.S. Constitution ratified, 1804

(See Data-Detail in Extra-Know-How Section, "Amendments to the U.S. Constitution.")

Explain that the amendment provided for the electors (not the voters) to vote for a president and vice-president on separate ballots; explore the significance of this ruling.

Investigate the process and implications of the entire electoral process.

Thomas Hunt Morgan, American zoologist and Nobel Prize winner in physiology and medicine, born 1866

(See Biography Data in Extra-Know-How Section.)

Investigate what Morgan's specific contributions were in the field of genetics; define what "genes" and "chromosomes" are.

Explore the career of a zoologist and of a physiologist.

(See activities under July 22, "Gregor Mendel ....")

William Faulkner, American writer and winner of both the Nobel and Pulitzer prizes, born 1897
(See Biography Data in Extra-Know-How Section.)
Obtain a copy of *The Sound and the Fury*; read sections to the class which describe the life-style of the Deep South.
Discuss Faulkner's statement, "If I were to choose between pain and nothing, I would choose pain."

Sandra Day O'Connor, first woman sworn in as a U.S. Supreme Court justice, 1981
Explain that O'Connor's area of expertise was within the judicial domain of the states rather than within the federal court system. Discuss the fact that there are various types of courts within the judicial system; identify which courts are under federal, state, or county jurisdiction, such as appellate courts, circuit courts of appeal, superior courts, and district courts, among others.

Barbara Walters, television newscaster and interviewer, born 1931
(See Biography Data in Extra-Know-How Section.)
Explain that Walters was the first woman to serve as an anchorperson on an evening television broadcast; investigate the career of a newscaster or TV host/hostess.
Learn the skills involved in the interview process; follow through with an actual interview with someone.

September 26

Johnny Appleseed Day (commemorates the birth of John Chapman, 1774)
(See Biography Data in Extra-Know-How Section.)
Obtain the film *Johnny Appleseed* from Walt Disney Films. (See Address Listing in Extra-Know-How Section.)
Explore the various kinds of apples that there are and plant apple seeds.
Obtain the Disney record, "Walt Disney Presents Dennis Day in the Story of Johnny Appleseed"; enjoy listening with the class.
Write to the Washington State Apple Commission for further information about apples. (See Address Listing in Extra-Know-How Section.)
Obtain a copy of *Johnny Appleseed*, by Eva Moore, to learn the extent of this legendary figure's planting of apple orchards across the nation.
Review Task Card #23 concerning activities with apples.

Cement patented, 1871
Find out how cement and concrete are related; investigate how cement is made.
Construct a wooden frame box for the purpose of filling with cement; discuss the precautions of working with cement and then mix the ingredients; fill the frame, and as it hardens, encourage students to set their handprints in the cement with a caption, such as "The Helping Hands of Room _____, 19_____."

T. S. Eliot, English poet, critic, and winner of the Nobel Prize, born 1888
(See Biography Data in Extra-Know-How Section.)
Investigate the background of the Nobel Prize and for which fields of endeavor the prizes are awarded.

John Philip Sousa's first band performance conducted, 1892
Obtain a recording of *The Stars and Stripes Forever*, one of about 100 of Sousa's marches and other compositions; practice marching to the music.
Invite a band teacher to class to discuss the responsibilities of a marching-band leader, especially in terms of arranging for formations on football fields and in parades.
Find out how a marching band is different from a dance band or an orchestra.
Investigate what training is needed to be a band major/majorette.

George Gershwin, American composer, born 1898
(See Biography Data in Extra-Know-How Section.)
Obtain recordings of his music and enjoy listening (*Porgy and Bess* with the song "Summertime"; *Rhapsody in Blue*; *An American in Paris*).

First Kennedy-Nixon televised debate broadcast, 1960
Discuss the impact that television and other media presentations have upon voters' perceptions of candidates; consider various forms of campaign persuasion techniques.

September 27

Samuel Adams, American Revolutionary patriot and signer of the Declaration of Independence, born 1722
(See Biography Data in Extra-Know-How Section.)
Trace the relationship between Samuel Adams and the John Adams family.
Discuss the point that Adams was considered an extremist; consider contemporary leaders who are identified generally as revolutionary or radical.

George Cruikshank, British caricaturist, born 1792
(See Biography Data in Extra-Know-How Section.)
Discuss what a caricature is, such as exaggerated facial characteristics, posture, stature of a particular individual.
Invite students to bring to class caricatures from newspapers and magazines.
Encourage students to create caricatures of people of their choice.

Hiram Rhoades Revels, first black U.S. senator (Mississippi), born 1822
(See Biography Data in Extra-Know-How Section.)
Read *Important Dates in Afro-American History*, by Lee Bennett Hopkins, to learn about other black leaders in America's history.
(See activities under February 25, "First black ....")

Thomas Nast, German-American cartoonist, born 1840
(See Biography Data in Extra-Know-How Section.)
Investigate which significant cartoon figures were creations of Nast.
Invite students to develop their original cartoon figures.
Discuss the impact that political cartoonists have had upon public opinion.
(See activities under January 15, " 'Donkey' emblem ....")

Joy Morton, founder of Morton Salt Company, born 1855
(See Biography Data in Extra-Know-How Section.)
Find out the effects of salt on the human body.
Discover what other uses salt has besides that of food seasoning.

Book matches patented, 1892
Consider book matches in terms of their covers' being an art form and as a medium for advertising.
Discuss accidents that can happen with safety matches.
Bring in samples of colorful book match covers and invite students to create their own.
Explore the career of a commercial graphics designer.

September 28

California first discovered by a European, Juan Rodríguez Cabrillo, a Portuguese-Spanish conquistador, 1542
Trace the route of Cabrillo's exploration from Spain and identify the area where he landed.
Locate on a map where the Cabrillo National Monument is.
Find out the English meaning of "conquistador."

Friedrich Engels, German social philosopher, born 1820
(See Biography Data in Extra-Know-How Section.)
Investigate what is meant by "dialectical materialism," the theme of much of Engels' writing.

Chicago White Sox indicted for having "thrown" the 1919 World Series in the "Black Sox Scandal," 1920
Discuss what is meant by "throwing a game" (bribing an individual player); consider the responsibility and code of ethics of a professional (or amateur) athlete.
Ask students to finish a story based upon the following situation:
    a) You are the pitcher in a world series game;
    b) your team is predicted to win;
    c) a private offer is made to you, a million-dollar bribe, to "throw the game."
Discuss the connotations of "white" and "black" in "standard" American English; make a list of expressions or terms using either "black" or "white."

Ed Sullivan, American entertainer and columnist, born 1902
    (See Biography Data in Extra-Know-How Section.)
    Hold a talent show and ask one student to act as host/hostess for the variety acts. (Encourage the student to mimic Sullivan's weekly toast, "A *rilly* big show ... ").

September 29

Scotland Yard established in London, 1829
    Find out the background of the name "Scotland Yard," as London's police headquarters.
    Compare and contrast the British law enforcement system with that of the United States.
    Suggest an oral, progressive story regarding a Scotland Yard detective case; encourage students to use a British accent.

Enrico Fermi, Italian-American physicist and Nobel Prize winner, born 1901
    (See Biography Data in Extra-Know-How Section.)
    Investigate the career of a physicist.
    Explain that Fermi was awarded the Nobel Prize for his contributions regarding radioactive substances; discuss the ways in which nuclear power can be used for peaceful means, as well as those which are ecologically sound.
    (See activities under July 16, "First atomic ....")

Gene Autry, American cowboy actor/singer, born 1907
    (See Biography Data in Extra-Know-How Section.)
    Investigate Autry's other areas of endeavor such as the "Angels" baseball team and his various media enterprises.
    Obtain a recording of Autry's popular version of "Rudolph, the Red-Nosed Reindeer" and share with the class.

September 30

Ether used in dentistry for the first time as an anesthetic by William Morton, American dentist, 1846
    Define the word "anesthesia"; name various anesthetics, such as ether, and explain how they are administered.
    Explain that Crawford Long, an American physician, used ether four years earlier for neck surgery; consider what surgery without anesthesia would be like.
    (See activities under November 1, "Crawford Long ....")

William Wrigley, Jr., founder of the chewing gum firm, born 1861
    (See Biography Data in Extra-Know-How Section.)
    (See activities under December 28, "Chewing gum ....")

Hans Wilhelm Geiger, German physicist, born 1882
    (See Biography Data in Extra-Know-How Section.)
    Explain that he introduced the Geiger counter, an effective device for detecting and measuring radioactivity; find out how the instrument operates and what its significance is.

Rayon, a synthetic fiber, patented, 1902
    Bring in sample of rayon or fabrics with rayon mixtures.
    Ask students to check clothing labels to find how much rayon is used.
    Discuss the word "synthetic," and make a list of other synthetic fibers, noting those which represent trademark names.

Babe Ruth hit his record-breaking 60th homerun of the season, 1927
    Gather data on World Series batting averages and develop math problems from the information.
    Find out which baseball player(s) have broken the homerun records formerly set by Babe Ruth.

Frisbee® design patented by Walter "Fred" Morrison, 1958
    Investigate the history of the Frisbee; read chapter 3, "The Frisbee," in *Made in America—Eight All America Creations*, by Murray Suid and Ron Harris.
    Review Task Card #41 for Frisbee golf activities.

OCTOBER

When October shifted from its place as the eighth month to the tenth month in the revised calendar, the Romans attempted to rename it "Antonius" after a Roman emperor, and "Faustinus" after his wife, and finally "Tactitus" after a Roman historian. However, the ancient Roman name, that which derived from the Latin word for "eight," prevailed.

Birthstone: *Opal*
Flower: *Marigold or Calendula*

Use the Find-a-Word Reproducible to preview happenings in October. (See Reproducible Section.)

MONTH-LONG OBSERVANCES

National Restaurant Month

Invite a restauranteur to come to class and discuss the business of owning and managing a restaurant.

Obtain copies of restaurant menus; discuss various terms, i.e., a la carte, antipasto.

Consult the yellow pages of the telephone directory; make a list of the local restaurants and classify them according to categories decided upon by the class.

Encourage students to design their own restaurant, along an imaginative theme; develop a menu to accompany the theme of the restaurant.

Write to the National Restaurant Association for information. (See Address Listing in Extra-Know-How Section.)

National Wine Festival Month

Trace the history of wine as a substitute for unhygienic drinking water and as a ceremonial drink for religious and official rituals.

Investigate the process of fermenting grapes and other substances.

Find out what the major wine-producing areas of the world are and locate them on a map.

Discuss the comment of Louis Pasteur, "Wine is the most healthful and most hygienic of all beverages"; investigate the positive attention that wine is receiving from the medical field in terms of the fructose value and its natural tranquilizing effect, among other factors.

Write to the Wine Appreciation Guild for information on wine-related items and information. (See Address Listing in Extra-Know-How Section.)

(See activities under December 27, "Louis Pasteur ....")

SPECIAL WEEKS

National Macaroni Week (Thursday toward mid-month)

Examine a variety of macaroni shapes; use food coloring to color the macaroni and create macaroni mosaics.

Find out where macaroni originated and how it is made.

Write to the National Macaroni Institute for information. (See Address Listing in Extra-Know-How Section.)

International Whale-Watching Week (Sunday of the week including October 21)

Investigate the whale as an endangered species; explore current abuses of international trade and ecology agreements.

Make a list of the marketable products which are derived from whales.

(See activities under October 21, "International Whale ....")

Fire Prevention Week (Sunday of the week including October 8)

Invite a representative from the local fire department to discuss fire prevention measures around the home; request that a home fire extinguisher and smoke detector be demonstrated.

Encourage students to develop a list and check their own homes for potential fire hazards.

Role-play an emergency call to the fire department; discuss the danger of false alarms.

Remind students that certain fires are not extinguished by water, i.e., grease fires which need bicarbonate of soda (baking soda) to extinguish them.

(See activities under April 1, "First salaried ....")

National 4-H Week (first Sunday)

Investigate what the 4-H Club is; obtain a copy of the insignia to find out what each of the *H*s represents in the name.

Write to the U.S. Department of Agriculture for further information. (See Address Listing in Extra-Know-How Section.)

(See activities under February Special Weeks, "Future Farmers ....")

National Pharmacy Week (Sunday of the week including October 7)

Write to the National Association of Retail Druggists for their NARD kit. (See Address Listing in Extra-Know-How Section.)

Invite a pharmacist to class to discuss pharmacy as a career; explore with him/her also the field of toxicology.

Investigate which colleges and universities offer programs in pharmacology.

Find out the modern methods of medication production as opposed to the former process of individualized mortar-and-pestle preparations.

Conduct a market research by comparing the prices of aspirin at different types of stores; find out the wholesale versus the retail prices of various medicines.

Explore why certain drugs require a prescription in order to be purchased.

Invite the school nurse to class to talk about the use and abuse of drugs.

National Newspaper Week (usually second Sunday)

Contact a local newspaper office in order to arrange for a visit.

Discuss the dynamics of news happenings which occur just before the production deadline; consider the working hours of those who help in the production of a morning paper.

Invite a reporter to class; explore with him/her the career of investigative reporting, as well as other press-related careers; ask about the jargon used in the field of journalism.

Trace the history of American newspapers since the early eighteenth century.

Send for a copy of the Sunday edition of the *New York Times*; study the various parts of the newspaper and the general editorial perspective it represents; consider the consumption of paper involved in the production of one copy of the newspaper; find out the extent of distribution, and create various math problems which indicate the amount of pages produced for one day's distribution of the Sunday edition.

Write to various foreign embassies for copies of their newspapers in order to compare newspaper styles and to examine various types of alphabets; cut out the headlines of those with foreign alphabets, noting on them the country from which they come, and create mixed collages of them.

Review Task Card #51 for newspaper activities.

(See activities under April 24, "First regularly ... " and April 29, "William Randolph ....")

National Forest Products Week (third Sunday)

Make a class list of products which come from forest areas.

Write to the following addresses: California Redwood Association for "Teachers' Conservation Kit"; Western Sawlog Wood Products Association for the booklet series, "Our Forests and You," Pamphlet #PR-10, in particular. (See Address Listings in Extra-Know-How Section.)

Investigate the state and federal regulations regarding the commercial use of forests.

Write a group letter to Smokey the Bear for information about fire prevention. (See Address Listing in Extra-Know-How Section.)

National Business Women's Week (third Sunday)

Find out what percentage of the work force is currently composed of women.

Discuss the implications for both men and women concerning the provisions for gender equality in the U.S. government's Affirmative Action program.

Write to the National Federation of Business and Professional Women's Clubs for further information. (See Address Listing in Extra-Know-How Section.)

National Popcorn Week (Sunday of the week including October 24)
(See activities under February 21, "Popcorn first ....")

United Nations Week (Sunday of the week including October 24)
(See activities under January 9, "U.N. Headquarters ... " and February Special Weeks, "Brotherhood Week ....")

American Education Week (Sunday before Veterans Day)
Explain that the United States is considered to be the most "schooled society" in the world by virtue of its commitment to free public education and the relatively late school-leaving age; discuss the drawbacks and benefits of America's commitment to universal public education.

Investigate other countries' provision for education; note that most education systems are nationally controlled as opposed to the American idea of local control; find out other cross-national differences, such as the number of hours a week in school, age levels for expected attendance, types of schools, etc.

Attend a local school board meeting.

Write to the National Education Association for information. (See Address Listing in Address Section.)

National Mushroom Week (last Sunday)
Investigate the various types of mushrooms such as the Death Angel, Inky Caps, and fungus.
Find out how to identify poisonous from nonpoisonous mushrooms.

Determine the relative nutritional and caloric value of mushrooms.

Create a story about mushrooms.

Write to the American Mushroom Institute for more information. (See Address Listing in the Extra-Know-How Section.)

Use the dictionary for the word derivation and meaning of such terms as "mycology" and "macrofungi."

VARIABLE DATES

Jewish High Holy Days—Rosh Hashanah and Yom Kippur (end of September, early October)
Investigate the significance of these holidays.
Obtain a copy of *Jewish Holidays*, by Betty Morrow and Louis Hartman.

World Series (date and location varies)
Research the history of the World Series.
Investigate the records of the competing teams in the forthcoming series.
Conduct a survey to determine the favorite of all the teams in the American and National leagues. (See Conducting a Survey Data in Extra-Know-How Section.)
(See activities under April Variable Dates, "Baseball season ....")

Columbus Day (usually second Monday)
Display and share various books about Columbus.
Investigate the various struggles encountered on Columbus' voyage; ask students to develop a fictional log of the journey across the Atlantic.
Find out what Columbus' major goal was for the exploration; trace the outcome as to whether the original goal was met.
Suggest that students find out whether Columbus actually was the first European to have discovered America; if not, consider other reasons as to why his explorations were significant.

Sweetest Day (third Saturday)
Explain that the day originated as a time to spread cheer among the unfortunate and developed into an occasion to remember anyone with a kind act.
Discuss the statement: "Let me be a little kinder, let me be a little blinder to the faults of those around me" (Edgar Guest).
Encourage students to think a kind thought of an individual or express a gesture of kindness toward someone in the class.

Veterans Day (usually the fourth Monday)
Invite a veteran (perhaps a student's parent) to discuss the meaning of Veterans Day; consider how a veteran might feel about employment, family, and friends after returning from military service.
(See Data-Detail in Extra-Know-How Section, "Veterans Day—History.")

Return of standard time (last Sunday) in which clocks are set back one hour
(See activities under April Variable Dates, "Daylight Saving ....")

DAYS OF THE MONTH

October 1

William Boeing, American aeronautics designer, born 1881
(See Biography Data in Extra-Know-How Section.)
Obtain pictures of the Boeing 707 and 747 airplanes; discuss the various features of each.
Trace the development of passenger carriers since the production of the 747; illustrate the findings.

First World Series game held, 1903
Find out what two teams played in the original competition.
(See October Variable Dates, "World Series ....")

Vladimir Horowitz, Russian-American pianist, born 1904
(See Biography Data in Extra-Know-How Section.)
Invite a student or guest to play a selection on the piano.
Introduce a piano keyboard to learn the basic keys, the concept of an octave, etc.
Find out the differences between a spinet piano, a baby grand, and a concert grand piano.
Investigate the instruments which were forerunners to the piano: clavichord, harpsichord, and pianoforte.

Model T automobile introduced by Henry Ford, 1908
Obtain a picture of the original Model T Ford; discuss particulars of the car; suggest to students that they personify the car in terms of an early twentieth-century Sunday drive, such as a description of feelings that the car may have had as people admired the car going over the roads—or the thirst the car may have had for gas, since there were few or no gas stations.
Determine the differences between the Model T and the Model A cars.
Create an illustrated timeline of the various automobiles that were developed within the first 30 years of the twentieth century.
Discuss the following: When asked what had helped him over his greatest obstacle in life, Henry Ford allegedly replied, "The preceding one."
(See activities under June 4, "First Ford ... " and July 30, "Henry Ford ... " and November 5, "First U.S. ....")

James Earl Carter, thirty-ninth president of the United States, born 1924
(See Biography Data in Extra-Know-How Section.)

First American parachute battalion in America organized by the U.S. Army, 1940
Investigate various free-fall records, such as the greatest number of feet fallen before opening the parachute or the highest number of participants in a free-fall configuration.
(See activities under March 12, "First parachute ....")

October 2

Nat Turner, leader of a slave revolt, born 1800
(See Biography Data in Extra-Know-How Section.)
Trace the details of the rebellion and the outcome of it.

Tin can with key-opener patented, 1866
Discuss the advantages and disadvantages of this invention.
Ask students to consider the various ways that containers are designed to be opened; brainstorm ideas yet to be developed.

Mahatma Gandhi, Indian statesman, born 1869
(See Biography Data in Extra-Know-How Section.)
Stage a sociodrama in which students display Gandhi's style of nonviolent resistance, based upon an issue of their choice; discuss various types of asceticism, such as fasting. Discuss the irony of Gandhi's having been assassinated.

Explain that Gandhi believed in the unity of humankind and preached Christian and Moslem scriptures along with Hindu ideas, all of which were practiced in India; discuss the point that he was so highly revered that he was called "Mahatma," meaning "great-souled."

Encourage interested students to develop a study of India, including the many languages and dialects that are spoken, an explanation of the caste system and the "untouchables," as well as other customs and facts about India. (Note: Gandhi vigorously espoused the abolition of "untouchability.")

Groucho Marx, American comedian, born 1895

(See Biography Data in Extra-Know-How Section.)

Discuss Groucho Marx's style of humor.

Invite students to cut out a large, black mustache; adhere it to just above the upper-lip with rolled tape; create a Groucho Marx cigar from brown paper; encourage students to imitate Groucho's gestures and style of humor.

Explain that four of the five Marx brothers, Groucho, Harpo, Chico, and Zeppo, performed together in various vaudeville and burlesque acts; trace the lives of this famous family of performers.

Rex Reed, film critic, born 1938

(See Biography Data in Extra-Know-How Section.)

Obtain several film critiques from the newspaper; compare and evaluate the style of each.

Encourage students to write their own critiques of current film.

Discuss what financial effect a positive or negative evaluation has upon a film; consider also the effect of film criticism in terms of artistic excellence.

October 3

Child Health Day

Obtain a copy of the *Child Health Encyclopedia* by Richard I. Feinbloom, M.D., or of another health reference book to investigate child health problems. Examine the various health magazines on newsstands. Subscribe to *Current Health* by writing to Curriculum Innovations, Inc. (See Address Listing in Extra-Know-How Section.)

Invite students to chart their own medical history by filling out medical or health forms; these may be obtained from the school nurse or from a local physician.

Conduct a speech or essay contest with the topic, "When You Have Your Health, You Have Everything!"

Ask students to write to UNICEF for information concerning worldwide infant mortality rates and other topics related to children's welfare. (See Address Listing in Extra-Know-How Section.)

Discuss possible solutions to various forms of pollution as they relate to a healthy heritage for future generations of children.

Invite a member of a local children's hospital to present various audiovisual programs concerning children's surgery, birth defects/handicaps, terminal illness, and other topics.

Write a class letter to the school nurse for information on positive health care habits and nutrition.

Black Hawk, American Indian leader, died 1838

(See Biography Data in Extra-Know-How Section.)

William C. Gorgas, American army surgeon-general, born 1854

(See Biography Data in Extra-Know-How Section.)

(See activities under January 7, "Panama Canal ....")

Thomas Wolfe, American writer, born 1900

(See Biography Data in Extra-Know-How Section.)

Discuss the concept behind the title of one of Wolfe's books, *You Can't Go Home Again.*

First female U.S. senator, Rebecca L. Felton, appointed to a short term, 1922

Find out how many women have been in the U.S. Senate and how many currently are senators.

Investigate the qualifications required for becoming a U.S. senator.

Woody Guthrie, American composer who wrote the song, "This Land Is Your Land," died 1967

Obtain a recording of the song and analyze the words; find pictures of America to match the lyrics, or make a slide showing to accompany the song.

Use Task Card #67 to learn how to make a slide/sound show.

Invite students to write lyrics to the melody entitled, "This Is Your School."

October 4

Frederic Remington, American artist of frontier life and horses, born 1861
(See Biography Data in Extra-Know-How Section.)
Obtain copies of Remington's art and share with class.
Paint scenes based upon American frontier life.

Rutherford B. Hayes, nineteenth president of the United States, born 1822
(See Biography Data in Extra-Know-How Section.)

Edward Stratemeyer, author of both the Nancy Drew and Hardy Boys mystery stories, born 1862
(See Biography Data in Extra-Know-How Section.)
Find out the two pseudonyms under which he wrote each of the series of books.
Encourage students to select one of the mystery story books to read and then have them make an oral presentation promoting the book.
Arrange a book display of the many Nancy Drew and Hardy Boys mystery stories; ask students to choose a title from one of the books to serve as a theme for story-writing, games, and art experiences.

Damon Runyon, American writer, born 1880
(See Biography Data in Extra-Know-How Section.)
Explain that "Damon Runyon" is a *nom de plume.* Ask students to define that phrase; find out the difference between *nom de plume* and pseudonym.

"Dick Tracy" comic strip first published, 1931
Obtain a newspaper copy of this particular strip; share with the class; eliminate the given captions and encourage students to substitute their own dialogues.
Discuss the point of why the adventures of Dick Tracy would be termed a "comic" strip.
Use Task Card #68 for information on comic-lifts.

Sputnik, **first "artificial" satellite** launched by the USSR, 1957
Review the events and impact of this feat in the post-*Sputnik* years in America, such as financial allocations from the National Science Foundation to stimulate research and the implementation of space technology; relate the nation's reaction to *Sputnik* to all areas of the American spirit of competition.
Explain that "Sputnik" in English means "fellow-traveler"; encourage students to trace the advances made in space technology since 1957—in both America and in Russia.

October 5

Gregorian calendar adopted by Britain and its American colonies, 1582
Present information about the Gregorian calendar (which months have 30 days, the reason for leap years, etc.).
Find out how the Gregorian calendar differs from the former Julian calendar.
Investigate how long it was before England and her American colonies accepted the change to the Gregorian calendar.
Discuss the point that specific dates in the world's history have necessarily been altered due to the various modifications in the calendars.
(See activities under September 14, "Gregorian calendar ....")

Jonathan Edwards, American preacher, born 1703
(See Biography Data in Extra-Know-How Section.)
Locate copies of Edwards' sermons which reflect messages of fire and brimstone; talk about the strict Calvinist teachings in the early years of New England.

Tecumseh, American Indian leader, killed in battle, 1813
(See Biography Data in Extra-Know-How Section.)

Chester A. Arthur, twenty-first president of the United States, born 1830
(See Biography Data in Extra-Know-How Section.)
Find out what specific event led to Arthur's becoming president.
Obtain a picture of Arthur; discuss what "mutton chops" are.

Ray A. Kroc, founder of McDonald's Corporation, born 1902
(See Biography Data in Extra-Know-How Section.)
Investigate the history of McDonald's. (An excellent source is to be found in the book *Made in America*, by Murray Suid and Ron Harris.)
Create an original advertising gimmick related to McDonald's foods.
Suggest a new item that might be added to McDonald's menu.
Find out the nutritional value of various fast foods.

6,000 push-ups performed by a 16-year-old male, 1965
Introduce the *Guinness Book of Records*, by Norris and Ross McWhirter; invite students to find a record in the reference book that they would like to try to surpass.
Explain the purpose of push-ups and the proper way to do push-ups; hold a school-wide physical fitness program.

October 6

George Westinghouse, American inventor, born 1846
(See Biography Data in Extra-Know-How Section.)
Encourage students to count the number of electrical appliances in their houses and garages.

LeCorbusier (Charles E. Jeanneret), Swiss architect, born 1887
(See Biography Data in Extra-Know-How Section.)
Explain that LeCorbusier introduced new and radical ideas concerning the technical and aesthetic problems of building; ask interested students to investigate LeCorbusier's famous "Citrohan" model which introduced totally new construction methods.
Find out what famous building in New York LeCorbusier helped to design.
(See activities under June 8, "Frank Lloyd Wright ....")

Thomas Edison's first motion picture shown, 1889
Show a motion picture on Edison's accomplishments in acknowledgment of this particular achievement.
Review Task Card #14 to learn more about film in motion.

Thor Heyerdahl, Norwegian explorer, born 1914
(See Biography Data in Extra-Know-How Section.)
Share Heyerdahl's book *Kon Tiki* with the class.

October 7

Carbon paper patented by Ralph Wedgewood, 1806
Encourage students to experiment with a piece of carbon paper; discuss the advantages and disadvantages of using carbon paper to produce multiple copies; consider whether carbon copies are less used since the advent of photocopy machines.
Investigate what the chemical element of carbon is and what it is called in its impure state; find out the many uses of carbon.

First double-decked steamboat arrived at New Orleans, 1816
Obtain a photograph of a steamboat; invite students to create a stylized drawing of a double-decked steamboat.
Investigate the operating principles of a steamboat.

First U.S. railroad (metal tracks for horse-drawn wagons) opened, 1826
Trace the development of railway transportation in America.
Find maps and other data for information about how many miles of major railroad track currently exist in the United States.

James Whitcomb Riley, American poet, born 1849
(See Biography Data in Extra-Know-How Section.)
Find out why Riley is referred to as the "Hoosier Poet."
Share selections from Riley's *Rhymes of Childhood.*

Ten-day Pony Express system officially discontinued (as a result of the new telegraph service which was able to transmit information within seconds), 1861

Name other practices or activities which have been eliminated as newer, more efficient means have been developed; consider, too, the increasing speed with which change is occurring, thus requiring adaptation.

Discuss modern media's effect upon information dissemination.

October 8

Great Chicago Fire, causing financial damages of $196 million, occurred, 1871

Trace the development of Chicago, the "Second City," since 1871.

(See Data-Detail in Extra-Know-How Section, "Mrs. O'Leary's Cow," [a song with words that describe the legendary cause of the fire.])

Trace the derivation of and define the word "conflagration."

Peshtigo Fire, considered to be the most disastrous forest fire in history, occurred in Peshtigo, Wisconsin and spread to Michigan, 1871

Explain that approximately 90% of forest fires are caused by accidents and only 10% by lightning; discuss the loss of life and the damage to watersheds as a result of forest fires. Talk about nature's occasional need to destroy in order to regenerate and restore the balance of nature.

Investigate modern methods of forest fire-fighting; find out what "controlled fires" are and their purposes.

Write to Smokey the Bear to find out information about fire prevention. (See Address Listing in Extra-Know-How Section.)

(See activities under October Special Weeks, "National Forest ... " and October Special Weeks, "Fire Prevention ....")

Edward Rickenbacker, American aviator, born 1890

(See Biography Data in Extra-Know-How Section.)

Explain that Rickenbacker was adrift in the Pacific Ocean for 27 days following his plane's crash in World War II; comment also upon the fact that Rickenbacker received the Congressional Medal of Honor; ask students to find out the background of this award and to name other famous recipients of the medal.

Write a creative account of being afloat in the Pacific Ocean for a number of days and the various feelings and thoughts experienced in the process; include innovative techniques of survival.

October 9

Leif Erikson Day (commemorates the alleged landing of the Viking explorer on the North American mainland, about 1000 A.D.)

Find supporting evidence to discuss the issue of whether Columbus or Erikson was the first European to have arrived on the American continent; consider the importance of accurate record-keeping to validate one's experiences.

Study Viking ships and look for the various ornamentations that were a part of the stern of each ship; ask students to design a similar ornamentation out of soap.

Alfred Dreyfus, French military officer, born 1858

(See Biography Data in Extra-Know-How Section.)

See activities under January 13, "J'accuse, Emile Zola's ....")

Otto Young Schnering, pioneer of the "nickel candy bar" and founder of the Curtis Candy Company, born 1891

(See Biography Data in Extra-Know-How Section.)

Ask students to make a graph representing the range of classmates' favorite candy bars.

Invite students to design a wrapper for a candy bar and then to create a commercial for it.

Examine the wrapper of a candy bar to learn of the ingredients, remembering that glucose, dextrose, and sucrose are all forms of sugar.

John Lennon, British singer, born 1940

(See Biography Data in Extra-Know-How Section.)

Review Task Card #27 to portray the Beatles.

Investigate the circumstances surrounding Lennon's death; discuss public figures' vulnerability to attacks by publicity seekers and others.

October 10

China's National Day, commemorating the anniversary of the overthrow of the Manchu Dynasty
 Discuss what a dynasty is; make a timeline of the Chinese dynasties. Make a second timeline representing the royal monarchies of England or other countries.
 Report on topics such as how long the United States was without diplomatic relations with China, the relationship between Taiwan (Formosa) and the People's Republic of China, the life and times of Chiang Kai-Shek.
 Make an in-depth study of the Manchu Dynasty, including the causes and effects of its overthrow.
 Explore Chinese folklore, customs, and culture.
 Experience Chinese foods; try making rice sticks.

Giuseppe Verdi, Italian opera composer, born 1813
 (See Biography Data in Extra-Know-How Section.)
 Familiarize students with the stories of *Rigoletto, La Traviata,* and/or *Aïda,* and enjoy listening to various selections.

U.S. Naval Academy opened in Annapolis, Maryland, 1845
 Write to the U.S. Naval Academy for brochures and other information. (See Address Listing in Extra-Know-How Section.)
 Invite a representative from the local U.S. naval recruiting office to speak about careers in the navy.

Tuxedos formally introduced in Tuxedo Park, New York, 1886
 Ask students to bring mail-order catalogs to class; examine them for the various pictures of evening and formal wear; talk about and find pictures of the various types of formal attire throughout American history.
 Discuss the various parts of a tuxedo; ask students to design a formal or casual piece of wearing apparel and to suggest a name for it in association with a given geographical place name.

Pledge of Allegiance to the American flag first written, 1892
 Investigate the various reasons that caused the writing of the pledge.
 Find out if any other nations have a formal pledge to their national flag.
 Discuss alternative activities that might substitute for a daily pledge to the flag, such as projects related to becoming better citizens in the school, nation, and the world.
 (See Data-Detail in Extra-Know-How Section, "U.S. Flag and Flag Day—History".)
 (See activities under December 28, "Pledge of ....")

Spiro Agnew, vice-president to Richard Nixon, resigned from office, 1973
 Find out the reason for Agnew's resignation; investigate who the one other vice-president was who resigned.
 Obtain the reference book *The Vice-Presidents of the United States,* by John and Emalie Feerick.

October 11

General Casimir Pulaski Memorial Day (commemorates the death of the Polish-American Revolutionary War figure, 1779)
 Discuss the motivation involved in people having left their homelands to fight as military commanders for the revolutionary cause in America (such as Pulaski, Lafayette, Von Steuben).
 Investigate the history of Fort Pulaski in the state of Georgia.

Henry John Heinz, founder of the H. J. Heinz Company, born 1844
 (See Biography Data in Extra-Know-How Section.)
 Remind students of the Heinz Company's advertising slogan, "57 varieties"; make a class list of the varieties.
 Read the biography of H. J. Heinz, *The Good Provider,* by Robert C. Alberts.

Eleanor Roosevelt, American humanitarian, born 1884
 (See Biography Data in Extra-Know-How Section.)
 Investigate the many accomplishments of this First Lady, such as her assistance in establishing UNICEF.
 Discuss her statement: "No one can make you feel inferior without your consent."

First European adding machine patented, 1887
 Invite a sales representative to demonstrate the various types of adding machines and calculators and their respective advantages and disadvantages.

Obtain an adding machine and encourage students to practice to improve their skills in speed and accuracy.

Investigate other forms of adding machines, such as the abacus, that have historically served as aids in computing numbers.

Use Task Card #69 for computation skills and activities that involve the paper rolls used in adding machines.

Daughters of the American Revolution formed, 1890

Investigate the background of the organization by inviting a member to class to discuss its purpose and accomplishments.

Jerome Robbins, American choreographer, born 1918

(See Biography Data in Extra-Know-How Section.)

Trace the derivation of the word "choreography."

Obtain a recording of a ballet or of another appropriate selection; ask students to listen to the music, to imagine various physical movements, to create the choreography, and to perform what they have created.

Ecumenical Council convened by Pope John XXIII, 1962

Explain that "ecumenical" refers to the entire Christian church, as opposed to the limits of denominations or sects; encourage students to think about various word derivations and to identify an existing word or to create a "neologism" that would encompass all religious and belief systems.

October 12

Columbus Day (commemorates the alleged discovery of America by Christopher Columbus — now generally observed on the second Monday of October)

(See activities under October Variable Dates, "Columbus Day.")

Mississippi Territory organized, 1798

Find out the area that was represented by the Mississippi Territory.

Locate the state of Mississippi; find the latitude and longitude of its capital city; trace the background of the name "Mississippi."

Initiate a study on the Gulf coastal plain in America.

Ten-million-dollar U.S. Treasury note issued, 1837

Investigate the background of a treasury note.

Ten electric generators installed at Niagara Falls by the Westinghouse Electric Corporation, forming the first large power grid, 1895

Define what hydroelectric power is.

Investigate how electricity is transmitted from power plants for daily use elsewhere.

Discuss the advantages and disadvantages of governmental and industrial joint enterprises; also talk about the cooperative effort between the United States and Canada that Niagara Falls represents.

October 13

U.S. Navy originated, 1775

Investigate the reasons at that time for establishing a navy.

(See activities under October 10, "U.S. Naval Academy ....")

Cornerstone of the president's house in Washington, DC laid by George Washington, 1792

Investigate what wording was used on the White House cornerstone.

Encourage students to create appropriate wording for the cornerstones of local official buildings.

Review Reproducible #22 for information about the structure of the interior of the current executive mansion.

Find out who the first president was to have lived in the original structure.

Investigate under which presidential administration the executive mansion became officially known as the "White House."

(See activities under September 18, "Cornerstone of ....")

Rudolph Virchow, German pathologist who discovered the disease of leukemia, born 1821

(See Biography Data in Extra-Know-How Section.)

Find out information about the disease of leukemia.

Investigate what preparation is necessary to become a pathologist.

(See activities under April Month-long Observances, "Cancer-Control ....")

B'nai B'rith (Sons of the Covenant), an organization of brotherhood, founded, 1843

Write to the Anti-Defamation League for catalogs that contain information on intergroup relations. (See Address Listing in Extra-Know-How Section.)

(See activities under February Special Weeks, "Brotherhood Week ....")

October 14

William Penn, American Quaker leader who endured much hardship due to his religious beliefs, born 1644

(See Biography Data in Extra-Know-How Section.)

Explain that the state of Pennsylvania was named after William Penn; find out the meaning of "sylvania"; encourage students to create place names, using unusual word units with their own names.

Dwight D. Eisenhower, thirty-fourth president of the United States, born 1890

(See Biography Data in Extra-Know-How Section.)

Investigate how many American presidents have been military generals; research Eisenhower's accomplishments as the Supreme Commander of Allied Forces in Europe during World War II.

E. E. Cummings (e. e. cummings), American poet, born 1894

(See Biography Data in Extra-Know-How Section.)

Discuss Cummings' use of lower-case letters for proper names; explore what the term "poetic license" means.

Create a poem, or copy a familiar poem, and replace the upper-case letters with lower-case ones.

Share selections of Cummings' poetry.

First flight faster than sound accomplished, 1947

Investigate how fast sound travels; find out how much faster the record flight was; investigate the effects of "breaking the sound barrier."

Discuss the "instantness" of sound waves as related to radio and television broadcasting, music concerts, conversation—as opposed to the length of time required in writing and reading.

First live U.S. television broadcast transmitted from an in-orbit spaceship (*Apollo 7*), 1968

Fantasize distant areas from which broadcasts may originate in the future.

October 15

World Poetry Day (commemorates the international ties which literature and poetry, in particular, represent)

Introduce poetry through poems which represent different styles and rhythm patterns.

Explain that much current poetry is in the form of popular music; invite students to listen to a favorite song and to record the words in poetry form.

C. P. Snow, English writer, born 1905

(See Biography Data in Extra-Know-How Section.)

Discuss Snow's thesis in *The Two Cultures* that literary scholars are reluctant to attempt to understand science.

Research Snow's role in terms of U.S.-China foreign policy relations.

Nikita Khrushchev deposed as head of the USSR, 1964

Find out how a leader in Russia is relieved of power.

Investigate the current political structure of the USSR.

October 16

Noah Webster, American lexicographer, born 1758

Define and trace the derivation of the word "lexicographer"; make a list of words which begin with the word unit "lexi" and which are related in meaning.

Find the background of the meaning of "sesquipedalian" (given to using long words).

(See activities under April 14, "First edition ....")

Marie Antoinette, queen of France, guillotined, 1793
Investigate the reign of Louis XVI and Marie Antoinette.
Find out if the response to the bread famine, "Let them eat cake," is justly attributed to her.
Research the historical practice of guillotine executions.

Harpers Ferry raided by John Brown, 1859
(See activities under May 9, "John Brown ....")

Eugene O'Neill, American playwright and winner of both Pulitzer and Nobel prizes, born 1888
(See Biography Data in Extra-Know-How Section.)
Explain that O'Neill's plays are known for stage effects such as masks and sound devices; encourage students to create their own script, using various stage effects, and then to act out their play.
Discuss play-related vocabulary, i.e., playwright, script, sets, props, stage lighting, stage fright, stage directions, director, make-up artist, producer, prompter, playbill.
Introduce the student magazine *Plays*; write to Colon Drama Plays & Co. for information concerning subscriptions. (See Address Listing in Extra-Know-How Section.)

Rita Hayworth, American actress, born 1918
(See Biography Data in Extra-Know-How Section.)

World Food Day (in commemoration of the establishment of the Food and Agricultural Organization of the United Nations—FAO, 1945)
Ask students to bring in articles from current newspaper and news magazines which refer to population and hunger problems in the world.
Find out what the meaning of the "green revolution" is; discuss what the advantages and disadvantages are of intensive farming techniques; brainstorm ideas for a "marine revolution."

October 17

Process for making steel patented by Sir Henry Bessemer, English inventor, 1855
Investigate what the Bessemer process is.
Develop a class list of products that are made of steel.

Charles Herbert Kraft, manufacturer of blended and pasteurized cheese, born 1880
(See Biography Data in Extra-Know-How Section.)
Discuss the various types of cheese and how cheese is made.
Encourage students to create a recipe using cheese.
(See activities under June 4, "Roquefort cheese ....")

Arthur Miller, American playwright and recipient of the Pulitzer Prize, born 1915
(See Biography Data in Extra-Know-How Section.)
(See activities under October 16, "Eugene O'Neill ....")

New York Times, Sunday edition, reported as weighing 7 pounds, 14 ounces, 1965
Find out how much a local Sunday newspaper weighs.
Invite a printer or paper manufacturer to class to display and discuss the variety of different weights of paper.
Initiate a class project involving the conservation of paper.
(See activities under October Special Weeks, "National Newspaper ....")

October 18

Mason-Dixon line established, 1767
On a U.S. map, trace the Mason-Dixon line.
Find out who Mason and Dixon were and why they established the theoretical line.

Football rules in America established, 1873
Discuss current football rules in both amateur and professional football.

Invite a football player from the local high school to come to class dressed in his football uniform to answer questions about rules and regulations.

(See activities under May 3, "Johnny Unitas ....")

Mata Hari, Dutch-Indonesian World War I spy, executed, 1917

Investigate the incident and the political implications of Mata Hari's execution.

Discuss what the life of a spy might be like; research the lives of other war spies and the underground network in France during World War II.

(See activities under August 7, "Mata Hari ....")

Melina Mercouri, Greek singer-actress, born 1925

(See Biography Data in Extra-Know-How Section.)

Enjoy selections of Mercouri's singing; find out in how many languages she is able to sing.

Use of cyclamates in foods halted by the U.S. Department of Health, Education and Welfare (HEW), 1969

Discuss the term "cyclamate," its make-up, and its purpose; name the various sugar substitutes which evolved once cyclamates were not available, such as saccharine and aspartame.

Hold a debate as to whether the government has the right/responsibility to intervene in consumers' freedom to purchase.

October 19

Yorktown surrendered in the American Revolutionary War by England's General Cornwallis, 1781

Find out the significance of this event. Locate Yorktown, Virginia; find out information about the Colonial National Historical Park in Yorktown.

Investigate the contribution made to the Continental Army by Admiral Grasse, a French naval officer, in the Battle of Chesapeake Bay.

Charles E. Merrill, investment banker, born 1885

(See Biography Data in Extra-Know-How Section.)

Explain that Merrill became successful by having initiated several innovations in his business; for instance, he was the first to pay stock brokers with salaries rather than commission, the first to provide brokerage counseling, the first to advertise in popular publications, and the first to provide service to small investors.

Find out in what year the Merrill, Lynch, Pierce, Fenner & Bean firm was formed; find out what the current name of the company is.

Review various stock quotations in the financial section of a newspaper; look into various investment opportunities.

Investigate the career of a stockbroker.

Exports to Cuba embargoed by the United States, 1960

Discuss the impact of this event.

Find out the meaning of the term "embargo"; create a sociodrama involving an act of embargo, as related to the classroom.

October 20

Christopher Wren, English architect of St. Paul's Cathedral, born 1632

(See Biography Data in Extra-Know-How Section.)

Explain that Wren is described as having been a very precocious youngster who was talented in many different fields of endeavor; ask students to define the word "precocious."

Develop a class list of Wren's many accomplishments in astronomy and other areas of science, as well as in architecture.

Find out what historic events have taken place in St. Paul's Cathedral.

Explain that Wren was buried in St. Paul's Cathedral and that his epitaph reads, "Si monumentum requiris, circumspice" (If you seek his monument, look around you); ask students to ponder what words they would one day like to have inscribed as their epitaphs.

Describe the basic aspects of Georgian architecture with which Wren is associated.

John Dewey, American educator/philosopher, born 1859
   (See Biography Data in Extra-Know-How Section.)
   Emphasize part of Dewey's educational philosophy involving the concept and practice of "learning by doing"; encourage students to teach the class a particular idea by involving the learners in the process of doing or experiencing.

Sir James Chadwick, English researcher on radioactivity, born 1891
   (See Biography Data in Extra-Know-How Section.)
   Explain that Chadwick won the Nobel Prize for his discovery of the neutron and the proof that neutrons carry no electrical charge.
   (See activities under July 16, "First atomic ....")

Art Buchwald, American columnist and humorist, born 1925
   (See Biography Data in Extra-Know-How Section.)
   Obtain copies of Buchwald's humorous writing, share with the class, and discuss his style of writing; encourage students to develop a parody.
   Invite a columnist from the local newspaper to discuss writing as a career.

October 21

International Whale-Watching Day
   Write to the First Society of Whale Watchers for information. (See Address Listing in Extra-Know-How Section.)
   Discuss the different types of whales; find out the purpose of water being emitted from the spout; draw pictures of whales.
   Investigate the uses of whale oil and whale skin.
   Refer to the theme of the story in the *Bible*, "Jonah and the Whale," and suggest to students to pretend that they have been swallowed whole by a whale; invite creative writing or discussion about their imagined experiences in that situation.
   (See activities under October Special Weeks, "International Whale ....")

First U.S. aqueduct water supply system designed and built by Benjamin Latrobe, 1801
   Define and trace the derivation of the word "aqueduct"; list other words which contain the word units of either "aqu" or "duct."
   Investigate other water supply projects, such as those associated with the Tennessee River, Owens River, Columbia River, Colorado River, and the Feather River.

Alfred Nobel, Swedish chemist/inventor, born 1833
   (See Biography Data in Extra-Know-How Section.)
   Explain that Nobel is often described as the inventor of nitroglycerine, which he was not (nitroglycerine was discovered in 1847 by Ascanio Sobrero); Nobel developed a detonator and a process of detonation which was patented as dynamite; he also combined nitroglycerine with guncotton which produced blasting gelatin; later he developed ballistite, another explosive. Alfred Nobel believed that his explosives were so destructive that they would serve as a deterrent to war; but very quickly he became concerned about the misuse of dynamite; this concern was one of the major factors involved in his decision to create the Nobel Prize, an award intended to recognize outstanding achievement in the areas of chemistry, medicine/physiology, physics, literature, and peace.
   Discuss the positive uses of dynamite; consider the term "dynamite" as it is used figuratively or colloquially; talk about the meaning of the related words, "dynamism," "dynamic," "dynamics."
   Explore the term "blowing-up" as related to an explosion of dynamite and also as related to a burst of temper; make a class list of other multiple-meaning words which are not considered to be homographs because they basically originate with the same meaning—as opposed to the homographs, such as "homer" (homerun) and "homer" (a unit of measure); make lists of various homophones (heir, air) and homonyms (meet, meat).

Islands of San Juan in Puget Sound, as claimed by both the United States and by England, awarded to the United States by an arbitrator, Emperor William I of Germany, 1872
   Locate Puget Sound on a map; find out the differences and similarities between the two geographical terms, "sound" and "strait."
   Discuss the word "arbitrator"; relate the discussion to playground disputes and the possibilities of arbitration in that setting.

First electric light demonstrated by Thomas Edison, 1879
  Investigate the parts of a light bulb.

October 22

Franz Liszt, Hungarian composer and pianist, born 1811
  (See Biography Data in Extra-Know-How Section.)
  Explain that Liszt is known for his études, concertos, and symphonic or tone poems; find out the meaning of these terms.
  Obtain recordings of Liszt's "Liebesträume," "The Hungarian Rhapsodies," or "Les Préludes" and enjoy listening.

Collis P. Huntington, American railroad magnate, born 1821
  (See Biography Data in Extra-Know-How Section.)
  Investigate Huntington's role in the development of the Southern Pacific Railroad.

Samuel Houston inaugurated as the first president of the Republic of Texas, 1826
  Investigate the Battle of San Jacinto in which Houston captured Santa Anna.
  Explain that Houston was governor of Texas several years after it had become a state, but Houston was removed from office due to his refusal to join the Confederacy; discuss the sacrifice/satisfaction experienced when one stands on principle; ask students to relate personal situations in which they chose to stand by their principles and what the outcome was.

Leon Trotsky, Russian revolutionary, born 1879
  (See Biography Data in Extra-Know-How Section.)
  Research bolshevism and the Bolshevik October Revolution of 1917.
  Name other individuals who have been considered revolutionaries during their time, such as Thomas Jefferson; include current personalities also.

First Metropolitan Opera House opened, 1883
  Obtain a children's book about opera; share the story of a favorite opera; enjoy a recording of that particular opera.
  Discuss why many operas are written in either German or Italian; ask students if they would prefer that operas be sung in English or if they think that something would be lost in the translation.

Naval blockade of Cuba ordered by President Kennedy, 1962
  Find out the background for Kennedy's decision to blockade Cuba.
  Discuss the components of both macro- and micro- decision-making, i.e., gathering all available data and information, seeking advice from various sources, considering the outcome, and being willing to take responsibility for the final decision.

October 23

First day of the zodiac period, Scorpio, the Scorpion (through November 21)
  (See Data-Detail in Extra-Know-How Section, "Notes on Astrology.")

Departure of the swallows from the Mission San Juan Capistrano, California, which, according to legend, marks the anniversary of the death of St. John Capistrano, 1456
  Discuss the significance of legends, myths, and old wives' tales in nearly all cultures.
  (See activities under March 19, "Swallows allegedly ....")

First plastic surgery operation performed, 1814
  Investigate the career of a plastic surgeon; find out about the specialist areas of implantations, neoplasty, osteoplasty.
  Find out about plastic surgery and its potential for helping victims of other skin problems, as well as for meeting various cosmetic needs.

Johnny Carson, American television entertainer, born 1925
  (See Biography Data in Extra-Know-How Section.)
  Discuss the impact of radio and television talk shows.

Pelé, Brazilian soccer player, born 1940
(See Biography Data in Extra-Know-How Section.)
Invite a representative from the American Youth Soccer Organization to visit class.
Investigate the playing records of various professional soccer teams.

October 24

United Nations Day (commemorates the adoption of the United Nations Charter, 1945)
(See activities under January 9, "U.N. Headquarters ....")

Anthony van Loeuwenhoek, Dutch inventor of the microscope, born 1632
(See Biography Data in Extra-Know-How Section.)
Discuss the advantages and disadvantages of a microscope.
Investigate the prefix "micro," and find other words which begin with this prefix.
Review Reproducible #23 to learn about the parts of a microscope.

Sarah J. B. Hale, author of "Mary Had a Little Lamb," born 1788
(See Biography Data in Extra-Know-How Section.)
Review the song "Mary Had a Little Lamb," and create parodies to accompany the melody.

Record of having been the first person to go over Niagara Falls in a barrel established by Anna Taylor, 1901
Discuss the motivation for attempting such feats; investigate the various challenges that Evel Knievel has attempted.
Encourage students to answer the following question, "If you could do one spectacular event, what would it be?"

October 25

Johann Strauss, Austrian composer and conductor who surpassed his father in popularity, born 1825
(See Biography Data in Extra-Know-How Section.)
Create a timeline of the famous Strauss family.
Explain that Strauss wrote more than 400 waltzes, including "The Blue Danube" and "Tales from the Vienna Woods," as well as operettas, such as *Die Fledermaus* (the bat); enjoy listening to selections of Strauss' music.
(See activities under February 13, " 'Blue Danube' ....")

Charge of the Light Brigade in the Crimean War staged, 1854
Investigate the dates, causes and effects, and the countries involved in the Crimean War.
Enjoy the poem *Charge of the Light Brigade,* by Alfred Lord Tennyson.

Pablo Picasso, Spanish artist, born 1881
(See Biography Data in Extra-Know-How Section.)
Play the recording of Paul McCartney's "Picasso's Last Words: Drink to Me" on the album *Band on the Run,* by Apple Records.
Obtain prints of Picasso's painting that represent the various periods of his career; discuss the reasons that contribute to artists' changes in style.

Richard E. Byrd, American aviator/explorer, born 1888
(See Biography Data in Extra-Know-How Section.)
(See activities under May 9, "North Pole ....")

U.S. coast-to-coast air service started by Trans World Airlines (TWA), 1930
Investigate what the early transnational passenger planes were like.
Invite a representative from TWA or from a local travel bureau to visit class to describe the background of air passenger service; request that the visitor bring a map showing the various flight patterns across the country; ask students to select a flight they would especially like to take and the reason for their choice.

October 26

Erie Canal opened, 1825
Find out where the Erie Canal is and the original purpose for having constructed it.
Introduce the song "Erie Canal" and discuss the meaning of the words.

Charles William Post, founder of Post breakfast cereals, born 1854
(See Biography Data in Extra-Know-How Section.)
Make a survey of the most popular cereals, according to students in the classroom. (See Conducting a Survey Data in Extra-Know-How Section.)
Design a cereal box for a Post cereal.
Create an original cereal treat.
Develop a script for a commercial to advertise a cereal product.

Mahalia Jackson, American gospel singer, born 1911
(See Biography Data in Extra-Know-How Section.)
Determine what a gospel singer is; investigate the background of gospel singing as related to the early experiences of many professional jazz singers.

October 27

James Cook, English explorer of the South Pacific, born 1728
(See Biography Data in Extra-Know-How Section.)
Explain that Cook, like several explorers, attempted to no avail to find a water passage through North America; however, Cook explored New Zealand and the east coast of Australia and, in so doing, disproved the rumor that there was an immense southern continent.
Find out how Cook was able to prevent the disease of scurvy during his expeditions.

Theodore Roosevelt, twenty-sixth president of the United States, born 1858
(See Biography Data in Extra-Know-How Section.)
Explain that Roosevelt's childhood experiences, due to physical disabilities of weak eyesight and a slight build, caused him pain and feelings of being discriminated against; as a young adult he managed to pursue a variety of sports and to make a success of himself professionally. Think of other individuals who have chosen to move beyond their individual handicaps. Consider how his earlier experiences may have led him to his over compensating actions, such as his commitment to "the strenuous life."
Investigate Roosevelt's various beliefs, such as regulation of big business ("trust busting"), conservation of natural resources, "big stick" policy, "dollar diplomacy," and an "Open Door" in China.
Trace the background of Roosevelt's statements and discuss the meaning: "There can be no divided allegiance here. We have room for but one flag.... We have room for but one language...." "Speak softly and carry a big stick."
Find out the accomplishment for which Roosevelt was awarded the Nobel Peace Prize.

Macy's Department Store in New York City opened, 1858
Conduct a discussion about the concept of a department store, the role and responsibility of a department store manager, the margins of profit, wholesale vs. keystone prices, increased prices to offset costs of shoplisting, advertising, window displays and other merchandising expenditures; explore such terms as "overhead" and "leader" items used to draw customers into a retail store.

Boss Tweed (William Marcy Tweed) arrested for Tammany Hall corruption, 1871
Discuss corruption as it is found in government, business, and other institutions.
Investigate the original purpose of the Tammany Society.

October 28

Statue of Liberty dedicated, 1886
Explain that the statue was presented to the United States by the Franco-American Union to commemorate the French and American revolutions; investigate the statue's original title.
Review Task Card #64 for a copy of the poem, "Give Me Your Tired, Your Poor," by Emma Lazarus; analyze the words of the poem in terms of immigration. (The music score was subsequently composed to fit the poem.)

Investigate the overall height and weight of the statue.
Review Reproducible #21 for math activities related to the statue.

Volstead Act, enforcing the Eighteenth Amendment on prohibition, passed by the U.S. Congress, 1919
Explain that the act was passed by Congress over President Wilson's veto; discuss the point that the word "veto" is Latin for "I forbid." Review the "balance of power" concept in American government — among the executive, legislative, and judicial branches.

Jonas Salk, American scientist and discoverer of antipolio serum, born 1914
(See Biography Data in Extra-Know-How Section.)
(See activities under January Month-long Observances, "March of ....")

October 29

James Boswell, Scottish biographer of Samuel Johnson (a dominant literary figure in London), born 1740
(See Biography Data in Extra-Know-How Section.)
Discuss what is involved in compiling extensive biographic data about one individual; explain that Boswell met Johnson; ask students what effect his having met Johnson might have had on the biographical work.
(See activities under September 18, "Samuel Johnson ....")

Othaniel Charles Marsh, American paleontologist, born 1831
(See Biography Data in Extra-Know-How Section.)
Discuss how fossil remains help scientists to learn about life in past geological periods; explain that Marsh discovered the pterodactyl and about 1,000 fossil vertebrates, and that his findings gave substantial support to Charles Darwin's evolutionary theory.
(See Data-Detail in Extra-Know-How Section, "Explanation of Geophysical Dating Instruments.")

Stock Market collapsed, 1929
Discuss the international impact of the stock market collapse; investigate or surmise what human interest events may have occurred that day.
Invite a stock broker to class to explain the concepts of private stocks and bonds, as well as federal and municipal bonds.

Men drafted according to a numbers lottery for the U.S. armed services, 1940
Discuss what other methods or what sets of criteria might be used in the selection of military recruits.
Stage a lottery concerning a particular job in the school.
(See activities under April 1, "First U.S. conscription ... " and September 16, "Selective Service ....")

National Organization for Women (NOW) established in America, 1966
Discuss the organization's goal of human liberation for both men and women.
Investigate the current inequities which exist concerning legal and financial privileges, as well as professional job factors.
Research an earlier women's organization, the National Woman Suffrage Association, founded in 1869
(See activities under August 26, "Nineteenth Amendment ....")

October 30

John Adams, second president of the United States, born 1735
(See Biography Data in Extra-Know-How Section.)
Make a class list and briefly identify the descendents of John Adams and his wife, who also became distinguished in American history.

Emily Post, American authority on etiquette, born 1873
(See Biography Data in Extra-Know-How Section.)
Obtain a copy of the *Blue Book of Social Usage*, written by Emily Post; review the etiquette standards at the time Emily Post wrote the book. Discuss how social behavior and practices have changed since that time.
Invite students to create their own book on social usage, describing etiquette for the class or for themselves.

Orson Welles' radio dramatization of H. G. Wells' *War of the Worlds* broadcast, 1938
Obtain a recording of the broadcast (recorded by Evolution Co.) and play it for the class; ask students to portray what they imagined while listening to the record.

Explain that the broadcast led some listeners to panic, thinking the Martians were actually invading the earth; discuss the necessity of investigating the source before overreacting to a particular incident or before perpetuating a false piece of information; introduce the game "Rumor Clinic." (A statement is communicated privately to one student, who in turn tells it to another student; the message is passed on, one to one, to all students; the final message is announced to compare the accuracy with the original statement.)

October 31

Halloween Day
(See Data-Detail in Extra-Know-How Section, "Halloween — History.")
Invite students to design original Halloween costumes and to participate in a parade.
Review safety rules of Halloween; urge students to consider the health significance of eating too much candy.
Encourage students to think of a magic or acrobatic trick to perform before expecting a free treat.
Write creative Halloween stories.

National UNICEF Day
Discuss what the acronym UNICEF stands for (United Nations International Children's Emergency Fund); think of other acronyms.
Write to the UNICEF Council for information. (See Address Listing in Extra-Know-How Section.)
Investigate whether local authorities allow UNICEF money to be collected door to door on Halloween as a substitute for trick or treating.

National Magic Day (since 1926)
Invite students to perform magic tricks.
(See activities under April 6, "Harry Houdini ....")

Juliet Lowe, founder of the American Girl Scouts, born 1860
(See Biography Data in Extra-Know-How Section.)
Trace the history of the organization back to England.
(See activities under March Special Weeks, "Girl Scouts ....")

Nevada admitted to the United States as the thirty-sixth state, 1864
(See States Admitted to the USA Data in Extra-Know-How Section.)

NOVEMBER

As the ninth month in the former calendar, November's name relates to novem, *the Latin word for "nine." The Romans suggested to their emperor, Tiberius Caesar, that the month be renamed in his honor; however, he modestly refused by commenting, "What will you do if you have thirteen emperors and only twelve months?"*

Birthstone: *Topaz*
Flower: *Chrysanthemum*

Use the Find-a-Word Reproducible to preview happenings in November. (See Reproducible Section.)

MONTH-LONG OBSERVANCES

Christmas Seal Campaign (second week of November through December 31)
   Make a list of various lung-related diseases, along with a short description of each.
   Write to the National Tuberculosis and Respiratory Disease Association for information concerning respiratory diseases. (See Address Listing in Extra-Know-How Section.)
   Ask students to bring in Christmas seals from past years.
   Encourage students to design original seals.
   (See activities under March 24, "Discovery of ....")

National Indigestion Season (from Thanksgiving through New Year's Day)
   Discuss what indigestion is, the causes of it, and how to prevent it.
   Suggest that students visit a drugstore or supermarket and make a list of the many products which claim to calm indigestion.
   Ask students to create a radio or television commercial which would advertise a self-designed product used for aiding digestion.
   Use Reproducible #24 to study the parts of the digestive system.

International Aviation Month (November 21 through December 17)
   Introduce a unit on aviation.
   Define the terms: gyroscope, tachometer, pitch indicator, compass, altimeter, bank indicator.
   Write to the Federal Aviation Administration for information concerning international agreements and regulations regarding international flights. (See Address Listing in Extra-Know-How Section.)
   Review Task Cards #36 and #58 for activities on flight.

SPECIAL WEEKS

Cat Week (first Sunday)
   Write to the American Feline Society for information about cats and about the organization. (See Address Listing in Extra-Know-How Section.)
   Collect pictures of cats and assemble a collage.
   Define and discuss the word "feline"; explain that the word unit "ine" refers to "of or pertaining to"; trace the meaning of other words, such as porcine (swine or rat), bovine (ox), equine (horse), porcupine (rodent), canine (dog).

National Children's Book Week (dates vary)

Ask the school librarian to hold a book festival.

Write to the Children's Book Council for information about Newbery and Caldecott award-winning books, as well as for general information about the organization. (See Address Listing in Extra-Know-How Section)

Hold a Book-Jacket Design Fair in which students design a book jacket (dust jacket) for one of their favorite books.

Review Task Card #42 for book activities.

(See activities under February 12, "Randolph Caldecott ... " and June 27, "First Newbery ...."

National Diabetes Week (third Sunday)

Find out the separate effects of sugar and insulin upon a person with diabetes.

Explain that insulin diabetics use insulin (a hormone extracted from the pancreas organ of pigs and calves) in order to reduce the amount of sugar in the system; investigate newer research that has isolated the gene which produces the hormone in rats, thus allowing the possibility of future bacterial "factories" that lessen the dependence upon pigs and calves; consider the significance of this research for diabetics who cannot use insulin due to allergies to pigs and calves; find out also about using human insulin for diabetics.

Investigate the use of the insulin pump.

Invite a diabetic to discuss diabetes and the discipline involved in regulating the diet—that of preventing an oversupply of sugar in the system.

Investigate what insulin shock is.

Write to the American Diabetes Association for further information. (See Address Listing in Extra-Know-How Section.)

Discuss the difference between being a noticeably handicapped person as opposed to being a person with a hidden handicap.

(See activities under April 15, "Insulin made ... " and November 14, "Frederick Banting ....")

National Stamp Collecting Week (third Monday)

Invite students to bring in their various stamp collections to share with the class.

Suggest that students select an individual or a particular cause for which they would enjoy designing a stamp.

Initiate a discussion on the value one might place upon a collection; ask students, in the case of fire, what possession or type of possession would they most want to rescue.

Trace the derivation of the word "philatelist"; initiate a philatelist club.

(See activities under February 15, "First adhesive ....")

National Doubletalk Week (first Sunday)

Discuss what double-talk is and such related terms as: double messages, euphemisms, hidden agendas, filibustering.

Latin America Week (Sunday before Thanksgiving)

Initiate a map or globe study as related to all of Latin America; discuss what countries constitute Latin America and what languages are spoken.

Invite interested students to choose a country, such as Mexico, and research the various Indian languages that are spoken in that country, some of which are not in written form.

Write to the Pan American Union or to the Organization of American States for further information. (See Address Listing in Extra-Know-How Section.)

(See activities under April Special Weeks, "Pan American ....")

VARIABLE DATES

Election Day (first Tuesday after first Monday)

Hold a mock election, including the preliminary activities of petitions, initiatives, referenda, preregistration, and the ballot voting and tallying.

Explain that in some countries where elections are held, many people cannot read or write; discuss alternative ways in which a vote might be cast which does not necessarily involve reading or writing.

Invite a representative from the League of Women Voters to explain the election process and various issues of a forthcoming election.

National Horse Show (first week)

Investigate the various criteria within each classification upon which horses are judged.

Research a unit on the evolution of horses, types of horses, and the care and training of horses.

Invite students to make drawings or paintings of horses and to write a story to accompany their illustrations. Define the word "equestrian."

Read a classic horse story, such as *Black Beauty, Man O' War*, or *The Red Pony*.

Thanksgiving Day (fourth Thursday)

Make a class list of items for which students suggest their gratitude.

Discuss the fact that nearly all cultures throughout the world traditionally have held harvest festivals; trace the particular history of America's celebration of Thanksgiving.

Investigate the relative wealth of natural resources among countries of the world; discuss the fact that America is exceedingly fortunate in having "one very good piece of geography."

(See activities under November 19, "*Mayflower* ship ... " and November 26, "First national ... " and December 4, "America's first ....")

DAYS OF THE MONTH

November 1

All Saints' Day, also known as "All Hallows' Day"

Investigate this holiday as it relates to ancient pagan beliefs and to Halloween.

Authors' Day

Request that the school librarian present a lesson on how to find a book by the author's name.

Invite students to write a letter to their favorite children's author to ask about the career of an author and related information. (Obtain addresses through particular publishers listed in *Books in Print* or through the listing of the author in *Current Biography* or one of the series of *Who's Who*.)

Discuss ideas as to how authors conceive ideas for stories; encourage students to become authors by creating their own stories, complete with a book jacket that highlights their own names. Read aloud *Conversations and Constructions*, by Toby Lurie, and invite students to compose their own poetry.

Suggest that students keep a daily journal to express their thoughts and feelings.

Investigate various types of writing that one might pursue, such as fiction, nonfiction, speechwriting, and journalism, among others.

(See activities under February 12, "Randolph Caldecott ... " and April Special Weeks, "National Library ... " and April 9, "First American ... " and June 27, "First Newbery ....")

Crawford Long, first physician to use ether in surgery, born 1815

(See Biography Data in Extra-Know-How Section.)

Define and trace the derivation of the word "anesthesia"; find out what ether is and how it is administered; name other anesthetics which are currently used.

Explain that Long used ether in surgery just shortly before William Morton used it in dentistry; ask students to consider why certain experiments or discoveries occur about the same time—ones which have not necessarily been developed in collaboration with another individual; discuss the statement, "There's nothing new under the sun."

(See activities under September 30, "Ether used ....")

First weather observation made by the U.S. Weather Bureau, 1870

(See activities under February 9, "U.S. Weather ....")

Stephen Crane, American author, born 1871

(See Biography Data in Extra-Know-How Section.)

Explain that Crane authored the well-known Civil War story *The Red Badge of Courage* without having participated in a war; encourage students to write a story about a particular event in history.

Barbed wire first manufactured in the United States, 1873

Discuss what barbed wire is, the purpose and danger of it, and whether its use is justified.

November 2

Daniel Boone, American frontiersman and wilderness explorer, born 1734

(See Biography Data in Extra-Know-How Section.)

Explain that Daniel Boone explored west on an Indian trail, the "Warrior's Path," and opened up an unsettled area of Kentucky for thousands of pioneers; discuss the quality which is associated with Daniel Boone—curiosity as to what was behind the next mountain.

Obtain a copy of *Daniel Boone*, by James Daugherty, or the recording and accompanying filmstrip, *Daniel Boone: Opening of the Wilderness.*

(See activities under June 7, "Exploration of ....")

Marie Antoinette, French queen, born 1755
(See Biography Data in Extra-Know-How Section.)
(See activities under October 16, "Marie Antoinette ....")

San Francisco Bay sighted by Gaspar de Portolá, 1769
Find out what the factors are that make San Francisco Bay one of the most sheltered natural harbors in the world.

Investigate what famous explorer in the sixteenth century preceded Portolá and others in the exploration of San Francisco Bay.

Trace the history of San Francisco since the days of the Gold Rush.

Write to the San Francisco Chamber of Commerce for information. (See Address Listing in Extra-Know-How Section.)

James K. Polk, eleventh president of the United States, born 1795
(See Biography Data in Extra-Know-How Section.)
Explain that Polk was the first "dark horse" presidential candidate; find out the meaning of this term.

Warren G. Harding, twenty-ninth president of the United States, born 1865
(See Biography Data in Extra-Know-How Section.)
Explain that Harding was the first president for which women were allowed to vote; find out what year the election was.

Investigate the Teapot Dome oil scandal.

North Dakota admitted to the United States as the thirty-ninth state, 1889
(See States Admitted to the USA Data in Extra-Know-How Section.)

South Dakota admitted to the United States as the fortieth state, 1889
(See States Admitted to the USA Data in Extra-Know-How Section.)

Balfour Declaration, pledging British support for a Jewish national home in Palestine, proposed by Arthur Balfour, British foreign secretary, 1917
Research the background of the Balfour Declaration in terms of its intent and its effect.
Investigate the formation of Israel in 1948 and Israel's development subsequent to that time.

Regularly scheduled radio broadcasting in America begun, 1920
Obtain recordings of earlier radio broadcasts and share with the class.
Encourage students to create a radio broadcast, including the use of many sound effects; tape record it for rebroadcast.

First U.S. newsreel theater opened, 1929
Ask students to film a newsreel in the school with either a videotape recorder or a Super 8 camera; suggest that they follow the format of the original "Movietone" newsreels—one world event, one local event, one sports event, and one human interest item; encourage various students to take responsibility for script writing and designing of costumes and props.

November 3

Stephen Austin, Texas patriot, born 1793
(See Biography Data in Extra-Know-How Section.)
Investigate Austin's role in the Texas Revolution.

William Cullen Bryant, American poet and journalist, born 1794
(See Biography Data in Extra-Know-How Section.)
Obtain a copy of the poem "Thanatopsis," a poem about death that Bryant wrote when he was young; study the poem's meaning with the class.

Explain that Bryant also translated Homer's *Iliad* and the *Odyssey* in blank verse; consider the responsibilities involved in translating another's work; find out what blank verse is.

Trace the derivation of the word "thanatopsis"; suggest that students pronounce the words "than" and "thanatopsis" to experience the difference between a voiced and unvoiced "th."

First vehicular tunnel from the United States to a foreign country (Canada) opened, 1830

Find out the location of this particular tunnel.

Investigate what a vehicular tunnel is, the advantages and disadvantages, and the process of constructing a vehicular tunnel.

Ask students to consider what constructive uses there might be for tunneled-out earth.

First national auto show held in America, 1900

Hold an automobile show of teachers' and staff members' cars; make signs which highlight various aspects of the cars; choose a panel of judges to decide upon the categories and to make the final decisions concerning the winners.

Explain that five years earlier, J. Frank Duryea had won the first U.S. automobile race held in Chicago; he drove his car at an average speed of seven and one-half miles per hour. Find out what the current record-setting speeds are in auto racing.

Obtain a copy of *Under the Hood: How Cars Work and How to Keep them Working*, by Robin Lawrie.

November 4

Artificial leg patented, 1846

Contact a local hospital to invite an orthopedist or prosthesis specialist to explain the development of prosthetics and the state of the art.

Discuss the advantages and disadvantages of having an artificial leg.

Create a story concerning the loss of a limb.

Consider the coordinated efforts involved in the development of prosthetics and modern hospital equipment—those of technologists and the medical profession.

James Fraser, American sculptor, born 1876

(See Biography Data in Extra-Know-How Section.)

Explain that Fraser designed the Indian head and buffalo on the pre-1938 five-cent coin; encourage students to bring in their coins so as to examine the designs on various coins, both domestic and foreign.

(See activities under April Special Weeks, "National Coin ....")

Cash register patented, 1879

Visit a local department store to observe a cash register which performs multiple tasks, i.e., totaling, identifying the purchased item, and registering inventory information.

Take a field trip to a supermarket where the goods are automatically coded and checked out by an electric eye.

Write to the National Cash Register Company for historical information and pictures of cash registers. (See Address Listing in Extra-Know-How Section.)

Obtain a toy cash register and arrange a mock store setting; encourage students to practice making change.

Will Rogers, American humorist, author, and actor, born 1879

(See Biography Data in Extra-Know-How Section.)

Enjoy a book of Rogers' famous sayings, such as "It's great to be great, but it's greater to be human"; "Nothing is so stupid as an educated man, once you get him off the subject he is educated in."

Walter Cronkite, American newscaster, born 1916

(See Biography Data in Extra-Know-How Section.)

Invite students to imitate Cronkite's words at the end of his television broadcasts, "And that's the way it is [November 4, 19--], Walter Cronkite, CBS News; Good night."

Listen to a variety of news broadcasters; compare and contrast various aspects of their styles in reporting news.

Investigate what training is necessary to become a radio or television newscaster or a narrator of film documentaries.

Trace the development of the word "news"; point out that coincidentally the letters represent the four directions from which news is generated—*n*orth, *e*ast, *w*est, and *s*outh.

First automobile with air-conditioning marketed, 1939
Discuss the advantages and disadvantages of air-conditioning in a car.

UNESCO established, 1946
Define the word "acronym" and then explain the meaning of each letter in UNESCO (United Nations Educational, Scientific and Cultural Organization).
Discuss the words contained in the Constitution of UNESCO: "Since wars begin in the minds of men, it is in the minds of men that the defense of peace must be constructed"; ask students to consider that global peace may well be dependent upon each individual's sense of inner peace, security, and well-being.
(See activities under January 9, "U.N. Headquarters ....")

November 5

Guy Fawkes Day (commemorates the unsuccessful attempt of Guy Fawkes and others to blow up British houses of Parliament and King James I, 1605)
Explain that the day is still celebrated by burning effigies of Guy Fawkes; define the word "effigy."
Discuss the justification, if any, for commemorating such events; question the wisdom of similarly considering an event such as "Watergate" as worthy of commemoration; ask students to think of other similar incidents.

Eugene V. Debs, American Socialist leader who was jailed for his beliefs, born 1855
(See Biography Data in Extra-Know-How Section.)
Discuss the democratic ideal of allowing citizens to live their lives according to their convictions and principles; consider what kinds of situations make this ideal a difficult one to adhere to.
Investigate what socialism is.
Explore the implications of constitutional rights as outlined in the Bill of Rights, First Amendment.

Will Durant, American historian, born 1885
(See Biography Data in Extra-Know-How Section.)
Explain that Durant and his wife, Ariel, wrote an entire history of the world (10 volumes); ask interested students to create a timeline of the history of the world.

First U.S. automobile patent granted to George B. Selden, 1895
Ask students to design and to describe a futuristic device, such as an individual flying belt. Appoint a student as patent officer; the first application for a patent which is considered acceptable is "stamped" with a patent number; other students who submit acceptable designs of a similar device receive a "patent pending" stamp, and if improvements and modifications are made on the original, new patent numbers can be assigned.
(See activities under October 1, "Model T ....")

Roy Rogers, American cowboy, actor/singer, born 1912
(See Biography Data in Extra-Know-How Section.)

Crossword puzzles first published in America, 1924
Explain the general procedures for working crossword puzzles; obtain a crossword puzzle dictionary and copies of various crossword puzzles, appropriate to the age-level, for students to solve.
Encourage students to create their own crossword puzzles or to investigate other forms of word puzzles.
Review Reproducible #20 for a sample crossword puzzle.
(See activities under April 18, "First crossword ... " and December 21, "First crossword ....")

Franklin Delano Roosevelt elected to this third term as U.S. president, 1940
(See activities under January 30, "Franklin Delano ....")

November 6

John Philip Sousa, American bandleader and composer, born 1854
(See Biography Data in Extra-Know-How Section.)
(See activities under September 26, "John Philip ....")

James Naismith, Canadian-American, founder of the game of basketball, born 1861
(See Biography Data in Extra-Know-How Section.)

(See Data-Detail in Extra-Know-How Section, "Basketball—History.")
Invite another class to play a game of basketball together.

First intercollegiate football game (Rutgers defeated Princeton) held, 1869
Find out the changes in rules and regulations that have developed in college football since 1869.
Discuss the difference between the prefixes "inter" and "intra"; hold an interclass sports activity.
(See activities under May 3, "Johnny Unitas ....")

Anna Sewell, English author of the book *Black Beauty*, born 1871
(See Biography Data in Extra-Know-How Section.)
Obtain a copy of *Black Beauty* and share with the class.

First electric shaver patented, 1923
Discuss the advantages and disadvantages of both the electric and the manual shaver.
Invite students to make fictitious magazine advertisements for electric shavers.
Suggest that students find pictures in magazines (which are printed on clay-bound base paper) and to use an eraser to "shave" off the beards or mustaches they find.
(See activities under March 18, "Electric dry ....")

November 7

Marie Curie, French scientist, born 1867
(See Biography Data in Extra-Know-How Section.)
Explain that Marie and Pierre Curie worked as a career-teaming husband and wife; think of other famous married couples who have teamed professionally.
Discuss the significance of Marie Curie's statement, "Nothing in life is to be feared; it is only to be understood." Encourage students to share various fears they have that perhaps could be eliminated if they were to be better understood. List the following fears or aversions on a chart or blackboard: claustrophobia (fear of closed, narrow spaces), agoraphobia (fear of being in open spaces), nyctophobia (fear of darkness), algophobia (fear of pain), autophobia (fear of being alone), cynophobia (fear of dogs or rabies); encourage students to find appropriate suffixes to attach to "phobia," or to make up various words for particular fears.
(See activities under April 20, "Radium isolated ....")

Cigarette manufacturing machine patented, 1876
Discuss the phenomenon of automation and how mass production can affect products which formerly have been made by hand.
Find out the cost of a package of cigarettes (or of one-tenth the cost of a carton); multiply the cost by 365 to discover how much money is spent annually by a pack-a-day smoker.
(See activities under March Variable Dates, "National Stop ....")

Isamu Noguchi, American-Japanese sculptor, born 1904
(See Biography Data in Extra-Know-How Section.)
Invite students to create their own unique sculptures out of a variety of materials, such as clay, soap, marble, paper, papier-mâché, or plaster-of-paris.

Albert Camus, French writer and Nobel Prize winner, born 1913
(See Biography Data in Extra-Know-How Section.)
Discuss Camus' statement about human relationships: "Don't walk in front of me; I may not follow. Don't walk behind me; I may not lead. Walk beside me and just be my friend."

Jeannette Rankin elected as the first woman to serve in the U.S. House of Representatives, 1916
Investigate the general status of women's rights at that time by indicating documented evidence of various statistics.

Museum of Modern Art in New York City opened, 1929
Discuss what modern art is and what period of time is generally considered to be the period of modern art.
Present samples of modern art to motivate students to create their own modern art.
Hold a debate on whether museums justify their costs of maintenance.
(See activities under April 13, "New York ....")

Women's Reserve of the U.S. Marine Corps established, 1942
    Investigate a career in the military.

Franklin Delano Roosevelt elected to his fourth term as U.S. president, 1944
    (See activities under January 30, "Franklin Delano ....")

November 8

Edmund Halley, English astronomer, born 1656
    (See Biography Data in Extra-Know-How Section.)
    Find out what a comet is.
    Explain that Halley studied the orbits of comets and accurately predicted that the great comet of 1682 would return in 1758; the discovery proved that the comet, now known as Halley's Comet, revolves around the sun; investigate about how often the comet returns, when its last appearance was, and when it is expected to return.

Louvre, the famous museum in Paris, opened, 1793
    Find out what the building was before it became a museum.
    Investigate what particularly famous paintings are exhibited in the Louvre.
    Learn what the training is to become a curator of a museum and what the responsibilities are of a museum curator.
    Develop a class list of the various kinds of museums, other than art museums.
    (See activities under January 12, "First United ... " and March 17, "National Gallery ... " and April 13, "New York's ... " and November 7, "Museum of ....")

Montana admitted to the United States as the forty-first state, 1889
    (See States Admitted to the USA Data in Extra-Know-How Section.)

Katharine Hepburn, American actress, born 1909
    (See Biography Data in Extra-Know-How Section.)

"Beer Hall Putsch" begun by Adolf Hitler and his Nazi followers, 1923
    Explain that the *Putsch* (revolt) was a situation which did not prove successful, largely due to Hitler's overconfidence; invite students to discuss examples of overconfidence they personally have experienced or that they are able to cite in history.

November 9

Benjamin Banneker, American inventor/mathematician, born 1731
    (See Biography Data in Extra-Know-How Section.)
    Explain that Banneker was a member of the commission appointed to lay out the streets of the District of Columbia. Obtain a street map of Washington, DC; ask students to locate various monuments and other areas of interest and to compute distances between various points.
    Investigate the history and various other information about the "Federal City."

Gail Borden, American inventor of the fruit-juice condensing process and various dairy product practices, born 1801
    (See Biography Data in Extra-Know-How Section.)
    Discuss the various types of milk; find out how condensed milk is made.
    Try various recipes using Borden's Eagle Brand milk.
    Find out whether raw milk must necessarily be pasteurized for it to be consumed safely and healthfully.

Theodore Roosevelt, the first U.S. president to leave the United States while in office, sailed through the Panama Canal Zone, 1906
    Discuss the advantages and disadvantages of a president's leaving the country. Explain that Roosevelt sought to keep an Open Door policy in China; discuss how long it would have taken Roosevelt to travel to China had he wished to do so as a diplomatic gesture.
    Consider the possible reasons why Roosevelt's predecessors chose not to leave the country, i.e., the time factor involved in surface transportation and domestic priorities as opposed to international concerns.

Electric neon tube sign patented, 1911

Explain that neon is a rare gaseous element which is colorless, odorless, and tasteless, and that it is used in airplane beacons; find out what is needed to convert the gaseous element into a glowing sign.

Invite students to design a neon sign for a place of business (real or fictitious), using fluorescent or phosphorescent chalk and paints.

Congress of Industrial Organizations (CIO) established, 1935

(See activities under May 24, "First strike ....")

New York and most of the northeastern United States blacked out due to an electric power failure, 1965

Explain that the power failure forced New Yorkers to become dependent upon neighbors they had not known before; discuss what anonymity is as related to living in a large city, working in a large organization, or attending a big school; consider how crises serve to bring people closer together out of need.

Explain that a considerable part of the economically developing world lives without the flow of electricity; invite students to imagine living without lighting and other electric conveniences.

November 10

Martin Luther, German leader of the Reformation, born 1483

(See Biography Data in Extra-Know-How Section.)

(See activities under October 31, "Reformation Day ....")

U.S. Marine Corps established by the Continental Congress, 1775 (celebrated as U.S. Marine Corps Day)

Investigate information about the rigorous training in the Marine Corps, a factor which has led to the Marines' reputation as a "tough" branch of the military.

Dial telephone service without the aid of an operator introduced coast-to-coast in America, 1951

Investigate the highly automated developments in telephone service.

Invite students to fantasize and design futuristic conveniences as related to telecommunication systems; investigate the meaning of the word unit "tele"; suggest that students name their creations using this word unit or one that is related to the field of communication.

November 11

Veterans Day (formerly observed as Armistice Day), sometimes celebrated on the last Monday in October

Find out the original reason for observing this holiday.

(See activities under October Variable Dates, "Veterans Day ....")

First school law (compulsory attendance) passed by Massachusetts, 1647

Investigate the attendance regulations of the school, according to state and local regulations; find out the requirements of the school-leaving age.

Contact the local school authorities to invite an appropriate representative to discuss truancy and such topics as the requirements and alternatives to attaining a high school diploma.

Consult the state's education code to find out the time allotments required in specific curriculum areas for each grade level.

Ask students to write about what they would elect to do were there not a law of compulsory school attendance.

Washington admitted to the United States as the forty-second state, 1889

(See States Admitted to the USA Data in Extra-Know-How Section.)

Tomb of the Unknown Soldier established, 1921

Find out where the monument is and the reasons for its having been established.

Independence from Great Britain declared by Rhodesia, 1965

Investigate Rhodesia's social-political situation since its independence.

Locate Rhodesia on a map of Africa; research information about Cecil Rhodes, the man after whom the country was named.

(See activities under May 25, "African Liberation ... " and April 4, "Rhodes Scholarship ... " and July 5, "Cecil John Rhodes ....")

November 12

Elizabeth Cady Stanton, American reformer and leader of the woman-suffrage movement, born 1815
(See Biography Data in Extra-Know-How Section.)
Explain that passage of the Fifteenth Amendment to the U.S. Constitution (a provision whereby former male slaves were granted the right to vote, but no woman was allowed to vote) motivated women to form the National Woman Suffrage Association in 1869, to which Elizabeth Stanton was elected as the president; find out what was achieved by this organization.

Develop a class list of restrictions that prevented women's equality during the nineteenth and early twentieth centuries, i.e., smoking, wearing long pants; then review the list in terms of what is currently considered acceptable for women to do.

Present the book *An Album of Women in American History*, by Claire Ingraham and Leonard Ingraham.
(See activities under October 29, "National Organization ....")

Auguste Rodin, French sculptor, born 1840
(See Biography Data in Extra-Know-How Section.)
Obtain a picture or copy of Rodin's famous sculpture *The Thinker*; encourage students to assume the identical posture. (Ask students to double-check one another's stance for accuracy as to which elbow on which leg.)

Present an art experience using clay; point out various techniques used to create different textures; experiment with using a variety of utensils to achieve more realistic-looking simulations of human features.

Discuss Rodin's comments: "Love your calling with a passion; it is the meaning of life"; "Nothing is ugly that has life. Whatever suggests human emotion, whether of grief, or pain, goodness or anger, hate or love, has its individual seal of beauty."

Judge Kenesaw Mountain Landis named first commissioner of baseball, 1920
Investigate the duties of a commissioner of baseball.
Review Task Card #17 and Reproducible #8 for activities about baseball.

Leon Trotsky replaced by Joseph Stalin as sole dictator of the USSR, 1927
Discuss the terms: dictator, autocrat, tyrant.
Compare and contrast three forms of government: democracy, monarchy, anarchy (according to some authorities, all other forms fit under these three or under a combination of them); compare the advantages and disadvantages of each, i.e., the expediency of a monarchy versus the cumbersome aspects of the democratic process.

National Cowboy Hall of Fame opened, 1965
Investigate the world of cowboys through books, film, and cowboy memorabilia/realia.

November 13

Robert Louis Stevenson, Scottish writer, born 1850
(See Biography Data in Extra-Know-How Section.)
Explain that Stevenson was afflicted with a lung disease as a child and was often confined to bed and was under the care of a nursemaid, to whom he dedicated his *A Child's Garden of Verses*; obtain a copy of this book and share, in particular, the poem "Land of the Counterpane."

Encourage students to read Stevenson's various novels: *Treasure Island, Kidnapped,* and *The Strange Case of Dr. Jekyll and Mr. Hyde*; discuss what is meant by "Dr. Jekyll and Mr. Hyde" behavior; ask students to pretend to take the serum that Dr. Jekyll took in order to become Mr. Hyde; ask them to make a list of things they would do as a Mr. Hyde; suggest they draw pictures of how their faces would change.

Louis Brandeis, American U.S. Supreme Court justice, born 1856
(See Biography Data in Extra-Know-How Section.)
Find out where Brandeis University is located.
(See activities under January 28, "First American ....")

First known sit-down strike conducted in the Hormel Meat Packing Company, 1933
Find out how a sit-down strike differs from other strikes.
Discuss the working factors which lead to strikes; investigate what the legalities are concerning strikes on company property.
(See activities under August 16, "George Meany ... " and May 24, "First strike ....")

Artificial snow introduced in America, 1946

Explain that the movie industry has used bleached cornflakes, white sand, and plastic shavings to simulate snow; ask students to consider other products which might be used for this purpose.

Discuss the various uses of artificial snow, other than for stage purposes.

Suggest that students create a snow diorama.

Vietnam moratorium demonstrations, in which thousands of people participated, begun, 1969

Find out the meaning and background of the word "moratorium."

Investigate the outcome of the moratorium demonstration as an effective nonviolent process of change and consciousness-raising.

Ask students to suggest various aspects of school life which they consider are in need of having a moratorium placed upon them.

November 14

Robert Fulton, American inventor, born 1765

(See Biography Data in Extra-Know-How Section.)

Explain that prior to the construction of his steamboat, Fulton had built a submarine; discuss the comment, "Achievement is not a station in life, it is a way of traveling."

(See activities under August 17, "Maiden voyage ....")

Claude Monet, French landscape artist, born 1840

(See Biography Data in Extra-Know-How Section.)

Study various prints of Monet's work to see how he achieved light effects without the use of black or brown.

Find out the background of the word "impressionist" as related to Monet.

Leo Hendrik Baekeland, American chemist and inventor of Bakelite—one of the first plastics, born 1863

(See Biography Data in Extra-Know-How Section.)

Discover when plastics first came into popular use; make a list of items made of plastic. Discuss the effects plastic has had on certain industries which produce parts for other manufactured products.

Obtain pieces of plastic and introduce a plastics-related art project.

Jawaharlah Nehru, prime minister of India, born 1889

(See Biography Data in Extra-Know-How Section.)

Discuss England's rule of India and Nehru's leadership in the struggle for independence.

Investigate how Nehru and Mahatma Gandhi differed in their economic views.

Frederick Grant Banting, Canadian scientist and Nobel Prize recipient who discovered insulin, born 1891

(See Biography Data in Extra-Know-How Section.)

Discuss the significance of having isolated the hormone, insulin.

Explain how insulin functions in the human body, both for diabetics and nondiabetics.

Investigate the home glucose testing devices, as well as other current methods for administering insulin.

Find out the ways in which one becomes diabetic.

Explain that several scientists helped in the discovery of insulin and that the honor of the Nobel Prize was shared with Banting's co-workers—a striking example of scientific fellowship working in the interest of humanity.

(See activities under November Special Weeks, "National Diabetes ....")

Aaron Copland, American composer, born 1900

(See Biography Data in Extra-Know-How Section.)

Obtain recordings of Copland's music and enjoy listening.

November 15

Sadie Hawkins Day

Explain that Sadie Hawkins is a character in the comic strip "Lil Abner." In the tradition of Sadie Hawkins Day, ask the boys to make a shoulder-to-shoulder line-up; at the starting signal, the boys are to run and the girls are to actively chase the boys; if caught, the boy must complete a favor for the girl.

Pike's Peak, a 14,110 foot mountain, cited by Zebulon Pike, 1806

Locate Pike's Peak on a map; study the significance of the Continental Divide.

Make a chart of the highest peaks in America and throughout the world, along with the respective elevations of each in metric measurements.

Discuss the difference between mountain hiking and mountain climbing; investigate the various records set by mountain climbers.

Felix Frankfurter, U.S. Supreme Court justice, born 1882

(See Biography Data in Extra-Know-How Section.)

Investigate Frankfurter's public record during his tenure as a judge in the Supreme Court.

November 16

W. C. Handy, American "Father of the Blues," born 1872

(See Biography Data in Extra-Know-How Section.)

Play recordings of blues-type music; encourage students to create a song in the style of the blues as related to a part of their own lives.

James Jordan, radio comedian known as "Fibber McGee," born 1896

(See Biography Data in Extra-Know-How Section.)

Share with the class the reference to Fibber McGee's overcrowded closet; ask students to clean out their classroom desks and their closets at home.

Speed of a mile a minute by an automobile first exceeded, 1901

Discuss the difference between a speedometer and an odometer; present various mathematical problems based upon speed and distance records.

Discuss the pros and cons of producing cars which travel faster than a mile a minute.

Investigate the fastest speed recorded by an automobile.

Oklahoma admitted to the United States as the forty-sixth state, 1907

(See States Admitted to the USA Data in Extra-Know-How Section.)

U.S. Federal Reserve banks opened, 1914

Investigate the significance of the federal reserve bank system.

Explain that the original federal reserve banks were not government-insured; find out when the change occurred and what prompted the government's greatest protection of the system.

(See activities under December 23, "U.S. Federal ....")

November 17

Louis Jacques Mande Daguerre, French painter and physicist, born 1789

(See Biography Data in Extra-Know-How Section.)

Explain that Daguerre invented the daguerreotype, the first practical method of photography; take photographs of the class.

Encourage students to create their own slides or filmstrips by drawing pictures and writing or tape-recording scripts.

Obtain the kit, "Draw Your Own Filmstrip and Slide Kit," from Scholastic Audio-Visual. (See Address Listing in Extra-Know-How Section.)

Encourage students to bring their cameras to take pictures around the school; once the pictures are developed, suggest that students create stories about their photographs.

Congress convened for its first session in Washington, DC, 1800

Obtain a picture of the capitol building; encourage students to draw a picture of the capitol, labeling the areas which house the Senate and the House of Representatives; invite students to pretend that they are the designers of the capitol; ask how they would design it differently.

Write to the U.S. Capitol Historical Society for the prices of the following pamphlets: "We, the People, the Story of the U.S. Capitol" and "Our Nation's Capital, Coloring Book." (See Address Listing in Extra-Know-How Section.)

Initiate a unit on the U.S. Congress, the legislative branch of the U.S. government.

Discuss the responsibility of writing to one's congressional representative concerning opinions and facts so that a legislator is more aware of the wishes of his/her constituency; explain also that a letter to one's representative prior to a visit to Washington, DC may result in a visitor's pass to tour his/her office.

Discuss the fact that many state capitol buildings are architecturally similar to the nation's capitol building; suggest that similar functions on a state level may be one of the reasons.

Suez Canal formally opened, 1869

Locate where the Suez Canal is; explain that both the Near East and Middle East are terms to refer to the area in which the Suez Canal is located; consider why both terms may have originated.

Investigate the significance of the Suez Canal in terms of Middle East political relations.

Research the structural challenges which both the Suez and Panama canals offered construction engineers; contrast the fact that the Panama Canal was built over mountainous areas which involved coping with uneven topography.

Review Task Card #9 to learn how to make a canal lock.

November 18

Puerto Rico first discovered by Europeans, 1493

Investigate the island of Puerto Rico; include information on the two forts, San Cristobal and El Morro; learn what responsibilities and privileges Puerto Rico has as a U.S. territorial possession; translate the name of Puerto Rico into English.

Ask students to pretend they are Puerto Ricans and are holding the following debate: "Puerto Rico should seek statehood in the United States."

Antarctica discovered by U.S. Navy Captain Nathaniel B. Palmer, 1820

Locate the continent of Antarctica.

Explore information about Antarctica regarding animals, vegetation, and climate.

Write a creative story of what it would be like to live in the Antarctic.

Obtain a copy of *Mr. Popper's Penguins*, by Richard Atwater.

Clarence Shepard Day, American author of *Life with Father*, born 1874

(See Biography Data in Extra-Know-How Section.)

Explain that a Clarence Day Award for "Outstanding Work and Love of Books and Reading" was established in 1960; find out what the word "bibliophile" means as opposed to "bibliophobe."

Encourage students to write a story of their lives with their fathers (either a realistic portrayal or a wishful one).

Standard Time adopted by railroads in the United States, 1883

Explain that this event preceded the world adoption of standard time the following year (see March 13, "World system ... "), probably because of the need for a uniform system of time for trains which crossed through differing time zones.

Obtain a large flat-surface map of the United States and enough clock faces with movable hands for each time zone; select a student to call out a particular time and zone ("Six p.m., Pacific Standard Time) and invite a volunteer to announce another time zone and adjust the appropriate clock to the corresponding time in that zone.

George Gallup, pollster, born 1901

(See Biography Data in Extra-Know-How Section.)

Find out information concerning the processes and criteria through which polls are established.

Compare the areas of interest, as surveyed by the Gallup Polls and the Harris Polls; discuss various other polls, such as the Nielsen Ratings.

Locate the results of a recent poll relating to education.

(See Conducting a Survey Data in Extra-Know-How Section.)

November 19

Mayflower **ship** docked off the coast of Massachusetts, 1620

Locate on a map where Plymouth Rock is and find out what the city is like today.

Explain that the arrival of the *Mayflower* represents the beginning of many traditions which have been sustained throughout the history of America; ask students to prepare a mural with a picture of the *Mayflower* on the left end and then draw pictures which sequentially represent the development of such items as clothing and transportation from 1620 to the present time.

(See activities under September 16, "Voyage of ... " and November 21, "Mayflower Compact ... " and December 21, "Pilgrims landed ....")

James A. Garfield, twentieth president of the United States, born 1831

(See Biography Data in Extra-Know-How Section.)

Explain that Garfield was assassinated only a few months after his inauguration by a disappointed job/office seeker; discuss the point that Garfield was opposed to the "spoils" system; encourage students to document with fact or simply to conjecture as to whether there was a direct connection between his assassination and his opposition to granting positions to political associates.

(See activities under September 6, "President McKinley ... " for information that relates to assassinated presidents.)

Gettysburg Address delivered by Abraham Lincoln, 1863

Investigate the background of the battle at Gettysburg for which the speech was a commemoration.

(See Data-Detail in Extra-Know-How Section, "Gettysburg Address.")

Familiarize students with the contents of the speech; ask students to compute what "four score" is; encourage interested students to deliver the speech.

Explain that the speech was supposedly not that well received at the time, perhaps due to its brevity of only 300 words. (The orator before Lincoln is reputed to have talked for two hours.) Explain that the speech has come to be regarded as one of the noblest expressions in American history; discuss how events of history and the passage of time change public opinion.

(See activities under July 1, "Battle of ....")

Machine which manufactured pencils introduced, 1895

Investigate approximately how many pencils per year the school consumes.

Explain the significance of the numerals on pencils as indicators of the softness-hardness of the lead; find out the many gradations of lead pencils that are used by draftsmen, engineers, architects.

(See activities under February Special Weeks, "National Pencil ... " and March 30, "Pencil with ....")

Indira Gandhi, India's prime minister, born 1917

(See Biography Data in Extra-Know-How Section.)

Investigate the strengths and weaknesses of Indira Gandhi's leadership of her country.

Find out the names of other female heads of state.

Roy Campanella, American baseball player, born 1921

(See Biography Data in Extra-Know-How Section.)

Discuss the fact that Campanella is a member of the Baseball Hall of Fame but that an automobile accident left him paralyzed and restricted to a wheelchair; read *The Roy Campanella Story*, by Milton Shapiro, and Campanella's own book, *It's Good to Be Alive.*

November 20

Peregrine White, first child born on the *Mayflower* while docked off Plymouth Rock, 1620

Explain that accurate records of births and deaths have not always been registered, but that this record may have been traced to the ship's log.

Encourage students to find their own birth certificates and examine them; discuss the purposes of birth certificates.

Passport photos made mandatory by the U.S. State Department, 1914

Ask students to conjecture as to why photos on passports were mandated.

Investigate what a passport is, its purpose, and how long it is valid.

Find out what agency one contacts locally to obtain a passport; consult the telephone directory concerning places where a passport photo can be taken.

Obtain a passport, examine it with the students, and encourage students to create their own.

Suggest that students write a story of intrigue regarding illegal entry into a country.

Learn what a visa is; investigate the different requirements in the United States for a visitor's visa and a resident visa; find out what the regulations are regarding visas for foreign students in America.

Determine the difference between the terms "emigration" and "immigration."

Talk about what customs and immigration regulations may be necessary in regard to interplanetary travel.

Robert F. Kennedy, U.S. senator and attorney general, born 1925

(See Biography Data in Extra-Know-How Section.)

Obtain a copy of *Robert F. Kennedy: Man Who Dared to Dream*, by Charles P. Graves, and read the book to the class.

Nuremburg (Nürnberg) trials (International War Crimes Tribunal) of Nazi leaders opened in Germany, 1945

Investigate the background of the trials; find out what extradition is and how it has affected the trying of war criminals.

Stage a debate on whether the statute of limitations ruling on Germany was fair.

November 21

Mayflower Compact signed, 1620

Obtain a copy of the compact and explain that the covenant was written to establish organization and structure of the new colony and to prevent unrest and disorder.

Ask students to write a classroom compact that would be appropriate for when a substitute teacher is responsible for the class.

(See activities under September 16, "Voyage of ... " and November 19, "*Mayflower* ship ....")

U.S. Constitution ratified by North Carolina, thus making it the twelfth state, 1789

(See States Admitted to the USA Data in Extra-Know-How Section.)

Pocket lighter patented, 1871

Discuss the various types of cigarette lighters and how they are designed to ignite.

Harpo Marx, American comedian, born 1893

(See Biography Data in Extra-Know-How Section.)

Investigate the musical instrument, the harp; find out the similarities between the harp, harpsichord, and the piano.

November 22

First day of the zodiac period, Sagitarrius, the Bowman or the Archer (through December 21)

See Data-Detail in Extra-Know-How Section, "Notes on Astrology."

Robert Cavelier LaSalle, French explorer, born 1643

(See Biography Data in Extra-Know-How Section.)

Explain that LaSalle sailed down the Mississippi River to its mouth and claimed the whole river valley for France; document the vestiges of French culture which have remained in the Mississippi area.

Distribute outline maps of the United States; color in the Mississippi River and its tributaries; research the pollution factor in the various rivers as a result of the chemical fertilizers used in the mid-west farming areas.

George Eliot (Mary Ann Evans), English author of *Silas Marner*, born 1819

(See Biography Data in Extra-Know-How Section.)

Investigate why Mary Ann Evans made use of a pseudonym; trace the derivation of the word units "pseudo" and "nym."

Discuss Eliot's comment, "He was like a cock who thought the sun had risen to hear him crow."

Charles DeGaulle, former president of France, born 1890

(See Biography Data in Extra-Know-How Section.)

Trace the development of France and Europe during his years as head of state.

SOS adopted as the international distress radio signal, 1906

Teach the Morse code; invite students to set up various codes between two or more parties (i.e., three eye blinks represent "Let's play four-square at recess," or unbuttoning one's shirt sleeve represents soccerball); suggest that students devise various written codes also.

Discuss the various ways in which distress can be communicated: flares, mirrors, flags, flashlights.
(See activities under April 27, "Samuel F. M. ....")

First transpacific airmail flight begun, 1935
Obtain a map which represents both Asia and North America; measure the distance from San Francisco to various major cities in Asia—Manila, Tokyo, Hong Kong, Singapore.

John F. Kennedy, thirty-fifth president of the United States, assassinated, 1963
Discuss the impact Kennedy's assassination had upon the country and upon the world; consider the charisma he had with people in foreign countries, due partly to speeches such as the one he delivered to the people of Berlin: "Ich bin ein Berliner!" (I am a Berliner).
(See activities under May 29, "John F. Kennedy ... " and September 6, "President McKinley ....")

November 23

Franklin Pierce, fourteenth president of the United States, born 1804
(See Biography Data in Extra-Know-How Section.)
Explain that Pierce was a "dark horse" candidate at the Democratic convention; find out what "dark horse" refers to in political campaigning.

Horseshoe manufacturing machine patented, 1835
Explain that horseshoes were originally made by blacksmiths; discuss the trade of a blacksmith; investigate the skills necessary, such as to design orthopedic horseshoes.
Play the game of horseshoes (hard rubber or plastic horseshoes are usually available).
Discuss the various superstitions related to horseshoes: "A horseshoe over one's door connotes good luck."
Consider the various types of feet represented by the animal world; invite students to design shoes for various other animals, such as pigs and ducks.

Boris Karloff, British actor, born 1887
(See Biography Data in Extra-Know-How Section.)
Explain that Karloff is famous for having portrayed monster figures by creating grotesque facial gestures and corresponding voice patterns; invite students to experiment with their facial and vocal expressions to create various moods.

SPARS, women's unit of the U.S. Coast Guard, authorized, 1942
Investigate what the acronym SPARS stands for.
Invite a representative from the U.S. Coast Guard to discuss the military as a career and also to talk about water safety.

November 24

Baruch Spinoza, Spanish-Dutch philosopher, born 1632
(See Biography Data in Extra-Know-How Section.)
Investigate such terms in philosophy as axiology, epistemology, and ontology.

Father Junípero Serra, Spanish missionary/explorer, born 1713
(See Biography Data in Extra-Know-How Section.)
Locate on a map of California the series of 21 missions which were established approximately a day's walk from one another; explain that the route came to be known as "El Camino Real," which means "The Royal Road."
Ask students to recollect the longest walk or hike that they have taken; discuss the practice of walk-a-thons for various causes.

Zachary Taylor, twelfth president of the United States, born 1784
(See Biography Data in Extra-Know-How Section.)
Find out why Taylor was called "Old Rough and Ready."

Henri de Toulouse-Lautrec, French artist, born 1864
(See Biography Data in Extra-Know-How Section.)

Explain that Toulouse-Lautrec is known for his lively, colorful posters, prints, and lithographs of the Parisian nightlife; it is alleged that his emphasis upon form and movement was partly a compensation for his own physical frailty, that of being crippled and deformed since early childhood.

Invite students to express themselves in some way which describes a fantasy, much as Toulouse-Lautrec did through his art.

Obtain prints of the artist's work and share with the class.

Scott Joplin, American black pianist and composer, born 1868
(See Biography Data in Extra-Know-How Section.)
Enjoy his ragtime music.

Investigate player pianos and piano rolls; explain that there are a few of his piano rolls published, but that there are no recordings of his works.

Create lyrics to accompany Joplin's music.

Hideyo Noguchi, Japanese-American bacteriologist and immunologist, born 1876
(See Biography Data in Extra-Know-How Section.)
Explain that in the course of Noguchi's work he contracted yellow fever and subsequently died. Discuss this situation in regard to occupational hazards involved in a variety of careers.

Investigate the profession of a bacteriologist and/or immunologist.

Tsung-Dao Lee, Chinese-American physicist, born 1926
(See Biography Data in Extra-Know-How Section.)
(See activities under September 22, "Chen Ning Yang ....")

November 25

First exhibition of sword swallowing occurred, 1817
Examine the spelling of the word "sword" as derived from middle and old English; consult a dictionary to find other words containing "sword."

Discuss feats such as sword swallowing and flagpole sitting; consult various reference books regarding records that have been established in similar feats.

Discuss what motivates people to participate in or to observe such events.

Andrew Carnegie, Scottish-American industrialist/philanthropist, born 1835
(See Biography Data in Extra-Know-How Section.)
Explain that Carnegie gained his money through the steel industry and that his multimillion dollar benefactions or charities totaled about $350 million, some of which went toward Carnegie Hall in New York City and to about 2,800 libraries; find out what current benefits are being derived from the Carnegie Foundation.

Treaty of Friendship and Commerce signed between Switzerland and the United States, 1850
Explore the cultural aspects of Switzerland (such as German, French, and Italian languages spoken in three different areas of the small country), as well as the physical features; explain that Switzerland has historically not been involved in wars, perhaps because of its being surrounded by mountains; ask students to investigate a topographical map of Switzerland.

Find out why foreign investors secure their money in Swiss banks.

Obtain a picture of the Matterhorn or of other mountain and meadow scenes in the Swiss Alps; encourage students to paint a mountain landscape.

Read *Heidi*, by Johanna Spyri, the story of a girl growing up in the Alps.

Evaporated milk patented, 1884
Bring in several types of milk, i.e., liquid homogenized, dried, condensed, evaporated; discuss the purposes of each and investigate the processes by which each is created.

Trace the etymology of the word "evaporated" to "vapor" and define it.

Find a recipe that calls for evaporated milk; make two separate preparations, one with evaporated milk and one with liquid homogenized milk; compare the results.

Joe DiMaggio, American baseball player, born 1914
(See Biography Data in Extra-Know-How Section.)

Decision made by the United States not to engage in biological warfare, 1969

Investigate what biological warfare is; discuss the least and the worst possible effects of this military strategy.

Initiate an oral interpretation activity based upon James Thurber's description in "The Last Flower." Encourage students to write a science fiction story involving the use of biological and chemical warfare; suggest that they be specific in terms of methods of distribution and to consider whether the victor would really be the victor; learn what a "Pyrrhic victory" is.

November 26

First lion in America exhibited in Boston, 1716

Compare and contrast the various zoos of the world.

Consider the profession of a veterinarian who treats rare animal diseases and travels around the world to treat animals in need.

Discuss why the lion is considered to be the "king of the jungle"; find out what is involved in taming a lion for a circus show.

Create pen and ink drawings of a male lion, with particular detail on the mane and tail.

First national Thanksgiving Day declared by George Washington, 1789

Explain that Thanksgiving was not widely celebrated in the early nineteenth century; research the efforts of Sara Josepha Hale in her campaign to make Thanksgiving a national patriotic holiday.

Choose a student to play the role of George Washington returning to the present day for a press conference. Invite students to interrogate the president with questions such as: "Have Thanksgiving celebrations through the years been observed as you had intended in 1789?" "Does it concern you that some people use processed canned turkey loaf and frozen corn?" "Have you any suggestions as to how the celebration of the day might be reevaluated in terms of its original purpose?"

(See activities under November Variable Dates, "Thanksgiving Day ... " and December 4, "America's first ....")

First social fraternity on a college campus established, 1825

Make available pictures of the Greek letters of the alphabet; invite students to break into small groups and to find Greek letters which meaningfully represent a name for their group, i.e., Kappa Epsilon Beta Tau (Kenmore Elementary Baseball Team).

Discuss the pros and cons of the exclusive nature of fraternities and/or sororities; find out the background of the practice of "blackballing."

Discuss the word "fraternity" as related to fraternal, supportive relationships, for both males and females.

First streetcar in the United States developed, 1832

Ask students to describe their concepts of a streetcar and to consider why the term "streetcar" evolved for this large vehicle.

Discuss other forms of current people-movers or people-carriers within metropolitan areas.

Charles M. Schultz, creator of "Peanuts" cartoon characters, born 1922

(See Biography Data in Extra-Know-How Section.)

Share some of Schultz's comic strips.

Write character descriptions for the cartoon personalities.

Encourage students to design a comic strip of their own, or else write a comic strip using Schultz's characters.

Explain that Schultz was born in Needles, California; on a U.S. map, locate the city.

Review Task Card #68 to learn how to make comic lifts with the "Peanuts" comic strip.

November 27

Anders Celsius, Swedish astronmer who devised the Celsius Centrigrade Scale, born 1701

(See Biography Data in Extra-Know-How Section.)

Begin a study unit on Celsius measurement; experiment with converting centigrade to fahrenheit temperatures and vice versa.

David Merrick, American theatrical producer, born 1912

(See Biography Data in Extra-Know-How Section.)

Ask students the following question: "If you could be a producer in the theater, what kind of production would you like to lead?"

The authors could find few other events of historical significance for November 27

It is suggested that the reader supply his or her own name with a creative thought or with a description of an invention that would warrant, respectively, a copyright or a patent.

Encourage students to go to the library to locate past issues of the *New York Times*; suggest that they look up issues of November 27 for randomly selected years to learn what was happening on that particular date. (Note: This activity is good for any day of the year, i.e., students' birthdays.)

November 28

First woman, Lady Astor, elected to the British Parliament, 1919

Investigate the requirements and the ceremony related to the honor of being accorded the title of "Lady," as was Lady Astor.

Find out the current number of women in the British Parliament.

Independence from France declared by the Chad Republic, 1958

Locate the Chad Republic on a map of Africa.

(See activities under May 25, "African Liberation ....")

November 29

Louisa May Alcott, American author, born 1832

(See Biography Data in Extra-Know-How Section.)

Explain the background of her famous book *Little Women*, a book she was asked to write for girls but would have preferred writing for boys; the publisher found it unacceptable until after he learned how much his own children enjoyed it. (Recommended version is the Caldecott Award-winning edition, as illustrated by Barbara Cooney.)

Introduce the biography by Cornelia Meigs *Invincible Louisa*.

First U.S. Army-Navy football game played, 1890

Find out who won the first game between the two teams (Navy, 24-0).

Explain that the teams represent two military academies in the United States, West Point (army) and Annapolis (navy); find out what the requirements are for entrance to these two schools and who is eligible to apply.

Invite students to form two teams, choosing to be on either the army or the navy team, and play a game of football, kickball, or soccer.

Vincent Edward Scully, sportscaster, born 1927

(See Biography Data in Extra-Know-How Section.)

Investigate the career of a sportscaster.

Invite a student to serve as a sportscaster for a school sports event.

Yugoslavia proclaimed as a republic, 1945

Name and locate on a map the six regions that were politically united once Yugoslavia became a republic.

Investigate Josip Broz Tito's break with the USSR and his concept of socialism.

Discuss various economic-political terms, such as private enterprise, collective cooperatives and state-owned farms and businesses, competition, nationalized medical programs, classless society, tax incentives.

November 30

Jonathan Swift, Irish writer, born 1667

(See Biography Data in Extra-Know-How Section.)

Introduce the book *Gulliver's Travels*.

Encourage interested students to write a similar adventure story but one based upon a land of giants.

Samuel Clemens (Mark Twain), American writer/satirist, born 1835
(See Biography Data in Extra-Know-How Section.)
Arrange an interest center which displays several of Twain's publications. Read to the class either *The Adventures of Huckleberry Finn* or *The Adventures of Tom Sawyer*; invite students to design their own book jackets for the books and then display the variety of interpretations.

Encourage students to create a story describing the mischievous activities that might occur if Huck and Tom were to be part of the classroom.

Discuss the autobiographic content represented in Twain's stories in that the Mississippi River setting and the activities were ideas from Twain's own childhood; discuss the advice to writers, "Write about that which you know and understand."

Find out how Clemens selected "Mark Twain" as a pen name; discuss the words "pseudonym" and *"nom de plume,"* and the reasons for using names other than one's own.

Think about Mark Twain's statements: "Schooling gets in the way of education"; "If you tell the truth, you don't have to remember anything."

Sir Winston Churchill, former prime minister of England, born 1874
(See Biography Data in Extra-Know-How Section.)
Encourage students to read biographies about Churchill and particularly note his many talents and skills (stone mason or bricklayer, prolific writer, amateur painter, reporter, army officer, world political leader), even through his parents considered him to be a poor student.

Investigate the requirements and the ceremony related to the honor of being accorded the title of "Sir," as Churchill was.

Explain that Churchill's mother was American-born and that the United States honored him as the nation's only "Honorary American."

Obtain recordings of Churchill's speeches from the library and note his speaking style.

Explain that Churchill planned his own funeral in great detail, all of which was carried out; invite students to write their own obituaries or epitaphs, either realistically as of the present time or imaginatively as of a later date. Consult *The New York Times' Obituary Index* to help locate Churchill's actual obituary.

Discuss Churchill's teasing comments on the English language: "This is something up with which I will not put"; "It is a riddle, wrapped in a mystery, inside an enigma."

Consider Churchill's term "Iron Curtain" as it relates to the Soviet-bloc countries.

Shirley Chisholm, black American politician, born, 1924
(See Biography Data in Extra-Know-How Section.)
Explain that Chisholm was formerly a nursery school teacher who later entered politics and became a candidate for the U.S. presidency in 1972; discuss the reasons why people may choose to change careers throughout their lives.

DECEMBER

Because December was originally the tenth month, it takes its name from the Latin word decem, *which means "ten." The month is traditionally a time of gift-bearing, due to the Christian holidays of St. Nicholas Day and Christmas and due to the Jewish celebration of Hanukkah.*

Birthstone: *Turquoise*
Flower: *Narcissus*

Use the Find-a-Word Reproducible to preview happenings in December. (See Reproducible Section.)

MONTH-LONG OBSERVANCES

See activities under November, Month-long Observances

SPECIAL WEEKS

Human Rights Week

Discuss the concept of what human rights are, the essence of which is the respect for the right of another to represent a particular belief (or condition) regardless of whether the belief itself is respected.

Consider the comment: "Your right to swing ends where my nose begins"; discuss the concepts of rights and privileges and the responsibilities that closely accompany them; talk about the situations in which rights are relinquished.

Invite a representative from the local chapter of the American Civil Liberties Union (ACLU) to discuss the legal protection of rights; trace the activities of Roger Baldwin, an early organizer of the association.

Discuss the following comments: "The liberty of discussion is the chief safeguard of all other liberties" (Thomas Macaulay). "The basic test of freedom is perhaps less in what we are free to do than in what we are free not to do."

Encourage students to add to the following list of groups whose rights often go unacknowledged: rights of children/students, parents, the profoundly handicapped, the less severely handicapped (stutterers, colorblind, learning disabled), the aged, women and men (in varying aspects), ethnically different individuals, left-handed people, exceptionally short or tall individuals, twins and other people of multiple births, single men and women, *ad infinitum*; suggest that students choose one of the above topics and form a group to list the rights to accompany that group of people; compare and contrast the lists. Talk about the acceptable methods that interest groups can use to bring visibility to their particular cause.

Consult an almanac, along with *Census Reports by the Decade* (published by the U.S. Bureau of the Census), to analyze various data about America's ethnically diverse population.

Find out about the purposes of Amnesty International, an organization founded by Peter Benenson that won the 1977 Nobel Peace Prize in its efforts to rescue "prisoners of conscience" throughout the world; discuss the meaning and significance of the term, "prisoner of conscience."

Consider the point that only when people are committed to the concept of human rights are they ready for international, inter-space/galactic relationships.

Read the book *Human Rights Day*, by Aileen Fisher and Olive Rabe.

(See activities under February Special Weeks, "Brotherhood Week ... " and March Special Weeks, "International Education ... " and July 2, "Civil Rights ... " and August 26, "Nineteenth Amendment ....")

VARIABLE DATES

Winter Solstice (on or about December 21)
Explain that "solstice" means "sun stands still." Ask students to investigate the scientific explanation of solstice and relate it to the phrase "sun stands still." Remind students that a summer solstice occurs on or around June 21.

Hanukkah, Jewish Festival of Lights
Obtain a book on such topics as the Menorah, the Dreidel game, and the making of latkes.

DAYS OF THE MONTH

December 1

Minoru Yamasaki, Japanese-American architect, born 1912
(See Biography Data in Extra-Know-How Section.)
Investigate the career of an architect.
Discuss Yamasaki's statement that there is delight in the elements of change and surprise.
Encourage students to make their own architectural drawings. Obtain blueprints; examine the legend and the scale of each and then ask students to try to imagine the structure in its constructed form.

Boys' Town founded by Father Edward Flanagan, 1917
Investigate the background of Boys' Town.
Discuss Father Flanagan's quoted comment, "There is no such thing as a bad boy."

First National Cornhusking Championship held, 1924
Distribute an ear of corn to each student and hold a cornhusking contest; with the cornhusks, make corn-husk dolls. (If fresh corn is unavailable, use dried corncobs, as used in table decorations, for the corn-husk dolls.)

December 2

Pan American Health Day
Ask students to complete the following: "A healthy body is _____."
Locate on a map the countries which are likely to be considered part of Pan America.
Write to the Pan American Health Organization for information. (See Address Listing in Extra-Know-How Section.)
Find out the meaning of the prefix "pan"; make a class list of words which are prefaced by this word unit. (See activities under April Special Weeks, "Pan American ....")

First savings bank to operate in the United States opened, 1816
Consider the benefits of a bank as opposed to hiding money in a stocking or under a mattress.
Investigate the federal reserve banking system.
Find out the difference between a bank and a savings and loan association.
Ask students to design their own account books and record their earnings (credit) and expenditures (debit).
Review Task Card #8 to learn more about banking.

Monroe Doctrine presented, 1823
Investigate the cause and effects of this doctrine which states that no foreign power can establish dominance over any country in the Western Hemisphere.
Find out who the current secretary of state is and research what the responsibilities of the position are.
Trace the history of how the doctrine has been interpreted, invoked, and subsequently viewed in terms of policies with Latin America.

John Brown hanged, 1859
Discuss the following words, as expressed by John Brown on the day of his death: "I ... am now quite certain that the crimes of this guilty land will never be purged away, but with blood.... "
(See activities under May 9, "John Brown ....")

Statue of Freedom set on the U.S. capitol dome, 1863
Write to the U.S. Capital Historical Society for a copy of "Our Nation's Capital, Coloring Book." (See Address Listing in Extra-Know-How Section.)

First atom split following the establishment of the first nuclear reactor which produced the first nuclear chain reaction, 1942

Initiate a unit on atoms and molecules.

(See activities under March 28, "Breakdown of ... " and July 16, "First atomic ....")

Peter Carl Goldmark, American inventor of color television and long-playing records, born 1906

(See Biography Data in Extra-Know-How Section.)

Trace the development of color television; name other people and their contributions in relation to the progress of color television.

Review Task Card #38 for further information about television.

(See activities under August 19, "Philo T. Farnsworth ....")

Joseph R. McCarthy censured by the U.S. Senate, 1954

Investigate the Senate hearings on the U.S. Army's charges against McCarthy.

Define and differentiate the two words "censure" and "censor."

Suggest that students write a creative story in which one of the characters is censured by a public authority.

December 3

Gilbert Stuart, American portrait painter of George Washington, born 1755

(See Biography Data in Extra-Know-How Section.)

Obtain a print of Stuart's famous portrait of George Washington; discuss why Stuart may have chosen the particular facial expression that he did.

Explain that it was customary for well-known people to have portraits painted in earlier times because the technology of photography was not available.

Encourage students to paint a portrait.

Illinois admitted to the United States as the twenty-first state, 1818

(See States Admitted to the USA Data in Extra-Know-How Section.)

First coeducational college established, 1833

Find out the meaning of the prefix "co"; make a class list of words which begin with the prefix "co."

Ask students which activities at school they would like to participate in with both males and females and those which they would prefer to do separately.

Charles Alfred Pillsbury, American manufacturer, born 1842

(See Biography Data in Extra-Know-How Section.)

Ask students to make a list of Pillsbury products.

Discuss the different types of flour and how each is milled and prepared for marketing.

First low-cost housing project in the United States dedicated, 1935

Discuss the economic situation of the Depression years and the need for low-cost housing; ask students to design a low-cost housing unit and to justify their ideas in terms of thrift and feasibility.

First successful heart transplant performed, 1967

Discuss the issue of when death occurs—at the cessation of the heartbeat or at the cessation of brain wave activity; investigate whether medical and legal authorities agree on this issue; research the various legal precedents and state statutes and document the findings.

Find out the meaning of the prefix "trans"; make a class list of words which begin with this prefix.

(See activities under February Month-long Observances, "Heart Month.")

December 4

America's first Thanksgiving celebrated in Plymouth, Massachusetts, 1619

(See activities under November 26, "First National ....")

Manila paper patented, 1843

Display various types of paper to help students become aware of the classifications (newsprint, construction, butcher, tracing, corrugated, tagboard, papyrus, crepe, tissue, onion skin, bond, manila); suggest that students create an art project with one of the types of paper.

Explain that manila paper was originally derived from Manila hemp but is now produced from wood-pulp substitutes; find out how paper is manufactured and how wood is converted to paper.

Painting in the Museum of Modern Art, New York, discovered as having been hanging upside down for 47 days, 1961

Discuss how this incident may have happened; suggest that perhaps the painting was of an abstract nature that made the image difficult to define.

Exchange ideas about the saying, "Beauty is in the eye of the beholder"; obtain copies of various modern abstract prints and invite students to form a panel of critics to discuss the works.

December 5

Phi Beta Kappa, U.S. college honor fraternity, founded, 1776

Explain what honor societies are and discuss the pros and cons of their existence.

Expose students to the Greek alphabet and other alphabets (Hebrew, Cyrillic, and various Asian written symbols) by writing to foreign embassies and consulates to request copies of newspapers; upon receipt of the copies, cut out and label various headlines and assemble a collage of alphabets on posterboard.

Martin Van Buren, eighth president of the United States, born 1782

(See Biography Data in Extra-Know-How Section.)

Explain that Van Buren is said to have been the first "machine-elected" president; ask students to find out the background of the election to understand the meaning of this term.

Gall (Pizi), American Indian leader, died 1894

(See Biography Data in Extra-Know-How Section.)

Walt Disney, American animator, film producer, futurist, born 1901

(See Biography Data in Extra-Know-How Section.)

(See activities under July 17, "Disneyland in ... " and September 19, "First animated ....")

Otto Preminger, American film director, born 1906

(See Biography Data in Extra-Know-How Section.)

Investigate the career of a movie director.

Simulate a setting between a director and the actor/actress; ask a student to imitate a movie director, in a director's chair, by directing a student actor/actress to refine a particular movement (such as sitting down in a chair a certain way).

Twenty-first Amendment to the U.S. Constitution ratified, ending Prohibition, 1933

(See Data-Detail in Extra-Know-How Section, "Amendments to the U.S. Constitution.")

Discuss the statement, "It takes an act of Congress," as related to altering various procedures and practices.

(See activities under October 28, "Volstead Act ....")

Four thousand people killed in catastrophic London fog, 1953

Investigate the meteorological aspects of fog.

Invite students to share personal experiences they have had with fog.

Talk about the expression, "I'm in a fog."

Find out why that many deaths were caused by the fog.

Discuss the various ways people and vehicles are victimized by fog.

Obtain a copy of Carl Sandburg's poem "Fog"; suggest that students write a creative story related to fog—perhaps with a futuristic beam that very efficiently is able to penetrate fog.

American Federation of Labor (AFL) and Congress of Industrial Organizations (CIO) merger negotiated, 1955

(See activities under August 16, "George Meany ....")

December 6

St. Nicholas Day

Investigate how this children's holiday is celebrated in several European countries, as separate from Christmas.

Henry VI of England, crowned king at the age of nine months, born 1421
(See Biography Data in Extra-Know-How Section.)
Find out how England was governed until the king was old enough to serve as the reigning king; investigate how he also claimed the crown of France.
Ask students to write a creative story in which they are kings or queens of a particular realm (of the school or of a fictional land or planet).
Suggest a homework assignment in which students ask their parents or guardians to relate certain anecdotes about the student when he or she was approximately nine months old.

Columbus' landing at Hispañola recorded, 1492
Locate the area where Columbus landed.
(See activities under October Variable Dates, "Columbus Day ....")

Dave Brubeck, American jazz pianist, born 1920
(See Biography Data in Extra-Know-How Section.)
Discuss various types of music (ragtime, Dixieland, blues, modern, progressive); enjoy various recordings of each type.

December 7

U.S. Constitution ratified by Delaware, thus making it the first state, 1787
(See States Admitted to the USA Data in Extra-Know-How Section.)
Suggest that students make a list of the first 13 colonies in the order in which the Constitution was ratified.

First concert by the New York Philharmonic Orchestra presented, 1842
Find out the responsibilities and honors associated with various positions in the orchestra, i.e., first violinist, concert maestro.
Investigate how orchestras are supported in America in contrast to how they are funded in other countries.

Richard Warren Sears, American retailer, born 1863
(See Biography Data in Extra-Know-How Section.)
Read the book *Sears, Roebuck, USA, the Great American Catalog Store and How It Grew,* by Gordon L. Weil.
Discuss the impact of mail-order houses on the purchasing public.
Invite a representative from Sears to share the opportunities for employment with the firm.
Obtain order forms from the Sears Catalog; guide students in filling out an order form.

Willa Cather, American novelist and short-story writer of the American Midwest, born 1873
(See Biography Data in Extra-Know-How Section.)

Pacific War opened by Japan's bombing of Pearl Harbor, 1941 (also known as National Defense Day)
Explain that the Japanese attack represented a foreign attack on the United States and that the U.S. defense procedures since that time have become highly sophisticated; investigate the current measures of America's national defense.
Research in the library for newspapers of early December 1941 to determine what communication transpired between Tokyo and Washington, DC prior to the bombing; investigate how many American lives were lost in the invasion.

China's Nationalist government exiled to Formosa (Taiwan), 1949
Investigate the life and career of Chiang Kai-shek.
Find out which European country is responsible for having named the land "Formosa" and what the word means in English.
Explore the culture of Taiwan and its international status.
Find out about the Chinese language—its tonal, one syllable-like names (as they sound to English-speaking people), the differences between Mandarin and Cantonese, the many other forms of the Chinese language, and its written form of ideographs.

Overdue book returned to the University of Cincinnati after 145 years, 1968
Explain that the fine was calculated to be $22,646; hold a debate on the pros and cons of charging fines for overdue books.

Find out what the revenue from fines is used for in most libraries.

Suggest that students check at home and school for overdue library books; discuss the privilege of borrowing books from a government-funded service agency; explain that some countries have rental libraries but that few maintain public-supported libraries.

Develop a class list of services and items, other than books, that most libraries offer.

(See activities under April Special Weeks, "National Library ... " and April 9, "First American ....")

December 8

Jan Ingenhousz, Dutch physician who discovered photosynthesis, born 1730
(See Biography Data in Extra-Know-How Section.)
Conduct a science experiment in order to understand the process of photosynthesis.

Eli Whitney, American inventor of the cotton gin, born 1765
(See Biography Data in Extra-Know-How Section.)
Discuss the impact that Whitney's contribution has had on industry—that of introducing a modern system of producing machines with interchangeable parts; make a class list of products which have interchangeable parts, i.e., oil filters in a car.
Read the Newbery Award-winning book *Eli Whitney: Great Inventor*, by Jean L. Lathan.
(See activities under March 14, "First cotton ....")

Delaware River crossed by George Washington, 1776
Obtain a copy of the famous painting by Emmanuel Leutze depicting this event; discuss the point that some paintings are better known than the artists who painted them.
Examine the painting to note an error (the flag in the painting had not been designed at the time of the crossing).
Explain that Washington crossed the Delaware not to fight the British, but the Hessians—the German mercenaries who were hired by the British; investigate the background leading up to the crossing of the Delaware.
Find out how Molly Pitcher (Mary Ludwig Hays McCauley) assisted at Valley Forge.

Jan Sibelius, Finnish composer, born 1865
(See Biography Data in Extra-Know-How Section.)
Obtain a recording of "Finlandia" and enjoy listening.

American Federation of Labor (AFL) founded, 1886
(See activities under August 16, "George Meany ....")

James Thurber, American humorist, born 1894
(See Biography Data in Extra-Know-How Section.)
Obtain copies of Thurber's stories; in particular, share the character of Walter Mitty and also the narrative prose "The Last Flower."

Sammy Davis, Jr., American entertainer, born 1924
(See Biography Data in Extra-Know-How Section.)

State of war declared upon Japan by the United States, 1941
(See activities under December 7, "Pacific War ....")

Shipments to China banned by the United States, 1950
Investigate the background of the U.S. government's decision.
Consider current U.S.-China diplomatic relations; trace the development of trade policies between the two countries since 1950.

December 9

Joel Chandler Harris, Amercan artist/writer, born 1848
(See Biography Data in Extra-Know-How Section.)
Explain that Harris recorded and illustrated folktales; tell a folktale about Uncle Remus; invite students to write the story down in their own words and illustrate it.

First ball-bearing roller skate patented, 1885

Discuss the activity of roller-skating, such as various types of skates (wooden, fiber glass wheels, key skates), roller derbies, and roller rinks.

Invite students to bring their roller skates to demonstrate various tricks.

Christmas seals first offered, 1907

(See activities under November Month-long Observances, "Christmas Seal ....")

Jerusalem captured from Turkish Moslem rule by the British in World War I, 1917

Investigate a current map of the Near East; locate Jerusalem on it, as well as other known place-names of the Near East.

(See activities under November 2, "Balfour Declaration ....")

John Birch Society founded, 1958

Investigate the evolution of the John Birch Society.

Discuss such political-economic labels as "right-wing," "left-wing," "conservative," "liberal"; consider the pros and cons involved in the U.S. government's declared ideal of maintaining both extremes in the political process.

Branch Rickey, American baseball executive, died 1965

Explain that Rickey hired Jackie Robinson as the first black in major league baseball, despite pressures to the contrary; relate this situation to currently observed acts of nondiscrimination in the school or community.

December 10

Nobel Prize Day (prizes are awarded this day, the anniversary of Alfred Nobel's death in 1896)

(See activities under October 21, "Alfred Nobel ....")

U.N. Human Rights Day (commemorates the adoption of the United Nations Declaration of Human Rights in 1948)

Suggest that students make a classroom "Bill of Rights" and commit themselves to observing it.

Explain that citizens in America are legally able to apply for all types of jobs, regardless of race, gender, or religion, due to policies of affirmative action; use Reproducible #25 to learn how to develop a resumé.

(See activities under December Special Weeks, "Human Rights ....")

Mississippi admitted to the United States as the twentieth state, 1817

(See States Admitted to the USA Data in Extra-Know-How Section.)

Emily Dickinson, American writer, born 1830

(See Biography Data in Extra-Know-How Section.)

Explain that Emily Dickinson led a secluded life and that her poetry was not found until after her death; find out what "posthumous" publishing is.

Discuss a comment in one of Dickinson's letters: "To live is so startling it leaves little time for anything else."

Share selections of Dickinson's poetry.

Red Cloud, last of the great Sioux chieftains, buried in South Dakota, 1909

Explain that the Sioux nation once occupied the north-central portion of what is now the United States; find the area on a map of the United States; trace the history of the seizure of their land and the slaughter of their food supply, the bison.

Find out how many people there currently are in America who are of Native American descent; investigate their standard of living.

(See activities under June 2, "American Indians ... " and August Variable Dates, "American Indian ....")

December 11

Junior Chamber of Commerce Day

Invite a representative from the local chapter of the Junior Chamber of Commerce to explain more about the organization.

Aurora Borealis first recorded, 1719
Explain that auroral displays are brilliant, colored lights high in the earth's atmosphere, usually seen in the polar regions and usually associated with magnetic storms and streaks of sunlight; the phenomena are named "Aurora Borealis" in the northern atmosphere and "Aurora Australis" in the southern atmosphere.
Suggest that students attempt to depict an aurora with brightly colored chalk.

Indiana admitted to the United States as the nineteenth state, 1816
(See States Admitted to the USA Data in Extra-Know-How Section.)

Robert Koch, German microbiologist who discovered the causes of tuberculosis and cholera, born 1843
(See Biography Data in Extra-Know-How Section.)
Explain that cholera is a highly infectious and fatal disease which is transmitted by polluted food or water; find out what preventative measures have helped to halt the spread of the disease.
(See activities under March 24, "Discovery of tubercle ... " and November Month-long Observances, "Christmas Seal ....")

John Augustus Larson, American psychiatrist who invented the lie detector, born 1892
(See Biography Data in Extra-Know-How Section.)
Invite a representative from the police department to discuss the use of a lie detector or polygraph.
Introduce an unfinished story that relates to lying; invite students to supply an ending to the story.

Alexander Solzhenitsyn, Russian writer and immigrant to America, born 1918
(See Biography Data in Extra-Know-How Section.)
Discuss the dynamics of being a writer of books which are politically unacceptable to the government of one's country; review the importance of America's upholding its commitment to the First Amendment of the U.S. Constitution.

December 12

John Jay, first chief justice of the U.S. Supreme Court, born 1745
(See Biography Data in Extra-Know-How Section.)
Investigate the background upon which much of the U.S. law is based.

U.S. Constitution ratified by Pennsylvania, thus making it the second state, 1787
(See States Admitted to the USA Data in Extra-Know-How Section.)

George S. Parker, American game manufacturer and founder of Parker Brothers, born 1866
(See Biography Data in Extra-Know-How Section.)
Make a list of games produced by the Parker Brothers firm.
Encourage students to create their own board games.
Find out how many sets of "Monopoly" have been sold.
Compare and contrast the games of the early 1900s with those currently played.
Discuss the effect that computer games have had on board games.

First golf tee patented, 1899
Discuss the purpose of a golf tee; experiment to find out the degree to which a tee is helpful.
Obtain golf tees for students to create art projects; review Task Card #24 for general art ideas.
Review Task Card #41 for activities on golf.

First radio signal sent across the Atlantic Ocean from England to Newfoundland in North America by Guglielmo Marconi, 1901
Consider the benefit that this accomplishment represented, the benefits of instant communication over vast distances by way of the wireless, radio wave transmission.
(See activities under April 25, "Guglielmo Marconi ....")

Frank Sinatra, American singer/actor, born 1915
(See Biography Data in Extra-Know-How Section.)

Half-billion dollars given to U.S. colleges and hospitals by the Ford Foundation, 1955
Investigate how a foundation is established, controlled, and perpetually funded.
Ask students to fictionalize a foundation, decide upon its purpose, and select appropriate beneficiaries.

Martial law imposed upon Poland by the Polish government, 1981

Discuss what martial law is; investigate what the implications of martial law were in the case of Poland.

Trace the background of the Solidarity delegation, as led by Lech Walesa.

December 13

New Zealand discovered by Abel Tasman of the Netherlands, 1642

Initiate a study of New Zealand, Tasmania, and Australia; in particular, study the culture of the native Polynesian Maoris.

Exploration begun by Sir Francis Drake, the first Englishman to circumnavigate the world, 1577

Make a large mural illustrating the continents of the world; trace on the mural the many extensive voyages made by Drake.

Investigate the "Spanish Armada" as related to Drake.

John Henry Patterson, American executive of the National Cash Register Company, born 1844

(See Biography Data in Extra-Know-How Section.)

Explain that Patterson was the founder of the NCR Company and that he is credited with having instigated the widespread use of cash registers.

Investigate the expanded capabilities of current cash registers.

Invite a member of the United Food and Commercial Works International Union (which includes members of the Retail Clerks' Union) to discuss careers in retailing.

Write to the National Cash Register Company for information about the firm. (See Address Listing in Extra-Know-How Section.)

December 14

First U.S. state road authorized by Kentucky, 1793

Discuss the various highway networks in America—federal interstate, and state, county, and private roads.

Find out the relationship between gasoline tax and road maintenance; investigate the purpose of truck-weighing stations.

Choose a city in northern Minnesota or northern Wisconsin; find out the annual cost of keeping the roads clear of snow and/or the cost or repairing roads that are damaged each year by heavy winter weather.

Nut and bolt/screw machine patented, 1798

Demonstrate how a nut and bolt operates; suggest to students that they devise a project which would make use of nuts and bolts; encourage them to visit a hardware store to view the many sizes and shapes of screw-type fasteners available and to buy the appropriate hardware for their projects.

Alabama admitted to the United States as the twenty-second state, 1819

(See States Admitted to the USA Data in Extra-Know-How Section.)

First table tennis tournament held, 1901

Investigate the game of table tennis (ping-pong) as related to the different types of paddles and the method of scoring.

Research world records that have been achieved in ping-pong.

Conduct a table tennis tournament.

South Pole reached by Roald Amundsen, Norwegian explorer, 1911

Explain that Roald Amundsen had originally wanted to be the first explorer to reach the North Pole, but he was beaten by Robert E. Perry.

Investigate the topography, animal life, and vegetation of Antarctica.

Explain that the earth's coldest recorded temperature was at the South Pole in 1957-58; find out what that temperature was.

Read the book *All about the Arctic and Antarctic*, by the Newbery Award-winning author, Armstrong Sperry.

December 15

Bill of Rights adopted by the U.S. Congress, 1791
   Investigate the first 10 amendments of the U.S. Constitution in order to learn the significance of each.
   (See activities under December Special Weeks, "Human Rights ....")

Street-cleaning machine first used, 1854
   Find out which sector of the city government is responsible for street cleaning; investigate also what agency is responsible for the collection of trash and garbage and how it is disposed of after it is collected.
   Discuss the comment, "A culture reveals itself by what it throws away"; explain that America is considered to be a "throw-away" culture; ask students to brainstorm ideas as to how packaging and the use of paper bags might be modified and how a greater percentage of refuse might be recycled.

Sitting Bull (Tatanka Iyotake), American Indian leader, shot by police, 1890
   Investigate this incident and the life of Sitting Bull.

John Paul Getty, oil magnate, born 1892
   (See Biography Data in Extra-Know-How Section.)
   Find the location of the J. Paul Getty Museum and investigate to what other public services Getty has contributed his money.

Miniature golf courses established by Garnet Carter, a Tennessee promoter, 1929
   Discuss the rules for miniature golf and, if possible, play a round of miniature golf.
   Design a miniature golf course.
   Create a new recreation pastime, just as Garnet Carter did.

Glenn Miller, American bandleader, disappeared, 1944
   Explain that Miller's plane vanished on a flight over the English Channel; discuss the topic of "missing persons" and how people can disappear without any trace of evidence. Find out how many years of absence are required for an individual to be considered legally deceased. (Example: if a military person is reported as "missing in action," how long a period of time is required before the spouse is legally allowed to remarry?)
   Contact the local Bureau of Missing Persons to invite a representative to class for more information.
   Discuss the responsibility of notifying parents or guardians on one's whereabouts; ask students to write a creative story concerning their own disappearance; include the imagined reaction of their families.

December 16

Ludwig van Beethoven, German composer, born in Bonn, Prussia, 1770
   (See Biography Data in Extra-Know-How Section.)
   Explain that Beethoven was hard of hearing much of his life, but that he continued to compose many works even after he became totally deaf at the age of 45; explain that Beethoven was considered to be a child prodigy; find out what is meant by the term "child prodigy."
   Make a class list and define each of the following terms: symphony, concerto, chamber music, aria, cantata, oratorio.
   Consider the effort and talent involved in creating each instrument's part in terms of an orchestrated whole; enjoy listening to a recording from Beethoven's Ninth Symphony, "Ode to Joy."

Boston Tea Party staged, 1773
   Explain that Boston's harbor became a giant teapot as the Sons of Liberty, dressed as Indians, dumped 342 cases of tea into the water; investigate what the specific reason for this protest was and what kind of group the Sons of Liberty was.
   Find out whether the incident served the purpose for which it was intended; explore further as to whether protest movements are warranted—whether the end justifies the means.

Margaret Mead, American anthropologist, born 1901
   (See Biography Data in Extra-Know-How Section.)
   Investigate the career of an anthropologist; find out how many different kinds of anthropologists there are.
   Trace the derivation of the word unit "anthro"; locate other words in the dictionary which begin with "anthro" and define them. Conduct a similar study for the word unit "ology," as in anthropology and physiology.

December 17

John Greenleaf Whittier, American poet, born 1807
(See Biography Data in Extra-Know-How Section.)
Obtain copies of Whittier's abolitionist works and/or of his New Engalnd ballads.

Oliver Willcox Norton, founder of a firm which became the American Can Company, born 1839
(See Biography Data in Extra-Know-How Section.)
Investigate the process of food preservation used in the commercial canning of foods.
Consult a cookbook for information about home canning of fruits and vegetables.
(See activities under January 19, "Process for ....")

First motor-powered airplane by Orville and Wilbur Wright flown, 1903
Obtain a book on aerodynamics to understand more fully the significance of this accomplishment.
Develop a pictorial timeline of the history of flight.
Discuss human's desire to fly, "to beat nature"; consider other aspirations of human beings, such as psychic transcendence.
Obtain the Walt Disney film, "Man in Flight."
Review Task Card #58 on Amelia Earhart and flight.
(See activities under March 15, "First commercial ....")

Willard Libby, American geochemist, born 1908
(See Biography Data in Extra-Know-How Section.)
Explain that Libby developed a technique which provided geologists and archaeologists with a scientific method for accurately dating ancient materials of biological origin; find out what newer methods are being used, such as "thermoluminescence" and the technology of molecular biology.
(See Data-Detail in Extra-Know-How Section, "Explanation of Geophysical Dating Instruments.")

Arthur Fiedler, conductor, born 1894
(See Biography Data in Extra-Know-How Section.)
Explain that Arthur Fiedler led the Boston Pops Orchestra for many years; find out information about the many presentations of this orchestra.
Describe to students what an "aficionado" is; explain that Fiedler was an aficionado of anything related to fire equipment—fire stations, trucks, and other fire-safety equipment.

December 18

U.S. Constitution ratified by New Jersey, thus making it the third state, 1787
(See States Admitted to the USA Data in Extra-Know-How Section.)

Thirteenth Amendment to the U.S. Constitution ratified, abolishing slavery, 1865
(See Data-Detail in Extra-Know-How Section, "Amendments to the U.S. Constitution.")
Trace the 200-year history of black slavery in America; in view of the years following 1865, discuss how legislation does not necessarily insure enforcement of a law.
Obtain a copy of *Great Slave Narratives,* by Arna Bontemps.

Paul Klee, German expressionist painter, born 1879
(See Biography Data in Extra-Know-How Section.)
Obtain prints of Klee's expressionist-abstract art work and share with the class; find out what expressionism in art means.
Discuss Klee's statement, "Becoming is superior to being."

December 19

Poor Richard's Almanac, by Benjamin Franklin, published, 1732
Explain that an almanac was formerly a yearly calendar of days, weeks, and months, with various useful data; obtain a copy of *Poor Richard's Almanac* and share the many sayings that Franklin entered in his almanac; encourage students to create their own almanac sayings.
Examine various current world almanacs and report findings in an interesting way to the class.

Washington's Continental Army encamped at Valley Forge, 1777
Investigate the difficult conditions in which the 11,000 men had to survive; ask students to talk about times when they personally have experienced physical inconvenience and hardship.

Mary Aston Livermore, suffragette, born 1821
(See Biography Data in Extra-Know-How Section.)
Discuss the term "suffragette" and the Woman's Suffrage Movement.

December 20

Louisiana Purchase negotiated, 1803
Explain Jefferson's motivation for the purchase of the territory; the need for additional land was not as important as was free navigation down the Mississippi River.
Ask students to outline on a current U.S. map the area which represents the territory purchased from France; explain that approximately one million square miles was involved at about $20 a square mile; compute the total cost of the negotiation. Consider what the current cost per square mile might be.

Sacagawea, American Indian guide for the Lewis and Clark expedition, died 1812
(See Biography Data in Extra-Know-How Section.)
Trace the route of the Lewis and Clark expedition.
(See activities under August 31, "Exploration of ....")

Bachelor Tax levied in Missouri, 1820
Discuss the reasons why a bachelor might be taxed more than others; investigate the background of this particular tax levy.
Explain that various taxes, tax "breaks," and tax schedules are developed partly to encourage or discourage various practices and life-styles; find evidence of this by citing various examples either currently or in the past.
(See activities under February 28, "Bachelor Day ....")

Harvey S. Firestone, American industrialist and founder of Firestone Tire Company, born 1868
(See Biography Data in Extra-Know-How Section.)
(See activities under June 15, "Vulcanized rubber ....")

Union of Soviet Socialist Republics (USSR) formed, 1922
Investigate bolshevism and the Russian Revolution of 1917.
Introduce a geographic study on Russia, with emphasis on its energy resources.
Ask students to list, in order, the three largest countries in the world in regard to area and population.

Electronic television system in the United States patented, 1938
Review Task Card #38 for activities about television.
Ask students to conduct a classroom survey of how many hours each student watches television a week; find the average number of hours for each student and for the whole class.
Suggest that at the first of the week, a student be selected as the class television programmer with the responsibility of studying the television guide for educational and special programs and then reporting the selected schedule to the class.

Uri Geller, an Israeli known for his telekinetic ability, born 1946
(See Biography Data in Extra-Know-How Section.)
Define what telekinesis is; consider the potential involved in concentration.
Discuss the topic that individuals commonly use only about ten percent of their mental ability.
Explore various forms of psychic phenomena.
Read the book entitled *Mystery*, written by Uri Geller.

December 21

First day of winter (on or about December 21)
Suggest that the class take a neighborhood field trip to look for the first signs of the season; collect materials for a science table display; return and compile a class list of words describing the winter season; ask a student to record and reproduce the word list to be distributed to class members as reference for ideas in creative writing throughout the season.

Pilgrims landed at Plymouth, Massachusetts, 1620

Find out how long the Pilgrims had to live on board ship before they were able to build shelter and plant seeds for food.

Research the Society of Mayflower Descendents and report any unusual data.

(See activities under September 16, "Voyage of ... " and November 19, *Mayflower* ship ... " and November 21, "Mayflower Compact ....")

Joseph Stalin, Russian leader, born 1879

(See Biography Data in Extra-Know-How Section.)

(See activities under November 12, "Leon Trotsky ....")

Radium discovered by Marie and Pierre Curie, 1898

Ask students the difference between discovering an element and isolating it; inquire as to which process occurs first.

(See activities under April 20, "Radium isolated ....")

First crossword puzzle designed, 1913

(See activities under November 5, "Crossword puzzles ....")

Nevada's six-week divorce law supported by the U.S. Supreme Court, 1942

Discuss divorce and dissolution laws and their effects upon all concerned.

Apollo 8 spacecraft launched by the United States, 1968

Explain that this particular flight allowed views of the far side of the moon; encourage students to trace the purposes and achievements of the *Apollo* space program.

December 22

First day of the zodiac period, Capricorn, the Goat (through January 21)

(See Data-Detail in Extra-Know-How Section, "Notes on Astrology.")

International Arbor Day

Review Task Card #52 for activities on Arbor Day.

(See activities under April 28, "Arbor Day.")

James Oglethorpe, English general, born 1696

(See Biography Data in Extra-Know-How Section.)

Explain that Oglethorpe defeated the Spanish in 1742 and subsequently founded Georgia as a refuge for imprisoned debtors.

Consider the practice of imprisoning debtors and therefore eliminating their ability to earn wages and pay back their debts; brainstorm ideas of how to improve upon this practice.

Alfred Dreyfus sentenced to Devil's Island in world-famous case, 1894

(See activities under January 13, "*J'accuse*, Emile ....")

U.S. Golf Association formed, 1894

Review Task Card #41 for activities on golf.

Discuss the issue that golf courses consume too much chemical fertilizer and water for maintenance of the greens, as propounded by the environmentalists; consider the golf enthusiasts' defense that golf courses supply the needed greenbelts for the local ecosystem.

Lincoln Tunnel under the Hudson River opened, 1937

Consider the engineering feat of building a tunnel beneath a river.

Discuss ideas concerning what constructive uses might be made of the displaced earth.

Brainstorm ideas regarding how vehicle fumes might be eliminated from the Lincoln Tunnel.

December 23

Jacquard Loom, produced by French inventor, J. M. Jacquard, patented, 1801

Find out how the Jacquard Loom was an improvement upon former looms.

Review Task Card #48 for activities on how to make looms and how to weave.
Encourage students to bring samples of women materials for the class to examine.

Joseph Smith, founder of the Church of Latter Day Saints, born 1805
(See Biography Data in Extra-Know-How Section.)
(See activities under June 1, "Brigham Young ....")

Sarah Breedlove Walker, black businesswoman "millionaire," born 1867
(See Biography Data in Extra-Know-How Section.)
Trace Walker's life from poverty to wealth.
Consider Walker's situation of having come from a poor family; discuss ways in which her life and values may have changed after she became a millionaire. Ask students to project as to the effect, if any, that becoming a millionaire would have on their lives.

U.S. Federal Reserve banks created, 1913
Explain that the Federal Reserve system serves as a clearinghouse for the nation's financial trading.
Write to the U.S. Federal Reserve Bank of New York for the booklet "The Story of Checks," which explains checks, credit cards, and the Federal Reserve system. (See Address Listing in Extra-Know-How Section.)
(See activities under November 16, "U.S. Federal ....")

José Greco, Spanish dancer, born 1918
(See Biography Data in Extra-Know-How Section.)
Introduce rapid-paced Spanish music; suggest that students choreograph and demonstrate their dance patterns; include rhythm instruments.

Transistor invented, 1947
Explain that a transistor is a miniature amplifying device that performs much the same functions as the electronic vacuum tube; find out the various ways transistors have been used.

December 24

Kit Carson, American frontiersman and Indian fighter, born 1809
(See Biography Data in Extra-Know-How Section.)
Find out which expeditions and which troops he guided through the frontier.

War of 1812 ended by the United States' and Great Britain's signing of the Treaty of Ghent, 1814
Investigate the causes of the War of 1812; explain that the diplomatic victory marked increased isolation from Europe and the growth of nationalism as the nation was free to expand westward.
Locate Ghent on a map of Europe; discuss what a treaty is; ask students to design a treaty with a student or family member over a real or fictitious issue.

"Silent Night" or **"Stille Nacht"** composed in Germany by Franz Gruber (melody) and Joseph Mohr (lyrics), 1818
Ask students to read and discuss the lyrics and enjoy singing the carol together.
Draw an illustration which is inspired by the words of "Silent Night."
Obtain a copy of the song as it is sung in German.
Encourage students to learn to play the chords of the song on the autoharp and to play the melody on the song bells.

Bicycle with back brake pedal patented, 1889
Discuss the advantages and disadvantages of pedal brakes and of hand brakes.
Demonstrate the principle of bicycle brakes (friction against the wheel).
Look in books for pictures of early bicycle designs.
Review Task Card #40 for information about bicycles.

Howard Hughes, American financier, born 1905
(See Biography Data in Extra-Know-How Section.)
Speculate what life might be like for a wealthy person who chooses to live in seclusion.
Suggest that students comment on various interests in which they would like to invest money if they were wealthy.
Discuss the confusion that developed over Hughes' will; explore the significance of every adult's having an explicit will.

December 25

Christmas Day
(See Data-Detail in Extra-Know-How Section, "Christmas Greetings throughout the World.")
Enjoy poems from *Sing Hey for Christmas Day*, as selected by Lee Bennett Hopkins.

Isaac Newton, English physicist and philosopher, born 1642
(See Biography Data in Extra-Know-How Section.)
Explain that Newton was reputed by many to have been the greatest scientist who ever lived; discuss Newton's quoted response to that reputation: "If I have seen a little farther than others, it is because I have stood on the shoulders of giants" (among the "giants" were Galileo, Descartes, Copernicus, Leonardo da Vinci).
Talk about the point that Newton supposedly spent many hours under apple trees; the fall of the apples initiated his monumental investigation of gravity—the invisible force that holds the universe together; demonstrate Newton's Theory of Gravitation—whatever goes up must come down—by tossing a coin in the air; discuss the principles of the law in view of new space-age developments; for example, must orbited satellites eventually come back down to earth?
Investigate Newton's other contributions, such as the development of calculus and the discovery of the spectrum.
Read *Universe of Galileo and Newton*, by William Bixby.

Clara Barton, organizer of the American National Red Cross, born 1821
(See Biography Data in Extra-Know-How Section.)
Obtain a copy of *Clara Barton: Founder of the Red Cross*, by Helen Dore Boylston.
(See activities under March Month-long Observances, "Red Cross ....")

First steam passenger train scheduled, 1830
Create mathematical story problems involving a train schedule. (If a train is due at 7:06 and is 20 minutes late, what time is its arrival time?) Experiment with using the international 24-hour clock for time specifications.

Conrad Hilton, American hotelier, born 1887
(See Biography Data in Extra-Know-How Section.)
Contact a local travel agency for brochures on the locations of Hilton hotels around the world; ask students to chart the locations on a world map.
Investigate how Japanese interests all over the world are leading to the construction of hotels with conveniences that Japanese travelers may prefer.
Explore hotel management as a career.
Ask students to design their own hotel with options they think might attract people.

Robert Ripley, creator of Ripley's Believe It or Not series, born 1893
(See Biography Data in Extra-Know-How Section.)
Enjoy reading some of the entries from the *Ripley's Believe It or Not* books.
Encourage students to create their own "Believe It or Not" situations.
Hold a "Believe It or Not Day." Ask students to portray some of the entries; consider certain parallels between Ripley's situations and the more modern counterparts to be found on television programs such as "That's Incredible" or "Real People."

December 26

Boxing Day, a holiday and gift-giving day in many parts of the world
Explain that in some areas, the day is called "Boxing Day," meaning a day to "box up" gifts for the servants.

George Dewey, American admiral in the Spanish-American War, born 1837
(See Biography Data in Extra-Know-How Section.)
Trace the causes of the Spanish-American War.
Explain that the Treaty of Paris freed Cuba to a tutelage arrangement with the United States; Puerto Rico and Guam were ceded to the United States and the Philippines was surrendered to the United States for $20 million; ask students to trace the development of both Cuba and the Philippines since that time.
Discuss the point that this war led the way for U.S. involvement in the course of events in both Latin America and in the Far East.

Coffee percolator patented, 1865

Discuss the various ways of making coffee; obtain a percolator to demonstrate that particular process. (See activities under April 3, "Coffee mill ....")

Mao Tse-tung, Chinese leader, born 1893

(See Biography Data in Extra-Know-How Section.)
Find a book of various sayings of Mao.

December 27

Louis Pasteur, French scientist, born 1822

(See Biography Data in Extra-Know-How Section.)
Explain that Pasteur experimented with the fermentation of wine to learn that the process was caused by airborne bacteria; he developed the pasteurization process, that of killing harmful germs by heating. He also worked with the field of vaccinations by producing resistance to disease through an injection of weakened germ cultures.

Obtain pictures of bacteria; talk about bacteria as the most numerous living things and as one-celled organisms that are both harmful and helpful to human beings; encourage students to draw pictures of the three types of bacteria: round, rod, and spiral-shaped; explore what antibodies are.

Ask students to make a list of how bacteria have helped human beings.

Consider various suffixes which represent a process, i.e., "ation" in pasteurization or "lysis" in electrolysis; invite students to create a new process and attach an appropriate suffix to their names, as was done with Pasteur's name.

Discuss the statement by Pasteur: "Wine is the most healthful and most hygienic of all beverages."

Johannes Kepler, German astronomer who discovered the Law of Motion of the Planets, born 1871

(See Biography Data in Extra-Know-How Section.)
Encourage interested students to examine the three basic laws of planetary motion and give examples using a solar system model.

Radio City Music Hall opened, 1932

Encourage students to create and perform a Rockette's dance routine.

World Bank chartered, 1945

Explain that the World Bank is an autonomous body associated with the United Nations; ask students to investigate the purposes of this organization.

December 28

Iowa admitted to the United States as the twenty-ninth state, 1846

(See States Admitted to the USA Data in Extra-Know-How Section.)

Woodrow Wilson, twenty-eighth president of the United States, born 1856

(See Biography Data in Extra-Know-How Section.)
Explain that Wilson was the only president with a Ph.D. degree and that he wrote political science texts; discuss his view that a war was necessary to make the world "safe for democracy."

Investigate the Fourteen Points of the League of Nations.

Chewing gum patented, 1869

Make a class list of all the types of chewing gum available (brands and flavors); invite students to create an original gum flavor and a corresponding wrapper.

Find out the ingredients that are in gum and how gum is manufactured; consider the value of chewing only sugarless gum.

Invite students to make a chain out of gum wrappers.

Talk about the many incidental uses of gum, i.e., gum on the end of a stick to retrieve lost coins; encourage students to develop a creative vignette which is based on one of these different uses of gum.

(See Data-Detail in Extra-Know-How Section, "Chewing Gum—History.")

John Van Neumann, Hungarian-American mathematician, born 1903
(See Biography Data in Extra-Know-How Section.)
Explain that Van Neumann dealt with computers and was director of an electronic computer program; explore the field of computer-related careers.
(See activities under March 11, "Vannever Bush ....")

John Y. Brown, American restauranteur and founder of the Kentucky Fried Chicken franchise, born 1933
(See Biography Data in Extra-Know-How Section.)
Investigate the career of a restaurant owner or that of the manager of a fast-foods franchise.
Obtain information about various facets of the fast-food retail industry.
Design an advertisement for Kentucky Fried Chicken.
Investigate to what political office John Y. Brown was elected.

Pledge of Allegiance officially sanctioned by the U.S. Congress, 1945
Find out whether it is custom, policy, or law which determines whether the pledge is said in schools and at various public functions.
(See activities under October 10, "Pledge of ....")

December 29

William Macintosh, developer of the raincoat, born 1776
(See Biography Data in Extra-Know-How Section.)
Consider the various types of raincoats, such as different fabrics and styles; encourage students to design an ideal raincoat.

Charles Goodyear, American inventor of the vulcanization process, born 1800
(See Biography Data in Extra-Know-How Section.)
(See activities under June 15, "Vulcanized rubber ....")

Andrew Johnson, seventeenth president of the United States, born 1807
(See Biography Data in Extra-Know-How Section.)
Explain that Alaska was purchased from Russia, against popular support under Johnson's administration and was therefore called "Johnson's polar bear garden."
(See activities under March 13, "Impeachment proceedings ....")

Texas admitted to the United States as the twenty-eighth state, 1845
(See States Admitted to the USA Data in Extra-Know-How Section.)

Pablo Casals, Spanish cellist, born 1876
(See Biography Data in Extra-Know-How Section.)
Obtain a cello or other string-family instruments and share with the class.
Discuss Casal's statement: " ... the capacity to care is the thing which gives life its deepest meaning and significance."

Billy Mitchell, American army officer and aviator, born 1879
(See Biography Data in Extra-Know-How Section.)
Explain that Mitchell strongly urged the military sector to develop an air force; his outspoken manner resulted in his conviction by a court-martial. Discuss the point that visionary people's ideas are often not accepted by their contemporaries; consider Mitchell's abrasive approach and think of positive alternatives for approaching authorities with the idea for change.

Massacre at Wounded Knee occurred, 1890
Investigate the background of this event.
Discuss current events which tend to reflect the nation's attempt to compensate for the abuse of Native Americans.
(See activities under June 2, "American Indians ....")

Cyrano de Bergerac play opened, 1897
Obtain a copy of the script and share it with the class.
Introduce an oral interpretation lesson using Cyrano's famous "nose speech."

December 30

Andrés Vesalius, Flemish anatomist who first described the human body in detail, born 1514
(See Biography Data in Extra-Know-How Section.)
Explain that many of Vesalius' discoveries overthrew many of the doctrines put forth by Galen, whose authority in the medical field had gone undisputed for about 1,400 years.
Introduce a model of the human body to initiate a study of physiology and anatomy; suggest that students personify various parts of the body by writing verbalizations, i.e., "Stomach, I ache; please stop eating so many rich foods."
Use Reproducibles #26-32 for a science-art project.

Gadsden Purchase negotiated, 1853
Outline on a U.S. map the area which was involved in the $10 million purchase (southern portion of Arizona and New Mexico).
Trace the development of this area.

Rudyard Kipling, British writer and Nobel Prize winner, born 1865
(See Biography Data in Extra-Know-How Section.)
Explain that Kipling grew up in India where his father was a British official; his writings about nature and the habitats of animals are very accurate. Share with students *Just So Stories,* as illustrated by Nicolas, *The Elephant's Child,* as illustrated by Leonard Weisgard, the *Jungle Books, Kim, Captains Courageous,* and the poems, "Gunga Din" and "Mandalay."
Encourage students to create their own "Just-So Stories."

Simon Guggenheim, American philanthropist, born 1867
(See Biography Data in Extra-Know-How Section.)
Explain that Simon Guggenheim was one of several in a family line of highly successful industrialists and philanthropists; several family members established separate foundations with the commitment to return the money to humankind; ask students to find out the specific type of foundation Simon Guggenheim established.
(See activities under June 8, "Frank Lloyd ....")

Sanford Koufax ("Sandy"), Jewish-American baseball pitcher, born 1935
(See Biography Data in Extra-Know-How Section.)
Explain that Koufax was expected to play in the World Series during a Jewish holiday—an act which would violate the Jewish tradition. Ask students to discuss other situations which might cause ethical conflict for various people.
Trace Koufax's professional record in baseball.

December 31

Lord Cornwallis, British general who surrendered to George Washington at Yorktown, thus ending the Revolutionary War, born 1738
(See Biography Data in Extra-Know-How Section.)
Discuss what it is to lose or to surrender in public.
(See activities under October 19, "Yorktown surrendered ....")

Henri Matisse, French post-impressionist painter, born 1869
(See Biography Data in Extra-Know-How Section.)
Obtain prints of Matisse's art work; explain that he is particularly known for his depiction of odalisques, which are female Moroccan slaves.
Trace the political relationship of Morocco (North Africa) and France.
Find out what post-impressionist art is.

Ellis Island, United States immigration depot, opened, 1890
Discuss what effect the Industrial Revolution had upon immigration; investigate the island's location, its significance in history, the purpose of immigration quotas, and such terms as "immigration" and "emigrants."
Review Task Card #64 for a copy of the poem, "Give Me Your Tired, Your Poor."

New Year's Eve Day, the last day of the year

Participate in committee work by planning a New Year's Eve party, complete with theme, invitations, decorations, refreshments, and entertainment.

Speculate what a New Year's Eve party may be like at the turn of the next century.

> Ring out the old, ring in the new,
>   Ring, happy bells, across the snow:
>   The year is going, let him go;
> Ring out the false, ring in the true.
>
> —Alfred Lord Tennyson
> from "Ring Out, Wild Bells"

PART 2

**EXTRA-KNOW-HOW
SECTION**

INTRODUCTION

In part 1, Events and Activities Section, the reader is often referred to one of several areas within the Extra-Know-How Section, as follows:

1. General Topics:

    Biography Data
    States Admitted to the USA Data
    Resource Person Data
    Conducting a Survey Data

    All of the four categories above are provided in this section as general teaching/learning techniques to apply to the information found in part 1 of the book. As an example, when a person's birth is recorded as one of the entries in part 1, the reader is directed to Biography Data for a wide variety of ways to find out more about the individual. It is hoped that the similar strategies described for the other three categories will aid teachers and librarians as they help students to implement the material found in part 1 of the book.

2. Data-Detail:

    The Data-Detail is intended to supply additional content information to a few selected entries in part 1. The items represent those to which students have responded the most enthusiastically and those which teachers have found to be the most helpful in the development of learning activities. The contents do not reflect any particular emphasis but, rather, a diverse range of subjects—from sports history to career resources to poetry writing. The intent is to have a number of both well- and lesser-known topics included within one volume. Additionally, the format of Data-Detail functions as a sample for students who choose to write or tape reports on particular items, as suggested in the contract approach in the Sample Packet—Student Folders Section of the book.

    Because most of the data contained in Data-Detail is information the authors have derived from the books listed in the Reference Sources (appendices), the reader is referred to that listing for citations and any additional information. However, quoted material is directly documented beneath each entry.

3. Address Listing:

    When readers are referred in part 1 to the Address Listing, they are provided with the addresses of various agencies and associations with which to make contact for materials and supplemental information.

GENERAL TOPICS

BIOGRAPHY DATA

When an event lists "Biography" as an activity, it is recommended that:

1. The class discuss the person whose name is listed. A good source of biographies about many well-known personalities is the Value Tales Series, published by Western Publishing, Box 848, Jamestown, OH 45335.
2. At sometime during the year the class explore the following:
   a) Consider the research and preparation required of a biographer;
   b) Investigate the derivation of the words "biography" and "autobiography";
   c) "If you could be a biographer, about whom would you write?"

After the students have familiarized themselves with the person's life, they may choose to do one or several of the following activities:

1. Cut a piece of paper in the shape of a large thumbnail. On the paper, write biographic information and illustrate the data. Mount on a bulletin board with the caption of "Thumbnail Sketches."
2. Design a book jacket which represents the personality.
3. Illustrate a biography of the person by sketching a series of pictures of the major events of his/her life.
4. Make a poster that would publicize the particular person or his/her accomplishment.
5. Write a play about an incident from the person's life.
6. Make a puppet show depicting some of the significant people in the person's life.
7. Make a 3-D picture or bulletin board about the person.
8. Make a paper-doll stand-up of the character.
9. Make a filmstrip about the person's life.
10. Show pictures from the person's life on an opaque projector and have a discussion.
11. Make a collage to depict scenes, events, etc.
12. Ask several people to relate the person's life story, having one student continue the story from the point where the other student has ended.
13. Depict the life story through flannel-board figures.
14. Stage a pantomime of the life story, using a narrator.
15. Make a shadow play of the life story.
16. Make a diorama depicting scenes from the person's life.
17. State a role-play of a favorite incident.
18. Model the main character in dough, soap, plaster, wood, apples.
19. Make a sand table or sand pan, using dolls or models to create scenery.
20. Make a wire or pipe-cleaner figure with a head and face to depict the character.
21. Make a simple stitchery of the character or his/her major accomplishment.
22. Do a chalk-talk (short talk with chalk illustrations).
23. Make a mural.
24. Make a simple tapestry or stained glass window.
25. Use the "fan" idea and unfold scenes from the person's life.
26. Make a newspaper story concerning the main character.

27. Design a rebus, criss-cross, find-a-word, or crossword puzzle about the person.
28. Report about the person through the medium of a comic strip.
29. Dress up as the famous personality and ask another student to conduct an interview or hold a large press conference, involving many students.
30. Report in the form of a radio or television newsflash (written or oral).
31. Make a radio show with sound effects and music accompaniment.
32. Write a letter to the class, as if you were the famous person, telling about an incident in your life.
33. Make a scrapbook about the person and his/her accomplishments.
34. Dress as the character in the book and relate parts of his/her life.
35. Make a storybook for younger children about this famous person.
36. Make a timeline of events in the person's life.
37. Write an original song, poem, or jingle about the person.
38. Make up a set of questions about the person, to be used as a game for others.
39. Prepare a diary that may have been written by that famous person.
40. Read a portion of a book to the class and follow with a discussion.
41. Prepare a speech that would serve as a nominating speech for the person's election to the Hall of Fame.
42. Construct a mobile concerning the character's traits or accomplishments or events in his/her life.
43. Make a box game related to the person.
44. Draw a cartoon about the person.
45. Do a mock television quiz show, using questions about the person.
46. Have a contest, "Design a Portrait," depicting the person.
47. Make a slide show or movie to show the class.
48. Play a "Who Am I?" game with others in the class, using facts about the person.
49. Make up a riddle about the character.
50. If the character is deceased, pretend that he/she returns for a day; discuss or write about his/her possible reactions.

STATES ADMITTED TO THE USA DATA

At the beginning of the year, designate a large bulletin board to be used for a study of the 50 states in the United States. Make an outline map of the United States, without the names of the states, and mount it on the bulletin board.

On the anniversary of the date that a state was admitted to the Union or to the United States, ask the students to color in the state and place the names of the state and its capital.

String or thread can be extended from each state to the margin of the bulletin board, leading to written information about the state. Ask students to research the following information, either as individuals or through committees:

State motto	State population
Flower	Major resources and products
Bird	Largest cities
Song	Capital city
Tree	Famous sightseeing areas
Nickname	

Discuss the origin of the state's name and teach the state song. Toward the end of the school year, students may fill in the information for states admitted during the summer months.*

---

*Students who wish to pursue an in-depth study of the states can develop notebooks with more extensive information and illustrations.

RESOURCE PERSON DATA

1. Consider the resource possibilities within the parent group of the class.
2. Ask the visitor what requests he/she may have regarding room arrangement and equipment (i.e., overhead projector, film projector).
3. Suggest that the resource person bring any possible items which are related to the topic.
4. Encourage the person to present the information informally and to make the material as appropriate to the grade level as possible.
5. Beforehand with the students:
   a) Prepare and list questions they may have concerning the visitor's topic.
   b) Discuss the difference between relevant comments and digressing stories.
6. Acknowledge the resource person's visit with a class-written note soon after the presentation.

CONDUCTING A SURVEY DATA

1. Materials needed:
   a) Clipboard (optional)
   b) Papers which include the following:
      1) Survey schedule on which to arrange and follow appointments
      2) Data collection sheet (spaces for identification of respondents, place, date, time, data responses)
      3) If necessary, individual questionnaires
      4) Tally and summary sheet

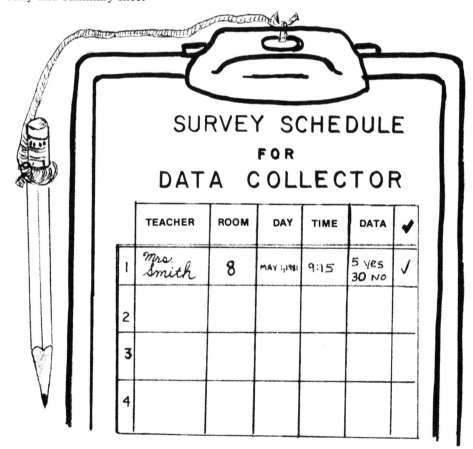

SURVEY SCHEDULE
FOR
DATA COLLECTOR

	TEACHER	ROOM	DAY	TIME	DATA	✔
1	Mrs. Smith	8	MAY 1, 1981	9:15	5 yes 30 NO	√
2						
3						
4						

2. Arrange ahead of time for convenient scheduling with teachers or any other target group which is to be surveyed.
3. Elicit from the students the appropriate behavior when visiting classes or particular people for the survey.

DATA-DETAIL

The following is an alphabetized list of the items included in the Data-Detail part of the book. The explanations about each item are provided in order to supplement information and to enhance interest and understanding of particular events and personalities.

AMENDMENTS TO THE U.S. CONSTITUTION*

The Bill of Rights: First 10 Amendments
Amendment 1: Freedom of Religion, Speech, and the Press; Right of Assembly and Petition

Amendment 2: Right to Keep Arms

Amendment 3: Quartering of Soldiers

Amendment 4: Regulation of Right of Search and Seizure

Amendment 5: Protection for Persons and Their Property

Amendment 6: Rights of Persons Accused of Crime

Amendment 7: Right of Trial by Jury in Suits of Common Law

Amendment 8: Protection against Excessive Bail and Punishments

Amendment 9: Constitution Does Not List All Individual Rights

Amendment 10: Powers Reserved to the States and the People

Amendment 11: Limitation of Power of Federal Courts

Amendment 12: Regulation of Electoral College—Separate Vote for President & Vice President

Amendment 13: Abolition of Slavery

Amendment 14: Guarantee of Protection to All Citizens

Amendment 15: Suffrage Not Denied because of Race, Color, or Servitude

---

*Source: *The Random House Dictionary of the English Language.* New York: Random House, 1966, pp. 1939-40.

Amendment 16:   Power to Levy Income Taxes

Amendment 17:   Election of Senators by Direct Vote

Amendment 18:   Prohibition of Manufacture and Sale of Liquor

Amendment 19:   Suffrage Rights Granted to Women

Amendment 20:   Terms of Office of President, Vice-President; Time Congress Shall Assemble

Amendment 21:   Repeal of Prohibition

Amendment 22:   Limitation of Terms of President and Vice-President

Amendment 23:   Regulation of Electoral College—Gave District of Columbia right to vote in presidential elections

Amendment 24:   Prepayment of Poll Tax or Other Taxes Not To Be Prerequisite for Voting in Federal Elections

Amendment 25:   Succession of Vice-President to Presidency

Amendment 26:   Lowering of the Voting Age to Age 18

APRIL FOOLS' DAY—HISTORY

There is no one agreed-upon explanation for the custom of playing practical jokes on the first day of April. In general, the custom has something to do with the observance of the spring equinox. April fooling became customary in France after the adoption of the reformed calendar in 1564, making the year begin on January 1. Under the old calendar, it had been common for the people to make new year's gifts and visits to friends on April first. The people who objected to the calendar change continued the original customs by extending quasi-gift giving and calls of "pretended" ceremony. It was not until the eighteenth century that April fooling became common in England. In Scotland, April fools are called April gowks, which means an April cuckoo. The early settlers of America brought the custom of April foolery with them; today it is observed by practical jokers in such ways as exchanging salt and sugar in the respective containers, as well as other tricks.

BASEBALL—HISTORY

Have you ever wondered how the game of baseball began? The name was given in 1835 when sacks filled with sand took the place of stakes or stones used to mark the spot players were to touch. They called these new sacks of sand "bases." A playing field called a diamond was first made in Cooperstown, New York in 1839. The game named "baseball," as we play it today, was really planned seven years later when a man named Abner Doubleday changed some of the rules and made it more of a sporting event. The first game was played in 1846, the score of which was 23 to 1. Until nine innings became the rule of the game, a winner was declared once the team had scored 21 runs. The Civil War slowed the development of baseball. When it ended, however, the Cincinnati Red Stockings became the first professional team. Baseball is so popular in the United States that it is known as the "American National Pastime." There is a museum and a Hall of Fame to honor baseball's best players.

BASKETBALL—HISTORY

Basketball is a made-in-America sport! It is one of the few major athletic games which was created by a certain person for a definite purpose. James Naismith, a YMCA instructor in Springfield, Massachusetts, wanted to develop a sport that could be played indoors in the wintertime when outdoor sports, such as soccer, could not be played due to inclement weather. The game was named basketball because the object of the game was to throw a ball into one or the other of two peach baskets which were set up at opposite ends of the playing court. In order to increase the challenge of "making a basket," the baskets were elevated on poles. However, that presented a problem when a basket was made because the players had to scale the pole to retrieve the ball. The difficulty was resolved by fashioning a drop-through hole in the peach baskets. Gradually the basket equipment evolved into its present-day form of a metal hoop and net. The game has become a rigorous and competitive sport, as well as a favorite participatory and spectator athletic activity in schools, universities, and athletic clubs throughout the United States and other countries.

CHEWING GUM—HISTORY

The practice of chewing gum dates back to approximately 50 A.D. when the Greeks are known to have chewed mastiche, the resin from the bark of the mastic tree; the Mayans used the chicle from the resin of the sapota tree for their chewing substance.

In North America, the native Indians introduced gum chewing to the early New England settlers in the form of resin from the spruce tree. In the early 1800s a type of paraffin gum was introduced in America; even today paraffin is used in gum, and paraffin alone is used for novelty types of gum.

Thomas Adams from New York City became interested in marketing chewing gum when he overheard a small girl asking a druggist for paraffin gum. It was by sheer coincidence then that he happened to meet Antonio Lopez de Santa Anna, the former conqueror of Mexico who was exiled and living in New York City. Santa Anna learned of Adams' interest and suggested he import the chicle from Mexico.

Others learned of the subsequent success that Adams was having, so they attempted to improve Adams' commodity by experimenting with flavors, with little success. It was William White, a popcorn salesman in Cleveland who found corn syrup to be one of the key ingredients in absorbing and maintaining flavors in gum. An Ohio physician had been working on pepsin power as an aid to digestion. His bookkeeper, Nellie Horton, suggested he combine the pepsin powder with gum "since so many people buy pepsin for digestion and gum for no reason at all." His blend of pepsin and chicle sold well once a financier helped him package his "medicine" product attractively.

Many other types of gums have emerged—those with aspirin, those with a variety of flavors, bubble gum, and sugarless gum.

People chew gum for a variety of reasons—to help clean the teeth, to aid digestion, to freshen the breath, and to enjoy a flavored taste. Some substance for chewing has been a relatively traditional habit throughout the world; for instance, the betel nut in several countries serves much the same purpose as chewing gum does. People simply tend to have an urge to chew, a process which begins in infancy when sucking for milk or when sucking one's thumb or pacifier. As people grow older, they can often be seen chewing on a pencil, a coarse blade of grass, or a piece of straw. Since its commercial introduction over a hundred years ago, chewing gum has been enjoyed by hundreds of millions of people around the world. (Note: Sugarless gum is strongly recommended over other types of gum.)

CHRISTMAS GREETINGS THROUGHOUT THE WORLD

Spanish:	Feliz Navidad	feh-LEES na-vi-DADTH
German:	Fröhliche Weihnachten	FREU-leesh-eh vi-nok-ten
French:	Joyeux Noel	jo-YEH no-EL
Italian:	Buon Natale	boo-ON na-TA-leh
Portuguese:	Feliz Natal	feh-LEES na-TAL
Danish:	Glaedelig Jul	GLA-da-lig U-el
Norwegian/Swedish:	God Jul	gud U-el
Finnish:	Hauskaa Joulua	HAUS-ka U-loo-a
Russian:	S Rozhdyestvom Khristovym	s ro-zhdye-STVOM krist-TOYM
Greek:	Kala Christougenna	ka-LA chris-TOU-yeh-na

COMMENTS ABOUT ALBERT EINSTEIN*

Part I: The following information was found to be in the school records of Albert Einstein:

> The boy is not a good all-around student; he has no friends; teachers find him a problem; father is ashamed of son's lack of athletic abilities; he has made a poor adjustment to school; the boy had odd mannerisms, makes up his own religion, chants hymns to himself; his parents regard him as "different."

---

*Source: W. Sullivan, "The Einstein Papers," *New York Times*, p. 1, Col. 1, March 27, 1972.

Part II: The following is a later record about the life of Albert Einstein:

> He didn't say his first word until he was three;
> At seven, his teacher said nothing good would ever come of him;
> When he was sixteen, he left his homeland (Germany) to avoid the draft;
> He couldn't get a job at nineteen because of his long hair, wrinkled clothes, and
> his accent.

> But ... before he was thirty, he had revolutionized the world of science.

DREYFUS AFFAIR

An incident of treason occurred in France shortly before the turn of the century. Alfred Dreyfus, a French army officer, was allegedly framed and then accused of having committed the crime. Dreyfus never ceased to protest his innocence, but his being a Jew weighed heavily against him. He was sentenced to life imprisonment on Devil's Island. The case was reopened, following Émile Zola's article which defended Dreyfus. Eventually Alfred Dreyfus was declared innocent and freed from prison.

EXPLANATION OF GEOPHYSICAL DATING INSTRUMENTS

Archaeologists and anthropologists are professionals who are interested in examining the material remains of former civilizations. They analyze the fossils, relics, artifacts, and monuments of cultures that existed long ago. From knowledge about the antiquities, they are able to infer what type of activities and belief systems the ancient cultures engaged in, as well as when they existed. There are many techniques by which they determine such information—from simple observation to cross-cultural comparisons to uranium-dating that pertains to radioactive elements and to even more sophisticated means.

Willard F. Libby, a geochemist, made a significant contribution to archaeology when, in 1945, he studied the element of carbon very extensively. Physicists had always believed that all carbon was a mixture of just carbon 12 (the most commonly found isotope) and carbon 13. Carbon 12 and carbon 13 are stable isotopes in that their atoms generally remain carbon atoms forever with no changes in their makeup. In 1941, another form, carbon 14, had been discovered, and three additional isotopes (carbon 10, carbon 11, and carbon 15) have since been produced in the laboratory. Willard Libby became interested in carbon 14 for a variety of reasons; carbon 14 is relatively long-lived in comparison to the other three radioactive isotopes; besides its relative long life, Libby learned that carbon 14 is uniformly distributed. He also learned that just as the carbon 14 level in the atmosphere remains unchanging, so also does the carbon 14 level remain constant within any living organism's body.

Every plant constantly accumulates very small amounts of carbon 14 that is taken from the air in the form of carbon dioxide. When animals eat plants, they build up amounts of carbon 14 in their bodies. Therefore, carbon 14 spreads throughout the chain of life in flowers, trees, frogs, shells, tigers, and—human beings.

The carbon 14 level remains constant within an organic unit, however, only when life continues. At the moment that death occurs within the organism, the intake of carbon ceases; all life processes halt and there is no further interplay between an organism and its environment. The carbon 12 that may be present in the trunk of a dead tree or in a dead animal remains where it is. But the radioactive isotope, carbon 14, begins to disintegrate, and the atoms become atoms of another kind. It is at this point of change that archaeologists can determine a measurement date for organic materials. They determine the amount of carbon 14 in a particular piece of organic material, figure the decay rate, and then count backwards to determine the date of the material. Charcoal and charred organic matter, such as heavily burned bone, have proved to be the most suitable for carbon 14 analysis. Wood, grass, cloth, seeds, antlers, and shells are also items able to be analyzed, but not artifacts of stone, metal, or clay.

A means of dating clay pottery would be extremely valuable to archaeologists; pottery provides an excellent beginning to the understanding of a culture, for three main reasons: 1) at any given time, nearly every ancient culture tended to produce pottery of the same general style (the coeval aspect); 2) because clay vessels break easily, the people had to make a great many of them so there are usually many pieces of clay artifacts to examine; 3) pottery pieces are generally indestructible and tend to be able to survive for thousands of years. Scientists are currently examining the phenomenon of thermoluminescence in order to adapt it as a means of aiding in the dating of pottery artifacts. Thermoluminescence is a process by which certain minerals are ground to powder and heated; for several seconds, the ground particles give off a bright glow. Potsherds (jagged fragments of broken pots) in powdered form also produce the luminescent effect. The color patterns are then measured on a spectograph, which, in turn, helps to determine the age of the artifact.

GETTYSBURG ADDRESS*

Fourscore and seven years ago our Fathers brought forth on this continent a new nation conceived in liberty, and dedicated to the proposition that all men are created equal. Now we are engaged in a great civil war, testing whether that nation, or any nation so conceived and dedicated, can long endure. We are met on a great battlefield of that war. We have come to dedicate a portion of that field as a final resting-place for those who here gave their lives that that nation might live. It is altogether fitting and proper that we should do this. But in a larger sense, we cannot dedicate — we cannot consecrate — we cannot hallow — this ground. The brave men, living and dead, who struggled here, have consecrated it far above our poor powers to add or detract. The world will little note nor long remember what we say here. It is for us, the living, rather, to be dedicated here to the unfinished work which they who fought here have thus far so nobly advanced. It is rather for us to be here dedicated to the great task remaining before us — that from these honored dead we take increased devotion to that cause for which they gave the last full measure of devotion; that we here highly resolve that these dead shall not have died in vain; that this nation, under GOD, shall have a new birth of freedom; and that government of the people, by the people, for the people, shall not perish from the earth.

Note: When Lincoln delivered his speech, it was criticized by many as being "flat and dishwatery." One of the few who did appreciate Lincoln's remarks was the speaker who had preceded him. He later wrote Lincoln, "I should be glad if I might flatter myself that I came as near the central point ... in two hours as you did in two minutes.

GREAT SEAL OF THE UNITED STATES OF AMERICA

On July 4, 1776, the day the Declaration of Independence was adopted, Congress appointed a committee to design the Great Seal of the United States of America. The Great Seal serves to attest to the authenticity of federal documents, by the authority of the United States government. Not until June 20, 1782, was the design of the seal agreed upon and adopted by the U.S. Congress.

The symbols in the design of the obverse side are as follows:

The crest forms the circular design of the seal;
Thirteen five-pointed stars represent the original thirteen states;
Ring of Light symbolizes God's guidance and protection of the new nation;
Coat of Arms
    Eagle — chosen as a national symbol because of its proud appearance, size, and strength;
    Shield on the breast represents Congress;
    Thirteen red and white vertical stripes stand for the first thirteen states;
    Scroll with the motto: *E Pluribus Unum* (one, of many) symbolizes the union of many states;
    Olive branch symbolizes peace;
    Bundle of thirteen arrows represents a commitment to defending the new and sovereign nation.

*Source: Betty Barclay, *Lamps to Light the Way*. Glendale, CA: Bowmar Pub. Corp., 1970, p. 164.

The entire design of the obverse side means, "We are a new and sovereign nation, a strong Union of many states, with a belief in God. We are powerful like the eagle. While we want peace with all nations, we are ready at the same time to defend ourselves against attack."

The symbols in the design of the reverse side are as follows:

> The pyramid represents the strength of the government; it was purposely left incomplete to indicate the potential for growth and for additional strength; the Roman numerals for 1776, the date of the nation's founding, are inscribed at the base of the pyramid.
> The eye symbolizes the watchful eye of God.
> The light around the eye symbolizes God.
> *Annuit Coeptis*, the Latin motto over the eye, means, "God has favored this undertaking."
> *Novus Ordo Seclorum*, another Latin motto, means, "A new order of the ages."

The entire design of the reverse side means, "Our nation was founded in 1776, with the help of God. It is strong and will continue to grow in size and power. For the first time in history, a nation is established with a government run by the people."

(Note: Both sides of the Seal are found on the back side of a U.S. one-dollar bill.)

GROUNDHOG DAY—HISTORY

According to an old legend, the groundhog, or woodchuck, comes out of his burrow on this day. If he sees his shadow, there supposedly will be six more weeks of winter, and he goes back to sleep. If the animal does not see his shadow, he stays up because winter is nearly over.

HALLOWEEN—HISTORY

Before Christianity came into Britain, the people had another religion, a pagan faith whose priests were called Druids. Because the Druid new year began on November 1, the night before was celebrated as a turn of the season. On that night, the Lord of Death, Saman, called together the wicked souls that had been condemned to inhabit the bodies of insects, birds, and animals. The ghoulish groups of owls, bats, cats, spiders, and other creatures went about bothering and teasing people. It was believed that those who had lived good lives on earth were given the souls of humans; these good ghosts supposedly returned to visit their relatives on this evening, called "All Hallows' Even," which over the years became known as Halloween.

When the Romans invaded Britain, they brought with them a less frightening observance of a similar holiday which they called "Halligan." The celebration was based upon the holiday in Rome named "Feralia," a religious day in which the dead heroes were prayed for and honored. All Saints' Day on November 1, as observed in many Christian countries, had its beginnings with this Roman holiday. In some Latin American cultures, the people set out food on the table at the church for the priest to say masses for the dead; they then go to the cemetery to pray on the graves of their ancestors. The people of China and Japan honor their dead in the "Feast of Lanterns." People in parts of West Africa practice a similar ceremony in which families go outside with torches to meet the ghosts of their ancestors and invite them to enter their homes.

Background of current customs:

Trick or Treat: Many years ago Irish farmers used to go from house to house begging for food for the Halloween feasting in the name of St. Colomba. Good wishes were extended to those who were generous, and threats were made to those who did not cooperate.

Witches: Some ancient cults believed in the devil, an individual who was believed to be sent to earth to corrupt human beings; witches and witchcraft were said to be associated with the devil.

Costumes: It is believed that the custom of masquerading derived from the court jesters who dressed in strange costumes and chanted unusual rhymes in English and Scottish parades.

Jack-o'-Lantern: There is an old Irish legend about a very stingy man named Jack who was kept out of heaven because of his unkindness; he also was not allowed in hell because of the jokes he played on the devil. He supposedly was condemned to walk the earth forever, carrying a hollowed-out pumpkin lighted from within by a candle.

Students may enjoy adapting the following words to the melodies of two familiar songs.

"Halloween Night" (Tune: "Three Blind Mice")
by Elaine Haglund

Witches, ghosts, and ghouls
Hear how they howl;
They all come out on a Halloween night
To screech and cry and give us a fright.
Did you ever see such a sight in your life
As witches, ghosts, and ghouls?

Bats, broomsticks, and owls
See how they fly;
They all come out on Halloween night
To hoot and flap and give us a fright.
Did you ever see such a sight in your life
As bats, broomsticks, and owls?

Lizards, toads, and spiders
See how they crawl;
They all come out on Halloween night
To slither and jump and give us a fright.
Did you ever see such a sight in your life
As lizards, toads, and spiders?

"Halloween Days" (Tune: "The Twelve Days of Christmas")
by Elaine Haglund

On the (first) day of Halloween
My ghoulfriend gave to me ...
A skeleton in a dead tree.

Second — two owls a-hooting
Third — three cauldrons bubbling
Fourth — four spiders spinning
Fifth — five vampire bats
Sixth — six cats a-hissing
Seventh — seven ghosts a-haunting
Eighth — eight pumpkins grinning
Ninth — nine monsters moaning
Tenth — ten broomsticks flying
Eleventh — eleven witches shrieking
Twelfth — twelve spooks a-lurking

HISTORY OF WRITING INSTRUMENTS*

EARLY DEVELOPMENTS

First tools of writing:	First refined instrument:	Egypt 4,000 B.C.:	China:
Flints to mark on cave or stone walls	Stylus, used by Greeks & Romans to write on waxen tablets	Hollow reed filled with ink*	Hair brushes dipped in ink

MODERN HISTORY

Era of Roman Empire:	1565 pencils:	1603 Steel point pen:	1869 First all-metal mechanical pencil:	1878 Ink pencil or Stylo-graphic pen:	1884 First fountain pen:	1888 Ball point pen patented:	1903 Fountain pen with a pump type filler:	1950 Ball point pen:
Quill pen (The best feathers for quills were the five outer wing feathers from geese, swans, or crows).	graphite sticks wrapped first in cloth and later enclosed in wood	on various holders, i.e., quill feathers	Known as a "magic pencil" which opened and closed like a telescope	The fore-runner of the ball point pen		(never produced due to lack of appropriate ink)	(basic concept of todays fountain pens)	became a universally used, high-performance writing tool

*The first inks, dating back to about 2500 B.C. consisted of lampblack, or soot, mixed with water or animal glue. Colored juices from many plant, animal, and mineral substances have been used as inks throughout the years. Early settlers in America often used the juice from the berries of inkberry and holly trees or the pokeweed plant.

*Source: Compiled and printed by Vernon U. Haglund

HOW WEBSTER CREATED THE DICTIONARY

Language is something you understand
and speak before you read, write, or
consult a dictionary.

Noah Webster had a very significant effect upon American English. He listened to the language of ordinary Americans and how it was being spoken. He wanted fervently to establish the identity of American English and to add dignity to the language that was being communicated in America. He was determined that American English not be locked into the tradition-bound English, as "ossified" in the dictionary of Samuel Johnson's *Dictionary of the English Language* in Britain.

Webster was already a well-known lexicographer and "word-smith" when he began preparing himself for the development of an American English dictionary, a feat which took him 28 years to complete. He studied 26 languages to learn the derivations of English words. He went through each entry of Samuel Johnson's dictionary and made notes on the dictionary pages of the deletions and additions he would make. One of his basic premises concerning language was that, "A national language is a bond of national union." Webster wanted a dictionary that would help eliminate the social and geographical class distinctions that language often serves to perpetuate.

Webster also had a goal of developing simpler, more rational spellings; Johnson's "harbour" became Webster's "harbor"; English "plough" became American "plow." He also introduced many words he was hearing in everyday usage, such as "applesauce," "skunk," "chowder." Such modifications would have been exceedingly upsetting to Jonathan Swift, who in 1712 complained that, "Our language is extremely imperfect; ... its daily improvements are by no means in proportion to its daily corruptions." Many of Webster's contemporaries in England and in America severely ridiculed Webster for his dictionary of "vulgar provincialisms of un-educated Americans." Critics called his work the "Merrykin Dikshunary" by "No-ur Webster eskwier junier." Even today Edwin Newman, author of *Strictly Speaking*, claims that "America will be the death of English.... The outlook is dire.... The evidence is all around us." Worse, the decay of the English language portends the decay of American society, since "the quality of our language is a reflection of the quality of our thought and character." Nonetheless, Webster's contribution has sustained itself as a log of *how* people actually speak in America, not necessarily how they *should* speak. Indeed, the cultural identity of the American idiom was firmly established through Noah Webster's original efforts.

Suggested activities: Invite students to list the types of assistance that most entries offer in a dictionary, such as spelling, pronunciation, definition, derivation, usage.

Encourage students to examine both a desk dictionary and a large dictionary to note:

1) the number of specialists and consultants involved in developing a dictionary;

2) the additional offerings in a dictionary, such as: maps, lists of geographical statistics, foreign language terms, famous documents, codes, signs, scientific charts, lists of colleges and universities, historical dates and names, lists of major reference works, abridged manual for English grammar and punctuation.

ICE-CREAM CONES — HISTORY

Ice-cream cones were first made in 1904 at a fair in St. Louis, Missouri by Ernest Hamwi. Hamwi, a pastry-maker, had a bakery booth at the fair which was next to an ice-cream booth. Hamwi observed that his neighbor had to wash dishes after each of the customers finished a serving of ice cream. Hamwi decided to design a pastry-holder for the ice cream so that dishes could be eliminated. He spread his batter, cooked it, and rolled it up in a cone shape, open at one end to hold the ice cream. The idea of the cone with ice cream was well received; soon a machine was designed and patented to make ice-cream cones.

INDEPENDENCE DAY (FOURTH OF JULY) — HISTORY

Independence Day is the birthday of the United States of America. On July 4, 1776, the Declaration of Independence was adopted by the Continental Congress; since that time the holiday has been celebrated as the founding of the United States, with speeches, parades, picnics, and fireworks.

Actually, the Continental Congress approved the resolution of independence on July 2, 1776, but it was not formally sanctioned until July 4. On July 8, it was publicly read in the yard of the Pennsylvania statehouse.

One year later on July 4, a celebration was held in Philadelphia by adjourning the Congress for a ceremonial dinner, several bonfires, and the ringing of bells and the displaying of fireworks. The custom quickly spread to other areas of the young nation. It serves as a day for citizens to consider the ideals on which the country was formed and to reevaluate to what degree the ideals are being practiced. (Note: Two of America's greatest statesmen, Thomas Jefferson and John Adams, died on July 4 of the same year, 1826.)

INFORMATION ABOUT PICKLES

A pickle is a food, usually a fruit or vegetable, which is preserved in vinegar and salt. Pickles are made with or without sugar and are usually seasoned with spices. Meats which are preserved in brine or vinegar are called pickled meats; pickled pigs' feet and corned beef are prepared in pickling solution or brine.

The most common vegetable to be pickled is the cucumber. Other fruits and vegetables are often used in making pickles or relishes, such as cauliflower, onions, tomatoes, beets, red and green peppers, cabbage, crab apples, peaches, pears, and watermelon.

In the process of pickling, the food substance is soaked in vinegar or brine. Then it is seasoned with things such as mustard, dill, horseradish, cinnamon, all-spice, cloves, celery seed, peppercorn, or pimiento. The pickle is then sealed tightly in jars. Some commercial firms prepare a mixture of many spices that is used for making particular types of pickles; the mixture is a product called pickle spice.

LABOR DAY — HISTORY

Labor Day is generally observed the first Monday in September as a legal national holiday to honor working people. Labor organizations sponsor various celebrations, but generally it is regarded as a day of rest and recreation to mark the end of summer.

Peter J. McGuire first recommended a national holiday to honor the country's working people in 1882. The workers in New York City staged the first labor parade in September of that year. Labor unions then urged the observance of a national holiday; in 1887, Oregon became the first state to make Labor Day a legal holiday. In 1894, President Cleveland signed a bill to authorize Labor Day as a legal holiday.

On varying dates, a labor holiday is observed in some European countries, Australia (where it is called Eight-Hour Day to commemorate the successful struggle for a shorter working day), and in Canada.

LEOPOLD-LOEB STORY

The following story took place in 1924. At that time, the newspapers named the event the "Crime of the Century." The public was shocked and horrified that such a crime had been committed.

Nathan Leopold was an intelligent 19-year-old from a wealthy family. He had just passed the bar exams of the legal profession and was planning soon to take a vacation in Europe. Richard Loeb was also a smart young man and was the son of a wealthy executive; he was only 18 years old but had already graduated from college.

Nathan Leopold and Richard Loeb were friends. Loeb was good looking and popular; Leopold was a quiet and scholarly person who worshipped Loeb. The two boys enjoyed "mind" games and often tried to think of ways to outsmart the public. Loeb, in particular, believed that some people were superior to others and that he, himself, was above the law.

In November 1923, the two friends began talking about committing a perfect crime. They decided that who the actual victim was was not really important, but that the individual should be a person from a wealthy family so that a ransom would be possible.

During the next six months, Loeb often brought up this particular discussion of their committing a crime. At first, Leopold thought it was just talk; but on May 23 Loeb informed Leopold that the plan was arranged and that the crime was to take place the following day. Despite Leopold's fear of blood,* his desire for Loeb's friendship was so great that he agreed to participate in the bizarre adventure.

---

*When Leopold was a child, other children had used red ink to make him think it was blood; when he would cry, they would call him a sissy.

So, on the afternoon of May 21, 1924 the two boys rented a Willys-Knight dark red touring car and cruised the town for their victim.

At a neighborhood school yard, some children were playing baseball. About 5 p.m. Bobby Franks needed to go home, so he began to leave the playground; Loeb was acquainted with Bobby and his family and decided that Bobby would indeed be the perfect victim.

Loeb rolled down the window and shouted, " ... like a ride home?"

Fourteen-year-old Bobby Franks, like most boys, thought it would be a treat to ride with older college graduates, so he agreed. By having so lured the unsuspecting Franks boy into the car, it was then easy to murder him—which they did; they then drove to a swampy field near Wolf Lake on the Illinois-Indiana border and hid the body. The two boys then drove on as if nothing had happened. Later that night, they drew up the ransom letter and called the Franks' home. As Mrs. Franks picked up the phone, she heard the following message: "Your son has been kidnapped; he is all right. There will be further news in the morning."

The following morning a man (Tony Mankowski) was walking through the marsh as a shortcut to work; he saw a foot sticking up in the culvert. He thought someone had drowned.

At the same time, the Franks family was receiving a special delivery letter with detailed instructions for the ransom.

The police were notified about both occurrences, but they did not connect the two incidents. A reporter for the *Chicago Daily News* went to the funeral home, however, to try to identify the swamp victim; he suspected that perhaps the two events were related. He contacted the Franks' home; soon after, the victim was identified as Bobby Franks.

It seemed a baffling mystery. The only clues were the ransom note and a pair of reading glasses found at the scene of the crime. During the police investigation, the game warden of the forest preserve at Wolf Lake was asked for a list of frequent visitors to the area. Nathan Leopold's name was on the list since he was an avid bird-watcher and even held classes in the area once a week. The police questioned him, but they found his story of "innocence" to be true; they also felt that since he was from a wealthy family, he would not be interested in ransom. However, when the pair of reading glasses turned out to be Leopold's and the typewriter that the ransom note had been typed on was identified, Leopold and Loeb were called in again for questioning. The state prosecutor played a trick on the two by claiming to each that the other had confessed; it was a trick which led each to actual confessions.

The two boys were labeled as "thrill killers." Public interest was high. At the trial on July 21, 1924, the courtroom was full. Clarence Darrow, a famous trial lawyer at that time, took the case. He was known as an attorney of the poor, but felt the rich should also have a chance. The boys pleaded "guilty." Many people felt Leopold and Loeb should be sentenced with the death penalty; however, the defense argued that the boys were victims of society and were insane at the time of the crime. The judge decided the boys were too young to be executed, so he gave the sentence of "Life Plus 99 Years" for each of them. They were sent to Joliet Penitentiary, with the recommendation that they never be paroled.

On January 28, 1936, Loeb was killed in a prison brawl; he had served 11 years of his term. Nathan Leopold served 33½ years. He tried hard to atone for his crime by setting up a prison library and school, and by volunteering for many service projects. His good record and public opinion won him his release from prison in 1958. He left the country to perform various social services in Puerto Rico, where he continued to feel guilty about the crime he had committed as a young man. He died on August 19, 1971.

Discussion topics: Can anyone force you to do anything but your own self? Has there been a time when a friend made you feel like you should do something wrong? Besides a desire for friendship (as in Leopold's case), what other types of circumstances lead people to knowingly commit a wrongdoing?

Additional references: *Life Plus 99 Years*, by Nathan Leopold; *Compulsion*, by Meyer Levin (a play); *The Crime of the Century*, by Hal Higdon.

"LOVE BALLAD TO MY LOVE, THE GREAT PICKLE"
by Marcia Sokol

It was in nineteen sixty-four
At the Disneyland General Store
Where I developed my first love
And I long to meet with him once more.

Oh, how I long for that great pickle!
It was there I met my friend
That I will love till no end;
He came out of his barrel
And my hunger he did mend.

Oh, how I long for that great pickle!
He was so marvelously delicious
And ever so dill and nutritious;
I could have eaten him in one bite
But now don't get suspicious.

Oh, how I long for that great pickle!
He was fat and green,
Yet the best sight ever seen,
And with that vinegar taste
I became a pickle fiend.

Oh, how I long for that great pickle!
My love was gone so very soon
It was like losing a balloon;
I was left with just a sick stomach
And it was my saddest afternoon.

Oh, how I long for that great pickle!
It will cost me a nickle and a dime
To have another next time;
Yet, will it be as good?
At that, I'll stop this rhyme.
    YET
  Oh, how I long for that great pickle!!!

MEMORIAL DAY – HISTORY

Memorial Day originated soon after the Civil War in the United States. In 1868, the date of May 30 was selected as the Memorial Day for the northern states to honor those who had recently died. Today it is generally celebrated the last Monday in the month of May, although some southern states also observe other days in commemoration of Civil War deaths.

Memorial Day is dedicated to the memory of all who have died in war for the United States. There are usually special ceremonies at the Tomb of the Unknown Soldier and at the American military cemeteries all over the world where World Wars I and II were fought and many lives were lost. More recently, Memorial Day generally serves as a time set aside in remembrance of any loved one who has died.

Memorial Day is also called "Decoration Day" because the graves of military people are decorated with flags and flowers; often there are also big parades to commemorate the occasion.

"MRS. O'LEARY'S COW"
from Camp O-Ongo Song Leader

According to legend, the Great Chicago Fire was caused by Mrs. O'Leary's cow, as described in the words below:

Late last night when we were all in bed,
    O' Mother Leary left a lantern in the shed.
The cow kicked it over and winked her eye and said,
    It will be a hot time in the ol' town tonight.
    FIRE, FIRE, FIRE
    WATER, WATER, WATER

MT. RUSHMORE DESCRIPTION

Mt. Rushmore National Memorial is located in the Black Hills in the southwest part of South Dakota. It is a mammoth sculpture that was started in 1929 by Gutzon Borglum and was completed in 1942. (Borglum's son completed the last year's work after Borglum's death in 1941.) On the mountainside are carved the heads of Presidents Washington, Jefferson, Lincoln, and Theodore Roosevelt.

Borglum first created a scale model of the project; then the measurements were laid out on the mountain. The appropriate areas were first dynamited; then men were lowered in seats from the top of the mountain to cut into the rock with compressed air drills and chisels.

Facts about the memorial:

The mountain sculpture can be seen from more than 60 miles away.

The eye of Jefferson is large enough for an adult to stand erect within it.

The heads are carved to the scale of people 465 feet tall.

The head of Washington is 60 feet from the chin up to the top of the head.

NOTES ON ASTROLOGY

March 21-April 19: Aries, the Ram
Active and ambitious nature
Natural leaders, eager to lead the way
Creative people
Loyal, will fight for what they think right
Anger quickly but calm down easily
Begin projects but are easily diverted
Able to get another to work with them on new projects but often quit before project is finished
Good sense of humor; enjoy music
Effective salespeople, actors, lawyers, and statesmen

April 20-May 19: Taurus, the Bull
Well-liked, become a good friend, generous, share own money
Usually trustworthy and faithful but can get furious
Strong and stubborn
Plan ahead and finish projects
Like games, sports, music, drama
Excellent memory
Led by emotion rather than reason
Good as engineers, builders, chemists, explorers

May 20-June 20: Gemini, the Twins
Imaginative, generous, and affectionate in nature
Adapt well to change but become easily dissatisfied soon after
Figure things out and act quickly
Learn new things quickly; clever, witty
Popular
Feel self-assured but tend to scatter his/her energy rather than focus it
Good business people; do well in advertising and publishing and as television writers and artists

June 21-July 22: Cancer, the Crab
Strong determination
Imaginative
Tend to be jealous
Home-loving, enjoy family life but also like to travel and have adventure

Sensitive but often do not show it
Loyal to family and friends
Enjoy the past or the old ways of doing things
Feelings hurt by criticism, crawl into own shell, moody
Do well in business as manufacturers and merchants; also good as teachers, librarians, scientists, and musicians

July 23-August 21: Leo, the Lion
Like activity, outdoors, and sun
Powerful personality, born leaders, ambitious, impulsive
Easily flattered
Generous and brave
Can become lazy
Stand up for friends and family, criticize people who disagree with them
Good doctors and nurses, famous actors, real estate developers

August 22-September 22: Virgo, the Virgin
Quick mind, alert, and hard working
Capable people but difficult personalities
Fearful of accidents, illness, and financial problems
Curious minds — really look into things, excellent memories
Do not like to think of unhappy things
Find fault with people and projects
Good as teachers, writers, editors, lawyers

September 23-October 22: Libra, the Scales
Original in ideas
Try to make friends, sympathetic, helpful to friends or strangers
Need to learn to accept criticism
Generous and expect that quality in others
Fond of music
Stand up for the underdog
Like amusements and excitement
Good in research
Do well as inventors, actors, musicians, singers

October 23-November 21: Scorpio, the Scorpion
Fearless nature, great self-control and self-confidence
Strong when roused to action
Ability to overcome problems
Can become domineering
Quiet people but know what is going on
Satisfied with self
Strong as business people and as doctors

November 22-December 21: Sagittarius, the Bowman
Cheerful, happy disposition
Very active and capable, work very hard to get things done
Outspoken and sometimes offensive in that way
Help charitable causes
Mind own business
Like to travel
Good as prospectors, air pilots, sea captains, and scientists

December 22-January 20: Capricorn, the Goat
Good organizing ability
Desire success
Appreciate solitude
Deep thinkers, have gloomy moods

Criticism worries them, may even make them stop trying
Good as managers in business and finance, writers, teachers, and lawyers

January 21-February 19: Aquarius, the Water Carrier
Friendly and popular, but also like to be alone
May tend to be lazy; self-reliant and confident
Good memories
Active in social causes
Do things in a quiet way
Good bargainers; do well in law and politics and as scientists and inventors

February 20-March 20: Pisces, the Fish
Calm, devoted to friends, and appreciated by friends
Modest, unselfish, interested in nature
Sincere and trustworthy but often fooled by others
Often doubt own ability and fear the future
Do well in government jobs, science, and engineering

RESOURCE GUIDE FOR PROFESSIONAL AND VOCATIONAL EDUCATION AND JOB PLACEMENT

General Occupational Information:

1. *Dictionary of Occupational Titles* (1980)
   Superintendent of Documents
   U.S. Government Printing Office
   Washington, DC 20402

2. *Encyclopedia of Careers and Vocational Guidance* (1975)
   Doubleday & Company
   501 Franklin Avenue
   Garden City, NY 11530

3. *Occupational Briefs* (1980)
   Chronicle Guidance Publications, Inc.
   Moravia, NY 13118

4. *Occupational Outlook Handbook* (1949)
   Superintendent of Documents
   U.S. Government Printing Office
   Washington, DC 20402

5. *Occupational Outlook for College Graduates* (1978)
   Superintendent of Documents
   U.S. Government Printing Office
   Washington, DC 20402

6. *Modern Vocational Trends Reference Handbook* (1970)
   Juvenal L. Angel
   Monarch Press
   Division of Simon & Schuster
   12 Floor, 1320 Avenue of the Americas
   New York, NY 10020

7. *What Color Is Your Parachute? (A Practical Manual for Job Hunters and Career Changers)* (1972)
   Richard Nelson Bolles/Ten Speed Press
   P.O. Box 7123
   Berkeley, CA 94707

8. *Be What You Want To Be* (1977)
   Phyllis and Noel Fiarotta
   Workman Publishing
   237 East Fifty-first Street
   New York, NY 10022

9. *A/V Media in Career Development* (1981)
   College Placement Council
   P.O. Box 2263
   Bethlehem, PA 18001

10. *Life Career Game*
    Sarane S. Boocock
    Sage Publications
    275 South Beverly Drive
    Beverly Hills, CA 90212

11. *Job Experience Kit*
    Science Research Associates
    Order Department
    155 North Wacker Drive
    Chicago, IL 60606

12. *Career Planning* (1973)
    Gerald Cosgrave
    Guidance Center Faculty of Education
    University of Toronto
    Ontario, Canada M58 1A1

13. *Life Work Planning* (1975)
    Arthur G. Kirn and Marie O. Kirn
    McGraw-Hill Book Company
    330 West 42nd Street
    New York, NY 10036

14. *Planning for Career Option* (1976)
    Hippocrene Publishing
    171 Madison Avenue
    New York, NY 10016

15. *Up Your Career* (1977)
    Dean C. Dauw
    Waveland Press
    P.O. Box 400
    Prospect Heights, IL 60070

College and University Resources:

16. *American Universities and Colleges* (1965)
    Otis A. Singletary and Jane P. Newman, Eds.
    American Council on Education
    1 Dupont Circle
    Washington, DC 20036

17. *The College Blue Book* (1962)
    Macmillan Information Corporation
    866 Third Avenue
    New York, NY 10022

18. *American Junior Colleges* (1940 to date)
    Edmund J. Gleazer, Ed.
    American Council on Education
    1 Dupont Circle
    Washington, DC 20036

Financial Aid Publications:

19. *Scholarships, Fellowships and Loans
    News Service* (1979-1980)
    Bellman Publishing
    P.O. Box 164
    Arlington, MA 02174

20. *Scholarships, Fellowships and Loans* (1977)
    Bellman Publishing
    P.O. Box 164
    Arlington, MA 02174

21. *Financial Aids for Higher Education
    1974-75)*
    William C. Brown Co., Publisher
    2460 Kerper Boulevard
    Dubuque, IA 52001

Continuing Education Information:

22. *Guide to Continuing Education in
    America* (1972)
    College Entrance Examination Board
    Quadrangle Books
    330 Madison Avenue
    New York, NY 10017

23. *So You Want to Go Back to School—
    Facing the Realities of Reentry* (1977)
    Elinor Lenz and Mar Hansen Shaevitz
    McGraw-Hill Book Company
    1221 Avenue of the Americas
    New York, NY 10036

**Vocational, Apprenticeships, and Internship
Resources:**

24. *Lovejoy's Career and Vocational Guide—
    A Handbook of Job-Training
    Opportunities* (1978)
    Clarence E. Lovejoy
    Simon & Schuster
    1230 Avenue of the Americas
    New York, NY 10020

25. *Directory of Internships, Work
    Experience Programs and On-the-Job
    Training Opportunities* (1976)
    Ready Reference Press
    Specialized Indexes
    100 East Thousand Oaks Boulevard,
    Suite 224
    Thousand Oaks, CA 91360

26. *First Supplement to the Directory:
    On-the-Job Training and Where to
    Get It* (1968)
    Robert Liston and Julian Messner, 1978
    Simon & Schuster
    1230 Avenue of the Americas
    New York, NY 10020

27. *Alternative to College* (1974)
    Miriam Hect and Lilian Traub
    Macmillan Information
    866 Third Avenue
    New York, NY 10022

Publications for Women, Minorities, and the Handicapped:

28. *Five Hundred Back-to-Work Ideas for Housewives* (1971)
   Barbara Prentice and Peter Sandman
   Macmillan Publishing
   Riverside, NJ 08075

29. *Career Guidance for Young Women: Considerations in Planning Professional Careers* (1974)
   John G. Cull and Richard F. Hardy
   Charles C. Thomas, Publisher
   301-327 East Lawrence Avenue
   Springfield, IL 62717

30. *I Can Be Anything: Careers and Colleges for Young Women* (1978)
   Joyce Slayton Mitchell
   Bantam Books
   414 East Golf Road
   Des Plaines, IL 60016

31. *Equal Employment Opportunity for Minority Group College Graduates: Locating, Recruiting, Employing* (1972)
   Robert Calvert, Jr.
   Garrett Park Press
   Garrett Park, MD 20766

32. *Your Handicap—Don't Let It Handicap You* (1974)
   Sarah Splaver, Ed., and Julian Messner
   Simon & Schuster
   1230 Avenue of the Americas
   New York, NY 10020

33. *Career Education for Handicapped Children and Youth* (1979)
   Donn E. Brolin and Charles Kokaska
   Charles E. Merrill Publishing
   Columbus, OH 43216

Work and Study Abroad Resources:

34. *Whole World Handbook: A Student Guide to Work, Study, and Travel Abroad* (1976)—$5.95
   Council on International Educational Exchange
   205 East Forty-second Street
   New York, NY 10017

35. *Academic Programs in Europe Sponsored by American Universities and Colleges* (published annually—free)
   Council on International Educational Exchange
   205 East Forty-second Street
   New York, NY 10017

36. *New Guide to Study Abroad* (1980)
   $7.95
   Lily von Klemperer and John A. Garraty
   Harper & Row Publishers
   10 East 53rd Street
   New York, NY 10022

The following references are published annually:

37. *Post-Secondary Education in the European Community* ($4.00)
   European Community Information Service
   2100 M Street, NW, Suite 707
   Washington, DC 20037

38. *Study Abroad* (free)
   The U.S. Department of Education, Office of International Education
   400 Maryland Avenue, SW
   Washington, DC 20202

39. *Study Abroad*
   UNESCO Publications
   7, place de Fontenay
   75700 Paris, France

40. *Handbook on International Study for U.S. Nationals*
   Institute of International Education
   809 U.N. Plaza
   New York, NY 10017

41. *U.S. College Sponsored Programs Abroad: Academic Year*
   Institute of International Education
   809 U.N. Plaza
   New York, NY 10017

SAINT PATRICK'S DAY — HISTORY

British-born Patrick became a beloved patron saint of Ireland, the country where he spread the Christian religion. The holiday marks the death of St. Patrick, a time after which it is said that the sun did not set for 12 days and nights. The day is now celebrated by wearing a "bit o' green" or by displaying the shamrock, the three-leafed clover symbol of the Emerald Isle (the Isle of Saints), Ireland.

Ireland allegedly has no snakes, and it is St. Patrick who is said to have been responsible. The legend is that once he had successfully driven out all of the snakes except one, he tricked that last large snake. Supposedly, Patrick obtained a box and tried to lure the snake into it, but the snake insisted the box was too small for him. Patrick coaxed and coaxed the snake to enter the box. To prove the box was too small, the snake stuck its head into it and gradually more of its body; at the right instant, patrick closed the lid and threw the box into the sea. Some Irish people believe the legend of the snake symbolizes Patrick's elimination of the pagan gods when he so thoroughly converted the Irish to Christianity.

In Ireland, Saint Patrick's Day is the day when the herds are turned out to pasture and the sun begins to be warm enough for the potatoes to be planted.

SAINT VALENTINE'S DAY — HISTORY

This day, intended for sweethearts, was once a festival about wolves. Its origin was really a legend from ancient Rome; the legend supposedly provided a way to help keep wolves away from sheep so that the sheep would not be hurt. The day can also be traced to a particular ceremony whereby a young man was to choose a young woman to join him in the festivities. That particular custom remained a popular holiday through Christian times. Its name originated with a priest named Valentine who helped people in prison. On the day he was to be executed for his services to the outcasts, he wrote a farewell note to the blind daughter of a jailor whom he had cured. He signed it, "From Your Valentine." Now, many people send valentines to those who are special to them.

Suggestion: Encourage students to create, instead of frilly valentines, personal expressions for their classmates which begin, "I like you because ... " in order to affirm one another and to celebrate friendship.

Choose a local agency to which to send handmade valentines (elderly people's home, hospital, prison).

SCHOOL RECORD OF THOMAS ALVA EDISON*

When Thomas Edison was first enrolled in school, he was diagnosed as abnormal. The following information was found to be in Edison's school records:

Boy, age six, head large at birth; thought to have brain fever; three siblings died before his birth; the mother does not agree with neighbors and family that the child is probably abnormal. Child sent to school and diagnosed as mentally ill by the teacher; Mother is angry, has withdrawn Thomas from school and says she will teach him herself.

SHOES — HISTORY

It is likely that prehistoric people devised footwear from pieces of animal skin that were tied to the feet with vines or strips of skin.

In North America, the first settlers wore simple styles of shoes that were tied across the instep with leather thongs called "shoe strynges." At that time, shoemakers, called "cordwainers," went from village to village and from house to house developing custom-made shoes for each member in the family from the supply of leather and tools which they carried with them. Shoemakers were also called "cat whippers" because the process of stitching the soles of the uppers with the heavy thread was called "whipping the cat."

For years, shoes were made to be worn on either foot and, therefore, were interchangeable. These "straight" shoes were purposely interchanged from one foot to the other each day to maintain their straight form rather than "giving into" the direction of either of the feet if each shoe was continually worn on the same foot.

---

*Source: *Newsletter*, Orange County, California, Association of School Psychologists, Spring, 1977, p. 2.

A pioneer in the field of shoemaking, John Adams Dagys, opened a shoe shop in Lynn, Massachusetts. His successful idea was to divide the production of a shoe into separate jobs, each of which was performed by a separate worker; this process allowed a modified assembly-line production to occur. He furthered his idea by distributing the basic soles of the shoes to people for them to complete the operations in their homes. Women usually bound the uppers together, men fastened the soles onto the uppers, and children learned to adhere the lining of the shoes. Even fishermen in the area were able to take parts of shoes to work on while at sea.

Throughout the eighteenth century, the most difficult part about shoemaking remained the sewing of the sole. Wooden pegs eventually replaced the sewing, but it was not until 1772 that wooden pegs began to be widely used by shoemakers. The pegs were carved from hard maple wood and more effectively served the function of fastening the soles to the uppers.

Another innovation during the eighteenth century (about 1750) was that of building up a stock of certain sizes, rather than custom-making each pair of shoes. The market for shoes which were not especially designed for each individual was slow in the beginning; however, the idea grew, and shoemakers were gradually able to send their surplus shoes into the distribution centers of large cities.

Elisha Hobart in 1812 introduced the manufacture of shoe nails which then replaced the wooden pegs; about 1850, Lyman R. Blake greatly facilitated the production of shoes by inventing the sole sewing machine.

Until about the time of the Civil War, "straight" shoes had been consistently worn; about 1860, shoemakers began making right and left shoes, or "crooked" shoes, as they were first called. Right and left shoes, as a pair, were more easily volume-produced for the soldiers; gradually the idea became popular with civilians, and since that time, nearly all shoes have been made and sold as pairs.

Today shoes are widely available and are within reasonable enough price ranges that shoe repair, as a career, is becoming somewhat of an "endangered occupation." Also, people generally have several types of footwear so that immediate repair is not essential to their daily activities. The purpose of wearing shoes has shifted somewhat since the time when people wore them primarily as protection. Today there are enough smooth or soft surfaces (floor tiling, carpets) that conceivably one could go barefoot much of the time. However, protection remains a major reason for using footwear; nowadays, though, people have shoes for different occasions and reasons—for style, for leisure, for formal wear. Consumer needs have been responsible for the development of unique designs in babies' and children's shoes; the various children's shoes are no longer just smaller designs of adult footwear, but are often created to respond to children's particular footwear needs. Many other types and specialties of shoes exist today, such as orthopedic, sports, and other kinds needed by people in particular professions.

SKIS—HISTORY

The word "ski" is an Icelandic word that means "piece of wood" in English. One of the ways the people in Iceland have been able to cross the vast ice fields is through the use of skis—long pieces of wood strapped onto their shoes to glide over the ice and snow. The first skis had highly curved tips similar to the prows of the Viking ships. In fact, Norsemen sometimes referred to their Viking ships as "the ski of the sea."

American ski manufacturers used to import wood from other countries, but now much of the strong white hickory wood in the state of Minnesota is used for constructing skis. White ash, a wood that American Indians used for making their bows, is also used in making good skis. Currently, other processed materials, such as metal and fiberglass, are also used in the manufacture of skis.

SOFT DRINKS—HISTORY

It is known that since the earliest times, people all over the world have been attracted to bubbling water from natural springs. But it was not until 1767 that effervescent water was produced artificially. Joseph Priestly, the English clergyman who discovered oxygen, found that by introducing carbonic gas into water, a pleasant taste sensation resulted.

In America, Benjamin Silliman, professor of chemistry at Yale University, began bottling and selling "soda water" in 1807. Two years later, Joseph Hawkins was granted the first U.S. patent for preparing artificial mineral water.

In 1832, John Matthews came from England to New York to supply stores with soda water; he also manufactured an apparatus, a fountain which was used in the carbonating process; his soda fountain is generally considered as the primary factor that led to converting soda water drinking into an industry.

A Frenchman, Eugene Foussel, who owned his own perfume shop in Philadelphia, regularly served plain carbonated water to his customers. It was Foussel who decided to add flavors to his customers' drinks. Soon after, the soda water manufacturers were competing with one another to develop flavored syrups. By 1880, more than 500 bottling plants were annually producing about 260 million bottles of carbonated beverages in a variety of flavors.

In the 1880s, two currently known brand names were introduced to the market of soft drinks: Coca-Cola® and Dr. Pepper®.

Coca-Cola: John S. Pemberton, an Atlanta pharmacist, had been experimenting with soft drink mixtures. In 1866, when he created a special formula that pleased him, he proceeded to mix the first batch in a three-legged iron pot over a wood fire in the back yard of a post-Civil War brick house. He was very satisfied with the results, but he had no name for his new blend. His friend, F. M. Robinson, suggested that he combine the names of two of the ingredients, "coca" (the dried leaves of a South American shrub) and "cola" (an extract of the kola nut). Robinson also wrote the new name in a flowing Spencerian script, much the same as the trademark name has appeared through the years. Pemberton spent $46 for advertising, thereby initiating a policy that has been continued by the company ever since; more money has been spent advertising Coca-Cola throughout the world than any other single commodity in the history of advertising.

Upon Pemberton's death in 1888, Asa G. Candler acquired ownership of Coca-Cola for the sum of $2,300 and by 1892, he had organized the Coca-Cola Company. To meet the demands of the consumers, the company began to establish plants under a franchise system to serve customers in a variety of geographic areas.

Around the turn of the century, Coca-Cola became bottled; at that point, the company then had the trademarks of its name and nickname, "Coke," and of the distinctive curved and fluted bottle. The company then developed the innovative six-bottle carton and then the crate or case. In the late 1920s, the cooler was introduced in stores so as to make the drink more immediately refreshing; the cooler was followed by mechanical refrigeration (and ice cubes) and automatic coin-control storage units, followed by disposable cans and caps, and automated dispensing machines with paper or synthetic cups. The marketing ideas lent much to the visibility and availability of the soft drink.

Today Coca-Cola is sold all over the world, often with the translated name inscribed on the bottle, along with the familiar script that F. M. Robinson originally designed for his friend, John S. Pemberton, the originator of Coca-Cola.

Dr. Pepper: In the state of Virginia, a drugstore soda fountain attendant was infatuated with the daughter of the owner of the store, a physician named Dr. Pepper. Unfortunately, Dr. Pepper did not appreciate the many soda concoctions that the young man was creating each day for the girl to receive her affectionate approval. The father also had higher aspirations for his daughter's future, so he fired her young suitor. Unhappy, the young man headed west until he stopped in Texas to become employed once again as a soda fountain attendant. He continued to concoct a wide variety of fountain flavors, all the time dreaming about and talking of the girl he had left behind. One day he created a soda mixture that turned out to be everyone's favorite; his regular customers, having learned about the romance with Dr. Pepper's daughter, teasingly named the new drink "Dr. Pepper."

At this point, the creator of the "Dr. Pepper" drink and the young girl from Virginia were able to come together once again and finally be married. Meanwhile, a customer at the Texas drugstore became interested in the "Dr. Pepper" flavor. The gentleman was a chemist and the owner of a bottling works. In 1885, shortly before Coca-Cola was getting its start, Mr. Lazenby, the bottler, managed to put Dr. Pepper on sale at the soda fountains in the local area. By 1910, Dr. Pepper syrup had begun to be distributed to several areas. In 1922, Mr. Lazenby's daughter married J. A. O'Hara, a young gentleman who saw great potential in Dr. Pepper and set up a wide sales and distribution program for the drink. From 1930 until the present time, Dr. Pepper has remained a prominently sold soft drink beverage.

The Dr. Pepper Company received a boost at one point when a physician, Dr. Walter Eddy, at Columbia University, claimed that the human diet needed three in-between meal boosters during the day when energy is known to slacken. He recommended that people avoid these particular low periods by restoring their energy quickly through a soft drink like Dr. Pepper. Eddy's "three times" of "10, 2 and 4 (o'clock)" were quickly incorporated into Dr. Pepper's trademark as a reminder to people about these let-down periods. The soft drink of Dr. Pepper has enjoyed the reputation ever since of being the "friendly pepper-upper."

"THE AMERICAN CREED"

I believe in the United States of America as a Government of the people, by the people, for the people, whose just powers are derived from the consent of the governed; a democracy in a republic; a sovereign Nation of many sovereign States; a perfect union, one and inseparable; established upon those principles of freedom, equality, justice and humanity for which American patriots sacrificed their lives and fortunes.

I therefore believe it is my duty to my country to love it; to support its Constitution; to obey its laws; to respect its flag, and to defend it against all enemies.

(This creed was written in 1917 by William Tyler Page. It was accepted for the American people, by the House of Representatives, on April 3, 1918.)

"THE BALLAD OF POOR INNOCENT BOBBY"
(as related to the "Crime of the Century")
by Marcia Sokol

Young Bobby Franks
He went to school one day
Everything seemed normal
It was 1924 on the 21st of May.

He left the school at 3 o'clock
and bid his friends good-bye
not one time did the poor guy think
he was going off to die.

POOR INNOCENT BOBBY

Leopold and Loeb met him
With a brutish heart and grin
"We're committing the perfect crime
You'll never see home again."

Little Bobby fell down on his knees
To Leopold and Loeb he pled
But Loeb picked up the chisel
and beat him over the head.

POOR INNOCENT BOBBY

Into the red rented car
and onto the little lake
They then drowned the body
and finished without a mistake.

They set up the ransom
then little Bobby was found
yet they had the perfect crime
and all the world it did astound.

POOR INNOCENT BOBBY

Then Leopold's glasses were discovered
It was his because of the special rim
yet he taught classes at the lake
so they couldn't blame him.

His conscience got to Leopold
He wanted to confess to kidnap and murder too
He talked with Rich Loeb
There was nothing else he could do.

POOR INNOCENT BOBBY

Loeb and Leopold were in the police station
after giving themselves in
They finally realized after hours of questions
that a loser can never really win.

They got a famous lawyer
Clarence Darrow to clear their name
Then came the trial of the century
While their families sat in shame.

POOR INNOCENT BOBBY

The trial was soon over
Darrow's work was to some avail
For they were not executed
just sent, for life, to jail.

In prison Loeb was killed
since then Leopold has done a great deal
in many fields, making up for his crime
yet his conscience he will never heal.

POOR INNOCENT BOBBY

UNCLE SAM—HISTORY

"Uncle Sam" is both a nickname for the United States and a figure that symbolizes the American nation.

The story of how "Uncle Sam" developed apparently originated during the War of 1812 when the American government contracted with Elbert Anderson to furnish supplies for the army. The inspector who checked the incoming supplies was named Samuel Wilson, known affectionately by his friends as "Uncle Sam." The boxes and crates of supplies were all marked with the initials of the contractor (E.A.) and with those of the United States (U.S.). When workman was asked the meaning of "U.S.," he replied that he did not know unless the letters referred to the name of the receiving inspector, "Uncle Sam." Even though it was later learned what the initials had originally been intended to mean, the story lingered on, and Uncle Sam became synonymous with the United States.

Thomas Nast is the first artist to have depicted the figure of Uncle Sam. He drew it in order to contrast the foolish cartoons that British caricaturists were drawing of American symbols in the 1860s. Thomas Nast's figure of Uncle Sam came to represent the qualities of the American ideal—hard work, honesty, wisdom, and good will.

Note: Prior to Uncle Sam, "Brother Jonathan" was considered as an affectionate symbol of the American people. This was a tribute to Jonathan Trumbull, the governor of Connecticut who was George Washington's friend and advisor. Supposedly, when Washington needed advice, he would "consult Brother Jonathan," an expression which came into common usage whenever anyone needed advice.

U.S. FLAG AND FLAG DAY—HISTORY

On June 14, 1777, the Continental Congress adopted a design for a flag which served as the basis of all later American flags: 13 stars and stripes, one for each of the original states. Prior to this design, many flags had been used in the American colonies. About 1707 and until the time of the Revolutionary War, the Queen Anne flag was flown; it had a field of red with the combined crosses of St. George and St. Andrew on a union of blue. Several other flags and banners were finally combined into the "Grand Union Flag" which flew over George Washington's Boston headquarters. It had 13 red and white stripes to represent the 13 colonies, and in the upper quarter were red and white crosses that had been adopted from the British flag.

On the first Flag Day in 1777, George Washington is quoted as having said, "We take the stars and blue union from Heaven, the red from our mother country, separating it by white stripes, thus showing we have separated from her, and the white stripes shall go down to posterity representing liberty."

As new states were admitted to the United States, stars and stripes were added. In 1791, the flag was changed to include 15 stars and 15 stripes to account for Vermont and Kentucky's entrance into the Union. This was the flag that flew over Fort McHenry and inspired Francis Scott Key to write *The Star-Spangled Banner*. In 1818, the third official flag had 20 stars and 13 stripes. In 1912, when New Mexico and Arizona joined the Union, the familiar flag design that is now used was adopted. In 1959, when Alaska and Hawaii were admitted to the United States, two new stars were added.

Developmental Stages of the Pledge to the U.S. Flag

The first pledge: "I give my hand and heart to my country, one nation, one language, one flag."

(author unknown, said at public ceremonies in the 1800s)

1892:   "I pledge allegiance to my Flag and to the Republic for which it stands—one Nation indivisible, with liberty and justice for all." (Francis Bellamy)

1923:   "I pledge allegiance to the Flag of the United States of America and to the Republic for which it stands, one Nation indivisible, with liberty and justice for all."

1954:   "I pledge allegiance to the Flag of the United States of America and to the Republic for which it stands, one nation under God, indivisible, with liberty and justice for all."

Two proposed pledges: "I pledge allegiance to the flag of the United States of America and dedicate myself to the principle that the Republic for which it stands shall be in truth one nation, under God, indivisible, dedicated to liberty and justice for all. (James E. Allen, Jr.)

"I salute the flag of the United States of America by committing myself to the principle that the nation for which it stands ever be indivisible and dedicated to liberty and justice for all." (Dr. Whitney Smith, Jr., director, Flag Heritage Foundation)

Interpretation of the Pledge to the U.S. Flag

I pledge
    means I promise

allegiance
    means to be true or loyal

to the flag
    means to the sign

of the United States of America
    means of our country

and to the Republic for which it stands
    means Republic is the kind of government in America—a government in which the people make laws through their elected representatives

one nation under God
    means one country whose people believe in God

indivisible
    means cannot be divided; it is one country

with liberty
    means with freedom; people are free but must obey laws that carry responsibility with them

and justice for all
    means fairness for all

VETERANS DAY—HISTORY

At 11:00 a.m., November 11, 1916, a truce was signed marking the end of World War I. In 1919 on the anniversary day of this event, President Woodrow Wilson proclaimed the day as Armistice Day in commemoration of the termination of the war. The day was to be observed by parades and religious services, with a special two-minute interval of silence beginning at 11 a.m.

In 1926, Congress ordered the president to proclaim each November 11 as Armistice Day. Since that time, it has been observed annually in the United States to honor those veterans, living and dead, who served with the U.S. military forces. It was in 1954 that Congress adopted this broader interpretation of the legal holiday and changed the name of the commemoration to Veterans Day. The day is currently celebrated at different times in the United

States—a day in late October or else on November 11. In France and in the United Kingdom, November 11 has been adopted and observed as Armistice Day since 1920, in honor of Allied soldiers who died in World War I.

"YES, VIRGINIA, THERE IS A SANTA CLAUS"
by Francis Pharcellus Church

Background information: A child, named Virginia, wrote a letter to the newspaper inquiring about whether a Santa Claus existed; the following is a copy of the reply in the Chicago *Sun Times* (1897).

Yes, Virginia, there is a Santa Claus. He exists as certainly as love and generosity and devotion exist, and you know that they abound and give to your life its highest beauty and joy. Alas! how dreary would be the world if there were no Santa Claus! It would be as dreary as if there were no Virginias. There would be no child-like faith then, no poetry, no romance to make tolerable this existence. We should have no enjoyment, except in sense and sight. The eternal light with which childhood fills the world would be extinguished.

Not believe in Santa Claus! You might as well not believe in fairies! You might get your papa to hire men to watch in all the chimneys on Christmas Eve to catch Santa Claus, but even if they did not see Santa Claus coming down what would that prove? Nobody sees Santa Claus, but that is no sign that there is no Santa Claus. The most real things in the world are those that neither children nor men can see. Did you ever see fairies dancing on the lawn? Of course not, but that's no proof that they are not there. Nobody can conceive or imagine all the wonders there are unseen and unseeable in the world.

You tear apart the baby's rattle and see what makes the noise inside, but there is a veil covering the unseen world which not the strongest man, nor even the united strength of all the strongest men that ever lived, could tear apart. Only faith, fancy, poetry, love, romance, can push aside that curtain and view and picture the supernal beauty and glory beyond. Is it all real? Ah, Virginia, in all this world there is nothing else real and abiding.

No Santa Claus! Thank God! he lives, and he lives forever. A thousand years from now, Virginia, nay ten times ten thousand years from now, he will continue to make glad the heart of childhood.

ADDRESS LISTING

The following alphabetized list of addresses is provided to aid in obtaining supplementary information. The addresses are furnished only as potential sources, the locations of which are, of course, subject to change—as are the types and the availability of the offered materials. Readers are encouraged to consult reference books which supply more extensive information related to current locations or various agencies and companies.

Academy of Motion Picture Arts and Sciences
9038 Melrose Avenue
Los Angeles, CA 90069

Aetna Life and Casualty Insurance
Special Services Librarian
Public Relations and Advertising
151 Farmington Avenue
Hartford, CT 06115

Alaska Division of Tourism
Bonnie Lang—Pouch E
Juneau, Alaska 99801

Allergy Foundation of America
801 Second Avenue
New York, NY 10017

American Association of Blood Banks
30 North Michigan Avenue
Chicago, IL 60602

American Cancer Society
219 East Forty-second Street
New York, NY 10017

American Chiropractic Association
Department of Public Affairs
2200 Grand Avenue
Des Moines, IA 50312

American Dental Association
211 East Chicago Avenue
Chicago, IL 60611

American Diabetes Association
18 East Forty-eighth Street
New York, NY 10017

American Feline Society
41 Union Square West
New York, NY 10003

American Field Service
313 East Forty-third Street
New York, NY 10017

American Foundation for the Blind
Publications Division
15 West Sixteenth Street
New York, NY 10011

American Heart Association
44 East Twenty-third Street
New York, NY 10010

American Indian Historical Society
Publications-Chautauqua House
1451 Masonic Avenue
San Francisco, CA 94117

American Mushroom Institute
P.O. Box 373
Kennett Square, PA 19348

American National Red Cross
17th and D Streets, NW
Washington, DC 20006

American Nature Study Society
Savannah Science Museum
4405 Paulsen Street
Savannah, GA 31405

American Numismatic Association
P.O. Box 2366
Colorado Springs, CO 80901

American Optometric Association
7000 Chippewa Street
St. Louis, MO 63119

American Quarter Horse Association
2736 West Tenth Street
Amarillo, TX 79168

American Rose Society
4048 Roselea Place
Columbus, OH 43214

Anti-Defamation League
315 Lexington Avenue
New York, NY 10016

Asphalt Institute
Asphalt Institute Building
College Park, MD 20740

Association on American Indian Affairs
432 Park Avenue South
New York, NY 10016

Association for Study of Negro Life and History
1407 Fourteenth Street, NW
Washington, DC 20005

Bankers Life
Department ETC
711 High Street
Des Moines, IA 50307

Blackhawk Films
The Eastin-Phelan Corporation
Davenport, IA 52808

Botanical Society of America
New York Botanical Garden
Bronx, NY 10458

Bureau of Indian Affairs
Department of Interior
C Street—between Eighteenth & Nineteenth
  Streets, NW
Washington, DC 20240

California Artichoke Advisory Board
P.O. Box 287
Santa Cruz, CA 95061

California Redwood Association
Service Library
617 Montgomery Street
San Francisco, CA 94111

Carter's Ink
Customer Service Department
Cambridge, MA 02142

Center for Disease Control
Attn: Bureau of Health Education
Atlanta, GA 30333

Cereal Institute of America
135 A. LaSalle Street
Chicago, IL 60603

Chamber of Commerce of Hawaii
Dillingham Building
Honolulu, HI 96813

Children's Book Council
175 Fifth Avenue
New York, NY 10010

Clowns of America
P.O. Box 3906
Baltimore, MD 21222

Colon Drama Plays
8 Arlington
Boston, MA 02116

Columbia Pictures
8mm Division
711 Fifth Avenue
New York, NY 10022

Cosom
Division of ITT Thermotech
P.O. Box 701
21850 Granada Avenue
Lakeville, MN 55044

Thomas Y. Crowell
Children's Department
666 Fifth Avenue
New York, NY 10019

Curriculum Innovations
3500 Western Avenue
Highland Park, IL 60035

Earth Action Council
UCLA—P.O. Box 24390
Los Angeles, CA 90024

Eastman-Kodak
343 State Street
Rochester, NY 14650

Edmund Scientific
555 Edscorp Building
Barrington, NJ 08007

Esmark
Corporate Affairs Department
55 East Monroe
Chicago, IL 60603

Experiment in International Living
Kipling Road
Brattleboro, VT 05301

Farragut Naval Camps
Box BC
Toms River, NJ 08753

Federal Aviation Administration
800 Independence Avenue
Washington, DC 20591

Federal Bureau of Investigation
Department of Justice Building
Washington, DC 20535

Federal Power Commission
825 North Capitol Street
Washington, DC 20426

First Society of Whale Watchers
P.O. Box 10312
Honolulu, HI 96816

Fitzgerald Publishing (Golden Legacy)
527 Madison Avenue
New York, NY 10022

Florida Department of Commerce
Direct Mail—Collins Building
Tallahassee, FL 32304

Food and Drug Administration
HFI-10
5600 Fishers Lane
Rockville, MD 20852

Footwear Bureau of Canada
Suite 711
1010 Saint Catherine Street, West
Montreal, PQ, Canada H3B 3R4

General Motors
Public Relations Staff
Room 1-101, General Motors Building
Detroit, MI 48202

Gerber Products
445 State Street
Fremont, MI 49412

Giant Photos
Box 406
Rockford, IL 61105

Glass Container Manufacturer Institute
1800 K Street, NW
Washington, DC 20006

Goodyear Tire & Rubber
Public Relations Department
Akron, OH 44316

Holy Fools
Box 1828
Springfield, IL 62705

Hunt Manufacturing
Dept. AC, Thirteenth Floor
1405 Locust Street
Philadelphia, PA 19102

Hunt-Wesson Kitchens
P.O. Box 3331
Fullerton, CA 92634

Inter-American Press Association
141 Northeast Third Street
Miami, FL 33132

International Film Bureau
332 South Michigan Avenue
Chicago, IL 60614

Italian Historical Society of America
111 Columbia Heights
Brooklyn, NY 11201

Jamestown-Williamsburg
Department of Educational Programs
Colonial Williamsburg Foundation
Williamsburg, VA 23185

Japan National Tourist Organization
651 Market Street
San Francisco, CA 94105
or
45 Rockefeller Plaza
New York, NY 10019

John Hancock Mutual Life Insurance
Community Relations Department, B-22
200 Berkeley Street
Boston, MA 02117

Johns Hopkins University
Thirty-fourth and Charles Streets
Baltimore, MD 21218

Kellogg
Home Economic Services
Department T-975
Battle Creek, MI 49016

Kiddie Kreations
906 North Woodward
Royal Oak, MI 48067

Knitted Outerwear Foundation
51 Madison Avenue
New York, NY 10010

Lead Pencil Manufacturing Association
600 East Forty-second Street
New York, NY 10017

George Q. Lewis
342 Madison Avenue
New York, NY 10017

Libby-Owens Ford Glass
811 Madison Avenue
Toledo, OH 43695

Library of Congress
Central Services Division
Publications Distribution Unit
Washington, DC 20540

Little League Baseball
P.O. Box 1127
Williamsport, PA 17701

March of Dimes National Foundation
1275 Mamaroneck Avenue
White Plains, NY 10605

Mayo Foundation
Rochester, MN 55901

Modern Maid Food Products
110-60 Dunkirk Street
Jamaica, NY 11412

Motor Vehicle Manufacturers Association of
the United States
Educational Services
320 New Center Building
Detroit, MI 48202

National Archives Trust Fund Board
National Archives Building
Washington, DC 20408

National Association of Audubon Societies
950 Third Avenue
New York, NY 10022

National Association of Broadcasters
1771 North Street, NW
Washington, DC 20036

National Association of Real Estate Boards
1300 Connecticut Avenue, NW
Washington, DC 20036

National Association of Retail Druggists
1 East Wacker Drive
Chicago, IL 60601

National Baseball Hall of Fame and Museum
Cooperstown, NY 13326

National Cash Register
Main and K Streets
Dayton, OH 45409

National Conference on Christians and Jews
43 West Fifty-seventh Street
New York, NY 10019

National Council of YMCA
291 Broadway
New York, NY 10007

National Dairy Council
6300 North River Road
Rosemont, IL 60018

National Easter Seal Society for Crippled
Children and Adults
2023 West Ogden Avenue
Chicago, IL 60612

National Education Association
1201 Sixteenth Street, NW
Washington, DC 20036

National Federation of Business and Professional
Women's Clubs
2012 Massachusetts Avenue, NW
Washington, DC 20036

National Future Farmers of America
P.O. Box 15160
Alexandria, VA 22309

National Macaroni Institute
P.O. Box 336
Palatine, IL 60067

National Museum of Racing
Union Avenue
Saratoga Springs, NY 12866

National Peanut Council Communications Division
1 Illinois Center
111 East Wacker Drive
Chicago, IL 60601

National Restaurant Association
1530 North Lake Shore Drive
Chicago, IL 60605

National Tuberculosis and Respiratory Disease
Association
1740 Broadway
New York, NY 10019

National Wildlife Federation
1412 Sixteenth Street, NW
Washington, DC 20036

Northern Great Lakes Area Council
P.O. Box 490
Libertyville, IL 60048

Organization of American States
Public Information Department
Seventeenth Street and Constitution Avenue, NW
Washington, DC 20006

Panama Canal Information Office
P.O. Box M
Balboa Heights, Canal Zone

Pan American Health Organization
Mr. Cesar A. Portocarrerro
Public Information Office
525 Twenty-third Street, NW
Washington, DC 20037

Pan American Union
Seventeenth Street and Constitution Avenue, NW
Washington, DC 20006

Pan American World Airways
Education Department
Pan Am Building
New York, NY 10017

Parker Pen
219 East Court
Janesville, WI 53545

Pasadena Tournament of Roses Association
391 South Orange Grove Avenue
Pasadena, CA 91109

The Pentagon
Washington, DC
Zip Codes: Defense—20301
            Army—20310
            Navy—20340
            Air Force—20330

Pickle Packers International
P.O. Box 31
St. Charles, IL 60174

Popcorn Institute
111 East Wacker Drive
Chicago, IL 60601

Poultry & Egg National Board
18 South Michigan Avenue
Chicago, IL 60603

Procter & Gamble
Cincinnati, OH 45202

Ramic Productions
4910 Birch Street
P.O. Box 7530
Newport Beach, CA 92660

Reedco
Box 345
Auburn, NY 13021

Register of Copyright
Library of Congress
Washington, DC 20540

Revere Copper & Brass
Advertising Department
605 Third Avenue
New York, NY 10016

Roquefort Association
41 East Forty-second Street
New York, NY 10017

San Francisco Chamber of Commerce
456 California Avenue
San Francisco, CA 94104

Scholastic Audio-Visual
906 Sylvan Avenue
Englewood Cliffs, NJ 07632

Scripps-Howard Newspapers
200 Park Avenue
New York, NY 10017

Smithsonian Institution
National Air and Space Museum Library
900 Jefferson Drive, SW
Washington, DC 20560

Smokey the Bear
United States Forest Service
Department of Agriculture
Washington, DC 20252

Snibbe Publications
140 Overbrook Boulevard
Belleaire Bluffs, FL 33540

Stephen Foster Memorial
White Springs, FL 32096

Taylor Instrument
Attn: Department A3 00 92692
Arden, NC 28704

Tuskegee Institute
Tuskegee, AL 36088

UNICEF Council
331 East Thirty-eighth Street
New York, NY 10016

United Methodist Communications
810 Twelfth Avenue, South
Nashville, TN 37203

United Nations
U.N. Plaza
New York, NY 10017

United Nations World Health Organization
1211 Geneva 27
Switzerland

University of California
Extension Media Center
Berkeley, CA 94720

U.S. Atomic Energy Commission
Technical Information Center
P.O. Box 62
Oak Ridge, TN 37830

U.S. Capital Historical Society
200 Maryland Avenue, NE
Washington, DC 20515

U.S. Committee for UNICEF
P.O. Box 5050
Grand Central Station
New York, NY 10017

U.S. Department of Agriculture
Washington, DC 20250

U.S. Department of Energy
Main Building—Forrestal Building
1000 Independence Avenue, SW
Washington, DC 20585

U.S. Department of Interior
C Street (between Eighteenth and Nineteenth
  Streets, NW)
Washington, DC 20240

U.S. Department of the Interior
Geological Survey
Chief, Branch of Visual Services
303 National Center
Reston, VA 22092

U.S. Department of the Treasury
Office of Public Affairs, Room 2313
Fifteenth and Pennsylvania Avenue
Washington, DC 20220

U.S. Federal Reserve System
33 Liberty Street
New York, NY 10045

U.S. Naval Academy
Annapolis, MD 21403

U.S. Olympic Committee
57 Park Avenue
New York, NY 10016

U.S. Patent Office
2021 Jefferson Davis Highway
Washington, DC 20231

U.S. Postal Service
Office of the Assistant to the Postmaster General
Washington, DC 20260

Walt Disney Productions
5000 Buena Vista
Burbank, CA 91503

Washington State Apple Commission
Sharon Klingenberg
P.O. Box 18
Wenatchee, WA 98801

Weights & Measures Associates
1 Thomas Circle, NW
Washington, DC 20005

Western Sawlog Wood Products Association
1500 Yeon Building
Portland, OR 97204

Western Union Corporation
Donn Dutcher
Public Affairs Department
85 McKee Drive
Mahwah, NJ 07430

Wilton Enterprises
833 West 115th Street
Chicago, IL 60643

Wine Appreciation Guild
1377 Ninth Avenue
San Francisco, CA 94122

Zenith Radio Corporation
6501 West Grand Avenue
Chicago, IL 60635

P A R T 3

TASK CARD SECTION

INTRODUCTION

The task cards are self-explanatory. Listed below in numerical order are the titles of the task cards. The date in parentheses indicates the date that the task card is first introduced in the Events and Activities Section of the book.

The task cards vary as to age levels. Some task cards are difficult and students may need assistance; others are quite easy. Many of the activities can be adapted for other days and events. For instance, Task Card #54 is designed as a Mother's Day art project but can be used as a Christmas gift idea as well.

TASK CARDS

Task Card #1—What Are Some Terms a Typographer Uses?

Things to Know Beforehand:

Every line of printing is created in one of three ways:
1) by setting individual foundry type by hand for each letter in the line;
2) by casting, mechanically, individual letters one at a time on the Monotype for the whole line (controlled by a roll of paper on which the operator at a keyboard sets the message);
3) by casting, mechanically, a slug for an entire line of type on the Linotype® or Intertype®. (There are usually two styles of letter—roman and italic.)

Type for printing was invented in China; movable type was used in Korea before its independent invention in Europe by Johann Gutenberg, about 1456. Since that time, there have been many new developments in the printing industry. The following list defines terms which are commonly used among typographers.

Black-face Letter: Dark or bold form of German text; also called Gothic.
Bleed: When the print extends beyond the trim edge of the paper.
Bodytype or Copy: Type used for the main body of a job.
Bold Face: The dark form of a type family in contrast to its light and medium forms.
B&W: Abbreviation for black and white.
Calligraphy: The art of fine handwriting, with brush or pen applied to lettering.
Caps: Short for capitals.
Copy: Manuscript material.
Galley Proofs: Proof of type material that is still in the galley and so is easily corrected.
Gutter: Edge of a page nearest the binding.
Italics: Script-like letters or type.
Linotype: Machine-set type, cast on slug.
Logotype: Signature or trademark.
Lower Case: Small letters usually found in the lower part of the type case.
Monotype: Machine-set type, cast from single matrices.
Offset: Lithography or other process which first prints the image in reverse on an off-setting "blanket." The blanket prints correctly on the paper.
Pica: Unit of measurement of column width, 6 per inch; also a size of typewriter letter, 10 per inch.
Positive: A photographic image giving the black and white relationship of the original copy.
Proof: Impression pulled from a cut or a body of type for examination or correction.
Script: Lettering based on handwriting.
Serif: A smaller line of a letter used to finish off a main stroke of the letter.
Slug: Leads of varying thickness used to separate lines to type.
Specs: Specifications on manuscript or layout.
Upper Case: Capital letters.

Directions:

Study these terms; find a partner and quiz each other about the meaning of the above terms.

* * * * *

Questions/Activities to Think and Write About:

1. Would you like to work in the printing industry?
2. Find out how a newspaper or book is printed.
3. Find out about the different weights of paper on which words are printed.
4. Try writing in a variety of styles, such as Roman, Gothic, Old English.
5. Obtain a calligraphy book and/or kit; study and practice the art of calligraphy.

Task Card #2—What Other Ways Are There to Print?

Materials:

Vegetables and fruits that can be cut to reveal a pattern inside or fruits and vegetables in which a design can be cut
Thick tempera paint
Paintbrush
Paper
Newspaper or cover sheets for the desks

Directions:

1. Cut vegetables and fruit in half or cut designs in the fruit or vegetables.
2. Paint the tempera onto the surface of the fruit with the paintbrush.
3. Gently stamp the vegetable or fruit-painted surface onto the paper.
4. Lift straight up and proceed. (Three or four printings are possible each time the surface is painted.)

* * * * *

Questions/Activities to Think and Write About:

1. How would your printing look if different types of paper were used?
2. Which fruit or vegetable did you find worked the best? Why?
3. How could your sheet of printed paper be used?

Task Card #3—How Would You Have Made the Flag?

Materials:

Paint or crayons or felt-tipped marking pens
Paper
Pencil

Information to Know Beforehand:

Legend has it that in 1777, George Washington asked his friend, Betsy Ross, a seamstress, to design a flag for the thirteen colonies. He suggested that she use six-pointed stars, but Betsy Ross decided upon five-pointed stars since they were easier to make. She carefully designed and stitched what she felt would be acceptable.

Directions:

1. Find a picture of the flag which Betsy Ross designed.
2. Fold a piece of paper in half; on one side, make a copy of Betsy Ross' flag.
3. Pretend that George Washington has asked you to design a flag; use the other half of the paper to draw your design.

* * * * *

Questions/Activities to Think and Write About:

1. Fill in the blanks by using whatever resource to help you learn more about the flag.
   a. The American flag today has _____ stripes.
   b. Betsy Ross' flag had _____ stripes.
   c. The American flag today has _____ stars.
   d. Betsy Ross's flag had _____ stars.
   e. The colors of the American flag are _____, _____, and _____.
   f. Which color stands for valor? _____
   g. Which color stands for purity? _____
   h. Which color stands for justice? _____
   i. The thirteen stripes represent what? _____
   j. In what year was the fiftieth star added? _____
2. Design a flag that would represent America if there were 51 states.

Task Card #4 — Is Butter Better?

Materials:

½ pt. heavy cream
Large mayonnaise jar, several baby food jars, or small milk cartons

Information to Know Beforehand:

How butter is made: When milk is churned, it is so violently knocked about, that the tiny skins that hold the fat break. The fat floats out, and the churning causes the little crops of fat to become joined together. That mass of fat, after proper treatment, becomes the butter that we eat.

It is believed that the Arabs first learned how to make butter. They put milk into skins and carried it on the backs of camels through the desert; but the milk was so jolted about that the fat became churned into butter; by accident, the Arabs had learned how to make this valuable food.

American pioneer women made butter with a wooden churn.

Directions:

You can make butter, too, using the following recipe:

Pour cream (½ pt.) in a jar or milk carton. Shake vigorously until the cream turns to butter. Taste and add a sprinkle of salt.

* * * * *

Questions/Activities to Think and Write About:

1. Compare and contrast butter and oleomargarine.
2. Find out the various ways that butter is used.
3. Design a commercial for butter.
4. Make a list of different types of butter.

Task Card #5 — Do You Know How to Play Box and Broom Hockey?

IDEA 1: YOU CAN PLAY BOX HOCKEY

Materials:

Carton box or large gift box
Black checker for a hockey puck
Black felt-tipped marking pen or black crayon
Scissors
Cardboard to serve as a hockey paddle, cut to the following shape (quantity — 2):

Directions:

1. In the carton box, cut out the goalie holes, as shown below.

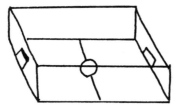

2. Draw a center dividing line across the box with black marker.

3. Place checker puck on the center line.

4. Begin playing, following these guidelines:

   With a paddle, Player A attempts to push the checker puck through Player B's goal while Player B attempts to push the puck back in the opposite direction. When the checker puck goes through a goal, a point is scored and the opposing player receives the chance to put the puck back in play.

IDEA 2: YOU CAN PLAY BROOM HOCKEY

Materials:

Household brooms (enough for each player)
Rubber ball or tennis ball (to be used as the puck)
Area marked off with goal markings, center circle or line
   *Game can be played on roller skates

Directions:

Find out the rules for ice hockey and play broom hockey the same way. Use a rubber ball or tennis ball instead of a puck and a broom instead of a hockey paddle.

Task Card #6—How Do You Take a Blind Walk?

Materials:

Blindfolds
Sensory materials, as described below (#3)

Introduction:

Remind the students that some people are born blind and that some people become blind through accident or disease. Explain that people who have lost their visual capacity usually develop other senses to sharpen their perception of the world.

Directions:

1. Divide the class into partners; blindfold one partner and have the sighted partner lead the "blind" person around the room in order to experience the feeling of insecurity and to attempt to develop a sense of trust in his/her partner. Have the students trade positions so that both may experience "blindness."
2. Ask the class to make a circle; blindfold one person in the middle of the circle and give directions to have that blindfolded person get out of the circle. Make up other similar tasks for other students.
3. While the students are blindfolded, ask them to feel such materials as glue, kitchen implements, a variety of coins, fabrics, textures; ask them to smell various fragrances such as cinnamon, flakes of milk chocolate; ask them to identify various samples of food as they taste them.
4. Ask the students to draw a picture while they are blindfolded.

* * * * *

Questions/Activities to Think and Write About:

1. When a blind person dresses in the morning, how does he/she know if everything matches?
2. How would your world be different if you were blind? If you were color-blind? If you were both blind and deaf?

Task Card #7—How Is Peanut Butter Made?

IDEA 1: YOU CAN MAKE PEANUT BUTTER

Materials:

1 cup raw peanuts
2 T. salad oil
¾ tsp. salt
Electric blender
Set of measuring spoons
Measuring cup
Crackers

Information to Know Beforehand:

George Washington Carver was an agricultural chemist who did many experiments with the peanut and the sweet potato. He discovered that many useful products could be made from each of these things. From peanut extractions, he developed metal polish, linoleum, vegetable milk, ink, grease, cooking oils, 19 shades of dyes and stains, food sauces, shampoo, cheese, and peanut butter.

You can try making peanut butter by following the recipe below.

Directions:

1. Shell the 1 cup of raw peanuts and remove the brown husks.
2. Place the peanuts in a blender. Add the 2T. salad oil and the ¾ tsp. salt.
3. Blend until proper consistency. (It may take 10-15 minutes). Watch the change.
4. When complete, enjoy tasting the peanut butter on a cracker.

* * * * *

Questions/Activities to Think and Write About:

1. Make a list of the brand names of peanut butter.
2. Find an advertisement or a label from any product that makes the following claims:
   Symbols: Some ads or labels try to make you remember a product by using a certain symbol. The company hopes that a picture of Aunt Lulu will remind you of good times and good food when you're shopping. Question: Does a symbol that you can remember always insure a good product?

   Personal Endorsement: This type of ad or label shows a famous person who claims that the product is very good. Companies hope that you will buy the product because you like or admire the famous person. Question: Does being an expert in swimming make one an expert in soft drinks?

   New and Improved: Some ads claim that something new and special has been added to a product. Question: If another ingredient has been added, is it necessarily better than other brands?

   Think of other ways which advertisers use on labels to encourage people to buy the products.
3. Design your own label for the peanut butter you have made.

IDEA 2: YOU CAN GROW YOUR OWN PEANUTS FOR YOUR NEXT BATCH OF PEANUT BUTTER

Materials:

Raw peanuts (preferably oblong Virginia type)
Sandy, loamy soil
Container for planting (paper cups work as starters)

Directions:

1. Carefully remove peanuts from their shells and plant in the sandy, loamy soil so that the pointed end is up and the nub or rounded end (sometimes called the germ) is down.
2. Space peanuts 3 to 5 inches apart and cover with soil (1 inch).
3. Place container in a warm, sunny location and keep soil moist.
4. Your peanuts should start to sprout in 5 to 7 days.

NOTE: You can write to the National Peanut Council, Communications Division, for additional ideas.

National Peanut Council
Communication Division
One Illinois Center
111 East Wacker Drive
Chicago, IL 60601

Materials:

Cardboard box cut out for bank teller window
Checkbook (sometimes a local bank will give checkbooks free of charge)

	_____ 19 _____ 151 $\frac{90-2196}{1222}$
PAY TO THE ORDER OF _____	$ _____
_____ DOLLARS	
COMMUNITY BANK	_____
MEMO _____	
⑅ 2ꞁ96⑆ ꞁ980ꞁ0736⑊ 0042	

Paper money (money can be drawn on a green spirit master and run off on green paper; or, a green stencil can be made with green ink)

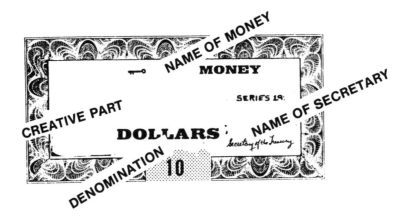

Bank record book (made from paper stapled together or composition book)

004 2881 2620
ACCOUNT NUMBER

SAVINGS PASSBOOK

SAVINGS & LOAN
INCORPORATED UNDER THE LAWS OF COMMUNITY
THIS CERTIFIES THAT

_____

HOLDS A SAVINGS ACCOUNT ISSUED AT

_____ CALIF. _____ THE

_____ DAY OF _____ 19 _____

BY _____
AUTHORIZED SIGNATURE

DATE	WITHDRAWAL	INTEREST	DEPOSIT	BALANCE
				FORWARDED

PERSONAL CHECKBOOK OF

CHECK NO.	DATE	DESCRIPTION	AMOUNT OF CHECK (−)	AMOUNT OF DEPOSIT (+)	BALANCE 350.00	
201	3-17-80	Gas Company	50.00		−50.00	
					300.00	
	3-18-80	PAYCHECK		800.00	+800.00	
					11,000.00	

Directions:

1. Choose a student banker; ask him/her to set up a bank area.
2. Invite other students to start an account with the bank.
3. The banker should record the name and signature of the student in the bank record book, assign him/her an account number, and issue a bankbook.
4. Throughout the year, money can be earned by completing various jobs, such as sweeping the floor, erasing, homework assignments, etc. Money could be used to buy various items or privileges.
5. The bank can be opened certain times during the day and bank customers can withdraw and deposit.
6. The banker should keep a record of withdrawals and deposits in his/her master record book.

Note: Interest can be earned if desired. (See Reproducibles #2 and #3 to learn how to write a check.)

Task Card #9—How Do You Build a Mini-Canal Lock?

Materials:

4 half-gallon milk cartons for the locks
Masking tape to seal the connections between the milk cartons
1 piece of aluminum foil, approximately 4x5 inches, for a small ship

Directions:

1. Remove one side of each milk carton.
2. Measure and cut the ends.

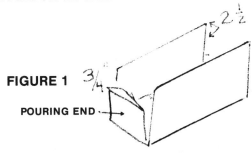

FIGURE 1

POURING END

3. Connect the milk cartons and staple in place.

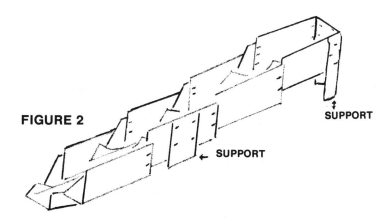

FIGURE 2

SUPPORT

SUPPORT

4. Use masking tape to cover area where the milk cartons are connected.
5. Staple supports to locks as indicated in figure 2, making sure the height of the supports will hold the bottoms of the cartons level. (The supports are cut from scrap material left from milk cartons.)
6. Form a small ship of aluminum foil.
7. Fill the canal with water and sail a ship.

Adapted from Long Beach Unified School District *Handbook for Industrial Arts Activities, Sixth Grade Unit: Latin America*, 1969.

Task Card #10 — Who Was Countee Cullen?

Materials:

Pencil
Paper

Knowledge to Know Beforehand:

Countee Cullen was actually born "Countee Porter" and then was adopted and grew up in Harlem, New York. As a young man, he wrote much poetry and studied under many great poets. Countee Cullen had most of his poetry published, and he received several top poetry awards. The following are titles of books written by Countee Cullen:

The Ballad of a Brown Girl	*Color*
The Black Christ	*Copper Sun*
Caroling Dusk	*The Lost Zoo*
The Media and Other Poems	*On These I Stand*

Countee Cullen is the poet considered to have started the "Black Renaissance" in poetry. He is most known for his brief epitaphs; the epitaphs were witty comments on human foibles. Most of the epitaphs were only four lines long; yet, they held deep meaning. The most quoted of these pseudo tombstone inscriptions is the one which follows:

> For a Lady I Know
> She even thinks that up in heaven
> Her class lies late and snores,
> While poor black cherubs rise at seven
> To do celestial chores.

Countee Cullen was also famous for children's verse, the most famous of which was "L. E. Phants Letter."

> Dear Noah: Please save me a spot
> Exposed to the sun, where the Mice are *not*;
> But if I *must* share my chamber, the Ant
> is the one I should welcome. Yours: L. E. Phant

Countee Cullen's poems usually deal with racial feelings, events in history, and human foibles. Cullen used simple, concrete words in his poetry and tried not to use "dictionary" words; often he used original words, as Dr. Seuss does in his books. Most of the critics found Cullen's poetry delightful.

Directions:

1. Sketch a picture which goes with the poems above.
2. Create a poem in the style of Countee Cullen.

Task Card #11—Do You Know How To Make Strawberry Rhubarb Sauce?

Materials:

2 lbs. fresh, young rhubarb
1 box strawberries, fresh or frozen
1½ cups sugar
Pan
Hotplate or stove

Directions:

1. Fresh strawberries must be hulled and sliced; frozen strawberries must be thawed.
2. Cut fresh rhubarb into 1-inch pieces.
3. Combine the 1½ cups of sugar with the strawberries and rhubarb in a pan.
4. Simmer over the heat until syrupy. Stir and watch closely; adding a small amount of water may be necessary.

* * * * *

Questions/Activities to Think and Write About:

1. Think of various foods on which the strawberry rhubarb sauce could be served.
2. Find out how much rhubarb costs and how it is grown.

Task Card #12— How Does Milk Get From the Cow to the Kitchen?

Materials:

Butcher paper
Overhead projector
Chalk or felt-tipped marker
Cardboard
Scissors
Paint
Rubber glove
1 or 2 cans of goat's milk
Bucket (to catch the milk)
Mop (for clean-up)

Directions:

1. Obtain a picture of a cow. With an overhead projector, draw the figure of the cow on the butcher paper; paint the picture and cut it out. Trace the picture on cardboard and cut it out. Paste the picture to the cardboard. Support the figure either by attaching it to the bulletin board or by propping it up with a sawhorse.
2. Staple the rubber glove where the cow's utter is. Fill halfway with the goat's milk; place the bucket under the utter-glove. Take a small pin to poke holes through each glove finger. Ask students individually to milk the cow.

* * * * *

Questions/Activities to Think and Write About:

1. Discuss different types of milk (condensed or evaporated, homogenized, powdered, chocolate, buttermilk, low-fat, etc.).
2. Discuss Pasteur's contribution (sterilization) and that of Borden's (condensation) to the dairy industry.
3. Ask the students to draw a diagram which shows the various steps involved in bringing milk from the cow to the kitchen (milking, pasteurizing, packaging, storage, transporting, retailing in the market, enjoying at home).

Task Card #13 — What Is It Like to Be a Traitor?

Directions:

1. Secretly invite a student to participate with you in an activity. Explain to him/her that he/she is to be a part of a lesson which is designed to help explain the concept of what it's like to be a traitor. Continue:

   During the course of the day, I will tell a secret to the entire class and warn the students not to tell anyone. Then, as a traitor to the class, you are to disclose the secret on the playground to people who are not members of our class.

   If the student agrees to act as a traitor, make sure he/she understands the situation fully.
2. Tell the class a special secret, such as:

   If no one find out, our class can have a special banana-split day. Make sure no other classes hear about it, though. And especially be sure that the principal does not find out. If anyone finds out, we won't be able to do this, Remember, keep it a secret!
3. Continue through the rest of the day, as usual, but check to find out if the chosen student has told the secret.
4. Once it has been discovered that the chosen student has betrayed the class, explain to the class that this was a sociodrama, planned and executed by you and the student to show what a famous person in history did. Then discuss Benedict Arnold and the word "traitor."

Additional Information about Benedict Arnold:

Benedict Arnold was an army officer, born in Connecticut (1741-1801). His name is synonymous with traitor. During the early years of the Revolutionary War, he distinguished himself as a true American, but the desire for money led to his plan for turning over Westpoint, a key post on the Hudson River, to the British. He became known as a traitor; he died in London, impoverished and disgraced.

* * * * *

Questions/Activities to Think and Write About:

1. How do you think (<u>name of student-traitor</u>) felt, acting as a traitor?
2. How did you, as a class, feel being betrayed?
3. How do you think Benedict Arnold felt before and after his act of treason?
4. Name other Americans who have betrayed their country.
5. Read *The Man without a Country* by Edward Everett Hale.

Materials:

Blank movie-leader or transparent film (preferably 16mm because it is easier)
Transparency marking pen which is waterproof and smearproof (brand names: Pentel® or Sanford Sharpie®)
Black or opaque movie-leader
Straight pins
Movie reel
Cellophane or masking tape
Movie projector

Directions for Design Method

1. Roll out the blank leader and tape down the ends.
2. Mark off the leader into sections about 24 inches long.
3. With colored pens, make designs on the film; also, use pins to poke holes or to make scratch marks. Caution: do not be too rough so that the film will be damaged and unable to travel through the projector.
4. Show the film and use appropriate musical records to accompany it.

Directions for Visual Picture Method

1. Roll out the blank leader and tape down the ends.
2. Draw pictures or designs within the sprocket frames; each image must be repeated 10 to 20 frames in order to be visible on the screen.
3. Show the film and use taped narration to accompany the film.

Simple animation can be done this way. Check library books to explore how animation can be created. Experiment and enjoy!

24 frames equal 1 second viewing time.

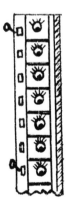

On a commercial film, observe:
- How fast the film runs through the projector
- Where the sound track is on the film
- What the purpose of the sprocket holes is

Task Card #15 — What Is It Like to Pan for Gold?

Materials:

Scissors or knife
Heavy-weight cardboard boxes, filled with a quarter of an inch of sand
Water
Gold glitter or cake decorator's gold pieces (pebbles painted gold can be used)
2 or 3 pie tins

Introduction:

Remind the class that this is a wet and disorderly activity, so ground rules need to be established beforehand.

Directions:

1. Cut boxes (as shown below) and place them in a trough formation. Place sand in each box; sprinkle glitter or gold pieces throughout the boxes. Place a garden hose in the water source area in order to generate a continued flow of water. (You may wish to cut an exit hole at the opposite end to allow the water to flow out.)
2. Ask students to line up as miners; ask the first student to take a pie tin and pan for gold by moving the pie tin along the sand and water, in an attempt to collect the gold glitter or pieces.
3. Select a student to serve as the assayer. Ask him or her to count the person's gold as he/she finishes panning. Give a related prize to the winner — "Bag O' Nuggets."

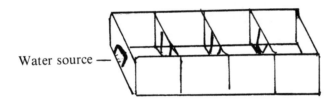

Water source —

To add interest to the activity, ask the class to come to school dressed as '49ers. While waiting, the students can sing miners' songs, such as "Clementine."

* * * * *

Questions/Activities to Think and Write About:

1. Mining provided a need for a special kind of clothing; investigate the history of how and why Levi® jeans were created.
2. Think how your life would have been different if you had lived during the gold rush time.

Task Card #16—How Do You Make Papier-mâché?

Materials:

Newspaper strips (3-inch strips for outer cover; 1-inch strips for tighter spots)
Flour
Mixing bowl
Boiling water
Oven or hot air to dry the project

Directions:

1. Cut newspaper strips so they will be ready to create the project when the mixture is ready.
2. Figure out a shape and decide if any molds need to be used. (To obtain a round shape, a balloon is a good starting base.)
3. Take a handful of flour and place it in a mixing bowl. Use a mixer (at low speed) and add some boiling water. Continue adding more flour and boiling water until the mixture is the consistency of hot wheat cereal.

Note: Mixture can be stored overnight in an airtight bag or bowl in the refrigerator. You can always thin the mixture with more water if it is too hard. The better the mixture, the better the finished project.

4. Dip a newspaper strip into mixture and smooth over the form so there are no lumps or air bubbles.
5. Cook the finished project in a slow oven to dry. Depending on the project, it may take 3 or 4 hours. The project can be placed to dry outside or in a warm place for a few days.
6. Paint the project and display it.

Note: If paper towels are used as the last coat of paper, it is easier to paint when dry since the dark newspaper print sometimes shows through with one coat of paint. Acrylic paints work the best, but poster paints may also be used.

Papier-mâché, found in hobby stores, or wallpaper paste mixed with water to the consistency of hot wheat cereal (thin) can also be used.

Materials:

Cardboard poster (see below)
Nine pieces of cardboard, numbered from 1 to 9 on the cards
Baseball score sheet pads or reproduced sheets, made as shown below
Poster with symbols and meanings (see below)

SAMPLE
SCORECARD

PLAYER	POSITION	CODE	1	2	3	4	5	6	7	8	9		H	RBI
GEHRIG, L.	First Base	1st ③	◆–											
BENCH, J.	Catcher	C ②	K①											
FOX, N.	Second Base	2nd ④	/BB											
BANKS, E.	Third Base	3rd ⑤	F–7②											
AARON, H.	Left field	LF ⑦	◆HR											
MAYS, W.	Center field	CF ⑧	6–3 ③											
MANTLE, M.	Right field	RF ⑨	3U①											
HARRIS, M.	Shortstop	SS ⑥	⟩≡											
KOUFAX, S.	Pitcher	P ①	6–5–3 ②③											
		Hits	2 / 1											
		Runs	2 / 0											

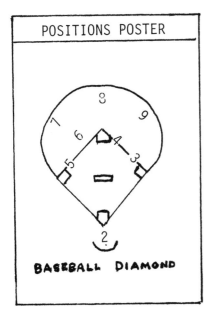

POSITIONS POSTER

BASEBALL DIAMOND

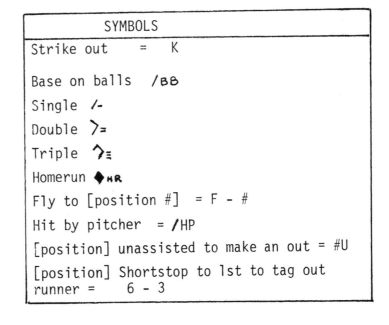

SYMBOLS

Strike out   =   K

Base on balls   /BB

Single /–

Double ⟩=

Triple ⟩≡

Homerun ◆HR

Fly to [position #] = F – #

Hit by pitcher = /HP

[position] unassisted to make an out = #U

[position] Shortstop to 1st to tag out
runner =   6 – 3

315

Directions:

1. Explain that each position has a number assigned to it; (Example: the right fielder is number 9, center fielder is 8, etc.).
2. Ask the students to place the number cards onto the poster in the correct order.
3. Ask students to draw on their own paper a diamond and to number the positions.
4. Explain the symbol-poster and ask students to try to remember the symbols.
5. Ask students to play a baseball game while others use a scoresheet to keep official score.

IDEA 1: YOU CAN MAKE ICE CREAM THE EASY WAY (1 GALLON)

Materials:

3 eggs (egg beater)
2 cups sugar
2 teaspoons vanilla flavoring
2 quarts half & half
Container to mix items in and freeze

Directions:

1. Beat eggs gradually adding sugar.
2. Add half & half.
3. Add vanilla flavoring and any other flavoring desired.
4. Pour into ice-cream freezer container and freeze.
5. Eat and enjoy.

IDEA 2: YOU CAN MAKE ICE CREAM AN EVEN EASIER WAY (½ GALLON)

Materials:

2 cans Eaglebrand® sweetened condensed milk
1 quart flavored soda pop (strawberry flavor is the best)
Ice-cream freezer container or Tupperware® containers

Directions:

1. Mix ingredients together (shake or stir).
2. Pour into container and freeze.
3. Eat and enjoy. (Create clever names for the flavors.)

IDEA 3: YOU CAN MAKE ICE CREAM THE HARD WAY

Obtain an old-fashioned ice-cream freezer and follow directions for homemade ice cream.

IDEA 4: YOU CAN MAKE ICE CREAM SUNDAES

Materials:

Ice cream, sauces and toppings, dishes to put sundaes in, cherries, whipped cream, nuts, bananas, etc.

Directions:

1. Place ice cream in a bowl and decorate with topping, making original creations.
2. Create menus and set up an ice cream parlor.

IDEA 1: YOU CAN HAVE A "SING DOWN"

Materials:

Paper and pencil

Directions:

1. Divide members into small groups.
2. Choose a recorder or secretary for each group and give him/her paper and pencil.
3. Explain rules of the game:
   - Rules:
     - a. Leader states the word to be located in the songs.
     - b. Team members will have a given amount of time to tell the secretary song titles that contain the word.
     - c. The secretary then writes the song titles down.
     - d. After the leader calls "stop," all pencils will be put away, and groups will be ready to sing.
     - e. The leader calls each group in a set order to sing one song at a time—up to the part where the word is located. (They must sing the complete sentence if the word is in the first sentence.)
     - f. No song may be repeated; if this occurs, the group will be eliminated.
     - g. The last group with songs still on the list is the winner.
4. Begin the game using the above rules. Some good starting words are: love, blue, boys' names, states' names, etc.

IDEA 2: YOU CAN PLAY "NAME THE TUNE" GAME

Materials:

Tape recording with various songs (or collection of records)
Answer sheet

Directions:

1. Pass out answer sheets on which students can place the names of the songs to be guessed.
2. The leader should say "Number One" and then play first song, or part of it, allowing students time to write the title of the song on their answer sheets.
3. Continue with additional songs.
4. Correct the answer sheets and find the winner with the most correct song titles.

Task Card #20 — What Can You Do with Teeth?

IDEA 1: YOU CAN TRY AN EXPERIMENT

Materials:

Glass of Coca-Cola or soda pop
Tooth (Obtain from your local dentist or from a youngster who has lost a tooth)

Directions:

1. Place the tooth in the glass of soda pop and set overnight; examine the next day for tooth decay.
2. Observe and record how long it takes for the tooth to become discolored.

IDEA 2: YOU CAN STUDY ABOUT TEETH AND ABOUT DENTISTRY

Materials:

Book on teeth and dentistry
Paper
Pencil

Directions:

A. Answer the following questions:
   1. What is amalgam?
   2. Explain what a malocclusion is.
   3. What is orthodontics?
   4. How is plaque related to tooth decay?
   5. How does tooth decay occur?
   6. What is the purpose of human teeth?
B. Mark your answer sheet as follows and then fill in the names of the various teeth.
   1. B – – – – – – – S
   2. I – – – – – – S
   3. C – – – – – S
   4. M – – – – S
C. Find out the answers to the questions below:
   1. What do you do to keep your teeth healthy?
   2. What are the causes and treatment for the disease known as pyorrhea?
   3. What is the most common disease of people — within the mouth?
   4. What other areas of the body might be affected if one's teeth are infected?
   5. What kind of a dental specialist is a pedodontist?
D. Read the following paragraph and consider various dentistry-related careers.

Most dentists are considered to be general practitioners who provide many kinds of dental care. They clean teeth, X-ray teeth, fill cavities, bond and cap teeth, and treat gum diseases. Dentists are often assisted by the services of either dental hygienists or dental assistants. Dentists usually send their laboratory work to commercial firms which make dentures, inlays, and other dental parts. Some dentists are specialists in certain areas; for instance, an oral surgeon performs surgery in the mouths of patients. All dentists try to educate their patients concerning preventative dental health, such as brushing teeth thoroughly and seeing one's dentist every six months.

IDEA 3: YOU CAN MAKE A SURVEY

Materials:

Paper and pencil

Directions:

1. Make a survey of the members of the classroom who have fillings, no cavities, etc.
2. Make a similar survey of the members of another classroom.
3. Compare and contrast the two groups.

IDEA 4: YOU CAN MAKE A POSTER ABOUT TOOTH DECAY OR ABOUT DENTAL HEALTH

Materials:

Posterboard
Marking pens

Directions:

1. Plan the information you wish to convey on the poster.
2. Draw the poster and then display it.

Task Card #21—How Do Businesses Really Work?

Materials:

Sign: CONSUMER
Sign: RETAILER
Sign: WHOLESALER
Sign: MANUFACTURER

An item which is manufactured (box of cookies, pencil, etc.)
A means of exchange (play money)

Directions:

1. Choose 4 teams:
   Team A—manufacturer (ones who produce the goods)
   Team B—wholesalers (ones who buy from the manufacturers)
   Team C—retailers (ones who sell items to the consumers)
   Team D—consumers (ones who buy the goods)
2. Role-play the actual sequence of buying and selling; rotate roles so that everyone understands the cycle.

   Optional ideas: include invoices, bookkeeping, business terminology;
   include information on the stock market, competitive business practices (advertising, etc.),
   and the concept of capitalism

Vocabulary:

capital gains	cost	goods and services
profit/loss	investment	salary/wages
expenditures	unemployment	patents and trademarks
advertising	economics	production
employee/employer	supply and demand	recession
means of exchange	resources	statements/billing

Conclusion of Unit:

Ask students to fill out the production/sales cycle:

_____ to _____ to _____ to _____.

Invite students to explain each aspect of the cycle.

Task Card #22 — How Do You Make Cookies with a Heart?

Materials (for about 8-10 cookies):

2½ c. unsifted flour
2 T. powdered cinnamon
1½ tsp. powdered ginger
½ tsp. ground cloves
¼ tsp. salt
1 stick margarine
½ c. dark brown sugar
⅓ c. dark corn syrup
1 egg

2 mixing bowls
Covering for the bowl
Spatula
Foil or waxed paper
Rolling pin
Knife
Heart-shaped cookie cutter or cardboard heart
Egg beater, or spoon
Cookie sheet

Directions:

In a mixing bowl, sift together the flour, cinnamon, ginger, cloves, and salt. In another bowl, cream and soften the margarine and add the brown sugar; stir until smooth. Add corn syrup and egg to the sugar mixture; beat until smooth, light, and fluffy. Add dry ingredients gradually (about one-fourth at a time), mixing until smooth. Cover the bowl and chill 1 hour.

On a lightly floured surface, roll out one-half of the dough to ¼ of an inch thickness. (Save other half for the decorations.) Use a cookie cutter or heart-shaped pattern to cut the dough into hearts. Decorate and then bake at 350° Fahrenheit for 15 minutes or until golden brown. Remove with spatula and cool.

Optional idea: Prepare the mixture ahead of time; cut and decorate the cookies in the classroom.

Decorations:

With the extra dough, make little balls, rolled in one's hands; for decoration, place the little balls around the edges of each cookie; or, coil and twist the dough and place around the cookie. Also, one can use the point of a knife to cut small designs.

Task Card #23 — What Can You Do with Apples besides Eat Them?

IDEA 1: YOU CAN MAKE APPLE PEOPLE

Materials:

Apples (hard cooking apples work best)
Knife or potato peeler
Paint or lemon juice
Needle and thread and material for costume (beads, sequins, etc.)
Items for hair (cotton balls, wig or real hair, steel wool)
Shellac, nail polish, or acrylic clear spray is optional to preserve the face
Straight pins or wire

Directions:

1. Peel the apple, leaving the stem and a bit of peel around it for a handle.
2. Use a knife to carve the features of the face (these should be exaggerated because shrinking will change the features).
3. Before the drying begins, soak the apple in lemon juice for 45 minutes for a lighter skin tone.
4. Remove the apple from the lemon juice and hang to dry in a well-ventilated area for two to four weeks (the apple will shrink and turn a carmel brown when it dries).
5. While the head is sitting, construct costume, add hair, and attach hair with pins or wire.
6. Display doll for others to see.

IDEA 2: YOU CAN BOB FOR APPLES

Materials:

Large trash can or barrel filled with water
Apples — enough for all participants

Directions:

1. Place apples in the barrel full of water.
2. Begin bobbing for apples by allowing two or three members at a time to dunk their heads in water, trying to catch an apple with their teeth (hands should be placed behind their backs).

Note: It is recommended that a time limit be established.

Toothpick art is making creations with toothpicks!

Materials:

Boxes of different kinds of toothpicks—round, flat, colored, depending upon the project
Glue
Cardboard or mounting board
Styrofoam balls

A. Board Designs

Directions:

1. Decide upon an idea for a creation.
    Decide whether it is to be flat or standing up.
2. Count the approximate number of toothpicks needed and begin.
3. Put glue on the area which is to be the starting point; then put the first toothpick down; hold until the count of 10. (Blowing on the glued area will speed the drying process.) Glue next toothpick and continue the process.
Allow overnight drying period.

Sample: [image: rectangle with toothpick] Sample toothpick glued on board

B. Toothpick Star

1. Glue together a diamond shape on the flat surface; ◇
2. Add a cross bar; ⇔
3. Make another of the same; ⇔
4. Connect the two shapes with a toothpick at the top and another one at the bottom. ⇔⇔
5. Glue together five, seven, or nine more structures in the same way.
6. Attach all structures together to form a star.
7. Spray paint or paste tissue paper in each triangle for an added effect.

C. Styrofoam Designs

1. Poke toothpicks into styrofoam balls.
2. Assemble the balls into a shape, such as a Christmas tree.

Task Card #25—How Do You Use the Yellow Pages of the Telephone Book?

Materials:

Telephone book—yellow pages section
Three-hole punch
Three-ring binder
Typing paper
Typewriter
Scissors

Directions:

1. Ask students to go through the yellow pages of the telephone directory and cut out about 20 different pages from throughout the book. (Obtain old copies of telephone directories from local telephone companies.)
2. Put the pages in alphabetical order, with a piece of white typing paper between each page.
3. Punch all sheets and put together into a notebook.
4. Design a notebook cover.
5. Put directions inside the cover (see "directions" sample below).

SAMPLE DIRECTIONS PAGE:

DIRECTIONS

1. Use paper and pencil.
2. Put your name on your paper.
3. Choose a page to work on.
4. Mark the yellow page number on your paper (Example: UNIFORMS-p. 753).
5. Do the task on the white sheet placed before each yellow page.
6. Write your answers on your paper.
7. Turn to another task!

GREAT! YOU ARE LEARNING HOW TO USE THE YELLOW PAGES!

6. Write on each white typing page some investigative tasks, as related to the next yellow page (see sample below).

SAMPLE WHITE PAGE:

UNIFORMS

A. You got a job! It is a position as a nurse. Find a place that sells nurses' uniforms and that takes Master-charge payment.
B. You are an executive who needs to buy uniforms for your construction workers; find four places that sell these types of uniforms, in order to compare prices.
C. You want to rent uniforms; find two places to call.

Task Card #26—How Do You Make a Pinhole Camera?

Materials:

Brass shim stock, from an automobile parts store (between two and six-thousandths of an inch is best); heavy-duty aluminum foil can be used, but it is fragile
#8 sewing needle
Pencil with an eraser
Cardboard box (shoe boxes are best)
Spray can of flat black paint
Photographic paper—4x5 inches (kept out of light)
Masking tape

Additional Materials—for developing pictures from the camera

3 pans (one with developer, one with water, one with fixer)—available at camera shop
A roller to wipe excess water and a paper towel
Unexposed sheet of paper same size as picture negative
A darkroom or photo studio

Directions:

1. Take the shim stock and the needle; insert the needle eye into the eraser on the pencil to make a drill; drill a hole in the center of the shim stock, the rounder the better.
2. Take the cardboard box and make a hole a little bigger than the pinhole in the front outside of the box.
3. Spray paint the inside of the cardboard box camera.
4. With masking tape, tape the pinhole over the larger hole in the front of the box.
5. In a totally dark room, secure a sheet of photo paper to the back of the camera—shiny side facing out.
6. Set the camera on a solid base (outside is better so that no lighting problems will result); put a weight on the camera to keep it steady; open the pinhole for about 2 minutes.

To Develop (in a totally dark room):

7. Put exposed photo paper into developer pan for 1½ to 2 minutes.
8. Slosh it back and forth in a second pan that has water.
9. Drop the photo paper in the third tray with fixer for about 2 minutes; turn on the lights to see negative and then set back in the fixer for about 5 to 10 minutes. Then put the photo paper in a large pan of water to wash for 20 minutes.

To Make a Print:

10. Blot out excess water with a paper towel; wet an unexposed sheet of paper and put on a flat surface with the glossy side up. Lay the negative facedown on top of the unexposed sheet of paper. Use a roller to press any water out. Turn on an overhead white light for about 10 seconds. Develop the bottom sheet just as was done with the negative.

Note: If the print is too dark, cut down the exposure time; if it is too light, increase the exposure time—same for the negative.

Most camera shops will help with additional information.

Task Card #27 – How Do You Create a Shadow Play?

IDEA 1: YOU CAN USE SHADOWS BEHIND A WHITE SHEET

Materials:

Two posts to attach sheet
One large, plain white sheet
A light to place behind sheet

Directions:

1. Staple or tape one edge of the sheet to one post (as shown below) and the opposite end of the sheet to the other post.
2. Put a backlight behind the sheet structure, with the light facing toward the sheet.
3. Turn off all other lights.
4. Have performers stand directly behind the sheet so the shadows will project for the audience.

Note: When using this technique to act out music groups, such as the Beatles, cardboard guitars can be cut out and they will appear as real guitars. Musical accompaniment will enhance the production.

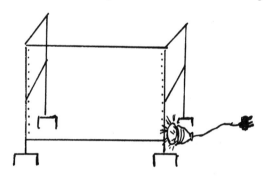

IDEA 2: YOU CAN USE A SCREEN AND PROJECT LIGHT IMAGES

Materials:

Overhead projector (screen is optional)
Rectangular glass baking dish
Cooking oil
Food coloring
Water
Stir stick

Directions:

1. Turn on the overhead projector.
2. Place dish on the overhead projector. Fill with water. (The amount of water will result in different images.)
3. Add a drop of cooking oil to the water.
4. Lightly sprinkle food coloring into oil spots in the water.
5. Swirl with the stir stick for extra effects (experiment with extra shapes).

Task Card #28 — What Can You Do with Pickles?

IDEA 1: YOU CAN MAKE PICKLES

Materials:

2 qt. jar with lid
Fresh dill
1½ tsp. kosher coarse salt
¾ cup vinegar
Water
Heating element
Cucumbers for pickling

Directions:

1. Fill the jar with washed cucumbers.
2. Put in stalks of fresh dill (3 or more).
3. Add 1½ tsp. salt and ¾ cup vinegar.
4. Fill with water and then pour liquid from the jar into a pan and heat to boiling.
5. Pour heated liquid back over cucumbers in the jar and add spices, garlic and peppercorns.
6. Seal the lid, then turn the jar upside down to see if there are any leaks.
7. Set for two weeks.
8. Open and eat.

IDEA 2: YOU CAN PLAY THE GAME "PICKLE"

Materials:

A ball and three players

Directions:

1. Stand one player at each of the two arbitrarily set bases (first and second bases) while the third player runs from base to base without being tagged out by one of the basemen. A player is considered tagged out when one of the basemen tags him/her with the ball when he/she is not on base.
2. Players can switch positions during the game after the runner has been tagged out (i.e., the runner takes the place of the baseman who tags him/her).

IDEA 1: YOU CAN MEASURE YOUR SMILE

Materials:

String
Scissors
Tape measure or ruler

Directions:

1. Take a piece of string and line it up with your smile.
2. Cut the string the exact size of your widest smile.
3. Place the string on the tape measure or ruler and detrmine how long a smile you have.
4. Make a survey or chart to find out who has the longest smile.

IDEA 2: YOU CAN MAKE A SHRINKING SMILE

Materials:

Shrinkable plastic (obtained at hobby stores) sheets
Oven art or permanent felt-tipped markers
Scissors or Exacto® knife
Oven to bake in (toaster ovens work well)
Foil and spatula
Hole punch if holes are needed

Directions:

1. Place plastic over the pattern and draw the outline on the plastic.
2. Add any words, such as "SMILE," etc.
3. Turn over the design and add color on the back side, using solvent base permanent marking pens or oven art pens.
4. Cut the excess plastic away from the outline.
5. Poke any pin holes or chain holes now, using a hole punch or knife.
6. Preheat oven to 400°. Place cut-out design on a cookie sheet or foil. Watch as it shrinks.

Note: The design will curl into a ball, then open and lay flat. When completely flat, remove it from oven and lay the design on a flat surface to cool. Press down with spatula. The colors will intensity and the small imperfections will disappear.

Helpful Hints:

The pattern will shrink to 15% of the original size.

Artex® and Liquitex® are the only other items that can be used to color plastic instead of permanent markers.

To curve the design, lay it on a curved surface when taking it out of the oven.

For added protection, spray the back of the design with an acrylic to prevent the color from coming off.

Task Card #30—Can You Spring into Spring?

SPRING is enjoying life, the sun, and a cold drink!

IDEA 1: YOU CAN GROW A HAPPY SPRING FRIEND

Materials:

Clay flowerpot and dish
Decorating supplies
Grass seed and soil

Directions:

1. Turn the flowerpot upside down and draw a spring happy face on one side of the pot.
2. Place the flowerpot in the dish and put a thin layer of soil on the top of the head.
3. Press the grass seeds gently into the head of soil.
4. Fill the dish with water and be sure to keep it full.
5. Watch and wait and the hair will grow. It might even need a trim.

IDEA 2: YOU CAN MAKE A SUN PILLOW

Materials:

Yellow butcher paper sheets (the larger the paper, the larger the pillow)
Scissors and decorating materials
Needle with thread or yarn to sew together
Nylons or pillow stuffing material

Directions:

1. Cut out a sun pattern on two sheets.
2. Decorate a happy sun face on the top sheets.
3. Sew together top and bottom sheet along one side.
4. Stuff the pillow and sew the other side together.

IDEA 3: YOU CAN MAKE ICED TEA—A DELICIOUS SPRING DRINK

Materials:

Teapot and oven to heat teapot
Pitcher filled halfway with ice
Pan with 4 tea bags hanging along side
Extra cold water, sugar and lemons if desired
Glass to drink tea

Directions:

1. Heat the water in the teapot to boiling and then pour it into pan, over the teabags. Add a drop of cold water to cool and remove teabags.
2. Pour tea water into the pitcher. The ice will melt but the tea will be ready to be put in the refrigerator or to be poured into a glass over additional ice cubes. Sugar and lemon can be added.
3. If tea is too strong, add additional cold water.

IDEA 4: YOU CAN MAKE SOLAR TEA

Materials:

3 tea bags and water
Large glass bottle container/jar

Directions:

Place tea bags in a jar; fill with water and then cover. Set in sunlight for 2-3 hours, and refrigerate.

Task Card #31 — What Do You Know about the Product JELL-O?

Did you know that the entire Jell-O company was offered for sale for $35 — but there were no takers! At the turn of the century, things changed for the Jell-O company and the dessert idea caught on. Today it is the largest-selling prepared dessert.

IDEA 1: YOU CAN TRY A JELL-O FINGER TREAT

Materials:

4 envelopes unflavored gelatin
3 packages (3 oz. size each) of flavored gelatin (If you want red, use cherry-flavored; green, use lime, etc.)
4 cups boiling water
Large mixing bowl and stir spoon
Shallow baking pan, 13x9 inches
Knife to cut the dessert into squares
Plate to display them and eat from

Directions:

1. In a large mixing bowl, combine the unflavored gelatin and the 3 boxes of flavored Jell-O in powdered form.
2. Add 4 cups of boiling water, and mix until gelatin is dissolved.
3. Pour into a shallow pan about ¼ of the way high. The higher you pour the mixture, the thicker your finger cubes will turn out.
4. Chill in refrigerator until firm.
5. Cut into cubes.
6. Enjoy and share with others.

IDEA 2: YOU CAN TRY CREATING JELL-O ADVERTISEMENTS

Jell-O was advertised as follows in a 1938 magazine:

America's Most Famous Dessert
   Jell-O is the dainty dessert that can be made in a minute. It does not require a cook to make it, for there is no cooking to be done. It is made by dissolving the contents of a package of JELL-O in a pint of boiling water. If fruit is to be added to the dessert, you push a little in here and there, to suit yourself. Fruited Jell-O desserts are exquisite.
   There are 7 Jell-O flavors: STRAWBERRY, RASPBERRY, LEMON, ORANGE, CHERRY, PEACH, and CHOCOLATE.
   Ten Cents Each, at all grocers!
Jell-O has had many campaigns and slogans such as "There is always room for Jell-O."

Materials:

Paper and writing utensils to design advertisements

Directions:

1. Investigate the Jell-O product today and design an advertisement.
2. Share with others.

IDEA 1: YOU CAN SOW SEEDS FROM A PACKET

Materials:

Aluminum-foil pans from pies, frozen foods, or egg cartons
Potting soil from a garden shop
Large plastic bags
Small watering can
Variety of seeds
Small corks
Large dishes

Directions:

1. Punch some holes in the bottom of each pan with the needle.
2. Fill each pan with potting soil and press down lightly.
3. Place the pan in a dish with a cork under each corner of the pan to form a bridge.
4. Sprinkle a few seeds on the top of the dirt and cover them with a very thin layer of additional soil. Press down lightly.
5. Soak the soil with water.
6. Poke holes in the plastic bags and place the bags over the seed trays.
7. Keep the soil moist, but do not let water come through the drainage wells into the dish. The pans must not sit in water.
8. When the seeds begin to sprout, place the plants near a window to allow them sun.

IDEA 2: YOU CAN GROW MUSTARD FARMS

Materials:

Paper towels
Dish
Mustard seeds
Water

Directions:

1. Place a few paper towels in the dish and soak them with water.
2. Sprinkle the mustard seeds on the towels and keep them moist.
3. Put the dish with the seeds in front of a window.
4. In about two weeks, you should have fresh mustard to add to salads, etc.

IDEA 3: YOU CAN PLANT FRUIT PITS

Materials:

Small pots to grow seeds in (yogurt cups or milk cartons can be used)
Pits (from oranges, lemons, grapefruit, melons, cherries, grapes, or apples)
Potting soil
Water

Directions:

1. Soak a few pits in water overnight.
2. Place them in a container or pot with a hole in the bottom, filled with potting soil.
3. Stand the pot in a saucer and keep the soil moist. The plants must not be in direct sunlight until they begin to sprout.

Note: You can obtain a plant water meter in stores to help determine plants' needs for water.

Task Card #33 – What Can You Do with a Parachute?

Materials:

Large parachute
Group of participants

Directions:

1. Ask students to stand in a square formation and put the parachute in the center.
2. Play each game below:

   INFLATION—The players all hold on to the parachute edges with their hands at waist level. The leader shouts "Inflate." This means the participants squat down to the ground and seal the parachute to the ground. Then on the count of 3, the participants shoot up their arms straight over their heads, raising the chute. Bounce down again and again trying to see how high the chute will inflate.

   IN & OUT—This game is played as above but, as the chute comes down, the players must run (still holding the chute) 3 steps in and under the chute. They try to get out without getting caught under the chute.

   Note: It is fun to have a student try various stunts, such as push-ups, sit-ups, jump rope, etc., before the chute deflates.

   BALL SHAKE—Divide the participants into two groups and hold the parachute like a blanket. The object is to knock off the ball on the opponents' side while they try to balance back onto the chute. No hands can be used to stop the ball, only teamwork.

3. Create your own parachute games or use familiar games and adapt them for play with the parachute. "Steal the Bacon" is a great game to play with a parachute. The chute can also be rolled and used for a "Tug-of-War."

Note: Experiment, but do not use the parachute as a body-catcher or trampoline for people. The chutes are not strong enough, and accidents could be serious.

Task Card #34 – What Can Oxygen Do?

IDEA 1: YOU CAN TRY AN EXPERIMENT TO FIND OUT WHAT OXYGEN CAN DO

Materials:

Drip pan or shallow bowl
Food coloring
Candle at least 1-inch thick
Jar or glass to put over candle
Matches to light candle
Water

Directions:

1. Heat the wax on the end of the candle and stand it up in a bowl or drip pan.
2. Pour water mixed with food coloring around the candle.
3. Light the candle.
4. Turn the glass or jar over the lighted candle.
5. Explain that oxygen is needed for fire to burn; when oxygen is taken away, the fire extinguishes.

IDEA 2: YOU CAN TRY ANOTHER EXPERIMENT

Materials:

Large test tube
Water
Iron filings or steel wool
Small pan with ½ cup water

Directions:

1. Fill the test tube with water and then empty the water.
2. Put in iron bits while the tube is still wet.
3. Shake the tube around and empty the iron bits that do not stick to the tube.
4. Turn the test tube upside down and stand it in the small pan with water.
5. Wait until the next day. The water will rise into tube.

Note: The part of the air that was used up and that causes rusting is a gas called oxygen. About 1/5 of our air is oxygen. Iron with oxygen = rust.

IDEA 3: YOU CAN SEE OXYGEN IMPACT YOUR LUNGS

Materials:

Roll of string and scissors to cut string

Directions:

1. Cut the string long enough to go around the rib cage of a body when exhaling.
2. Inhale and see how much difference there is in the size of the string, first when breathing in oxygen and then when exhaling carbon dioxide.

Task Card #35—What Is the Time?

Time is the period between two events or during which something exists, happens, or acts. It is a measurable interval.

IDEA 1: YOU CAN MAKE A PLATE CLOCK AND TEACH SOMEONE TO TELL TIME

Materials:

Paper plate
Construction paper and scissors
Paper fastener or brad
Marker to write numbers on clock
12 checkers to teach minutes

Directions:

1. Cut clock arms to fit the surface of a clock.
2. Insert a paper fastener through the arms of the clock and paper plate. Make sure they are movable.
3. Number the clock.
4. Teach someone the hours on a clock.
5. Take a checker and mark 5 minutes on the first checker, 10 minutes on the second checker, 15 minutes on the third checker, etc.
6. Place the 5-minute checker on the number 1 on the clock and help someone learn that the 1 is also five minutes past the hour. This way you help the person learn to tell time by minutes as well.

IDEA 2: YOU CAN DESIGN YOUR OWN ORIGINAL TIMEPIECE

Materials:

Anything you would need to design a timepiece (real or fictional)

Directions:

Be clever and create!

IDEA 3: YOU CAN LEARN THE DIFFERENT TIME ZONES OF THE UNITED STATES

Materials:

Large map of the United States
7 plate clocks or clocks with movable hands
Marker to draw time zones

Directions:

1. Mark the time zones on a USA map.
2. Set a time in the East and all the zones will be one hour earlier as you move toward the West. Set all clocks.
3. Have a caller shout a time in one time zone and see if others can set their clocks accordingly.

Materials:

1 piece of balsa wood, 1/8-inch thick to fit pattern
2 pieces of balsa wood, 1/16-inch thick to fit patterns
Metal clip for the nose of the glider (a paper clip will work)
Decorative materials
Tool for cutting balsa wood
Water, in order to soak the wing

Directions:

1. Trace the fuselage and rudder pattern, below, onto the 1/8-inch balsa wood and cut out.
2. Cut out the slits, as shown on the pattern.
3. Cut out the stabilizer (the 1/16-inch balsa wood) and insert it in the fuselage slit.
4. Cut out a wing, using the pattern below. Make the wing 1/16-inch thick.
5. Soak in water to get the bend in the wing.
6. Insert the wing into the fuselage slit.
7. Decorate and attach the metal clip to the front of the fuselage, as shown.
8. Enjoy flying the glider.

Note: You can make a pilot in the cockpit, among other variations. Remember safety rules when flying the glider!

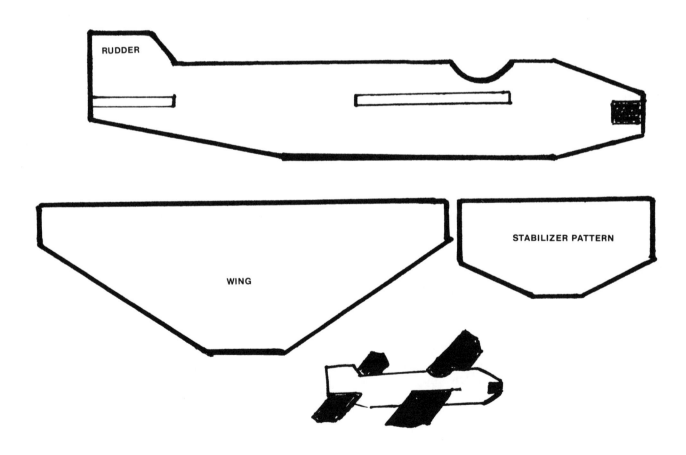

Task Card #37— What Can You Do for Earth Day?

You can always clean up your environment and ...

IDEA 1: YOU CAN EXAMINE THE EFFECTS OF WIND ON THE EARTH

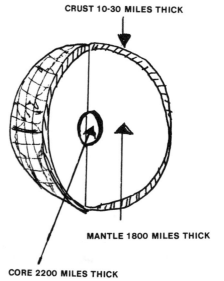

CRUST 10-30 MILES THICK

MANTLE 1800 MILES THICK

CORE 2200 MILES THICK

Materials:

5 shoe boxes or tins:
    1 filled with clay
    1 filled with damp sand
    1 filled with dry sand
    1 filled with sand and gravel
    1 filled with damp clay
A hair dryer or air blower

Directions:

1. Blow for 6 seconds at the same angle and distance on each box of earth. Observe the effects.
2. Write down your observations and experiment with different angles.

IDEA 2: YOU CAN STUDY THE DIFFERENT EARTH PERIODS

Materials:

Encyclopedia or book on the earth
Paper for notes or a chart

Directions:

Make a chart as shown:

NAME OF ERA	NUMBER OF YEARS AGO	LENGTH OF SEA	CHARACTERISTICS OF ERA
Cenozoic	Has not ended yet; began 65 million years ago	65 million years	Erosion of continents; mountain-building volcanic activity
Mesozoic			

IDEA 3: YOU COULD MAKE A DISPLAY ABOUT THE EARTH

Materials:

Anything you would need for your display

Directions:

Take what you already have or learn more and create a display telling about the earth and its history.

Task Card #38 — What Do You Know about Television?

IDEA 1: YOU CAN TRY MAKING A TELEVISION SET (pretend of course)

Materials:

Cardboard box
Tool to cut cardboard box
Roll of shelf paper (white) or butcher paper
Two paper towels or wrapping paper roller insets
Tape
Decorative materials
Tagboard for tubes, size of the cardboard box back
TV repair manual for a TV set
Paints or decorative materials

Directions:

1. Place the box with the open side facing opposite you.
2. Cut an area for the screen on the side of the box that is opposite the opening.
3. Cut a hole to insert towel rollers on the top of the box.
4. Insert 1 paper towel roller into the box top and tape the other paper to the roller; tape the other end of the paper to the second inserted roller.
5. Turn the paper roller so the picture passes across the screen image. Draw your TV show.
6. Examine a TV manual and make mechanical parts, dials, etc. (Pipe cleaners or straws make good antennas.)

IDEA 2: YOU CAN MAKE TELEVISION GRAPHICS AND CUE CARDS

Materials:

6x12-inch card stock or tagboard
Lettering materials (felt marker, stencils, or other lettering tools)
Ruler

Directions:

1. Place card stock on the table. Draw a light pencil line for a 2-inch margin around the card stock. Draw guidelines for the print in between lines of print. All words should have 2-inch letters, with ½-inch to 1-inch space between each word.
2. Draw your graphics.
3. Erase pencil marks.

S T E V E ' S

S H O W

T I M E

338

X-ray art is many things. It could mean using old X-rays and making art projects from them. It could also mean making art projects that are like X-rays.

TRY THE 3 WAYS TO HAVE X-RAYS LIKE ART!

IDEA 1: DIAZO X-RAY

Materials:

Diazo paper (obtain from an art or photo store)
Tupperware or plastic rectangular-shaped container with a top
Ammonia
Blocks or two thick books
Cut-out shapes or items to print
Floodlight or spotlight
Timer (by the seconds)
Plate for the ammonia

Directions:

1. Place items on the back or yellow side of the diazo paper.
2. Place light so it shines directly on the paper. Turn on for 1½-2 minutes or until unexposed paper turns white.
3. Put ammonia in a plate and then place the plate inside the box. Put blocks on each side of the dish to create a bridge support for the diazo paper.
4. Take the items off the paper; put the paper across the blocks and over the ammonia dish that is inside the rectangular box.
5. Leave the paper inside the developing box until it turns a blue color with the images remaining white; mount on a frame.

Note: Direct sunlight will fade prints.

IDEA 2: SUN X-RAY

Materials:

Photographic paper
Objects to create images
Sunlight or hot lights

Directions:

1. Place the paper outside or under hot lights, with objects on the top of the photo paper, for 5 to 10 minutes. Images will appear.
2. Frame and display.

IDEA 3: CHALK X-RAY

Materials:

Black construction paper
White chalk
Objects to be "X-rayed"

Directions:

Place object to be "X-rayed" under black paper and color over the item with the chalk. Be sure to feather the edges as you use the chalk.

IDEA 1: YOU CAN LEARN THE PARTS OF A BIKE

Materials:

Bicycle (top grade)
Index cards and writing tool

Directions:

1. Review all the parts of the bicycle on the picture below.
2. Fold index cards in half; number the outside of as many cards as there are parts to be named.
3. Label the inside of the card with the name of the bicycle part.
4. Quiz fellow students.

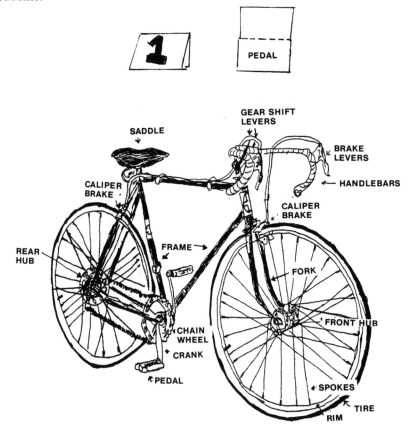

IDEA 2: YOU CAN LEARN BICYCLE TERMINOLOGY

Materials:

Dictionary or bicycle book

Directions:

Define the following bike terms: ankling, banana seat, derailleur, wheelie, rattrap pedal, five-speed, ten-speed, unicycles, folding bikes, and reflective tape.

Task Card #41 – What Can You Do with Golf?

IDEA 1: YOU CAN INVESTIGATE THE GAME AND DEFINE THE FOLLOWING TERMS

Clubs	Sand trap	Irons
Caddies	Water hazards	Woods
Scoring	Golf balls	Putter
Par	Tee	Golf shoes
Handicap	Green	Birdie
Golf course	Hole	Hole in one

IDEA 2: YOU CAN SET UP A MINIATURE PUTTING GREEN

Materials:

Paper cups
Putters
Golf balls
Construction-paper flags
Scorecards

Directions:

1. Distribute the paper cups throughout the grass playing area.
2. Place numbered flags in sequential order by each cup.
3. Putt from hole to hole, marking the scorecards as you go (remember that the lowest score wins).

IDEA 3: YOU CAN PLAY FRISBEE GOLF

Materials:

Frisbees
9 chairs or posts
9 sheets of construction paper
Marking pen and tape

Directions:

1. Spread out the chairs across the playing area.
2. Tape a piece of construction paper on each chair back and number each chair 1 to 9.
3. Stand at the starting point, throw a frisfee, aiming for a chair. If the chair is hit on the first throw it is scored as a hole in one. If a frisbee reaches only partway, a player's next turn is thrown from the spot where the frisbee landed and a stroke is counted. The lowest score wins.

   If a frisbee does not hit a chair, a stroke is counted; on the player's next turn, he/she again tries to hit a chair from where the frisbee landed.

Do you know that books were originally hand-written by scribes? It took a great deal of time to complete one book; then Johann Gutenberg developed the printing press so books could be printed.

YOU CAN EXPLORE THE PRINTED BOOK

Materials:

Discarded books you can examine and tear apart
Materials for students to create their own books
Large sheet of newsprint or construction paper marked as:

(front side)   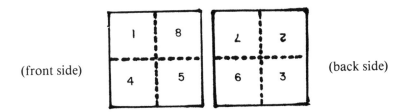   (back side)

Directions:

1. Locate the following parts of a book preceding the main text:
    a. Half-title page (page with only the title of the book)
    b. Title page (contains author's name, publisher, etc.)
    c. Copyright date (date found on title page or on verso [back] of the title page)
    d. Dedication
    e. Table of Contents
    f. Introduction
    g. Acknowledgments
2. Locate the parts of the book following the main text:
    a. Bibliography
    b. Index
    c. Appendix
    d. Glossary or key to abbreviations

Note: Not all books will have all items above.

ALL PAGES OF A BOOK ARE PRINTED IN MULTIPLES OF FOUR. EACH GROUP OF FOUR IS CALLED A "SIGNATURE."

3. Take the newsprint paper and fold back numbers 1 and 8; then fold numbers 4 and 5 closed so that number 1 is on top. Cut across the top and open the signature.
4. Create your own book—fiction or nonfiction. Learn the Dewey Decimal number for your book. Make sure your book has all the necessary elements of a book.

Task Card #43—Do You Know about the Olympics?

IDEA 1: YOU CAN HAVE A MOCK OLYMPICS

Materials:

Track and field equipment, or equipment for events to be held
Meter measuring tools
Awards

Directions:

1. Create an Olympics Committee.
2. Have a sign-up sheet with events you plan to simulate.
3. Invite participants to choose a country they plan to represent.
4. Set up the events.
5. Begin the competition.

IDEA 2: YOU CAN FURTHER STUDY THE OLYMPICS

Materials:

Drawing and writing paper

Directions:

1. Design an Olympic medal.
2. Do a research project on one of the following Olympic events and be sure to find out who won each event each year! (See sample chart below.)

SUMMER GAMES

Men's Track
Women's Track
Gymnastics
Swimming—Diving
Water Polo
Boxing
Wrestling
Judo
Weightlifting
Rowing
Canoeing-Kayaking
Yachting

Shooting
Equestrian Sports
Fencing
Archery
Cycling
Volleyball (men's/
 women's)
Field Hockey
Handball
Football
Basketball

WINTER GAMES

Skiing
Biathlon
Figure Skating
Speed Skating
Tobogganing
Bobsledding
Ice Hockey

SAMPLE CHART:

SPORT—BOXING SECTION—HEAVYWEIGHT			
Year	Location	Name	Country
1904	St. Louis	Sam Berger	USA
1908	London	A. L. Oldman	UK
1968	Mexico City	George Foreman	USA

Materials:

3 or more copies of the same picture per project (old history or reading books that can be cut up make great sources)

Frame paper (black construction paper a little larger than the picture to be made into 3-D)

Glue

Balsa wood sticks ⅛-inch thick to be cut into little pieces or toothpicks, or paper to roll (wood works more effectively)

Directions:

1. Place black construction paper down and glue one copy of the picture on the paper.
2. Cut a second picture so that certain pictures will stand out.
3. Glue wood bits in center of the area where the next picture will be placed.

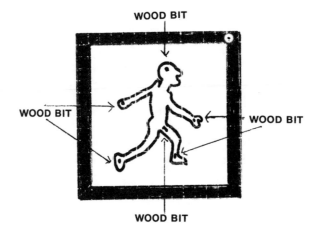

4. Patch the second picture over first picture and wood bit. Continue following this procedure until the picture has the depth desired.
5. Fold up the sides of the black construction paper ½ inch and pinch the corners to obtain the appearance of a frame.
6. Display the 3-D art.

Task Card #45 — How Do You Organize a Pet Show?

Materials:

Tables or booths
Signs describing animals
Ribbons and awards
Judges
Animals and their special foods and cages

Directions:

1. Introduce the idea of a pet show.
2. Ask students to fill out applications (sample shown below).
3. Assign a number to each pet.
4. Ask students to create a sign for their pets, containing the following information: Classification of animal
   Scientific name
   Pet's family name
   Paragraph report on the animal
   Owner's name
5. Choose judges to award prizes to the animals on the day of the show.
   Note: Judges can award prizes for a variety of categories, such as: Best behaved pet; Most tricks; Most unusual pet; Best in category; Smallest within category; Best habitat; Best name of pet; etc.
6. On the day of the pet show, set up tables or booths in a horseshoe fashion, placing pets and signs in proper order.
7. Ask a master of ceremonies to introduce each pet and owner; have the judges circulate to evaluate.
8. Announce the winner and award prizes.

Note: A good resource and research book on pets is: *Pets*. By Verne N. Rockcastle. Racine, Wisconsin: Western Publishing Co. (No date).

APPLICATION #	PLEASE PRINT	FOR OFFICIAL USE ONLY:
NAME OF OWNER: _____ ADDRESS OF OWNER: _____ PHONE NUMBER OF OWNER: ( )_____		ACCEPTED _____ REJECTED _____ REASON: _____
NAME OF PET: _____ TYPE OF PET: _____ TYPE OF CAGE TO BE CONTAINED IN: _____ SIZE OF PET: _____ SPECIALTIES OF THE PET: _____ _____		ASSIGNED BOOTH: _____
I, _____, promise to be responsible for my pet, _____. _____		_____ Signature (of pet show director)

Task Card #46—How Are Prices Controlled?

IDEA 1: INTERVIEW A BUSINESS PERSON IN THE COMMUNITY

Materials:

Paper and pencil
Questions to ask about price control
Business person

Directions:

1. Make arrangements to interview a business person regarding price control (either in person or over the telephone).
2. Conduct the interview.
3. Share data with others.

IDEA 2: ESTABLISH A STORE AND EXPERIENCE PRICE CONTROLS

Materials:

Two businesses, such as candy stores
Price tags (index cards with prices for each item)
Each store must have a fair trade item, such as a Hershey® bar selling for 20¢
Store signs

Directions:

1. Invite a wholesaler to sell items to each store.
2. The store managers then must put a price on the items.
3. People may buy and sell items throughout the store until a timer of "X" amount of minutes goes off. At that time, one store (it is best to pick randomly which store) is asked to put a control, or freeze, on its items. The other store can continue without controls.
4. Discuss what happened.

Task Card #47 — Do You Know How to Play "Capture the Flag"?

Materials:

Chalk or something to designate boundaries
2 flags (if you are playing the game in terms of the Civil War, a Confederate flag and a Union flag should be used)
Whistle for the referee
Color strips 12 to 18 inches long (material works best or flag football strips); each player is to have a strip; two different colors are needed, one color for each team. If you are playing the Civil War version, one team could have gray and the other blue.

Directions:

1. Set up the playing field as shown.
2. Divide the players into two teams. Each team has its own court with its own flag. Each team has its own jail.
3. Team captains are chosen. If you are playing the Civil War version, one captain is Jefferson Davis and the other is Abraham Lincoln. Captains must choose guards for their jails and flags. These guards are the only players to go behind the back field line.
4. All the players put on their color strips. The flags must be placed in their areas.
5. Team members, or soldiers, line up at the starting line and when the referee blows the whistle, the game may begin.
6. Every time a whistle is sounded, all players must freeze or they are out of the game.
7. Each time, members try to conspire to steal the opponent's flag and return safely across the battlefield line to their own camp. If the color strip is pulled from the player, he/she must go to the opponent's jail. A player may be rescued by having another teammate reach the prison safely and take back one prisoner across enemy lines. If tagged, they both go back to jail. STRATEGY is important. There are NO jail breaks.
8. A player running into the flag hiding place may wait free in the marked-off area or else return immediately. If a player is tagged with the flag in his/her possession, everything starts over. If he/she makes it across the center line safely, the game ends. If you are playing the Civil War version, the battle is won. A new battle may start.

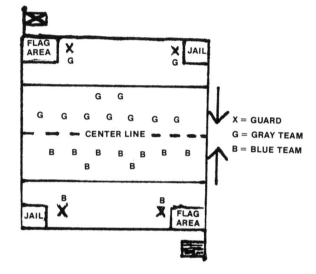

Note: A basketball court with chalked-in boxes makes a good area for this game. Caution: practice safety rules ahead of time. Do not allow pushing and pulling.

Variations:

In addition to being color-stripped and sent to jail, you may vary the game, as follows: If a player is tapped on the arm, he/she is wounded and must hold his/her arm behind the back throughout the game. Tagged on the leg means the leg has been shot and the player must hop on one leg for the duration of the game. If players are given two color strips at the start of the game, 1 strip pulled = jailed; 2 strips pulled = dead and out of the game. You can also create your own variations — HAVE FUN!

IDEA 1: YOU CAN WEAVE A PAPER PLACE MAT STRIP

Materials:

Construction paper, 18x20 inches (1 per place mat)
Construction paper cut up in strips, 12x2 inches (6 per placement)
Razor blade or cutting tool and protective board underneath

Directions:

1. Cut construction paper with a razor or paper cutter as shown:

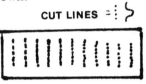

2. Take the colored strips and weave a pattern. Over-under-over, etc., for first strip then under-over-under for second, etc.

Note: A zigzag cut will give a unique effect —

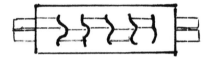

IDEA 2: YOU CAN WEAVE A POT HOLDER

Materials:

Plastic loom kit and loops from hobby store
or
Wood board 10x10x1 inch and nails to construct your own looms

Directions:

1. Take the frame and hook loops across it.
2. Weave each loop in and out (over and under), alternating each time across the secured loops. Make sure they are tight. (See figure A on opposite page.)
3. Lift off frame by inserting 1 loop hole into the other and pulling up to form the next loop hole. Start at one corner and continue until entire pot holder is lifted from the frame. The final loop becomes a hanging loop and stays up. (See figures B and C on opposite page.)

Note: If you are making your own loom, hammer 10 nails 1/10 of an inch apart on all 4 sides of the wood block. (See opposite page.)

FIGURE A

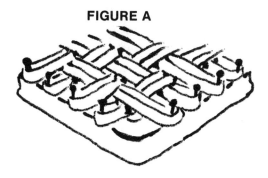

FIGURE B

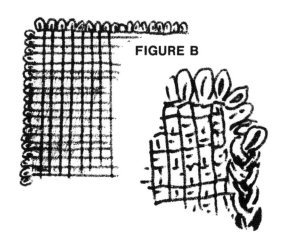

FIGURE C

You can do many things! You can pick up litter and be a water-watcher conservationist ...

IDEA 1: YOU CAN MAKE A WATER USAGE CHART

Materials:

Paper for chart
Pencil to record data on chart

Directions:

Copy the chart below on your chart paper and keep the data filled in each week. You and your friends may wish to compare charts. Be aware of the water you use.

WATER USAGE CHART by _____
For the Week of _____

HOW THE WATER WAS USED	AVERAGE AMOUNT FOR ONE USE	MON	TUES	WED	THURS	FRI	SAT	SUN
Taking a bath	30 gallons							
Taking a shower	20 gallons							
Flushing toilet	3 gallons							
Washing hands	2 gallons							
Getting a drink	¼ gallon							
Brushing teeth	¼ gallon							
Cooking a meal	5 gallons							
Using a washer	32 gallons							
Washing dishes (per meal)	8 gallons							
OTHER _____	estimate							
	TOTALS							

IDEA 2: YOU CAN TURN WASTE PRODUCTS INTO USEFUL ITEMS

Materials:

Aluminum can (empty)
Scissors
Black spray paint

Directions:

1. Take the can and cut off the top ¼ of the way from the top.

2. Cut strips down about ¼-inch wide to the bottom, leaving an inch or so border.

3. Curl up each strip to form a curled edge.

4. Spray paint and when dry use the item as a catsup bottle holder, a candle holder, an ash tray, etc.

Note: A pin cushion can be made by stuffing or attaching padded felt or other material to the top of the can.

William Shakespeare was an English poet. Dramatists called him the "Bard of Avon," one who clearly defined the good and evil of his characters and situations.

SOME FAMOUS QUOTES FROM SHAKESPEARE:

"Never a borrower or a lender be.... "

"To be or not to be, that is the question."

"The whole world's a stage and we are but actors upon it."

SOME QUESTIONS TO THINK ABOUT:
(All answers can be found in the encyclopedia.)

1. Why was so much music used in Shakespeare's plays?
2. Into what groups are Shakespeare's plays usually divided? What is an example of each type?

IDEA 1: YOU CAN TRY SOME OF HIS PLAYS

Materials:

Versions of his plays (comical, satirical, revised, or natural)
Items for the costumes and scenery

Directions:

1. Go over the story outlines, characters, and scenes.
2. Assign parts and act them out. enjoy!

IDEA 2: YOU CAN TRY MAKING A MODEL OF THE GLOBE THEATER

1. Find a picture of the Globe Theater (the place where Shakespeare's plays were originally staged).
2. Choose the materials with which you want to work.
3. Construct the model.

Task Card #51—What Can You Do with a Newspaper?

IDEA 1: INVESTIGATE NEWSPAPER TERMINOLOGY

Materials:

Dictionary
Newspaper

Directions:

1. Define the terms below.
2. Locate an example of each term in the newspaper.

   NEWSPAPER TERMS:

Alley	Dummy layout	Paste up
By-line	Editor	Reporter
Caption	Exclusive story	Syndicated columnist
Column	Filler	Typo
Copy	Jump	UPI
Dateline	Lineage	

IDEA 2: YOU CAN CHECK THE PET COLUMN IN THE CLASSIFIED SECTION FOR ONE WEEK AND MAKE A GRAPH SHOWING HOW MANY PETS ARE SOLD OR GIVEN AWAY; DETERMINE THE AVERAGE PRICE OF THOSE BEING SOLD ON A GIVEN DAY

Materials:

Pet column in classified section

Directions:

See idea.

IDEA 3: YOU CAN CHOOSE A LETTER FROM A "DEAR ABBY" COLUMN AND PLAY THE GOSSIP GAME

Materials:

Letters from "Dear Abby"

Directions:

1. Ask students to sit in line formation.
2. The person at the front of the line reads one of the letters and whispers the story to the second person.
3. The second person passes the story on to the third person, etc. The final person relates the story out loud.

IDEA 4: YOU CAN USE THE HOROSCOPE COLUMN FROM YESTERDAY'S NEWSPAPER; FIRST, WRITE ABOUT WHAT HAPPENED TO YOU YESTERDAY AND THEN CHECK YESTERDAY'S HOROSCOPE TO SEE IF IT WAS RIGHT.

Materials:

Horoscope column from previous day

Directions:

See idea.

IDEA 5: YOU CAN USE A GROCERY STORE ADVERTISEMENT AND MAKE UP A CROSSWORD PUZZLE, USING THE DIFFERENT FOODS ADVERTISED

Materials:

Grocery store ad from food section of the paper

Directions:

1. See idea.
2. Let friends work your puzzle.

IDEA 6: YOU CAN USE AUTO ADS AND PRETEND YOU ARE A CAR SALESMAN SELLING THE CAR

Materials:

Auto ads from newspaper

Directions:

See idea.

IDEA 7: YOU CAN PRETEND YOU HAVE "X" AMOUNT OF DOLLARS TO SPEND FOR YOUR FAMILY; GO THROUGH THE ADS OF THE NEWSPAPER AND MARK DOWN ITEMS YOU ARE CONSIDERING BUYING

Materials:

Ads from newspaper

Directions:

1. See idea.
2. Describe the amount of dollars to spend.
3. Be sure to stay within your budget.

IDEA 1: YOU CAN LEARN ABOUT TREES

Directions:

1. Learn the parts of a tree.
2. Make a list of the types of trees (or draw various types).
3. Make a list of the functions and uses of trees, such as trees keep the air supply fresh, etc. When you finish your list, rank the items according to importance.

IDEA 2: YOU CAN MAKE A PRESSED LEAF COLLAGE

Materials:

Paper
Glue
Scissors
Pencil
Leaves from a tree

Directions:

1. Press various leaves of trees between dictionary pages; glue them on construction paper, and label them.
2. Display and share with class.

IDEA 3: YOU CAN EXPLORE TREES THROUGH POETRY

Directions:

1. Create poetry about trees, using the style of Haiku poetry.
2. Read poems about trees, such as Joyce Kilmer's *Trees*.

IDEA 1: YOU CAN CREATE A SIMULATED RACETRACK

Materials:

6 large cardboard cut-outs of horses
2 dice
Playground roped or chalked as shown below

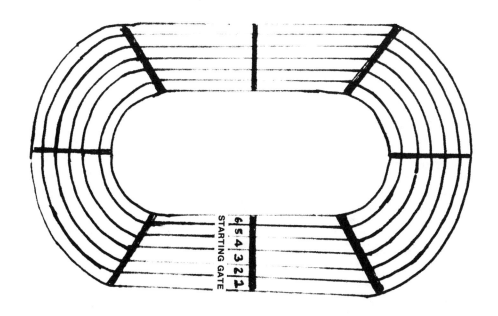

Directions:

1. The jockeys straddle their legs over their horses and wait at the starting gate.
2. The announcer begins the race by rolling one die to determine the horse number. For instance, if a 6 is showing on the die, it designates horse #6. Then the announcer rolls both dice to designate the number of spaces each horse can move ahead toward the finish line.
3. Announcer continues rolling the dice and narrating the race until a winner reaches the finish line.

IDEA 2: YOU CAN USE A COMMERCIAL VIDEO GAME ON HORSE RACING

Materials:

Intellivision® "Horse Racing" cartridge
Intellivision video unit

Directions:

See directions on cartridge and play the game.

YOU CAN MAKE A FANCY GIFT THAT CAN ALSO BE PRACTICAL! MAKE APPLE JELLY GOBLETS.

Note: The following recipe *cannot* be doubled! The recipe makes approximately five to six 8-oz. goblets.

Ingredients:

1 box SURE-JEL®
5 cups of sugar (2¼ lb.)
Decorations (i.e., glitter, plastic straw, plastic flowers)
Food coloring (if desired)
3 blocks of paraffin (and crayons to add color to wax, if desired)
4 cups commercially prepared, bottled apple juice

Materials:

6- or 8-qt. heavy kettle (large enough to prevent boiling over)
Waxed paper (enough to cover kettle top)
5 or 6 goblets, mugs, or glasses (baby food jars can also be used)
1 pound coffee can (empty)
Sauce pan for melting
Aluminum foil (enough to cover tops of goblets)
Electric beater
Butter knife
Heating element to heat pan (camping stoves can be used)
Large metal stirring spoon
Measuring cup
Cleanser for cleaning wax drippings

Directions:

1. In the heavy skillet, place 1 box of SURE-JEL and the 4 cups of apple juice. Add food coloring at this point, if desired.
2. Bring to a boil over high heat and add, at once, the sugar. Boil and stir for one minute to a rolling, full boil and boil hard for one minute. Stir constantly.
3. Remove from heat.
4. Skim off foam with a large metal spoon.
5. Immediately ladle the jelly into *hot* glasses or jars, leaving a ½-inch space at the top of glasses and a ⅛-inch space at the top of jars. Be sure the containers are hot when placing the jelly into them. (If plastic goblets are used, be careful that the goblets do not crack when pouring the hot jelly into them.)
6. In a coffee can, place one block of paraffin. Place the coffee can in a sauce pan with hot water to melt the paraffin. Place ⅛ inch of paraffin on top of the jelly to secure jelly in the glass. Make sure that the paraffin touches all sides; prick any air bubbles.
7. Cut foil the size of the mouth of the glasses and place it on the top of the paraffin in the sealed jelly glass.
8. Melt 2 blocks of paraffin in the coffee can. Take the coffee can from the water and allow the paraffin to cool until it turns "milky." Whip the paraffin with an electric beater, starting at high speed immediately.
9. With a butter knife, place the whipped wax on top of the foil in a decorative foam fashion. Insert a straw and any decorations while wax is still warm; sprinkle glitter, if desired. (Note: The wax hardens fast.)
10. Set to harden and clean off any drippings with cleanser.

Note: The jelly does not have to be stored in the refrigerator until it is opened. To eat jelly, pop off the decorative foam and coating wax.

Task Card #55 — What Can You Do for May Day?

IDEA 1: YOU CAN HOLD A MAYPOLE DANCE

Materials:

Large pole (tether pole is an excellent source)
Crepe paper streamers or colored material strips
Masking tape

Directions:

1. Tape crepe paper streamers to top of pole.
2. Ask students to hold strips out from the pole.
3. Invite students to alternate by an in-and-out pattern so that the pole becomes braided.
4. The students can chant the old song:

"Here we go 'round the maypole
   The maypole
The maypole
   Here we go 'round the maypole
This the first day of May! HURRAH!

IDEA 2: YOU CAN MAKE MAY BASKETS

Materials:

Construction paper 12x18 inches
Scissors and ruler
Glue or tape
Items to decorate and fill basket

Directions:

1. Cut construction paper in a 12x12-inch square.
2. Measure and cut as shown.

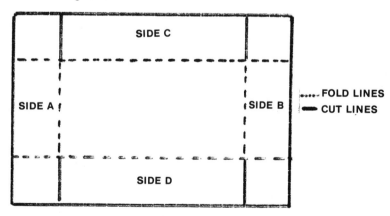

3. Fold side A in and crease. Fold side B in and crease. Stand edges up. Fold D and C up and crease. Fold at corners to shape box form.

4. Glue corners to flaps to shape a box formation.

5. Cut a 2-inch strip from excess paper and glue it to use for a handle.
6. Decorate and fill baskets.

Task Card #56—What Can You Do with Old Nylons?

IDEA 1: YOU CAN MAKE A DOLL STUFFED WITH NYLONS

Materials:

Material for doll pattern and a pattern
Scissors, needle, and thread
Old nylons and decorative doll supplies

Directions:

1. Cut out material into a doll pattern.
2. Sew one side together and stuff with nylons to give shape to the doll.
3. Sew up the other side and decorate as a fancy doll.

IDEA 2: YOU CAN BRAID A RUG FROM OLD NYLONS

Materials:

Nylons (number used depends on size of rug)
Bleach and a pan or bowl to pour bleach into
Scissors to cut off panty hose tops
Needle and thread to sew ends of braided nylon strips

Directions:

1. Cut all panty hose pant parts off so as to have legs only.
2. Put nylons in bleach so they will all turn out one color.
3. Take 3 legs and braid together and sew ends.
4. Repeat step 3 again and again until you have enough braided strips to sew together into a rug.

Task Card #57—What Do You Know about the Stock Exchange?

Materials:

Paper to print stock certificates
Newspaper containing New York Stock Exchange transactions
Play money
Booth for transaction
Chalkboard and chalk

Directions:

1. Learn how to read stock exchange transactions.

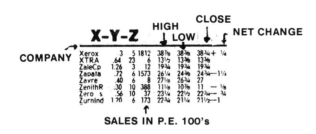

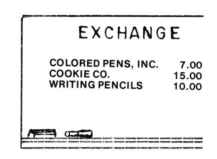

2. Investigate the following terms: dividends, stocks, shares, liquidation, certificates, transaction opening, transaction closing, company name, stock exchange.
3. Find names of specific exchanges: New York Exchange and Pacific Stock Exchange, etc.
4. Create a company or corporation. (*See* Task Card #60.)
5. Choose a person to operate the exchange.
6. Representatives should go to the exchange official and obtain a seat on the exchange (official writes company name on chalkboard and lists costs per share and sales).
7. As the companies operate, people can buy and sell shares; at the same time, the stock market exchange official continually updates the chalkboard.

Task Card #58 — Who Was Amelia Earhart?

Amelia Earhart was a famous pilot who enjoyed flying and the entire field of aviation. Amelia Earhart was born on July 24, 1898 in Atchison, Kansas. She had a dream to be a pilot and fulfilled her dream. On May 20, 1932 she flew across the Atlantic on a daring solo flight. President Herbert Hoover presented her with a medal for being the first woman to fly alone across the Atlantic. She set all types of flight records. They on July 2, 1937 Amelia's plane was lost around Howland Island in the Pacific. There are many rumors as to what happened, but no one really knows.

IDEA 1: AMELIA EARHART LOVED TO STUDY FLIGHT AND THE AIR; YOU CAN TRY SOME FLIGHT EXPERIMENTS

Materials:

Vacuum cleaner air tube
Ping-Pong balls
Cardboard weather vane
String and a rock
Glue and a round stick
Propeller (you can buy or make from 2 spoon tops)

Directions:

Follow the directions below for three different activities to learn more about the flow of air.

A.   Use a tank-type vacuum cleaner. Turn it on and hold the outlet end upward, keeping two Ping-Pong balls or balloons riding on the airstream in midair. The balls or balloons will be pushed into the low pressure of the airstream.

B.   A simple weather vane can be made out of string and cardboard. When a cardboard arrow is placed in the wind, the larger drag of the tail is forced back, thus making the arrow point into the wind.

C.   A toy helicopter can be made by gluing a plastic propeller to a small, round stick. When twirling the stick in one's hands, it should rise into the air.

IDEA 2: CREATE PAPER AIRPLANES TO UNDERSTAND HOW A PILOT CONTROLS THE FLIGHT OF A PLANE

Materials:

Paper to fold into airplanes
Airplane book for fancy paper airplanes (obtain from library)

Directions:

1.   Fold the paper as shown:

2.   Throw the plane and let it glide. Notice how it flies and then turns back and ends up as shown. The plane may "nose" upward. If the ends are turned up sharply, the plane may nose up until it stalls and then falls. If the plane is thrown fast enough, it may even make a complete circle, called an "inside loop."

Note: Eye safety should be considered when flying the planes.

You can make relief maps from salt and flour and show examples of various geographical terms.

Materials:

2 cups flour
Mixing bowl
Stir stick or spoon
1 cup water
Dash of salt or saw dust to help preserve
Dictionary or geography terms book
Wood or heavy cardboard base (to build relief maps on)
Paints to decorate
Acrylic spray to give protective finish (or hair spray)

Directions:

1. Place flour in a mixing bowl, add a little water, and stir. Continue this process until the mixture is the consistency of hot wheat cereal.
2. Design the type of relief map outline you would like to make.
3. Form the map on the board by slowly pouring mixture, then molding it with your hands. To obtain mountains, simply pinch area. To form lakes, carve a line deep into the mixture with your finger.
4. Allow to dry 2 or 3 days. Stick a toothpick in the map to see if it is completely dry. (Oven baking will make cracks.)

   Note: If your mixture needs added substance or is to be a permanent display, it is best to add sawdust or salt to keep bugs away. (Inside the pencil sharpener you can find sawdust mixed with lead).

5. Paint and label all forms.
6. After paint and labels are added and dried, spray with acrylic lacquer or hair spray.

GEOGRAPHICAL TERMS THAT CAN BE USED IN A SALT AND FLOUR RELIEF MAP DESIGN

Bay	Desert	Mountain	Sea
Beach	Field	Mountain range	Shore
Brook	Forest	Ocean	Stream
Canal	Glacier	Pasture	Swamp
Canyon	Gulf	Peak	Tributary
Cape	Harbor	Peninsula	Tunnel
Cave	Hill	Pond	Valley
Coast	Iceberg	Prairie	Volcano
Continent	Island	Reservoir	Waterfall
Country	Isthmus	River	Waves
Crater	Lake		

Task Card #60 — What Is a Corporation?

Materials:

Dictionary
Paper for contractual agreement
Company sign logo
Company registration form
Products for company

Directions:

1. Investigate the terms: corporation, company, management, employer, employee.
2. Create an idea for a company and get together with several other people to form a corporation.
3. Draw up a contractual agreement for your corporation (obtain samples from a local attorney or from books).
4. Fill out an application for a business license (see sample below).
5. Set up a business (review Task Card #21).
6. Enjoy your profits or cry over your losses.

Application # _____   DATE OF APPLICATION_____
                            BUSINESS APPLICATION
                                PLEASE PRINT

NAME OF OWNER _____

ADDRESS OF OWNER _____
                            Street   City   State   Zip Code

PHONE NUMBER (   )_____ AGE _____ BIRTHDAY _____

TYPE OF BUSINESS TO BE ESTABLISHED _____

NAME OF COMPANY _____

BOOKKEEPER _____

TYPE OF INVENTORY TO BE SOLD _____

_____
                                                    Signature of applicant

---

For OFFICIAL use ONLY:

    Accepted _____   Rejected _____   Reason: _____

BUSINESS LICENSE GRANTED FOR _____ days. License will terminate on the _____ day of
_____, 19_____.

Task Card #61 – How Can You Find Out about Copyrights?

A copyright is a form of protection given by law of the United States government to the authors of literary, dramatic, musical, artistic, and other works.

IDEA 1: YOU CAN INVESTIGATE INFORMATION FROM THE COPYRIGHT OFFICE

Materials:

Paper and pencil
Envelope and a stamp for mailing

Directions:

1. Write to the Copyright Office, Library of Congress, Washington, DC 20559, and ask for General Information on Copyrights.
2. After receiving your booklet from the Copyright Office, answer the following questions:
   a) Who can claim a copyright?
   b) What can be copyrighted?
   c) What cannot be copyrighted?
   d) What is the symbol used for "copyright"?

IDEA 2: YOU CAN LOCATE COPYRIGHT NOTICES IN BOOKS

Materials:

Paper and pencil
Old books

Directions:

1. Look in various books for the copyright notice.

   SAMPLE: © copyright 1972 John Doe
2. Make a chart as shown below. When you locate a copyright notice record the data.

BOOK TITLE	PUBLISHED BY	COPYRIGHT	FOUND ON
The Bedtime Book of 365 Nursery Rhymes	The HAMLYN PUBLISHING GROUP	© copyright 1972, Hamlyn Publishing Group	4th page of book
The Tale of Two Cities	Random House	copyright 1950 Random House, Inc.	4th page of book

IDEA 1: YOU CAN MAKE A TIE HOLDER

Materials:

Cardboard cylinder from paper towels or foil roll
Decorative rope or yarn
Decorating supplies (paint, glitter, stars, etc.)
Scissors
Shellac

Directions:

1. Notch the cardboard cylinder at each end at the top.
2. Decorate the cylinder.
3. Shellac the finished product.
4. Run decorative yarn through the cylinder, hooking onto notches and tying a knot at the top, leaving room for hanging as shown.

IDEA 2: YOU CAN MAKE A PENCIL HOLDER

Materials:

Small cylinder can (6-oz. juice cans cardboard)
9 wooden clothespins (with metal clip)
2 rubber bands
Spray paint

Directions:

1. Break the clothespins apart (18 half pieces)
2. Press the clothespin against the can, with the rounded edge on top.
3. Slip rubber band over the pins in the grooves to hold them on the can.
4. Spray paint inside and outside of the can.
5. Put in the pens and pencil.

IDEA 3: YOU CAN MAKE A TIE-SHAPED FATHER'S DAY CARD

Materials:

Construction paper
Decorative supplies
Pen or pencil
Scissors

Directions:

1. Fold construction paper in half.
2. Draw a tie shape so that the edge of the tie is on the fold of paper.
3. Cut out all edges except the folded side.
4. Decorate and write a verse inside.

Task Card #63 — What Can You Do with Sandpaper?

Sandpaper is a substance used to grind, smooth, sharpen, and polish various materials. Sandpaper is a very valuable tool used at home and in industry.

IDEA 1: YOU CAN USE SANDPAPER TO SAND SOMETHING

Materials:

Sandpaper
Piece of wood

Directions:

Take your piece of sandpaper and work with the grain of the wood item to be sanded.

IDEA 2: YOU CAN DO SANDPAPER ART DESIGNS

Materials:

Sandpaper (the rougher the sandpaper, the better the image)
Wax crayons
Cloth (muslin or old sheets)
Iron and iron surface

Directions:

1. Draw the design on the rough side of the sandpaper. Use wax crayon and press hard.
2. Turn the sandpaper with the crayon design over and place it on cloth.
3. Iron so that the design is transferred to the cloth.
4. Display the cloth pieces or sew together for a blanket.

IDEA 3: YOU CAN MAKE A SANDPAPER INSTRUMENT

Materials:

Sandpaper
Blocks of wood
Tacks or nails

Directions:

1. Take a piece of sandpaper and fold over the top of the wood block.
2. Tack or nail to hold firm.
3. Repeat steps for the second sand block.
4. Hold one sand block in the left hand and other block in the right hand and scrape together by moving hands abruptly up and down.
5. Try various musical songs and keep the rhythm with the sandpaper blocks.
6. Create songs that need sandpaper rhythm instruments.

Task Card #64 — What Do You Know about the Statue of Liberty?

The Statue of Liberty was a gift of the people of France for the Centennial Celebration. The statue was dedicated on October 28, 1886.

The statue represents many things. The torch in her hand represents the Light of Liberty. The law book represents the Declaration of Independence. The statue is dressed in long, flowing robes and standing among broken chains to represent freedom and to commemorate the French and American revolutions.

The statue was designed by Frederic Auguste Bartholdi.

An American poet named Emma Lazarus wrote the poem "The New Colossus," which is engraved on the tablet affixed to the pedestal of the statue.

> Not like the brazen giant of Greek fame,
> With conquering limbs astride from land to land;
> Here at our sea-washed, sunset gates shall stand
> A mighty woman with a torch, whose flame
> Is the imprisoned lightning, and her name
> Mother of Exiles, From her beacon-hand
> Glows world-wide welcome; her mild eyes command
> The air-bridged harbor that twin cities frame.
> "Keep ancient lands, your storied pomp!" cries she,
> With silent lips. "Give me your tired, your poor,
> Your huddled masses yearning to breathe free,
> The wretched refuse of your teeming shore,
> Send these, the homeless, tempest-tossed to me.
> I lift my lamp beside the golden door!"
>
> (From *I Am an American*,
> by Books 2000 (eds.). New York: Western Pub. Co., Inc.,
> 1972, p. 15).

In the 1920s, it was very popular to have one's photo taken with the Statue of Liberty in the background. You can try this:

Materials:

Large paper and felt markers to draw the statue
Camera with black-and-white film (Polaroid® works best)
Sepia-Toner (can be purchased at any camera shop for under $1.00)
Pan filled with bleach
Water to rinse photo

Directions:

1. After drawing the statue, put it up against a wall and dress yourself in the styles of the 1920s or 1930s. Stand in front of the poster about 5 feet away to create a depth effect.
2. Have someone take the picture with black-and-white film.
3. When the picture is developed, wash it in water, then set it in bleach, then in the toning solution.

Note: You do not need a darkroom. The process takes only a few seconds and you have an old tintype sepia photo of you in front of the Statue of Liberty.

Task Card #65 — Who Was Julius Rosenwald?

Julius Rosenwald was a philanthropist born in Springfield, Illinois on August 12, 1862. When he was 17 he went to New York to learn the clothing business. He then returned to the Midwest to set up his own business. He believed in high-quality merchandise at the lowest possible prices.

In 1895, Rosenwald became vice-president of Sears, Roebuck & Co. It was his idea to develop the Sears mail-order catalog.

Rosenwald once said, "The aim of my life is to have an income of $15,000 a year—$5,000 to be used for personal expenses, $5,000 to be laid aside, and $5,000 to go to charity."

IDEA 1: YOU CAN PRETEND YOU ARE JULIUS ROSENWALD

Materials:

Copies of the Sears Roebuck Catalog around the early 1900s
Copies of the modern catalog
Paper and pencil
Imagination

Directions:

1. Pretend you have $5,000 to spend. Go through the catalogs and pretend to buy items; design a sample form, as shown below.
2. Pretend you have $5,000 to give to a charity. What charity would you choose? What items would you buy for the chairty from the catalogs?

1906 SEARS ROEBUCK CATALOG SEARCH				Name:_____ Date:_____		
PAGE	ITEM	#	COLOR SIZE	PRICE PER ITEM	BUYING FOR	TOTAL
126	Bike	ASO4	Blue Boy's 26"	$28.00	Son	$28.00

IDEA 2: YOU CAN MAKE A MAIL-ORDER CATALOG

Materials:

Booklet to paste or draw items in
Magazines to cut up pictures
Pencil to write the data

Directions:

1. Create your own mail-order catalog. Remember the policies of Julius Rosenwald—high-quality merchandise at the lowest possible prices.

You simply make homemade instruments for musicians to play.

Materials:

2 pan lids or trash-can lids for large cymbals
Blocks of wood can be used for galloping-horse sounds
Small cans or boxes filled with rice or beans to make shake cans
Water glasses filled with different levels of water and a tap stick for making a xylophone
Table or barrel top to pound for a drum sound
Jug or Clorox® bottles to whistle into
Waxed paper over combs for kazoo sound
Coat hanger triangle with a nail for the striker
Metal spoons back to back, held in between fingers for castanet sound
Pop bottle tops (castanet)
Kettle or box harp (see below)
Washtub fiddle (see below)
Washboard and a thimble
Additional instruments of your choice

Directions:

1. Combine all the instruments and decide on a song to create the rhythm. You may want to add a singer. "Yankee Doodle" is an easy song with which to begin.

TO MAKE THE WASHTUB FIDDLE

Materials:

Metal washtub basin
Clothesline cord or venetian blind cord
Broomstick
Eye screws
Metal cutter

Directions:

1. Cut a hole in the tub and place the broomstick in securely.
2. Screw the eyehook into the top of the broomstick and thread the cord from the top of the broomstick to the second eyehook secured in the washtub.

TO MAKE THE BOX HARPS

Materials:

Cardboard box or a sheet-cake-sized pan
Monofilament fishing line, 10 to 20 pound weight to button cord
Something to poke a hole through the tin or cardboard base
Bridge made from cardboard or wood
Pencil or stick and tape

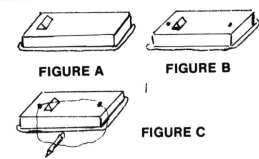

FIGURE A

FIGURE B

FIGURE C

Directions:

1. Turn the tin upside down and glue the bridge, as shown.
2. Poke 2 string holes through the tin; thread the fishing line through the hole, across the bridge and back around through the other hole.
3. Place a stick or pencil on the underside to allow room for sound and line tension.

Materials:

Camera (Instamatic with slide film works well)
Slide film
Proper lighting for your shots
Material to photograph
Tape recorder and blank cassette or reel
Slide projector carousel
Carousel slide tray
Screen or white wall
Paper and pencil to write script
Graphics titles and credits

Directions:

1. Draw a story board script (as shown below) and/or create a detailed script.
2. Plan and take photo shots.
3. Develop.
4. Sequence shots in a carousel slide tray.
5. Record sound track and sequence the slides.

Note: Pictures from books can be used by putting the book on the ground and placing black construction paper around the book. Stand at least 3 feet above the picture and shoot the slide.

Note: Popular songs make excellent sound tracks and easy sources for slide-show material because pictures can be matched up with the words and music.

STORYBOARD

1. Title "Big Red"
2. Boy and dog facing front
3. Boy and dog going for a walk
4. Boy stops—dog sits up

SCRIPT

	Audio	Visual	Directions
1	Background MUSIC	TITLE CARD	Center on card
2	Announcer says, "Big Red"	Boy and Big Red	Front face, full body
3	ONCE UPON A TIME... DOG.	Boy walking dog.	Profile side-view (full)
4	MUSIC	Boy stops; dog sits up.	Full shot centered
	Narrator says:	Narrator and dog sitting	Front face

Materials:

Sunday comics or comic books with color characters
Roll of cellophane clear tape (the wider the better)
White construction paper or typing paper
Scissors

Directions:

1. Find a favorite comic character and tape a piece of cellophane tape over the picture. If the picture is too wide, use several strips of tape, being careful to overlap a little on each piece of tape so that the picture can be lifted as a whole.
2. With your fingers, rub hard over the taped area. The better the rubbing, the better the lift.
3. Carefully peel off the tape; the comic picture should be transferred to the tape.
4. Place the picture on white construction or typing paper. Rub down so wrinkles do not appear. You may want to remove excess tape.
5. Try another one. It is fun to combine characters from different strips and create original comic stories. (Example: Dick Tracy meets Spiderman).

Task Card #69 — Do You Know How to Make Math Rolls?

Math Rolls can be used to practice the basic mathematical computation skills.

Materials:

Adding machine roll paper
Clear plastic covering with adhesive back
Fine point felt marker
Erasable crayon or grease pencil
Tissue
Rubber band

Directions:

1. Cut a strip of paper at least 2 feet long from the adding machine roll of paper.
2. Mark on top of the strip "Watch the Signs."
3. Create a beginning problem and continue as shown (see example).
4. When you reach the end of the strip, turn it over and print the final answer.
5. Cover with clear plastic or laminate so other students can try to work the roll. They will write the answers with the erasable crayon or grease pencil; wipe off with tissue when finished.
6. Roll and put a rubber band around the math roll.

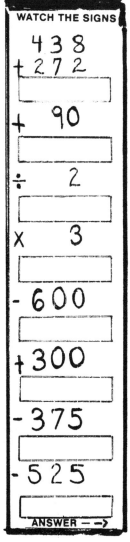

(Front of Strip)

(Back of Strip)

PART 4

REPRODUCIBLE SECTION

INTRODUCTION

The following is a list of reproducibles, arranged in numerical order. The directions for how to use each reproducible, along with the answer sheets, follow this list. The information within the parentheses specifies the dates that the reproducibles are first introduced in the Events and Activities Section of the book.

FIND-A-WORD MONTHLY PUZZLES

DIRECTIONS AND ANSWERS

Reproducible #1: Bring in a guitar or a large picture of a guitar. Tell the names of the parts and then pass out the sheets. Ask students to label the parts, as follows:

A.	Tuning key	F.	String numbers
B.	Guitar head	G.	Capo d'astro
C.	Space between fret	H.	Sound hole
D.	Brass strip fret	I.	Guitar base
E.	Names of strings	J.	Bridge

Reproducible #2: First half—explain the parts of a check. Ask students to turn the sheet over and letter a column A-J; then dictate the list of parts.

A. Name and address of check writer
B. The bank's computer number
C. Receiver's name
D. Amount of check in manuscript or cursive writing
E. Name and address of bank
F. Signature of check writer
G. Date the check is written
H. Amount of check in numerals
I. Checkbook number of check writer
J. Account number in the bank

Second half—explain how to fill out a check. Ask the students to practice the process on the "Pretend Check."

Reproducible #3: First half—use the top half of the sheet to show how to record checks that have been written and deposits that have been made.

Second half—ask the students to design their own personalized checks; discuss the wide variety of colors and designs which are currently available.

Reproducible #4: First part—obtain a set of chess pieces. Discuss the various pieces. Ask students to record the name and movement of each piece.

Sample: (Picture) = *Rook* = ✛

Second part—ask students to draw a line from each represented piece to the space on the chess-board where it belongs at the start of the game.

Third part—Suggest that the students design an elimination tournament schedule.

Reproducible #5: Distribute the worksheets and ask the students to find the member nations of the United Nations.

Reproducible #6: Ask the students to read the information and then discuss it. Suggest that students make up their own thesaurus words.

Reproducible #7: Ask the students to follow the written directions and create the envelope as directed.

Reproducible #8: Distribute the worksheet and ask students to try the questions. Answers are as follows:
1. cork and rubber
2. 90 feet
3. 60 feet, 6 inches
4. Dodgers = Brooklyn
   Braves = Milwaukee, Boston
   Athletics = Kansas City, Philadelphia
5. Gloves have separate slots for each finger; mitts do not
6. 60 homers
7. Hank Aaron
8. George Herman Ruth
9. RBI — Runs Batted In
   MVP — Most Valuable Player
   DH — Designated Hitter
10. Check baseball encyclopedia
11. a. Edward C. Ford
    b. Jay Hanna Dean
    c. Vernon Gómez
    d. Lou Gehrig

Reproducible #9: Distribute the worksheet and ask students to label the parts.

a. Aorta
b. Pulmonary artery
c. Right auricle
d. Pulmonary vein
e. Left auricle
f. Vena Cava
g. Left ventricle
h. Right ventricle
i. Septum

Reproducibles #10 and #11: Distribute worksheets 10 and 11. Ask the students to attach the bottom of Reproducible 10 to the top of Reproducible 11, covering the title of Reproducible 11. Invite the students to fill in additional historic events inbetween those provided. Encourage the students to decorate the top of the timeline with appropriate pictures.

Reproducible #12: Distribute the worksheet; an option is to split the activity into two games. To play the first game, each student must put one letter of his/her name in each square of the letter column. (See picture below.) After the letter column is completed, the leader of the game picks five categories, such as musicians, instruments, songs, terms, theme songs, etc. The players are given five minutes to fill in the chart. At the end of five minutes, answers are read aloud and scored. There are five points per correct answer, horizontally and vertically. The highest score wins.

GAME 1

CATEGORIES

LETTER	A SONGS	B MUSICIANS	C INSTRUMENT	D TV THEME	E TERMS	SCORE
M	"MICHELE"	MOZART		"MR. ED"	MUSIC	20
A	"AMERICA"				ALTO	10
R	"RAINDROPS KEEP FALLIN'..."				ROUND	10
C			CLARINET	"CHARLEY'S ANGELS"		10
I	"ITSY BITSY SPIDER"					5
SCORE	20	5	5	10	15	TOTAL 110

(Total of horizontal and vertical score columns = 110)

To play the second game, the instructor makes flashcards with various music terms and symbols. Students fill in the Bingo board with these terms and symbols in mixed order. Then the leader calls out a symbol and players play Bingo.

Reproducible #13: Distribute the worksheet and ask students to examine the basic fingerprint patterns and fill in the top part of the fingerprint card. Use a stamp pad and ask students to fill in their fingerprints.

Reproducible #14: Cut out the license and distribute to the students. Ask them to fill in the parts, using metric measures.

Reproducibles #15 and #16: Distribute the worksheets and follow the directions on part I.

Reproducible #17: Distribute the worksheet and ask the students to follow the directions. The answers for the parts of the bird are:

A. Top of head
B. Eye
C. Forehead
D. Bill
E. Cheek
F. Chin
G. Side of neck
H. Throat
I. Wings back
J. Breast
K. Rump
L. Tail
M. Belly
N. Leg
O. Foot

The answers for the lower half of the reproducible can be found in a variety of reference books.

Reproducible #18: Ask students to clear their desks of everything but a pencil. Distribute the "Friendship Test" and stress the importance of following directions. Direct students to read the paragraph above the test. Write on the chalkboard the starting time for the test. Tell the students that they will have ten minutes to complete the test and that you will be watching carefully. Allow students to begin. After the test, explain how important it is to follow directions. Ask students to fill in the lower portion of the reproducible.

Reproducible #19: Distribute the worksheets and allow time for the students to complete their answers. Answers are as follows:

1. One hour because alarm clocks do not work on the basis of a.m. or p.m.
2. Yes, they also have a third and second, as well.
3. Because he is living.
4. One; all the rest are anniversaries of that day.
5. The match.
6. All of them.
7. White because it has to be on the North Pole.
8. Halfway because then he would be running out.
9. Six—three on each team.
10. A 50¢ piece and a nickle (one is not a nickel).
11. 9
12. 70
13. They didn't play each other.
14. Two (the two you took).
15. No, because the coins wouldn't be marked "B.C."
16. It was not Moses, but Noah.
17. The beggar is a woman.
18. No, he is dead if his wife is a widow.

Reproducible #20: Distribute the crossword puzzle and allow the students to work.

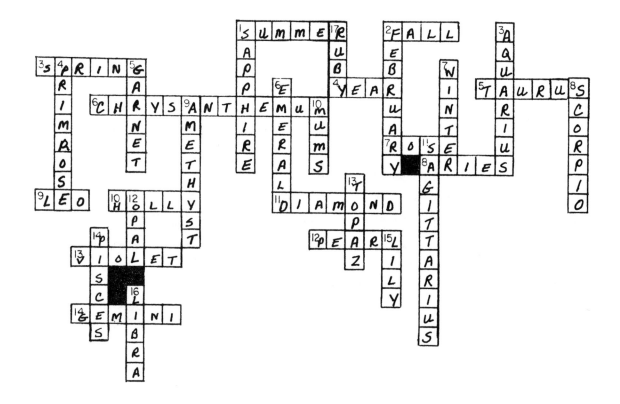

Reproducible #21: Distribute the worksheet and paper for students to figure out the answers. Answers are as follows:

1. Subtract 1886 from current date to figure answer.
2. Subtract 1776 from current date to figure answer.
3. Subtract 1924 from current date to figure answer.
4. $900,000
5. 305 feet
6. Answers will vary.
7. Substract from current decade to figure answer.
8. 156,000 windows
9. 200 feet
10. 13,000,000 ÷ 365 = answer
11. 186 days
12. 1,324 feet
13. $2.50
14. Answers will vary.

Reproducible #22: Obtain a book on the interior of the White House, such as *The White House*, White House Historical Association. Distribute the worksheets, asking students to label the rooms of the White House. Answers are as follows:

1. Queens' Bedroom
2. Lincoln Sitting Room
3. Lincoln Bedroom
4. Treaty Room
5. Yellow Oval Room
6. State Dining Room
7. Cross Hall
8. Entrance Hall
9. Green Room
10. East Room
11. Red Room
12. Blue Room
13. South Portico
14. Office Curator
15. Library
16. Vaulted-Arch Corridor
17. Vermeil Room
18. China Room
19. Diplomatic Reception Room

Reproducible #23: Distribute and follow directions. Answers for the parts of the microscope are as follows:

A. Eyepiece
B. Objective slides
C. Coarse adjustment knob
D. Stage
E. Arm
F. Mirror
G. Bases

Answers to questions are as follows:

1. Anthony van Leeuwenhoek
2. A scientist that deals with microorganisms
3. Little, small, minute
4. Petri dish, culture, specimen

Reproducible #24: Distribute the worksheets and follow the directions. The answers are as follows:

A. Tongue
B. Salivary glands
C. Esophagus
D. Stomach
E. Liver
F. Gallbladder
G. Pancreas
H. Large intestine
I. Small intestines
J. Appendix
K. Colon

The digestive system changes FOOD into FUEL ENERGY for the body.

Reproducible #25: Distribute the worksheets and ask the students to fill out the top portion by putting their names on the first line; street address on the second line; city, state and zip code on the third line; and their telephone number on the fourth line; invite students to fill out the rest of the resumé.

Reproducibles #26 through #32: Pass out all of the worksheets and review the directions on Reproducible #26 with the class.

Monthly Puzzles: The Find-a-Word puzzles are provided for each month of the year, with some of the happenings of the month chosen at random. The directions are on top of each Find-a-Word puzzle, and the answers are below each puzzle. Encourage students to create Find-a-Words with events that are not included.

JANUARY

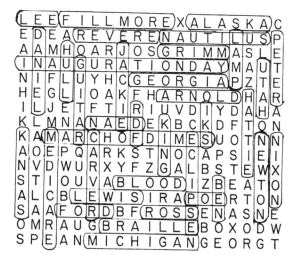

FEBRUARY

MARCH

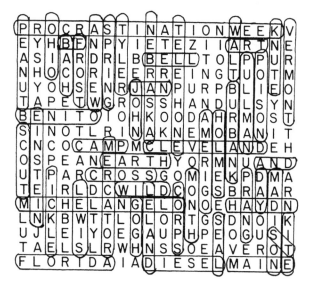

APRIL

MAY

```
CONSTITUTIONMJGOODMANBRAHMS
HOPECINCODEMAYOEDBAOMLASRBH
AABEDPOSTURECULLNIGHTENGALE
PCFJULIAWARDHOWEOKOEEAAODPN
MHARRYSTRUMANMARCEARARKBIQR
APROLSJROMMOPSPANCHOLSEZORY
NAHINDENBURGDISASTERTSMITHT
RNFLORNBASMARLASPWPEHDAYCIB
HPLANONCUISTELLIEIEDMAOMAY
OPWELLESMCCVESAPESACULLENWR
DQARSTRADEIAHODECCLRYITZIEL
ETYFOUNTAINPENNAHOPOLICEBEI
UVNXYKENNEDYUNITASLSZACMANN
WKENTUCKYDERBYTIONASENIORPE
WHITMANWISCONSINSJACOBRIIST
```

JUNE

```
KENTUCKYFATHERSLSDAYBK
LOUEGOLFWEEKTLLMARBLEA
HPGNFRANKARKANSASAIIJEM
UEENPEJAUEAVYKHYIGCYCH
ORKTSNACVBUNRPLSBOECIHA
RIHSULKTTMDGALLPAVLIM
ANBEEEIFTMMIUEDEWIETM
NSUERROLEEJNLRUBENSHE
ECELIKARREIARNRRTADA
ERKANMAGNALASTBTORNADO
WEISMULLERLTWAACSNDIAK
DSOUSTYPEWRITERTEIIRVE
TLIBERTYAMONROETOLAYIY
SFORAGONEWITHTHEWINDSES
DOUBLEDAYHALLOFFAMEEVS
```

JULY

```
BASTILLEIWLOBNVPOTTERH
OMEYOCUYIYTZAEEARHARTO
AAGERALDHOWERWHGREGORT
TYIIBLADAMSIBYAETEESWD
FORDEDNYOIUREOMARCOCHTO
OWTAPEIJONESRINONRATB
SHNHGRSLIGKEUKTTHEGRHB
TIMOONCOLTQGEUILDTEBAL
RAJPDISNEYLANDCAESARC
BROCOHANNLEASEIIURSRMK
BLSKEUAGONONDLIEIIUNSS
TEHETGLEDIONGSOMDBNUTI
GRAIBHOJESSEJAMESEGMRT
AMELPMUHAWTHORNETYRTYOUNGE
MEFORBTCOOLIDGEEVEYRAGE
```

AUGUST

```
TENNYSONESCALATORAWBHE
AVIATIONFCFKGSABINADIJ
DEBATESLLIWNILLEOPRQLJU
IALLERGYEMSJBEWRIGHTLU
CROCKETTMWIOGDENSOOWHIL
EMLOVEYCIHSHOENSSALAIU
ITISOAPLGOCSTAJESSEFKS
LRSSHWVOSOCOOHRAICKOKR
OOSTOAWRCTANNIEMCPEOSO
NNOEOIAAHVSSETHIECOGE
TGUVLUTDBOKDTCOGLORMGN
WOREAYHOOVERHHOHVATADW
RRIPARKAWAYENCVTIRSRON
SHREDDEDWHEATORALPHILA
SANDWICHAHOLUCILLEBALL
HARRISONCLOWNKPDERBYLD
```

SEPTEMBER

```
C O N S T C O O P F R H I S P A N I C H O M
O A C R E E P E A C E H O L A L L E R X A E
N C O N S T I T U T I O N A A L L E R B R E
S A M S Z L I H T Y O M P R E E O N U P O D
T L E T A O Y T U S W E A T E R W O N E O B
I I D E N V O R M E C E N Y O G E P I A N O
T F Y V U E U E N W M V C P W Y L G T C E H
D O G E C P H A N I E J A M E S B A J A N E
B R E A K F A S T N T A K A N F S T P O G N
M N Y M I N P U L G C M E D S R S L H O L R
H I A I N F P R I M A H K F K A M I C K E Y
L A B O R O I Y R A N G E R N N A N C A P R
D A G S I R N D B C T R N A O C R G R G E C
H E R A B T E E E H E E N N P I S O I G I O
O W E R B A S P T I R A Y C F S H A C B C O
J A M E O F S T U N I T E D S T A T E S A P
C E M E N T V E J E W I S H O O L Y V O P E
E O D D O A P P L E S E E D L O L P B N P R
```

OCTOBER

```
R E S T A U R A N T V E T E R A N S L I S
N L E E U W E N H O E K H A O N B O E I N
O O C H I C A G O F I R E R A N O B E L W H A
A M A E L E A N O R A L L L N F E O A I H A
H A L L O W E E N G R O U C H O I I N S
A L I T W E T P O N P O P C O R N N L Z L
D O F C V E E H M I L L E R T E G L E T E
A S T O C K M A R K E T R Y M S E R I E S
M H A L T H O R A N D G S T A T U E F R O
S T E U Y E A M U D G D A Y H A M A G I C
C R A M L L R A P N E W S P A P E R S E H
M P O B U E N C S E L I E E Y N D T C N W I
O A A U N N E Y E V E G T N E A E H C A R L
D B U S I N E S S A V H G N S V W U R S I
E L T I T O W N T D O T R A C Y E R S L N
L O L E E N A D M A C A R O N I Y O O L N E
T H E O D O R E A P R E V E N T I O N N E
```

NOVEMBER

```
N O R T H D A K O T A W R C A B R A H B C A
D O U B L E T A L K T I O U D O O B E A N R
A V M I Q E G A R F I E L D R U O D R L N C A R
U M O N R R O Y S E A L L I I R N I A L N N E
T O T I H A L L E Y E R N E A E B N E E G I
H N E S S T O E A T H E R Y N C A D Y K G
O R A T S O E R H W I E L E C T I O N O E R E
R S N W I F T H A N K S G I V I N G E P R E
S W T T A C R O N K I T E C D O I I S A M
D E I A Y D L A E H A W K I N S E L I X
I A U N L M E N L T B O O K L B G E C U E
A B N N A M K I G P O L K L E B S I R E U
B E E L O S G I U X B A A A L S T A M P L M
E T N A M N I H U O B R E H R T E R I C O O S A
T E C R E I A S A D T M O N T A N A E U E E
E S O U T H D A K O T A N N A T A M B X Z A
```

DECEMBER

```
I L L I N O I S M I S S I S S I P P A J O H
O V A N I A O G L E T H R O N E W P A U L A N
W L E D O O G L E T H R O P E E B A B N H U K
A E L I V J A L A B A M C H W S A U L I I K A
H U M A N A N D R E S A R L T G R E C O L K A
P E N N S Y L V A N I A S P O S T U A R T H
G F R A N K D E L A W A R E N O O L L A O N H
O S G I E W V H A E R R I N G L N G U M N H A
I E A T H U R B E R G E S O S O L D A E A A
D N A N G I G M A W I T M A L T E E W R W U
Y E T H K R T H A A L J O L I S C T O G O L F
A R W A S I I D I S N E Y K L E E O T T O R A
R O I N W E R A J O H N S O N A A T A E U A N
V E N J I R C O R N A E O C O R H T U B I N C
R E F R I G E R A T O B C H R I S T M A S C H
R E F R I G E R A T O R H E A L T H E A P H
```

REPRODUCIBLES

Name: _____
Date: _____

MATCH WORDS WITH APPROPRIATE LETTER

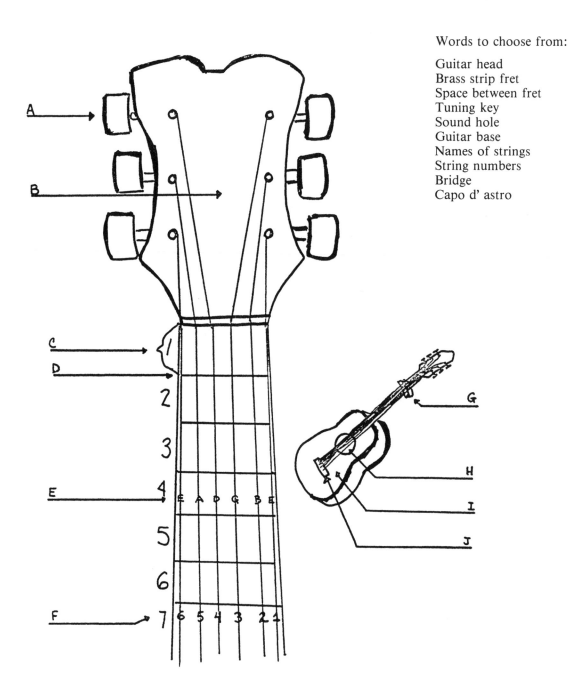

Words to choose from:

Guitar head
Brass strip fret
Space between fret
Tuning key
Sound hole
Guitar base
Names of strings
String numbers
Bridge
Capo d' astro

Name: _____
Date: _____

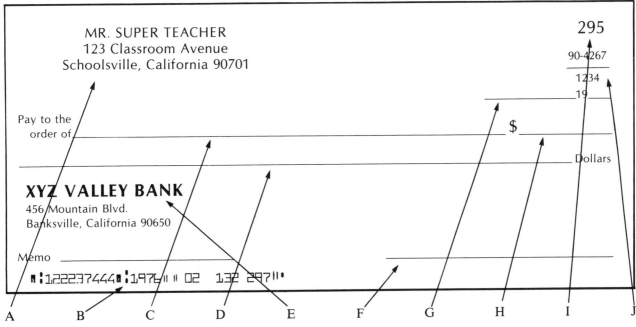

MR. SUPER TEACHER
123 Classroom Avenue
Schoolsville, California 90701

295

90-4267

1234

19___

Pay to the
order of _____ $ _____

_____ Dollars

XYZ VALLEY BANK
456 Mountain Blvd.
Banksville, California 90650

Memo _____   _____

⑆1222374440⑈1976⑉ ⑉ 02   132 297⑈

A   B   C   D   E   F   G   H   I   J

100

90-4367

1244

19___

Pay to the
order of _____ $ _____

_____ Dollars

PRETEND BANK
123 American Avenue
Schoolsville, California 90701

Memo _____   _____

⑆1222374440⑈1976⑉ ⑉ 02   132 297⑈

Reproducible #3 — How to Write a Check, Part 2

Name: _____
Date: _____

Check Number	Date	Check issued to or description of deposit	(-) Amount of check	✓	(+) Amount of deposit	Balance	

PERSONALIZED CHECK

Name: _____
Date: _____

CHESS PIECE	NAME OF PIECE	WAY IT CAN MOVE
	ROOK	vertical & horizontal linear movement

Draw a line from chess piece below to place on board where they are put at start of game.

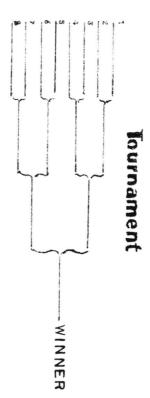

Tournament

WINNER

389

Name: _____
Date: _____

DIRECTIONS: Find and circle the names of the countries of the United Nations. There are over 100 names. The names may be placed horizontally, vertically, backwards, or diagonally. GOOD LUCK! Make a list of members of the United Nations that are not in the puzzle below.

```
D C A M E R O O N E G C A M B O D I A M A L A Y I S A U E
O Z A M B I A L G E R A U S T R A L I A U I L U N W F G C
M E K U W A I T U R C N O R W A Y I S L S B B G D A G A U
I C Y P R U S Y R S H A B O A T G O R I T Y A O O Z H N A
N H E I C U B A L W I D E N M A R K A L R A N S N I A D D
I O M V E N E Z U E L A L I E S E T E V I T I L E L N A O
C S E O Y I L O X D E V G G X E A U L J A S A A S A I D R
A L N R L T G R E E C E I E I E T H I O P I A V I N S A G
N A E Y O E H O M N Y F U R C C B O O R O N R I A D T H A
R V T C N D A M B A R I M I O U R N C D L G G A P O A O M
E A H O E S N A O T O J J A P D I D O A A A E S F I N M B
P K E A W T A R U S S I A B O B T U S N N P N U A R E E I
U I R S Z A P O R T P T P E R U A R T E D O T D S A G Y A
B A L T E T E M G C A A A T T R I A A T A R I A O N I U S
L L A U L E G F O H I L N Y U M N S R H H E N N M O R H E
I G N N A S Y R I A N Y U O G A O O I E O J A M A I C A N
C E D I N O P A C D O H E G A B O N C H I N A O L R O I E
U R S S D M T N E C U A B O L I V I A U N T T R I E N T G
K I S I S A O C L N E P A L A B A D O N D O U O A L G I E
R A O A I N B E A F G O R R O M A N I G I B R C L A O M L
A B U F I N L A N D E R B O S T W N A A A A F C G N E A G
I E L S A L V A D O R T A N Z A N I A R U G O O E D E U S
N B R A Z I L B U R U N D I T A B C U Y S O M A B O B R O
I U C B R A L R G C O L U M B I A A S B O T S W A N A I U
A L P H I L I P P I N E S A R T U R U G U A R Y O F H T T
N G A U R E B A A B I O G N L L T A G F B K Q A T A R A H
I A R T O B E N K C G U I N E A U G U A T E M A L A A N A
C R A A M A R A I D E F N O S Y R U Y I T N A Z I P I I F
A I G N A N I M S I R A Q A O U K A A T N Y L O V E N A R
R A U E N O A A T T I V O L T A E F N S I A A M A L T A I
A R A P I N E P A T A E L O H T Y G A X O R W A N D A N C
G G Y A A O M O N G O L I A O L O A S A U D I A R A B I A
```

Name: _____

Date: _____

A THESAURUS is a book of words grouped by ideas. With the dictionary, a person generally knows the word but needs to find out more information about the word. With a thesaurus, the person generally has an idea about what a word means but wants to find a more specific word to express a concept.

Some thesaurus editions are made alphabetically like the dictionary, but generally the book is divided into two sections. The back section is an alphabetical index which directs the reader to a number in the front section of the book. In other words, a person first looks up the idea in the alphabetical index and then finds the closest synonym listed beneath. Then he/she turns to the numbered section and chooses the best word from all those listed.

Suppose, for example, we need another word for the word "book." We would look up the noun "book" in the index and find:

> book
> > n. book part 605.13
> > publication 559.1
> > edition 605

Since "edition" is the most appropriate word for our use, we would turn to the numbered section 605 and find:

nouns: edition, book, volume, tome, opus

Because we need a word to substitute for "book" in the following sentence, we would probably choose "volume": "The library has 500 volumes in its collection."

The THESAURUS can help you develop a better vocabulary!

Roget's Thesaurus is the most popular synonym-finder. Peter Mark Roget, the originator, was a famous doctor and researcher in London. Just for fun, he started keeping a list of words that could be used for other words. In the year 1852 he brought out his *Thesaurus of English Words and Phrases Classified and Arranged so as to Facilitate the Expression of Ideas and Assist in Literary Composition.*

In 1911 the Thomas Crowell Company published the first completed edition. It became extremely popular and everyone called it "Roget's Thesaurus."

Peter Roget died on September 12, 1869, at the age of 90, saying, "I hope my thesaurus will help everyone who writes or speaks from now on!"

On the back of this sheet, make a list of 10 words that you use daily. Try to find different ways to express the same thought by using the thesaurus. Mark the new word in a column next to the idea you look up. Also be sure to use the thesaurus from now on in all your work; you will be more scholarly.

EXAMPLE: WORDS I USE   NEW WORD FROM THESAURUS

1. Scholarly   1. Educated (474.21)

2.   2.

Name: _____
Date: _____

FOLD = - - - -

C

E

B

D

glue

glue

A

Directions:

1. Cut out pattern
2. Fold flap *a* into *b*
3. Fold flap *c* into *b*
4. Put paste or glue along border on flap *d* and then fold up *d* to *b* on top of flaps *c* and *a*.
5. Crease *e* for top flap.

Name: _____

Date: _____

DIRECTIONS: Try to answer all the questions below!

1. The inside of a baseball is made of:

   cork & rubber   aluminum   felt   stones

2. The official distance between the bases is:

   105 feet   99 feet   90 feet   90 inches

3. The official distance between the pitcher's box and home plate is:

   32 feet 4 inches   66 feet   60 feet 6 inches   3 yards

4. Name the cities the baseball teams below originally had as their home.

   Dodgers =
   Braves =
   Athletics =

5. What is the difference between a mitt and a glove?

6. How many homers did Babe Ruth hit in 1927?

7. Who broke Babe Ruth's record of 714 homeruns?

8. What was Babe Ruth's real name?

9. What do the abbreviations below stand for?

   RBI =
   MVP =
   DH =

10. Define the terms below:

    a. diamond   g. fly ball
    b. mound   h. triple
    c. bullpen   i. stolen base
    d. line drive   j. error
    e. strike   k. umpire
    f. dugout   l. balk

11. Name the real names for the players below:

    a. "Whitey" Ford
    b. "Dizzy" Dean
    c. "Lefty" Gomez
    d. "The Iron Horse"

Name: _____
Date: _____

DIRECTIONS: Label the parts of the heart.

A

B

C

D

E

F

G

H

I

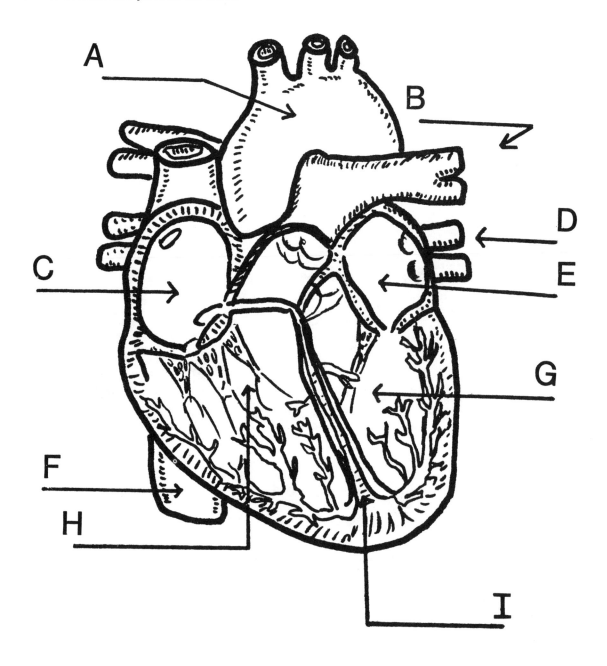

Name: _____
Date: _____

TIMELINE
of
AMERICAN HISTORY

| COLUMBUS | 1492 |

| PILGRIMS | 1620 |

Declaration of Independence — 1776

"Star Spangled Banner" written   War of 1812 — 1812

California Gold Rush — 1849

Western Movement – Pony Express — 1850

Civil War — 1861

Union Pacific Railroad — 1869

Coca Cola Invented – Telephone Invented — 1889

Henry Ford invented Horseless Carriage — 1902

(Timeline continues on page 396.)

Name: _____

Date: _____

Wright Brother's Flight — 1903

World War I — 1917

"Roaring 20's" — 1920

Stock Market CRASH — 1929

World War II — 1941

T.V. "Rock & Roll" — 1950

Space Age — 1960

Beatlemania — 1964

Surfing – Protests – Riots — 1968

Ecology – Energy Crisis — 1970

Name: _____

Date: _____

GAME 1

CATEGORIES

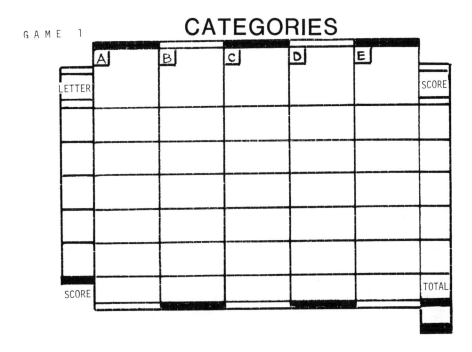

GAME 2

"MUSIC BINGO"

FREE

SPOT

Name: _____
Date: _____

DIRECTIONS: Fill in the fingerprint card below. Use an ink pad to roll your fingerprints.

EIGHT BASIC FINGERPRINT PATTERNS

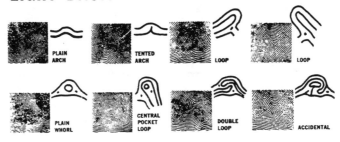

PLAIN ARCH   TENTED ARCH   LOOP   LOOP

PLAIN WHORL   CENTRAL POCKET LOOP   DOUBLE LOOP   ACCIDENTAL

PERSONAL IDENTIFICATION	LAST NAME	FIRST NAME	MIDDLE NAME	SEX	RACE
FINGERPRINTS SUBMITTED BY	SIGNATURE OF PERSON FINGERPRINTED			HT.(Inches)	WT.
				HAIR	EYES
FINGERPRINTED BY	RESIDENCE OF PERSON FINGERPRINTED			DATE OF BIRTH	

Person to be Notified in Case of Emergency

NAME _____

ADDRESS _____

See Reverse Side for Further Instructions

DATE FINGERPRINTED	LEAVE THIS SPACE BLANK
PLACE OF BIRTH	CLASS. _____
CITIZENSHIP	REF. _____
SCARS AND MARKS	

1. RIGHT THUMB	2. RIGHT INDEX	3. RIGHT MIDDLE	4. RIGHT RING	5. RIGHT LITTLE

6. LEFT THUMB	7. LEFT INDEX	8. LEFT MIDDLE	9. LEFT RING	10. LEFT LITTLE

LEFT FOUR FINGERS TAKEN SIMULTANEOUSLY   LEFT THUMB   RIGHT THUMB   RIGHT FOUR FINGERS TAKEN SIMULTANEOUSLY

Source: Identification Division, Federal Bureau of Investigation, "Fingerprint Identification" and form FD-353, Personal Identification Fingerprint Card.

Name: _____

Date: _____

DIRECTIONS: Fill in the blanks on the license below. You will need metric measuring tools.

Metric Measuring License

This license entitles _____, upon completion of the form below,
to be an OFFICIAL METRIC MEASURER, authorized to measure, at any time, using any OFFICIAL
METRIC UNITS (such as cm, dm, m, km, g, or kg), ANYTHING that can be measured either with
OFFICIAL MEASURING TOOLS or by ESTIMATION.

height _____ cm   arm spread _____ cm   nose to fingertip _____ cm   elbow to fingertip _____ cm   handspan _____ cm

palm _____ cm   thumb _____ cm   index finger _____ cm   middle finger _____ cm   ring finger _____ cm   pinkie _____ cm

knee to floor _____ cm   foot length _____ cm   foot width _____ cm   shoe length _____ cm   shoe width _____ cm

plain step _____ cm   giant step _____ cm   most gigantic step _____ cm   circumference of head _____ cm

circumference of neck _____ cm   circumference of chest _____ cm   circumference of wrist _____ cm   circumference of wrist _____ cm   circumference of waist _____ cm

circumference of thigh _____ cm   circumference of ankle _____ cm   weight _____ kg   weight of shoe _____ g

weight of relaxed hand _____ g   age _____ years   signature _____   date _____

ALL OF THESE MEASUREMENTS WILL CHANGE—KEEP YOUR METRIC MEASURING LICENSE UP TO DATE

Copyright © 1979 by Education Development Center, Inc.

Source: The METRIC MEASURING LICENSE was developed by Project TORQUE, Education Development Center, Inc., Newton, MA 02160.

399

Name: _____
Date: _____

DIRECTIONS: Color, cut, and glue into a globe shape. Use part 2 with this sheet to complete the globe.

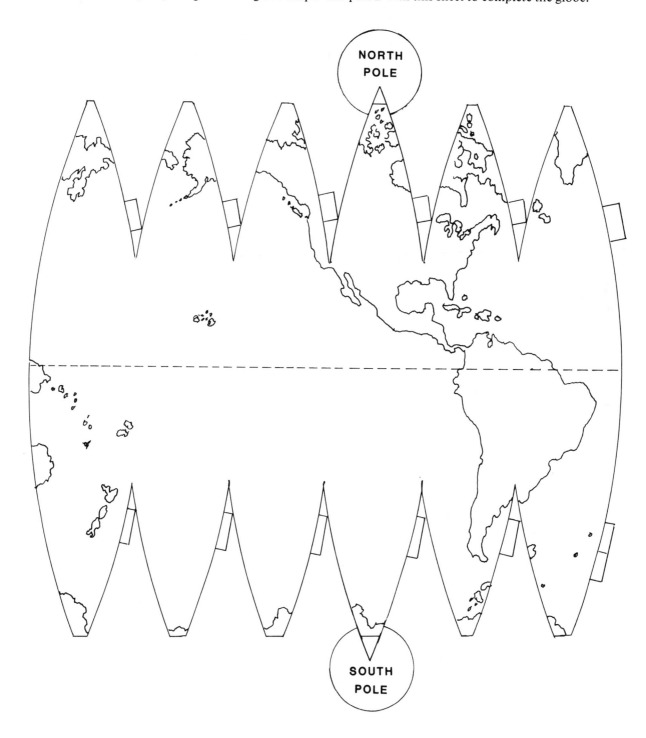

Name: _____
Date: _____

DIRECTIONS: See directions on part 1 (page 400).

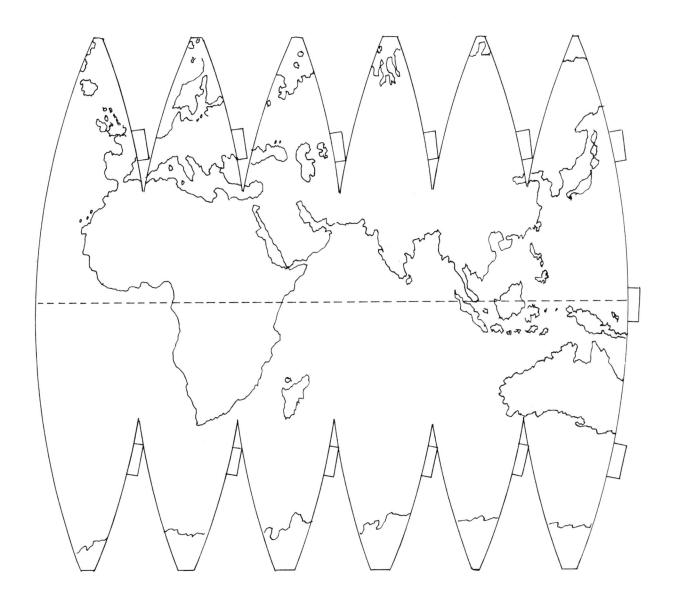

Name: _____
Date: _____

DIRECTIONS: Label the parts A-O.

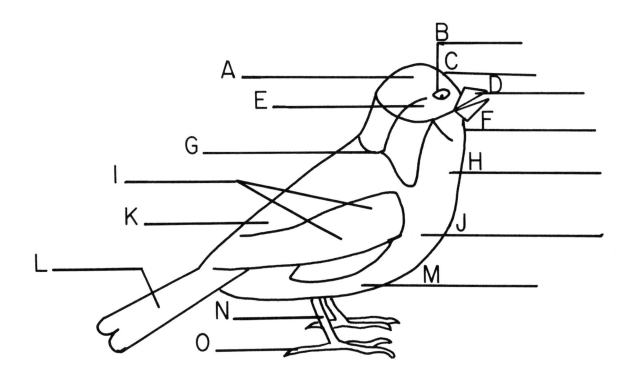

DIRECTIONS: Answer the questions below on another sheet of paper.

1. Name a bird of the woodland or forest.
2. Name a bird of the desert.
3. Name a water bird.
4. Name a beach or ocean bird.
5. Name a jungle bird.
6. Name a bird of the Antarctic.
7. How and why do birds migrate?
8. Name the 4 types of bird flight.
9. Name some prehistoric birds.
10. A scientist who studies birds is called an _____.

DIRECTIONS: Paint a watercolor of a bird on another sheet of paper.

DIRECTIONS: Do a project on a special bird or build a birdhouse.

Name: _____

Date: _____

This is a timed test. It is fairly easy. Do not begin until directed. If you are friendly or know the rules of friendship, you can probably pass this test. Be sure not to be SHY! Be sure to read entire test before doing exactly what is asked. There are several different versions of this test so do not worry if your neighbor is doing something different. Mind your own business! GOOD LUCK!

FRIENDSHIP TEST

1. Jump up and say, "HELLO WORLD, I FEEL FRIENDLY!"
2. Yell your name aloud so all can hear.
3. Name a person in your group you like. (aloud)
4. Name something you love. (aloud)
5. Go touch the teacher's desk and return to your seat.
6. Spell the word FRIENDSHIP backwards. (aloud)
7. Sing or hum a short song.
8. Count to 10 and say, "It is fun to be friendly!"
9. Act like an animal from Noah's Ark.
10. Turn around in circles and yell, "I'm halfway through this test."
11. Yell out a phone number.
12. Yell the exact time on the clock.
13. Think of something funny and laugh aloud.
14. Name an event in American history.
15. Imitate an actor or actress. (aloud)
16. Name your favorite TV show. (aloud)
17. State your name and say, " _____ is GREAT!"
18. Now do not do problems 1 through 17 or you will look silly.
19. Smile and say your name aloud.
20. Watch the others politely making fools of themselves.

SOME HELPFUL HINTS IN TEST TAKING ARE:

Name: _____

Date: _____

1. If you went to bed at 8 o'clock at night and set the alarm to get up at 9 o'clock in the morning, how many hours of sleep would you have?

2. Do they have a 4th of July in England?

3. Why can't a person living in Winston-Salem, North Carolina be buried west of the Mississippi River?

4. How many birthdays does the average person have?

5. If you had only one match and entered a room where there was a kerosene lamp, an oil burner, and a wood-burning stove, which would you light first?

6. Some months have 31 days; some have 30. How many have 28?

7. A person builds a house with 4 sides to it, rectangular in shape. Each side has a southern exposure. A big bear came by. What color is the bear?

8. How far can a dog run into the woods?

9. How many outs are there in an average inning during a baseball game?

10. Two coins total 55¢ in value; one isn't a nickel. What are the coins?

11. A farmer had 17 sheep; all but 9 died. How many did he have left alive?

12. Divide 30 by ½ and add 10. What is the answer?

13. Two people were playing checkers. They played five games and each won the same number of games. No ties. How do you figure this?

14. Take two apples from three apples and what do you have?

15. An archeologist claimed he found some coins dated 46 B.C. Do you think he did? Why?

16. How many animals of each species did Moses take aboard the Ark with him?

17. A woman gives a beggar 50¢. The woman is the beggar's sister but the beggar isn't the woman's brother. How come?

18. Is it legal in North Carolina for a man to marry his widow's sister?

ALL QUESTIONS HAVE LOGICAL ANSWERS!

17 correct — GENIUS
12 correct — NORMAL
8 correct — SUBNORMAL
0 correct — IDIOT

Name: _____

Date: _____

ACROSS

1. Season beginning June 21
2. Season where leaves turn brown & yellow
3. Season with flowers in bloom (around March 21)
4. There are 12 months in a _ _ _ _ _
5. The zodiac name for the BULL symbol
6. Flower for the month of November
7. Flower for the month of June
8. The zodiac name for the RAM symbol
9. The zodiac name for the LION symbol
10. The flower for the month of December
11. The gem or birthstone for the month of April
12. The gem or birthstone for the month of June
13. The flower for the month of February
14. The zodiac name for the TWINS symbol

DOWN

1. The gem or birthstone for the month of September
2. The second month of the year
3. The zodiac name for the WATER BOY symbol
4. Flower for the month of June with prefix PRIM
5. The birthstone for the month of January
6. The gem or birthstone for the month of May
7. The season of the year (around December 21)
8. The zodiac name for the SCORPION
9. The gem or birthstone for the month of February
10. Flower for the month of November (nickname)
11. The zodiac name for the ARCHER symbol
12. Birthstone or gem for the month of October
13. Birthstone or gem for the month of November
14. The zodiac name for the FISH symbol
15. Flower for the month of May
16. The zodiac name for the SCALES symbol
17. The birthstone or gem for the month of July

Name: _____

Date: _____

DIRECTIONS: Answer the questions below. (Think—What mathematical operation is it?)

1. The Statue of Liberty was a gift of the people of France to the people of the United States. It was dedicated on July 4, 1866. How many years ago was the statue dedicated?

2. The Statue of Liberty has in her left hand a law book with the date 1776. How many years ago was that?

3. The Statue of Liberty became a national monument in 1924. How many years ago was that?

4. The U.S. government raised $300,000 to build a suitable pedestal for the Statue of Liberty. Today the pedestal would probably cost 3 times that amount to build. If so, how much money would be needed?

5. The height of the Statue of Liberty is 151 feet. The height of the base is 154 feet high. How high is the monument?

6. The Statue of Liberty's face is 10 feet wide. How much larger is her face than your face?

7. King Kong climbed the Empire State Building in the 1930s. How many decades ago was that?

8. The Empire State Building has 6,500 windows to wash twice a month. How many windows would be washed each year?

9. The 86th floor is 1,050 feet high. How many more feet would one need to climb to reach the top floor (102) at 1,250 feet)

10. 13,000,000 visitors come to see the Empire State Building every year. There are 365 days in a year. What is the average number of people per day that visit the building?

11. The Empire State Building has 1,860 steps. If you climbed 10 steps a day, how many days would it take you to reach the top?

12. The Empire State Building is 1,472 feet tall and the Statue of Liberty is 151 feet tall. How much taller is the Empire State Building than the Statue of Liberty?

13. In 1968, to visit the Empire State Building it was $1.60 for adults. To visit the Statue of Liberty it was $0.90 for adults. How much money was needed to visit both monuments in one day (not counting souvenirs, etc.)?

14. MAKE UP YOUR OWN STORY WORD PROBLEM ABOUT THE STATUE OF LIBERTY OR THE EMPIRE STATE BUILDING BELOW:

Score

14

Name: _____

Date: _____

DIRECTIONS: Number your paper from 1-19 and name the rooms of the White House.

Name: _____
Date: _____

DIRECTIONS: A) Fill in the parts of a microscope below; B) Answer the questions below.

"PARTS of a MICROSCOPE"

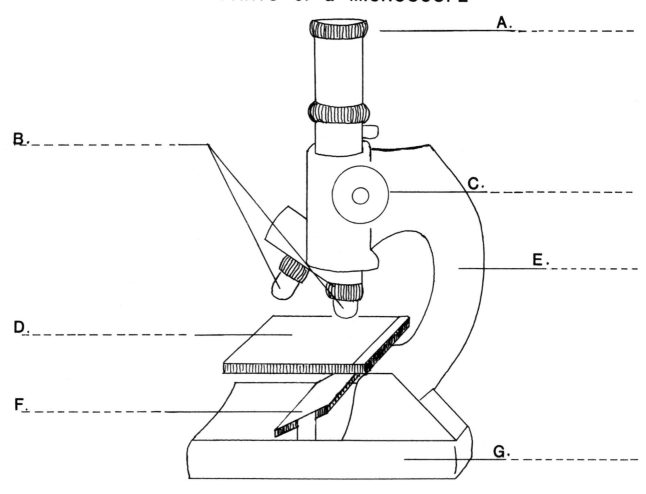

A. _____

B. _____

C. _____

E. _____

D. _____

F. _____

G. _____

1. The microscope was invented by _____.

2. Define the term "microbiologist":

3. The prefix "micro" means:

4. List some terms you would need to know when using a microscope:

Name: _____
Date: _____

DIRECTIONS: Fill in the parts of the digestive system and the statement below:

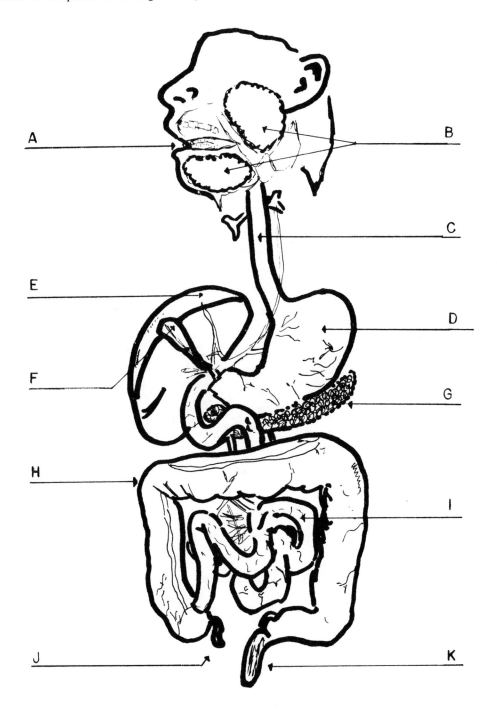

A _____

B _____

C _____

E _____

D _____

F _____

G _____

H _____

I _____

J _____

K _____

THE DIGESTIVE SYSTEM CHANGES F __ __ D INTO F __ __ L E __ __ __ __ __ Y FOR THE BODY.

Name: _____

Date: _____

RESUMÉ

_____

_____

_____

_____

_____

OBJECTIVE:

EDUCATION:

WORK EXPERIENCE:

HONORS & ACTIVITIES:

PERSONAL:
    MARITAL STATUS:
    WEIGHT:
    HEIGHT:
    DATE OF BIRTH:

REFERENCES:

Name: _____

Date: _____

DIRECTIONS

Objective: In using the following reproducible outlines (pages 412-17), you will be able to see various relationships and the interaction of the various anatomical parts of the human body. You will also be able to understand 1) that the bones protect the organs, 2) that the muscles attach to the bones, and 3) how the skin serves as the outer covering of the body. The project will also serve as a health record for you.

Directions: Obtain a large sheet of construction paper, coloring tools, glue, scissors, an ink pad for fingerprints, and a paper fastener.

1. Color all parts. The outer body (figure D, page 417)) should be colored in your favorite outfit—to look like you. (Coloring guides are just suggestions.)
2. Cut out the internal organs and circulatory system outline (figure 1, page 412) and the skeletal back view (figure 2, page 413).
3. Glue together figure 1 on top of figure 2, turned over so that the organs are on the front of the bones showing on the back.
4. Cut out the other figures—A, B, C, and D (pages 414-17).
5. Place the back view (A) muscular system on the construction paper so that the muscles face the construction paper. DO NOT GLUE.
6. Place double glued figure from step 3 next on top of the view of the muscles. DO NOT GLUE.
7. Place the skeletal system, front view (figure B, page 415), on top of the organs system figure. DO NOT GLUE.
8. Place the muscular system, front view (C, page 416), on top of the skeletal system. DO NOT GLUE.
9. Place the outer skin, drawn with your favorite outfit, figure D, on top of the muscular system. DO NOT GLUE.
10. Take a paper fastener and put it through the stack of systems; hook the fastener through the construction paper so that the body becomes attached to the construction paper. Leave room on the construction paper for the Personal Body Data sheet and the title. See sample below.
11. Make a title for the poster. Suggestion: The Inside Body of _____
12. Fill out the Personal Body Data sheet; cut it out and then glue it on the poster.
13. Hang the project up for display or save it for later years!

PERSONAL BODY DATA

AGE:
HEIGHT:
WEIGHT:
HAIR COLOR:
SKIN COLOR:
EYE COLOR:
CONDITION OF HEALTH:
BIRTHMARKS:
BROKEN BONES:

THUMBPRINT

DATE RECORDED:

_____
Signature

SAMPLE POSTER FORMAT

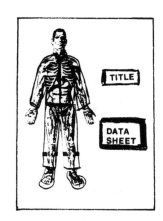

411

Name: _____
Date: _____

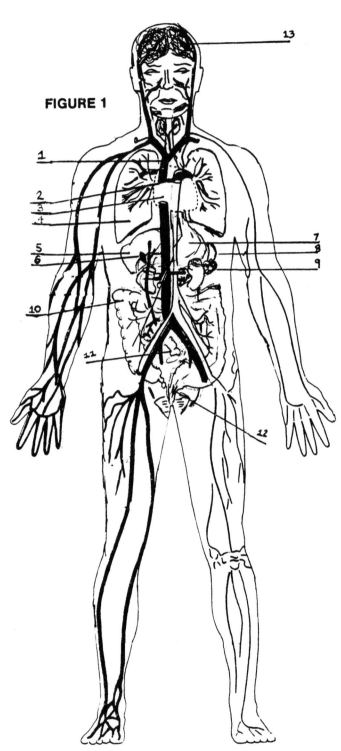

FIGURE 1

BASIC COLORING GUIDE

 1 veins — BLUE
 2 arteries — RED
 3 heart — PURPLE
 4 lungs — ORANGE
 5 liver — BROWN
 6 gallbladder — GREEN
 7 stomach — PINK
 8 spleen — YELLOW
 9 pancreas — YELLOW
10 large intestines — RED
11 small intestines — PINK
12 colon — RED
13 brain — GRAY

Name: _____
Date: _____

FIGURE 2

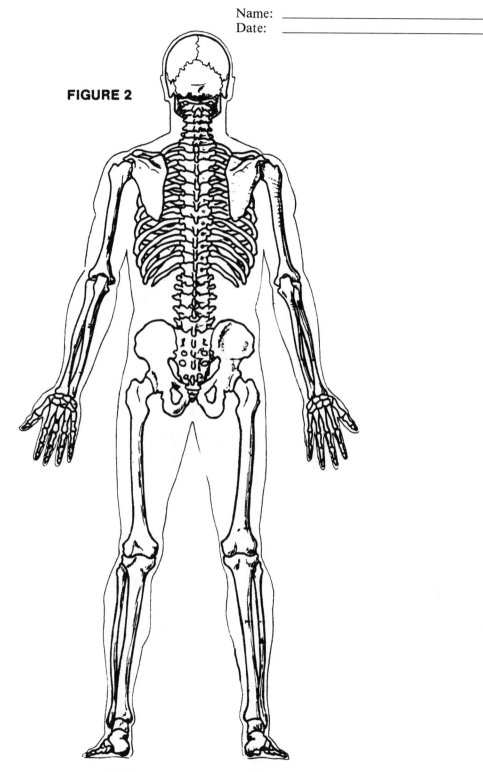

BASIC COLORING GUIDE
Bones should be a light yellow.

Name: _____
Date: _____

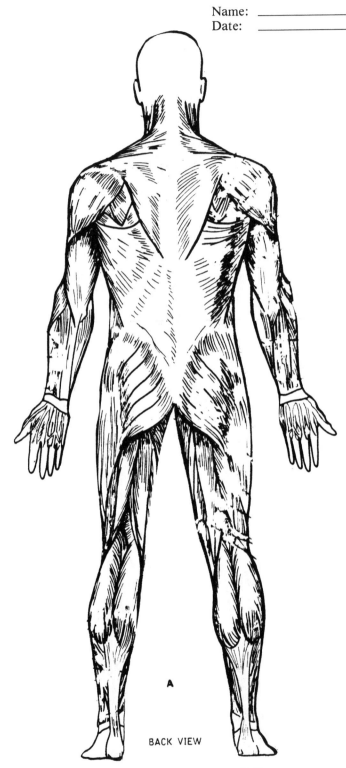

A

BACK VIEW

BASIC COLORING GUIDE
Color muscles light red or pink.

Name: _____
Date: _____

Diaphragm

B

BASIC COLORING GUIDE
Bones should be a light yellow.

415

Name: _____
Date: _____

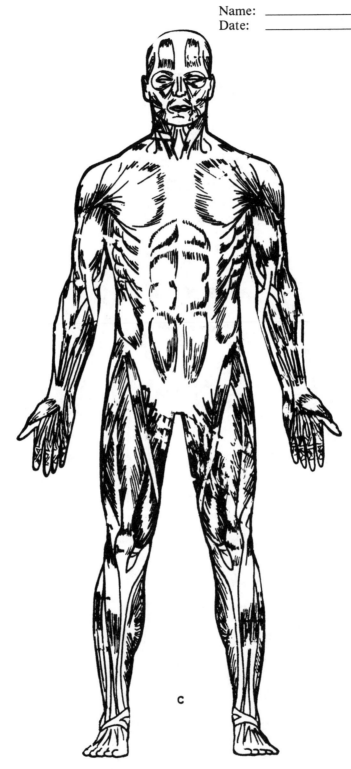

c

BASIC COLORING GUIDE
Color muscles light red or pink.

Name: _____
Date: _____

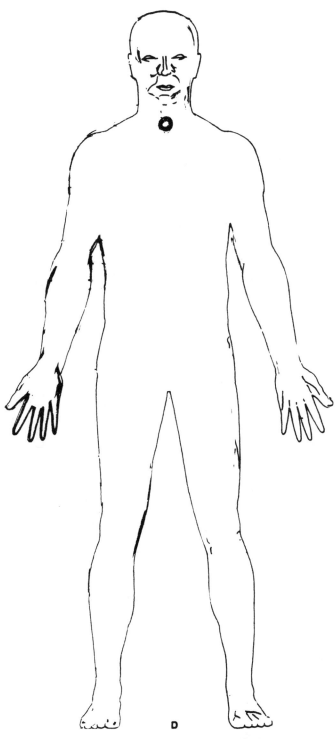

BASIC COLORING GUIDE
Human body to be colored to look like you.

Name: _____
Date: _____

DIRECTIONS: Find the words of famous people and events in January (words in dark print only). Words may be horizontal, vertical, backwards, or diagonal. Good luck!

JANUARY

```
L E E F I L L M O R E X A L A S K A C
E D E A R E V E R E N A U T I L U S P
A A M H O A R J O S G R I M M A S L E
I N A U G U R A T I O N D A Y M A U T
N I F L U Y H C G E O R G I A P Z T E
H E G L I O A K F H A R N O L D H A R
I L J E T F T I R I U V D I Y D A H A
K L M N A N A E D E K B C K D F T O N
K A M A R C H O F D I M E S U O T N N
A O E P Q A R K S T N O C A P S I E I
N V D W U R X Y F Z G A L B S T E W X
S T I O U V A B L O O D I Z B E A T O
A L C B L E W I S I R A P O E R T O N
S A A F O R D B F R O S S E N A S N E
O M R A U G B R A I L L E B O X O D W
S P E A N M I C H I G A N G E O R G T
```

FAMOUS PEOPLE

Benedict **Arnold**
Louis **Braille**
Hattie Caraway
George Washington **Carver**
Lewis Carroll
Dizzy **Dean**
Millard **Fillmore**
Ben Franklin
Jacob **Grimm**
Bobby **Hull**

Martin Luther **King**
Robert E. **Lee**
Isaac **Newton**
Richard **Nixon**
Edgar Allan **Poe**
Paul **Revere**
Jackie Robinson
Peter Roget
Betsy **Ross**
Daniel Webster
F.D.R.

EVENTS

March of Dimes Month
Guitar Month
Blood Month
Ski Week
Henry **Ford** inaugurated "assembly line"
Submarine *Nautilus* launched
Incandescent **lamp** patented
Eclipse of the moon
Inauguration Day
Medicare signed
Alaska, Connecticut, **Georgia, Kansas, Utah, Michigan**
   and New Mexico admitted to the United States

418

Name: _____

Date: _____

DIRECTIONS: Find the words of famous people and events in February (words in dark print only). Words may be horizontal, vertical, backwards, or diagonal. Good Luck!

FEBRUARY

```
C R I M E W W J O H N G A L I L E O
H O C W D O U G L A S S S H O L O M
A C Y E I O R X A N E B C O G L D A
R K R E S D U E P K G F H G E I G R
L W U K O H T I E J O R E G O N K I
E E S A N T H O N Y V L A M R U N O
S L O B P Q R S C T I U R V G S W H
D L X R Y Z P L I Q A X T V E R N E
I L L A A B C P L U T O D E F G H N
C E C H O P I N I I K H E A L T H R
K A L A R I Z O N A T H I S T O R Y
E P M M N O P Q R D S C H I N E S E
N U V N U W X W Y L E A R T H D A Y
S Z B R O S O B L A C K W E L L A B
H A R R I S I S S I N I C H O L A S
D A V I D S X C O B A S E B A L L Y
```

FAMOUS PEOPLE

Hank Aaron
Sholom Aleichem
Mario Andretti
Susan B. **Anthony**
Elizabeth **Blackwell**
Frederick **Chopin**
Nicholas Copernicus
Charles **Dickens**
Frederick **Douglass**
Thomas A. **Edison**
Galileo
John Glenn
William **Henry** Harrison

Abraham Lincoln
Charles Lindbergh
Cyrus McCormick
Linus Pauling
Norman **Rockwell**
Babe **Ruth**
David Sarnoff
André **Segovia**
Adlai Stevenson
Jules **Verne**
George Washington
Grant **Wood**

EVENTS

Heart Month
American **History** Month
American **Music** Month
Crime Prevention Month
Brotherhood Week
National **Pencil** Week
National Engineer's **Week**
Children's Dental **Health** Week
Valentine's **Day**
Groundhog Day
Leap Year
Chinese New Year
Baseball's National League formed
Planet **Pluto** discovered
Big California **earth**quake happened
Arizona, Massachusetts, and Oregon admitted to the United States

Name: _____

Date: _____

DIRECTIONS: Find the words of famous people and events in March (words in dark print only). Words may be horizontal, vertical, backwards, or diagonal. Good luck!

MARCH

```
P R O C R A S T I N A T I O N W E E K V
E Y H B F N P Y I E T E Z I I A R T N E
A S I A R D R L B B E L L T O L P P U R
N H O C O R I E E R R E I N G T U O T M
U Y O H S E N R J A N P U R P B L I E O
T A P E T W G R O S S H A N B U L S Y N
B E N I T O I O H K O O D A H R M O S T
S I N O T L R I N A K N E M O B A N I T
C N C O C A M P M C L E V E L A N D E H
O S P E A N E A R T H Y O R M N U A N D
U T P A R C R O S S G O M I E K P D M A
T E I R L D C W I L D C O G S B R A A R
M I C H E L A N G E L O N O E H A Y D N
L N K B W T T L O L O R T G S D N O I K
U J L E I Y O E G A U P H P E O G U S I
T A E L S L R W H N S S O E A V E R O T
F L O R I D A I A D I E S E L M A I N E
```

FAMOUS PEOPLE

Johann Sebastian **Bach**
Alexander Graham **Bell**
Luther **Burbank**
Grover **Cleveland**
Rudolph **Diesel**
Albert **Einstein**
Robert **Frost**
Vincent Van **Gogh**
Franz Josef **Haydn**
Justice Oliver Wendell **Holmes**
Andrew Jackson
Benito Juarez
Jerry **Lewis**

James **Madison**
Jan Matzeliger
Gerhard **Mercator**
Michelangelo
Louis **Prang**
George M. **Pullman**
John D. Rockefeller
Knute Rockne
B. F. Skinner
Leland Stanford
John **Tyler**
Amerigo Vespucci
Walt Whitman

EVENTS

Red **Cross** Month
Hamburger **Month**
Youth **Art** Month
Pickle Month
Easter **Seal** Campaign Month
Kite Month
Weights **and** Measures Week
National **Procrastination Week**
National **Peanut** Week
Girl **Scout** Week

Campfire Girls Birthday
National **Wild**life Week
Poison Prevention Week
Spring begins
Peace **Corps** established
Telephone patented
St. Patrick's Day
Earth Day
Meteorology **Day**
Florida, Maine, Nebraska, Ohio, and **Vermont** admitted to the United States

Name: _____
Date: _____

DIRECTIONS: Find the words of famous people and events in April (words in dark print only). Words may be horizontal, vertical, backwards, or diagonally. Good Luck!

APRIL

```
A T B Z C Y P X E X F L G V H U I T J
K C R O S S W O R D L E M M T N O O S
P E A R T H Q U A K E O Q S R S E D E
L O U I S I A N A C D N R E F G X I C
G A R D E N F B H A H A R V E Y P C R
S T E A U D U B O N E R V S E B R T E
I L A W C O I N R H I D L H O U E I T
W I S H O U D I N I E O A A Z C S O A
A S S A S S I N A T E D U K I H S N R
S T O N O P R T L L A G E P A O A Y
H E H S N H V A I E L V H S P N H R H
I R L L J D I X B R I I L P E A L Y L
N X C L A Y N Y R B N N Z E R N P Q R
G L H O E V G E A I G C R A D I U M P
T G R A N T E A R K T I C R I D E E S
O E X M U I R A Y E O C R E E D H A P
N H J E F F E R S O N M O N R O E O U
S E W E W M A R Y L A N D T O N I G H
```

FAMOUS PEOPLE

Hans Christian Andersen
John James **Audubon**
James **Buchanan**
Henry **Clay**
Leonardo da Vinci
Dorthea **Dix**
Duke **Ellington**
Ulysses S. **Grant**
William **Harvey**
William Randolph **Hearst**
Sonja Henie

Adolf **Hitler**
Harry **Houdini**
Washington **Irving**
Thomas **Jefferson**
Joseph **Lister**
James **Monroe**
Samuel **F. B.** Morse
John **Muir**
William **Shakespeare**
Booker T. **Washington**
F. W. Woolworth

EVENTS

National **Laugh** Week
Library Week
Coin Week
Secretary Week
Garden Week
Bike Safety Week
Pony **Express** service
  began
Zipper patented
American **Creed** written
Patent **Law** adopted

Webster's **dictionary**
  copyrighted
Lincoln **assassinated**
U.S. income **tax due**
Paul Revere's **ride**
San Francisco **earthquake**
First **crossword** puzzle
  published
Radium discovered
Louisiana and **Maryland**
  admitted to the United
  States

421

Name: _____
Date: _____

DIRECTIONS: Find the words of famous people and events in May (words in dark print only). Words may be horizontal, vertical, backwards, or diagonal. Good luck!

MAY

```
C O N S T I T U T I O N M J G O O D M A N B R A H M S
H O P E C I N C O D E M A Y O E D B A O M L A S R B H
A A B E D P O S T U R E C U L L N I G H T E N G A L E
P C F J U L I A W A R D H O W E O K O E E A A O D P N
M H A R R Y S T R U M A N M A R C E A R A R K B I Q R
A P R O L S J R O M M O P S P A N C H O L S E Z O R Y
N A H I N D E N B U R G D I S A S T E R T S M I T H T
R N F L O R N B A S M A R L A S P W P E H D A Y C I B
H P I A N O N C U I S T E L L I E I E D M A O M A Y E
O P W E L L E S M C C V E S A P E S A C U L L E N W R
D Q A R S T R A D E I A H O D E C C L R Y I T Z I E L
E T Y F O U N T A I N P E N N A H O P O L I C E B E I
U V N X Y K E N N E D Y U N I T A S L S Z A C M A N N
W K E N T U C K Y D E R B Y T I O N A S E N I O R P E
W H I T M A N W I S C O N S I N S J A C O B R I I S T
```

FAMOUS PEOPLE

Frank **Baum**
Irving **Berlin**
Johannes **Brahms**
Countee **Cullen**
Salvador **Dali**
Pancho González
Benny **Goodman**
Patrick **Henry**
Bob **Hope**
Julia Ward Howe
Edward **Jenner**
John F. **Kennedy**

Edward **Lear**
Horace **Mann**
Florence **Nightengale**
Jacob Riis
Beverly **Sills**
Kate **Smith**
Harry S Truman
Johnny **Unitas**
John **Wayne**
Orson **Welles**
Walt **Whitman**

EVENTS

Senior Citizen Month
National **Radio** Month
Correct **Posture** Month
Bike Month
Hearing & **Speech** Month
Salad Month
National **Music** Week
Police Week
World **Trade** Week
Kentucky Derby
Mother's **Day**
May Day

Cinco de **Mayo**
Hindenburg disaster
World **Red Cross** Day
Constitution Day
Fountain pen patented
Piano patented
Minnesota, **Rhode** Island,
South Carolina and **Wisconsin** admitted to the
United States

Name: _____
Date: _____

DIRECTIONS: Find the words of famous people and events in June (words in dark print only). Words may be horizontal, vertical, backwards, or diagonal. Good Luck!

JUNE

```
K E N T U C K Y F A T H E R S L S D A Y B K
L O U E G O L F W E E K T L L M A R B L E A
H P G N F R A N K A R K A N S A S A I J E M
U E E N P E J A U E A V Y K H Y I G C U C E
M R N E W H A M P S H I R E I O D O Y D H H
O K T S N A C V B U N R P L S B O E C Y E A
R I H S U L K T T M D G A L L P A V L H R M
A N B E E E I F T M M I U E D E W I E T M E
N S U E R R O L E E J N L R U B E N S H E H
N E C E L I K A R R E I A R N R R T A D A A
E R K A N M A G N A L A S T B T O R N A D O
W E I S M U L L E R L I W A A C S N D I A K
D S O U S T Y P E W R I T E R T E I I R V E
T L I B E R T Y A M O N R O E T O L A Y I Y
S F O R A G O N E W I T H T H E W I N D S E
D O U B L E D A Y H A L L O F F A M E E V S
```

FAMOUS PEOPLE

Pearl S. **Buck**
Jefferson **Davis**
Jack Dempsey
Abner **Doubleday**
Paul Lawrence **Dunbar**
Errol Flynn
Anne Frank
Judy Garland
Lou Gerhig
Nathan **Hale**

Helen Keller
John Maynard **Keyes**
Paul McCartney
William James **Mayo**
Marilyn **Monroe**
Elisha **Perkins**
Peter Paul **Rubens**
Harriet **Beecher** Stowe
Johnny **Weismuller**
Frank Lloyd Wright

EVENTS

Dairy Month
National **Rose** Month
National **Humor** Month
Little League Baseball
   Week
Golf Week
National Spelling **Bee**
Father's Day
National **Marble**
   Tournament
Baseball's **Hall of Fame**
   opened
Flag Day
Sandpaper patented
Statue of **Liberty** arrived
Great **Seal** of the United
   States adopted

Typewriter patented
Custer's **last** stand
Bicycle patented
Paul Bunyon **Day**
Gone with the Wind
   published
Magna Carta Day
Summer begins
Kamehameha Day
First American **tornado**
   recorded
**Arkansas, Kentucky, New
   Hampshire, Tennessee,
   Virginia** and West Vir-
   ginia admitted to the
   United States

423

Name: _____

Date: _____

DIRECTIONS: Find the words of famous people and events in July (words in dark print only). Words may be horizontal, vertical, backwards, or diagonal. Good luck!

JULY

```
B A S T I L L E I W L O B N V P O T T E R H
O M E Y O C U Y I Y T Z A E E A R H A R T O
A A G E R A L D H O W E R W H G R E G O R T
T Y I I B L A D A M S I B Y A E T E E S W D
F O R D E D N Y O I U R E O M A R C O C H O
O W T A P E I J O N E S C R I N O N R A T G
S H N H G R S L I G K E U K T T H E G R H B
T I M O O N C O L T Q G E U I L D T E B A L
E S A J P D I S N E Y L A N D C A E S A R A
R T R O C O H A N N L E A S E L V L S R M C
B L S K E U A G O N O N D L I E I I U N S K
T E H E T G L E D I O N G S O M D B N U T S
G R A I B H O J E S S E J A M E S E G M R T
A C L C O N E S A B A T T L E N N R K E O O
M E L P M U H A W T H O R N E T Y T O U N N
E F O R B T C O O L I D G E E V E Y R A G E
```

FAMOUS PEOPLE

John Quincy **Adams**
Louis **Armstrong**
P. T. **Barnum**
Sir William **Blackstone**
David Brinkley
Julius **Caesar**
Alexander **Calder**
Marc Chagall
George M. **Cohan**
Samuel **Colt**
Calvin **Coolidge**
Amelia **Earhart**
George Eastman
Gerald Ford

Henry **Ford**
Stephen **Foster**
John **Glenn**
Oscar Hammerstein II
Nathaniel **Hawthorne**
Elias **Howe**
John Paul **Jones**
Thurgood **Marshall**
Charles **Mayo**
Gregor Mendel
Clement Moore
Beatrix **Potter**
James **Whistler**

EVENTS

Hot Dog Month
National **Barbecue** Month
Tennis Week
Safe **boating** Week
Joke Exchange Week
Miss Universe **Pageant**
All-Star Baseball **Game**
Battle of Gettysburg
Song "America" **sung** for
first time
Liberty Bell Day
Doughnut cutter patented

Bastille Day
Tape measure patented
Atomic **bomb** exploded
Disneyland opened
Neil Armstrong landed on
Moon
Jesse James held first
train robbery
Ice-cream **cones** created
Idaho, Wyoming, and **New
York** admitted to the
United States

424

Name: _____

Date: _____

DIRECTIONS: Find the words of famous people and events in August (words in dark print only). Words may be horizontal, vertical, backwards, or diagonal. Good luck!

AUGUST

```
T E N N Y S O N E S C A L A T O R A W B H E
A V I A T I O N F C F K G S A B I N A D I J
D E B A T E S L L I W N I L L E O P R Q L J
I A L L E R G Y E M S J B E W R I G H T L U
C R O C K E T T M W I O G D E N S O O W H L
E M L O V E Y C I H S H O E N S S A L A I I
C S M I T H S O N I A N N B D T A D O F C U
I T I S O A P L G O C S T A J E S S E F K S
L R S S H W V O S O C O O H A I O A S L O R
O O S T O A W R C T A N N I E N M C P E K O
N N O E O I A A H V S S E T H I E C O L O S
T G U V L I T D B O K D T C O G L O R M G E
W O R E A Y H O O V E R H H O H V A T A D N
R R I P A R K A W A Y E N C V T I R S R O W
S H R E D D E D W H E A T O R A L P H I L A
S A N D W I C H A H O L U C I L L E B A L L
H A R R I S O N C L O W N K P D E R B Y L D
```

FAMOUS PEOPLE

Neil **Armstrong**
Lucille Ball
Leonard **Bernstein**
Clara **Bow**
Ralph Bunche
Davy **Crockett**
Cecil B. DeMile
Sir Alexander **Fleming**
Benjamin **Harrison**
Wild Bill **Hickok**
Alfred **Hitchcock**
Herbert **Hoover**

Lyndon B. **Johnson**
Francis Scott **Key**
Herman **Melville**
Maria Mitchell
Ogden Nash
Annie Oakley
Julius Rosenwald
Dr. Albert **Sabin**
Alfred Lord **Tennyson**
Seth Thomas
Andy **Warhol**
Orville **Wright**

EVENTS

Sandwich Month
National **Allergy** Month
National **Clown** Week
Soap Box **Derby**
Sports Day
Shredded Wheat biscuits patented
Escalator patented
Smithsonian Institution founded
National **Aviation** Day

Lincoln-Douglas **debates** begun
Soap (liquid) patented
National **Park** Service established
Waffle iron patented
Sacco and Vanzetti executed
Colorado, Hawaii, and **Missouri** admitted to the United States

425

Name: _____

Date: _____

DIRECTIONS: Find the words of famous people and events in September (words in dark print only). Words may be horizontal, vertical, backwards, or diagonal. Good Luck!

SEPTEMBER

```
C O N S T C O O P F R H I S P A N I C H O M
O A C R E E P E A C E H O L A L L E R X A E
N C O N S T I T U T I O N A A L L E R B R E
S A M S Z L I H T Y O M P R E E O N U P O D
T L E T A O Y T U S W E A T E R W O N E O B
I I D E N V O R M E C E N Y O G E P I A N O
T F Y V U E N W M V C P W Y L G T C E H
D O G E C P H A N I E J A M E S B A J A N E
B R E A K F A S T N T A K A N F S T P O G N
M N Y M I N P U L G C M E D S R S L H O L R
H I A I N F P R I M A H K F K A M I C K E Y
L A B O R O I Y R A N G E R N N A N C A P R
D A G S I R N D B C T R N A O C R G R G E C
H E R A B T E E E H E N N P I S O I I A O
O W E R B A S P T I R A Y C F S H A C B C O
J A M E O F S T U N I T E D S T A T E S A P
C E M E N T V E J E W I S H O O L Y V O P E
E O D D O A P P L E S E E D L O L P B N P R
```

FAMOUS PEOPLE

Jane Addams
Edgar **Rice** Burroughs
John Chapman (Johnny **Appleseed**)
James Fenimore **Cooper**
Richard J. **Gatling**
Charles Dana **Gibson**
Jesse **James**
Sister Elizabeth **Kenny**
Alfred A. **Knopf**
John **Marshall**

J. P. Morgan
Jesse **Owens**
Francis Parkman
William Sydney Porter **(O. Henry)**
Walter **Reed**
Mickey Rooney
Ed Sullivan
William Howard **Taft**
H. G. Wells
Darryl F. **Zanuck**

EVENTS

National **Allergy** Month
National Better **Breakfast** Month
National **Pancake** Month
Home Sweet Home Month
Comedy Appreciation Month
Hispanic Heritage Week
Constitution Week
National **Dog** Week
National **Sweater** Week
Share the **Happiness** Week
Labor Day

Jewish High Holy Days
Treasury Department established
V-J Day
Name of **United States** adopted
Sewing machine patented
Typewriter **ribbon** patented
World **Peace** Day
Electric **range** patented
Cement patented
Autumn begins
California admitted to the United States

426

Name: _____
Date: _____

DIRECTIONS: Find the words of famous people and events in October (words in dark print only). Words may be horizontal, vertical, backwards, or diagonal. Good Luck!

OCTOBER

```
R E S T A U R A N T V E T E R A N S L I S
N L E E U W E N H O E K H A O N B O E I N
O O C H I C A G O F I R E R A N O B E L W
A M A E L E A N O R A L L N F E O A I H
H A L L O W E E N G R O U C H O I I N S A
A L I T W E T P O N P O P C O R N N L Z L
D O F C V E E H M I L L E R T E G L E T E
A S T O C K M A R K E T R Y M S E R I E S
M H A L T H O R A N D G S T A T U E F R O
S T E U Y E A M U D G D A Y H A M A G I C
C R A M L L R A P N E W S P A P E R S E H
M P O B U E N C S E L I E E Y N D T C N G
O A A U N N E Y E V E G T N E A E H A W E
D B U S I N E S S A V H G N S V W U R I O
E L T I T O W N T D O T R A C Y E R S L R
L O L E E N A D M A C A R O N I Y O O L G
T H E O D O R E A P R E V E N T I O N N E
```

FAMOUS PEOPLE

John **Adams**
Chester A. **Arthur**
William **Boeing**
Johnny **Carson**
John **Dewey**
Dwight D. Eisenhower
Rutherford B. **Hayes**
Thor Heyerdahl
Anthony Van
   Leeuwenhoek
John **Lennon**
Franz **Liszt**

Juliet **Low**
Groucho Marx
Arthur **Miller**
Alfred **Nobel**
William **Penn**
Pablo Picasso
Eleanor Roosevelt
Theodore Roosevelt
Noah Webster
George Westinghouse

EVENTS

National **Restaurant** Month
Macaroni Week
Whale-Watching Week
Fire **Prevention** Week
National 4-H **Week**
National **Pharmacy** Week
National **Newspaper** Week
National **Forest** Products
  Week
Business Women's Week
Popcorn Week
United Nations Week
American Education Week
Columbus Day
Model T auto introduced
"Dick **Tracy**" strip
  published

Chicago fire
Leif Erikson Day
National **Magic** Day
Pledge of Allegiance
  written
U.S. **Navy** originated
Erie Canal opened
Stock market crashed
UNICEF **Day**
Statue of Liberty dedicated
"**War** of the Worlds" broadcast
Halloween
World **Series**
Veterans Day
Nevada admitted to the
  United States

Name: _____
Date: _____

DIRECTIONS: Find the words of famous people and events in November (words in dark print only). Words may be horizontal, vertical, backwards, or diagonal. Good luck!

NOVEMBER

```
N O R T H D A K O T A W R C A B R A H B C
D O U B L E T A L K T I O U D O O B E A A
A V I O E G A R F I E L D R U O D R L N R
U M N R R O Y S E A L L I I R N I A L N N
T O T I H A L L E Y E R N E A E B N E E E
H N E S S T O F A T H E R Y N C A D Y K G
O T R O W E R H W I E L E C T I O N O E I
R A N E I T H A N K S G I V I N G E P R E
S N A A F N C R O N K I T E C D O I I S F
S W T T A R D L A E H A W K I N S E A E
D E I A H I A I T B O O K L B G E C R M L
I E O Y A S N N L R K H O R S E W V C U I
A U N L N M E G P O L K L E B S I R E E X
B N A M K I S U X B A A A L S T A M P L M
E E L O S T O B R E H R T E R I C O O S A
T S E N G H U O C R O L I C C O A N G U Y
E C R E I A S A D T M O N T A N A E U E E
S O U T H D A K O T A N N A T A M B X Z A
```

FAMOUS PEOPLE

Louisa **May** Alcott
Benjamin **Banneker**
Daniel **Boone**
Louis **Brand**eis
Andrew **Carnegie**
Sir Winston Churchill
Samuel L. Clemens
Stephen **Crane**
Walter **Cronkite**
Marie **Curie**
Will **Durant**
Felix Frankfurter
James **Garfield**
Edmund **Halley**
Warren G. **Harding**

Boris Karloff
Claude **Monet**
James **Naismith**
Franklin **Pierce**
James **Polk**
Auguste **Rodin**
Roy Rogers
Will Rogers
Father Junipero Serra
Anna Sewell
John Philip **Sousa**
Elizabeth **Cady** Stanton
Robert Louis Stevenson
Jonathan **Swift**
Zachary **Taylor**

EVENTS

Christmas **Seal** Campaign
Indigestion Season
International Aviation
  Month
Cat Week
National Children's **Book**
  Week
National **Diabetes** Week
National **Stamp** Collection
  Week
National **Doubletalk** Week
Latin America Week
Thanksgiving
Election Day

National **Horse** Show
Authors' Day
Artificial **leg** patented
UNESCO established
Guy Fawkes Day
Sadie **Hawkins** Day
Suez Canal opened
Puerto **Rico** discovered
Montana, North Carolina,
  North Dakota, Okla-
  homa, South Dakota and
  Washington admitted to
  the United States

Name: _____
Date: _____

DIRECTIONS: Find the words of famous people and events in December (words in dark print only). Words may be horizontal, vertical, backwards, or diagonal. Good luck!

DECEMBER

```
I L L I N O I S M I S S I S S I P P A J O H
O V A N I A O G L E T H R O N E W P A U L A
W L E D O O G L E T H R O P E E B A B N H N
A E L I V J A L A B A M C H W S A U L I I U
H U M A N A N D R E S A R L T G R E C O L K
P E N N S Y L V A N I A S P O S T U A R T K
G F R A N K D E L A W A R E N O O L L A O A
O S G T E W V H A E R R I N G L N G U M N H
O I E A T H U R B E R G E S O S O L D A E A
D N R N G I G M A W I T M A L T E E W R W U
Y A S U E T L E M I S S I S S I P P I T T S
E T H K R T H A A L J O L I S C T O G O L F
A R W A S I I D I S N E Y K L E E O T T O R
R O I N W E R A J O H N S O N A A T A E U A
V E N J I R C O R N A E O C O R H T U B I N
R E F R I G E R A T O B C H R I S T M A S C
R E F R I G E R A T O R H E A L T H E A P H
```

FAMOUS PEOPLE

Clara **Barton**
Ludwig van Beethoven
Emily Dickenson
Walt **Disney**
Ira **Gershwin**
John **Paul** Getty
Charles **Goodyear**
Jose **Greco**
Conrad **Hilton**
John **Jay**
Andrew **Johnson**
Paul **Klee**
Robert **Koch**

Margaret **Mead**
Isaac **Newton**
Louis Pasteur
Otto Preminger
Frank Sinatra
Gilbert **Stuart**
James **Thurber**
Martin **Van** Buren
Andres Vesalius
Eli Whitney
John Greenleaf **Whittier**
Woodrow **Wilson**

EVENTS

Human Rights Week
Winter **Solstice**
Hanukkah
Christmas
Cornhusking Championship
Pan American **Health** Day
Gas **refrigerator** patented
Junior Chamber of Commerce Day
Golf **tee** patented
Boston **Tea** Party
U.S. **Golf** Association formed
Chewing **gum** patented
Alabama, Delaware, Illinois, Indiana, Iowa, Mississippi, New Jersey, **Pennsylvania** and Texas admitted to the United States

PART 5

SAMPLE PACKET — STUDENT FOLDERS SECTION

INTRODUCTION

The sample sheets found in this section may be reproduced and used each month to create a monthly folder for each student. The names of the sheets are listed below in the order in which they appear in the packet. A set of directions and an explanation of each sheet follow.

DIRECTIONS AND EXPLANATIONS

DIRECTIONS TO MAKE STUDENT FOLDERS

Toward the end of each month, students are given materials with which to create a monthly folder for the forthcoming month. Students are each given a piece of construction paper (12x18 inches) to make their folders. The students are to label the folder cover with their own name, followed by "Folder for the Month of _____."

It is recommended that the instructor present a few of the highlights of the upcoming month, as found in the Events and Activities Section—the Month-long Observances, the Special Weeks, and the Variable Dates. Students then may choose to illustrate the cover of their folders with a drawing appropriate to the particular month.

The Contract sheet should be stapled on the inside cover of the student folder; and the Outline sheet should be stapled on the back inside cover (see examples below). The top portion of the Contract should be filled out and the Outline sheet completed. (See directions that follow as to how to use the Contract and Outline sheets.)

EXPLANATION OF THE CONTRACT ITEMS AND/OR
THE SAMPLE PACKET SHEETS

Contract: The Contract, stapled to the inside of the folder cover, is an agreement between the instructor and the student. It functions as a reminder to the student as to what he/she has contracted individually to do for the month; the Contract also serves as a record sheet for the evaluation of the student's work.

Most of the projects which are listed in the first column of the Contract are each represented by the remaining sheets in the packet and are explained below. The ✓ column is the space for the student to check what he/she has completed. The "Student Points" column is to be filled in by the instructor, using the "Possible Points" column as a guideline. The criteria for evaluation should be jointly established, at the outset, with the students—creativity, resourcefulness, thoroughness, the amount of effort and time represented, legibility, and so on. The "Scale" of the Contract refers to a grade based upon a scale, such as below:

850-900+	= A		850-900+	=	Excellent
700-849	= B	*or*	700-849	=	Very Good
500-699	= C		500-699	=	Average
400-499	= D		400-499	=	Needs Improvement

The following Sample Packet sheets are listed as they relate to the items in the first column of the Contract Sheet.

Outline: The Outline sheet is accounted for on the Contract as Behavior, Participation, and Listening to Events. At the first of each month, the appropriate introductory data from the Events and Activities Section of the book are read aloud for the students to fill in on their Outline sheets. The Outline sheet, stapled to the inside of the back folder cover, is easily referred to as a reminder of the month's major features and as a source for project ideas throughout the month.

Item 2 of the Contract refers to the *cover* of the student folder. Students are encouraged to design an innovative cover for their monthly folders—one which relates to the information entered each month on the Outline sheet.

Calendar: The Calendar sheet may be used in a variety of ways. Once students have filled in their own names, the month, and the year, and have appropriately numbered the days, they may opt to use the sheet in whatever way they wish; they may choose to use the sheet as a daily diary to record each day's historical events—just those which appear most interesting; or they may wish to make note of additional events which they discover in their independent research activities.

Telegram: Students may use the Telegram sheet to send information related to a historical event of the month. Those who write telegrams are encouraged to be as creative as possible as to the message, the timing, and the names of the receiver and sender. Remind students to write in "telegraph-ese" ... eliminating the less important words!

Biography Project: The Biography Project sheet is provided for students to write an essay about one of the famous people who was born or who died on one of the month's days in history. Students are to complete the information at the top of the page and then create original titles for the essays. The following sign · · · ·⟩ indicates where to indent and begin the biographical sketch. The lines along the side of the paper represent margins. The "Source(s)" indicate where the student's references for information are to appear (i.e., *World Book Encyclopedia,* Vol. 1, 1980, p. 242).

Historical Project: Similar to the Biography Project sheet, the Historical Project sheet is provided in order for students to present a report on an event that occurred on one of the month's days in history—other than that of the birth or death of a famous personality.

States Project (3 sheets—includes the Outline Map and the Data Map of the United States): The form for gathering information on a particular state in the United States is best used in connection with the two maps (Outline and Data) which follow the States Project sheet. Once students complete the necessary information on the States Project sheet,they can locate the particular state on the Data Map, double-check the year the state was admitted, and print the place-name of the capital by the dot provided on the map. Students are encouraged to use the blank Outline Map, using any variety of legends to symbolize topics such as topography, demography, vegetation, etc.

Find-a-Word: The Find-a-Word sheets are to be found in the Reproducible Section of the book rather than in the Sample Packet, largely because the Find-a-Word puzzles are referred to in a number of places throughout the book. It is recommended that the appropriate Find-a-Word sheet be handed out at the outset of each month; while in the process of locating the month's events and people's names in the puzzle, students will become familiar with potential topics for their other projects, such as the Biography, Historical, States, and Book Reports.

Items 9, Task Card(s), and 10, Reproducible(s), are provided on the Contract so as to keep a record of the quality and amount of task cards/reproducibles that are completed during a given month.

Items 11, Month-long Project(s), and 12, Special Weeks or Variable Dates Project(s), on the contract represent the spaces on which to record the appropriate information about completed work in either of these areas.

Book Report: Throughout the Events and Activities Section of this book, references are made to particular books. The class may choose to have the book read aloud in class or to read the title on an individual basis. Also, it is assumed that students will encounter many interesting books in their related research that are not mentioned in *On This Day.* In any case, the Book Report sheet is provided with directions for students to follow in describing a book that they have read—one which relates to an event or personality represented on one of the days of the given month. In part IV of the form, students are invited to be as imaginative, ingenious, and resourceful as possible in their projects.

Items 14 and 15 (Extra Credit) on the Contract allow for greater latitude concerning extra projects either assigned by the instructor (Item 14) or else extra credit projects that are pursued by individual students (Item 15).

SAMPLE PACKET—
STUDENT FOLDERS

CONTRACT

_____ hereby agrees with _____ to
　　　Student　　　　　　　　　　　　　　　　　Instructor

complete on or before _____ the items below for a letter

grade of "___". If there is a breach of contract, the party of the

second has the right to lower grade according to scale.

_____　　_____
Signature of 1st party (STUDENT)　　　　　　Witness

PROJECT DESCRIPTION	POSSIBLE POINTS	✓	STUDENT POINTS
1. BEHAVIOR, PARTICIPATION & LISTENING TO EVENTS	0 - 100		
2. COVER DESIGN RELATING TO THE MONTH	0 - 25		
3. CALENDAR	0 - 25		
4. TELEGRAM	0 - 25		
5. BIOGRAPHY PROJECT	0 - 100		
6. HISTORICAL PROJECT	0 - 200		
7. STATE REPORT	0 - 100		
8. FIND-A-WORD FOR THE MONTH	0 - 50		
9. TASK CARD(S) # _____	0 - 100		
10. REPRODUCIBLES(S) # _____	0 - 100		
11. MONTH LONG PROJECT	0 - 100		
12. SPECIAL WEEKS or VARIABLE DATE PROJECT	0 - 100 (per project)		
13. BOOK REPORT	0 - 100		
14.			
15. EXTRA CREDIT	VARIES		
SCALE:	TOTAL		
			EVALUATION:

438

OUTLINE FOR THE MONTH

OF_____ BY_____.

I. MONTH-LONG OBSERVANCES

II. SPECIAL WEEKS

III. VARIABLE DATES

CALENDAR

SUNDAY	MONDAY	TUESDAY	WEDNESDAY	THURSDAY	FRIDAY	SATURDAY

TELEGRAM

WESTERN UNION

TELEGRAM

W. P. MARSHALL, PRESIDENT

1213 (7-58)

DOMESTIC SERVICE

Check the class of service desired; otherwise this message will be sent as a fast telegram

TELEGRAM

DAY LETTER

NIGHT LETTER

INTERNATIONAL SERVICE

Check the class of service desired; otherwise the message will be sent at the full rate

FULL RATE

LETTER TELEGRAM

SHORE-SHIP

$

S

E

NO. WDS.-CL. OF SVC. | PD. OR COLL. | CASH NO. | CHARGE TO THE ACCOUNT OF | TIME FILED

Send the following message, subject to the terms on back hereof, which are hereby agreed to

To _____ 19____

_____ Destination _____

Street and No.

Care of or

Apt. No.

Sender's name and address .(For reference)

Sender's telephone number

Name:

Date:

Topic: Biography Project
on _____

Title:

· · · · · · ▶

Source(s):

Name:

Date:

Topic: Historical Project
on _____

Title:

· · · · · ▶

Source(s):

443

Name:

Date:

Topic: States Project

Facts on States for the Month of _____

STATE:

ADMITTED:
as the _____ state to the United States.
GEOGRAPHIC LOCATION:
CAPITAL:
NICKNAME:
STATE FLOWER:
INDUSTRIES:
PRODUCTS:
SIGHTS:
AREA:
GOVERNOR:

SOURCES WHERE INFORMATION WAS LOCATED:

More about the State:

Outline of State

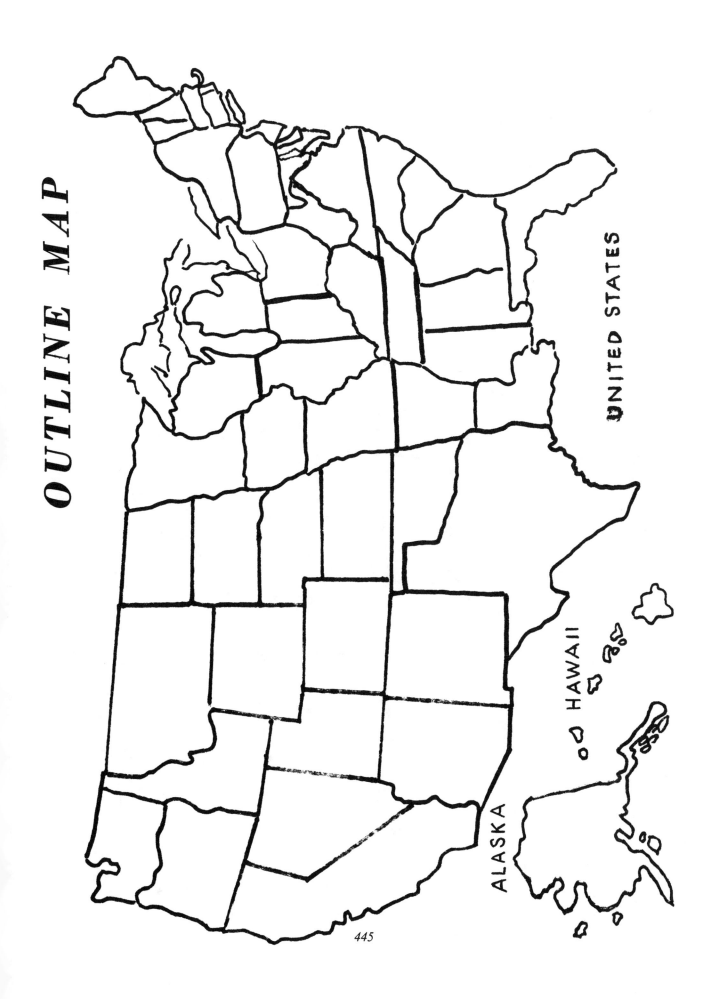

OUTLINE MAP

UNITED STATES

HAWAII

ALASKA

445

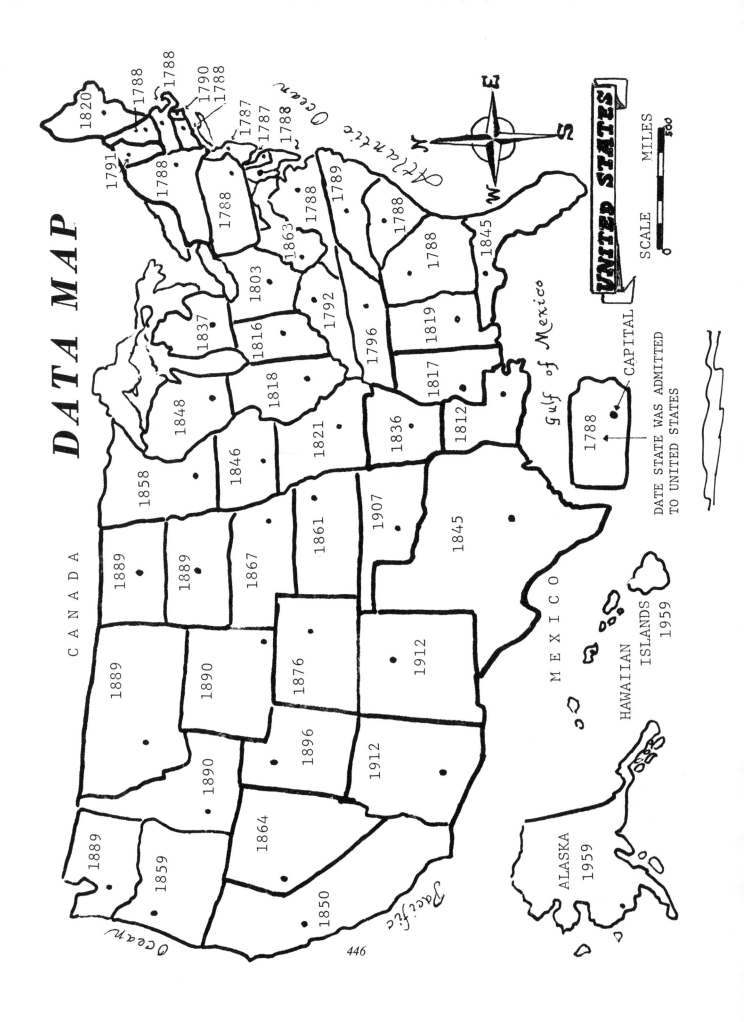

DATA MAP

BOOK REPORT

Prepared by:_____

Date:_____

I. Fill in the following information:

    A. Title:

    B. Author:

    C. Publisher:

    D. City of publication:

    E. Date of publication:

    F. Number of pages in the book:

    G. Classification of the book (fiction or nonfiction, etc.)

    H. Library call number:

    I. Illustrator:

    J. Main characters:

    K. Main idea or theme of book:

II. Write a short summary of the book:

III. Write your opinion of the book:

IV. Complete *one* of the following projects:
    A. Make a book jacket for the book.
    B. Make a collage to depict scenes, people, places, etc., from the book.
    C. Make a diorama or display of the book.
    D. Create an advertisement for the book.
    E. Create a puzzle, find-a-word or game based upon the book.
    F. Write a letter recommending the book to a friend.
    G. Demonstrate something learned from the book.
    H. Design an original project, based upon the book.

APPENDIX A:
Notable Black Personalities

The following is a list of names of various black personalities referred to in this book. The names are alphabetically arranged within each of the months, so as to correspond with the entries found in part 1, Events and Activities Section, of this book.

JANUARY
Muhammad Ali
Edward Brooke
Ralph Bunche
George Washington Carver
Countee Cullen
Martin Luther King, Jr.
Eartha Kitt
Jackie Robinson
Robert Weaver

FEBRUARY
Hank Aaron
Marian Anderson
Frederick Douglass
Langston Hughes
Sidney Poitier
Hiram Revels
Malcolm X

MARCH
Ralph Abernathy
Muhammad Ali
Crispus Attucks
Pearl Bailey
Edward M. Bannister
Edward J. Dwight, Jr.
Robert Flemming
Aretha Franklin
Joe Frazier
Jan Matzeliger
Norbert Rillieux
Sugar Ray Robinson
Harriet Tubman

APRIL
Duke Ellington
Ella Fitzgerald
Matthew Henson
Martin Luther King, Jr.
Jackie Robinson
Robert Smalls
Lincoln Steffens
Booker T. Washington

MAY
Gwendolyn Brooks

Countee Cullen
Joe Louis
Willie Mays
Malcolm X

JUNE
Charles Drew
Paul Lawrence Dunbar
Thurgood Marshall
Wilma Rudolph

JULY
Louis Armstrong
Arthur Ashe, Jr.
Mary McLeod Bethune
Thurgood Marshall
Leroy "Satchel" Paige
O. J. Simpson

AUGUST
James Baldwin
Count Basie
Ralph Bunche
Wilt Chamberlain
Althea Gibson
Alex Palmer Haley
Jesse Owens
Roy Wilkins

SEPTEMBER
Jesse Owens
Hiram Revels

OCTOBER
Mahalia Jackson
Pelé
Nat Turner

NOVEMBER
Benjamin Banneker
Roy Campanella
Shirley Chisholm
W. C. Handy
Scott Joplin

DECEMBER
Sammy Davis, Jr.
Sarah Breedlove Walker

APPENDIX B:
Notable American Indians

The following is an alphabetical list of names of famous Native Americans, some of whom are referred to in part 1, Events and Activities Section, of the book.

Black Hawk, 1767-1838

Cochise, 1812?-1874

Crazy Horse (Tashunea-Uitee), 1849?-1877

Gall (Pizi), 1840-1894

Geronimo (Geyathlay), 1829?-1909

Keckuk (means "the watchful"), 1788?-1848?

Massasoit, 1590?-1661

Osceola, 1805?-1838

Philip, 1639-1676

Pocahontas, 1596?-1617

Pontiac, 1720-1769

Powhatan, 1550?-1618

Quanini, 1845?-1911

Red Cloud, 1822-1909

Red Jacket (Otetiani or Sagoyewath), 1756-1830

Sacagawea, 1787-1812?

Samoset (Osamoset—means "he who walks over much"), ?-1653

Sequoya (George Guess), 1770?-1843

Sitting Bull (Tatanka Iyotake), 1831?-1890

Smohalia, 1815?-1907

Spotted Tail (Sinte-galeshka), 1833-1881

Squanto (Tisquantus), ?-1622

Tecumseh, 1768-1813

Thorpe, James Francis (Jim), 1888-1953

Washakie, 1804?-1900

Wovoka, 1858?-1932

Note: The birth dates of Native American Indians were often not recorded; therefore, when a question mark (?) is indicated, the year can only be considered an approximate date.

APPENDIX C:
Notable Women

The following is a list of names of various women referred to in this book. The names are alphabetically arranged within each of the months, so as to correspond with the entries found in part 1, Events and Activities Section, of this book.

JANUARY
Joan Baez
Hattie Caraway
Carrie Chapman
Mary Mapes Dodge
Joan of Arc
Eartha Kitt
Carrie Nation
Betsy Ross
Nellie Ross
Maria Tallchief

FEBRUARY
Marian Anderson
Susan B. Anthony
Elizabeth Blackwell
Judy Blume
Betty Friedan
Lucy B. Hobbs
Julia Ward Howe
Lydia Estes Pinkham
Laura I. Wilder

MARCH
Pearl Bailey
Joan Crawford
Aretha Franklin
Belva Ann Lockwood
Phyllis McGinley
Liza Minnelli
Dinah Shore
Harriet Beecher Stowe
Harriet Tubman
Lillian Wald

APRIL
Charlotte Brontë
Carol Burnett
Bette Davis
Ella Fitzgerald
Jan Van Kawick-Goodall
Sonja Henie
Mrs. Oveta Culp Hobby
Ali MacGraw
Mary Pickford
Pocahontas

Lily Pons
Debbie Reynolds
Barbra Streisand
Anne Sullivan
Shirley Temple

MAY
Amelia Bloomer
Gwendolyn Brooks
Catherine the Great
Ellen Church
Jacqueline Cochran
Amelia Earhart
Janet Guthrie
Julia Ward Howe
Dolly Madison
Golda Meir
Florence Nightingale
Queen Victoria
Beverly Sills
Kate Smith

JUNE
Lizzie Borden
Gwendolyn Brooks
Pearl S. Buck
"Babe" Zaharias Didrikson
Anne Frank
Judy Garland
Helen Keller
Ada H. Kepley
Margaret Mitchell
Marilyn Monroe
Tricia Nixon
Rose Cecil O'Neill
Jeannette Rankin
Wilma Rudolph
Harriet Beecher Stowe

JULY
Mary McLeod Bethune
Emily Brontë
Phyllis Diller
Amelia Earhart
Mary Baker Eddy
Emma Lazarus

Jacqueline Kennedy Onassis
Beatrix Potter
Ann Stevens
Abigail Van Buren

AUGUST
Lucille Ball
Clara Bow
Virginia Dare
Gertrude Ederle
Edna Ferber
Althea Gibson
Mata Hari
Maria Montessori
Annie Oakley
Mary Shelley
Lucy B. Stone

SEPTEMBER
Jane Addams
Sister Elizabeth Kenny
Grandma Moses
Sandra Day O'Connor
Margaret Sanger
Barbara Walters

OCTOBER
Rebecca Felton
Sarah J. B. Hale
Rita Hayworth
Mahalia Jackson

Juliet Lowe
Marie Antoinette
Mata Hari
Emily Post
Eleanor Roosevelt

NOVEMBER
Louisa May Alcott
Lady Astor
Shirley Chisholm
Marie Curie
Mary Ann Evans
Indira Gandhi
Sadie Hawkins
Katharine Hepburn
Marie Antoinette
Carrie Nation
Jeannette Rankin
Anna Sewell
Elizabeth Cady Stanton
Peregrine White

DECEMBER
Clara Barton
Willa Cather
Emily Dickinson
Mary Aston Livermore
Margaret Mead
Sacagawea
Sarah Breedlove Walker

APPENDIX D:
Notable Jewish Personalities

The following is a list of names of various Jewish personalities referred to in this book. The names are alphabetically arranged within each of the months, so as to correspond with the entries found in part 1, the Events and Activities Section, of this book.

JANUARY
Isaac Asimov
Jules Feiffer
Samuel Gompers
Danny Kaye
Arthur Rubinstein
Haym Solomon

FEBRUARY
Sholom Aleichem
Jack Benny
Judy Blume
Jascha Heifetz
Robert Oppenheimer
David Sarnoff

MARCH
Albert Einstein
Betty Friedan
Dinah Shore
Barbra Streisand
Lillian Wald
Irving Wallace

APRIL
Sol Harry Goldberg
Harry Houdini
Levi Strauss

MAY
Irving Berlin
Moshe Dayan
Sigmund Freud
Benny Goodman
Golda Meir
Beverly Sills

JUNE
Anne Frank
Allen Ginsberg
Oscar Hammerstein

JULY
Milton Berle
Marc Chagall
Phyllis Diller
Emma Lazarus
Isaac Bashevis Singer
Isaac Stern
Albert Warner

AUGUST
Bernard Baruch
Leonard Bernstein
Sam Goldwyn
Albert Sabin
Leon Uris

SEPTEMBER
George Gershwin
Walter Lippmann
Barbara Walters

OCTOBER
Art Buchwald
Groucho Marx
Arthur Miller
Vladimir Horowitz
Jonas Salk
Leon Trotsky

NOVEMBER
Louis Brandeis
Aaron Copland
Felix Frankfurter
Harpo Marx
Baruch Spinoza

DECEMBER
Alfred Dreyfus
Arthur Fiedler
Uri Geller
Simon Guggenheim
Sanford ("Sandy") Koufax

APPENDIX E:
Reference Sources

Arbuthnot, May Hill, and Shelton L. Root, Jr., eds. *Time for Poetry.* Glenview, IL: Scott, Foresman, 1968.

Banks, James A. *Teaching Strategies for Ethnic Studies.* Boston: Allyn & Bacon, 1975.

Barclay, Barbara. *Lamps to Light the Way: Our Presidents.* Glendale, CA: Bowmar, 1970.

Beadle, Jeremy. *Today's the Day.* New York: New American Library, 1981.

Bernardo, Stephanie. *The Ethnic Almanac.* Garden City, NY: Dolphin Books—Doubleday, 1981.

Blassingame, Wyatt. *The Look-It-Up Book of Presidents.* New York: Random House, 1968.

Book of Knowledge: The Children's Encyclopedia. New York: The Grolier Society, 1934.

Brasch, R. *How Did It Begin?* New York: Pocket Books, 1970.

Britannica Encyclopaedia of American Art. Chicago: Encyclopaedia Britannica, 1981.

Campbell, Hannah. *Why Did They Name It?* New York: Fleet Publishing, 1964.

Cary, Sturges. *Arrow Book of Presidents.* Englewood Cliffs, NJ Scholastic Book Services, 1972. (Also send to the publisher for the giant game poster, "So You Want to Run for President"; Scholastic Book Services, 50 W. 44th St., New York, NY 10036.)

Chase, William P., and Helen Chase. *Chase's Calendar of Annual Events* (annual). Flint, MI: Apple Tree Press, 1971.

Churchill, E. Richard, and Linda R. Churchill. *Twentieth Century America Activity Reader.* Portland, ME: J. Weston Walch, Publisher, 1978.

Clemens, James R. *Creative Holidays: 100 Unusual Holiday Ideas.* Inglewood, CA: Educational Insights, 1971.

Compton's Encyclopedia. Chicago: Compton, 1980.

Coy, Harold. *Presidents.* New York: Watts (Franklin), 1973.

Current Biography. New York: H. W. Wilson Publication, 1973.

Dictionary of American Biography. New York: Charles Scribner's Sons.

Donaldson, Elizabeth, and Gerald Donaldson. *The Book of Days.* New York: A & W Publishers, 1979.

Emrich, Duncan, ed. *The Hodgepodge Book: An Almanac of American Folklore.* New York: Four Winds Press, 1972.

Encyclopaedia Britannica. Chicago: Encyclopaedia Britannica, 1981.

Ethridge, James M., and Barbara Kopala, eds. *Contemporary Authors.* Detroit: Gale Research, 1967.

Fiarotta, Phyllis, and Noel Fiarotta. *The You and Me Heritage Tree.* New York: Workman, 1976.

Golden Book Encyclopedia. New York: Golden Press, 1959.

Golenpaul, Dan, ed. *Information Please Almanac Atlas and Yearbook.* New York: Dan Golenpaul Associates, 1979.

Gregory, Ruth. *Anniversaries and Holidays.* 3rd ed. Chicago: American Library Association, 1975.

Hart, Michael H. *The 100: A Ranking of the Most Influential Persons in History.* New York: Hart Publishing, 1978.

Hochman, Stanley. *Yesterday and Today: A Dictionary of Recent American History.* New York: McGraw-Hill, 1979.

Hopkins, Lee Bennett. *Important Dates in Afro-American History.* New York: Watts (Franklin), 1969.

Hopkins, Lee Bennett, and Misha Arenstein. *Do You Know What Day Tomorrow Is? A Teacher's Almanac.* New York: Scholastic Book Services, 1975.

Hurwitz, Howard L. *An Encyclopedic Dictionary of American History.* New York: Washington Square Press, 1974.

Jones, E. Willis. *The Santa Claus Book.* New York: Walker, 1976.

Kane, Joseph N. *Famous First Facts and Records.* New York: Ace Books, 1973.

Karp, Theodore. *Dictionary of Music.* New York: Dell, 1973.

King, Edith. *Teaching Ethnic Awareness.* Santa Monica, CA: Goodyear, 1980.

Krythe, Maymie R. *All about American Holidays.* New York: Harper & Row, 1962.

Krythe, Maymie R. *All about the Months.* New York: Harper & Row, 1966.

Larrick, Nancy, ed. *More Poetry for Holidays.* Champaign, IL: Garrard Publishing, 1973.

Larrick, Nancy, ed. *Poetry for Holidays.* Champaign, IL: Garrard Publishing, 1966.

Lee, Nancy, and Linda Oldham. *Hands on Heritage.* Long Beach, CA: Hands on Publications, 1978.

Linton, Calvin D., ed. *The Bicentennial Almanac.* Nashville, TN: Thomas Nelson, 1975.

McGraw-Hill Yearbook of Science and Technology. New York: McGraw-Hill, 1972.

McWhirter, Norris. *Guinness Book of Records.* New York: Sterling Publishing, 1980.

Menke, Frank. *Encyclopedia of Sports.* Garden City, NY: Doubleday, 1977.

Mirkin, Stanford M. *When Did It Happen: A Noted Researcher's Almanac of Yesterdays.* New York: Ives Washburn, 1957.

Pasternak, Michael. *Helping Kids Learn Multi-Cultural Concepts.* Champaign, IL: Research Press, 1979.

Pictorial Encyclopedia: People Who Made America. Skokie, IL: United States History Society, 1973.

Ploski, Harry A., and Warren Marr. *The Negro Almanac—A Reference Work on the Afro-American.* New York: The Bellweather Company, 1976.

Robbins, Ireene. *Elementary Teacher's Arts and Crafts Ideas for Every Month of the Year.* West Nyack, NY: Parker Publishing, 1970.

Robertson, Patrick. *The Book of Firsts.* New York: Bramhall House, 1974.

Ross, Wilma S. *Fabulous Facts about the 50 States.* New York: Scholastic Book Service, 1976.

Sanders, Sandra. *Easy Ways with Holidays.* New York: Scholastic Book Services, 1970.

Sechrist, Elizabeth Hough. *Red Letter Days: A Book of Holiday Customs.* Philadelphia: Macrae Smith, 1965.

Sechrist, Elizabeth Hough, and Janette Woolsey. *New Plays for Red Letter Days.* Philadelphia: Macrae Smith, 1953.

Siegel, Richard, and Carl Rheins. *The Jewish Almanac.* New York: Bantam Books, 1980.

Sills, David L. *International Encyclopedia of the Social Sciences.* New York: Free Press, 1977.

Smith, Godfrey, ed. *1000 Makers of the Twentieth Century.* Great Britain: Sir Joseph Causton & Sons Limited, 1971.

Spinrad, Leonard, and Thelma Spinrad. *Instant Almanac of Events, Anniversaries, Observances, Quotations, and Birthdays for Every Day of the Year.* New York: Parker Publishing, 1972.

Suid, Murray, and Ron Harris. *Made in America — Eight Great All-American Creations.* Reading, MA: Addison-Wesley Publishing, 1978.

Sullivan, W. "The Einstein Papers," *New York Times*, March 27, 1972, p. 1, Col. 1.

Thernstrom, Stephan, et al. (eds.). *Harvard Encyclopedia of American Ethnic Groups.* Cambridge: Harvard University Press, 1980.

U.S. Postal Service. *Stamps and Stories.* Published yearly. (See also "Stamp Collecting Kits"; the kits are arranged according to categories, such as sports, animals, nature, history, foreign stamps, all of which are available at a local U.S. Post Office.)

Wallechinsky, David; Irving Wallace; and Amy Wallace. *The Book of Lists.* New York: William Morrow, 1977.

Weast, Robert C. *Handbook of Chemistry and Physics.* Boca Raton, FL: CRC Press, 1980.

Webster's American Biographies. Springfield, MA: G & C Merriam, 1975.

Webster's Biographical Dictionary. Springfield, MA: G & C Merriam, 1976.

Who Was Who in America. Chicago: Marquis Who's Who Publication, 1973.

Who's Who in America. Chicago: Marquis Who's Who Publication, 1972.

World Almanac and Book of Facts, 1981. New York: Newspaper Enterprise Association, 1980.

World Almanac (eds.). *World Almanac Book of Who.* New York: World Almanac, 1980.

World Book Encyclopedia. Chicago: World Book Childcraft, 1980.

Worth, Fred L. *The Trivia Encyclopedia.* New York: Tempo Books — Grosset & Dunlan, 1975.

Index

The index provides access to the information found in part 1, Events and Activities Section. Names of events, persons, or observances can first be located through the following alphabetized index; any related information can be followed up by cross-references within the Events and Activities Section which direct the reader to other parts of the book. *Note:* Most of the index listings refer to the actual headings found in the entries of part 1; however, a number of index listings refer the reader to information contained *within* the entry.

The index is arranged according to various types of dates following the entries:

Month and day preceded by the letter "b"—birthday.
Month followed by no other notation—listed in the introductory information at the beginning of the month.
Month followed by "MLO"—listed in the month-long observances at the beginning of the month.
Month followed by "SW"—listed in Special Weeks at the beginning of the month.
Month followed by "Var"—listed in Variable Dates at the beginning of the month.
Month and day alone—event, activity, or observance.

*Throughout the Index, a numeral inside parentheses refers to the number of related items within the one entry in part 1 of the Events and Activities Section.